# Fresh Perspectives on the 'WAR ON TERROR'

# Fresh Perspectives on the 'WAR ON TERROR'

Miriam Gani
Penelope Mathew
(editors)

E PRESS

Published by ANU E Press
The Australian National University
Canberra ACT 0200, Australia
Email: anuepress@anu.edu.au
This title is also available online at: http://epress.anu.edu.au/war_terror_citation.html

National Library of Australia
Cataloguing-in-Publication entry

| | |
|---|---|
| Title: | Fresh perspectives on the war on terror / editors Miriam Gani, Penelope Mathew. |
| ISBN: | 9781921313738 (pbk.)  9781921313745 (web) |
| Subjects: | Terrorism. |
| | War on Terrorism, 2001- |
| | National security--Law and legislation. |
| | Islam and world politics. |
| Other Authors/Contributors: | |
| | Gani, Miriam. |
| | Mathew, Penelope. |
| Dewey Number: | 363.325 |

All rights reserved. No part of this publication may be reproduced, stored in a retrieval system or transmitted in any form or by any means, electronic, mechanical, photocopying or otherwise, without the prior permission of the publisher.

Cover design by ANU E Press

Cover image: "Eye of the Storm" by Sven Geier. Available from http://www.sgeier.net/fractals/fractals/02/Eye%20of%20the%20Storm.jpg

This edition © 2008 ANU E Press

# Table of Contents

| | |
|---|---:|
| Acknowledgements | vii |
| Contributors | ix |
| Table of Cases | xi |
| Table of Statutes | xv |
| Table of International Instruments | xix |
| Chapter 1. Introduction: Letters from the Front<br>*Miriam Gani and Penelope Mathew* | 1 |

## Part One – Identifying the Threat and Choosing the Weapons

| | |
|---|---:|
| Chapter 2. Islam and the Politics of Terrorism: Aspects of the British Experience<br>*John Strawson* | 9 |
| Chapter 3. Another Modest Proposal: In Defence of the Prohibition against Torture<br>*Desmond Manderson* | 27 |
| Chapter 4. Protecting Constitutionalism in Treacherous Times: Why 'Rights' Don't Matter<br>*W Wesley Pue* | 45 |

## Part Two – Preparing the Ground: Balance, Proportionality, and Public Perceptions

| | |
|---|---:|
| Chapter 5. Balancing Security and Liberty: Critical Perspectives on Terrorism Law Reform<br>*Simon Bronitt* | 65 |
| Chapter 6. Lay Perceptions of Terrorist Acts and Counter-Terrorism Responses: Role of Motive, Offence Construal, Siege Mentality and Human Rights<br>*Mark Nolan* | 85 |
| Chapter 7. The Proportionality Principle in the Context of Anti-Terrorism Laws: An Inquiry into the Boundaries between Human Rights Law and Public Policy<br>*Christopher Michaelsen* | 109 |

## Part Three – Rules of Engagement: Beyond the Limits of the Law

| | |
|---|---:|
| Chapter 8. More Law or Less Law? The Resilience of Human Rights Law and Institutions in the 'War on Terror'<br>*Andrew Byrnes* | 127 |

Chapter 9. Black Holes, White Holes and Worm Holes: Pre-emptive
Detention in the 'War on Terror'  159
*Penelope Mathew*

Chapter 10. Forgiving Terrorism: Trading Justice for Peace, or
Imperiling the Peace?  189
*Ben Saul*

## Part Four – Reports from Two Theatres of War: Legislation, Sanctions and Prosecutions in Europe and Australia

Chapter 11. The European Union as a Collective Actor in the Fight
against Post-9/11 Terrorism: Progress and Problems of a Primarily
Cooperative Approach  209
*Jörg Monar*

Chapter 12. The European Union, Counter-Terrorism Sanctions against
Individuals and Human Rights Protection  235
*Gabriele Porretto*

Chapter 13. How Does it End? Reflections on Completed Prosecutions
under Australia's Anti-Terrorism Legislation  269
*Miriam Gani*

Chapter 14. Executive Proscription of Terrorist Organisations in
Australia: Exploring the Shifting Border between Crime and Politics  297
*Russell Hogg*

## Part Five – Calling a Halt: The Role of Bills of Rights

Chapter 15. Strapped to the Mast: The Siren Song of Dreadful Necessity,
the United Kingdom Human Rights Act and the Terrorist Threat  327
*Colm O'Cinneide*

Chapter 16. The ACT Human Rights Act 2004 and the Commonwealth
Anti-Terrorism Act (No 2) 2005: A Triumph for Federalism or a Federal
Triumph?  361
*Andrew Byrnes and Gabrielle McKinnon*

Bibliography  379

Acronyms and Abbreviations  413

Index  415

# Acknowledgements

The editors would like to acknowledge the following people and organisations for their important contributions to this book. The Australian Research Council awarded a substantial grant that funded the work of a number of the authors in this book.[1] We thank our fellow Chief Investigators under this grant, Simon Bronitt, Andrew Byrnes, Russell Hogg and Mark Nolan and our Research Associate, Gabriele Porretto, for their collegiality, lateral thinking and hard work in helping us bring this part of our larger project to fruition. The Australian Academy of Social Sciences also provided a smaller grant that assisted in the holding of an expert workshop that led to this volume.

Thanks are also due to the ANU College of Law for supporting the research effort of the six researchers funded by the ARC grant, particularly the ANU E Press Editorial Board, Margaret Thornton, Stephen Bottomley, Matthew Rimmer and Fiona Wheeler, and other colleagues at the ANU, including Gregor Urbas, Hilary Charlesworth, and Peter Grabosky. Most importantly, we thank Jennifer Braid for the final editorial work on the manuscript. Jenny's tireless work, endless patience and good sense and humour were the essential ingredients for completion of the manuscript. We are grateful to our Dean, Michael Coper, for ensuring that Jenny could do this work. We would also like to thank two former students at the ANU College of Law, David Easteal and Jessica Giovanelli, for their assistance with the preparation of the manuscript. Finally, we thank our partners and children for graciously enduring countless working morning teas and dinners at our homes and other vicissitudes associated with the book. Thank you, Shaun, Isabelle, Luke, Don and Tom.

**Miriam Gani and Penelope Mathew**
The Australian National University
Canberra

   ARC Discovery Project DP0451473

---

[1] 'Terrorism and the Non-State Actor After September 11: the Role of Law in the Search for Security', ARC Discovery Project DP0451473.

# Contributors

**Professor Simon Bronitt**

Professor of Law, ANU College of Law and Director of the National Europe Centre, The Australian National University, Canberra, Australia.

**Professor Andrew Byrnes**

Professor of International Law, Faculty of Law and Australian Human Rights Centre, The University of New South Wales, Sydney, Australia.

**Miriam Gani**

Senior Lecturer in Law, ANU College of Law, The Australian National University, Canberra, Australia.

**Russell Hogg**

Associate Professor of Law, School of Law, University of New England, Armidale, NSW, Australia.

**Gabrielle McKinnon**

Research Associate, Regulatory Institutions Network, Centre for International Governance and Justice, The Australian National University, Canberra, Australia.

**Professor Desmond Manderson**

Canada Research Chair in Law and Discourse, Faculty of Law, McGill University, Montreal, Canada.

**Dr Penelope Mathew**

Reader in Law, ANU College of Law, The Australian National University, Canberra, Australia. From August 2008, Visiting Professor and Interim Director, Program in Refugee and Asylum Law, University of Michigan.

**Christopher Michaelsen**

Visiting Fellow, Faculty of Law, University of New South Wales, Sydney, Australia. Formerly Human Rights Officer (Anti-Terrorism), The Organization for Security and Co-operation in Europe (OSCE), Office for Democratic Institutions and Human Rights (ODIHR), Warsaw, Poland.

**Professor Jörg Monar**

Professor, Marie Curie Chair of Excellence, Université Robert Schuman de Strasbourg, Strasbourg, France and Director of the European Union-funded SECURINT project on EU internal security governance.

**Dr Mark Nolan**

Senior Lecturer in Law, ANU College of Law, The Australian National University, Canberra, Australia.

**Colm O'Cinneide**

Senior Lecturer in Law, Faculty of Laws, University College London, London, United Kingdom.

**Dr Gabriele Porretto**

Formerly Research Associate and Sparke Helmore Lecturer, ANU College of Law, The Australian National University, Canberra, Australia.

**Professor W Wesley Pue**

Nathan Nemetz Chair in Legal History, Faculty of Law, University of British Columbia, Vancouver, Canada. Currently serving as Vice-Provost and Associate Vice-President Academic Resources, University of British Columbia, Vancouver, Canada.

**Dr Ben Saul**

Senior Lecturer and Director of the Sydney Centre for International Law, Faculty of Law, University of Sydney, Australia.

**John Strawson**

Reader in Law, School of Law, University of East London, London, United Kingdom.

# Table of Cases

*A and Others v Secretary of State for the Home Department, X and another v Secretary of State for the Home Department* [2005] 2 AC 68 (*Belmarsh Detainees*): 110, 111, 119, 120, 121, 122, 123, 124, 173, 174, 175, 334, 335, 336, 339, 347, 352, 353, 357, 358, 359, 360

*A v Australia*, UN Doc. CCPR/C/59/D/560/1993: 181

*A v Secretary of State for the Home Department (No 2)* [2005] UKHL 71; [2005] All ER (D) 124 (Dec); [2006] 1 All ER 575: 343

*Abdul Jaber al-Kubaisi v Iraq and United States of America*, Opinion No 44/2005, 30 November 2005, A/HRC/4/40/Add 1: 145, 146

*Abu Qatada v SSHD* SC/15/2005, 26 February 2007: 336, 344, 355

*Aksoy v Turkey* (1996) 23 EHRR 553: 111, 359

*Al-Nashif v Bulgaria* [2002] 36 EHRR 655: 336

*Australian Communist Party v Commonwealth* (1951) 83 CLR 1: 298, 299

*Ayadi v Council* (T-253/02) [2006] ECR II-2139: 230, 257, 258, 259, 260, 261, 262

*Barrios Altos (Interpretation of Merits Judgment)*, IACHR (3 September 2001): 192

*Bdurahman Nacer Addullah al-Dahmane al-Chehri et al v Saudi Arabia*, Opinion No 12/2006, 11 May 2006, A/HRC/4/40/Add.1: 145

*Belilos v Switzerland* (10328183) [1988] ECHR 4 (29 April 1988): 170

*Bismullah v Gates*, 501 F.3d 178, 196 (D.C. Cir. 2007), 2007 WL 2067938: 162

*Bosnia Case* [1993] ICJ Rep 440: 203, 251

*Bosphorus v Ireland* [2005] 42 EHRR 1: 251

*Boumedienne v Bush*, 476 F 3d 981 (DC Cir. 2007): 162

*Brannigan and McBride v United Kingdom* (1993) 17 EHRR 539: 110, 111, 115

*Brogan v UK* (1989) 11 EHRR 117: 333

*Bundesverfassungsgericht*, Judgment of 18 July 2005, BVerfG, 2 BvR 2236/04: 225

*Canada v Pharmaceutical Society (Nova Scotia)* [1992] 2 SCR 606 (SCC): 60

Case C-354/04 P, *Gestoras pro Amnestia* [2007] ECR I-1579: 229

Case C-355/04 P, *Segi* [2007] ECR I-1657: 229

*Case Concerning Armed Activities on the Territory of the Congo (Democratic Republic of the Congo v Uganda)* ICJ Judgment of 19 December 2005: 145

Case T-228/02, *Modjahedines* [2006] ECR II-4665: 228, 229, 230

*Castillo Páez (Reparations) Case* (27 November 1998) Ser C, No 43: 192, 197

*Chahal v UK* (1997) 23 EHRR 413: 334, 336, 339, 343, 344, 359

*Chahal v United Kingdom* (1996) 23 ECR 1996-V 1831: 265, 266

*Charkaoui v Canada (Citizenship and Immigration)* [2007] SCC 9: 52

*Chumbipuma Aguirre et al v Peru (Barrios Altos)* (2001) Series C, No 75: 192

*Ciancimino v Italy* (1991) 70 DR 103: 328

*Commission v Council* [1998] ECR I-2763: 228

*DD and AS v SSHD*, SC/42 and 50/2005, 27 April 2007: 344

*Donnelly and Others v UK*, Application 5577, 5583/73, Decision of the Commission, 5 April 1973: 333

*Dorsch Consult Ingenieurgesellschaft mbH v Council and Commission* ((C-184/95) [1998] ECR I-1443: 239

*DPP (Cth) v Thomas* [2005] VSC 85: 277

*DPP v Thomas* [2006] VSC 120: 287, 288

*DPP v Thomas* [2006] VSC 243: 289

*Drescher Caldas v Uruguay*, UN GAOR Supp. No. 40 (A/38/40) at 192 (1983): 184

*Edwards v United Kingdom* (2002) 35 EHRR 487: 253

*European Parliament v Council* [2006] ECR I-4721: 231

*Faheem Khalid Lodhi v R* [2007] NSWCCA 360 (unreported): 290

*Gestoras Pro Amnistía and Others v Council of the European Union* (T-333/02) (unreported; a summary of the order is available in [2004] OJ C 228/40: 245

*Golder Case* (1975) 18 Eur Court HR (ser A) 4: 245

*Götz Leffler v Berlin Chemie AG*, Case C-443/03, Grand Chamber, Decision of 8 November 2005, ECR 2005-1, 9611: 261

*Greek Case* (1969) 12 Yearbook ECHR 1: 111, 112, 113, 114

*Gregg v Georgia* (1976) 428 US 153 (US): 38

*Guzzardi v Italy* (1980 Series A No 39); (1980) 3 EHRR 333: 338, 341, 354

*Hamdan v Rumsfeld*, 126 S Ct 2749 (2006): 161, 162, 163, 165

*Hamdan v Rumsfeld*, 415 F 3d 33 (DC Cir. 2005): 163

*Hamdi v Rumsfeld*, 542 US 507 (2004): 55, 161, 162

*Handyside v United Kingdom* (1976) 1 EHRR 737: 113

*Haneef v Minister for Immigration and Citizenship* [2007] FCA 1273: 98, 186, 376

*Hassan v Council* (T-49/04) [2006] ECR II-52: 230, 257, 258, 259, 260, 261, 262

*Hyam v DPP* [1975] AC 55: 90

*Ireland v United Kingdom* (1978 Series A No 35) 2 EHRR 25: 110, 111, 115, 116, 117, 333, 359

*Jasper v United Kingdom* (2000), unreported: 265, 266

*Kaunda and others v President of the Republic of South Africa* (CCT 23/04) [2004] ZACC 5: 261

*Kioa v West* (1985) 159 CLR 550: 314

*Landinelli Silva v Uruguay* (1981) HRC Comm No 34/1978: 117

*Lawless v Ireland* (1960) 1 EHRR 1: 359

*Lawless v Ireland* (No 3) (1961) 1 EHRR 15: 111, 112, 117

*Lawless v Republic of Ireland* (No 3), [1961] ECHR 2 (1 July 1961): 180, 182

*Liversidge v Anderson* [1942] AC 206: 331, 352, 356, 357

*Lodhi v The Queen* (2006) 199 FLR 303: 90, 106, 107, 273, 274, 275, 276

*McCann and Others v United Kingdom* (1995) 21 EHRR 97: 113, 114, 333

*Minister for Immigration and Multicultural Affairs v Singh* (2002) 209 CLR 533: 316

*Mourad Benchellali et al v United States of America* Opinion No 5/2003, 8 May 2003, UN Doc E/CN.4/2004/3/Add.1, 33: 145

*O'Neill v Canada (Attorney-General)* (2006), OJ No 4189: 52

*OK, et al v George Bush, et al*, US District Court for the District of Columbia, Case 1:04-cv-01136-JDB: 47

*Organisation des Modjahedines du peuple d'Iran v Council of the European Union* (T-228/02) [2006]: 228, 229, 280, 262

*Osman v the United Kingdom* (1998) VIII Eur Court HR 3169: 257

*Padilla v Hanft*, 547 U.S. 1062 (2006): 161

*Philip Morris International v Commission* (T-377/00) [2003] ECR II-1: 244

*Prosecutor v Furundzija* IT-95-17/1-T (10 December 1998): 203

*Prosecutor v Kondewa* SCSL-2004-14-AR72(E) (25 May 2004): 195

*Prosecutor v Morris Kallon and Brima Buzzy Kamara (Jurisdiction)* (*Lomé Amnesty Case*), SCSL-2004-15-AR72(E) and SCSL-2004-16-AR72(E), Appeals Chamber, 13 March 2004: 192, 193

*R (Al-Jedda) v Secretary of State for Defence* [2006] EWCA Civ 327: 192

*R (Gillan) v Commissioner of Police for the Metropolis* [2006] UKHL 12: 345, 357

*R (Q) v Secretary of State for the Home Department* [2006] EWHC (Admin) 2690: 339

*R (Saadi) v Secretary of State for the Home Department* [2001] EWCA Admin 670: 341

*R v Demirian* [1989] VR 97: 89

*R v Dudley and Stephens* (1884) 14 QBD 273: 67

*R v F* [2007] 2 All ER 193: 74

*R v Halliday* [1917] AC 260: 357

*R v Joseph Terrence Thomas* [2006] VSCA 165: 73

*R v Khawaja* (2006), 214 CCC (3d) 399, WL 3031774 (Ont SCJ): 51, 52, 59, 61, 62

*R v Khazal* [2004] NSWSC 548: 97

*R v Lodhi* (2005) 199 FLR 236: 274

R v Lodhi (2006) 199 FLR 364: 276, 290, 292, 293, 294

R v Lodhi [2005] NSWSC 1377: 301

R v Lodhi [2006] NSWSC 584: 107, 274, 275, 276, 293

R v Mallah [2005] NSWSC 317: 276, 285, 286

R v Mallah [2005] NSWSC 358: 284

R v Secretary of State ex parte Hosenball [1977] 1 WLR 776: 357

R v Secretary of State for the Home Department, ex parte Rehman [2001] UKHL 47, [2003] 1 AC 153: 339

R v Thomas (2006) 14 VR 475: 288

R v Thomas (No 3) (2006) 14 VR 512: 288

R v Ul-Haque (Unreported, NSW Supreme Court, Bell J, 8 February 2006): 302, 303, 304

Raimondo v Italy App 12954/87 (1994 Series A 281-A) 18 EHRR 237: 338, 341, 354

Rameka v New Zealand, CCPR/C/79/D/1090/2002: 180

Ramzy v the Netherlands, Observations of the Governments of Lithuania, Portugal, Slovakia and the United Kingdom Intervening in Application No 25424/05 (Eur Court HR 2005): 176, 186

Rasul v Bush, 542 US 466 (2004): 55, 162

Re Bullivant [2007] EWHC 2938 (Admin): 342

Re JJ [2006] EWCA Civ 1141; [2007] QB 446: 341, 342

Re MB [2006] EWHC (Admin) 1000: 341, 342

Roberts v Parole Board [2005] UKHL 45: 336, 349

Saadi v Italy, App. No. 37201/06 (Eur Court HR 2008): 344

Saadi v United Kingdom, App. No. 13229/03 (Eur Court HR 2006): 339

Saddam Hussein al-Tikriti v Iraq and United States of America, Opinion No 46/2005, 30 November 2005, A/HRC/4/40/Add 1: 145

Secretary of State for the Home Department v E [2007] EWHC (Admin): 341, 358

Secretary of State for the Home Department v E and S [2007] UKHL 47; [2007] 3 WLR 720: 342

Secretary of State for the Home Department v JJ [2007] UKHL 45; [2007] 3 WLR 643: 341

Secretary of State for the Home Department v MB [2007] UKHL 46; [2007] 3 WLR 681: 342

Secretary of State for the Home Department v Rehman [2001] UKHL 47; [2002] 1 All ER 122; [2003] 1 AC 153: 336, 339, 357

Secretary of State for the Home Department v MB [2006] EWCA (Civ) 1140: 341

Segi and Others v Council of the European Union, (T-338/02) [2004] II-1647: 245

Simón Case, Argentine Supreme Court, causa No 17.768 (14 June 2005) S.1767.XXXVIII: 193

SSHD v AF [2007] EWHC 651: 342

SSHD v Bullivant [2008] EWHC B2 (Admin): 342

SSHD v Rideh and J [2007] EWCA Civ 804: 342, 344

T v Home Secretary [1996] AC 742: 316

Tariq Aziz v Iraq and the United States of America, Opinion No 45/2005, 30 November 2007, A/HRC/4/40/Add 1: 144

Terminiello v City of Chicago, 337 US 1 (1949): 56, 351

Thomas v Mowbray [2007] HCA 33: 53, 183, 288, 376

United States of America v Omar Ahmed Khadr, 4 June 2007: 162

United States of America v Salim Ahmed Hamdan, 4 June 2007: 162

Viro v The Queen (1978) 141 CLR 88: 38

Waite and Kennedy v Germany (1999) I ECtHR 393: 257

Walid Mohammed Shahir Muhammed al-Qadasi et al v Yemen, Opinion No 47/2005, 30 November 2005, A/HRC/4/40/Add.1: 145

Wilkerson v Utah (1878) 99 US 130 (US): 38

Y v SSHD, SC/36/2005, 24 August 2006: 344

Yassin Abdullah Kadi v Council and Commission (T-315/01) [2005] ECR II-3649: 230, 238, 239, 247, 248, 249, 250, 252, 253, 254, 256, 257, 258, 259, 260, 264, 265

Yusuf and Al Barakaat International Foundation v Council and Commission (T-306/01) [2005]

ECR II-3533: 230, 238, 239, 247, 248, 249, 250, 252, 253, 254, 255, 256, 257, 258, 259, 260, 264, 265

*Zecevic v DPP* (1987) 162 CLR 645: 35

# Table of Statutes

AUSTRALIA
Commonwealth
Anti-Terrorism Act (No 2) 2005 (Cth): 74, 75, 271, 273, 283, 362, 366, 373
Anti-Terrorism Act 2004 (Cth): 271, 277, 278, 290
Anti-Terrorism Act 2005 (Cth): 271, 272, 273
Anti-Terrorism Bill (No 2) 2005 (Cth): 374
Australian Capital Territory (Self-Government) Act 1988 (Cth): 368
    s 35(2): 368
Australian Security and Intelligence Organisation Act 1979 (Cth)
    s 34ZO: 97
    s 34ZP: 97
    s 34ZQ(9): 97
    s 34ZQ(2): 97
    s 34ZQ(10): 97
Crimes Act 1914 (Cth): 96
    s 19AG: 290
    s 23C: 96
    s 23CA: 96, 185
    s 23DA: 185
Crimes Legislation Amendment (National Investigative Powers and Witness Protection) Bill 2006 (Cth): 96
Criminal Code Act 1995 (Cth): 66, 67, 73, 74, 75, 79, 81, 89, 269, 270, 271, 272, 274, 278, 286, 290, 292, 294, 303, 310, 366, 367
    Ch 2: 272
    Pt 5.3: 269, 270, 271, 273, 277, 280, 283, 294, 376
    Div 100.8: 366
    Div 103: 283
    Div 104: 96, 183, 288
    Div 105: 96, 178
    s 2.1: 272
    s 4.1(1)(c): 276
    s 5.2: 275
    s 5.2(1): 276, 286
    s 5.2(2): 276
    s 5.3: 293
    s 5.4: 290
    s 5.6: 286, 289
    s 11.2(1): 274
    s 11.3: 274
    s 11.4: 272

s 11.5: 273
s 11.6(1): 274
s 15.4: 274, 284, 306
s 100.1: 89, 90, 270, 274, 287
s 100.1(1): 74, 89, 90, 91, 178, 301, 303
s 100.1(1)(c)(ii): 100
s 100.1(2): 275, 290, 301
s 100.1(3): 275, 301
s 100.1(4): 302
s 100.8: 366, 376
s 101.1: 271, 272, 273, 302
s 101.1(2): 274
s 101.2: 271
s 101.2(3): 272
s 101.2(4): 274
s 101.4: 271, 291, 302
s 101.4(1): 291, 293
s 101.4(3): 272
s 101.4(4): 274
s 101.5: 97, 271, 291, 302
s 101.5(1): 291, 293
s 101.5(3): 272
s 101.5(4): 274
s 101.6: 271, 272, 273, 284, 285, 286, 291, 302
s 101.6(2): 272
s 101.6(3): 274
s 102.1: 303
s 102.1(1): 278, 279, 280, 282, 303
s 102.1(17): 300
s 102.1(1A): 281, 282, 303
s 102.1(2): 280
s 102.1(2)(a): 282
s 102.1(2A): 281, 305
s 102.1(3): 300
s 102.1(4): 281, 300
s 102.1(5): 300
s 102.1A: 281, 300
s 102.2: 277, 299, 305
s 102.3: 277, 305
s 102.4: 277, 305
s 102.5: 278, 305
s 102.6: 277, 278, 287, 288, 305
s 102.6(1): 287
s 102.7: 185, 276, 277, 278, 289, 305
s 102.7(1): 287
s 102.8: 278, 279, 305
s 102.9: 274, 306
s 103.1: 283
s 103.2: 283

s 103.3: 288
s 104.4: 282
s 105.2: 179
s 105.4: 178
s 105.4(5): 178
s 105.4(6): 178
s 105.4(6)(a): 178
s 105.8(5): 178
s 105.8(6)(c): 180
s 105.8(6A): 180
s 105.10: 178
s 105.11: 179
s 105.12: 179
s 105.12(5): 179
s 105.12(6)(d): 180
s 105.12(6A): 180
s 105.18(2): 179
s 105.28(2)(a): 180
s 105.32: 180
s 105.51(1): 179
s 105.51(2): 179
s 105.51(5): 179
s 105.52: 179
s 106.3: 273, 291
s 147.2: 284, 285, 286
s 147.2(2): 284
Criminal Code Amendment (Hamas and Lashkar-E-Tayyiba) Act 2003 (Cth): 280, 300
Criminal Code Amendment (Hizballah) Act 2003 (Cth): 280, 300
Criminal Code Amendment (Terrorism) Act 2003 (Cth): 299
Criminal Code Amendment (Terrorist Organisations) Act 2004 (Cth): 280, 300
Criminal Code Amendment (Theft, Fraud, Bribery and Related Offences) Act 2000 (Cth): 286
Defence Act 1903 (Cth): 80
  Pt IIIAAA: 79
  s 51SE: 80
  s 51SE(2): 80
  s 51SE(3): 80
  s 51T: 80
  s 51T(3): 81
Defence Force Discipline Act 1982 (Cth): 81
Defence Legislation Amendment (Aid to Civilian Authorities) Bill 2006 (Cth): 79

Migration Act 1958 (Cth)
  s 501: 186
National Security Information (Criminal and Civil Proceedings) Act 2004 (Cth): 180, 291
Passports Act 1938 (Cth): 288
  s 9A(1)(e): 288
Security Legislation Amendment (Terrorism) Act 2002 (Cth): 269, 299
Security Legislation Amendment (Terrorism) Bill 2002 (Cth): 73, 299
Security Legislation Amendment (Terrorism) Bill 2002 [No 2] (Cth): 272, 274

## Australian Capital Territory
Civil Law (Wrongs) Amendment Bill 2005 (No 2) (ACT): 365
Civil Unions Act 2006 (ACT): 368
Human Rights Act 2004 (ACT): 70, 77, 361, 362, 363, 365, 366, 367, 368, 369, 370, 371, 372, 373, 374, 375, 376
Human Rights Amendment Act 2008 (ACT): 361
Parentage Bill 2003 (ACT): 368
Sexuality Discrimination Legislation Amendment Bill 2003 (ACT): 368
Terrorism (Extraordinary Temporary Powers) Act 2006 (ACT): 96, 179, 184, 363, 373
Terrorism (Extraordinary Temporary Powers) Bill 2006 (ACT): 371, 373
Terrorism (Preventative Detention) Bill 2006 (ACT): 373

## New South Wales
Bail Act 1978 (NSW)
  s 8A: 97
Crimes (Administration of Sentences) Regulation 2001 (NSW)
  cl 22: 97, 98, 290
Law Enforcement (Powers and Responsibilities) Act 2002 (NSW): 75
  s 87B: 75
  s 87C: 75
  s 87D: 75
  s 87E: 75
  s 87I: 75
  s 87J: 75
  s 87K: 75
  s 87L: 75

s 87M: 75
s 87N: 75
Law Enforcement Legislation Amendment (Public Safety) Act 2005 (NSW): 75, 76
Terrorism (Police Powers) Act 2002 (NSW): 79, 96

Pt 3: 96

Terrorism (Police Powers) Amendment (Preventative Detention) Act 2005 (NSW): 373, 374

## Northern Territory
Terrorism (Emergency Powers) Act 2003 (NT): 96

## Queensland
Terrorism (Preventative Detention) Act 2005 (Qld): 96

## South Australia
Terrorism (Preventative Detention) Act 2005 (SA): 96

## Tasmania
Terrorism (Preventative Detention) Act 2005 (Tas): 96

## Victoria
Terrorism (Community Protection) Act 2003 (Vic): 96

Charter of Human Rights and Responsibilities Act 2006 (Vic): 70

## Western Australia
Terrorism (Preventative Detention) Act 2005 (WA): 96

## CANADA
Anti-Terrorism Act SC 2001 (Can): 50, 51, 52, 57

The Constitution Act 1982, being Schedule B to the Canada Act 1982 (UK): 52, 54

Public Safety Act SC 2001 (Can): 50

## FIJI
Reconciliation, Tolerance and Unity Bill 2005 (Fiji): 198

## UNITED KINGDOM
Anti-Terrorism, Crime and Security Act 2001 (UK): 119, 173, 334, 336, 337, 353

Pt 4: 334, 335, 336
s 21: 119
s 23: 119, 120, 121, 122, 123, 124

Criminal Justice Act 2003 (UK): 177

s 306: 346

Human Rights Act 1998 (UK): 70, 119, 120, 173, 330, 340, 354, 356, 359, 360, 361

s 4: 173, 335

Immigration Act 1971 (UK): 339

Northern Ireland (Emergency Provisions) Acts 1973–96 (UK): 331-332

Prevention of Terrorism Act 2005 (UK): 173, 336, 341, 353

Ch 2: 173

Prevention of Terrorism Bill 2005 (UK): 336

Prevention of Terrorism (Temporary Provisions) Act 1974 (UK): 332, 334

s 2(1)(a): 336

Prevention of Violence (Temporary Provisions) Act 1939 (UK): 332

Special Immigration Appeals Commission Act 1997 (UK): 336

Terrorism Act 2000 (UK): 74, 177, 334, 345, 349, 353

s 1: 344
s 1(4)(a): 345
s 40: 177
s 41: 177
s 44: 345
s 57: 346
Sched 8: 177

Terrorism Act 2006 (UK): 345, 353, 354

s 1: 346
s 5: 346
s 23: 177
s 24: 177

## UNITED STATES OF AMERICA
Detainee Treatment Act 2005 (USA): 162

Military Commissions Act 2006 (USA): 162

Uniting and Strengthening America by Providing Appropriate Tools Required to Intercept and Obstruct Terrorism Act of 2001 (USA PATRIOT Act) Public Law No 107-56, 115 Stat 272 (2001): 52

# Table of International Instruments

Canadian Charter of Rights and Freedoms 1982: 52, 54, 55, 56, 57, 58, 59

Convention Against Torture and Other Cruel, Inhuman or Degrading Treatment or Punishment 1984: 33, 138, 147, 168

Convention Based on Article K.3 of the Treaty on European Union, on the Establishment of a European Police Office (Europol Convention) 2003: 222

Convention between the Kingdom of Belgium, the Federal Republic of Germany, the Kingdom of Spain, the French Republic, the Grand Duchy of Luxembourg, the Kingdom of the Netherlands and the Republic of Austria (Prüm Convention (Schengen III)) 2007: 218

Convention for the Creation of an International Criminal Court 1937: 201

Convention on the Rights of the Child 1989: 143, 149

Convention Relating to the Status of Refugees 1951: 176, 181, 317

Convention Relative to the Treatment of Prisoners of War (Geneva Convention III) 1950: 145, 161, 164, 171

European Convention for the Protection of Human Rights and Fundamental Freedoms 1950: 69, 70, 71, 111, 112, 113, 114, 116, 117, 118, 119, 120, 121, 123, 153, 236, 238, 246, 247, 249, 250, 251, 253, 255, 256, 257, 259, 260, 262, 265, 268, 330, 333, 334, 335, 336, 338, 339, 341, 342, 344, 346, 353, 354, 356, 357, 359, 360

European Union Charter of Fundamental Rights 2000: 231, 233, 246

Geneva Convention Relative to the Protection of Civilian Persons in Time of War (Geneva Convention IV) 1950: 145, 164

International Covenant on Civil and Political Rights 1966: 38, 69, 81, 111, 112, 113, 116, 117, 118, 119, 123, 138, 144, 145, 147, 148, 149, 160, 163, 164, 165, 166, 168, 169, 174, 180, 181, 182, 183, 255, 256, 361, 369, 371

La Gomera Declaration 2002: 212

Peace Agreement between the Government of Sierra Leone and the Revolutionary United Front of Sierra Leone 1999: 193

Rome Statute of the International Criminal Court 1998: 191, 202, 203, 204, 205

Treaty Establishing the European Community 1957: 210, 226, 228, 231

Treaty of Amsterdam amending the Treaty on European Union, the Treaties establishing the European Communities and certain related acts 1997: 206, 226

Treaty on European Union 1992 (Maastricht Treaty): 209, 210, 215, 226, 227, 228, 229, 233, 240, 241, 245, 246, 262, 267

United Nations Charter 1945: 131, 192, 202, 235, 239, 248, 249, 255, 260

Universal Declaration of Human Rights 1966: 140, 145, 184

Vienna Convention on the Law of Treaties 1969: 166, 170, 172

# Chapter One

# Introduction: Letters from the Front

Miriam Gani[*] and Penelope Mathew[**]

On 20 September 2001, in an address to a Joint Session of Congress and the American people, President George W Bush declared a 'war on terror'.[1] He did so, of course, in the immediate aftermath of the events of 9/11, when the United States and most of the world was reeling with shock and horror.

That address still reverberates for more reasons than the famous declaration of war. It was here that President Bush both characterised the parties to the 'war' and set the parameters of the combat:

> Our response involves far more than instant retaliation and isolated strikes. Americans should not expect one battle, but a lengthy campaign, unlike any other we have ever seen. It may include dramatic strikes, visible on TV, and covert operations, secret even in success. We will starve terrorists of funding, turn them one against another, drive them from place to place, until there is no refuge or no rest. And we will pursue nations that provide aid or safe haven to terrorism. Every nation, in every region, now has a decision to make. Either you are with us, or you are with the terrorists … From this day forward, any nation that continues to harbor or support terrorism will be regarded by the United States as a hostile regime.

The concept of the 'war on terror' — a war between the white hats, the harried victims of aggression and the black hats, ideological extremists who threaten our democratic way of life — has proven to be both an attractive and a potent rhetorical device. It has been adopted and elaborated upon by political leaders around the world, particularly in the context of military action in Afghanistan and Iraq. As President Bush's ally, former British Prime Minister Tony Blair stated in a television interview on 16 September 2001: 'the fact is that we are at

---

[*] Senior Lecturer in Law, ANU College of Law, The Australian National University, Canberra, Australia.
[**] Reader in Law, ANU College of Law, The Australian National University, Canberra, Australia. Human Rights Legal and Policy Adviser, Human Rights Commission (Australian Capital Territory). From August 2008, Visiting Professor and Interim Director, Program in Refugee and Asylum Law, University of Michigan, Ann Arbor, USA.
[1] The full text of the speech is available at <http://www.whitehouse.gov/news/releases/2001/09/20010920-8.html>.

war with terrorism ... it is a war, if you like, between the civilised world and fanaticism'.[2]

But use of the rhetoric has not been confined to the military context. The 'war on terror' is a domestic one, also, and the phrase has been used to account for broad criminal legislation, sweeping agency powers and potential human rights abuses throughout much of the world. Just as George W Bush declared, in his address that: '[w]e will take defensive measures against terrorism to protect Americans,' so too the 'fight against terrorism'[3] was invoked to justify a 'swift and firm'[4] legislative response to the perceived threat by the previous Australian federal Government. In the domestic 'war on terror', the competing needs of highly effective anti-terrorism laws and protection of human rights are conceived as a balancing act, with the metaphor of war and the state of emergency it engenders allowing the scales to be tipped in favour of laws that would be seen as overbroad in less turbulent times. So, whilst it is acknowledged that 'it is critical that our efforts do not come at the expense of our basic human rights'[5] nevertheless, the law must be used 'to its fullest effect'.[6]

Just as the 'war on terror' pervades the modern consciousness, so too, the academic landscape is littered with reflections upon the latest iteration of the phenomenon of terrorism. This collection of essays, however, seeks to bring fresh perspectives to the 'war on terror'.

The contributors to this book first came together as a group of experts from Australia, Canada, the United Kingdom, France and Germany at a workshop entitled 'Ensuring Accountability: Terrorist Challenges and State Responses in a Free Society' held at the Australian National University in Canberra in April 2006. (Readers should note that the law in the book is current up to June 2007.) The workshop was organised as part of a research project, 'Terrorism and the Non-State Actor After September 11: The Role of Law in the Search for Security' funded by the Australian Research Council.[7] The aim of the workshop was to bring together scholars researching and writing about terrorism from a variety of disciplinary perspectives including international law and international relations, public and constitutional law, criminal law and criminology, legal theory, and psychology and law.

Academics do not write from the front-line of the 'war against terror'. Rather they seek to write about it from a more detached and reflective point of view,

---

[2] This statement is quoted and discussed in C McInnes, 'A Different Kind of War? September 11 and the United States' Afghan War' (2003) 29 *Review of International Studies* 165, 171.
[3] P Ruddock, Federal Attorney-General, 'International and Public Law Challenges for the Attorney-General' (Speech delivered 8 June 2004, at the ANU, Canberra) [7].
[4] Ibid [51].
[5] Ibid [79].
[6] Ibid [57].
[7] ARC Discovery Project DP0451473.

acknowledging that writing about what Australian war correspondent Charles Bean called the 'bare and uncoloured story'[8] requires many perspectives and is particularly elusive when the use of the very term 'war' is largely hyperbole. This collection seeks both to draw on and to engage critically with the metaphor of war in the context of terrorism. It does so by breaking the concept down into what could be seen as distinct phases or concerns of conflict.

In Part One, entitled 'Identifying the Threat and Choosing the Weapons', the three authors address topics as diverse and provocative as the British experience of Islam and the politics of terrorism (John Strawson); a critique of the proponents of torture as a weapon in the 'war on terror' (Desmond Manderson); and a critical perspective on the utility of rights language in countering the excesses of counter-terrorism laws (Wesley Pue). Each of these chapters seeks to make a point that is often overlooked in the mainstream debates about terrorism. Strawson's chapter concerns the construction of a monolithic 'Islam' by outsiders and insiders that leads to Islam's conflation with terrorism. He discusses ways of stimulating more inclusive and sophisticated conversations within and about the many forms of Islam. Manderson defends the prohibition on torture against those who argue that torture is a necessary and moral tool in the fight against terrorism. He attacks the hypothetical presented by proponents of torture in the name of counter-terrorism, which assumes that intelligence that saves lives will result, and reasserts the need to regard torture as an unthinkable, insupportable practice. Finally, Pue runs against the grain of most contemporary arguments concerning counter-terrorism, and, indeed, much of this volume, by looking at the limitations of legislated rights in preserving freedom. He argues, using the example of Canada, that bills of rights can be co-opted in support of draconian counter-terrorism measures. All three of these chapters therefore zero in on language and ideas, rather than the power of force or violence, as being at the core of terrorism and responses to it.

Part Two, 'Preparing the Ground: Balance, Proportionality, and Public Perceptions', contains three chapters that examine common perceptions of terrorism and efforts to combat it. Simon Bronitt critiques the common motif that liberty must be 'balanced' against security. He demonstrates that there is no 'balance': rather, liberties are lost in a chimerical pursuit of security. Christopher Michaelsen turns our attention to whether the courts, particularly domestic courts, should limit themselves to examining the 'proportionality' of counter-terrorist measures in human rights terms without taking on the role of judging the seriousness of the threat to which the measures seek to respond. He exposes the logical gap left by the courts that the political arms of government are then free to exploit when the courts stop short of examining the seriousness

---

[8] Charles Bean, quoted in K S Ingles, 'Bean, Charles Edwin Woodrow (1879-1968)', *Australian Dictionary of Biography vol 7* (1979) 227.

of the 'terrorist threat'. Mark Nolan's chapter presents data obtained through an empirical study of lay perceptions of terrorism and legislative responses to it. He demonstrates that the seriousness of particular actions are coloured by the perception that the action has a terrorist 'motive.' All three chapters assist in explaining why there is such a strong tendency to knee-jerk reactions in counter-terrorism.

Part Three is entitled 'Rules of Engagement: Beyond the Limits of the Law'. The chapters collected in this Part deal with the complex relationships between law and politics set in motion by counter-terrorist measures. Andrew Byrnes examines ways in which law may be enlisted in, or excluded from, responses to terrorism, and the capacity of human rights law and institutions to resist both co-option and irrelevance. Penelope Mathew's chapter takes a detailed look at so-called preventative detention in three jurisdictions. She provides a case study of Byrnes' themes, exploring the ways in which detention is justified as beyond the law, an exception to the law or as permitted by the law. Finally, Ben Saul discusses the complexities of one political solution to terrorism — the amnesty.

Part Four of the book, 'Reports from Two Theatres of War: Legislation, Sanctions and Prosecutions in Europe and Australia' incorporates chapters examining: the response to terrorism of the European Union as a collective actor (Jörg Monar); the role of the European Court of Human Rights in protection of human rights when dealing with sanctions imposed by the political organs of the European Union (Gabriele Porretto); the complexities of Australian terrorism offences as they have emerged through the handful of terrorist prosecutions in Australia (Miriam Gani); and the shifting border between crime and politics exemplified by executive proscription of terrorist organisations in that country (Russell Hogg).

Finally, Part Five, 'Calling a Halt: the Role of Bills of Rights' brings together two chapters that analyse the role of human rights protection in the United Kingdom and the Australian Capital Territory (Colm O'Cinneide, and Andrew Byrnes and Gabrielle McKinnon respectively). These two chapters provide evidence that bills of rights can be useful tools to mitigate the harms of counter-terrorist measures. They provide a counterpoint to the earlier chapter by Pue.

Throughout the book, major themes emerge: the precipitous and reflexive passage of anti-terrorism laws in the wake of 9/11 in multiple jurisdictions; the over-breadth, over-severity and over-inclusiveness of the resulting laws; the inexorable legislation-creep as temporary measures become permanent and the political pressure to be hard on terror leads to more and more law; the real nature of the threat, its psychology and the role of the structures of government both in assessing and responding to it; the role of rhetoric and hypotheticals; the dangers inherent in human rights discourse and the very real possibility of radicalisation of targeted communities.

These common themes unite the chapters of the book, but each chapter has something different and important to say. The publication of them as an e-book is designed to allow readers to choose to read any particular chapter that interests them, or, alternatively, to engage with the volume as a whole.

# PART ONE

Identifying the Threat and Choosing the Weapons

# Chapter Two

# Islam and the Politics of Terrorism: Aspects of the British Experience

## John Strawson[*]

## Introduction

The debate about the relationship between Islam and terrorism is at a critical stage. While crass Orientalist arguments[1] that Islam is essentially violent have been largely removed from the agenda, the attempt to construct a distinction between moderate and extremist Islam has been revealed as overly simplistic. Since 11 September 2001 (9/11) most governments have attempted to distinguish between Islam as a religion practised by millions and the tiny minority of Muslims who subscribe to an interpretation of Islam that authorises the use of violence against its enemies.[2] However, this approach fails to engage with the complexities of Islam as a social category, which has a long and varied history.

Moreover, Islamic history is one of disputation. There is not one Islamic category, but many 'Islams'. As a result there are trends within Islam that have an ambiguous relationship to violence and offer justifications for its use or even extol it. There is in fact an intense conflict within Islamic discourse over the issue, which since the late nineteenth century has been connected to the position of Muslims in a world that has been perceived to be dominated by colonialism and since 1945 increasingly by the 'West'. In this discourse Muslims as a community are portrayed as marginalised and humiliated by a materialist powerful West.[3] In this chapter I want to suggest that making the distinction between Islam and terrorism requires an active engagement in an ideological battle rather than a passive identification of a neat sociological distinction between moderates and extremists. There is a genuine terrorist threat and it is nourished by an international political current, which while it has roots in Islam, is aggressively opposed to the great contribution of Muslim civilisation to law,

---

[*] Reader in Law, School of Law, University of East London, London UK. I would like to thank the editors for their most helpful comments on this chapter.
[1] On Orientalism generally see E W Said, *Orientalism: Western Conceptions of the Orient* (London: Routledge and Kegan Paul, 1978).
[2] See J Strawson, 'Islamic Law and the English Press', in J Strawson (ed), *Law after Ground Zero* (London: Routledge-Cavendish, 2002) 205-14.
[3] See, eg, T Honderich, *Humanity, Terrorism, Terrorist War: Palestine, 9/11, 7/7* (London, New York: Continuum Books, 2006).

philosophy and the arts. Its strategy to acquire legitimacy is based thus not on the defence of this rich Islamic heritage but through an essentialist campaign against 'the West', which is portrayed as anti-Muslim. The challenge, I will argue, is to engage in an ethical political campaign that eschews the West's past stereotypes of Muslims and Islam and yet offers a robust alternative to the legitimisation of violence. Policy-makers in Britain, however, have constructed a model of the issue that is highly problematic.

## The British Government's Approach

My starting point is the British Government's attempts to grapple with the issue. The British Government's approach to the issue of terrorism 'in the name of Islam' has been the attempt to make a distinction between 'Islamist terrorism' and the mainstream Islam of the 'Muslim communities'. This position is well summed up in one of the opening paragraphs of a document tabled in Parliament by the then Prime Minister, Tony Blair, in July 2006, *Countering International Terrorism: The United Kingdom's Strategy*:

> The principal current terrorist threat is from radicalized individuals who are using a distorted and unrepresentative version of Islam to justify violence. Such people are referred to in this paper as Islamist terrorists. They are, however, a tiny minority within the Muslim communities here and abroad. Muslim communities themselves do not threaten our security; indeed they make a great contribution to our country. The Government is therefore working in partnership with Muslim communities to help them prevent extremists from gaining influence here.[4]

In this account there is a clear distinction between 'Muslim communities here and abroad' and 'a tiny minority' who 'are using a distorted and unrepresentative version of Islam to justify violence'. The slippage between the 'radicalized individuals' to the 'tiny minority' perhaps hints at the difficulty of deciding what the critical test of 'a distorted and unrepresentative version of Islam' actually is. In this and other related government documents there appears to be a view that individuals in the Muslim community are in danger of being won over to this form of Islam. If this is so then we must assume that there is a distinct form of Islam that already exists, and indeed the text of the strategy document names the threat as emanating from 'Islamist terrorists'.[5] This term is explained in a footnote in rather problematic terms:

---

[4] HM Government, *Countering International Terrorism: The United Kingdom's Strategy* (July 2006), com 6888, 1 <http://www.intelligence.gov.uk/upload/assets/www.intelligence.gov.uk/countering.pdf>.
[5] Ibid [25].

> The majority of groups usually referred to as Islamists are not terrorists. Islamism is a term with no universally agreed definition, but which is usually used to suggest that a particular group or movement is seeking to build political structures it deems Islamic.[6]

This definition is rather confused as it conflates movements that regard Islamic political structures as a necessary condition for the practice of Islam with those who advocate models of Islamic governance as a possible choice. However, Islamism is useful in identifying a form of political Islam that is categorical, makes no distinction between politics and religion, regards Islam as a complete, unchangeable and finished system and is usually associated with authoritarianism.[7] The choice of Islamism as a way of describing such movements was on the whole adopted by scholars to avoid the misleading description of 'fundamentalism', which became common in the media following the Iranian Revolution in 1979.

The Government is also keen to stress the assumption that there is a genuine, undistorted and representative form of Islam, which can be identified and used as a counterweight to the Islamist version. This approach in my view produces a confused and contradictory policy towards the 'Muslim communities'. I will argue that the Government's binary division between an assumed genuine Islam and a distorted version is flawed.

In the same year *Countering Islamic Terrorism* was produced, the Department of Education and Skills published a government guidance document entitled *Promoting Good Campus Relations*, which is aimed at helping administrators of universities and colleges engage with Muslim students. The document seeks to help Higher Education Administrators (working with 'the vast majority of students on campus') to isolate and challenge what it calls 'violent extremism'.

> Unacceptable extremism can range from incitement of social, racial or religious hatred, to advocating the use of violence to achieve fundamental change to the constitutional structure of the UK, to carrying out terrorist acts. Individuals can and do hold extreme views without espousing violence. The authorities are concerned with any form of extremism that espouses, promotes or leads to violence: 'violent extremism'.[8]

The document then explains that 'violent extremist activity in the name of Islam is justified by using a literal, distorted and unrepresentative interpretation of Islamic texts to advocate and justify violence in order to achieve fundamental

---

[6] Ibid 6.
[7] See generally, F Halliday, *Islam and the Myth of Confrontation: Religion and Politics in the Middle East* (London, New York: I B Tauris, 1996) especially 110-12.
[8] Department for Education and Skills (UK), *Promoting Good Campus Relations: Working with Staff and Students to Build Community Cohesion and Tackle Violent Extremism in the Name of Islam at Universities and Colleges* (2006) 6 <http://www.dfes.gov.uk/pns/pnattach/20060170/1.txt>.

change in society'.⁹ This view is further emphasised by adding that a 'clear distinction should be made between these extremist individuals and the faith that they might claim to be associated with or represent ... Moreover propagating false perceptions about the values and beliefs of Islam potentially adds to a vicious circle that may fuel discrimination and Islamophobia'.¹⁰ Such statements reinforce the view expressed in *Countering International Terrorism* that terrorist danger arises from those who propagate 'false perceptions' of Islam, which are to be regarded as 'distorted and unrepresentative'. In this narrative the character of the distortion of Islam is identified as 'a literal' interpretation. Again the character of the terrorist threat is named as 'Islamist terrorism'.¹¹

The document then outlines the way in which the Government thinks that such ideas spread in universities. It suggests that there are several catalysts that individually, or in combination, can be responsible for propelling individuals towards violent extremism. Amongst these it cites:

> the development of a sense of grievance and injustice; a negative and partial interpretation of history and recent events and of the perceived policies of 'the West'; a sense of personal alienation or community disadvantage arising from socio-economic factors such as discrimination, social exclusion and lack of opportunity; and exposure to extremist ideas, whether from the internet, peers or a forceful and inspiring figure already committed to extremism.¹²

These factors, it is suggested, create a pool of individuals who will attract the attention of existing extremists who will then, in the terms of the document, 'groom' individuals into their agenda. Universities and colleges, it is said, provide environments in which extremist individuals can develop networks through student societies and the like. This pool of potential extremists is composed, according to this view, of both those who are just interested in exploring their faith and those who actively seek extremist views. In either case the involvement of such students in faith-based societies or attendance at Friday prayers can expose them to recruiters who might be 'charismatic radical speakers', or whose 'scholarly background' might be 'emphasized in order to give them greater credibility in the eyes of students'.¹³ There is concern that through these societies and religious activities students might be subject to peer pressure and bullying as those 'who have a differing viewpoint can be afraid to speak and differentiate themselves from the majority'.¹⁴ The sudden turn from individual recruiters peddling a 'literal, distorted and unrepresentative interpretation of Islamic texts'

---

⁹ Ibid.
¹⁰ Ibid.
¹¹ Ibid [2(4)].
¹² Ibid 7.
¹³ Ibid 8.
¹⁴ Ibid 9.

to a majority within a given student society is not explained. Nevertheless, according to the process described in the document, the views have become representative at least of this group, which will now attempt to pressure the individual into accepting the majority view. This scenario is in reality quite likely, as the many Islamic societies may well be within the orbit of one variant or other of political Islam or indeed Islamist groups. Unfortunately, instead of tackling this sensitive issue, the document falls back on pathology. In this account the individual is constructed as prey to be seized by the clever extremist. The student is seen as an individual at risk from infection. Extremism is a virus that appears to be capable of being passed from one individual to another. The remedy is to break the cycle of infection. University administrators must therefore vet literature on the campus, note speakers being invited to meetings and consider inappropriate use of the internet.[15] Strangely, university administrators are directed to these technical issues rather than to the more complex task of how to deal with an influential political movement, which while not necessarily in itself violent, may have an ambivalent attitude to violence in some circumstances.

## Islamism's Place in Political Islam and its Relationship to Violence

The implication of the regular references to 'Islamist terrorism' in the Government literature is simply not thought through. Islamism is a form of political Islam that is a well-established and growing trend both within Muslim communities in Europe and particularly in the Islamic world. Political Islam comes in many strains and certainly not all are marked by an attachment to violence.[16] As we have noted, the term 'Islamism' has been used especially since the early 1990s to identify movements that are based on an assumption that Islam has a predominant political mission. The essence of such movements is their view that the ability to practise Islam fully as a religion is dependent upon the ability to create an Islamic political system. Western political systems, as well as the current political systems in the Muslim world, are seen as obstacles to this. Some variants of Islamism, such as the Muslim Brotherhood, which is powerful in the Middle East, and of which the Palestinian Hamas is a component, do subscribe to violence as a method of establishing their aims. In the Middle East, Islamist parties have had great success at the polls in the recent past, as evidenced by elections in Palestine, Egypt and Bahrain. This prominence gives supporters of the Islamist movement in Europe a high degree of legitimacy. The Muslim Brotherhood works within Mosques and is well represented in Britain through the Muslim Association of Britain, which is a component of the Muslim Council of Britain,

---

[15] Ibid 9-10.
[16] On political Islam see G Kepel, *Jihad, The Trail of Political Islam* (London: I B Tauris, 2006). For a fascinating account of contemporary political Islam in Egypt see R W Baker, *Islam Without Fear: Egypt and the New Islamists* (Cambridge Massachusetts, London: Harvard University Press, 2003) esp 165-211.

a group often seen by the Government as representative of the Muslim communities. This is not to say that the Muslim Brotherhood in Britain supports terrorism within the country. However, its support for terrorism in the Middle East, in particular against Israel, does show that there is a great blurring at the boundaries of where 'violent extremism' begins and ends.

An example of this problem is Sheikh Yusef Al-Qaradawi, who is associated with the Muslim Brotherhood. Is he a moderate because he condemns terrorism in Britain or an extremist because he supports it against Israel? In July 2004, Al-Qaradawi was asked on the BBC why he supported suicide bombings in Israel. His answers were instructive:

> It's not suicide, it's martyrdom in the name of God, Islamic theologians and jurisprudents have debated this issue. Referring to it as a form of jihad, under the title of jeopardizing the life of the mujahideen. It is allowed to jeopardize your soul and cross the path of the enemy and be killed.[17]

The enemy in the case of Israelis can be civilians as he explains in a highly gendered statement, 'Israeli women are not like women in our society because Israeli women are militarized'. As a result he continues, 'I regard this type of martyrdom operation as justice of Allah almighty. Allah is just. Through his infinite wisdom he has given the weak what the strong do not possess and that is the ability to turn their bodies into bombs like the Palestinians do.'[18] Al-Qaradawi has a major influence on Muslims through his teachings, which are broadcast through his web site (*Islamonline*), and his regular television program on Al Jazeera, 'Law and Life'. He has been regarded by many as a moderate and has shared platforms with many Western politicians including former United States President Bill Clinton and the former Mayor of London Ken Livingstone. The latter has made an extensive defence both of Al-Qaradawi and of his own association with him. At the time of the BBC interview, Al-Qaradawi appeared at a London conference organised by the Mayor and when objections were made to his presence due to his position on suicide bombing, Livingstone's defence was posed in these terms:

> Like many people in the Middle East, he is a strong supporter of the rights of the Palestinians. He takes the view that in the specific circumstances of that conflict that, where Israel is using modern missiles, tanks and planes in civilian areas to perpetrate the illegal occupation of Palestinian lands, it is justified for Palestinians to turn their bodies into weapons.[19]

---

[17] BBC News, 'Al-Qaradawi Full Transcript', *Newsnight*, 7 July 2004.
[18] Ibid.
[19] Mayor of London, *Why the Mayor of London will Maintain Dialogue with all London's Faiths and Communities: A Reply to the Dossier Against the Mayor's Meeting with Dr Yusuf Al Qaradawi* (London: Greater London Authority, 2005) 3.

This statement from the Mayor of London, while not constituting approval of the position of Al-Qaradawi, as he later makes clear, nonetheless presents a rather neutral rendering of it. As Livingstone explains his own position, he appears to equate suicide bombings with the military policy of Israel: 'it would be impossible to refuse to speak to a person like Dr Al-Qaradawi who has no personal involvement in violence of any kind, but at the same time speak to an Israeli Government, which kills Palestinian civilians with modern weapons every week'.[20] Despite Livingstone's disavowal in the same interview of violence in the Palestinian-Israeli conflict ('I condemn violence in Israel and Palestine'), the Mayor is rather gentle with Al-Qaradawi's position. Thus, support for suicide bombings in the Israeli-Palestinian conflict is constructed as just one opinion amongst others. As such, Livingstone appears to legitimise it as a policy choice. This policy choice if applied to Britain would no doubt come under the Government's view of 'violent extremism'.

Al-Qaradawi's support for suicide bombing as a legitimate tactic against Israel is not an isolated position but is commonly held amongst many segments of political Islam. It is a position that has its roots in the methodology of a political movement that is founded on the distinction between Muslims and Non-Muslims, as well as the distinction between full Muslims and failed Muslims. The prominent leader of the Muslim Brotherhood, Sayyid Qutb, sought to create a Muslim vanguard that would overcome the false Muslims and offer new leadership to Non-Muslims.[21] Central to his argument is the use of the concept of *Jahilliyyah*, which originally referred to the period of ignorance before the Prophet's mission in the seventh century. Qutb adapts this concept to the contemporary period: in this account the leadership of the Muslim world, both political and religious, is in the state of *Jahilliyyah*. As a result the Muslim community is

> buried under the debris of the man-made traditions of several generations, and ... crushed under the weight of those false laws and customs which are not remotely related to the Islamic teachings and, which in spite of all this, calls itself the 'world of Islam'.[22]

Qutb contrasts the state of the Muslim world with

> the era during which Europe's genius created its marvelous works in science culture, law and material production, due to which mankind has progressed to great heights of creativity and material comfort. It is not easy to find fault with

---

[20] Ibid.
[21] See D Cook, *Understanding Jihad* (Berkley, Los Angeles, London: University of California Press, 2005) 102-6.
[22] S Qutb, *Milestones* (Dehli: Markazi Maktaba Islami, first published 1964, 1991 ed) 11-12.

the inventors of such marvelous things, especially since what we call the 'world of Islam' is devoid of all this beauty.[23]

However, while material issues are not unimportant, Muslims must 'have something to offer besides material progress' and this 'faith and a way of life must take concrete form in human society — in other words, in a Muslim society'.[24] The main obstacle to achieving this is that the 'whole world is steeped in *Jahilliyyah*'.[25] Qutb explains his very modernist use of the term. First, according to this view, it takes the form of a 'rebellion against God's sovereignty on earth'.[26] Second, 'it is now not, in that simple and primitive form of the ancient *Jahillyyah*, but takes the form of claiming the right to create values to legislate rules of collective behaviour, and to choose any way of life rests with men, without any regard to what God has prescribed'.[27] He regards both capitalism and communism as being similar in emphasising the priority of mankind over God. The task of Muslims is to aim for international leadership to liberate humanity from this secular materialism through a revival of Islam. A revival of a genuine Muslim society can become a model for the whole world. As all Muslim countries have been infected by *Jahilliyyah* the central task is to remove the corrupt leaderships.

To prove this point, Qutb contrasts the actions of politicians of his day with the practices of the Prophet, as developed during his leadership in Medina and then in Mecca (622-632 AD). It is at this point in the seventh century that Qutb constructs the pure Islamic society and it is to this pure moment that Muslims need to return. The means of doing this is Jihad, which is seen as both a religious and a military struggle. Nor does he see the use of Jihad as confined to defensive action, as 'this diminishes the greatness of the Islamic way of life'.[28] Rather Jihad 'is a means of establishing the Divine Authority'.[29] Initially this will be within a Muslim country that then becomes the 'headquarters for the movement for Islam',[30] which can in turn be the springboard to bring Islamic rule to the rest of the world. Qutb emphasises that Islam uses force to remove all the barriers to the creation of a Muslim society. The '*Jahili*' leadership is such a barrier and exists in both Muslim and non-Muslim countries. The aim is to create a society in which individuals will be 'free from the servitude to men and have gathered together under the servitude of God and to follow only the Shari'ah of God'.[31]

---
[23] Ibid 12.
[24] Ibid.
[25] Ibid.
[26] Ibid 15.
[27] Ibid.
[28] Ibid 130.
[29] Ibid 131.
[30] Ibid.
[31] Ibid 135-36.

This is a universal struggle in which national and ethnic differences are to be disregarded.

Qutb's approach is a program for an international political Islam, the purpose of which is the creation of a universal Islamic political system. Violence can be justified. Indeed it is an indispensable means to the achievement of such a system.

The Muslim Brotherhood was founded in Egypt in 1928, and although it was banned there, through its front organisations it is a powerful opposition in society and in the National Assembly. It also received a boost when its Palestinian affiliate, Hamas, won the Palestinian election in 2006.[32] It has branches in most Arab countries. It has an influence amongst Muslims throughout the world. Al-Qaradawi is not therefore simply an individual of some prominence within the Muslim world but rather part of a political movement that, like all other political movements, vies for support and attempts to create organisations.

## Islamist Politics and 'The West'

Islamist politics are not, however, reducible to the Muslim Brotherhood, but are varied and heterogeneous. In South Asia, movements inspired by the late Sayyid Abdul Ala Mawdudi,[33] who founded the Jamaat-e-Islami in colonial India in 1941, have had great influence. Mawdudi advocated an Islamic state based on Islamic law. His views are very similar to Qutb's and the two are often thought of as the founders of modern political Islam. The Jamaat is a powerful political force in Pakistan and has branches in India, Bangladesh and Afghanistan. Organisations that support these views are also active in Britain and have a dominant presence in many Mosques. The Jamaat has gained its influence through working through a variety of organisations in Britain, including the United Kingdom Islamic Missions, Dawatul Islam, the Young Muslims Organisation and the Islamic Forum Europe. Saudi Arabia's Wahabi movement has also created an international network of organisations that espouse the *salafi* (or purist) form of Islam — a current that also has a strong political element. Among organisations working in Britain in support of the Wahabi movement are the Muslim World League and the World Assembly of Muslim Youth. The success of the Islamic revolution in Iran has been a springboard for the development of political Islam amongst *shi'a*. The most prominent organisation that supports a version of the politics associated with Khomeini is the Islamic Human Rights Commission. In addition there are many other smaller organisations such as Hizb-ut-Tahrir (Party of Liberation), which is organised on an international basis and projects a united Islam under a restored Caliphate.[34]

---

[32] On Hamas see S Mishal and A Sela, *The Palestinian Hamas: Vision, Violence and Coexistence* (New York: Columbia University Press, 2006).
[33] 1903-1979.
[34] The Caliph was the combined religious and political leader that replaced the Prophet. In Islamic history there has rarely been agreement on one center of authority, nonetheless the Ottoman Empire

Hizb-ut-Tahrir's organisation has much in common with far-left methods of party building; it is highly disciplined, revolves around frenetic levels of activity and holds out the prospect of an imminent breakthrough in one Muslim country or another.[35] It is very active amongst students and offers not only a political vision but also a way of life, as members spend most of their time with each other. The organisation is careful to make public statements against violence in Britain, but it has been suggested that its radical ideology can provide a conveyor belt to violent activities, which is the reason that the British Government was considering banning the organisation.[36]

The Islamist insistence that Islamic religious values can only be safeguarded within an Islamic state of some sort is accompanied with an attack on democracy. This view is based on two levels of critique. The first is that democracy represents the rule by human beings and this is counter-posed to God's rule. The second attempts to appeal to contemporary political discourses and concentrates on flaws in democracy, particularly with democracy as practised by Western states, including their human rights records. The main critique of democracy and human rights is linked to an analysis of colonialism and current Western international relations.[37] In this account, democracy and human rights are sham products of the West as evidenced by centuries of colonialism and all its attendant evils.[38] It is certainly the case that the excessive claims within the West to the patrimony of democracy and human rights with deep roots in the West's history, is highly problematic.[39] It is also the case that much of the Muslim world did experience European colonialism. However, this was not true of Iran or of most of the Ottoman Empire.[40] Nevertheless, under this account, the history of subordination to Western interests in the colonial period becomes entangled with current Western policy in the Muslim world. The tendency is to construct Muslims as continuing victims of Western intrigue. The West's responsibilities are not limited to direct interventions such as in Afghanistan and Iraq, but also for the bolstering of authoritarian regimes in Egypt and Pakistan. The international failure to solve long-running conflicts, such as in Kashmir and the

---

maintained the Caliphate as a feature of its rule. The office was abolished in 1924 when the Ottoman Empire was dismantled in its entirety with the formation of the secular Republic of Turkey under Mustafa Kemal.

[35] For an account of the organisation from the inside see E Husain, *The Islamist: Why I Joined Radical Islam in Britain, What I Saw Inside and Why I Left* (London: Penguin Books, 2007).

[36] According to reports, the police opposed the idea of a ban, as it would merely drive the organisation underground.

[37] See K Dalacoura, *Islam, Liberalism and Human Rights* (London, New York: I B Tauris, 2003) esp 65-8.

[38] See A S Moussalli, *The Islamic Quest for Democracy, Pluralism and Human Rights* (Gainesville: University Press of Florida, 2001) 1-28.

[39] See J Strawson, 'A Western Question to the Middle East: Is There a Human Rights Discourse in Islam?' (1997) 1 *Arab Studies Quarterly* 10, 31-58.

[40] The European powers arrived late in this part of the world with the British Occupation of Egypt in 1882, and then after the First World War with the British and French Mandates for Palestine (and Jordan), Iraq, Syria and Lebanon.

Israeli-Palestinian conflict, are offered as evidence of the Western complicity in Muslim suffering. Western interventions on the side of Muslims such as in Bosnia or Kosovo are either edited out of this account or seen as even more suspicious. Equally, states within the Muslim world that are occupiers, such as Turkey in Cyprus or Morocco in Western Sahara, are passed over. The humanitarian tragedy in Darfur at the hands of an Islamist regime is a situation usually too inconvenient to mention.

The construction of the Muslims into a community of victims by Islamism has the purpose of instilling a high degree of Muslim solidarity. It also creates an all-powerful single enemy, the West, which stands behind all the disasters of the Muslim world. The radically different causes of the conflicts, which the Islamists list on their roll call of victims, are ignored. Palestinians are reconstructed from a people struggling for self-determination into Muslims under attack by the Western supported Israel. In the same way, Egypt is not seen as a society torn between supporters of authoritarian rule and a movement for democracy, but as Muslims bearing the weight of Western-backed oppression.

## Creating a Space where Islam can Define Itself

The British Government's policy of attempting to isolate 'violent extremism' in the same way it might deal with bird flu, fails to take into account the character of Islamism, and indeed of politics within Islam itself. In its approach, the Government assumes that there must be an Islam that is the opposite of the 'distorted' Islam it says leads to violence. In this account the Government appears to presume that there is a core Islam that is widely accepted and capable of being represented. In this presumption there is an uncanny echo of Qutb's distinction between the real Islam that he is fighting for and the fake or *Jahili* version that the current authorities project. Furthermore, the Government's analysis that certain views are 'unrepresentative' is quite untested. Indeed it can be argued that one of the great strengths of Islam is that the divine message in the Qur'an is addressed to the individual, which means that there is no established singular point of authority.[41] Islamic history has been a series of challenges, rebellions and conflicts precisely over this issue since the death of the Prophet. Islamic law (*shari'a*) to which political Islam appeals as the basis of the future of the Islamic state is not reducible to a singular code. Indeed no such code exists. Rather Islamic law is a rich discourse that is not only divided into major schools, but also into differing trends of interpretations within those schools.[42] The Government wisely refers to 'Muslim communities' rather than to the Muslim

---

[41] There are several sources of authority within Islam such as the Al Azhar University in Egypt for Sunnis and the Najaf Schools in Iraq for the Shi'a, but these exercise influence over and indeed compete with other centres. This situation does mean that there are many interpretations of Islam and no single arbiter of which is correct. For an enlightening discussion of this issue see K A El Fadl, *Speaking in God's Name: Islamic Law, Authority and Women* (Oxford: Oneworld, 2001).
[42] See, eg, S Zubaida, *Law and Power in the Islamic World* (London: I B Tauris, 2003).

community. It does not, though, draw the conclusion that this is to some extent because Islam itself is not reducible to a singular essence.[43] However, in the search for the Islam that rejects 'violent extremism' the existence of a single Islam is nonetheless assumed. The view that there is an essentialist Islam that operates according to strict identifiable principles derives from Orientalist discourse. For Said, Western constructions of Islam are to some extent the fear of the closeness of Europe to the Islamic world. As he says: 'the whole history of the creation of the Orient involves a continuous diminishment, so that now … in the Western press, the things you read about Islam and the Arab world are really horrendously simplified and completely belie the two or three hundred years of close contact'.[44] Close contact is equally rejected by the Islamists who fully utilise the space created by this distance to stake out their own 'Islam'. While the Western stereotyped Islam may have little traction within Muslim communities, the Islamists buttress their appeal by narrating familiar Islamic concepts, but through the prism of Islamist politics.

Islamism just reverses the Orientalist construction of a singular Islam. Instead of embracing an Islam open to interpretation and application, an authoritarian closure is imposed. This strangely mirrors the way in which the British Government's discourse, in its desire to construct a violence-free Islam, offers a stable and unchanging Islamic core. This choice between two rigid visions is highly problematic. However, as we see the British discourse unfold, its Orientalist roots often mean it leaves core Islamic principles to the Islamists. It is this approach no doubt that led a former Home Secretary, Charles Clark to say:

> There can be no negotiation about the re-creation of the Caliphate; there can be no negotiation about the imposition of Sharia law; there can be no negotiation about the suppression of equality between the sexes; there can be no negotiation about ending free speech. These values are fundamental to our civilization and simply not up for negotiation.[45]

Such statements assume both that there is a singular content to *shari'a* and that this content is inimical to 'our civilization': civilisation exemplified here by gender equality and freedom of speech. It should be said that if Clark is referring to 'our civilization' as the West, both gender equality and freedom of speech are of relatively recent acquisition. Such observations apart, on this view *shari'a* is necessarily opposed to both gender equality and freedom of speech. Both propositions ignore the lively debate within Islamic law and jurisprudence over

---

[43] See generally A Al-Azmeh, *Islams and Modernities* (London: Verso, 1993).
[44] G Viswanathan (ed), *Power, Politics and Culture: Interviews with Edward Said* (New York: Vintage, 2001) 238.
[45] C Clarke, 'Contesting the Threat of Terrorism' (Speech delivered at The Heritage Foundation, 5 October 2005).

both issues — debates which have a long lineage.[46] Clark therefore delivers *shari'a* to the Islamists and in so doing implies that all Muslims who disown violent extremism must do the same. A similar fate has befallen the concept of Jihad. Once seized by Islamism, and in particular by its extremist fringes, the concept has become a byword for terrorism. Indeed it is now common for Islamist organisations that support terrorism to be described as 'Jihadi' organisations and for individual terrorists to be labeled Jihadis. This must delight Osama bin Laden and all other extremists in the Muslim world. Their definition of Islam has come to be accepted.[47]

One of the main features of Islamist movements is the wholesale rejection of Islamic civilisation. This is a common feature of many different groups including the Muslim Brotherhood and the Wahabi movement in Saudi Arabia. In the latter's case the religious authorities teach that the mere existence of buildings associated with the Prophet, even his house and grave, can lead to idolatry. Accordingly, many of these sites are being progressively destroyed. This is symbolic of the Islamist approach to Islamic history much of which is dismissed as human corruption of the true message of Islam. The early Islamic empires of the Umayyads and Abbasids are also characterised as essentially corrupt systems. This results in the rejection of the elaborate jurisprudence that was established during these periods.[48] It was particularly in the early Abbasid period that the schools of law appeared and the Islamic world made its contribution to international law through the Siyar works.[49] Islamic law was formed through different schools with competing interpretations and applications.[50] This pluralism within legal discourse does not appeal to those movements that think Islam teaches only one path. The consequences of the rejection of the development of Islamic jurisprudence are highly significant. It means that when the Islamist exponents speak of *shari'a* they do not mean a sophisticated legal system based on highly complex jurisprudential arguments, but rather a newly invented rigid legal system that would justify authoritarian rule. At the same time, by removing the *Siyar* (Islamic international law) from their agenda, the Islamists very conveniently also remove the Islamic legal restraints on the use of force from their obligations. Amongst these restraints are that civilians are not legitimate targets. As Khadduri comments in his introduction to *Shaybani's*

---

[46] For a progressive Islamic approach to these issues see F Esack, *Qur'an, Liberation and Pluralism: An Islamic Perspective of Interreligious Solidarity Against Oppression* (Oxford: Oneworld, 1997).
[47] For a discussion on this issue see J Strawson, 'Holy War in the Media: Images of Jihad' in S Chermak, F Y Bailey, and M Brown (eds), *Media Images of September 11* (Westport and London: Praeger, 2003) 17-28.
[48] See W H B Hallaq, *A History of Islamic Legal Theories* (Cambridge: Cambridge University Press, 1997).
[49] See M Khadduri, *The Islamic Law of Nations: Shaybani's Siyar* (Baltimore: The Johns Hopkins Press, 1966).
[50] See, eg, M Khadduri (ed), *Al-Shafi'i's Risala: Treatise on the Foundation of Islamic Jurisprudence* (Cambridge: Islamic Texts Society, 1987).

*Siyar*, 'unnecessary damage in the prosecution of war was disapproved and practices such as killing noncombatants, mutilation, and treacherous attacks were prohibited'.[51] Al-Qaradawi would thus find no legal justification for his position on Israeli civilians from these sources. Nor would Osama bin Laden and the Al Qa'ida groups he has inspired find legal sanction for the long lists of attacks on civilians since 9/11.[52] Indeed such groups are not even permitted to use Jihad at all as it is a collective and not individual obligation and can only be authorised by Muslim authorities.[53] In other words, the question of the use of force in Islam is neither decided by the individual Muslim nor by the individual scholar. Within Islamic history, Jihad can only be decreed by those with recognised authority within whatever political state structure exists. This necessity derives from both the legal position of the government and the requirement for an organised collective effort.[54] Islamist ideology thus rests on a rejection not just of Western civilisation but of Islamic civilisation.

The ability of Islamist organisations to gain influence within the Muslim communities and in Mosque leaderships is due in part to the weakness of Islamic education. The portrayal of Islam in Orientalist terms as being backward during the colonial period, had a major impact on the approach to education as a whole in which a Western narrative of history and culture tended to predominate. Education within the colonies, such as India, was also seen as playing a major part in attaching the colonised peoples to the Imperial project. This had two long-term effects. First, mainstream education in the schools and universities tended to replicate the syllabus of the metropolitan countries. Within this context Islam was seen as a break on modernisation and progress. As a result, several generations of the elite within the colonised countries became detached from their own societies — often sharing the same prejudices about Islam as their colonisers. Consequently, a second effect took root: the continuation of Islamic education at the periphery in a form that was largely unregulated and certainly ignored by both the colonialists and the local elites. The combination has been lethal. By the twenty-first century most Islamic schools within a country like Pakistan are effectively controlled by Islamist groups, including the Taliban. While most of the elites remain 'Western educated' the masses have received an Islamic education at the hands of Islamists. While there are no doubt many examples of good Islamic schools with an enlightened syllabus, most have a rigid and highly ideological approach to Islam.

---

[51] Khadduri, above n 49, 53.
[52] On Al Qa'ida see J Burke, *Al-Qaeda: Casting a Shadow of Terror* (London: I B Tauris, 2003).
[53] See H M Zawati, *Is Jihad a Just War? War Peace, and Human Rights under Islamic and Public International Law* (Lewiston, Queenston, Lampeter: The Edwin Mellen Press, 2001).
[54] See I Rushd, *The Distinguished Jurist's Primer* (I A K Nyaze trans, Reading: Garnet, 1994) vol 1, 454-78 [trans of: *Bidayat al-Mujtiahid*].

Meanwhile in the West, Islamic studies for the most part have remained highly esoteric and confined to a few institutions. While the hold of Orientalism has weakened greatly, its effects still remain. There are few experts in the field with the result that those who do exist can exert a powerful influence on policy-making.[55] There is virtually no broad Islamic education within the school system. Where there are attempts to introduce the topic to the syllabus, the construction of Islam tends to be highly reductive and narrowly rigid. In education, as in the media, the imperative seems to be the production of 'an Islamic position'.[56]

Islamic education in many parts of the Islamic world, as well as within the West, is thus in need of great intellectual and financial investment. Western intellectual arrogance all too often has sought to claim exclusive patrimony over science, politics and law. As we have noted the same has been true for democracy and human rights, which, far from being seen as recent universal gains, are rather viewed as essentially part of an exclusively Western heritage. This has also played a part in undermining a rigorous assessment of the development of ideas across all civilisations and their impact on one another. In the case of Islam this arrogance has assisted in producing its mirror image.

## A Humanist Response to the Authoritarianism of Terrorism

While the West's history and current policies have played a role in the rise of Islamism, it would be an error to assume that it is the main factor in its formation or influence. The idea that the current incarnation of terrorism is mainly the result of Western policies in Afghanistan or Iraq, for example, is erroneous.[57] The emergence of Al Qa'ida and like organisations is a political phenomenon that predates these policies. The political ideas that sustain these organisations have been in circulation for many decades and sometimes, as with the Wahabis, for centuries.[58] The lazy politics that have laid the blame for the emergence of Islamist terrorism on 'justified anger' at Western policies are merely a form of Orientalist re-inscription of Western centrality in international politics. In particular, such politics draw on the stereotype of Islam as a violent religion. It is one thing to be critical of Western policies in relation to the Middle East and quite another to kill civilians on trains and buses in London or Madrid. Furthermore, it needs to be stressed that the main victims of Islamist terrorism

---

[55] An example is Daniel Pipes who has extremely essentialist views of Islam, in particular about its alleged violent nature. He writes frequently in the press and is an advisor to the Bush Administration. For an example of his work see D Pipes, *The Path of God: Islam and Political Power* (New Brunswick and London: Transaction Publishers, 2003).

[56] I know this personally as someone often asked by both students and the media to provide single line answers to such questions as: 'Is e-commerce compatible with Islamic Law?' or 'Does Islamic law permit husbands to beat their wives?' The questioner wants a yes or no answer — or at most a sound bite.

[57] See, eg, T Ali, *Bush in Babylon: the Recolonisation of Iraq* (London: Verso, 2004); for a spirited reply to such views see N Cohen, *What's Left? How Liberals Lost Their Way* (London: Fourth Estate, 2007).

[58] See, eg, A Rahnema (ed), *Pioneers of Islamic Revival* (London: Zed Press, 1994).

have been Muslims, not in Europe, but in Iraq itself. In Iraq, the deaths of hundreds of thousands of civilians are not the result of United States or United Kingdom military action, but of the calculated decision by Al Qa'ida in Mesopotamia and by like-minded organisations that bombing mosques, markets, hospitals, universities and other civilian targets will bring them political advantage. Yet these actions have been reconstructed as a form of 'resistance to occupation' not just by Islamist organisations, but also by segments of the Western left. This further complicates the delineation of the divide between ideas and violence.

Responding to Islamist terrorism involves grasping that Islamism is a major factor in international relations. Islamism has become the fastest growing movement in the Middle East. As soon as free elections took place in Iraq, Islamic-based parties won the lion's share of the Arab vote. As we have noted, in the past two years, Islamist political parties have won the Palestinian legislative elections and have polled well in Egypt and Bahrain. If free elections were to be held in all the countries of the Middle East and North Africa, Islamist parties would probably be the largest groups in most legislatures.[59] Islamism and the parties themselves are composed of many trends and factions. Many are opposed to violence. Nonetheless, the categorical politics that the movement espouses create a space that too often legitimises violent acts. In this space notions of resistance to oppression, martyrdom and God's immutable law play a key role. The politics of Islamism thus provide the space in which toleration of violence becomes acceptable. The problem for governments in their attempt to combat violent extremism is that they have to deal with not just tiny groups of radicalised individuals, but with a major political movement that is well rooted and which circulates through mosques, schools and above all the media and the internet. The battle of ideas is not therefore engaged with tiny unrepresentative groups, but rather with a broad and influential current, which takes different political colourations. It has spawned groupings that are mobilised as supporters of different centres; the Wahabi leadership in Saudi Arabia, the Islamic Republic of Iran, Hezbollah in Lebanon, the Sudanese Government, Hamas in Palestine, the Muslim Brotherhood in Egypt, the Jamaat-e-Islami in South Asia. It is within these movements that the possibility of terrorism can be debated as a policy option. If, as Al-Qaradawi suggests, the killing of Israeli civilians in Israel is justified, then perhaps it would be equally justifiable to kill Israelis abroad, or indeed, to kill supporters of Israel anywhere. It is a short step from this to argue that the suffering of the Palestinians is the result of the policies of the West and that therefore all people in the West are implicated and thus potential targets.

---

[59] See C R Ryan, 'Jordan: Islamic Action Front Presses for Role in Governing' (2006) 4(3) *Arab Reform Bulletin* http://www.carnegieendowment.org/publications/index.cfm?fa=view&id=18233&prog=zru#ryan.

The British Government's attempt to focus on isolated violent extremism as a distinct phenomenon underestimates the forces that produce it.

Terrorism involves relatively few people, and, within the West, terrorist acts cause terrible suffering to their victims, but they do not threaten governments or the political system. This is not true in some parts of the Islamic world where the alliance between terrorism and powerful Islamist political organisations does pose a serious threat to the existing political regimes. Western countries and governments in the Islamic world do have a common interest in developing a coherent response to these threats.

Islamist-based terrorism does not, however, mean that the threat we face is Islam itself.[60] Indeed it is Islamic civilisation that is perhaps the main resource that can be mobilised against terrorism and extremism. Islamist movements were not created as a reaction to Western power, but rather a response to the perception of corruption within Islam. Nonetheless, they have become adept at using the West's (often inept) policies opportunistically to mobilise their supporters. The old Orientalist images that portrayed Islam as backward, incapable of change, if exotic, play into the hands of the Islamists whose reverse discourse categorises Islam as a fixed tradition with stable values. Its attempt to appropriate the Prophetic period as an essentialist mimetic moment is an interesting re-inscription of the Orientalist account. Like Orientalism, however, it deadens Islam and reduces this critical period to a reified mythic trope.[61]

Islamic civilisation with its great contributions to theology, jurisprudence, philosophy, science, architecture and literature is itself under attack from such movements. Islamic civilisation's great dynamism and energy is in stark contrast to the narrow restrictions of the Islamist perspective. The West and the Islamic world both have an interest in investing in a major intellectual effort to overcome the effects of colonialism and Orientalism as a contribution to restoring the critical role that Islam has played within world civilisation. The intellectual project to overcome the Orientalist prism offers more than just an end to the exclusion of Islam, as Said seductively wrote:

> For the first time, the history of imperialism and its culture can now be studied as neither monolithic nor reductively compartmentalized, separate, distinct. True, there has been a disturbing eruption of separatist and chauvinist discourse whether in India, Lebanon, or Yugoslavia, or in Afrocentric, Islamocentric, or Eurocentric proclamations; far from invalidating the struggle to be free from empire, these reductions of cultural discourse actually prove the validity of the

---

[60] See J J Esposito, *Terror in the Name of Islam* (Oxford, New York: Oxford University Press, 2002).
[61] See A Dashti, *23 Years: A Study of the Prophetic Career of Mohammad* (Costa Mesa: Mazda Publishers, 1994).

fundamental liberationist energy that animates the wish to be independent, to speak freely, and without the burden of unfair domination.[62]

For the Islamic world and the West this has a special significance. It also demonstrates that colonialism and its consequences are equally problematic for the former Imperial powers as for the former colonised peoples.

The British Government, in common with most other Western powers, faced terrorism 'in the name of Islam' within a dominant intellectual environment connected to Orientalism. Despite this it was important to note the efforts that were made after 9/11 to avoid connecting terrorism to Islam in a crass way. However, the problem came as these governments attempted to identify the root problem of terrorism while at the same time 'engaging' with Muslim communities and seeking their genuine representatives. At this point, there was a relapse to an essentialist view that there was a core Islam and that terrorist extremism could be isolated as if it were a virus. The recognition within British Government documents that 'Islamism' and 'Islamist terrorism' are the threat should alert us that a political battle on an international scale is now required. Bio-security is not a model for human security.

Marginalising the Islamist current and narrowing the intellectual space for terrorism should be the aim of this political campaign. The importance of Islamic civilisation should be its core message.

---

[62] E W Said, *Culture and Imperialism* (London: Chatto and Windus, 1993) xxiii.

# Chapter Three

# Another Modest Proposal: In Defence of the Prohibition against Torture

### Desmond Manderson[*]

## Introduction

François Marie Arouet was born in 1694 when the *Ancien Régime* — the iron fist of Louis XIV in the velvet glove of Versailles — seemed insouciant, eternal, and impervious to change. Yet by the time of Arouet's death in 1778, the Enlightenment had wrought such a destabilising effect upon the old order that it was on the point of collapse. Arouet, writing under the nom de plume Voltaire,[1] was a pivotal figure in the development of modern Western ideas about government and justice. Playwright, essayist, and critic, he was above all a relentless fighter against cruelty and superstition. I doubt many would disagree with me when I say that we still have need of such fighters. But sometimes we find the advocates of cruelty and superstition in surprising places.

Voltaire's battle cry against the enemies of Enlightenment was '*Écrasez l'infâme*'.[2] You must wipe out infamy. But what was so infamous as to mandate utter obliteration? On one level, the Catholic Church of his day; on another, the whole system of absolutism that held France, and most of Europe, in thrall. What they had in common was this: a power that was entirely unaccountable, entirely unlimited, and which instilled a climate of fear through the measured dosage of cruelty.

---

[*] Professor and the Canada Research Chair in Law and Discourse, Faculty of Law, McGill University, Montreal, Canada. Recent books include *Songs Without Music: Aesthetic Dimensions of Law and Justice* (Berkeley: University of California Press, 2000) and *Proximity, Levinas and the Soul of Law* (Montreal: McGill-Queen's University Press, 2006). Research for this essay was initially undertaken at the International Institute for the Sociology of Law in Oñati, Spain, and at the National Europe Centre, The Australian National University. Additional work was undertaken with the support of the John Fleming Centre for the Advancement of Legal Research, ANU. The collegiality and intellectual commitment of these bodies is enormously appreciated. A version of this essay was originally published in (2005) 10 *Deakin Law Review* 640. Permission to reproduce is gratefully acknowledged.

[1] T Besterman, *Voltaire* (London: Longmans, 1969); A O Aldridge, *Voltaire and the Century of Light* (Princeton, NJ: Princeton University Press, 1975). See also R Pearson, *Voltaire Almighty: A Life in Pursuit of Freedom* (London: Bloomsbury, 2005).

[2] J Herrick, *Against the Faith: Essays on Deists, Skeptics, and Atheists* (Buffalo, NY: Prometheus Books, 1985, ch 3: Voltaire: *Écrasez l'infâme*, 56); B R Redman (ed), *The Portable Voltaire* (New York: Viking Press 1949 ed).

Voltaire had in mind, in particular, State practices of torture, both private and public, which were common in France. This barbarism sickened him and he knew, father of the Age of Reason though he was, that there was no reasoning with or controlling it. We cannot argue about such cruelty for that is already to dignify it as reasonable. We can only commit ourselves to its destruction. *Écrasez l'infâme.*

One of the cases that most profoundly disturbed Voltaire was the death of Damiens. Convicted of attempting to assassinate Louis XV, he was disgustingly tortured and finally executed over the course of several hours in the main square of the Paris townhall. Michel Foucault wrote at length about this gruesome event, and treated it as emblematic of the world of early modernity.[3] Under the *Ancien Régime*, the power of the state was absolute, exercised through public spectacles and through terrors, designed to establish the total control of the state and the total subjection of all those who resisted it. Torture, no less than the great castles and glorious pageantry of the monarchy, was a way of representing that spectacular power.

> Antiquity had been a civilization of spectacle. "To render accessible to a multitude of men the inspection of a small number of objects": this was the problem to which the architecture of temples, theatres and circuses responded. With spectacle, there was a predominance of public life, the intensity of festivals, sensual proximity. In these rituals in which blood flowed, society found new vigour and formed for a moment a single great body.[4]

Terrorism, implies Foucault, is above all an attack on the state and its exclusive right to the legitimate use of violence. Unlike a murderer or robber, the terrorist or assassin does not just kill: he claims a legitimacy, even a lawfulness, in doing so. Such acts do not 'break' the law, but seek to impose a new or higher law. In the days of the *Ancien Régime*, public execution re-appropriated that violence to the state, and turned the victim into an unwilling agent of the sovereign's power.[5] The very bodies of the tortured, such as Damiens, became abject puppets forcibly made to act a part in this pageant play of complete authority. The reduction of a person to a body and a body to the puppet of another's will, as much as pain, defines torture. Torture and execution 'did not re-establish justice; it re-activated power'.[6] Its point, ultimately, was not to exact retribution or, it goes without saying, to extract information, but to show us all just who was boss.

---

[3] M Foucault, *Discipline and Punish: The Birth of the Prison* (A Sheridan trans, New York: Vintage, 1995 ed), 3-31 [trans of: *Surveiller et Punir: Naissance de la Prison* (first published Paris: Gallimard, 1975)].
[4] Ibid 216-17.
[5] Ibid 48-49.
[6] Ibid 49.

Yet ironically, as the case of Voltaire demonstrates, the very brutality of torture undermined the stability of the state. Many people were naturally horrified by events like the death of Damiens. Many more recalled, or had occasion to experience the *lettres des cachets*, which entitled the French state to lock their opponents up without trial, without explanation, and at His Majesty's pleasure. Thus torture and arbitrary punishment became imbued with a wholly different set of meanings than that intended by the state. It came to show not the power of the state, but its insecurity; to suggest not the divinity of the sovereign but his partiality; to instil not a kind of passivity and submission in the population but on the contrary to generate activity and resistance. These provocations exploded into life at the end of the eighteenth century, wiping out not just these notorious practices but the regime with which they had become synonymous.

## Torture in Theory

Foucault argues that since the Enlightenment, power has been exercised in quite different ways: not by the punishment of bodies, but through the disciplining of minds; not through dramatic acts that destroy us utterly, but through tiny daily pressures that encourage us to conform; not in a public square and periodically, but every day in homes, schools, factories, armies, hospitals. The end of torture as a state institution was coupled by the rise of other institutions, less violent and more subtly committed to moulding 'docile bodies'.[7]

But perhaps we have written off the *Ancien Régime* too quickly. In 2005, two Australian academics, Professor Mirko Bagaric and Julie Clarke, attracted widespread attention by arguing that torture is a 'permissible' and even a 'moral' action in certain circumstances.[8] Within days, Peter Faris, one-time head of the now defunct National Crime Authority, was reported as supporting the 'call'.[9] And of course in the United States, arguments for the necessity of occasional and exceptional acts of torture or unlimited detention circulate regularly in the halls of government as well as in the pages of the law reviews.[10]

---

[7] Ibid 135-69.

[8] M Bagaric and J Clarke, 'The Yes Case Can Outweigh the No', *Sydney Morning Herald* (Sydney), 17 May 2005 (hereinafter Bagaric and Clarke, *SMH*); M Bagaric, 'A Case for Torture', *The Age* (Melbourne), 17 May 2005. See also M Bagaric and J Clarke, 'Not Enough Official Torture in the World? The Circumstances in which Torture is Morally Justifiable' (2005) 39 *University of San Francisco Law Review* 3 (hereinafter Bagaric and Clarke, *USFLR*). I continue to refer in many places to the newspaper articles, particularly *The Sydney Morning Herald* because, perhaps surprisingly, they present both a more explicit and a more coherent argument for why torture is morally justifiable. *USFLR*, though larded with literature reviews, makes the case in a more peremptory and indirect fashion.

[9] 'Torture Acceptable, Says Former NCA Chief', *Sydney Morning Herald* (Sydney), 22 May 2005.

[10] In addition to Bagaric and Clarke, above n 8, see also Gonzales, below n 18; Wolf Blitzer interview with Alan Deroshowitz, 'Dershowitz: Torture can be justified', 3 March 2003, at <http://edition.cnn.com/2003/LAW/03/03/cnna.Dershowitz>; A Dershowitz, 'The Torture Warrant: A response to Professor Strauss' (2004) 48 *New York Law School Review* 275.

In good lawyerly fashion, Bagaric and Clarke discuss the question in abstractions entirely shorn of any social context. The necessity of torture is presented in purely theoretical terms. Torture, they say, is only justifiable where 'it is used as an information-gathering technique to avert a grave risk'.[11] Elsewhere, while not ruling out the torture of an 'innocent person' to obtain vital information, they focus on the archetypal hypothesis in which 'torturing a wrongdoer ... is the only means, due to the immediacy of the situation, to save the life of an innocent person'.[12] Now they caveat this argument by conceding that 'none of the recent high profile cases of torture appear to satisfy these criteria'.[13] Well isn't that nice to know. So the question is presented as a thought experiment designed to help us interrogate, so to speak, our moral instincts; to approach them in a reasoned rather than a merely emotional way. The thought experiment is meant to encourage us to think more clearly about a subject that is often, they tell us, a prey to fuzzy passions,[14] and unfairly tainted by irrational and inappropriate 'pejorative connotations'.[15] Their stated goal is to normalise torture, to encourage us to see it as no different from any other tool of social policy.[16]

But it is not remotely plausible to attempt to disassociate the article's reflections on the legality of torture from a social context in which the use of torture by governments is in fact on the rise, and is openly being presented as legitimate and even necessary in the 'post-9/11 world': by government spokesmen and soldiers, television producers and talk-show hosts. The top-rated television show '24' has depicted no less than 67 instances of torture on the part of its heroes in its five years, and the untrammelled sovereignty exhibited by its counter-terrorist star, Jack Bauer, is beginning to exercise a considerable sway over the minds and imagination of many trainee soldiers and interrogators.[17] The legitimacy of torture is undoubtedly back on the agenda.

Neither of course is there anything in the least fictional or coincidental about the discussion of torture at this moment in time. We are familiar with the dismal story of Abu Ghraib. But this was no isolated instance. In pursuit of the so-called 'global war against terrorism', the United States has not only been involved in cases of torture itself, but has routinely sent — the term used is 'rendered' —

---

[11] Bagaric and Clarke, *USFLR* above n 8, 611.
[12] Bagaric and Clarke, *SMH* above n 8; *USFLR* above n 8, 612-14.
[13] Ibid 616.
[14] See in particular Bagaric and Clarke, *SMH* above n 8.
[15] Bagaric and Clarke, *USFLR* above n 8, 583.
[16] Ibid 584-85.
[17] J Mayer, 'Whatever it Takes', *New Yorker* (New York), 19 February 2007; see also 'Prime Time Torture' study by Human Rights First organisation:
<http://www.humanrightsfirst.org/us_law/etn/primetime/index.asp>.

suspects to third countries in order that they might be tortured there.[18] So too allegations of the kind of practices and calculated cruelties that take place at Guantánamo Bay have surfaced recently with worrying regularity.[19]

Above all, the United States Government has over the past several years clearly indicated its desire to claim an absolute sovereignty worthy of the Sun King. The Bush Administration insists on its right, as the executive, to act as *it* sees fit in the 'war on terror', including by the use of torture and unconstrained by either domestic or international law. In 2003, the Working Group Report on Detainee Interrogations in the Global War on Terrorism, authorised by then Secretary of Defense Rumsfeld, insisted that the President's 'ultimate authority' in a time of self-proclaimed and self-defined war was not capable of curtailment by any laws, including United States statutes, against torture. Consequently, 'the prohibition against torture must be construed as inapplicable to interrogations undertaken pursuant to his Commander-in-Chief Authority'.[20] Alberto Gonzales, at that time Legal Counsel to the White House, advised in 2002 that the 'new paradigm' of counter-terrorism 'renders obsolete Geneva [Convention]'s strict limitations on questioning of enemy prisoners and renders quaint some of its provisions'.[21] Alberto Gonzales was appointed United States Attorney-General in 2005. In the celebrated words of Lord Steyn, a 'legal black hole'[22] has been created in two ways. On the one hand, unrestricted sovereignty is now claimed in interrogating terror suspects. On the other, the United States President has himself declared that the detainees at Guantánamo and elsewhere (over 70,000 people at last count) fall into no cognizable legal category and are

---

[18] J Barry, M Hirsh and M Isikoff, 'The Roots of Torture', *Newsweek International*, 24 May 2004 at <http://www.msnbc.msn.com/id/4989481/>; J Mayer, 'Outsourcing Torture', *New Yorker* (New York), 14 February 2005. See also US Department of Defense, *Working Group Report on Detainee Interrogations in the Global War on Terrorism: Assessment of Legal, Historical, Policy and Operational Considerations*, 6 March 2003; Office of Legal Counsel US Department of Justice, *Memorandum For Alberto R. Gonzalez, Counsel to the President, and William J. Haynes II General Counsel of the Department of Defense, Re: Application of Treaties and Laws to Al Qaeda and Taliban Detainees*, 22 January 2002. And see Amnesty International, *Guantanamo and Beyond: The Continuing Pursuit of Unchecked Executive Power (Report on the United States)* (2005) at <www.amnesty.org>.
[19] See Amnesty International, *Iraq: Amnesty International Reveals a Pattern of Torture and Ill-Treatment*, 26 May 2004, at <http://web.amnesty.org/web/web.nsf/prnt/irq-torture-eng>; Amnesty International Report 2004, *United States of America*, at
<http://web.amnesty.org/web/web.nsf/print/2004-usa-summary-eng>; J Margulies, *Guantánamo and the Abuse of Presidential Power* (New York: Simon & Schuster, 2006); C Butler (ed), *Guantanamo Bay and the Judicial-Moral Treatment of the Other* (West Lafayette, Ind: Purdue University Press: Published in cooperation with the Institute for Human Rights, Indiana University-Purdue University Fort Wayne, 2007); S Miles, *Oath Betrayed: Torture, Medical Complicity and the War on Terror* (New York: Random House, 2006).
[20] US Department of Defense, above n 18, 20-21. See 18 USC § 2340A.
[21] A Gonzales, 'Memorandum for the President: Decision Re Application of the Geneva Conventions on Prisoners of War', 25 January 2002, in K Greenberg and J Dratel (eds), *The Torture Papers: The Road to Abu Ghraib* (New York: Cambridge University Press, 2005) 118, 119.
[22] Lord Steyn, 'Guantanamo Bay: The Legal Black Hole' (F A Mann Lecture, 25 November 2003), at <http://www.statewatch.org/news/2003/nov/guantanamo.pdf>.

therefore unprotected under international law.[23] In the vacuum caused by the infinity of sovereignty and the nullity of its targets, anything is now possible.

Let us be clear about this: the only reason Bagaric and Clarke's article was worth publishing — in the *University of San Francisco Law Review*, let alone in the opinion pages of *The Age* and the *Sydney Morning Herald* — is because the actions of the United States Government in particular has made the subject topical and relevant. Despite their protestations to the contrary, the argument for the legitimacy of torture matters not because it is an intriguing little exercise in moral philosophy, but because it intervenes directly into a real social context. Bagaric and Clarke propose a hypothetical case in which the extraction of information from a suspect must be accomplished urgently so as to avoid the execution of a hostage; Peter Faris refers to the imminent explosion of a bomb. The very same hypotheticals were used by Attorney-General Gonzales to justify discarding the Geneva Convention. 'The nature of the new war places a high premium on other factors, such as the ability to quickly obtain information from captured terrorists and their sponsors in order to avoid further atrocities against … civilians.'[24] Yet as we know, this 'torture memo' encouraged the very practices that Bagaric and Clarke themselves judge 'reprehensible'.[25] These practices include not only Abu Ghraib,[26] but a wide range of interrogation techniques through which, according to Amnesty International's 2005 report, the US Government is even now engaging in torture dressed up in bureaucratic newspeak 'in pursuit of unfettered executive power'.[27] Thus a purely theoretical idea about torture gives credence to the very rhetoric that has far from theoretical consequences.

The authors dismiss this as a 'slippery slope' argument. But the use of arguments like those of Bagaric and Clarke to justify ever-expanding practices of torture is not a possibility but a fact, engineered, according to US Government sources, as part of 'a calculated effort to create an atmosphere of legal ambiguity'.[28] These Australian academics are seriously implicated in the creation of that atmosphere: that too is not just my fear or my opinion, but a fact. The context in which an argument is made is part of its meaning. This is not a complex point. One is responsible not only for one's words but also for their inevitable and predictable effects.

---

[23] US White House, *Memorandum: Humane Treatment of Al Qaeda and Taliban Detainees*, 7 February 2002, in Greenberg and Dratel, above n 21, 134-5.
[24] Gonzales, above n 21.
[25] Bagaric and Clarke, *SMH*, above n 8.
[26] S M Hersh, 'Torture at Abu Ghraib', *New Yorker* (New York), 10 May 2004; M Danner, *Torture and Truth: America, Abu Ghraib, and the War on Terror* (London: Granta Books, 2005); and see also Greenberg and Dratel, above n 21.
[27] Amnesty International, above n 18 at 2.
[28] Barry, Hirsch and Isikoff, above n 18.

Neither do the authors *themselves* sincerely believe that the argument they make is so limited and hypothetical. They attack the 'misguided', 'alarmist', 'reflexive', 'absolutist' and 'short-sighted' 'moral indecency' of our belief that torture is always wrong.[29] They describe torture as suffering from 'pejorative connotations' [sic] and its critics as 'illogical' while their own defence of torture is 'dispassionate' and 'analytical'.[30] Poor Voltaire. He has been accused of many things, but rarely all at once. Whatever else we may say of Bagaric and Clarke, their argument is rich in emotion and rhetoric. True enough, they say that their defence of torture is so cautiously phrased that 'a real-life situation where torture is justifiable [might] not eventuate'. But in the very next paragraph they conclude: 'the argument in favour of torture in limited circumstances needs to be made because it will encourage the community to think more carefully about moral judgments we collectively hold that are the cause of an enormous amount of suffering in the world'.[31] I wonder what hasty moral judgments they have in mind as being responsible for 'an enormous amount of suffering'? The sole example they provide is our fanatical, woolly-headed prohibition of torture. So this is what their argument must mean: the prohibition against torture is doing our society enormous harm and causing enormous suffering not only in some hypothetical thought-world, but *right* now.

Even if we take Bagaric and Clarke's very modest proposal for torture at face value, it is logically inseparable from the real-world practices they disavow. Torture by its very nature deals with uncertainty; ignorance is the problem that it claims to solve through the exercise of violence. Yet torture produces such exceptionally unreliable information that it is thought to be largely useless.[32] All Western legal systems acknowledge this by excluding as unreliable the fruit of torture.[33] But the authors blandly assert, in one short paragraph and on the basis of a single strangely unconvincing anecdote, that 'the main benefit of torture is that it is an excellent means of gathering information. Humans have an intense desire to avoid pain ... and most will comply with the demands of a torturer to avoid the pain.'[34] They appear oblivious to how far short of convincing this 'argument' is; nor do they appear to grasp the difference between 'compliance' and 'truth'. Let alone 'evidence'. The central reason that Australian suspect Mamdouh Habib was finally released from US custody is that he had been tortured, and therefore any confession he made was legally inadmissible in any court.[35] Having been tortured, Habib could never be put on trial. Bagaric

---

[29] Bagaric and Clarke, *SMH*, above n 8.
[30] Bagaric and Clarke, *USFLR*, above n 8, 583-4.
[31] Bagaric and Clarke, *SMH*, above n 8.
[32] For an historical understanding, see P duBois, *Torture and Truth* (New York: Routledge, 1991).
[33] See, eg, *Convention Against Torture and Other Cruel, Inhuman or Degrading Treatment or Punishment* (10 December 1984) 1465 UNTS 85, art 15.
[34] Bagaric and Clarke, *USFLR*, above n 8, 588.
[35] CBS News, 11 January 2005; *Sydney Morning Herald* (Sydney), 11 January 2005.

and Clarke do not explain why they believe that torture produces good evidence. On the contrary, under current law, it produces no evidence at all. Bagaric, at least, apparently thinks that in such circumstances the rules of evidence are hopelessly outdated and irritatingly inconvenient;[36] but that is at the very least an argument that would have to be made with some care, and Bagaric and Clarke do not bother to do so.

Now let us look at the problem of ignorance and uncertainty from the torturer's point of view. A licensed torturer cannot *know* that a supposed terrorist (for example) is the only way to locate a bomb; or that there is a bomb; or that he will tell the truth under torture; or even that he is a terrorist. The torturer suspects these things or rather he says he knows these things, and of course he has every reason to say he knows these things, because that is the approach that justifies his actions. It is human nature to see the confused and ambiguous world in the way that is most convenient to us. Suppose our supposed terrorist denies knowing anything. Do we let him go or torture him some more? When exactly do we stop? When exactly do we believe what the victim is telling us when the justification of torture is precisely that we only believe him when he tells us what we want to know, without our already knowing it?

There is a paradox here that leads inexorably to the kind of grey areas or 'slippery slope' in the use of torture by interrogators for which Bagaric and Clarke attempt to deny all responsibility. Given the existence of criteria under which torture becomes acceptable, even the narrow criteria that Bagaric and Clarke provide, the pressure on someone in a volatile and violent situation to see his enemy in a way that *will* justify torture is irresistible. So the question is: how much useless torture is justifiable in these troubled times? The authors concede that their modest proposal may not lead to torture that saves a life. But they do not tell you the logical corollary: it must and will lead to torture, and therefore by their own reasoning it must and will lead to torture that does *not* save a life. I have seen no-one in the whole current debate over the role of torture in counter-terrorism even address this issue. Instead we have fallen victim to the Jack Bauer fallacy. Of the 67 instances of torture on '24', Jack extracts 67 crucial pieces of life-saving information. But that is not our world and never, ever, will be.

## Torture in Practice

In our world, it is duplicitous to describe torture, as Bagaric and Clarke do, at least in their newspaper articles, as 'inflicting a relatively small level of harm on a wrongdoer'.[37] The article, which appeared in the *University of San Francisco Law Review*, does not repeat this reasoning though the authors argue that once

---

[36] M Bagaric, 'Not everyone is entitled to a trial', *Canberra Times* (Canberra), 8 February 2007.
[37] Bagaric and Clarke, *SMH* above n 8.

a threshold of justifiability has been reached 'the higher the figure the more severe the forms of torture that are permissible.'[38] In the first place, there seems to be a real lack of understanding as to how the physical aspects of torture work. How effective would a regulated, prescribed, and 'relatively small' dose of torture be? Torture is not like paying a parking fine. The terror and the threat of torture does not come from the pain by itself. Many of us can tolerate a finite dose of pain, even if it is severe: ask a woman what childbirth is like.[39] There is surely no reason to think that highly motivated terrorists would find the suffering of a specific 'level of harm' impossible to bear. The power of torture, in most instances, comes instead from the promise that the torturer makes that the pain *will not stop* unless you talk and *will get worse* until you do. It is a logical contradiction to imagine that torture can be regulated, as Bagaric and Clarke seem to imagine, because it is part of its essence as torture that the victim is beyond protection and that resistance is futile. In addition, it is an essential and well-documented part of its psychology that the torturer is the sole arbitrator of life and death.[40] The whole dynamic of torture involves the reduction of one party to pure power and the other to pure powerlessness. In short, and I believe this is a central point that the authors have not understood, torture gets people to talk (not, of course, to tell the truth, but certainly to talk: you will recall that the authors confuse 'comply with the demands of a torture' and 'an excellent means of gathering information'[41] ) if and only if the *torturer* is sovereign. I suspect that a torturer-cum-bureaucrat is a contradiction in terms.

It is frankly appalling that so many writers are prepared to trivialise the very practice they advocate. Perhaps Bagaric and Clarke have read nothing about the nature of pain, memory, and fear.[42] Perhaps they have not read a single thing about the experience of torture and its implications on those who suffer it and those around them.[43] Torture is not simply pain. It is an experience of absolute powerlessness that reduces the victim, in their own eyes as well as their torturer's, to an animal, a bare life without will or dignity of any kind.[44] It is the destruction of identity. Torture is rape just as rape is torture. It is not something to shrug off or even, most of the time, to get over.

---

[38] Bagaric and Clarke, *USFLR* above n 8, 614.
[39] See E J Cassell, 'Pain and Suffering' in W T Reich (ed), *Encyclopedia of Bioethics* vol. 4 (New York: Macmillan Library References USA, 1994) 1897-1905; E Cassell, *The Nature of Suffering and the Goals of Medicine* (New York: Oxford University Press, 1991).
[40] E Scarry, *The Body in Pain: The Making and Unmaking of the World* (New York: Oxford University Press, 1987 ed) .
[41] Bagaric and Clarke, *USFLR*, above n 8, 588, 616.
[42] Ibid.
[43] P Elsass, *Treating Victims of Torture and Violence: Theoretical, Cross-cultural, and Clinical Implications* (New York: New York University Press, 1997).
[44] G Agamben, *Homo Sacer: Sovereign Power and Bare Life* (D Heller-Roasen trans of *Homo sacer: Il potere sovrano e la nuda vita*, (first published Turin: Einaudi, 1995) Stanford: Stanford University Press, 1998).

Neither should we limit our analysis to the impact of torture on a single individual during a single finite emergency, a limiting of the actual costs and effects of torture that Bagaric and Clarke engage in quite explicitly.[45] In the world we live in and in which Bagaric and Clarke's argument actually matters, torture is never about the emergency rescue of an innocent life. It is used to extract a wide range of information about the functioning of many outlaw groups. But because of the inherent unreliability of its evidence, this is not its main purpose. Torture is used to punish and humiliate dissidents, terrorists, and members of ethnic minorities. And it is used as a calibrated dose of cruelty through which to terrorise the whole community to which they belong.[46] Just as in the case of Damiens, torture is a demonstration of what the state can do to you and what it can get you to do. The effect is to create a generalised fear about the infinite and random power of the state to destroy lives, and an intense sense of vulnerability in victim populations.

We need to think about the effects of torture not merely on the bodies that suffer pain but on the families and communities around them who live under its constant and unavoidable shadow. Torture affects whole societies: it terrorises them and ultimately, as we saw in Voltaire's Europe, the powerlessness it instils shifts from passivity to rage. The turning point in the lives of many Al Qai'da operatives was their imprisonment and torture in Egyptian, Syrian, and other Middle Eastern prisons: this same Egypt to which the United States *still* 'renders' suspects in order to soften them up.[47] Torture is in real danger of producing terrorists: whole families and villages of them. That is why the prisoners in Guantánamo Bay — according to the Secretary-General of Amnesty International, part of the 'gulag of our times'[48] — are proving to be an increasingly insoluble problem for the US, and many fear now that they may never be able to be released. How can they be? Bystanders or warriors initially, they are much greater risks to us now.

To these real and far-reaching consequences, which our society would have to understand, accept, and somehow combat if we were ever to accept Bagaric and Clarke's argument, the authors have paid no attention at all.

## Defending It

I have argued, first logically and then practically, that it is impossible to accept this modest proposal for torture in its own neatly limited terms. We still have to imagine to what consequences such a principle would actually lead. But for

---

[45] Bagaric and Clarke, *USFLR*, above n 8, 613-4.
[46] See, eg, J Conroy, *Unspeakable Acts, Ordinary People: The Dynamics of Torture* (London: Vision Paperbacks, 2001).
[47] Mayer, above n 18. See also Human Rights Watch Reports for 2005, particularly in relation to Egypt; and S Grey, 'America's Gulag', *New Statesman* (London), 17 May 2004.
[48] *New York Times* (New York), 26 May 2005.

the sake of argument let us look a little closer at the ways in which Bagaric and Clarke, amongst others, attempt to defend an entitlement to torture.[49] Thus it is said that the prohibition against torture has only served, by its unnecessary absolutism, to drive it 'beneath the radar screen of accountability'; legalisation 'would reduce the instances of torture'.[50] It is difficult to see why this assertion would be true. Our societies are not without experience of legal torture. Was there less of it then? Moreover, the emotions that lead to real torture — fear, crisis, hatred — will not be reduced by legality. In what sense will 'accountability' make a difference to the practice of torture except to provide a helpful framework in which it can be organised, carried out and defended?

I admit that the radar argument sounds plausible: illegality does not always work and sometimes seems to make matters worse.[51] This is particularly the case, for example, in relation to so-called victimless crimes such as drug use. Indeed, Bagaric and Clarke are explicit in adopting for themselves a discourse of 'harm minimisation' drawn from that literature.[52] But torture is hardly victimless. Let us look a little closer to see where the analogy falls down. With drug use or prostitution, the argument is that legalisation will clean up the secretive conditions in which they occur and therefore not lessen the incidence of them but instead make them safer. In general, the scholars of what is called 'harm minimisation' *do not contend* that a more open approach to drugs will lead to less use; only that it will dramatically improve the social and health conditions of users.[53] But it is not the *conditions* under which torture is practised that are the problem. Danger and pain are not a by-product of torture (as they are, for example, to a considerable degree a by-product of the current regime of drug prohibition); they are the purpose of it. Were torture done in public, were it supervised by a qualified medical practitioner in an hygienic environment, were it made respectable — tell me, would any of this make torture better? Once again Voltaire comes to mind: 'If we believe absurdities, we shall commit atrocities.'[54]

The centre-piece of Bagaric and Clarke's defence offers as obvious example of begging the question as I have seen. They argue by analogy to 'the right to

---

[49] I leave aside their criticism of the 'slippery slope' argument to which I have referred above.
[50] Bagaric and Clarke, *USFLR*, above n 8, 615; their argument here draws strongly on Dershowitz, 'Torture Can be Justified' and 'The Torture Warrant', above n 10.
[51] I have written about this at considerable length elsewhere: D Manderson, *From Mr Sin to Mr Big: A History of Australian Drug Laws* (Melbourne: Oxford University Press, 1993).
[52] Bagaric and Clarke, *USFLR*, above n 8, 583, 608.
[53] A Wodak and T Moore, *Modernising Australia's Drug Policy* (Sydney: UNSW Press, 2002); A Wodak and R Owens, *Drug Prohibition: A Call for Change* (Sydney: UNSW Press, 1996); M Hamilton et al (eds), *Drug Use in Australia: A Harm Minimisation Approach* (Melbourne: Oxford University Press, 1998); P Erikson et al (eds), *Harm Reduction: A New Direction for Drug Policies and Programs* (Toronto: University of Toronto Press, 1997).
[54] Translation of '*Certainement qui est en droit de vous rendre absurde est en droit de vous rendre injuste.*' Voltaire, *Questions sur les Miracles* (1765) (Louis Moland (ed), *OEuvres complètes de Voltaire*, Paris: Garnier, 1877-1885, tome 25 (357-450)).

self-defence, which extends to the right to defend another'.[55] Just as we are entitled to respond with violence to a murderous attack, they say, we are entitled to protect others; if the only way to protect them is by torturing somebody for information, then torture must be legitimate too. But the analogy falls down in at least three ways. First, the principle of self-defence recognises a reality: when it is 'him or me' a law that said I could not respond to an attacker would be simply unenforceable.[56] Here the violence of torture is a choice deliberately made and carried out, and not purely responsive.

Second, their analogy assumes the only point it needs to prove. One can legally defend oneself; one can even kill an attacker if necessary; but what legal system has ever authorised a case of torture 'in self-defence'? Why do the authors assume that self-defence, which is strictly limited to a direct, minimal and reasonable response to threat,[57] is in any way equivalent to torture, which is by its very nature indirect and maximal? In fact, our societies have, at least since the Enlightenment, feared pain more than death,[58] believed that human dignity requires absolute protection under all circumstances, and for that very reason thought torture a more serious act than execution. Legal systems throughout the world outlawed torture long, long before capital punishment. In the US, torture has always been contrary to the 8th Amendment; it is the paradigmatic example of 'cruel and unusual punishment'.[59] Yet the death penalty continues to be applied — as painlessly as possible.[60] So clearly in the US, throughout the world, and by most people, it is generally considered worse to torture than to kill.[61] As Bagaric and Clarke go to some lengths to point out, we do indeed often ask many people, including civilians, to make the ultimate sacrifice for the good of others, for example in times of war.[62] Bagaric and Clarke think it obvious that if we can kill someone in self-defence, or require them to die for us, *therefore* it must be all right to torture them. But this is precisely what the absolute prohibition of torture rejects. Bagaric and Clarke could certainly make an argument against this orthodoxy. But neither they nor, to the best of my knowledge, other apologists for torture have attempted to do so. They simply assert their position as self-evident. It is nothing of the kind.

---

[55] Bagaric and Clarke, *USFLR*, above n 8, 603. The argument is developed more clearly in the newspaper articles: see *SMH*, above n 8.
[56] See L Fuller, 'The Case of the Speluncean Explorers' (1949) 62 *Harvard Law Review* 616.
[57] *Viro v The Queen* (1978) 141 CLR 88; *Zecevic v DPP* (1987) 162 CLR 645.
[58] See P Ariès, *The Hour of Our Death* (H Weaver trans of *L'homme devant la mort* (first published 1981) New York: Knopf: distributed by Random House, 1981).
[59] *Constitution, Amendment VIII* (US); see *Wilkerson v Utah* (1878) 99 US 130 (US).
[60] *Gregg v Georgia* (1976) 428 US 153 (US).
[61] See *International Covenant on Civil and Political Rights* (16 December 1966) 999 UNTS 171, art 6, which likewise permits the death penalty but (in art 7) outlaws torture.
[62] Bagaric and Clarke, *USFLR*, above n 8, 606-9.

There is a third, and to my mind even more important way in which the analogy between self-defence and torture fails. Self-defence is about individual action, torture is about government action: the limits are not necessarily the same. There is a profound difference between individual acts of violence and a system of government-regulated torture. There is a difference between kidnapping and government sponsored 'disappearance'. There is a difference between murder — even mass murder — and genocide.[63] The difference is the government sanction and the government power that stands behind it in each case.[64] Government action — law — carries a mark of legitimacy with it. Self-defence, which leads to murder, or even revenge, might elicit our sympathy. We might even in some way excuse it. But it is not the same thing as a government program, which establishes, institutionalises, administers, and authorises torture. No matter how limited, torture is thereby made *right* in a way that no act of personal self-defence ever makes murder right. We hold governments to higher standards for a good reason.

So too, the reach and mechanisms of government power make torture a weapon from which no member of the community will feel immune. If the state could torture any one of us — they probably would not but they *could* — what sort of a society would we live in? Now Bagaric and Clarke attempt to avoid this problem by implying that torture would only affect the very few that in some sense deserved it. Although they admit that there may be situations in which 'torturing the innocent' to extract information would be justifiable if enough lives were thereby saved, the purchase of their argument as to the moral justifiability of torture rests on distinguishing those who are in danger and 'blameless', from those who are 'wrongdoers.'[65] In the newspaper articles written at the same time, the authors make this distinction central to their construction of the moral basis for torture. There, they insist that it is 'verging on moral indecency … to favour the interests of wrongdoers over those of the innocent'.[66] One way or another, the notion of wrongdoing underlies their assumption that we have the right person; that their suffering can be used to save another's life; and that even if the torture fails to elicit information the loss is not in the end so very terrible.

But who are these 'wrongdoers' who, according to the general assumptions that underscore this whole debate, can be legitimately made to suffer so that the innocent might live? Perhaps they are only the associates of terrorists, or family members; and in any case any torture that takes place will very probably precede

---

[63] G Andreopoulos, *Genocide: Conceptual and Historical Dimensions* (Philadelphia: University of Pennsylvania Press, 1994).
[64] In relation to genocide, see D Manderson, 'Apocryphal Jurisprudence' (2001) 26 *Australian Journal of Legal Philosophy* 27.
[65] Bagaric and Clarke, *USFLR*, above n 8, 584, 607-9, 612-13.
[66] Bagaric and Clarke, *SMH*, above n 8.

a trial that might establish just how culpable they are. After all, as both Bagaric and Clarke along with Gonzales insist, the whole point of the argument in favour of torture is our need 'to *quickly* obtain information from captured terrorists [sic] and their sponsors'.[67] So much for the rule of law: another suspicion has been magically converted into something we just happen to know. In fact, Bagaric and Clarke's own argument shows us exactly how, under the pressure of time, and the urge to get immediate results, even the most modest regime of torture will inexorably corrupt what one might have thought to be core values of this society and of our legal system. 'The investigation and trial process is simply one way of distinguishing wrongdoers from the innocent,' they cheerfully muse. 'To that end, it does not seem a particularly effective process. There are other ways of forming such conclusions.'[68] Torture, for example?

In the real world, which again I realise it might be considered bad form to bring up, there are many reasons why we might all live in fear of a government that had reserved to itself some kind of right to torture suspects who it has determined in some way are 'wrongdoers'. Perhaps it might just be a case of mistaken identity, or maybe you happened to be born with a foreign sounding name, or maybe you look suspicious or are the wrong colour, or come from a country with a violent history, or are otherwise associated with the wrong people, or perhaps you were just known for holding unpopular opinions at one time or other. How much torture might it take to show that you were not really a 'wrongdoer' after all? And what effect would that endemic, nagging fear have on all our lives and our relationship to the state? Peter Faris, former head of the National Crime Authority, says it would be alright 'to pull out a fingernail of a terrorist in order to save a couple of million lives'.[69] But the government legitimisation of torture, whatever the reason, would ultimately serve only to cripple a few million lives and corrupt our understanding of law and of justice. Bagaric and Clarke try and avoid these profoundly serious consequences by insisting that 'our decisions in extreme situations will be compartmentalised to desperate predicaments'.[70] But it is precisely this effort to quarantine our thinking about torture that is inevitably doomed to failure.

## Opposing it

The apologists cannot see the difference between self-defence and torture because they are concerned only about outcomes and never about means. For Bagaric and Clarke, it is simply a mathematical calculation: a tortured terrorist versus one innocent life or many. They even offer us a comforting formula at the end:

---

[67] Gonzales, above n 21.
[68] Bagaric and Clarke, *USFR*, above n 8, 612.
[69] Bagaric and Clarke, *SMH*, above n 8.
[70] Bagaric and Clarke, *USFR*, above n 8, 607.

W+L+P/T x O = torture.[71] This effort at calculation no doubt underpins *any* argument for the expediency of torture in a 'state of exception'.[72] It is, of course and as they argue, a version of utilitarianism.[73] The authors are at pains to defend the validity of utilitarianism as a moral theory. But they do so dishonestly because they have made no serious effort to take into account the *actual* costs of the balancing act they propose. In most versions of the utilitarian calculus, which one hears in defence of such extreme measures, and Bagaric and Clarke's version is no exception, the real benefits are a sheer fantasy and the real costs are wholly and shamefully ignored.

Against utilitarianism, there is not much to say that has not been said many times before. Ethics means that there are some things you do not do *even though* it might advantage you (or the whole society) to do them. Ethics means that we impose limits on our actions that cannot be reduced to a calculation about winners and losers. Slavery, for example, would not be less wrong if more people gained from it than lost. It would not be less wrong even if we only enslaved 'wrongdoers'. The wrong is intrinsic and irredeemable. It is not negotiable in terms of costs and benefits.[74] Bagaric and Clarke argue that the problem with absolutist theories is that there is no fundamental virtue that grounds them.[75] This misses the point. The particular instances are the virtues. The prohibition of slavery is one, irreducible to some other more abstract principle. The prohibition against torture is another.

So too, human rights protect not just good people but all people, and not just some of the time but all of the time: they are not to be weighed up, or sacrificed. It is in the nature of a human right that it is incalculable. We might feel that certain people have acted in such a way that they no longer *deserve* to be treated humanely, and if society as a whole were to gain by torturing them a little, then we should be allowed to do so. But human rights are not something we deserve. They protect each of us from abuse by protecting all of us unconditionally. These rights recognise as inviolable the core of our autonomy as human beings, *regardless* of the temptation or the need to violate them. The argument is undoubtedly partial and problematic[76] and Bagaric and Clarke are right to draw our attention to how nebulous, fluid and ambiguous the claims of rights (like

---

[71] Ibid 613.
[72] G Agamben, *State of Exception* (K Attell trans of *Stato di eccezione*, (first published Turin: Bollati Boringhieri, 2003) Chicago: University of Chicago Press, 2005).
[73] Bagaric and Clarke, *USFLR*, above n 8, 605-11; J S Mill, *Utilitarianism* (G Sher (ed), Indianapolis: Hackett, 2001, original work published 1861); P Singer, *Practical Ethics* (Cambridge: Cambridge University Press, 1993).
[74] J Rawls, *A Theory of Justice* (Oxford: Oxford University Press, 1971); B Williams, *Ethics and the Limits of Philosophy* (Cambridge, Mass: Harvard University Press, 1985).
[75] Bagaric and Clarke, *USFLR*, above n 8, 602.
[76] C Douzinas, *The End of Human Rights* (Oxford: Hart, 2000); M Glendon, *Rights Talk: The Impoverishment of Political Discourse* (New York: Maxwell Macmillan, 1990).

any theoretical claim at all) often are.[77] Nevertheless, if there is anything at all that we have a right to protect against the government and against all of society, it is not just our bodily integrity but our sanity, our very self. That is the absolute right of which torture threatens to deprive us. Simply in terms of 'weighing up' the costs and benefits, in order to evaluate *seriously* the prohibition against torture in utilitarian terms, rather more than a fingernail is at stake.

Torture is wrong under all circumstances, not because it leads to certain bad outcomes, but for no reason: simply and inherently. This is not a perverse argument. Love, for example, is good not because it might lead us to wealth or happiness, but for no reason.[78] It just is. In fact, to continue to look for reasons, to ask 'what is love good *for*?' or 'how does loving someone benefit *me*?' is the logic of a psychopath. Now if Bagaric and Clarke, amongst many others, cannot see the inherent wrong of torture, it is hard to see how to communicate with them. But let me suggest two possible approaches intended to communicate what I see as intrinsically true to those who clearly do not see it that way.

The first approach is literary. When Voltaire was a relatively young man, Jonathan Swift, author of *Gulliver's Travels*, wrote 'A Modest Proposal' of his own. What will we do about the poor children of Ireland, he asked, who are such a burden to their parents?

> I have been assured by a very knowing American of my acquaintance in London, that a young healthy child well nursed is at a year old a most delicious, nourishing, and wholesome food, whether stewed, roasted, baked, or boiled; and I make no doubt that it will equally serve in a fricassee or a ragout.[79]

There's a solution to famine for you, and what after all is wrong with it? If children seem too innocent, we could just eat those in the reformatories, wrongdoers each and every one. Without a sense of our limits, the calibration of costs and benefits is unstoppable: and we *shall* be led to commit atrocities. It strikes me that the current modest proposal for torture makes the same mistakes: slipping seamlessly and without argument across fundamental distinctions, ignoring the social context it echoes, blind to the horrific practical implications of the system it envisages, far too confident of the reliability and accuracy of its own judgments. But Swift's modest proposal was satire, while Bagaric and Clarke's is not.

---

[77] Bagaric and Clarke, *USFLR*, above n 8, 597-604.
[78] See E Levinas, *Totality and Infinity* (A Lingis trans of *Totalite et infi* (first published 1961, Pittsburgh: Duquesne University, 1969); E Levinas, *Otherwise Than Being* (A Lingis trans of *Autrement qu'être* (2nd ed, 1978) Hague; Boston: M Nijhoff; Hingham, MA: Distributors for the US and Canada, Kluwer Boston, 1981); D Manderson, *Proximity, Levinas and the Soul of Law* (Montreal; Ithaca: McGill-Queen's University Press, 2006).
[79] J Swift, 'A Modest Proposal' (1729) in *A Modest Proposal and Other Satires* (Amherst, MA: Prometheus Books, 1994), 257 at 259.

The second approach is historical. Both proposals, above all, display that dangerous human quality of arrogance, which assumes that we can and should weigh up one person's pain and a community's fear, against another's life. It is the economists' approach to life and the tyrant's approach to politics: everything is a calculation, and no calculation is too ambitious to be foresworn. The use of such formulae will offer an easy answer to all our problems, but the easy answers are usually wrong. We know all about the Western history of state-sanctioned torture, *l'amende honorable* and the Inquisition. It is not a tradition worth reviving.

Our repugnance is not simply the instinctive and 'reflex rejection of torture' that Bagaric and Clarke disparage.[80] Disgust, like shame, is not a pointless emotion. On the contrary, it is an exceptionally powerful way to change the behaviour of people and of communities.[81] A great deal of effort and thought has been expended giving torture the 'pejorative connotations' it has today. We have *learnt* this feeling of disgust over several centuries. Voltaire would weep to read the arguments now being used to justify a new-found tolerance of torture and tyranny. He saw torture and he knew what it smelled like. And he also knew that at some point the arguments must stop so that the disgust might begin. *Écrasez l'infâme.* Don't negotiate: wipe it out.

---

[80] Bagaric and Clarke claim that when faced with the kind of hypothetical on which their argument is built, 'not many' people would find torture unacceptable. But the statistic they cite does not even remotely justify this particular lithe assertion: see *USFLR*, above n 8, 583 fn 8. If Bagaric and Clarke's idea of 'not many' people is 53 per cent then I fear for the way in which they would put in practice the neat mathematical calculation called 'The Formula' they think will clarify for us when torture is justified. The point is not trivial. When investigators justify torture, as when intellectuals interpret statistics, they are prone to see what they want to see, to justify the result they want to achieve.
[81] M Nussbaum, *Hiding from Humanity: Disgust, Shame and the Law* (Princeton, NJ: Princeton University Press, 2004); J Braithwaite, *Crime, Shame, and Reintegration* (Cambridge, UK; New York: Cambridge University Press, 1989).

# Chapter Four

# Protecting Constitutionalism in Treacherous Times: Why 'Rights' Don't Matter

W Wesley Pue[*]

## Introduction

The twenty-first century begins obsessed with matters of security and the supposed need to 'trade-off' security and liberty. So pervasive is this obsession that a recent Hollywood movie, known more for its state-of-the-art special effects and tortured plot lines than for its thought-provoking quality begins, dramatically, with the reading of an Emergency Proclamation.

The setting is Bermuda, a British overseas possession, in the eighteenth century. Its opening scene portrays a mass hanging, conducted with military efficiency. The victims are an array of hapless souls including men and women of all ages and a pre-pubescent boy. The first words spoken in *Pirates of the Caribbean: At World's End* are delivered in the crisply upper-class accent of a British officer:

> In order to effect a timely halt to deteriorating conditions and to ensure the common good, a State of Emergency is declared for these Territories, by Decree of Lord Cutler Beckett, duly appointed Representative of His Majesty the King.
>
> By Decree according to Martial Law, the following statutes are temporarily amended:
>
> - Right to Assembly. Suspended.
> - Right to *Habeas Corpus*. Suspended.
> - Right to Legal Counsel. Suspended.
> - Right to verdict by a jury of peers. Suspended.

---

[*] Nathan Nemetz Chair in Legal History, Faculty of Law, University of British Columbia, Vancouver, Canada. Currently serving as Vice-Provost and Associate Vice-President Academic Resources, University of British Columbia, Vancouver, Canada. I wish to acknowledge the detailed advice of Robert Diab, the encouragement of colleagues at the University of British Columbia, the indispensable research assistance and critical insights of Robert Russo, and the intellectual provocation and collegiality of participants at an important conference on 'Ensuring Accountability: Terrorist Challenges and State Responses in a Free Society', Australian National University, Canberra, 20-21 April 2006. I am especially indebted to Miriam Gani, Penelope Mathew, and Simon Bronitt for their equal measures of intellectual leadership, critical insight and generosity of spirit. None of the above share blame for the views expressed herein.

> By Decree all persons found guilty of piracy or aiding a person convicted of piracy or associating with a person convicted of piracy shall be sentenced to hang by the neck until dead.

The words are punctuated with dramatic pauses at all the right places. On each utterance of the word 'suspended', the camera focuses beneath the gallows as the trap is released. Shackled feet appear, swinging, as each suspension of constitutional propriety is announced. Bodies pile high on crude carts, hauled off as the officer's last words are delivered. In Hollywood convention, his impeccable English accent marks him as a scoundrel, an evil-doer, of the worst sort.

One presumes that a United States (US) viewing audience is expected to derive a moral lesson of sorts from this. The King evokes, dimly perhaps, collective memory of the overseas monarch whose 'oppressions' provoked the American Revolution. The actions of the authorities are marked as utterly 'un-American'. Viewers are invited to identify with pirates, presented here as sympathetic and well-meaning sorts who struggle against unchecked power, undemocratic and unconstitutional assertions of authority, and the evils of Empire. The clipped British accent, the mechanical efficiency of the gallows permit no other association. Middle America, raised for half a century now on Disney-land rides such as that which inspired the 'Pirates of the Caribbean' series, consigns 'piracy' to a romantically amusing past. We are invited to focus on the excesses of duly constituted authority, personified in Lord Cutler Beckett and his officers. The bodies of the downtrodden accumulate too hastily to permit alternative interpretation. The camera lingers on a small boy, too short to reach the noose. His beefy executioners helpfully resolve the dilemma by hoisting him onto a barrel, fortuitously raising him to just the right height to reach his noose.

This set-up clearly marks the movie's antagonist as evil. Disappointingly, the fuller implications of this startling starting sequence are left unexplored. Nonetheless, it is hard to miss the resonances. President Bush, like the fictional British imperial authority of another time and place, has decreed that the common good requires long established constitutional principles to be set aside. *Habeas corpus*, the right to counsel, the right to a jury trial, and freedom of association are all threatened, qualified, constrained, or impeded during the 'War on Terror' just as in Disney's fictional past.

As in Lord Cutler Beckett's administration, the measures are temporary, limited to the duration of a 'war' on terror. Like the past empire of US fiction, contemporary America has created zones in which authority operates without constraint of law. Contemporary America, like the fictional eighteenth-century colonial administration vilified in the Disney Corporation's movies, draws no distinction, in pursuit of enemies, between children and adults.[1]

One should not make too much of popular culture, of course. Nonetheless, it is telling that a rather blunt critique of the 'War on Terror' has gained sufficient foothold to frame even an action movie. It is the brutality of the 'War on Pirates' and an authoritarian state administration's derogation of long-established 'rights' that serves to delineate 'good' from 'bad', 'hero' from 'villain', the virtuous from the 'evil-doer' for movie-viewers. Who, we wonder, can protect us from modern-day Lord Cutler Becketts?

Even highly manipulated, powerful, visual images such as those in *Pirates of the Caribbean: At World's End*, lack persuasive power, however, for those who take the threat of terrorism seriously. The killing of children at the gallows, like the killing of children by bomb, bullet, or bayonet, evokes one response if we presume the action to have been taken by a capricious, avaricious, and evil empire; quite another if common decency and, perhaps, civilisation itself, is viewed as utterly vulnerable to the threat represented by the particular children and those behind them. Though *World's End* does not pause to consider the violations of human dignity, property, livelihood, and life perpetrated by pirates, anyone seeking to 'read' the movie against contemporary circumstances cannot fail to register, powerfully, the real pain inflicted by terrorists. Images of airliners being flown into office towers, nightclub bombings in Bali, and attacks on railways, buses or subways in Spain, Mumbai, or London are seared into twenty-first-century Western consciousness. The fear that dirty nuclear devices, chemical or biological weapons might be unleashed on major cities in order to wreak damage and death on an unprecedented scale cannot be ignored. Such things *will* happen.

Confronted with the spectre of real terror, death, and destruction, and of real enemies quite unlike the playful pirates of fiction, most contemporaries are willing to trade a little freedom for a little security. In the world of realpolitik, terrorist threats must be taken seriously. Niceties such as the right to counsel, *habeas corpus*, privacy, or trial by jury, acquire an abstract character. Nice if you can have them, these lawyers' obsessions seem less important than life, property, or democracy: second order priorities, or luxuries perhaps.

But, is it lawyers' obsessions that are at issue?

So conceiving things seriously misconstrues the matter. The linguistic usages of lawyers have taken over much public discourse during the past half-century. Curiously, this has narrowed the range of consideration on immensely important

---

[1] See, eg, the case of Canadian Omar Khadr and his US *habeas corpus* proceedings: *OK, et al v George Bush, et al*, US District Court for the District of Columbia, Case 1:04-cv-01136-JDB <http://www.nightslantern.ca/law/omarkhadr13june07.htm>.

public matters and blunted critique of even draconian laws. In most liberal democracies, discussions of the virtues of this or that 'anti-terrorism' law have been cast in terms familiar to legalistic-minded civil libertarians. The analysis of anti-terrorism law has most often been championed by professionals whose detailed knowledge and focused critiques, as often as not, serve to confound. By focusing too much on particulars, larger shifts in the way power operates under the guise of the 'War on Terror' are obscured.

In this brief commentary, I hope to avoid confusing the trees for the wood, by taking the discussion of contemporary anti-terrorism law[2] to a level somewhat above the forest canopy, to a point from whence the full contours of the forest can be perceived, its breadth, depth, and height discerned. I hope to draw upon the perspective so attained in order to reveal a surprising truth. The violation of 'rights', at least as we now understand that notion, forms a surprisingly small portion of what is wrong with 'anti-terrorism' legislation in major Western countries. Consequently, the presence or absence of constitutionally entrenched 'rights' protections ('charters', 'bills', or 'human rights' legislation) determines only a small degree of the variance of outcomes when draconian state powers are subjected to judicial review. In substantiating this second point, it is necessary to attain a bird's-eye view of anti-terrorist law, but also to engage in some realism about constitutionally entrenched rights. One final point bears emphasis, though it cannot be developed in this essay: only the tiniest sliver of state action is ever subjected to judicial review. This gives any discussion of what happens in the courts a somewhat abstract, other-worldly character, grotesquely distanced from the quotidian routine in which subjects encounter state authority.

## Bird's Eye View: Anti-Terrorism Law and the Principle of Legality

In his classic work, *The Morality of Law*,[3] Lon Fuller offers a compelling account of the minimum conditions of legality. Much, it turns out, follows from the simple proposition that law serves to guide human conduct by means of rules. Fuller illustrates his understanding of law through an extended parable concerning a bumbling but well-meaning 'King Rex,' who makes a complete hash of governance because he is unable to appreciate the virtue and nature of law. 'Eight routes to disaster' emerge from Rex's failures:

---

[2] My central reference point throughout is Canada's anti-terrorism legislation, which I discuss at greater length in W W Pue, 'War on Terror: Constitutional Governance in a State of Permanent Warfare' (2002 Laskin Lecture in Public Law, Osgoode Hall Law School); (2003) 41 *Osgoode Hall Law Journal* (Special Issue on *Civil Disobedience, Civil Liberties, and Civil Resistance*, edited by H Glasbeek and J Fudge) 267, 267-92 (see also sources cited therein). Problematic aspects of Canada's legislation mirror features of similar statutes in the US, UK, and Australia, as contributions to this volume amply demonstrate.
[3] L L Fuller, *The Morality of Law* (New Haven: Yale U P, revised ed, 1969).

1. a failure to achieve rules at all, so that every issue must be decided on an ad hoc basis;
2. a failure to publicise, or at least to make available to the affected party, the rules he is expected to observe;
3. the abuse of retroactive legislation, which not only cannot itself guide action, but undercuts the integrity of rules prospective in effect, since it puts them under the threat of retrospective change;
4. a failure to make rules understandable;
5. the enactment of contradictory rules;
6. rules that require conduct beyond the powers of the affected party;
7. introducing such frequent changes in the rules that the subject cannot orient his action by them; and
8. a failure of congruence between the rules as announced and their actual administration.[4]

Fuller's *desiderata* are widely considered to embody the essence of the rule of law. Few could argue against the virtue of generality, promulgation, prospectivity, clarity, absence of contradictions, performability, constancy over time, or congruence of rules with actions.[5]

Casual observers of contemporary legal systems can be forgiven for thinking it unlikely that any of these 'routes to disaster' can be present in notoriously law-bounded modern democracies. Anyone who has ploughed through the mind-numbingly complex, elaborate, voluminous, legislation that emerged from Western legislatures in the aftermath of 11 September 2001 (9/11), would be forgiven for thinking it unlikely that failure to achieve rules — the first 'route to disaster' — could be at issue. Moreover, it seems entirely obvious that blowing up office buildings, trains, buses, and so on should be illegal. This, along with massive media attention on the 'War on Terror' makes it seem, at first glance, that none of routes two, four, six or seven (failure to publicise; incomprehensible rules; impossible-to-obey rules; unstable law) can be of concern. It would be logical to think that there can hardly be any question of one law authorising what another prohibits when it comes to terrorism. Hence, the fifth disaster route, 'contradictory rules', seems unlikely. Similarly, the third route to disaster, retroactivity, seems an unlikely reef on which anti-terrorism law might flounder. Indeed, it is commonly asserted that much anti-terrorism law only prohibits things that were previously illegal (killing civilians, conspiring to do so, etc). Finally, given the paramount importance of preventing terrorist attacks, one would think state authorities at all levels would be determined to ensure

---

[4] Ibid 39.
[5] See, eg, N E Simmond, 'Law as a Moral Idea' (2005) 55 *University of Toronto Law Journal* 61, 87. See also the remarkable book by M Ribeiro, *Limiting Arbitrary Power* (Vancouver: UBC Press, 2004).

congruence between anti-terrorism rules and state action: the eighth disaster route seems unlikely.

Closer inspection overturns each assumption. The very complexity of anti-terrorism statutes, which seemingly inoculates against failure to achieve rules (disaster route one), is our first clue. If we take Canada's anti-terrorism legislation[6] as representative of the genus, surprising results begin to emerge. The deeper one probes the language, structure, and workings of anti-terrorism law, the clearer it becomes that *each and every one of Fuller's eight routes to disaster* is taken. As is commonly the case in human endeavour, the road to disaster is paved with good intent. Unfortunate consequences arise from the desire to 'name' global terrorism as a distinct category of criminal activity, from the intent to disrupt terrorist organisations (rather than merely prosecute criminal activities after the fact), and from the desire to draft legislation so as to ensure that no future terrorist can ever shelter in legal loopholes.

Anyone who has given the matter any thought knows the difficulty of giving a precise definition to 'terrorism'. The term is invoked for its rhetorical power and denunciatory effect rather than analytical coherence. 'Terrorist' actions are invariably prohibited under ordinary criminal prohibitions on violence, intimidation, or extortion. It is a crime to blow people up deliberately, with or without special 'anti-terrorism' laws. So too, conspiracies to do such things, aiding and abetting individuals doing them, and so on, are criminal under ordinary law. It may be that 'anti-terrorism' gives emphasis to the denunciation of all non-state violence, bolstering the moral power of law, perhaps. Nonetheless, the urge to denounce imports lack of clarity: how does one distinguish ordinary murder from terrorist murder? The issue is made murkier still when two additional elements are taken into account.

First, following Bush doctrine,[7] Canadian legislators sought to prohibit not just terrorist acts against Canadians (a relatively straight-forward matter), or even against Canada and its allies (designated from time to time by delegated legislation, perhaps), but terrorism against *any* state authority *anywhere*.[8] This, of course, is nonsense. No country that plays on the world stage wishes to forego the possibility of destabilising its enemies by aiding and abetting violent opposition ('terrorism') within their borders. The stated objective on the face of anti-terrorism law is, thus, one that no one seriously intends. Even countries (such as Canada?) who would be blameless bystanders in world affairs endorse

---

[6] Although much law-making is somewhat affected by 'anti-terrorism' intent, the most prominent of Canada's 'anti-terrorism' statutes are the *Anti-Terrorism Act*, SC 2001, c 41 and the *Public Safety Act*, SC 2004, c 15.
[7] A concise retrospective on the Bush administration's 'War on Terror' including a discussion of its key elements is provided in S Power, 'Our War on Terror', *New York Times* (New York), 29 July 2007.
[8] This point is elaborated more fully in Pue, above n 2.

ally-sponsored terrorism through their silence.[9] To be blunt, we have deliberately passed statutes that do not mean what they say. This is the legislator's equivalent of making promises with fingers crossed: the statute book is liberally peppered with discretionary powers in order to allow the law to mean whatever officials might, from time to time, wish it to mean. Discretion permeates anti-terrorism law's genetic code: the widest possible latitude is accorded to state authorities (senior police officers, Ministers of Justice, and the like) when it comes to intervening against 'terrorism'. This is specifically because no one wants vigorous prosecution of everyone and every group, association or institution that violates the letter of our law. We have, in short, a deliberate, structural 'failure of congruence between the rules as announced and their actual administration' (disaster route eight). It is as if the legislators who passed these laws had their fingers crossed behind their backs the whole time.

Second, anti-terrorism law seeks to disrupt the networks on which terrorists rely. So far, so good. Complexities intrude, however, when we move from targeting the generals and ground-troops who initiate terrorist violence, to reach into the wider networks of more or less passive supporters, financial backers, bankers, financial institutions, and agents. Cognisant of the cellular organisation of the 9/11 attackers and knowing that several of those individuals held imperfect knowledge of their mission, Canada introduced an extremely broadly defined offence of 'facilitating' terrorism.[10] In another piece, I have summarised certain aspects of the facilitation offence this way:

> Bizarrely, *knowing* facilitation can happen even though no terrorist activity was in fact carried out, where the 'facilitator' does not know "that a particular activity is facilitated", and where no particular terrorist activity was foreseen or planned at the time it was facilitated.[11]

Though learned judges are capable of 'reading down' facilitation provisions so as to render them both intelligible and, perhaps, tolerable, the statutory language is extraordinarily, unnecessarily, imprecise. It is hard to know which of Fuller's requirements of legality is left inviolate in such statutory schemes. A system founded, at every critical juncture, on official discretion fails to achieve rules at all: the first and essential requirement of legality is absent. 'Umpire's Discretion' prevails.[12]

---

[9] It is salutary to recall that the Taliban was much aided by the West in the days when their war was with Russia and that both Nelson Mandela and George Washington meet the Canadian definition of terrorists.

[10] See *R v Khawaja* (2006), 214 CCC (3d) 399, WL 3031774 (Ont SCJ, Rutherford J); 2006 CarswellOnt 6551 [30]ff, for a summary of the immediate background at the time the *Anti-Terrorism Act* was drafted. Canadians had prior experience of cellular terrorist organisations in the Federation for the Liberation of Quebec (FLQ), however.

[11] Pue, above n 2, 278.

[12] S Arnold, 'Umpire's Discretion: States of Insecurity and Canada's Anti-Terrorism Legislation' (manuscript of summer, 2007).

## Rights Don't Matter

This perspective is obtainable only from a bird's eye view. It is as hard to discern from 30,000 feet as it is from ground level. Too distanced a perspective dulls perception, leading to jingoistic, utterly illogical, defences of the statutory scheme. Prime examples of jingoism include the surprisingly common assumption that the Act passes muster either because 'Canada is a pretty decent country' or because it lacks one or more offensive provisions found in similar legislation elsewhere (the USA PATRIOT Act[13] is a favourite whipping boy, here). Others, displaying stunning capacity for non sequitur, conclude that otherwise objectionable laws are acceptable because 'our political leaders are trustworthy' or 'our security personnel are well-meaning'.

Conversely, viewing the matter from a position too close to the ground of criminal law practice or 'constitutional' law doctrine obscures the larger story. The particular camouflages the general; the wood is lost for the trees. A sloppy habit of thought that common lawyers have fallen prey to during the past half-century compounds the problems of perceptions dimmed by complacency on the one hand or too intense a focus on detail on the other. We have become inured to a degree of imprecision in statutory drafting that routinely far exceeds the requirements of pragmatic governance, much less the requirements of the rule of law.

I do not wish to be understood as implying that the many *specific* objections to anti-terrorism law have no bite. An impressive line-up of eminent scholars has laboured since 2001 to identify profound problems with many particular aspects of Canada's *Anti-Terrorism Act*, for example.[14] Some challenges have begun to find their way to court.[15]

When problems are identified in the scope or operations of anti-terrorism legislation, the hope is commonly expressed that the *Canadian Charter of Rights and Freedoms* (the '*Charter*')[16] will knock off the roughest edges. Similarly, scholars, lawyers and rights activists in countries lacking an entrenched bill of rights often take the view that one or other bad outcome could be avoided 'if only' they enjoyed similar constitutional structure.[17] Among the more

---

[13] *Uniting and Strengthening America by Providing Appropriate Tools Required to Intercept and Obstruct Terrorism Act of 2001 (USA PATRIOT Act)* Public Law No 107-56, 115 Stat 272 (2001).

[14] A good amount of scholarship that has stood the test of time was published during the very short period of time in which Canada's *Anti-Terrorism Act* was before Parliament. See R J Daniels, P Macklem, and K Roach (eds), *The Security of Freedom: Essays on Canada's Anti-Terrorism Bill* (Toronto: University of Toronto Press, 2001).

[15] See *R v Khawaja* (2006), 214 CCC (3d) 399, WL 3031774 (Ont SCJ, Rutherford J); 2006 CarswellOnt 6551; *O'Neill v Canada (Attorney-General)* (2006), OJ No 4189; *Charkaoui v Canada (Citizenship and Immigration)* [2007] SCC 9.

[16] *The Constitution Act 1982*, being Schedule B to the *Canada Act 1982* (UK) c 11.

[17] An enormously important and careful comparative study makes such arguments, though in a subtle and nuanced fashion in comparing rights protection in three areas (double jeopardy, same-sex

thoughtful scholars making this argument, Australia's George Williams, is unambiguous:

> I should state clearly my position on a Bill of Rights. My view is that we do need better formal legal protection for human rights at the national level and in each of the States and Territories ... [I]t has become all too clear that Australia does have a range of serious human rights problems, such as the detention of young children seeking asylum, the indefinite detention of asylum seekers who cannot be deported and our overreaching terror laws (which in some respects like the new powers for ASIO [the Australian Security Intelligence Organisation] go beyond even the laws enacted in the United States). There are also problems in regard to the undermining of our most important political freedoms. A good example is the right to vote ... a so-called 'electoral integrity' measure, removes the vote from prisoners and also forces the closure of the electoral roll on the day that the election is issued, thereby denying thousands of Australians the chance to change their enrolment details and many young Australians the chance to vote for the first time.[18]

Similarly, Senator Trish Crossin is on record to the effect that entrenched rights protection would have ameliorated the worst effects of Australia's anti-terrorism legislation: 'A Bill of Rights would ensure that those fundamental freedoms are written down, and provide courts with the ability to examine and rule on instances where those rights may have been breached'.[19] Again, when the High Court upheld Australia's use of 'interim control orders' under its anti-terrorist regime in the case of 'Jihad Jack',[20] one response was to call for an entrenched bill of rights. *The Age* reported:

> Human rights lawyer Greg Barns ... [said] the ruling highlighted the need for Australia to have a bill of rights ... "This is the high point of the capital-C conservatism of the current High Court", Mr. Barns said ... [I]n the absence of a bill of human rights, the High Court in the past had been prepared to check

---

relationships, hate speech) in Australia, Canada, New Zealand, and the UK. See L McNamara, *Human Rights Controversies: The Impact of Legal Form* (Abingdon & New York: Routledge-Cavendish, 2007).

[18] G Williams, 'Victoria's Charter of Human Rights and Responsibilities' (Speech delivered at the Senate Occasional Lecture, Parliament House of Australia, 7 July 2006). The fact that the Australian High Court has recently accepted that a blanket ban on prisoners' right to vote is unconstitutional qualifies, but does not fundamentally contradict Williams' more general point. George Williams has been a passionate advocate for entrenched rights protection in Australia. See, amongst his many publications, *A Charter of Rights for Australia* (Sydney: UNSW Press, 2007); *What Price Security? Taking Stock of Australia's Anti-Terror Laws* (Sydney: UNSW Press, 2006) (with Andrew Lynch); *The Case for an Australian Bill of Rights: Freedom in the War on Terror* (Sydney: UNSW Press, 2004); *A Bill of Rights for Australia* (Sydney: UNSW Press, 2000).

[19] T Crossin, 'The Rights of the Human Rights Act' (Paper presented to the Darwin Launch of the Campaign by New Matilda for a Human Rights Act for Australia, 21 July 2006).

[20] *Thomas v Mowbray* [2007] HCA 33 (2 August 2007).

the power of Australian governments. "Today the High Court has abrogated that responsibility."[21]

It is hard to know what to make of such arguments in the abstract. Entrenched rights' codes undoubtedly set out a certain level of constitutional aspiration against which citizens, officials, and judges alike are asked to evaluate their actions. The standards can be taken as consensual and are, in any event, 'binding'. Here lies the rub, however.

The formal theory of the thing apart, the 'bindingness' of constitutionally entrenched rights is a good deal less certain than is often thought. This is not because we presume bad faith on the part of officials or judges. Nor is it only because some courts are, as Barns suggests, more inclined to 'capital-C conservatism' than others.

The inherent ambiguity of language intrudes powerfully, destabilising the content of even the most 'certain' rights. Section 2 of the *Charter*, for example, protects the 'fundamental freedoms' of 'thought, belief, opinion and expression', along with freedom of 'conscience and religion', 'peaceful assembly', and 'association' for 'everyone'.[22] No weasel words are used. In practice, however, these seemingly unqualified 'fundamental freedoms' can be restricted in myriad ways without constitutional rupture. Free expression does not licence defamation or 'hate speech'; freedom of religion does not protect the use of prohibited narcotics in sacramental rites; and the freedom of peaceful assembly is violated by state authorities with surprising regularity.[23]

Other rights are explicitly qualified even in their utterance. Thus, deprivation of 'life, liberty and security of the person' is entirely allowable under the terms of Canada's *Charter* provided it is done 'in accordance with the principles of fundamental justice' and it is only 'unreasonable search or seizure' and arbitrary detention and imprisonment that are prohibited (*Charter* ss 7, 8, and 9, respectively). The point is *neither* that these words are meaningless nor that judges, officials, and law-makers fail to take them earnestly to heart on a daily basis. They are not, however, unambiguous, not absolute and, as words on paper, can never be self-enacting. These conditions apply to all constitutionally entrenched rights, everywhere, even if no further words of explicit limitation are found.[24] It is naïve to hope for too much in the way of certainty merely

---

[21] B Nicholson, 'Kirby Lashes Judges over Terror Case Ruling', *The Age* (Melbourne), 2 August 2007.
[22] *The Constitution Act 1982*, being Schedule B to the *Canada Act* 1982 (UK) 1982 c 11, s 2.
[23] On one side of this see, W W Pue, 'Trespass and Expressive Rights' (Paper prepared for the Ipperwash Inquiry) <http://ipperwashinquiry.ca/policy_part/research/pdf/Pue.pdf>.
[24] Canada's *Charter* contains a further qualification: '1. The *Canadian Charter of Rights and Freedoms* guarantees the rights and freedoms set out in it subject only to such reasonable limits prescribed by law as can be demonstrably justified in a free and democratic society.'

because a statement of rights has been constitutionally entrenched. Lawyers love the ambiguity of language and, always, can make much of it.

All of this provides considerable grist for the lawyers' mill, of course. What effect it has on channelling anti-terrorism law along more, rather than less, desirable courses is less clear. The necessary imprecision of language leaves any marginally competent lawyer enormous room to manoeuvre, an effect accentuated in times of crisis or perceived crisis. As a result, the presence or absence of constitutionally entrenched 'rights' protections ('charters', 'bills', or 'human rights' legislation) determines only a small degree of the variance of outcomes when harsh or extraordinary state powers come to judicial review.[25]

This does not dispose of the issue of the utility of formal rights protection however. A constitutional bill of rights has undoubted educational value. Bills of rights and charters are displayed as posters in schools and offices, 'charter values' are invoked in public discourse and rights issues enter into public consciousness in a different way than they do in countries without entrenched 'rights protection'. When all is said and done, it is not unreasonable to assert, modestly, that the constitutional entrenchment of 'rights' can do no harm, and might actually lead to the enhancement of rights.

The Canadian experience of living with both a *Charter of Rights and Freedoms* and an overreaching anti-terrorism regime, suggests otherwise, I think. There is, at a minimum, reason for caution in this regard. I wish to assert that the presence of a charter in Canada has distorted public discourse about civil liberties and rights. Recognising that it is notoriously hard to identify cause and effect in the realm of law and social change, I do not want to enter into the complexities of the wider field of enquiry that this opens up, nor to assert that the *Charter* is *primarily* to blame for any particular evils. My more modest claim is that the quality of rights protection in any given culture, its commitment to the principle of the rule of law, and the substantive outcomes are not 'determined' by the presence or absence of a charter. I do assert that the presence of a charter in Canada has co-existed with a diminution in the quality of public discourse and that specific, identifiable, features of charter politics and charter law tug in this direction. I would not wish for a moment, however, to suggest that other factors are not in play, nor that the *Charter* is the *causa causans* in any of this. Others, no doubt, would point to declining union membership or church participation, falling newspaper readership, television's narcotic effect, the decline of political

---

The quagmire of Constitutional interpretation that this opens up cannot be entered into here. Suffice it to say that with or without such an explicit statement, *all* entrenched rights in all countries are subject to 'reasonable limits', however established.

[25] Many seemingly dramatic outcomes in US courts have as much to do with the limits on the constitutional division of power between the federal executive on the one hand and the federal legislative branch or the state's powers on the other, rather than with 'rights' as such. See *Hamdi v Rumsfeld*, 542 US 507 (2004); *Rasul v Bush*, 542 US 466 (2004).

parties, a general dumbing down of politics, consumerism, the evils of public education, 'Americanisation' of Canadian culture, or the perfection of politics by polling consequent on the publication of Theodore White's *The Making of the President, 1960*.[26]

Those qualifications noted, I wish to suggest three interrelated ways in which charters distract from the mission of attaining governance by the rule of law, much less 'rights protection'. In order to appreciate the ways in which this happens it is helpful to visualise 'entrenched' rights protections in three different, but compatible ways: as a Paper Tiger, a Trojan Horse, and a Narcotic Substance.

## Paper Tiger

Entrenched rights are Paper Tigers because the inherently open texture of words combines with the obvious necessity of incorporating a large 'fudge factor' in any document purporting to crystallise *anything* for all time. These factors have been canvassed above. Their effect is compounded considerably in times of perceived crisis if only, as legal cliché has it, because the constitution cannot become a 'suicide pact'.[27] The ambiguity of language makes entrenched charters or bills of rights Paper Tigers that roar, like ventriloquists' puppets, only when people give them voice.[28] Despite much fuss about a purported leftward tilt of 'activist judges',[29] the Supreme Court of Canada has yet to strike down a statute that the federal government is earnestly determined to defend. The Paper Tiger has roared most loudly in modifying laws that the government has little interest in sustaining, but that are too 'hot' to touch politically (abortion regulation and the exclusively heterosexual definition of marriage, for example). No statute considered crucial and staunchly defended by a committed federal government of Canada has yet been struck down.[30]

---

[26] T H White, *The Making of the President, 1960* (New York: Atheneum Publishers, 1961).
[27] This much-abused formulation was first articulated by US Supreme Court Justice Jackson, in dissent, in *Terminiello v City of Chicago*, 337 US 1, 37 (1949): 'This Court has gone far toward accepting the doctrine that civil liberty means the removal of all restraints from these crowds and that all local attempts to maintain order are impairments of the liberty of the citizen. The choice is not between order and liberty. It is between liberty with order and anarchy without either. There is danger that, if the Court does not temper its doctrinaire logic with a little practical wisdom, it will convert the constitutional Bill of Rights into a suicide pact.'
[28] This, in effect, is the critique of both left and right critics of judicial approaches to *Charter* 'rights' in Canada.
[29] See, eg, F L Morton and R Knopff, *The Charter Revolution and the Court Party* (Peterborough, Ontario: Broadview Press, 2000); R I Martin, *The Most Dangerous Branch: How the Supreme Court of Canada Has Undermined Our Law and Our Democracy* (Montreal: McGill-Queen's University Press, 2005); H White, *Judge Who Gave Canada Homosexual 'Marriage' Had Conflict of Interest Says Women's Rights Group* (2006) LiveSiteNews <http://www.lifesite.net/ldn/2006/jul/06071907.html>.
[30] A similar point is made in Joel Bakan's groundbreaking work, *Just Words: Constitutional Rights and Social Wrongs* (Toronto: University of Toronto Press, 1997).

## Trojan Horse

The *Charter's* deployment as a Trojan Horse was strikingly apparent in the events leading up to the passage of Canada's *Anti-Terrorism Act*. Despite the hurried introduction and passage of the legislation immediately following the 2001 terrorist attacks on the US, substantial and sustained criticism of the legislation emerged before the Bill could be passed. Critics ranged from the Evangelical Fellowship of Canada (which prepared a stunning brief)[31] to an elite group of legal experts mobilised by the University of Toronto Law Faculty.[32] In response the *Charter* was dusted off by Ministers and their most senior advisors to provide cover for the *Anti-Terrorism Act*. The Attorney-General of the day defended the legislation on the basis that it had been carefully reviewed by legal experts in the government's employ, who declared it safe from *Charter* review. In Orwellian fashion, Ottawa's upper echelons spoke of the Bill as having been so cleverly drafted as to be '*Charter*-proof'. Politics, unlike law, is unconstrained by logic. This declaration was spun effectively to support an altogether different proposition: because the Bill could not be challenged under the *Charter* it had to be good law. With studied cynicism, the *Charter* was used to bat away any and all substantial questioning of the constitutional propriety or wisdom of the Bill. 'Politics' of the crassest sort, the bar was set very low, deflecting attention entirely from the wisdom of the statute.[33] A focus on *Charter* compliance as, in effect, the only relevant 'rights' concern, says nothing about the way in which police or security officials will use the Act, nothing about the likelihood of the Bill attaining its desired ends, and nothing about its consonance with Canadian standards of civil liberties, justice, constitutionalism or the rule of law.

The strategy worked. The vehicle used to import unwise legislation that does profound violence to civil liberties into Canada's statute books (legislation, by the way, that is remarkably similar to Australia's in key aspects) was the *Canadian Charter of Rights and Freedoms*.

---

[31] Evangelical Fellowship of Canada, *Submission to the Standing Committee on Justice and Human Rights on Bill C-36, An Act in Order to Combat Terrorism*
<http://files.efc-canada.net/si/Religious%20Freedom%20in%20Canada/EFC/Anti-Terrorism%20Bill%20C-36.pdf>.
[32] R J Daniels, P Macklem, and K Roach (eds), *The Security of Freedom: Essays on Canada's Anti-Terrorism Bill* (Toronto: University of Toronto Press, 2001) 99.
[33] K Roach, *September 11: Consequences for Canada* (Montreal, Quebec & Kingston, Ontario: McGill-Queen's University Press, 2003): 'Such a strategy may deceive a public who thinks that consistency with the Charter means that rights are not infringed ... Constitutionalism in Canada before the Charter was built on the notion that those in power should not exercise their legal powers to the fullest extent possible even in times of perceived crisis. It was fundamental to British constitutionalism that what was legal might nevertheless be improper and unconstitutional ... we are losing sight of this older sense that power must be restrained by decency, prudence, and tradition, not just the legal limits that lawyers and courts impose on us.'

## Narcotic Effect

If a charter serves to camouflage the unpleasantness of certain laws, it also has a longer-term narcotic effect, numbing citizens to important matters of public governance. It does this over the long-term partly in the same way the 'Trojan Horse' strategy works in the short-term. Charters, bills of rights, and their ilk remove key issues from the domain of informed public debate, 'professionalise' rights-talk to an astonishing degree, and segregate matters of rights and liberties from the legitimate ambit of lay knowledge. Democratic governance is eviscerated under such conditions. This disempowering of the citizenry on issues related to liberty works in part because, through the stunning effectiveness of the Trojan trick, 'charter compliance' is offered as proof positive of legislative wisdom, obscuring issues of constitutional propriety lying below the charter threshold. The trick works only because charter talk professionalises, abstracts and removes from politics.[34] Citizens quickly become lost in discussions of section numbers, qualified rights, matters that are 'demonstrably justifiable in a free and democratic society', non obstante clauses, 'reading down', and multiple-stage tests. At each point in such discussions *the point* of particular issues gets lost in a sea of technicality. Even the simplest principles (you should not imprison someone in secret and indefinitely on executive command) is lost sight of.

A charter can serve to distract attention from what are in fact foundational constitutional questions: *who* should be able to do *what* to *whom*, *when*, and under *which* circumstances. These questions are the core of constitutionalism and working them out has been a constant struggle over centuries encompassing at least the period from the *Magna Carta* to the present. The 'working out' has not been exclusively or even principally a matter of the interpretation of written constitutions in any country derived from a Westminster model of governance (including the US).[35] Though much disparaged by scholars for a half-century or more, the 'rule of law' remains the *sine qua non* of constitutional governance. Bizarrely, the Canadian experience, with rare exception, has been to focus critique on this or that '*Charter*' violation to such a degree as to miss entirely the massively undefined and largely secret powers vested in officials under the rubric of the 'War on Terror'. This is the 800-pound gorilla in the room. The violation of 'rights', at least as we now understand that notion, forms a surprisingly small portion of what is wrong with 'anti-terrorism' legislation.

---

[34] Such outcomes are often welcomed by elected officials, who can conveniently avoid their responsibilities by fobbing tough questions off to the courts. McNamara, above n 17, 255, aptly observes that: 'A feature of the Canadian model as it has taken shape, that may have been unanticipated in 1982, is the tendency for the Charter to be regarded as a tool of the judiciary, and for litigation to be seen as the default strategy of Charter engagement. As a result, governments have not always been proactive in fulfilling their own obligations to advance human rights goals.'

[35] The real 'activist judges' in both Canada and Australia were able to protect rights rather vigorously during the immediate post-Second World War years by drawing on British Constitutional tradition in articulating a sort of implied Bill of Rights appended to federalism in each country.

Space precludes a full exploration of these themes, but one recent case serves to illustrate the general point. In *R v Khawaja* [36] (*Khawaja*) the Ontario Superior Court of Justice heard an application questioning the constitutional validity of Canada's anti-terrorism scheme. Mohammad Momin Khawaja had been charged with various offences involving participation in a terrorist group and 'facilitating' terrorism. Counsel for the accused sought a declaration that various sections of the statutory scheme were:

> of no force and effect pursuant to section 52(1) of the *Constitution Act, 1982*, on the basis that the provisions are vague and/or over-broad, they dilute the essential fault requirements of criminal law, and they infringe his rights to freedom of association, freedom of conscience and religion, and freedom of thought, belief, opinion, and expression pursuant to section 2 of the *Charter*.[37]

Similar objectives might have been expressed without invoking the *Charter*, of course. Long-standing principles of statutory interpretation — each designed to protect freedom — such as that criminal statutes should be strictly construed, that ambiguity should be resolved in favour of the accused, that the legislature should be presumed to intend minimal infringement of liberty and, conversely, be explicit as to its liberty-infringing intent, and so on, apply. Such principles have been diminished in application in Canada during the period in which all attention has focused on the *Charter* as the most important vehicle for protecting rights.

The allegation of over-breadth in *Khawaja* provides a stunning illustration of how ineffective 'rights protections' can be in a charter regime. Mr Justice Rutherford concluded that the impugned provisions were neither overbroad nor void for vagueness because 'they can be read, construed and applied in conformity with the principles of fundamental justice'[38] (ie, in a fashion that rendered them constitutionally acceptable). His Lordship's ruling is carefully reasoned and seemingly in conformity with the law as established by the Supreme Court of Canada in these respects. What is interesting about the reasoning offered and the result reached in *Khawaja* is not any error on the part of the deciding judge, but the shocking possibility that he may be absolutely correct. Even the casual observer will note the glaring illogic of the approach taken: the fact that a Superior Court Judge, who has enjoyed both the luxury of time to reflect and the benefit of learned submissions of counsel, is capable of 'reading', 'construing' and 'applying' vague or broad words in a lawful fashion rather begs the more important question of how the law serves to guide citizens and state officials alike. Statutory language that is only rendered lawful after it is interpreted in court violates almost every principle of legality that frustrated the blundering

---

[36] *R v Khawaja* (2006), 214 CCC (3d) 399, WL 3031774 (Ont SCJ, Rutherford J); 2006 CarswellOnt 6551.
[37] Ibid [3].
[38] Ibid [6].

King Rex in Lon Fuller's fable: the police officer is likely to misconstrue the extent of her power; the citizen to suffer accordingly. A modicum of realism suggests that lawful state conduct requires clarity in statutory drafting, not the sort of *ex post facto* rationalisation that reading down permits.

On the vagueness arm of the ruling, his Lordship noted the rule of law rationale for proscribing vague laws, citing authority to the effect that '[a] citizen is not to be deprived of liberty under a law that is vague'.[39] The rub comes, however, not because of a failure to recognise the importance of principles relating to liberty, but because of how they have been translated into constitutional practice by the Canadian courts. The Supreme Court of Canada has fallen into habits of extreme 'deference' to the legislature, to such an extent that it requires almost nothing back in terms of clarity of statutory drafting. Its doctrines relating to 'void for vagueness' fatally compromise the principle: so much so that Peter Hogg, the 'dean' of Canadian constitutional law experts has said that 'almost any provision, no matter how vague' would pass the test.[40] The treatment of the Supreme Court of Canada's test in *Khawaja* confirms Hogg's insight and is worth quoting at length:

> 17. The degree of precision required in our laws is not, however, to lay out a prescription such that one can predict with certainty the outcome of all conceivable factual situations. There are not enough draftspersons to accomplish anything like that; and who could read the volumes that would be required? A framework delineating the area of risk is what is required. The standard was described in *Canada v. Pharmaceutical Society (Nova Scotia)*, [1992] 2 S.C.R. 606 (S.C.C.) by Gonthier J. at 638-9 in these terms: "Legal rules only provide a framework, a guide as to how one may behave, but certainty is only reached in instant cases, where law is actualised by a competent authority. In the meanwhile, conduct is guided by approximation. The process of approximation sometimes results in quite a narrow set of options, sometimes in a broader one. Legal dispositions therefore delineate a risk zone, and cannot hope to do more, unless they are directed at individual instances."
>
> "By setting out the boundaries of permissible and non-permissible conduct, these norms give rise to legal debate. They bear substance, and they allow for a discussion as to their actualisation. They therefore limit enforcement discretion by introducing boundaries, and they also sufficiently delineate an area of risk to allow for substantive notice to citizens."
>
> "Indeed, no higher requirement as to certainty can be imposed on law in our modern state. Semantic arguments, based on a perception of language as an unequivocal medium, are unrealistic. Language is not the exact tool some may

---

[39] Ibid [16].
[40] Ribeiro, above n 5, 4.

*think it is. It cannot be argued that an enactment can and must provide enough guidance to predict the legal consequences of any given course of conduct in advance. All it can do is enunciate some boundaries, which create an area of risk. But it is inherent to our legal system that some conduct will fall along the boundaries of the area of risk; no definite prediction can then be made. Guidance, not direction, of conduct is a more realistic objective."* [Emphasis added by Mr Justice Rutherford]

18. I am not persuaded that the provisions in question are vague to the point of being unconstitutional. They describe conduct in a fashion that provides notice of what is prohibited and set an intelligible standard for both citizen and law enforcement officials. The fact that we were able to debate the potential boundaries of the provisions in court supports this conclusion. I shall return to the motivation clause later in another context, but the fact that the prohibited action may be motivated "in whole or in part" by a political, religious or ideological purpose, objective or cause does not, in my view, open the door to all kinds of actions. The prohibited actions are all spelled out with reasonable precision in terms of their intended harmful consequences in 83.01(1)(b)(ii)(A)-(E) of the definition. These intended, harmful consequences are all clearly undesirable, adequately comprehensible and not at all surprising objectives of criminal sanctions.

19. It is not sufficient in my view to conceive of hypothetical circumstances that test the periphery of a legislated prohibition. If a provision clearly identifies and applies to a core of misconduct but its application to peripheral conduct is uncertain, that does not mean that the provision is impermissibly vague. In such a case the law provides a basis for legal debate and the judiciary must determine the extent of its application.[41]

With respect, this mischaracterises the relevant issues considerably. To portray (paragraph 17) absolute linguistic certainty as the only alternative to utter imprecision is to proffer a *reductio ad absurdum* that could justify virtually any degree of drafting sloppiness or deliberate overreach. The dismissal of 'hypothetical circumstances that test the periphery of a legislated prohibition' sounds reasonable enough (there is, after all, danger in *reductio ad absurdum*) but is too dismissive by half. It is not, in fact, hard to imagine circumstances in which the wide discretion conferred on state officials by Canada's anti-terrorism legislation might be misused, and not all of them are fanciful.[42] Such 'hypotheticals' are particularly likely to give cause for concern to people who engage in charitable work in conflict zones (such as the Evangelical Fellowship of Canada) or whose families and connections reside in such areas. Elementary realism about charity and conflict, about state officials and minority groups

---

[41] *R v Khawaja* (2006), 214 CCC (3d) 399, WL 3031774 (Ont SCJ, Rutherford J); 2006 CarswellOnt 6551, [17], [18], [19].
[42] I develop this point much further in Pue, above n 2.

would suggest a more careful approach to 'hypothetical circumstances that test the periphery of a legislated prohibition' than Mr Justice Rutherford undertakes in this judgment. Curiously, his Lordship 'read down' the motive provision of the terrorism offence in Canadian law for just such reasons, citing legal scholar and one-time Justice Minister Irwin Cotler to the effect that 'the criminalisation of motive runs the risk of politicising the investigative and trial processes, while chilling the expression of "identifiable groups," and marks a departure from the general principles of criminal law in this regard'.[43]

The most unfortunate feature of Mr Justice Rutherford's approach in *Khawaja*, however, is not that he introduced errors of logic in his analysis, but that he was compelled to do so by the case law emanating from the Supreme Court of Canada. Stunningly, though accurately, he concludes that '[t]he fact that we were able to debate the potential boundaries of the provisions in court' renders them constitutionally valid. It is hard to imagine any form of wording, however vague, that well-paid lawyers could not 'debate'. The test of voidness for vagueness is exposed for what it is: a constitutional 'protection' that can mean nothing in practice.

And yet, if the courts cannot, *at a minimum,* insist that penal statutes (and penal-like statutes) be clear enough as to provide real-life guidance, first, to state officials as to who should and who should not come under their scrutiny and, second, to citizens, as to which overseas charities, causes, or liberation groups they are entitled to support, assist, or donate to, the protections of law are rather hollow. The *Charter* has not helped us to avoid this unfortunate outcome. It may have helped us to get here.

The *Charter* has not significantly affected the substance of Canada's anti-terrorism legislation. It may have diverted attention from the main play, sidelined concerned citizens from active participation in debate and mystified members of the public as to the issues raised by that legislative package. 'Rights' matter little if official discretion buttressed by overbroad legislation cast in the vaguest possible terms substitutes for governance in accordance with intelligible legal rules. Lord Cutler Beckett would be pleased.

---

[43] *R v Khawaja* (2006), 214 CCC (3d) 399, WL 3031774 (Ont SCJ, Rutherford J); 2006 CarswellOnt 6551, [62].

# PART TWO

Preparing the Ground: Balance, Proportionality, and Public Perceptions

# Chapter Five

# Balancing Security and Liberty: Critical Perspectives on Terrorism Law Reform

### Simon Bronitt[*]

## Introduction: The Balancing Model

Much of the debate post-September 11 (9/11) about expansion of state power to combat terrorism has been framed as striking a balance between security and liberty.[1] The 'balancing approach', whereby security is reconciled with respect for fundamental liberal rights and values, has been very influential in counter-terrorism law reform in Australia.[2] As the former federal Attorney-General Philip Ruddock pointed out:

> We don't live in an ideal world. We live in a world of trade-offs. And now we live in a world where we must accept the costs associated with protecting ourselves from terrorism ... There will always be a trade-off between national security and individual rights. The task of government is to recognise these trade-offs and preserve our security without compromising basic rights and liberties.[3]

The balancing paradigm has been a touchstone even for critics of the terrorism laws enacted since 2002. The Sheller Committee (the Security Legislation Review Committee), which undertook the five-year review of the first wave of terrorism

---

[*] Professor of Law, ANU College of Law and Director, National Europe Centre, The Australian National University, Canberra, Australia. This research has been supported by a Discovery grant from the Australian Research Council: 'Terrorism and the Non-State Actor After September 11: The Role of Law in the Search for Security' (DP0451473). I am grateful for the research assistance provided by Niamh Lenagh-Maguire. All errors are mine.
[1] J Waldron, 'Security and Liberty: The Image of Balance' (2003) 11(2) *The Journal of Political Philosophy* 191.
[2] The balancing approach was adopted in the Senate Standing Committee on Constitutional and Legal Affairs, *Report of Inquiry into the Security Legislation Amendment (Terrorism) Bill 2002 [No 2] and Related Bills – Interim Report* (3 May 2002). It is also adopted by G Williams, 'Australian Values and the War on Terrorism', *Australian Financial Review* (Melbourne), 7 February 2003, 6-7 (edited version of National Press Club Address, 29 January 2003); G Williams, *The Case For An Australian Bill of Rights: Freedom in the War on Terror* (Sydney: UNSW Press, 2004); G Williams, 'Balancing National Security and Human Rights: Assessing the Legal Response of Common Law Nations to the Threat of Terrorism' (2006) 8(1) *Journal of Comparative Policy Analysis* 43.
[3] P Ruddock, 'The Commonwealth Response to September 11: The Rule of Law and National Security' (Speech delivered at the National Forum in the War on Terrorism and the Rule of Law, New South Wales Parliament House, 10 November 2003) [26]-[29].

offences inserted into the *Criminal Code Act 1995* (Cth) ('Criminal Code'), conceived its task in the following terms:

> an appropriate balance must be struck between, on the one hand, the need to protect the community from terrorist activity, and on the other hand, the maintenance of fundamental human rights and freedoms.[4]

Likewise, the Australian Law Reform Commission's recent review of sedition approached the process of reform as one of 'balancing anti-terrorism measures with human rights'.[5] A similar approach also characterises the legal policy environment in the United Kingdom (UK), the United States (US) and elsewhere.

## The Critique of Balancing

Although a pervasive feature of public policy in the field of counter-terrorism, the balancing approach has been subject to significant academic criticism. As Jeremy Waldron points out, the concept of balancing must be subjected to careful analytical and empirical scrutiny in the context of counter-terrorism measures.[6] Notwithstanding the intuitive appeal of balancing, there are many objections to its use to guide terrorism law reform.[7] For criminal justice scholars, the balancing debate resonates with the pre-9/11 critique of balancing models applied to guide criminal justice reform.[8]

Rather than security versus liberty, the criminal justice debate was framed as striking a balance between crime control and due process, or variants thereof.[9] In both contexts, several objections may be levelled at balancing.[10] A common objection is that balancing promotes consequentialism in which the 'ends justify

---

[4] Security Legislation Review Committee (SLRC), *Report of the Security Legislation Review Committee* (2006) 3. See also p 47 where the SLRC notes '[s]triking this balance is an essential challenge to preserving the cherished traditions of Australian society'.

[5] Australian Law Reform Commission, *Fighting Words: A Review of Sedition Laws in Australia*, Report No 104 (2006) 101, 105.

[6] Waldron, above n 1.

[7] For criticism of these balancing models see S Bronitt, 'Constitutional Rhetoric v Criminal Justice Realities: Unbalanced Responses to Terrorism?' (2003) 14 *Public Law Review* 76, 76-80; M Gani, 'Upping the Ante in the "War on Terror"' in P Fawkner (ed), *A Fair Go in an Age of Terror* (Victoria: David Lovell Publishing, 2004) 80-91; and G Carne, 'Brigitte and the French Connection: Security Carte Blanche or A La Carte' (2004) 9(2) *Deakin Law Review* 573, 613-14.

[8] For an overview of the debate about balancing see L Zedner, 'Securing Liberty in the Face of Terror: Reflections from Criminal Justice' (2005) 32(4) *Journal of Law and Society* 507; S Bronitt and B McSherry, *Principles of Criminal Law* (Sydney: LawBook Co, 2nd ed, 2005) 871-6. In the criminal justice context, see earlier articles by A Ashworth, 'Crime, Community and Creeping Consequentialism' [1996] 43 *Criminal Law Review* 220, 220-30; S Bronitt, 'Electronic Surveillance, Human Rights and Criminal Justice' (1997) 3(2) *Australian Journal of Human Rights* 183.

[9] In the criminal justice context, the balancing metaphor is a powerful image, linking to the scales of justice and our adversarial system of justice. For a review of the key contributions to this debate by Herbert Packer, Doreen McBarnet and Andrew Ashworth, see Bronitt and McSherry, above n 8, 36ff.

[10] Feminists have also critiqued the bipolar or binary construction of this balancing model, which conceals the significant legitimate interests of victims: see P Easteal, 'Beyond Balancing' in P Easteal (ed), *Balancing the Scales: Rape, Law Reform and Australian Culture* (Sydney: Federation Press, 1998).

the means', a calculus in which individual interests are sacrificed for community gains. The logic of such utilitarian approaches[11] has even led some US and Australian scholars to propose that torture, if regulated through judicial supervision, may be justified to avert imminent terrorist attacks.[12] Such preventive measures are justified in terms either of self-defence (a doctrine which extends to defence of others and property) or of necessity. In reality, however, in respect of self-defence, this defensive action is not likely to be directed against the perpetrators of terrorism, but rather against 'soft targets' such as the suspected terrorist's associates or family members. A further point of distinction from the typical self-defence scenario here is that the defensive action is not being performed by a private citizen, but by law enforcement officials or defence personnel, thus invoking what amounts to a broader claim of legal justification based on necessity.

The defence of necessity, which admits that there will be circumstances where a person may legitimately break the law, involves the weighing of lesser evils. There is little case law on the defence, though the courts have held that necessity and duress are unavailable in murder cases — the courts are seemingly hostile to utilitarian calculations in cases that have involved the intentional sacrifice of one person's life to ensure the survival of many.[13] Recognising necessity in torture cases would similarly deny the autonomy and moral existence of the subject as a human being.[14] Even if the torture is 'regulated' so as to avoid the risk of death, the victim of torture is not only subjected to serious pain but also experiences a form of moral death.[15] Respect for human life and human dignity is a paramount value, and in modern times, the common law has not been willing to entertain legal argument about the relative value of one human life over many.

---

[11] 'Utility', for Jeremy Bentham, meant the greatest happiness (or welfare) of the greatest number with its maximisation being the proper end of humankind. The implications of utilitarianism for law is discussed in S Bottomley and S Bronitt, *Law in Context* (Sydney: Federation Press, 3rd ed, 2006) 45ff.

[12] See A Dershowitz, *Why Terrorism Works: Understanding the Threat, Responding to the Challenge* (New Haven: Yale University Press, 2002); M Bagaric and J Clarke, 'Not Enough Official Torture in the World? The Circumstances in Which Torture is Morally Justifiable' (2005) 39(3) *University of San Francisco Law Review* 1. It is not surprising that the father of utilitarian philosophy, Jeremy Bentham wrote an essay on the utility of torture, concluding that its use depended in each case on its 'overall utility': see W Twining and P Twining, 'Bentham on Torture' (1973) 24 *Northern Ireland Law Quarterly* 307; discussed in J Kleinig, 'Ticking Bombs and Torture Warrants' (2005) 10(2) *Deakin Law Review* 614, 614. In the modern law, torture is strictly prohibited, as it is subject to an absolute ban under international human rights law and prohibited under the *Criminal Code Act 1995* (Cth) ('Criminal Code').

[13] In *R v Dudley and Stephens* (1884) 14 QBD 273, the English common law established the limits of the defence, denying its availability as a defence to murder in a case of survival cannibalism where the crew, consistent with maritime custom of the time, had drawn lots to determine who they would kill in order to ensure their survival. Similar limitations apply to the availability of the defence of duress under common law.

[14] D Manderson, 'Another Modest Proposal' (2005) 10(2) *Deakin Law Review* 640, 651.

[15] As Manderson points out 'our societies have, at least since the Enlightenment, feared pain more than death, believed that human dignity requires absolute protection under all circumstances, and thought torture a more serious act than execution': ibid 649.

Another objection relates to the weight attached to these competing values. Jeremy Waldron reposes the question as how these two societal 'goods' in tension (namely security and liberty) should be justly distributed?[16] A recurrent problem with these balancing models is that there is no indication of the relative weight that should be attached to the competing interests. As a leading criminal justice scholar, Lucia Zedner, put it:

> Typically, conflicting interests are said to be 'balanced' as if there were a self-evident weighting of or priority among them. Yet rarely are the particular interests spelt out, priorities made explicitly, or the process by which a weight is achieved made clear. Balancing is presented as a zero-sum game in which more of one necessarily means less of the other ... Although beloved of constitutional lawyers and political theorists, the experience of criminal justice is that balancing is a politically dangerous metaphor unless careful regard is given to what is at stake.[17]

As Michael Freeman points out, the distributive effects between security and liberty are uneven: security is typically enhanced not through interference with *our* own liberty, but by sacrificing the freedoms of others, typically young Muslim males.[18]

Balancing becomes more problematic when we move beyond physical harm to less tangible and direct interests, such as individual or communal security. In this context, security is measured not only by the actual state of being secure, but also the psychological need to feel secure. These feelings will be based in part on a *perception* of the nature of the security threat and what works to address that insecurity — matters which are rarely determined by empirical evidence but dictated by political imperatives and priorities. Promoting the happiness of the majority (whether or not the policies are evidence-based) necessarily tips the balance heavily in favour of the state over the individual.

In the balance between liberty and security, security is invariably viewed as paramount. Security looms larger in this equation for a number of reasons. First, security threats are not confined to national borders or interests, but have a global reach. This aspect of globalisation, which is acute in the context of terrorism law, attaches further weight to the security side of the scales.[19] Second, our capacity to enjoy freedom rests on security. Indeed, Phillip Ruddock, the former federal Attorney-General, justified broader security measures as upholding

---

[16] Waldron, above n 1.
[17] Zedner, above n 8, 510-11.
[18] M Freeman, 'Order, Rights, and Threats: Terrorism and Global Justice' in R A Wilson (ed), *Human Rights in the 'War on Terror'* (Cambridge: Cambridge University Press, 2005) 48.
[19] A point made by Carne, above n 7: 'The national security aspect in the balance is inevitably given special weighting, producing a structural inequality in that "balance". These considerations suggest a general unsuitability of the balancing paradigm for reconciling national security and democratic interests.'

the right to 'human security', which he views as the paramount human right.[20] This 'new' approach, however, distorts the conventional understandings of the right to liberty and to security of person. It also corrupts the new paradigm of human security being advocated by influential human rights and development scholars. Before this recasting by the Attorney-General, the concept of human security had been developed to shift the focus of debate from the security of the state to the security of the people.[21] However, as previously noted, 'in this new era, fundamental human rights related to liberty and security can acquire radically new meanings'.[22] A cursory review of the case law under the 'right to security' in international human rights law would reveal a basic concern with confining the power of the state to coerce its citizens through powers of arrest and detention.[23] Indeed the correct approach, since human rights are not absolute, is to view national security as a competing public interest that may place some necessary and proportionate restriction on the exercise of a particular human right. To be sure, the idea of feeling safe should not be underestimated — there are social, legal and economic dimensions to this, but the promotion of such a feeling can hardly be paramount. Indeed, treating security as paramount can be disastrous, as the International Commission of Jurists noted in the Berlin Declaration:

> A pervasive security-oriented discourse promotes the sacrifice of fundamental rights and freedoms in the name of eradicating terrorism. ... [S]afeguarding persons from terrorist acts and respecting human rights both form part of a seamless web of protection incumbent upon the state.[24]

A further objection to balancing relates to the inverse relationship between liberty and security, namely that more of one thing (liberty) means less of another (security) and vice versa. This underlies the assumption that higher levels of human rights protection or due process *necessarily* will impede the effectiveness of law enforcement. To promote maximum collective security we must sacrifice

---

[20] P Ruddock, 'A New Framework – Counter-Terrorism and the Rule of Law' (2005) 16 *The Sydney Papers*, 113, 116-17.

[21] Commission on Human Security, *Human Security Now. Protecting and Empowering People* (New York: United Nations Human Security Unit, 2003). The concepts underlying human security are discussed by M Robinson, 'Connecting Human Rights, Development and Human Security' in Wilson above n 18, 313ff.

[22] Bottomley and Bronitt, above n 11, 414.

[23] The case law on art 5 of the *European Convention for the Protection of Human Rights and Fundamental Freedoms* (ECHR) 213 UNTS 222 (entered into force 3 September 1953) is reviewed in M Macovei, *The Right To Liberty and Security of the Person*, Human Rights Handbooks, No 5 (Strasbourg: Council of Europe, 2002) <http://www.coe.int/T/E/Human_rights/hrhb5.pdf>. The right to liberty and security of person under art 9 of the *International Covenant on Civil and Political Rights* (ICCPR), 999 UNTS 171 (entered into force 23 March 1976) 'guarantees against arbitrariness in relation to arrest and detention', rather than some broader right to safety: see N O'Neill, S Rice and R Douglas, *Retreat from Injustice: Human Rights in Australia* (Sydney: Federation Press, 2nd ed, 2004) 214.

[24] *The Berlin Declaration: the International Commission of Jurists Declaration on Upholding Human Rights and the Rule of Law in Combating Terrorism*, adopted 28 August 2004.

our civil liberties: sadly it seems that human rights and due process prove too costly precisely at the moment that they are needed most. However, these assumptions are contestable. Recent procedural reforms to the law governing criminal investigation suggest that some innovations, such as the mandatory recording of interviews and custodial access to lawyers, do not unreasonably fetter law enforcement. The practice of taping, though resisted by police initially, has in fact proved to deliver significant benefits for law enforcement, reducing the number of disputed confessions and providing credible evidence to refute suspect allegations of improper or oppressive treatment during investigation.[25]

In light of these insights from the field of criminal justice, it is not unrealistic to propose that effective counter-terrorism law can be promoted *with* high levels of human rights and due process. Indeed, it is important to avoid symbolic legislation, and ill-considered knee-jerk responses that prove to have limited impact or, worse still, to have potential counterproductive effects or unintended consequences.

Human rights law is not a straitjacket for effective counter-terrorism measures. As many human rights lawyers and organisations have pointed out, human rights are rarely unqualified or absolute, with permissible limitations in the name of security on rights such as privacy and fair trial provided they are both necessary and proportionate.[26] Since the *legal* expression of human rights is rarely unqualified,[27] the correct approach to policy development is to promote strict compliance with (rather than wide derogation from) fundamental human rights protected under international law or contained in domestic human rights legislation.[28] The problem is that this approach to necessary and proportionate qualification is regularly misunderstood by the courts and legislature. As Laurence Lustgarten has pointed out in the context of British courts addressing the human rights standards in the *European Convention on Human Rights* (ECHR) through the *Human Rights Act 1998* (UK):

> It often seems something is lost in the transition (or is it translation?) from Strasbourg to the UK courts, a process in which the ECtHR's [European Court of Human Rights] references to the necessary 'balance' between individual rights

---

[25] See generally, D Dixon, *Law in Policing: Legal Regulation and Police Practices* (Oxford, New York: Clarendon Press, 1997) on the relationship between law and policing, and recognition that due process is not necessarily antagonistic to crime control.

[26] This point has been made recently in a submission by the Human Rights and Equal Opportunity Commission to the SLRC, discussed in its Report, above n 4, 39. See also C Gearty, *Principles of Human Rights Adjudication* (Oxford: Oxford University Press, 2004) ch 2.

[27] There are only a few absolute rights, such as torture. Though even in this area, as Gearty notes, the prohibition 'is shown by the jurisprudence of the European Court of Human Rights to have plenty of grey areas around its fringes in which disputes have been able to thrive': Gearty, ibid 9.

[28] Australia has not yet adopted a bill of rights, though the Australian Capital Territory and Victoria have adopted human rights legislation modelled on the *Human Rights Act 1998* (UK): *Human Rights Act 2004* (ACT), *Charter of Human Rights and Responsibilities Act 2006* (Vic).

and public interest has led — not only in the context of terrorism — to the 'balancing away' of defendant's rights in a manner that arguably fails to comply with convention requirements ... the practical import is that the seductive metaphor of 'balance' can readily be used to override convention and other protections when the public clamour is loud enough.[29]

What this suggests is that both the courts and those responsible for legislative policy in these fields must develop a more sophisticated grasp of human rights law. Furthermore, an understanding of these obligations should inform their decision-making.

As well as fostering legitimacy, strict adherence to human rights law and due process may pay dividends in terms of wider compliance with these laws among the citizenry. There is a strong argument from social psychological research that individual compliance with even unpopular and harsh laws can be promoted by the belief that the processes of enforcement and adjudication are legitimate (that is, procedurally fair and just). As the social psychological research on procedural justice reveals, legal systems with a highly punitive criminal justice system, can deliver high levels of compliance with the law when combined with the processes that are perceived to be fair to accused persons.[30]

A common claim is that human rights observance is too costly in cases involving terrorism.[31] But a wider sweep of the history of criminal justice supports the above hypothesis about the importance of procedural justice to compliance. It is important to recall that 'due process' rights were not forged in the lower courts in relation to minor misdemeanours, but rather were first articulated in relation to serious security offences, such as treason and sedition. The history of the Star Chamber is often misrepresented by common lawyers as one of inquisitorial oppression and torture, overlooking its critical role in forging many of the key

---

[29] L Lustgarten, 'National Security, Terrorism and Constitutional Balance' (2004) 75(1) *The Political Quarterly* 4, 14. Ashworth makes a similar point that 'balancing' of interests is used indiscriminately, an approach he believes is simply wrong. He criticises the UK application of the ECHR, arguing that the broad brush approach taken does not take into account the hierarchy of rights that is explicit from the Convention structure (created by art 15), and thus a more precise approach is required to correctly apply the protections provided. Specifically, he suggests that although some rights may be 'outweighed' as necessary under a democratic society, others are not to be defeated by public interest, including the right to liberty and security (Art 5) and the right to a fair trial (Art 6): A Ashworth, 'What Have Human Rights Done for Criminal Justice in the UK?' (2004) 23 *University of Tasmania Law Review* 151.
[30] The key research in this field has been undertaken by T Tyler: *Why People Obey the Law* (New Haven: Yale University Press, 1990). This research is discussed by J Braithwaite, 'Crime in A Convict Republic' [2001] 64(1) *Modern Law Review* 11, 21, in the context of his study of convict justice in the eighteenth and nineteenth centuries. The commitment to procedural justice in an otherwise harsh legal system not only constrained abuses of power by officials, but also assisted convicts realign their identities to law abiding citizens. In his view, it was these features of the system, overlooked by many historians, that explains high levels of reintegration and low levels of re-offending, during this period.
[31] For a recent article making this claim, see G Rose and D Nestorovska, 'Australian Counter-Terrorism Offences: Necessity and Clarity in Federal Criminal Law Reforms' (2007) 31 *Criminal Law Journal* 20.

procedural protections that underwrite human rights law today.[32] As Geoffrey Robertson has pointed out, the key elements of modern Anglo-American justice (such as the right to counsel and the privilege against self-incrimination) are products of periods of intense political repression. Robertson contends that the more serious and inherently political the crime, the greater the legal quest for legitimacy through procedural safeguards, reminding us that it was in trials of treason that prisoners were first permitted defence counsel. Indeed, Robertson has argued that the seventeenth century trial of Charles I — the first trial of a head of state for tyranny and a precursor to modern war crimes trials — provided common lawyers and judges with the opportunity to fashion many significant legal innovations.[33]

Indeed, a similar point about the importance of the ideology of justice was made by Doug Hay in his study of eighteenth century English criminal justice, and the operation of the 'Bloody Code' under which an increasing number of offences were made felonies punishable by death.[34] In his view, the approach of the ruling class was to manipulate the ideology of law, to use it as 'an instrument of authority and a breeder of values' in order to maintain the legitimacy of the existing social order. Since fear alone could not establish deference to the law, the structures of the law itself might be used ideologically, to establish deference without force, to legitimate the class structure, and to maintain the domination of the holders of property. Hay emphasises how the elements of majesty, justice and mercy, embodied in the practices of the criminal law, served these ends.[35]

By looking to legal history, albeit briefly, we see that due process of law (with its symbolic and instrumental aspects) was considered more (not less) important during periods of insecurity and state repression. Why is this so? As foreshadowed above, the answer must be legitimacy — put simply, in cases where the political taint of the crime and the threat to security is manifest, the state must play and be seen to play scrupulously by the rules. This has

---

[32] Geoffrey Robertson highlights the role of the Star Chamber in Jesuitical persecution in the 1600s, which led to its demise during Cromwell's Commonwealth: G Robertson, 'Fair Trials for Terrorists' in Wilson (ed), above n 18, ch 8; G Robertson, *The Tyrannicide Brief* (London: Chatto & Windus, 2005). This is the period in which most of the fundamental due process protections were forged — trial by jury (absent in the Star Chamber), open justice and privilege against self-incrimination. The oppressive features of the Star Chamber can be overstated. As Barnes points out, many of the modern features of due process we associate with the common law were established in the Star Chamber procedure — foremost, the right to counsel (which was denied to the common law courts in relation to felony). Moreover, the Star Chamber placed much value on procedural regularity — namely the rigour of pleadings to define issues — and copious legal argument before judgment. An enduring myth, that the chamber promoted confession by torture was not entirely true either: treason was investigated and torture was used, but never by the judges, rather it was the officers working for the Privy Council who used these methods. See further T Barnes, 'Star Chamber Mythology' (1961) 5(2) *American Journal of Legal History* 1.

[33] Robertson, *The Tyrannicide Brief*, ibid.

[34] D Hay, 'Property, Authority and the Criminal Law' in D Hay et al, *Albion's Fatal Tree* (London: Allen Lane, 1975) 17; discussed in S Bottomley and S Bronitt, above n 11, 217-19.

[35] Ibid.

implications for modern terrorism offences. Rather than advocate for terrorism crime to be defined widely and to incorporate strict or absolute liability elements supported by extensive use of reverse onus provisions, legislatures should maintain fidelity to the default standards of criminal justice: namely the burden of proof resting with the prosecution, and offences requiring proof of subjective fault. This would be consistent with the principles of responsibility applied to the Criminal Code and the published federal guidelines on the appropriate use of absolute (no fault) liability.[36] Robertson argues that 'the justice we dispense to alleged terrorists cannot be exquisitely fair, but need not be rough. Above all, it must be justice that conforms with our inherited Anglo-American traditions.'[37] Indeed, the quashing of the conviction in the Jack Thomas case in 2006, on the basis that the confession evidence used against him at trial was obtained in coercive circumstances and in derogation of the requirements of Australian law, may be viewed as the judiciary seeking to uphold these values scrupulously in trials for offences that have been widely condemned as exceptional and draconian.[38]

## The Making of Terrorism Law: Uncivil Politics of Law Reform

Drawing from this vein of social psychological research discussed above, I would further argue that legitimacy in law is not simply about how the law is *enforced* by the executive and the judiciary — it is supported by beliefs about the propriety of the process by which the applicable laws are *made* and *reformed*. Harsh laws that divide the community may nevertheless be obeyed where there is a genuine effort to consider the concerns and interests in the legislative process. There is much scepticism, in the current political climate, as to whether the existing scrutiny of terrorism law through parliamentary committees or, indeed, through law reform agencies is effective in addressing these concerns and interests.[39]

The political imperative to act in order to reassure the electorate proves to be irresistible in the aftermath of a terrorist attack. Prior to the 2002 reforms, the Attorney-General's Department undertook no systematic review of the reach of

---

[36] The federal government's first proposals relating to terrorism offences contained in the Security Legislation Amendment (Terrorism) Bill 2002 departed from its own guidelines and were drafted as absolute liability offences: this egregious departure from the presumption of subjective fault in relation to offences of such a serious nature was justified in the Explanatory Memorandum. Whilst these provisions (as proposed) did not pass into law, the terrorism offences have strict liability elements.
[37] Robertson, 'Fair Trials for Terrorists', above n 32.
[38] *R v Joseph Terrence Thomas* [2006] VSCA 165 (18 August 2006). The implications of this case are discussed in J McCulloch, 'Australia's Anti-Terrorism Legislation and the Jack Thomas Case' (2006) 18(2) *Current Issues in Criminal Justice* 357.
[39] For an assessment of this trend in the context of sedition, see S Bronitt and J Stellios, 'Sedition, Security and Human Rights: 'Unbalanced' Law Reform in the "War on Terror"' (2006) 30(3) *Melbourne University Law Review* 923.

existing laws; there was no consideration of whether minor adaptation (with sentence enhancement for crimes with a terrorist motive) could achieve a result more consistent with the existing fabric of our criminal laws.[40] Despite its immense importance, forging new terror legislation has occurred largely 'on the cheap'. With limited time and resources, government has been encouraged to draw on 'off the shelf' solutions. In the Australian context, the legislature has borrowed heavily from UK models in relation to key definitions, and to new legal measures such as control orders and preventative detention.[41] The core definition of 'terrorist act', which triggers many of the counter-terrorism powers and forms an element of a number of the terrorism offences in the Code, was drawn directly from the *Terrorism Act 2000* (UK). In one respect, not highlighted in the debates in federal Parliament, the UK definition significantly extends the normal jurisdictional reach of the criminal law. The effect of this borrowed definition is that the terrorist act extends to behaviour that has no connection with Australia. Under the Criminal Code the terrorist act must be done, or the threat made, with the intention of (inter alia):

> coercing, or influencing by intimidation the government of the Commonwealth or a State, Territory *or foreign country* [42] [emphasis added].

While this definition of terrorism bears similarity to conventional political crimes such as treason and sedition, the extension to *any* foreign country is a clear manifestation of the globalisation of the concept of security. The recognition that the security of Australia is now dependent upon the security of other states (not just allies) justifies the adoption of expanded offences and powers that promote *global* rather than exclusively *national* security. The extended definition has another effect, potentially criminalising persons who support resistance movements that oppose tyrannical and undemocratic regimes. As the English Court of Appeal has noted in a recent case upholding the conviction of a person engaged in action to overthrow the Libyan dictatorship of Colonel Gaddafi:

> the terrorist legislation applies to countries which are governed by tyrants and dictators. There is no exemption from criminal liability for terrorist activities which are motivated or said to be morally justified by the alleged nobility of the terrorist cause.[43]

---

[40] The lack of a proper process to review or assess the current laws was a feature in both Australia and Canada: A Goldsmith, 'The Governance of Terror: Representing Terrorism in Canadian and Australian Counter-Terrorist Law Reform After September 11' (Paper presented at Crime, Community and the State: 18th Annual Conference of the Australian and New Zealand Society of Criminology, Wellington, New Zealand, 9-11 February 2005).

[41] In late 2005, in the wake of the London bombings, the Council of Australian Governments agreed to enact powers to impose preventative detention and control orders on a person without charge, trial or conviction, which were modelled directly on the measures inserted into the *Terrorism Act 2000* (UK). See *Anti-Terrorism Act [No 2] 2005* (Cth).

[42] Criminal Code s 100.1(1).

[43] *R v F* [2007] 2 All ER 193, [32].

These new offences, which apply universal jurisdiction under Category D extended jurisdiction provisions in the Criminal Code, define terrorism in terms of threats to international security (which have no bearing on our own domestic security). With the adoption of such far-reaching definitions (in both senses of the term), there is a further blurring of the traditional distinction between internal and external security, and a significant extension of the mandate of the Australian Federal Police (AFP). Surely such a significant shift in scope for counter-terrorism law and policy deserved greater critical consideration and public debate! This form of covert law reform is simply unacceptable in modern parliamentary democracies.

This pattern of expedited law reform has prevailed over the past five years.[44] The damage to the integrity of the parliamentary process is most evident in the most recent round of reforms: amendments introducing preventative detention and control orders and reframing the offence of sedition in the *Anti-Terrorism Act (No 2) 2005* (Cth). Despite allowing only one week for public submissions, the Senate Standing Committee on Legal and Constitutional Affairs received submissions from 294 individuals and organisations. At the close of submissions the Senate Committee had only 11 business days to review and make recommendations on the Bill. Not surprisingly, few significant changes were made to the Bill before its enactment.

Federal Parliament is not the only institution compromised by this climate of fear. Another example of how the normal law reform processes are distorted by political exigency is the 2005 Cronulla riots. Following a series of violent confrontations at Cronulla, the New South Wales Parliament introduced and passed on the same day an emergency package of powers for police, allowing them to 'lock down' suburbs.[45] Without the involvement of any judicial officer or court, senior police can declare an area they define as 'locked down', in which case the following powers apply: police may close licensed premises; declare an emergency alcohol-free zone for up to 48 hours; set up roadblocks and employ stop and search (without warrant) powers to persons, vehicles, and anything in the possession of those persons; and seize and detain any vehicle, mobile phone or similar device. Outside the realm of locked down areas, the amendments also empower any police officer to stop a vehicle if the officer has reasonable grounds for believing there is large-scale public disorder occurring or threatening to occur and that such action is reasonably necessary.[46] In the immediate aftermath of the violence, charges of riot and violent disorder were laid, though the

---

[44] A Lynch, 'Legislating With Urgency – The Enactment Of The *Anti-Terrorism Act [No 1] 2005*' (2006) 30 *Melbourne University Law Review* 747.
[45] *Law Enforcement Legislation Amendment (Public Safety) Act 2005* (NSW).
[46] *Law Enforcement (Powers and Responsibilities) Act 2002* (NSW) ss 87B, 87C, 87D, 87E, 87I, 87J, 87K, 87L, 87M, 87N, inserted by Schedule 1 of *Law Enforcement Legislation Amendment (Public Safety) Act 2005* (NSW).

overwhelming majority related to minor traffic infringements.[47] Most significantly, in the context of our discussion of terrorism laws, these extraordinary police powers were enacted hastily, without proper review of the adequacy of existing laws or objective analysis of the underlying causes of these disturbances.[48]

With limited time to review such proposals before passage, legislatures are often content to reassure themselves by mandating a review of the law's operation after a specified number of years. This form of post hoc review takes two forms: oversight and periodic review by the Ombudsman; and/or review by independent committees reporting to Parliament. The outcomes of these reviews have thus far not been promising. The first wave of terrorist offences introduced in 2002 has recently been the subject of review by the Sheller Committee; however, confidence in the review process was undermined when the Committee's recommendations were dismissed by the Government.[49] The legitimacy deficit in relation to both the content of terrorism laws, and the processes by which these laws are made and reviewed, is manifest.

There remains a strong belief that our democratic processes, in particular our system of legislative scrutiny and parliamentary committees, can produce laws in a time of emergency that balance the competing interests of security with liberty.[50] It is a strength of our system that citizens and organisations can indeed express concern about the breadth and impact of new counter-terrorism laws, and that scrutiny committees can make significant changes to legislation. Indeed, the Senate Committee reviewing the first wave of terrorism offences introduced in 2002 objected strenuously to the overuse of absolute liability, which resulted in significant remodelling of the Bill.

The post-9/11 environment, however, seems to have privileged some stakeholders in that process, particularly those members of the security and law enforcement communities who are viewed as more knowledgeable about the nature and scale of the threats faced, and expert about the range of legal reforms required to neutralise these threats effectively. While the former claim may be true, the latter is certainly contestable. The deference to counter-terrorism specialists over legal and criminal justice experts manifested itself in the way witnesses were 'oriented' before giving evidence to the Australian Capital Territory (ACT) Legislative Assembly Committee on a scheme of preventative detention. The

---

[47] A Clennell, 'Labor Soft After Riots: Debnam', *Sydney Morning Herald* (Sydney), 13 January 2006, 1.
[48] The *Law Enforcement Legislation Amendment (Public Safety) Act 2005* (NSW) was introduced, assented to and commenced on the same day: 15 December 2005.
[49] SLRC, above n 4.
[50] Rose and Nestorovska, above n 31, who deride international human rights laws for their 'uncertain applicability in the counter-terrorism context, as fundamental questions arise as to their own universality, immutability, interpretation and application'. They argue instead that the legitimacy of counter-terrorism laws lies 'in their collective approval through a democratic process that enfranchises and effectively reflects the values of the majority of persons who are addressed by those laws': 20-21.

first substantive question (directed to all witnesses) was whether they had been privy to various AFP or Australian Security Intelligence Organisation (ASIO) briefings on the nature of the terrorist threat to Australia. The import of this line of questioning was unsettlingly clear to the witnesses — clearly the proposers of preventative detention (namely the Prime Minister and Premiers who form the Council of Australian Governments) had received such a briefing, and on the basis of this intelligence were prepared to adopt these measures, with only the ACT Chief Minister willing to impose higher standards of due process because of the *Human Rights Act 2004* (ACT). By implication, those who opposed the Bill without such knowledge were simply not qualified to know the seriousness of the threat and what drastic steps are needed to avert devastating terrorist acts.[51] The line of questioning illustrates the power of security culture to sideline critical voices. It is, of course, also disingenuous since the true nature and risk of the terrorist threat is probably unknowable, as the 9/11 Commission itself found to be the case.[52]

What this discussion supports is the emergence of an uncivil politics of law reform.[53] Those committed to high standards of respect for human rights (even those who have experienced the abuse of emergency powers in liberal democracies in Europe) occupy a very narrow ledge of legitimacy. Commentators arguing for wider powers and laws tend to deride human rights law as vague and illegitimate, echoing Bentham's famous jibe against natural law rights as 'nonsense upon stilts'.[54] On this view, the legitimacy of counter-terrorism laws lies in their democratic origins, and if any critique is entertained, a narrow set of liberal concerns, such as necessity and clarity, are applied to new offences.[55] The criticism that international human rights law lacks democratic foundations overlooks the fact that these human rights are legal rules, which have been ratified by the Australian Parliament! The claim of inherent vagueness also overlooks the significant detailed body of jurisprudence, which has been built up through the cases, particularly those coming out of the European Court of Human Rights and the United Nations Human Rights Committee. This commonsense approach to counter-terrorism, which purports to distance the critics from any moral or political standpoints, embraces a model of law reform

---

[51] Apart from the federal police, most witnesses appearing before these Committees had not been privy to those briefings.
[52] D Luban, 'Eight Fallacies about Liberty and Security' in Wilson (ed), above n 18, 247.
[53] This is adapted from the phrase 'uncivil politics of law and order', coined in the pre-9/11 context, to describe the trend in Australia to drive criminal justice reform by reference to 'law and order commonsense' rather than informed expert opinion or available data: R Hogg and D Brown, *Rethinking Law and Order* (Sydney: Pluto Press, 1998) ch 1; see generally, D Weatherburn, *Law and Order in Australia: Rhetoric and Reality* (Sydney: Federation Press, 2004).
[54] Rose and Nestorovska, above n 31, 20-21. On natural rights see generally J Waldron (ed), *'Nonsense upon Stilts', Bentham, Burke and the Rights of Man* (London, New York: Methuen, 1987).
[55] Rose and Nestorovska, above n 31.

that focuses on prevention, pre-emption and precaution, which are examined in the next section.

## Preventative, Pre-emptive and Precautionary Models of Counter-Terrorism Law

Prevention is presented by politicians as the principal driving force behind our new laws. The former Commonwealth Attorney-General, Philip Ruddock, justified the 2005 package of anti-terrorism legislation on the basis that it 'ensures we are in the strongest position possible to prevent new and emerging threats'.[56] In Jude McCulloch's view, this package is suggestive of a new paradigm based on 'pre-emption' in the sense that it involves 'prevention of the perceived *risk* of terrorism':[57]

> Under this model it is legitimate to punish and coerce without evidence and before any terrorist act, even a 'terrorist act' under the legislation that involves no harm or plan to do harm. The *rationale of* prevention takes priority over other considerations including the rights of the accused and the need for reliable and convincing evidence of guilt prior to punishment. Anti-terrorism legislation is 'preemptive' in that it seeks to punish or apply coercive sanctions on the basis of what it is anticipated might happen in the future.[58]

In similar terms, Andrew Goldsmith has argued that the counter-terrorism strategies adopted post-9/11 are part of a wider culture of prevention and risk management in society, and the movement to a 'world risk society' and 'government through fear'. He argues that this cultural change gives rise to pressure towards legal exceptionalism, as fear of the unknown (and unknowable) leads to enhanced powers of proscription — a 'small price to pay for greater security'. He suggests that the precautionary principle may be used by governments to implement draconian measures: 'Extreme caution is justified as prudent in response to profound uncertainty. For some however, it merely provides a convenient cover for adopting conservative or even repressive responses.'[59]

The precautionary principle, which was first developed in the field of environmental regulation, posits that where the risk of a harm (in this case through terrorist attack) is unpredictable and uncertain, and where the damage that would be brought about by that harm is irreversible, any lack of scientific certainty in relation to the nature of the harm or consequences should not justify inaction. This promotes what Cass Sunstein calls the 'Laws of Fear', in which

---

[56] Commonwealth, *Parliamentary Debates,* House of Representatives, 3 November 2005, 102 (Philip Ruddock, Attorney-General) during the 2nd Reading Speech to the Anti-Terrorism Bill (No 2) 2005 (Cth).
[57] McCulloch, above n 38, 359 (emphasis in original).
[58] Ibid (emphasis in original).
[59] Goldsmith, above n 40.

the precautionary principle displaces risk-based or evidence-based approaches to public policy.[60] Whether this principle should be applied to counter-terrorism policy is highly contentious. Unlike the field of environmental policy, no state has claimed to have embraced the precautionary model for terrorism law.[61] Indeed, much of the language of counter-terrorism policy continues to be expressed in terms of either prevention or pre-emption rather than precaution. Nevertheless, upon closer scrutiny the discourse of public policy has shifted from one based on risk assessment and risk management (where policy-makers claim to weigh the likelihood of attack against the costs and benefits of particular strategies) to one based, in the face of uncertainty, on the need for precautionary action. It is possible to detect new counter-terrorism strategies, particularly those using technologies that permit surveillance of suspect 'places' rather than individual suspect persons, and displace or by-pass traditional protective safeguards.[62]

Indeed, the recent creation of new powers allowing the military to use lethal force to deal with serious aviation incidents is best understood in terms of moving beyond preventative to precautionary models of legal action. The recent amendments to Part IIIAAA of the *Defence Act 1903* (Cth) create a legislative framework for prospective authorisation of force — including lethal force — by the military in aid of civil power. These amendments give Australian Defence Force (ADF) personnel a range of powers, including the power to destroy an aircraft.[63] The Act now provides an expanded legislative basis for military action. Previously, such action would be limited to use of force falling within the ADF's (largely untested) powers to use force within the framework of general defences relating to self-defence (which includes defence of others), necessity, sudden/extraordinary emergency or lawful authority under the Criminal Code. The constitutional legitimacy of using such force would be supported by the defence powers in s 51(vi) of the *Commonwealth Constitution*. However, a review in 2004 noted that the existing powers were too reactive (modelled around a

---

[60] C Sunstein, *Laws of Fear: Beyond the Precautionary Principle* (Cambridge: Cambridge University Press, 2005).

[61] Like 'zero tolerance' policing in relation to drug law enforcement, precaution is not an official (that is, legislatively endorsed) principle guiding policy, though particular strategies and approaches conform more closely to a precautionary approach. For a discussion of the concept of zero tolerance policing, see Bronitt and McSherry, above n 8, ch 13.

[62] On the recent adoption of B Party warrants and powers to access stored data without warrants see S Bronitt and J Stellios, 'Regulating Telecommunications Interception and Access in the Twenty-First Century: Technological Evolution or Legal Revolution?' (2006) 24(4) *Prometheus* 413, 417-21. Also see the new powers in New South Wales (discussed above) and the broad powers to stop and search etc under the *Terrorism (Police Powers) Act 2002* (NSW).

[63] See Revised Explanatory Memorandum, Defence Legislation Amendment (Aid to Civilian Authorities) Bill 2006, 2, noting that this Part provides for 'the use of reasonable and necessary force when protecting critical infrastructure designated by the authorising Ministers' and enables a 'call out' of the ADF to respond to incidents or threats to the Commonwealth in the air environment' as well as ensuring that 'powers conferred on the ADF under Part IIIAAA can be accorded to the ADF in the course of dealing with a mobile terrorist incident and a range of threats to Australia's security'.

siege situation) and that there needed to be a more proactive model — hence the 2006 amendments. These include powers to take defensive action to protect critical infrastructure within Australia, and specifically to take action against hijacked aircraft.[64]

In using force or other measures against a vessel or aircraft, or ordering such, the ADF member must conform to the requirements of s 51SE(2) or (3), which require that:

- the order was not manifestly unlawful;
- the member has no reason to believe that circumstances have changed in a material way since the relevant order was given;
- the member has no reason to believe that the order was based on a mistake as to a material fact, and
- taking the measures was reasonable and necessary to give effect to the order.

The purpose of these provisions is to ensure that defence personnel are under strict control, through a chain of command, when they are receiving orders. Subsections 51SE(2) and (3) draw heavily, according to the Explanatory Memorandum, on the principles of the defence of acting under lawful authority (paragraph 37). However, it is probably best described as a hybrid between lawful authority and necessity.

Most contentious, under Division 3B, is the power to use lethal force in order to protect critical infrastructure designated by the authorising Ministers. Section 51T of the *Defence Act 1903* (Cth) provides:

> (2B) Despite subsection (1), in exercising powers under subparagraph 51SE(1)(a)(i) or (ii) or Division 3B [action against aircraft], a member of the Defence Force must not, in using force against a person or thing, do anything that is likely to cause the death of, or grievous bodily harm to, the person unless the member believes on reasonable grounds that:
>
> (a) doing that thing is necessary to protect the life of, or to prevent serious injury to, another person (including the member); or
>
> (b) *doing that thing is necessary to protect designated critical infrastructure against a threat of damage or disruption to its operation*; or
>
> (c) doing that thing is necessary and reasonable to give effect to the order under which, or under the authority of which, the member is acting. [emphasis added]

---

[64] *Defence Act 1903* (Cth) s 51SE allows ADF members operating under orders given by the Chief of the Defence Force to do certain things in relation to persons, vessels, aircraft or offshore facilities. These include destroying a vessel or aircraft (or ordering it to be destroyed) and preventing, or putting an end to acts of violence. For a review of these powers see M Head, 'Australia's Expanded Military Call-Out Powers: Causes For Concern' (2006) 3 *University of New England Law Journal* 125, and S Bronitt and D Stephens, '"Flying Under the Radar" — The Use of Lethal Force Against Hijacked Aircraft: Recent Australian Developments' (2007) 7(2) *Oxford University Commonwealth Law Journal* 265.

By contrast, the law relating to self-defence in the Criminal Code expressly excludes this level of force to protect property. The purpose of the new provisions in relation to aviation security incidents under the Act is to provide clear legal authority for the military to act. The provisions obviate the need to engage in the deliberative exercise of weighing competing interests as required under the law relating to necessity; to evaluate the imminence of the threat posed as required for self-defence; or to resort to the vagaries of prerogative or executive powers in order to defend the realm. The provisions seek to structure the decision-making process — and also to move beyond the reactive 'call-out' model — to designate a set of circumstances where the Chief of Defence is already pre-authorised or prospectively authorised to act (whether in Australia or offshore). In these cases, the military can act without ministerial authorisation or the Governor-General's order.

While the precautionary rationale is apparent in these powers, there are some further features of the legislation that pull *against* precautionary action. For example, the call-out powers have always raised a concern about excessive or disproportionate force by the military against civilians. To address this, specific measures were included to limit the use of force. Thus, s 51T(3) imposes a duty on defence personnel, where practicable, to first call on someone to surrender before using force likely to cause death or grievous bodily harm. Significantly, the Act seeks to promote more legal certainty for defence personnel by conferring immunity from state and territory criminal law (criminal offences such as murder, causing grievous bodily harm, etc) and ensuring that defence personnel will be dealt with only by reference to offences under the Commonwealth criminal law, and military discipline offences available under the *Defence Force Discipline Act 1982* (Cth).

These new counter-terrorism laws move beyond a conventional preventative to a more precautionary model — under this new legislation, key decision-makers are not weighing up competing harms (choosing the lesser of evils) but rather authorising and taking action (including the intentional use of lethal force) where the level of danger to life or limb is unknown or uncertain. This new legislation permits pre-emptive designation of places as critical infrastructure, which authorises the use of lethal force even though there is no prospect that this action would save a greater number of people, and may even foreseeably involve the killing of a significant number of people on the ground where the plane crashes. It is this particular scenario that presents the most serious challenge for human rights law and the right to human life and dignity, which is protected under international human rights law.[65]

---

[65] The right to life is protected by ICCPR, opened for signature 16 December 1966, 999 UNTS 171, art 6 (entered into force 23 March 1976). Following this line of argument, the German Constitutional Court recently held that the *Aviation Security Act* (11 January 2005) authorising the direct use of military force against hijacked aircraft was contradictory to the paramount rights in the federal Constitution:

## Conclusion

> As governments erode established procedures, the lawlessness of terrorism is being met with the lawlessness of counter-terrorism.[66]

In undertaking research for this chapter, I repeatedly came across statements that we now live in an 'Age of Terror' in both political and scholarly literature. Although some scholars have argued that this best fits the US experience and may not be replicated around the globe,[67] it seems that many liberal democracies are facing very similar challenges. In the US, Australia and the UK, an uncivil politics of law reform prevails in the field of counter-terrorism. Security culture leaves little space for human rights language and instruments. Under the sway of balancing models and the rationale of promoting preventative or precautionary measures, human rights tend to be traded away as a threshold issue.

The impact of 9/11 on the legitimacy of the law reform process has been highly deleterious: community consultation on draft legislation; the involvement of professional law reform agencies, as well as parliamentary oversight, have been seriously debased (if not sidelined entirely). The question is how long these trends will continue and how best to promote strategies for the civil politics of law reform in which human rights are protected and respected, rather than trumped by security considerations.

The problem in the current and future law reform context will be the likely 'trickle down' effect of this uncivil culture — the normalisation of emergency powers seems inevitable. Indeed, this trend has long been evident in the UK, where exceptional measures (such as the abolition of the right to silence) in Northern Ireland in the 1980s were subsequently brought to the mainland in the 1990s.[68] In Australia, the trend toward the enactment of preventative powers will continue — in relation both to combating terrorism and to ordinary crimes, which target suspect classes or groups rather than individuals.

This chapter has exposed the subtle but significant shift from preventative to precautionary models in the field of counter-terrorism. Prevention no longer seems the objective or end game. Rather, consistent with the precautionary model, in a security environment characterised by uncertainty, the law

---

art 2 II 1 GG (which guarantees the right to life), and art 1 I GG (which guarantees the right to human dignity): see O Lepsius 'Human Dignity and the Downing of Aircraft: The German Federal Constitutional Court Strikes Down a Prominent Anti-terrorism Provision in the New Air-transport Security Act' (2006) 7(9) *German Law Journal* 761; M Bohlander, 'In Extremis – Hijacked Airplanes, "Collateral Damage" and the Limits of Criminal Law' [2006] *Criminal Law Review* 579; and S Hufnagel, 'German Perspectives on the Right to Life and Human Dignity in the "War on Terror"' (2008) 32 *Criminal Law Journal* 100.

[66] J Hocking, *Terror Laws: ASIO, Counter-Terrorism and the Threat to Democracy* (Sydney: UNSW Press, 2004) xiii.

[67] R Falk, 'Human Rights: A Descending Spiral' in Wilson (ed), above n 18, ch 11.

[68] The normalisation of emergency powers, and the work of Paddy Hillyard, is discussed in Bronitt and McSherry, above n 8, 877.

increasingly favours pre-emptive action, mass surveillance and disruption tactics. The sense of an impending apocalyptic disaster, whether it be environmental or security related, promotes a fatalism in which liberalism and established legal norms are viewed as simply too costly. In truth, there is a serious risk of irreversible harm — not just the harm that terrorism presents to our security, but also the threat that counter-terrorism measures themselves pose to human rights.

As the International Commission of Jurists noted in its Berlin Declaration:

> Since September 2001 many states have adopted new counter-terrorism measures that are in breach of their international obligations. In some countries, the post-September 2001 climate of insecurity has been exploited to justify long-standing human rights violations carried out in the name of national security.[69]

One solution might be to invert the precautionary principle so that protection of human rights (like protection of the environment) is the principal value or objective prioritised. In the face of harm being done to human rights by opportunistic governments around the world, we must act to promote higher levels of protection of human rights even though we may lack knowledge that particular measures will be effective in this respect. There remains a broader debate, for example, over whether the adoption of bills of rights or the existing common law presumptions in favour of liberty provide an effective mechanism for upholding these important rights. Precautionary logic might suggest that we should act now to implement such measures, whilst remaining careful to monitor whether such reforms are having the desired impact. In relation to both the making and the enforcement of counter-terrorism laws, a re-modelled precautionary principle serves to uphold rather than to trade away human rights. It would certainly place human rights protection (and its various institutions) at the heart of regulatory design. In light of the arguments above, this attention to human rights would enhance both the legitimacy and effectiveness of our responses to terrorism (objectives that should be viewed as mutually reinforcing rather than antagonistic in the way that the balancing model presumes). The decision to prioritise human rights is ultimately a political rather than a strictly legal choice, especially so in the Australian system, which lacks an entrenched bill of rights. Somewhat pessimistically, my conclusion is that it is unrealistic to expect any significant policy change in the near future — the prevailing uncivil politics of law reform will regrettably continue to marginalise such unorthodox perspectives.

---

[69] *The Berlin Declaration*, above n 24.

# Chapter Six

# Lay Perceptions of Terrorist Acts and Counter-Terrorism Responses: Role of Motive, Offence Construal, Siege Mentality and Human Rights

Mark Nolan[*]

## Introduction

This chapter reports data from an empirical study of lay perceptions of terrorist acts and counter-terrorism initiatives in Australia. Relationships were measured between the following independent variables: perpetrator motive, offence construal (how an incident was described by a police spokesperson), siege mentality beliefs (the belief that you are alone in the world and under siege), and human rights beliefs. The measured dependent variables were: perceived blameworthiness of the perpetrator and perceived appropriateness of counter-terrorism initiatives. Measurement of human rights beliefs were also made, including whether participants agreed that violations of civil and political rights were justified in response to a food tampering incident due to an overarching 'right to human security' (derived from the right to life). A 'right to human security' had been asserted in Australia by the former Commonwealth Attorney-General in statements preceding data collection.[1]

---

[*] Senior Lecturer in Law, ANU College of Law, The Australian National University, Canberra, Australia <mark.nolan@anu.edu.au>. This research was funded by an Australian Research Council grant *'Terrorism and the Non-State Actor After September 11: The Role of Law in the Search for Security'* (DP0451473 awarded for 2004-2007, http://law.anu.edu.au/terrorismlaw/). Thanks to Prita Jobling for her assistance in collecting and entering these data and conducting data analyses. Thanks to Dr Kristina Murphy and Professor Craig McGarty for allowing us to invite their psychology students to participate in this study as approved by the ANU Human Research Ethics Committee, Protocol Number 2005/219.

[1] For example, statements made by former Attorney-General Phillip Ruddock in the 2004 Deakin Law School Oration as published, P Ruddock, 'National Security and Human Rights' [2004] *Deakin Law Review* 14. See other statements by Ruddock such as in press interviews: <http://www.abc.net.au/worldtoday/content/2005/s1497863.htm>; G Carne, 'Reconstituting "Human Security" in a New Security Environment: One Australian, Two Canadians and Article 3 of the Universal Declaration of Human Rights' (2006) 25 *Australian Year Book of International Law* 1, note 11, citing P Ruddock, 'Recent Developments in National Security' (Press Release, 6 February 2004). In this press release, Ruddock supported the views of Irwin Cotler, then Attorney-General of Canada, stating: 'Cotler has been a prominent human rights advocate over time and he made in a number of addresses, an examination of this question about how you get the balance right between security and what are seen often as civil and political rights. But his starting point was to emphasise the importance of the civil and political

Participants in this sample were generally not in favour of increasing the police or state's ability to counter terrorism with unprecedented criminal processes. Participants were also not in favour of a 'right to human security' that would trump other civil and political rights. However, even in this sample, participants perceived the perpetrator to be *more blameworthy* if motivated by a jihadist cause *rather than by* an anti-corporate motive, *despite the fact that the remaining facts surrounding the terrorist act were identical in all four experimental conditions*. The implications of this effect are discussed for jurors' perception of blameworthiness in Australian terrorist cases that incorporate motive-like elements such as perpetrating an act or issuing a threat of action *with the intention of advancing a political, religious or ideological cause* in Australian counter-terrorism offences.[2]

The chapter begins by outlining the main reasons for conducting this empirical study: (i) the tendency to describe post-September 11 political violence as exceptional examples of criminality, and (ii) the concern over inclusion of motive elements in terrorist offence definition.

## Exceptionalism and Siege Mentality

In this so called 'age of terror', much of the rhetoric used to justify changes to procedural and/or substantive criminal law suggests that the 'world has changed', sometimes 'forever'.[3] As the rhetoric goes, the old ways of policing, prosecuting and imprisoning are simply inadequate. Much of the tradition and principle of criminal law and procedure is thought by some to be less relevant now and to create undue risks in the prevention or regulation of political violence. Such arguments proceed by suggesting that if we are to counter terrorism in this new age, investigative powers and criminal sanctions must be broadened if our efforts are to be effective in the face of new threats. This emphasis could be captured in the phrase 'exceptional law for exceptional times'. The use of this phrase, or arguments consistent with it, was a key motivation for conducting this empirical work measuring perceptions of politically-motivated violence *and* perceptions of the public responses to the use of such violence.

Insights into the social psychology of exceptionalism exist in research conducted before the attacks on America on 11 September 2001 (9/11). For example, the social psychological dynamics surrounding politically-motivated violence in the Middle East has been investigated by Israeli social psychologist Professor Daniel Bar-Tal from Tel Aviv University and colleagues. Bar-Tal has attempted to explain

---

right that citizens are entitled to expect in a civilised society and that is to be safe and secure, to be safe and secure from terrorist activities in which citizens are targeted.'

[2] See M Gani, Chapter 13 this volume, for a review of these offences.

[3] For example, then Prime Minister John Howard stated in a radio interview, 'I want people to be more alert to understand the world has changed but I don't want them to stop living their normal lives': Radio 2UE, *Interview With John Laws*, 21 November 2002.

some of the social relationships in the Middle East in terms of the ongoing socialisation of Israeli Jews with a 'siege mentality'. A siege mentality is a socialised psychological belief orientation that shapes conceptions of the other, especially conceptions of those Palestinians perpetrating politically-motivated violence. Bar-Tal has described the orientation in the following terms:

> A belief held by group members stating that the rest of the world has highly negative behavioural intentions toward them.[4]

Also,

> a significant and influential part of the group believes that outsiders have intentions to do wrong to or inflict harm on their group ... this belief is usually accompanied with additional thoughts by group members such as that they are 'alone' in the world, that there is a threat to their existence, that the group must be united in the face of danger, that they cannot expect help from anyone in time of need, and that all means are justified for group defence.[5]

One striking aspect of this belief orientation is that it suggests more than simply feeling under threat by an outgroup and more than being motivated to promote your ingroup identity and to denigrate your opponent. In addition, those with a siege mentality believe that the rest of the world will not or cannot help them; those under siege perceive that they face this threat alone and in relative isolation from other potential allies and coalition members.

In light of this belief orientation, Bar-Tal lists four consequences of adopting siege mentality beliefs as being: (i) negative attitudes against 'the world', (ii) intergroup mistrust, (iii) pressure toward intragroup conformity, and (iv) self-protection and self-reliance. It is interesting to note that the perceived isolation consequent upon holding negative attitudes against 'the world' is likely to have a chilling effect on the perceived utility of international institutions and concepts such as international human rights norms. This retreat from rights is one measurable consequence of the adoption of siege mentality beliefs and that relationship was tested in this empirical study. Bar-Tal describes such a collective retreat from established norms in the face of siege in the following way:

> [the group] may take drastic measures, even out of the range of the accepted norms for the intergroup behaviours, to prevent possible danger and avert the threat.[6]

---

[4] D Bar-Tal and D Antebi, 'Siege Mentality in Israel' (1992) 16(3) *International Journal of Intercultural Relations* 251, 251.
[5] D Bar-Tal and D Antebi, 'Beliefs about Negative Intentions of the World: A Study of the Israeli Siege Mentality' (1992) 13(4) *Political Psychology* 633, 634; D Bar-Tal, 'The Masada Syndrome: A Case of Central Belief' in N Milgram (ed), *Stress and Coping in Time of War* (New York: Brunnor/Mazel, 1986) 32.
[6] Bar-Tal and Antebi, 'Beliefs about Negative Intentions of the World: A Study of the Israeli Siege Mentality', above n 5, 643.

There is one further point to note about this perceived isolation and negative attitude against 'the world': that, in principle, it would appear to be a belief that could be held plausibly by the victims of politically-motivated violence just *as well as* by those using politically-motivated violence. However, in the present study the cognition and belief orientation of politically active 'terrorists' was not measured. Instead, the attitudinal response of members of hypothetical victim groups to a threat of politically-motivated violence was measured.

Bar-Tal and colleagues have made empirical, social psychological measurements of a 'siege mentality' orientation in Israel by asking participants to indicate their level of endorsement of the following statements presented as questionnaire items with Likert-scales (eg, 1 = strongly disagree to 7 = strongly agree):

- There is no place for internal criticism in times of danger.
- Anyone who opposes the majority opinion weakens the strength of the nation.
- In order to continue to exist we have to act according to the rule 'if anyone comes to kill you, kill him first'.
- We can't rely on advice from other nations, because they do not necessarily have our welfare at heart.
- There have always been countries which looked for closeness and friendship with us.
- Because of the persistent danger to our existence, we must end internal disagreements.
- Our existence is the end which justifies the means.
- The whole world is against us.
- Only demonstration of force will deter our enemies from attacking us.
- Only unity will save us from external enemies.
- When neighbouring countries get into conflicts, we will often be blamed for it.
- Most nations will conspire against us, if only they have the possibility to do so.[7]

This work by Bar-Tal and colleagues is an example both of social scientific work conducted well before 9/11 and of work that had begun to describe and even explain some of the dynamics of fearing terrorism and justifying counter-terrorism responses. Simple generalisation of psychological belief orientation across time and political context is neither simple nor desirable. However, even if some new dynamics are observed, measured and understood, it is interesting to test whether the contemporary social manifestation of exceptionalism and the more modern justifications of counter-terrorism responses can ever be said to be entirely new. For these reasons, it was considered timely

---

[7] Ibid.

to manipulate and measure exceptionalism in Australia using questionnaire items akin to Bar-Tal's siege mentality scale.

## Use of 'Motive' in the Definition of Australian Terrorist Act Offences

Even if the phenomenon of politically-motivated violence appeared new to some but not to others following 9/11, it is arguable that Australia's legislative response to terrorism to date has been exceptional. The Australian government avoided the urge to make amendments to Australia's substantive and procedural criminal law after the Hilton bombing on 13 February 1978,[8] and, for example, following an attempted bombing of the Turkish Consulate in Melbourne in 1986.[9] However, following 9/11, the federal Parliament made extensive amendments to both offence definition and criminal procedure. As a result of these amendments, terror suspects can be treated very differently to other types of offenders.

Perhaps the most controversial aspect of our domestic response has been the inclusion of political, religious or ideological motive, alongside an intention to coerce or influence by intimidation a government or the public, as a key part of the definition of a terrorist act in s 100.1(1) of the *Criminal Code Act 1995* (Cth) ('Criminal Code'). At first blush at least, this legislative decision seems exceptional according to common law criminal doctrine.[10] The relevant drafting appears in the keystone definition of terrorist act in s 100.1 of the Criminal Code as follows:

> s 100.1
>
> (1)
>
> ...
>
> *terrorist act* means an action or threat of action where:
>
> ...
>
> (b) the action is done or the threat is made with the *intention of advancing a political, religious or ideological cause*; and
>
> (c) the action is done or the threat is made with the intention of:
>
> (i) coercing, or influencing by intimidation, the government of the Commonwealth or a State, Territory or foreign country, or of part of a State, Territory or foreign country; or
>
> (ii) intimidating the public or a section of the public.
>
> [Emphasis added.]

---

[8] R M Hope, *Protective Security Review* (Canberra: Commonwealth of Australia, 1979).
[9] *R v Demirian* [1989] VR 97.
[10] B McSherry, 'The Introduction of Terrorism-Related Offences in Australia: Comfort or Concern' (2005) 12(2) *Psychiatry, Psychology and Law* 279, 282.

The *Hyam v DPP* [11] common law position on motive versus intention leads to concern over the drafting of the terrorist act definition. In that case a distinction was drawn between proof of intention and evidence of motive, insofar as motive is thought to be 'an emotion prompting an act that is quite separate from an intention'.[12] In this sense, motive, at best, may constitute some form of circumstantial evidence for proof beyond reasonable doubt of intention as the requisite *mens rea* element. The fault element as expressed in the s 100.1 definition of a terrorist act appears to require proof of the intentional advancement of a cause; perhaps dressing up proof of motive by using the more accepted *mens rea* language of intention. This drafting seems to require the fact finder to consider the perpetrator's emotional reasons prompting them to act (though see the conclusion to this chapter, and Gani, Chapter 13 this volume, where *Lodhi* is discussed).

Some may argue that the drafting defines a form of acceptable specific intent, as seen in aggravated assault with the intent to have sexual intercourse or even violence offences by those possessing higher order genocidal intent. On this view, the intention of advancing a political, religious or ideological cause appears more mainstream rather than it being an attempt to criminalise behaviour based on motive rather than intention. Taking this approach normalises the use of motive in s 100.1(1) and deems this intention to be a specific intent rather than a motivating emotion as described in *Hyam*. In that sense, the need to prove intention to advance a political, religious and ideological cause via terrorist acts would not be all that different from the way we have been criminalising specific intents as part of the definition of many (non-terrorism) offences predating 9/11. The case of *Hyam* does appear to legitimise the use of motive evidence as one way to prove intention indirectly in circumstantial cases. When this is allowed, then perhaps the distinction between motive and intention will be lost in the minds of the (lay) legal decision-maker, and, the conceptual integrity of 'intention' and 'motive' is blurred at the level of proof in any event.

Nonetheless, one possible conclusion is that s 100.1(1), as extracted above, is a significant departure from the relevant common law position on motive and consequently its use in the prosecution of offences is an example of exceptionalism.[13] A realistic view, prompting empirical interest in the impact of motive on blameworthiness, would be that jurors may simply understand the proof required to be an invitation to judge blameworthiness based on motive rather than applying a more formal legal test of intention to the facts as condoned by *Hyam*.

---

[11] [1975] AC 55.
[12] Ibid 73 (Lord Hailsham).
[13] McSherry, above n 10, 282-3, citing Bronitt, points out that status offences have criminalised characteristics possessed by some defendants and this may be conceptually close to the use of motive to criminalise physical acts.

Some criticism of the drafting in s 100.1(1) is made by Gani and Urbas who have commented on the inadequacy of the phrase 'the intention of advancing a political, religious or ideological cause'.[14] Gani and Urbas see technical problems making it difficult for a prosecutor to prove such an intention. Their arguments also suggest that the defendant's motive will not always be used fairly, based on the current approach. The rather clumsy way of criminalising motive here, if that is what the legislature intended to criminalise, is illustrated by Gani and Urbas via reference to more difficult cases. For example, could a rather peripheral actor, such as an Australian medical worker in Sri Lanka, be charged with a terrorist offence. Gani and Urbas conclude their paper by noting that:

> The focus on the technicalities of intention may, in the end, mean that legislation in the area of terrorism does not adequately deal with the problem at its core, the problem of motive. In the area of terrorism, we can never escape the question of the motives of the accused. In reality, it will be the touchstone to which juries will intuitively turn when reaching their decisions.[15]

The use of this 'touchstone' by juries is the main rationale for studying lay evaluations of criminal blameworthiness in this study. What level of perceived blameworthiness will be used if evidence suggests that perpetrators sought to advance *particular* political, religious or ideological causes? Will all such causes be considered equally blameworthy or are some causes perceived to be more heinous than others, *even if the action or threat of action is the same* and only the motives differ? If some motives will be considered more blameworthy than others, it is important to determine the extent to which that difference may impact on verdict decisions of lay jurors. In the context of the current 'war on terror', assertion of a religious motive, rather than other political or ideological motives, as the emotion prompting the alleged terrorist act may have more impact upon decision-makers.

## The Empirical Research

### Design

The study was designed to investigate the effect that *exceptionalism* has upon legal attitudes, and the reactions lay decision-makers have to the use of *'motive'* in the definition of criminal offences. These two independent variables formed the basis for the design of this experimental study and four separate experimental conditions were created according to a 2 × 2 fully-factorial experimental design. This design can be described formally as a 2 (*offence construal by police spokesperson*: exceptional crime, standard crime) by 2 (*motive of the perpetrator*: jihadist, anti-corporate) between-participants design, where each independent

---

[14] M Gani and G Urbas, 'Alert or Alarmed? Recent Legislative Reforms Directed at Terrorist Organisations and Persons Supporting or Assisting Terrorist Acts' (2004) 8(1) *Newcastle Law Review* 19.
[15] Ibid 50.

variable has two levels. Each participant was randomly assigned to one of these resultant four conditions. The design and procedure are further described below and the labels for the conditions are set out in Table 1.

Four different sets of stimulus materials were designed and one set of stimulus material was given to each participant in each of the four experimental groups. The variables were manipulated by changing the information provided to participants in an incident report and in a police statement. The motive of the criminal (jihadist or anti-corporate) was varied between conditions as needed by changing the information in the incident report (see below in 'Materials/Procedure'). The different types of offence construal ('standard crime' or 'exceptional crime') were created by providing different police statements to participants.

**Table 1: Design of the study and explanation of the four experimental conditions**

| | Motive of the Perpetrator | |
|---|---|---|
| | *Jihadist* | *Anti-corporate* |
| **Police Statement** | | |
| *Exceptional crime* | Jihadist/exceptional crime (j/e) | Anti-corporate/exceptional crime (a/e) |
| *Standard crime* | Jihadist/standard crime (j/s) | Anti-corporate/standard crime (a/s) |

Other dependent variables measured in this study included: (i) the use of a siege mentality belief orientation when responding to the report of the incident, (ii) the perceived appropriateness of counter-terrorism powers, and (iii) the perceived appropriateness of human rights norms.

## Adapting Bar-Tal's Siege Mentality Scale

In discussion with Daniel Bar-Tal, the Israeli Siege Mentality Scale was adapted so that the focus of each item became Australian counter-terrorism policy. Such contextualisation of the siege mentality scale has not been attempted in past research, but it was hoped to create a sensitive measure of *terrorism siege mentality beliefs*. The siege mentality scale has not been administered to Australian participants to date, so this attempt was also a test of the generalisability of such belief items across cultures and across different political scenarios. The items used in the present study, in the order they were presented to participants, are as follows (the starred items were reverse-scored, meaning that higher ratings on those items mean *low* siege mentality rather than *high* siege mentality as per the other items):

- There is no place for internal criticism of Australia's counter-terrorism policy.
- Anyone who opposes increasing Australia's counter-terrorism powers weakens the strength of the nation.
- Most nations care about our security and welfare.*

- In order to maintain Australia's security from terrorism we have to act according to the rule 'if people come to kill you, kill them first'.
- Most nations are eager to cooperate with Australia and to achieve closer political and strategic relationships with us.*
- Many nations would be happy to see Australians suffer as the result of terrorist acts.
- Security from terrorism does not justify unprecedented and broad counter-terrorism powers as the means to that end.*
- Sometimes it feels as though large parts of the world are against us.
- Only the demonstration of force and harsh punishments for terrorists will deter them from attacking us.
- Only unity will save us from terrorist attacks.
- When other countries suffer terrorist attacks, Australia is usually not blamed.*
- Many terrorists will conspire against Australia if they have the possibility to do so.

## Participants and Data Collection

Data were collected in the week of the Council of Australian Governments' (COAG) Special Meeting on Counter-Terrorism held on 27 September 2005. During that week, 124 undergraduate psychology students studying a psychology and criminology course at the Australian National University participated in the study.

## Materials/Procedure

In the *jihadist conditions* (ie, *both* the jihadist/standard crime (j/s) condition *and* the jihadist/exceptional crime (j/e) condition) participants were asked to imagine that they had read the following report of a hypothetical incident set in Australia.

> *The Reported Incident*: Police are investigating a possible food-tampering incident affecting supplies to a leading multinational hamburger chain established in Australia.
>
> There has been no claim of responsibility as yet but police report that anonymous threats have been made to restaurant owners that state: 'Don't trust the safety of any of your food supplies today. Action has been taken so that infidels will be stopped in the name of Allah!'
>
> The media reports detail that all unsold raw materials received from suppliers have been destroyed. Restaurants have closed. Customers who have consumed food from these restaurants today have been urged to have health checks immediately. This has resulted in high demand and long waiting times in hospital emergency departments and consulting rooms of doctors around the country. People are reporting a range of symptoms to hospitals and doctors including severe stomach cramps, nausea, and vomiting. A number of people have collapsed with, as yet, undiagnosed conditions. Emergency hotlines have been established to monitor the situation.

In the *anti-corporate conditions* (ie, *both* the anti-corporate/standard crime (a/s) condition *and* the anti-corporate/exceptional crime (a/e) condition) the incident report was as for the above except for the fact that the anonymous threat in the second paragraph was replaced with the following:

> Don't trust the safety of any of your food supplies today. Action has been taken so that people will stop trusting the lies of multinational corporations who control our diets!

Participants were asked to express the 'apparent motive of the perpetrator(s)' in their own words after reading through the incident report. They then rated on a 7-point Likert rating scale (anchored by 1 = strongly disagree, 4 = no opinion, and 7 = strongly agree) 'the extent to which you agree that the motive you described above as held by the perpetrator(s) of the food-tampering incident is the most important factor in judging the blameworthiness of the act'.

In the *standard crime conditions* (ie, *both* the jihadist/standard crime (j/s) condition and the anti-corporate/standard crime (a/s) condition) the police report read as follows:

> *The Police Statement*: 'This is a clear example of how inappropriate political protest can endanger lives. From time to time we as a society have to manage such criminal acts in the best way we know how, according to long-standing norms of our criminal justice system. These actions are unjustified and deserve the full force of the criminal law in order to bring those responsible to justice. We will deploy the standard share of available resources proportionate to such events to swiftly identify the culprits. Our investigation of this incident and our willingness to prosecute these criminal acts must be evident to all.'

In the *exceptional crime conditions* (ie, *both* the jihadist/exceptional crime (j/e) condition *and* the anti-corporate/exceptional crime (a/e) condition) the police report read as follows:

> *The Police Statement*: 'This is a clear example of how the world has changed since 9/11. We must face this threat of terrorism head on and not bow to the terrorists responsible for these attacks. These actions are unjustified and deserve the full force of Australia's counter-terrorism law and policies in order to bring those responsible to justice. We have diverted all available resources to the investigation of these incidents and are working with counter-terrorism agencies to swiftly identify the culprits. Our investigation of this incident and our willingness to prosecute these terrorist acts will be evident to all.'

After reading the police statement the participants rated (on the same 7-point scale as above) 'the extent to which you agree with the police spokesperson's statement' and 'the extent to which you think that the police spokesman's statement was appropriate in the circumstances' (scale anchors were: $1 =$ not at all appropriate, $4 =$ no opinion, and $7 =$ extremely appropriate). Those participants who thought that the spokesperson's statement was inappropriate (having made a rating less than 4) were invited to suggest in their own words 'the theme of a statement you think would have been more appropriate'. Participants were next asked the forced choice question 'Would you describe the food-tampering incident described above as a terrorist act?' (answer options = yes/no) and were invited to 'explain the reason for your last answer' in one sentence.

Participants then rated their agreement (on a 7-point Likert rating scale anchored by $1 =$ strongly disagree, $4 =$ no opinion, and $7 =$ strongly agree) with each of the 12 adapted siege mentality scale items as listed above.

In the next section of the questionnaire, participants were asked to make ratings (on a 7-point Likert rating scale anchored by $1 =$ not at all appropriate, $4 =$ no opinion, and 7 = extremely appropriate) of 'how appropriate each of the following [16] measures would be to deal with people suspected of the food tampering incident described above and any threat their actions represent'. It should be noted that as a result of the 27 September 2005 COAG meeting, or otherwise, some of the measures indicated below as *not* being current practice in Australian states and territories at the time of data collection have been implemented subsequently (see footnotes to the items below for examples of such amendments but such citations were not provided to participants). Also, legislation passed after the COAG meeting introduced powers to make preventative detention orders and control orders,[16] often broader than some of the items below relating to detention without charge and travel restrictions.

The list of powers and measures rated by the participants was as follows:

- Allow covert search warrants to be issued to investigating police officers whereby the owners of premises searched do not need to be told of execution of the search warrant until 90 days after the search takes place *(NB: These powers are given currently to some Australian state police).*[17]
- Allow police to conduct random bag searches in public places such as restaurants, on public transport, and in crowds at large sporting or recreational events *(NB: Such powers are currently not used much in Australia).*
- Demand that citizens carry a national identity card that includes a photo and biometric information (such as a fingerprint), and to produce the card when requested to do so by police under risk of arrest for not producing the card *(NB: This is not current practice in Australia).*
- Allow a default maximum of 4 hours detention for questioning before charging suspects with offences, this period being extendable any number of times up to a total of 20 hours maximum detention *(NB: This is current practice for police interviewing of terror suspects in Australia. Interviews of those not suspected of committing terrorist offences can only be extended once or twice up to 8 hours of total questioning).*[18]

---

[16] See the regime of control orders and preventative detention orders in Division 104 and 105 respectively of the *Criminal Code Act 1995* (Cth); State and Territory legislation allowing for preventative detention without charge for up to 14 days has also been enacted: *Terrorism (Extraordinary Temporary Powers) Act 2006* (ACT); *Terrorism (Emergency Powers) Act* (NT); *Terrorism (Police Powers) Act 2002* (NSW); *Terrorism (Community Protection) Act 2003* (Vic); *Terrorism (Preventative Detention) Act 2005* (Qld); *Terrorism (Preventative Detention) Act 2005* (SA); *Terrorism (Preventative Detention) Act 2005* (Tas); *Terrorism (Preventative Detention) Act 2005* (WA).

[17] *Terrorism (Police Powers) Act 2002* (NSW), pt 3, especially s 27U regarding notice of execution of covert search warrant; at the time of writing, the Crimes Legislation Amendment (National Investigative Powers and Witness Protection) Bill 2006 (Cth) had not been enacted though it proposed to introduce a regime of covert search warrants ('delayed notification search warrants') into the *Crimes Act 1914* (Cth) for the investigation of federal offences.

[18] Compare ss 23C and 23CA of the *Crimes Act 1914* (Cth). It is also worth noting that the detention of Mohamed Haneef in July 2007 demonstrated that the combination of s 23DA extensions of time to detain and question without charge, as well as 'dead time' provisions allowing time to stop running, such as s 23CB, did mean that detention for lengthy periods such as 12 days without charge was possible.

- Allow a default maximum of three months detention for questioning before charging suspects with offences *(NB: This is not current practice in Australia)*.
- Allow the police to determine if a suspect can have their lawyer present during an investigative interview *(NB: This power is currently not available to police in Australia)*.
- Allow the police to determine which particular lawyers can be present during investigative interviews *(NB: This power is currently given to some Australian Security Intelligence Organisation (ASIO) officers conducting intelligence-gathering interviews with people who have information relevant to terrorism)*.[19]
- Allow the police to eject a lawyer from investigative interviews if the police believe the lawyer is being too disruptive of the questioning of the suspect *(NB: This power is currently given to some ASIO officers conducting intelligence-gathering interviews with people who have information relevant to terrorism)*.[20]
- Allow police to monitor private discussions between suspects and their lawyers *(NB: This power is currently given to some ASIO officers conducting intelligence-gathering interviews with people who have information relevant to terrorism)*.[21]
- Automatically deny bail to any suspect charged with criminal offences relating to the food tampering as described above *(NB: This is a possible outcome under some Australian state and federal laws)*.[22]
- Place those suspects who are denied bail after being charged with criminal offences relating to the food tampering as described above into maximum security prisons whilst awaiting trial *(NB: This has occurred in some Australian states)*.[23]
- Place those suspects who are denied bail after being charged with criminal offences relating to the food tampering as described above into maximum security prisons where solitary confinement is used for most of the day *(NB: This has occurred in some Australian cases)*.[24]

---

[19] See *Australian Security and Intelligence Organisation Act 1979* (Cth) (ASIO Act) ss 34ZO and ZP, governing questioning warrants.

[20] ASIO Act s 34ZQ(9), though note s 34ZQ(10) that directs the interviewer to explain that the interviewee may contact another lawyer.

[21] ASIO Act s 34ZQ(2).

[22] Eg, the presumption against bail for terrorism offences in s 8A of the *Bail Act 1978* (NSW) where the person charged with a terrorism offence must prove why bail should not be refused. Note that this presumption can be rebutted and was done so in *R v Khazal* [2004] NSWSC 548 where bail was granted following a charge under s 101.5 of the Criminal Code, an offence of collecting, or making a document connected with preparation for, or assistance in a terrorist act punishable by imprisonment for 15 years.

[23] There has been a new inmate classification introduced for remandees charged with terrorism offences or for prisoners convicted of terrorism offences, see *Crimes (Administration of Sentences) Regulation 2001* (NSW) cl 22, as also discussed in Gani, Chapter 13 this volume.

[24] *Crimes (Administration of Sentences) Regulation 2001* (NSW) cl 22 and Gani, Chapter 13 this volume.

- Automatically deny a non-parole period (ie, denying the possibility of early release) to anyone convicted of criminal offences relating to the food tampering as described above *(NB: This is not a normal sentencing outcome in Australia)*.[25]
- Imprison anyone convicted of criminal offences relating to the food tampering as described above in maximum security prisons *(NB: This has occurred in some Australian cases)*.[26]
- Strip Australian citizenship, Australian residency or visa status from anyone convicted of criminal offences relating to the food tampering described above *(NB: Not the standard result in Australia)*.[27]
- Deny prisoners access to special facilities and special diets consistent with religious obligations *(NB: There have been some complaints of such treatment made by some prisoners currently held in Australian prisons)*.[28]

In the final section of the questionnaire, participants answered some questions about human rights and standard criminal practice. First, they rated the appropriateness of the following two scenarios:

- To ensure security of the nation, allowing general treatment of suspects by the police and by the courts in ways inconsistent with international human rights law *(NB: Liability for human rights complaints made against Australia still exists)*.
- To ensure security of the nation, allowing general treatment of suspects by the police and by the courts in ways inconsistent with standard criminal practice *(NB: Liability for human rights complaints made against Australia still exists)*.

An open-ended question followed, asking participants to 'please describe what you think is the main purpose of human rights law when societies are faced with food-tampering incidents as described above'. These questions relate to previous measurement of the perceived purpose of human rights law in Australia as collected by me in 2003.[29] However, the current measures extend such inquiry

---

[25] Though subsequent to data collection, the non-parole period set for Faheem Lodhi was 75 per cent of his total sentence.
[26] *Crimes (Administration of Sentences) Regulation 2001* (NSW) cl 22 and Gani, Chapter 13 this volume.
[27] Though note the legal debate surrounding the cancellation of Mohamed Haneef's visa by the Minister of the Department of Immigration and Citizenship following his release from custody without charge: *Haneef v Minister for Immigration and Citizenship* [2007] FCA 1273 (21 August 2007).
[28] Prisoner Jack Roche first made such allegations in 2004 relating to his incarceration in Hakea Prison in Western Australia and this claim was eventually settled out of court by the West Australian government in May 2006: 'Convicted Terrorist Settles Food Claim', *Sydney Morning Herald* (Sydney), 16 May 2006.
[29] M A Nolan, *Construals of Human Rights Law: Protecting Subgroups as well as Individual Humans* (unpublished doctoral thesis, the Australian National University, 2003) <http://thesis.anu.edu.au/public/adt-ANU20050324.155005/index.html>; M A Nolan and P J Oakes, 'Human Rights Concepts in Australian Political Debate' in T Campbell, J Goldsworthy and A Stone (eds), *Protecting Human Rights: Instruments and Institutions* (Oxford: Oxford University Press, 2003).

to whether there is any support for the notion of a right to human security (derived from the right to life) that can be asserted as a justification for other violations of human rights in the interest of counter-terrorism and security.[30]

Participants then answered two further forced (yes/no) choice questions:

- Do you think a right to human security enjoyed by all Australians allows us to disregard any human rights complaints made against Australian police officers by those suspected of the food-tampering described above?
- Do you think a right to human security enjoyed by all Australians allows us to disregard any human rights complaints made against Australian correctional services officers by anyone convicted of and imprisoned for the food-tampering described above?

Finally, some demographic information was collected including: age, gender, whether the participant or a close relative or close personal friend had ever been a victim of a violent crime. Participants were invited to comment generally about the study and were fully debriefed as to the aims and design of the experiment.

## Results

We had sought to test the following hypotheses:

- Those who agree that the incident should be described as a terrorist attack and agree with the exceptionalist rhetoric will be more likely to justify extended counter-terrorism powers and believe in a right to human security.
- These beliefs should also relate to high scores on the Terrorism Siege Mentality Scale.
- These relationships should be the strongest in the jihadist/exceptional crime condition but it was thought interesting to investigate whether the framing of an anti-corporate food-tampering incident as an exceptional crime in turn causes participants to justify broader criminal justice responses, even in the anti-corporate/exceptional crime condition.
- The standard crime description by police in the jihadist condition would lead people to think that this incident poses only a standard or normal level of criminal threat that would neither result in high siege mentality beliefs nor result in endorsement of exceptional criminal procedures.

In order to test these hypotheses, a range of relationships were investigated between participants' attitude ratings, and the themes emerging from their qualitative responses were also analysed. Relationships tested between quantitative measures included between: offence construal, perpetrator motive, siege mentality beliefs, perpetrator blameworthiness, perceived appropriateness

---

[30] Ruddock, above n 1. See a review of the asserted legal basis for a right to human security by Carne, above n 1.

of counter-terrorism initiatives, and beliefs about the importance of human rights.

## Description of Motive and Importance of Motive for Blameworthiness

Participants' open-ended descriptions of perpetrator motive in each condition confirms that participants understood the motive to be jihadist or anti-corporate when the motive was described as such in the stimulus materials. However, an interesting unexpected result was that a few participants (n = 4) simply stated that the perpetrator(s) had 'terrorism' rather than jihad or an anti-corporate protest, as a motive. These motive descriptions, all made by participants in the jihadist conditions, were as follows:

- 'terrorism: strike fear and panic into a large segment of the population' (Participant 56, j/e condition);
- 'terrorism' (Participant 63, j/e condition);
- 'terrorism, selfish' (Participant 93, j/e condition);
- 'terrorism in the food industry: fanatics attempting to discourage the use/consumption of certain food' (Participant 105, j/s condition).

Other descriptions of motive by participants were couched in terms more consistent with one or more of the elements of the Australian definition of a terrorist act, notably the intention of intimidating the public or a section of the public in s 100.1(1)(c)(ii) of the Criminal Code. Examples of these motive descriptions as being the creation of chaos and collective fear in the minds of the public rather than simply as jihadist or anti-corporate motives were seen across all conditions, for example:

- 'to disrupt the everyday lives of citizens, create disorder and fear and get their message heard' (Participant 5, j/s condition);
- 'to injure as many people as possible to make a statement' (Participant 12, j/e condition);
- 'to scare the Australian public' (Participant 19, a/s condition);
- 'to put the Australian public in a state of fear for their own safety by eating at a well-known restaurant' (Participant 12, a/e condition).

An analysis of variance revealed a main effect for the motive of the criminal variable (see Figure 1).[31] In other words when the food-tampering incident was associated with the anonymous threat made to restaurant owners stating 'don't trust the safety of any of your food supplies today, action has been taken so that infidels will be stopped in the name of Allah!', rather than as the anti-corporate threat, then participants believed that the jihadist motive was 'the most important

---

[31] Mean importance of motive for blameworthiness by condition: j/s = 4.83 ($sd$ = 1.34, $n$ = 29), j/e = 5.03 ($sd$ = 1.22, $n$ = 31), a/s = 4.32 ($sd$ = 1.68, $n$ = 31), a/e = 4.23 ($sd$ = 1.59, $n$ = 30); $F(1, 117)$ = 5.94, p <.05.

factor in judging the blameworthiness of the act'. This was significantly more than was the case when the motive of the food tamperer was an anti-corporate ideology.

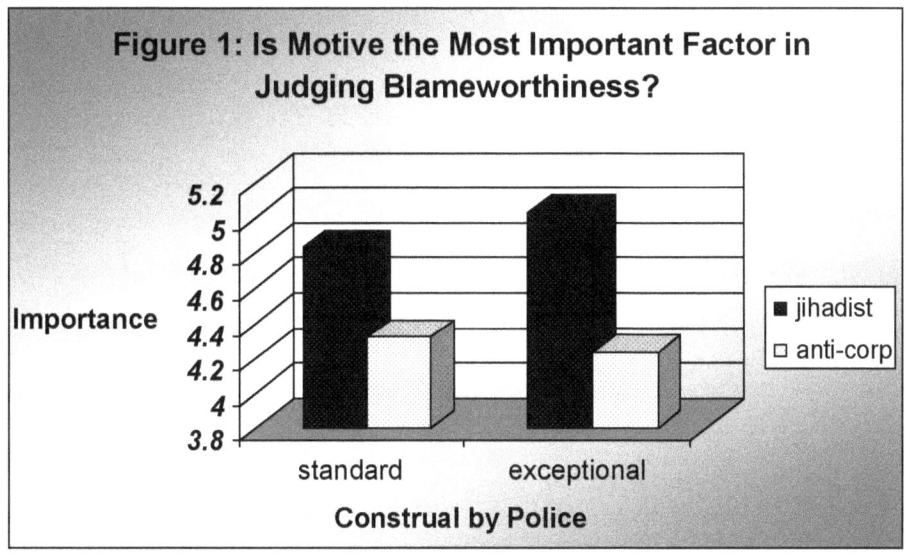

Figure 1: Is Motive the Most Important Factor in Judging Blameworthiness?

This finding is interesting in light of the fact that other results (discussed below) suggest that these participants as a group did not endorse broadening powers in order to counter terrorism. In other words, even people with low Terrorism Siege Mentality scores, who did not support the idea that civil and political rights could be weakened by asserting a right to human security, still believed that religious jihadist motives rendered the same physical food-tampering acts more blameworthy than food-tampering with anti-corporate political or ideological motives.

## Agreement With and Perceived Appropriateness of the Police Statement

Analysis of variance revealed a main effect for the construal of the crime used in the police statement (Figure 2).[32] In other words, participants agreed with the police statement significantly more when the standard crime description was used in contrast to when the food tampering incident was described as an exceptional crime indicative of how the world has changed since 9/11. This preference was the same irrespective of the motive of the perpetrator provided in the stimulus materials.

---

[32] Mean agreement with the construal of crime by police by condition: j/s =5.38 ($sd$ = .98, $n$ = 29), j/e = 4.26 ($sd$ = 1.59, $n$ = 31), a/s = 5.45 ($sd$ = 1.59, $n$ = 31), a/e = 4.27 ($sd$ = 1.51, $n$ = 30); $F(1, 117)$ = 10.25, p <.001.

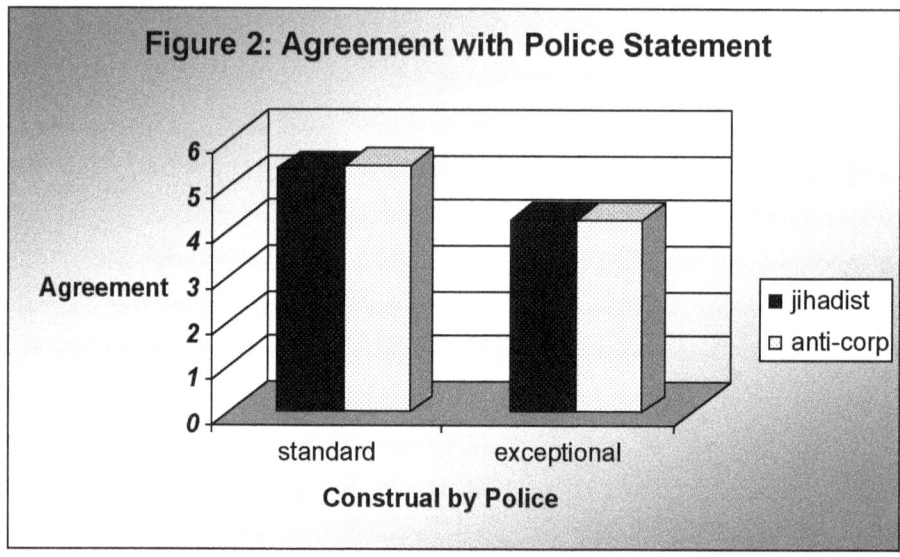

Figure 2: Agreement with Police Statement

This effect was the same for the perceived appropriateness of the police statement.[33] Some alternative themes for the police statement as suggested by those perceiving the exceptional crime statement to be inappropriate included the following (from a total of 23 responses in the exceptional crime conditions and from a total of 33 open-ended responses across all conditions):[34]

- 'that we must look at the larger picture and understand what it is these people are complaining about. That we won't engage with them but will seek to solve the problem' (Participant 29, j/e condition);
- 'that the police were diverting all resources to determine who the perpetrators is/are, rather than simply assuming that it was an act of terrorism' (Participant 34, j/e condition);
- '[that] this may be an example of a terrorist act and at present resources have been diverted so that definite conclusions can be drawn' (Participant 38, j/e condition);
- '[stating that] "These actions are unjustified" is an incorrect statement. Better to state the importance of solving the problem by identifying why they did it' (Participant 72, j/e condition);

---

[33] Mean level of perceived appropriateness of the police statement by condition: j/s =5.07 ($sd = 1.07$, $n = 29$), j/e = 4.16 ($sd = 1.39$, $n = 31$), a/s = 5.35 ($sd = 1.60$, $n = 31$), a/e = 4.40 ($sd = 1.65$, $n = 30$); $F(1, 117) = 12.45$, $p < .01$.

[34] The number of participants suggesting an alternative theme for the police statement having thought the theme in the provided statement was inappropriate was as follows: j/s = 4; j/e = 12, a/s = 5, a/e = 11; meaning that from this sample more people had solutions to the poor choice of theme in the police statement in the exceptional crime conditions ($n = 23$) than participants had in reaction to the theme of the police statement in the standard crime conditions ($n = 9$).

- 'I don't think the acts were done for religious/terrorist reasons. [It] is unclear whether the acts were targeting a particular group of people or aimed to interfere with [the] everyday life for all. [The statement] should have been aimed at catching the people' (Participant 106, j/e condition);
- 'changing [the] world means changing society, terrorism is so extreme, would use something else. Aim of speech should be about freedom of people' (Participant 36, a/e condition);
- 'it is possible that terrorists are responsible for these attacks, as such, this avenue should and will be more deeply investigated by police and counter-terrorism agencies will be mobilised if need be' (Participant 40, a/e condition);
- 'I believe that the police should not have used the act to justify certain laws or policies, but simply assured the public that there would be an investigation' (Participant 87, a/e condition);
- 'perhaps just refer to the perpetrator, bringing in the subject of terrorism when there is no substantial evidence to suggest it is only provocative' (Participant 100, a/e condition);
- 'acknowledging this person/people are upset, but highlighting the means which they have chosen is inappropriate, and that is why efforts will be put into finding/prosecuting them' (Participant 104, a/e condition).

## Should this Act be Called a Terrorist Act and Why?

Across the entire sample of 122 participants who responded to this question, 84 participants (68.9%) considered the food tampering incident to be a terrorist act and 38 participants (31.1%) did not. The frequency (and percentage) of participants in agreement that the incident was a terrorist act by condition is as follows: j/s = 21 (67%), j/e = 23 (79%), a/s = 21 (67.7%), a/e = 19 (61.3%); meaning that 43 (71.7%) of participants in the jihadist conditions and 40 (66.7%) of participants in the anti-corporate conditions agreed that the incident should be called a terrorist act.

Some examples of why the food-tampering incident *was not* considered a terrorist act in each condition were as follows:

- 'because it is aimed at everyone not a specific group: everyone eats' (Participant 42, j/s condition);
- 'it was criminal and wrong but not necessarily a terrorist act' (Participant 6, j/e condition);
- 'I view terrorism as actually killing people, not just harming them' (Participant 26, a/s condition);
- 'terrorism is an extreme act, would target the superpower — America — and not national Australian food companies' (Participant 36, a/e condition).

## Perceived Appropriateness of Counter-Terrorism Powers

Participants' attitudes towards the appropriateness of the listed counter-terrorism powers did not vary according to whether the power was held by police (or others) at the time of administering the questionnaire or not.[35] All participants as a group believed that, on average, all of the powers presented were inappropriate for dealing with the perpetrators of the food incident.[36] Analysis of variance revealed no significant main effects for either the motive or the construal variables, and the interaction between motive and crime construal was not significant. In other words, neither the motive nor the police spokesperson's statement (or some combination of these variables) produced differences in the perceived inappropriateness of the rated counter-terrorism powers.

## National Security as a Justification for Counter-Terrorism Responses

When thinking about dealing with the perpetrators of the food-tampering incident, all participants in all conditions rejected the suggestion that national security allows 'general treatment of suspects by the police and courts in ways inconsistent with international human rights law'.[37] This rejection of national security as a justification was replicated when participants were asked if national security could allow 'general treatment of suspects by the police and the courts in ways inconsistent with standard criminal practice'.[38]

## A Right to Human Security?

Only four of 123 participants who answered the question thought that 'a right to human security enjoyed by all Australians allows us to disregard any human rights complaints made against Australian police officers by those suspected of the food-tampering incident'. Similarly, only four of the 122 participants answering the question thought that a right to human security would excuse complaints of human rights violations made 'against Australian correctional services officers by anyone convicted of and imprisoned for the food-tampering described above'.

---

[35] Cronbach's $\alpha = .87$.

[36] Entire sample mean appropriateness of the 16 listed powers (as a combined measure) = 3.00 ($sd = .97$, $n = 124$); mean appropriateness by condition: j/s =3.12 ($sd = .98$, $n = 29$), j/e = 2.88 ($sd = .87$, $n = 31$), a/s = 3.10 ($sd = 1.09$, $n = 31$), a/e = 2.90 ($sd = .96$, $n = 30$).

[37] Entire sample mean endorsement = 1.9 ($sd = .1.5$, $n = 124$); mean endorsement by condition: j/s = 1.77 ($sd = 1.45$, $n = 29$), j/e = 1.94 ($sd = 1.94$, $n = 31$), a/s = 2.13 ($sd = 1.69$, $n = 31$), a/e = 1.77 ($sd = 1.52$, $n = 30$).

[38] Entire sample mean endorsement = 2.02 ($sd = 1.5$, $n = 124$); mean endorsement by condition: j/s =1.81 ($sd = 1.30$, $n = 29$), j/e = 2.19 ($sd = 1.51$, $n = 31$), a/s = 2.19 ($sd = 1.68$, $n = 31$), a/e = 1.87 ($sd = 1.48$, $n = 30$).

## What is the Purpose of Human Rights Law when Faced with Terrorist Acts?

Some examples of the open-ended responses from participants in each condition of the study are as follows:

- 'to balance the power of the state with the rights of individuals' (Participant 1, j/s condition);
- 'to ensure that citizens are not abused by the authorities. Creating some sort of police state will only engender more anti-Australian [feeling] and lead to support for terrorists' (Participant 10, j/e condition);
- 'to ensure respect for dignity, personal freedoms, faith and human life when in police custody, jail or other types of confinement' (Participant 7 a/s condition);
- 'to ensure that, in the rush for the society to protect its own interests, the rights of the criminal party are not discarded' (Participant 4, a/e condition).

One reason given appeared to blend derision and respect for perpetrators:

- 'to make sure we don't mistreat the offender since they are humans too and have their own reasons for their stupid acts' (Participant 31, a/e condition).

One response obtained came close to the rhetoric used by those endorsing a right to human security:

- 'everybody should be able to have access to safe food and water, so if a group of people are responsible for the illness/death of others they should be held accountable' (Participant 106, j/e condition).

## Can any of these Attitudinal Results be Explained by Siege Mentality Beliefs?

Participants' scores on the siege mentality scale did not vary by experimental condition, suggesting that the motive and crime construal variables used in this hypothetical scenario study alone were not enough to produce differences in measured siege mentality beliefs. An alternative explanation is that our participants were simply never disposed to adopt the terrorism siege mentality belief orientation as operationalised. In any event, endorsement of siege mentality beliefs (as a single combined measure)[39] was low across all conditions and no significant effects were revealed by analysis of variance.[40]

Correlational analysis reveals some significant relationships between these low scores on the siege mentality scale and other variables of interest. For example, significant correlational results based on the entire sample include those between:

- low Terrorism Siege Mentality scores (SM) and low levels of perceived appropriateness of the 16 rated counter-terrorism measures;[41]
- low Terrorism Siege Mentality scores and low endorsement of national security as a justification for treatment by the police and the courts that is inconsistent with human rights (incon HRs)[42] or standard criminal procedure (incon SCP).[43]

The size of these significant correlations is around the same magnitude when the analysis is done by condition.[44]

## Conclusions

In this study the motive of the perpetrator to advance *a particular* cause, jihadist rather than anti-corporate views, resulted in participants perceiving *greater* blameworthiness. This was the case *even* when the participants, on the whole, *neither* strongly endorsed terrorism siege mentality beliefs *nor* supported the expansion of counter-terrorism powers at the expense of violating human rights in the interest of ensuring human security. This result alone is intriguing. It is of particular interest in terms of the possible impact on juries of evidence of the intention to advance political, religious or ideological causes. These data suggest that judges may need to use jury instructions to combat such attitudinal biases against defendants alleged to be pursuing *particular* motives.

However, as discussed by Gani, Chapter 13 this volume, a decision in *Lodhi*[45] handed down after the data collection has clarified the legal test to be used when

---

[39] Use of combined Terrorism Siege Mentality Scores in this study should be treated with caution as Cronbach's $\alpha = .65$ and principle components analysis with varimax rotation revealed multiple factors that were difficult to interpret. A deeper problem is the lack of normality of responses to each of the Terrorism Siege Mentality scale items. These psychometric properties are in contrast to the more reliable one factor response solutions obtained by Bar-Tal and colleagues: Cronbach's $\alpha = .88$ in Bar-Tal and Antebi, above n 5.

[40] Mean combined siege mentality score by condition: j/s = 2.88 ($sd = 67$, $n = 29$), j/e = 2.82 ($sd = .69$, $n = 31$), a/s = 3.01 ($sd = .54$, $n = 31$), a/e = 2.97 ($sd = .66$, $n = 30$).

[41] $r = .32$, $p < .01$.

[42] $r = .29$, $p < .01$.

[43] $r = .31$, $p < .01$.

[44] Eg, in the anti-corporate motive condition (n = 62): $r$ (SM, appropriateness of all CT powers) = .44, $p < .01$; $r$ (SM, incon HRs) = .34, $p < .01$; $r$ (SM, incon SCP) = .35, $p < .01$. When the offence was construed as a standard crime: $r$ (SM, incon CP) = .26, $p < .05$. When the offence was construed as an exceptional crime: $r$ (SM, incon HRs) = .33, $p < .01$; $r$ (SM, incon SCP) = .36, $p < .01$; $r$ (SM, appropriateness of all CT powers) = .41, $p < .01$.

[45] *Lodhi v R* (2006) 199 FLR 303 (Spigelman CJ, with McClellan CJ at CL and Sully J agreeing).

determining the requisite intention. It was held in that case that the advancement of the political, religious or ideological cause attaches to the terrorist act itself *and not to the state of mind of the accused as he or she was engaging in the conduct that constitutes the offence*.[46] This means that the blameworthiness bias result in this study is most relevant to what Gani describes as the 'simple cases': where the accused actually shares the intention to advance the cause via the use of the coercive violence. In Gani's 'difficult cases' where the accused does not share the intention to advance the cause, the blameworthiness effect for motive demonstrated here is less relevant to juries' liability decisions. However, in 'simple cases' the demonstrated bias (that jihadist motives are more blameworthy than anti-corporate protest motives) remains concerning in terms of its residual impact on liability judgments *despite* the decision in *Lodhi* and the use of judicial instructions about the relevant legal test. In other words, what will be the 'touchstone to which juries will intuitively turn when reaching their decisions'[47] in those simple cases? Will it be the view that jihadist motives are more blameworthy intentions than other examples of politically-motivated violence?

It is perhaps unsurprising that the sample surveyed in this study rejected extension of counter-terrorism powers beyond those powers consistent with established principles of criminal justice for non-terrorism offences and those consistent with civil and political rights. It is also perhaps unsurprising that our first attempt to develop a Terrorism Siege Mentality Scale did not produce the same psychometric simplicity as the more general siege mentality scale developed with Israeli samples in the Middle East. However, perhaps a stronger test of the Terrorism Siege Mentality construct would occur with samples of participants *likely to endorse siege mentality beliefs to a high level*. Based on this sample at least, some Australian undergraduates do not feel alone in the world due to the terrorism threat. It remains to be seen whether the socialisation of siege in other samples at other times can be measured; including measurement of the socialisation of siege amongst political elites responsible for counter-terrorism policy post-9/11, and, perhaps, also amongst perpetrators themselves.

---

[46] *Lodhi v R* (2006) 199 FLR 303, Spigelman CJ (with McClellan CJ at CL and Sully J agreeing) quoted extensively at [80] and endorsed at [90] Whealy J's judgment of 14 February 2006 (*R v Lodhi* [2006] NSWSC 584 (Unreported, Whealy J, 14 February 2006) [83] and [103] (see Gani, Chapter 13 this volume).
[47] Gani and Urbas, above n 14.

# Chapter Seven

# The Proportionality Principle in the Context of Anti-Terrorism Laws: An Inquiry into the Boundaries between Human Rights Law and Public Policy

### Christopher Michaelsen[*]

## Introduction

A key question in the political and academic discourse on the legislative response to the threat of international terrorism has been the question of proportionality. While some have argued that the laws enacted to counter terrorism strike the right balance between national security imperatives and concerns for civil liberties and human rights, others have regarded them as disproportionate and as an overreaction.[1] What both sides have in common, however, is that they generally approach the question of proportionality without examining the nature and quality of the terrorist threat and by accepting the executive's assertion that the threat may warrant a range of comprehensive counter-measures.

I would argue that this approach is logically flawed. What proportionality generally requires is that there is a reasonable relationship between the means employed and the aims sought to be achieved. Essentially proportionality requires one to determine whether a measure of interference, which is aimed at promoting a legitimate public policy, is either unacceptably broad in its application or has imposed an excessive or unreasonable burden on certain individuals. A decision

---

[*] Visiting Fellow, Faculty of Law, University of New South Wales, Sydney, Australia <c.michaelsen@unsw.edu.au>.
[1] In Australia, commentators who consider Australia's anti-terrorism laws balanced and proportionate include: P Ruddock, 'Australia's Legislative Response to the Ongoing Threat of Terrorism' (2004) 27(2) *University of New South Wales Law Journal* 254; R Cornall, 'A Strategic Approach to National Security', (Address to the Security in Government Conference, Canberra, 10 May 2005). Authors questioning the proportionality of some of the Australian laws include: G Williams, 'Australian Values and the War against Terrorism' (2003) 26(1) *University of New South Wales Law Journal* 191; G Carne, 'Brigitte and the French Connection: Security Carte Blanche or A La Carte' (2004) 9(2) *Deakin Law Review* 604; C Michaelsen, 'International Human Rights on Trial – The United Kingdom's and Australia's Legal Response to 9/11' (2003) 25(3) *Sydney Law Review* 275; J Hocking, 'Counter-Terrorism and the Criminalisation of Politics: Australia's New Security Powers of Detention, Proscription and Control' (2003) 49(2) *Australian Journal of Politics and History* 355; C Michaelsen, 'Antiterrorism Legislation in Australia: A Proportionate Response to the Terrorist Threat?' (2005) 28(4) *Studies in Conflict & Terrorism* 321.

that takes into account proportionality principles should, inter alia, impair the right in question as little as possible, be carefully designed to meet the objectives in question, and not be arbitrary, unfair or based on irrational considerations.

In order to establish whether counter-terrorism laws and measures meet the objectives in question it is imperative to identify clearly what those objectives are. The objective of anti-terrorism laws is, in most cases, the reduction of the threat of terrorist attacks or activities. Thus it is logically necessary for a thorough proportionality analysis to consider or assess the quality and nature of the threat. I would argue that in the absence of such analysis, any proportionality assessment is incomplete.

Nonetheless, both the European Court of Human Rights (ECrtHR) and national courts, most recently the House of Lords, have taken a deferential approach and granted national authorities a wide 'discretionary area of judgment',[2] or, in the terminology of the ECrtHR, a 'wide margin of appreciation' with regard to the existence and analysis of the threat of terrorism that may constitute a so-called 'public emergency'.[3] One rationale behind this deferential approach, especially in common law countries, seems to be that in terms of both constitutional competence and expertise in the area of national security it is for government (and perhaps Parliament) rather than the courts to assess whether a public emergency exists.[4]

While not addressing the constitutional implications of this position, I will argue that in the context of international terrorism this rationale is flawed in its logic. Courts can and should be in a position to assess the nature and size of the terrorist threat without necessarily having to have access to specific intelligence. This is not to say that courts should not have access to specific intelligence or classified information held by the government. On the contrary, access to such information may be essential to fulfil fair trial requirements in proceedings against persons accused of terrorism offences. However, the difficulties and challenges that classified information poses for the courts shall not be the subject of analysis here. The argument I am trying to make in this chapter is that in spite of any access to specific intelligence information, courts can and should submit general policy decisions about the threat of terrorism to judicial scrutiny.

The argument has both an international and a domestic dimension (although the domestic dimension is related to the international one). First I will argue that developments in international human rights law provide ample justification for an 'extension' of the competency of the courts — especially the ECrtHR — to

---

[2] *A and Others v Secretary of State for the Home Department* [2005] 2 AC 68, [37], [39] (Lord Bingham) ('*Belmarsh Detainees*').
[3] See, eg, *Ireland v United Kingdom* (1978) Series A No 35, [78]-[79]; *Brannigan and McBride v United Kingdom* (1993) 17 EHRR 539, [41].
[4] See below n 22-38 and accompanying text.

assess the nature and quality of the terrorist threat that is seen to constitute a 'public emergency'. Second, I will argue that an 'extension' of competency of domestic and national courts would also be possible and desirable and, further, that it would also be the logical consequence of findings by the House of Lords in the *Belmarsh Detainees* decision of December 2004.[5]

## The Proportionality Principle in the Context of Derogation from the European Convention of Human Rights

An inquiry into the boundaries between human rights law and public policy in the context of counter-terrorism benefits from examining the proportionality principle in light of the international system for protecting rights during states of emergency.[6] The threat of terrorism has been invoked by governments in the past to justify restricting human rights and/or derogating from obligations contained in international human rights instruments.[7] It was in the context of the United Kingdom's (UK) derogation from the European Convention of Human Rights (ECHR)[8] in the aftermath of September 11 2001 (9/11) that the question of proportionality was addressed by the House of Lords in *Belmarsh Detainees*.

Both the ECHR and the International Covenant on Civil and Political Rights (ICCPR)[9] allow for derogation from certain rights enshrined in these instruments. Article 15 (1) of the ECHR reads:

> In time of war or other public emergency threatening the life of the nation any High Contracting Party may take measures derogating from its obligations under this Convention to the extent strictly required by the exigencies of the situation, provided that such measures are not inconsistent with other obligations under international law.

Article 4 (1) ICCPR reads:

---

[5] *Belmarsh Detainees* [2005] 2 AC 68.
[6] For accounts of the international system for protecting rights during states of emergency see R Higgins, 'Derogations Under Human Rights Treaties' (1976-77) 48 *British Yearbook of International Law* 281; T Buergenthal, 'To Respect and Ensure: State Obligations and Permissible Derogations' in L Henkin (ed), *The International Bill of Rights: The Covenant on Civil and Political Rights* (New York: Columbia University Press, 1981) 72-91; C Schreuer, 'Derogation of Human Rights in Situations of Public Emergency' (1982) 9 *Yale Journal of World Public Order* 113; J F Hartman, 'Working Paper for the Committee of Experts on the Article 4 Derogation Provision' (1985) 7 *Human Rights Quarterly* 89; D J Harris, M O'Boyle and C Warbrick, *Law of the European Convention on Human Rights* (London: Butterworths, 1995) 489-507; J A Frowein and W Peukert, *Kommentar – Europäische Menschenrechtskonvention* (2nd ed, 1996) 479-85; A-L Svensson-McCarthy, *The International Law of Human Rights and States of Exception* (The Hague, Boston: M Nijhoff Publishers, 1998).
[7] See, eg, *Lawless v Ireland* (No 3) (1961) 1 EHRR 15; *Greek Case* (1969) 12 Yearbook ECHR 1; *Ireland v United Kingdom* (1978) Series A No 35; *Brannigan and McBride v United Kingdom* (1993) 17 EHRR 539; *Aksoy v Turkey* (1996) 23 EHRR 553.
[8] *European Convention for the Protection of Human Rights and Fundamental Freedoms*, 213 UNTS 222 (entered into force 3 September 1953).
[9] *International Covenant on Civil and Political Rights*, 999 UNTS 171 (entered into force 23 March 1976).

> In time of public emergency which threatens the life of the nation and the existence of which is officially proclaimed, the States Parties to the present Covenant may take measures derogating from their obligations under the present Covenant to the extent strictly required by the exigencies of the situation, provided that such measures are not inconsistent with their other obligations under international law and do not involve discrimination solely on the ground of race, colour, sex, language, religion or social origin.

The principle of proportionality constitutes a general principle of international law and includes elements of severity, duration and scope.[10] It applies to Article 15 ECHR as well as to Article 4 ICCPR. Both provisions essentially require a derogating state to satisfy two tests. First, the derogating state is required to establish that exceptional circumstances of war or other public emergency threatening the life of the nation do in fact prevail (the *'designation* issue'), and second, that measures taken in consequence of such an emergency are 'strictly required by the exigencies of the situation' (the *'interference* issue').[11]

As to the *designation* issue, the ECHR and the ICCPR both lack a specific definition of a 'public emergency threatening the life of the nation'. Nevertheless, the international monitoring organs established under the treaties, notably the ECrtHR (and previously the European Commission of Human Rights), have extensively interpreted the term and provided jurisprudence valuable for determining its meaning and scope. As the Strasbourg authorities construe the terms of Article 15 according to their natural and ordinary meaning (as required by principles of treaty interpretation), and the derogation clauses of the ICCPR and the ECHR are similar, European decisions and findings are readily applicable to cases arising under the ICCPR.

The first substantive interpretation of Article 15 of the ECHR was made in *Lawless v Ireland*.[12] Confirming the determination by the European Commission of Human Rights that Article 15 should be interpreted in the light of its 'natural and customary' meaning, the ECrtHR defined 'time of public emergency' as 'an exceptional situation of crisis or emergency which afflicts the whole population and constitutes a threat to the organised life of the community of which the community is composed'.[13] The definition was further developed and clarified in the *Greek Case*.[14] Reaffirming the basic elements of the Court's approach in *Lawless v Ireland*, the Commission emphasised that the emergency must be actual

---

[10] See, eg, M Eissen, 'The Principle of Proportionality in the Case-Law of the European Court of Human Rights' in R St J Macdonald, F Matscher and H Petzold (eds), *The European System for the Protection of Human Rights* (Dordrecht, Boston: Martinus Nijhoff, 1993) 125-37.
[11] See, eg, S Tierney, 'Determining the State of Exception: What Role for Parliament and the Courts?' (2005) 68(4) *Modern Law Review* 668.
[12] *Lawless v Ireland* (No 3) (1961) 1 EHRR 15.
[13] Ibid 31.
[14] *Greek Case* (1969) 12 Yearbook ECHR 1.

or at least 'imminent'.[15] In order to constitute an Article 15 emergency, the Commission held that a 'public emergency' must have the following four characteristics:[16]

- it must be actual or imminent;
- its effects must involve the whole nation;
- the continuance of the organised life of the community must be threatened;[17] and
- the crisis or danger must be exceptional, in that the normal measures or restrictions, permitted by the Convention for the maintenance of public safety, health and order, are plainly inadequate.[18]

As to the *interference* issue, a fundamental requirement for any measures derogating from the ECHR or the ICCPR is that such measures are limited 'to the extent strictly required by the exigencies of the situation'. Derogation measures must thus be strictly proportionate. In *Handyside v United Kingdom* the Strasbourg Court expressly differentiated the 'strictly required' standard in Article 15 from the ordinary standard of 'necessity' or proportionality that is found in some provisions of the ECHR. The Court articulated three tiers of standards found in the Convention: 'reasonableness' (see, eg, arts 5(3) and 6(1) ECHR), 'necessity' (see, eg, art 10(2) ECHR) and 'indispensability'.[19] Indispensability was associated with the phrase 'strictly required' in Article 15 ECHR and the phrase 'absolutely necessary' in Article 2(2). The Court has since stated in *McCann and Others v United Kingdom* that:

> the use of the term 'absolutely necessary' in Article 2(2) indicates that a stricter and more compelling test of necessity must be employed from that normally applicable when determining whether state action is 'necessary in a democratic

---

[15] The notion of imminence is present in the Merits judgment in French (authentic version) but not in the English version. The relevant part of the Merits judgment in French reads: '*Une situation de crise ou de danger public exceptionnelle et imminente ...*'.

[16] *Greek Case* (1969) 12 Yearbook ECHR 1, [153].

[17] Some members of the Commission argued that when the organs of the state are functioning normally, there is no grave threat to the life of the nation and, therefore, emergency measures are not legitimate. However, the majority in the Commission did not follow this reasoning. In practice, both the second and third criteria are generally applied in a rather relaxed way.

[18] Evidence of these requirements being recognised as general legal standards in the process of determining the meaning of 'public emergency' can also be found in the *Siracusa Principles on the Limitation and Derogation Provisions in the International Covenant on Civil and Political Rights* ('*Siracusa Principles*'), reproduced in 'Siracusa Principles on the Limitation and Derogation Provisions in the International Covenant on Civil and Political Rights' (1985) 7(1) *Human Rights Quarterly* 3. The *Siracusa Principles* were drafted by a group of 31 distinguished experts in international law convened in Siracusa, Italy, in Spring 1984, by a number of well-respected organisations such as the International Commission of Jurists. In addition, these criteria are contained in the International Law Association's (ILA) work on the issue: ILA, *Paris Minimum Standards of Human Rights Norms in a State of Emergency* ('Paris Minimum Standards'), reproduced as 'The Paris Minimum Standards of Human Rights Norms in a State of Emergency' (1985) 79 *American Journal of International Law* 1072.

[19] *Handyside v United Kingdom* (1976) 1 EHRR 737, [48].

society' under paragraph 2 of Articles 8 to 11 of the Convention. In particular, the force used must be strictly proportionate to the achievement of the aims set out in sub-paragraphs 2(a), (b) and (c) of Article 2.[20]

By contrast to Article 2 ECHR, the stricter standard of necessity is justified in the context of Article 15 ECHR not by the importance of the right at stake but by the nature of the measure, which is to take a state outside the human rights regime. Any derogation measure must fulfil the following five basic requirements:

- the measures must be strictly required (ie, actions taken under ordinary laws and in conformity with international human rights obligations are not sufficient to meet the threat);
- the measures must be connected to the emergency (ie, they must 'prima facie' be suitable to reduce the threat or crisis);
- the measures must be used only as long as they are necessary (ie, there must be a temporal limit);
- the degree to which the measures deviate from international human rights standards must be in proportion to the severity of the threat (ie, the more important and fundamental the right which is being compromised, the closer and stricter the scrutiny);
- effective safeguards must be implemented to avoid the abuse of emergency powers. Where measures involve administrative detention, safeguards may include regular review by independent national organs, in particular, by the legislative and judicial branches.

As stated by the European Commission in the *Greek Case*, and by the Human Rights Committee in its *General Comment 29*, the states parties bear the burden of proof in establishing the existence of a 'public emergency'.[21] However, in assessing whether a 'public emergency' exists and what steps are necessary to address it, states are granted a so-called 'margin of appreciation'. The doctrine of margin of appreciation embodies the general approach of the Strasbourg Court to the difficult task of balancing the sovereignty of contracting parties with their obligations under the Convention.[22] As Ronald St James Macdonald, a former judge of the ECrtHR, observed, it is the doctrine of margin of appreciation that allows the Court to escape the dilemma of 'how to remain true to its responsibility to develop a reasonably comprehensive set of review principles appropriate for application across the entire Convention, while at the same time recognising the

---

[20] *McCann and Others v United Kingdom* (1995) 21 EHRR 97, [149].
[21] Human Rights Committee, *General Comment 29, States of Emergency* (Article 4), [4], [5], UN Doc CCPR/C/21/Rev.1/Add.11 (2001).
[22] See R St J Macdonald, 'The Margin of Appreciation' in Macdonald, Matscher and Petzold (eds), above n 10, 83.

diversity of political, economic, cultural and social situations in the societies of the Contracting Parties'.[23]

In the context of derogation in times of 'public emergency threatening the life of the nation', the margin of appreciation represents the discretion left to a state in ascertaining the necessity and scope of measures of derogation from protected rights in the circumstances prevailing within its jurisdiction.[24] In *Ireland v United Kingdom*, the ECrtHR held that:

> it falls in the first place to each Contracting State, with its responsibility for 'the life of [its] nation', to determine whether that life is threatened by a 'public emergency' and, if so, how far it is necessary to go in attempting to overcome the emergency. By reason of their direct and continuous contact with the pressing needs of the moment, the national authorities are in principle in a better position than the international judge to decide both on the presence of such an emergency and on the nature and scope of derogations necessary to avert it. In this matter Article 15(1) leaves the authorities a wide margin of appreciation.[25]

In *Brannigan and McBride v United Kingdom* the Court held that:

> it falls to each Contracting State, with its responsibility for 'the life of [its] nation,' to determine whether that life is threatened by a 'public emergency' and, if so, how far it is necessary to go in attempting to overcome the emergency. By reason of their direct and continuous contact with the pressing needs of the moment, the national authorities are in principle in a better position than the international judge to decide both on the presence of such an emergency and on the nature and scope of derogations necessary to avert it. Accordingly, in this matter a wide margin of appreciation should be left to the national authorities ...[26]

The margin of appreciation is thus granted to the national authorities both in relation to the existence of a public emergency — the *designation* issue — and in determining whether derogation measures are strictly required by the exigencies of the situation; the *interference* issue.

## Justifications for the Margin of Appreciation

Three main reasons have been advanced by the Court and commentators for applying a wide margin of appreciation in the context of derogations. First, it was argued by Michael O'Boyle, for instance, that given their perceived vital interests were at stake, governments could respond to an adverse decision by the Court regarding derogation by denouncing the Convention, or withdrawing

---

[23] Ibid.
[24] See, eg, T A O'Donnell, 'The Margin of Appreciation Doctrine: Standards in the Jurisprudence of the European Court of Human Rights' (1982) 4(4) *Human Rights Quarterly* 474.
[25] *Ireland v United Kingdom* (1978) Series A No 35, [78]-[79].
[26] *Brannigan and McBride v United Kingdom* (1993) 17 EHRR 539, [41].

recognition of the Court's jurisdiction or competence to receive individual petitions. To avoid losing state support in this way, the Court should reject derogation only in the most transparently spurious cases.[27]

Second, the ECrtHR held in *Ireland v United Kingdom*, that it was inappropriate to decide with the benefit of hindsight on issues that a government must necessarily address urgently and on the basis of information that it may not be capable of publicising.[28] This view is shared by J G Merrills, for instance, who argues that the determination that an emergency existed, and what measures were necessary to counter it, was a political judgment in relation to which judges were 'ill-equipped and improper arbiters'.[29] In addition, national authorities, Merrills argued, were in a much better position than a supranational institution like the Court to assess the situation on the ground. The government's discretion thus needed to be respected, especially as it was the government's responsibility to ensure law and order. The Court, on the other hand, served the public interest in effective government by ensuring that the government's conduct in relation to a proclaimed emergency is at least 'on the margin' of the powers conferred by Article 15 ECHR and Article 4 ICCPR.[30]

Third, and related to the second argument, emergencies exert great pressures against continued adherence to protection of human rights. As Oren Gross and Fionnuala Ní Aoláin pointed out, governments often consider protecting human rights and civil liberties to their fullest extent as a 'luxury that must be dispensed with if the nation is to overcome the crisis it faces'.[31] Moved by perceptions of physical threat both to the state and to themselves and motivated by growing fear and by hatred toward the 'enemy', the citizenry may support the government to employ more radical measures against the perceived threats. In these circumstances, notions of the rule of law, rights, and freedoms are legalistic niceties that bar effective action by the government. Exigencies tend to provoke the 'rally around the flag' phenomenon,[32] or, as Mark Nolan has pointed out, a 'siege mentality', in which governmental actions perceived as necessary to fight off the crisis garner almost unqualified popular support.[33] In this situation there was no role for a supranational institution, like the ECrtHR, to play.

---

[27] See, eg, M O'Boyle, 'Torture and Emergency Powers under the European Convention on Human Rights: Ireland v the United Kingdom' (1977) 71 *American Journal of International Law* 705.
[28] *Ireland v United Kingdom* (1978) Series A No 35, 214.
[29] See, eg, J G Merrills, *The Development of International Law by the European Court of Human Rights* (Manchester, New York: Manchester University Press, 1988) 37.
[30] Ibid.
[31] O Gross and F Ní Aoláin, 'From Discretion to Scrutiny: Revisiting the Application of the Margin of Appreciation Doctrine in the Context of Article 15 of the European Convention on Human Rights' (2001) 23 *Human Rights Quarterly* 625, 638-39.
[32] Ibid.
[33] Nolan, Chapter 6 this volume.

## Critique of the Justifications for the Margin of Appreciation

I would argue that all three arguments need to be revisited and ultimately rejected in the context of legislation enacted to counter the current threat of terrorism.

First, the ECHR and the Court in Strasbourg — like the Council of Europe itself — have become cornerstones of modern-day Europe. As such it is unthinkable in the realm of contemporary international politics that a Council of Europe member state would withdraw its recognition of the Strasbourg Court's jurisdiction or competence to receive individual petitions as a result of an unfavourable decision. This argument is supported, inter alia, by various unfavourable judgments of the Court in relation to the conflicts in Chechnya and South-Eastern Turkey, for instance. A similar argument can be made in relation to the ICCPR, which has become a universally accepted core instrument of international human rights law.

Second, the Strasbourg authorities themselves have confirmed that states do not enjoy an unlimited discretion in relation to the determination of a public emergency and that the domestic margin of appreciation is accompanied by 'European supervision'.[34] It is noteworthy that dissenting votes in the case law have repeatedly questioned the practice of granting states a wide margin of appreciation. In *Lawless v Ireland*, a minority of the Commission members rejected the margin of appreciation doctrine altogether, arguing that evaluation of the existence of a public emergency ought to be based solely on existing facts without regard to any account of subjective predictions as to future development.[35] They also argued that the Commission ought to review de novo the existence of a public emergency in a given situation without assuming an a priori deferential attitude towards the respondent government.

Interestingly, the Human Rights Committee also seems reluctant to grant a wide margin of appreciation, if it recognises the application of such a doctrine at all. In *Landinelli Silva v Uruguay*, for instance, the Committee found that 'the State Party is duty-bound to give a sufficiently detailed account of the relevant facts when it invokes Article 4(1)' and that it is the Committee's function 'to see to it that States parties live up to their commitments under the Covenant'.[36] Similarly, the *Siracusa Principles* explicitly state that the principle of strict necessity shall be applied in an 'objective manner' and, moreover, that 'the judgment of the national authorities cannot be accepted as conclusive'.[37]

But perhaps most questionable in the context of international terrorism is the argument that national authorities are in a better position to assess whether

---

[34] *Ireland v United Kingdom* (1978) Series A No 35, 207.
[35] *Lawless v Ireland* (No 3) (1961) 1 EHRR 15, 32.
[36] *Landinelli Silva v Uruguay* (1981) HRC Comm No 34/1978, [8.3].
[37] See No 54 and 57 of the *Siracusa Principles*, see above n 18.

circumstances that constitute a public emergency do in fact prevail. Unlike its previous manifestations, contemporary terrorism is hardly attributable to a confined number of terrorist organisations, even though it has been mainly associated with Al Qa'ida.[38] In other words, the threat is much more diffuse and abstract. In most circumstances the existence of a 'public emergency threatening the life of the nation' is or will be claimed in relation to a threat. In consequence, there has to be an assessment of the risk of the realisation of the threat, as well as its seriousness. Because the terrorist threat is usually 'international' and non-specific, the government's burden of justification in respect of the existence of a 'public emergency' is particularly high. The margin of appreciation granted to individual states in assessing the existence of a 'public emergency' and the proportionality of response measures thus need to be reconsidered and adjusted. The more global and non-specific the threat, the less the amount of discretion left to the state. As the threat of international terrorism is global, national authorities are not necessarily in a better position to decide on the imminence of a 'public emergency'. Quite the opposite: other countries might even have superior intelligence on specific terrorist threats.

It is equally debatable whether the highly politicised discourse on terrorism and counter-terrorism is conducive to rational and calm consideration and an appropriate balancing of the competing interests at stake. Thus, it may well be that a supranational institution like the ECrtHR, detached and removed from the immediate political debate, is better placed to judge matters more clearly and more accurately. It is the Court, therefore, that is in a better position than the national government to decide both on the presence of such an emergency and on the nature and scope of the derogations necessary to avert it.

The Court should also be less deferential to a government's assessment that a state of emergency exists where the emergency is possibly a permanent one, given that the concept of an emergency permitting derogation, which is embodied in the relevant clauses of the ECHR and ICCPR, is necessarily a temporary one, the logic being that rights may be temporarily suspended, not that they may simply be destroyed.[39] This is particularly the case in the context of international terrorism and the aftermath of 9/11 where the threat that is supposed to constitute a public emergency has become permanent. The Court should refrain from granting a wide margin of appreciation but rather should submit governmental

---

[38] For an assessment of the threat of contemporary terrorism see, eg, J Burke, 'Think Again: Al Qaeda' (2004) 142 *Foreign Policy* 18; B Hoffman, 'The Changing Face of Al Qaeda and the Global War on Terrorism' (2004) 27(5) *Studies in Conflict & Terrorism* 549; B Hoffman, 'Al Qaeda, Trends in Terrorism, and Future Potentialities: An Assessment' (2003) 26(6) *Studies in Conflict & Terrorism* 588; P Bergen, *Holy Terror, Inc.: Inside the Secret World of Osama bin Laden* (New York, Simon & Schuster, 2001).
[39] O Gross, '"Once More unto the Breach": The Systemic Failure of Applying the European Convention on Human Rights to Entrenched Emergencies' (1998) 23 *Yale Journal of International Law* 437.

claims to strict scrutiny, in relation to both designation and interference issues: the longer the emergency, the narrower ought the margin of appreciation be.

## The Question of Proportionality and the *Belmarsh Detainees* Decision

The ECrtHR has yet to address the question of whether the post-9/11 threat of terrorism may constitute a 'public emergency threatening the life of the nation' as well as the issue of what domestic measures might be necessary and proportionate to counter it. Both issues, however, were addressed by the House of Lords in the recent *Belmarsh Detainees* decision. From an international human rights perspective, the case is of particular interest as it deals with both the *designation* and *interference* issues in the context of the *Human Rights Act 1998* (UK), which incorporates the ECHR into domestic British law.

The case was brought by nine foreign (non-UK) nationals who had been certified by Britain's Home Secretary under s 21 of the *Anti-Terrorism, Crime and Security Act 2001* ('ATCSA') as suspected international terrorists and who had been detained under s 23 of the Act which allowed for detention without charge.[40] Section 23(1) ATCSA reads as follows:

> a suspected international terrorist may be detained under a provision specified in subsection (2) despite the fact that his removal or departure from the United Kingdom is prevented (whether temporarily or indefinitely) by (a) a point of law which wholly or partly relates to an international agreement, or (b) a practical consideration.[41]

The claimants challenged the legality of both these provisions and the Government's decision to derogate from Article 5 ECHR in respect of the detention provision.[42] The challenge had previously been unsuccessful before the Court of Appeal.

The Lords essentially had to address two central issues. The first was whether the Government's derogation from the ECHR in respect of the detention measures was lawful. The second was whether the statutory provisions under which the

---

[40] A Tomkins, 'Legislating against Terror: the Anti-Terrorism, Crime and Security Act 2001' (2002) (Summer) *Public Law* 205; H Fenwick, 'The Anti-Terrorism, Crime and Security Act 2001: A Proportionate Response to September 11?' (2002) 65 *Modern Law Review* 724.
[41] Section 23 has been repealed in the wake of the House of Lord's decision in *Belmarsh Detainees* [2005] 2 AC 68.
[42] In asserting the existence of a public emergency in the UK, the British Government stated that: 'There exists a terrorist threat to the United Kingdom from persons suspected of involvement in international terrorism. In particular, there are foreign nationals present in the United Kingdom who are suspected of being concerned in the commission, preparation or instigation of acts of international terrorism, of being members of organisations or groups which are so concerned or of having links with members of such organisations or groups, and who are a threat to the national security of the United Kingdom.' See the *Human Rights Act 1998* (Designated Derogation) Order 2001, No 3644, which came into force on 13 November 2001.

appellants had been detained were incompatible with the ECHR. The Lords thus addressed the *designation* issue as well as the *interference* issue. By an eight-to-one majority, the derogation by the UK Government from the ECHR was quashed and a declaration issued to the extent that s 23 ATCSA was incompatible with the *Human Rights Act 1998* (UK).[43]

The House of Lords judgments can be divided into three camps. Seven members of the Court — Lords Bingham, Nicholls, Hope, Scott, Rodger, Carswell, and Baroness Hale — held that, while a 'public emergency threatening the life of the nation' could be said to exist, the detention provision could not be said to be 'strictly required' by that emergency. It was disproportionate and discriminatory and hence unlawful. One judge — Lord Walker — dissented. He held both that there was a public emergency threatening the life of the nation and that the detention provision of s 23 ATCSA was neither discriminatory nor disproportionate to the aim the measure sought to achieve. Lord Hoffmann agreed with the majority that the provisions in question were incompatible with the ECHR. However, he was the only judge who held the derogation unlawful on the ground that there was no 'war or other public emergency threatening the life of the nation' within the meaning of Article 15 ECHR.

## The Majority Approach to the Threat of Terrorism

Lord Bingham's lead judgment represents the *ratio decidendi* as it had the agreement of six of the Lords. Unlike Lord Hoffmann, Lord Bingham was not prepared to hold that no public emergency threatening the life of the nation existed. Nevertheless, he upheld the appeal on the grounds that the detention powers were disproportionate and discriminatory. In relation to the *designation* issue, Lord Bingham's approach essentially absolved the Government from advancing clear and convincing evidence to Parliament (and the courts) to demonstrate that a public emergency threatening the life of the nation actually existed.

Lord Bingham approved and applied the case law of the ECrtHR on Article 15 ECHR granting a wide margin of appreciation. He found that to hold that there was no public emergency in cases where, 'a response beyond that provided by the ordinary course of law was required, would have been perverse'.[44] This reasoning, however, is illogical as it essentially bases the determination of the question of whether a public emergency exists on the measures taken to address it. As Tom Hickman has observed, 'if one is to infer from the fact that exceptional

---

[43] *Belmarsh Detainees* [2005] 2 AC 68, [73] (Lord Bingham). See also the judgments of Lords Nicholls, Hope, Scott, Rodger, Carswell, and Baroness Hale at [85], [139], [160], [190], [240] and [239] respectively.
[44] Ibid [28] (Lord Bingham).

measures have been taken that such measures are legitimate then the criteria of legitimacy (ie, public emergency) is relieved of substance'.[45]

Lord Bingham went on to hold that it was for the appellants to demonstrate that the Government's claim that there was an emergency that required derogation from the ECHR was 'wrong and unreasonable'.[46] The appellants, however, had 'shown no ground strong enough to warrant displacing the Secretary of State's decision on this important threshold question'.[47] Lord Bingham's reasoning is highly problematic. This reversal of the burden of proof in relation to the existence of a public emergency threatening the life of the nation raises serious concerns from a purely practical perspective. It is difficult to see how individuals will ever be able to disprove the government's view that an emergency exists, not least because the relevant evidence will be in the hands of the government.[48] Lord Bingham's view also runs contrary to the approach taken by the ECrtHR. As indicated earlier, the Strasbourg authorities have repeatedly confirmed that the burden is not upon the individual, but upon the government to demonstrate that there exists a national emergency that requires derogation from international human rights obligations.[49] It is noteworthy that the Human Rights Committee in its *General Comment 29* has taken a similar view.[50]

With regard to the *interference* issue, Lord Bingham held that the detention power was not rationally connected to the objective of addressing the imminent threat of terrorism as it did not correspond to that objective in several respects. First, and assuming that the terrorist threat constituting a national emergency stemmed from Al Qa'ida, the detention power set forth in s 23 ATCSA powers applied to non-Al Qa'ida terrorists as well. Second, it applied to Al Qa'ida supporters who posed no direct threat to the national security of the UK. Third, it did not apply to the threat from terrorists who were UK nationals. And fourth, it allowed any 'suspected international terrorist to leave our shores and depart to another country, perhaps a country as close as France, there to pursue his criminal designs'.[51] This, said Lord Bingham, was 'hard to reconcile with a belief in [the terrorists'] capacity to inflict serious injury to the people and interests of this country'.[52] As a result, the measure taken (ie, s 23 ATCSA) was not strictly required by the exigencies of the situation and the derogation was hence unlawful.

---

[45] T R Hickman, 'Between Human Rights and the Rule of Law: Indefinite Detention and the Derogation Model of Constitutionalism' (2005) 68(4) *Modern Law Review* 655.
[46] *Belmarsh Detainees* [2005] 2 AC 68, [29] (Lord Bingham).
[47] Ibid.
[48] See also Hickman, above n 45, 663.
[49] See above n 20 and accompanying text.
[50] Human Rights Committee, *General Comment 29*, above n 21, [4]-[5].
[51] *Belmarsh Detainees* [2005] 2 AC 68, [33] (Lord Bingham).
[52] Ibid.

From a purely logical perspective, Lord Bingham's reasoning with regard to the *interference* issue is not entirely consistent, especially in light of his findings in relation to the *designation* issue. He essentially held that it was not for the Court but for government to assess whether the threat of terrorism constituted a public emergency. Nonetheless, Lord Bingham then went on to hold that s 23 ATCSA was not rationally connected to the emergency and thus not suitable to reduce the imminent threat. He failed to explain, however, how he was able to conclude that a measure was not connected to the national emergency, or not suitable to reduce the imminent threat, when the nature and quality of the threat itself was not something that the Court was able to examine or determine. I would argue that this is a logical gap in the majority decision of the House of Lords in *Belmarsh Detainees* and also in the case law of the ECrtHR in the area of emergency derogations more generally. From a logical standpoint, it is simply impossible to determine whether an emergency measure is suitable to address a threat or a crisis without establishing what the nature or quality of the threat or crisis is in the first place.[53]

## The Dissentient Approach to the Threat of Terrorism

Lord Hoffmann, on the other hand, chose to undertake an examination of the quality and nature of the threat of terrorism to the UK and found that it did not constitute a 'war or other public emergency threatening the life of the nation'. He further held that it was insufficient merely to produce evidence of a credible plot to commit terrorist outrages since that did not meet the need to show that the threat of terrorism constituted a public emergency threatening the life of the nation. According to Lord Hoffmann:

> The Armada threatened to destroy the life of the nation, not by loss of life in battle, but by subjecting English institutions to the rule of Spain and the Inquisition. The same was true of the threat posed to the United Kingdom by Nazi Germany in the Second World War. This country, more than any other in the world, has an unbroken history of living for centuries under institutions and in accordance with values which show a recognisable continuity ... I am willing to accept that credible evidence of such plots exists. The events of 11 September 2001 in New York and Washington and 11 March 2003 in Madrid make it entirely likely that the threat of similar atrocities in the United Kingdom is a real one ...This is a nation which has been tested in adversity, which has survived physical destruction and catastrophic loss of life. I do not underestimate the ability of fanatical groups of terrorists to kill and destroy, but they do not threaten the life of the nation. Whether we would survive Hitler hung in the

---

[53] I acknowledge that it is possible — for practical reasons — to deal with the issue of proportionality solely by focusing on the discrimination issue in cases where blatantly and invidiously discriminatory measures are adopted. Nonetheless, the lack of consideration of the nature of the threat still leaves an undesirable hole and makes a thorough proportionality analysis incomplete.

balance, but there is no doubt that we shall survive Al-Qaeda. The Spanish people have not said that what happened in Madrid, hideous crime as it was, threatened the life of their nation. Their legendary pride would not allow it. Terrorist violence, serious as it is, does not threaten our institutions of government or our existence as a civil community.[54]

Lord Hoffmann explicitly held that there were legal limits to the Government's capacity to determine when a situation of public emergency existed, and further, that the Government was in fact wrong to declare a situation of public emergency in the aftermath of 9/11. In doing so, he did not grant the Government a wide margin of appreciation with regard to the *designation* issue. As a consequence, he also did not address the question of whether the Government's measures adopted in s 23 ATCSA were 'strictly required' (ie, the *interference* issue).

What is remarkable about Lord Hoffmann's judgment is that he is able to determine, without access to specific intelligence information, that the current threat of terrorism to the UK does not threaten the life of the nation. In fact, he explicitly accepts that there is a serious terrorist threat to the UK. But this threat is put into perspective by drawing comparisons both to historical threats to the UK and more recent manifestations of terrorism like the 9/11 attacks and the Madrid train bombings. And so the Government's general policy decision about the nature and quality of the threat of terrorism is submitted to judicial scrutiny despite lack of access to specific intelligence information.

## Conclusion

The ECrtHR as well as the House of Lords in the *Belmarsh Detainees* decision have taken a deferential approach in relation to the *designation* issue in the context of Article 15 ECHR and have granted national authorities a 'wide margin of appreciation' or 'discretionary area of judgment' with regard to the existence and analysis of the threat of terrorism that constituted a public emergency threatening the life of the nation. Leaving this discretion to national authorities absolved the courts from examining in greater detail the nature and quality of the threat that justified derogating from international (or domestic) human rights obligations. However, a closer analysis of the rationale behind the margin of appreciation doctrine reveals that several arguments that have been advanced to justify granting national governments a 'wide' margin are outdated as well as inapplicable in the context of the threat of international terrorism. Developments in soft law such as the *Paris Minimum Standards of Human Rights Norms in a State of Emergency* or the *Siracusa Principles on the Limitation and Derogation Provisions in the International Covenant on Civil and Political Rights*, which in some cases find their origins in dissenting opinions by judges of the Strasbourg authorities, as well as observations by the Human Rights Committee,

---

[54] *Belmarsh Detainees* [2005] 2 AC 68, [91], [94], [96] (Lord Hoffmann).

suggest that the discretion left to governments should be re-considered and adjusted. This is particularly the case in circumstances where the emergency becomes 'entrenched' with the threat of terrorism likely to remain present for several years.

In addition, I would argue that granting government a wide discretionary power (with little judicial supervision) in relation to the existence of a public emergency is problematic in light of a further requirement of lawful derogation, that is, that the measures taken pursuant to such derogation need to be 'strictly required by the exigencies of the situation' (the *interference* issue). From a logical perspective, it is difficult to see how it is possible to assess whether measures are 'strictly required' to address an emergency effectively when an analysis of the nature and scope of the threat that constitutes such emergency is not undertaken. This is a logical gap which is evident particularly in Lord Bingham's judgment in *Belmarsh Detainees*.

An analysis of the nature and size of the terrorist threat that may constitute a public emergency does not necessarily require the courts to have access to specific or classified intelligence that governments are understandably reluctant to release. Lord Hoffmann's opinion in the *Belmarsh Detainees* decision is a case in point. While not questioning the existence of a serious terrorist threat to the UK, he nonetheless remained to be convinced that atrocities like the 9/11 attacks or the Madrid train bombings of March 2003 threatened the 'life of the nation'.[55] As a result, Lord Hoffmann did not see a need to examine whether the UK Government's counter-measures (ie, s 23 ATCSA) were 'strictly required by the exigencies of the situation'. Lord Hoffmann's approach is refreshingly progressive. It remains to be seen, though, what impact it will have on future decisions of national courts as well as of the European Court of Human Rights.

---

[55] Ibid [96] (Lord Hoffmann).

# PART THREE

Rules of Engagement:
Beyond the Limits of the Law

# Chapter Eight

# More Law or Less Law? The Resilience of Human Rights Law and Institutions in the 'War on Terror'

## Andrew Byrnes[*]

## Introduction

In the years since the events of September 2001 shocked the United States (US) and many other states into the adoption of wide-ranging measures to respond to actual and perceived threats of international terrorism, the deployment of law has been a central part of the design and justification of those responses, as well as of attempts to moderate and restrain their excesses. While legal responses at the international and national levels have only been a part of the array of measures adopted, the volume of law-making that has taken place has been remarkable.[1] At the international level the extent of regulatory activity around terrorism has been striking: it includes new regulations for container shipping, civil aviation, financial transactions, customs, immigration and passports, use of the internet, and cyberterrorism, as well as provisions for the designation of many new criminal offences and the establishment of transnational law enforcement cooperation arrangements.

The number of institutions involved in efforts to respond to terrorism is also impressive. Nearly every international or regional institution has been caught up in the regulatory network in one way or another, and many have adopted new programs or considerably expanded existing ones in the area.[2] Much of the activity of these organisations has involved the adoption and implementation of new norms, frequently embodied in new international instruments.

---

[*] Professor of International Law, Faculty of Law and Australian Human Rights Centre, The University of New South Wales, Sydney, Australia. This research was funded by the ARC Discovery Project DP0451473 'Terrorism and the Non-State Actor: the Role of Law in the Search for Security'.

[1] See United Nations Working Group on Arbitrary Detention, *Report of the Working Group on Arbitrary Detention*, UN Doc E/CN.4/2004/3 (2004), [50].

[2] Eg, the OSCE Action Against Terrorism Unit lists 43 international or regional partner bodies and organisations with which it is cooperating on the subject. The Unit, established in 2002, 'is the Organization's focal point for the co-ordination and facilitation of OSCE initiatives and capacity-building programmes relevant to the struggle against terrorism': <http://www.osce.org/atu/>. The United Nations Counter-Terrorism Implementation Task Force, established in 2005 to coordinate counter-terrorism activities across the UN system, lists 24 parts of the UN system that are members of the Task Force: <http://www.un.org/terrorism/cttaskforce.html>.

The forms of legal responses seen in the prosecution of the so-called 'war on terror' can be broadly seen as falling into two categories: (a) the *regulation* of terrorism and terrorist activities; and (b) the *amelioration* of counter-terrorism measures.

The category of *regulation of terrorism* encompasses those measures relating to the prevention, investigation and punishment of acts relating to terrorism. It includes the development and application of new legal standards and procedures to aid in identifying persons engaged in terrorist acts or acts preparatory to them, and in investigating and prosecuting, or rendering them harmless. It also involves measures to protect infrastructure and particular forms of social activity from terrorist attacks, or at least to attempt to reduce the risk of such acts, to minimise their impact, and to be prepared to cope with the aftermath of terrorist attacks.

The *ameliorative* category comprises measures that involve efforts to moderate or restrain the excesses of the regulatory measures referred to above, from a number of perspectives, including:

- from a human rights or rule of law perspective (challenging many of the measures as unjustifiable limitations on the enjoyment of fundamental human rights and freedoms);
- from a regulatory impact perspective (resisting the additional burden in terms of red tape/regulatory impact and additional expense that counter-terrorism laws and policies may impose);
- from an instrumentalist and pragmatic perspective (questioning whether the measures are likely to be effective in reducing the threat of terrorism); and
- from other perspectives such as the broader political perspective of questioning whether the allocation of public and private resources to counter-terrorism and security measures is justifiable in the light of other equally or more pressing social problems.

Many factors have contributed to the speed and vigour with which governments have acted to adopt wide-ranging counter-terrorist measures: powerful political imperatives at the international and national level to respond to attacks and to be seen to provide as high a level of security for their populaces as possible against the perceived threats of serious terrorist attacks; the political and financial incentives offered by the United States; the domestic political expediency of being able to invoke a counter-terrorist discourse to legitimate a policy of political repression of minorities or political opponents; and the reputational advantages of being seen to be 'robust' in dealing with terrorists.[3] In justifying these measures, many governments have unapologetically challenged accepted

---

[3] See R Foot, 'Human Rights and Counterterrorism in Global Governance: Reputation and Resistance' (2005) 11 *Global Governance* 291, 299-302.

frameworks for the protection of human rights and existing assumptions and interpretations of the limits they impose.

Actions that violate rights and cause immediate (and longer-term) injury to individuals and institutions can be taken very quickly.[4] On the other hand, the (re)assertion of human rights and rule of law values in response to serious violations of human rights, may require time: to establish facts, to hold governments accountable, and to provide reparation to victims.

The development of new structures to pursue the counter-terrorist agenda and to stimulate states to adopt effective measures to achieve specific goals towards that end, have presented critical challenges to human rights norms and institutions. The priorities of counter-terrorism bodies and programs are not the same as those of human rights bodies, and counter-terrorism mandates frequently make no explicit reference to the role that human rights standards might or should play in the struggle against terrorism. The surge of political energy, and financial and other resources devoted to counter-terrorism efforts, and the associated claims to normative priority of the counter-terrorism agenda, have presented human rights institutions and actors with major challenges.

## Counter-Terrorism Strategies and Human Rights Responses: An Overview

This chapter is organised around an analysis of three types of counter-terrorism strategies, and examines the manner in which specific human rights responses to these strategies have been developed at the international level through a combination of institutional, procedural or normative engagement by different international actors. While the three strategies reflect different approaches to the relevance of international law to the counter-terrorism enterprise, they all fall into the category of regulatory measures described earlier. They involve the regulation of terrorism:

a. *through international law* — by the development of new international norms and procedures with a specific focus on addressing terrorism issues;
b. *despite international law (distorted legalism)* — by engagement with the human rights discourse, seeking to argue that counter-terrorist measures are in conformity with human rights law by invoking extreme or distorted interpretations of the law, or by disregarding authoritative interpretations or rulings on particular issues or in individual cases; or
c. *outside, or in disregard of, international law* — by adopting pragmatic measures without regard to, or in flagrant disregard of, their illegality under international (human rights) law.

---

[4] O Gross and F Ní Aoláin, *Law in Times of Crisis: Emergency Powers in Theory and Practice* (Cambridge: Cambridge University Press, 2006) 8.

The human rights responses to these strategies are examined in the light of actions taken by a number of international human rights bodies. These counter-strategies, each roughly corresponding to the strategies set out above, can be characterised as:

a. *mainstreaming* of human rights norms and expertise into counter-terrorism mandates and bodies;
b. *critical engagement* with states through existing human rights procedures over disputed issues of law; and
c. *fact-finding and exposure* of activities outside the law as a form of exacting public accountability.

These types of responses overlap, and the same actors may employ the various strategies at different times and in relation to different bodies. But they provide useful categories for understanding some of the major forms of reaffirmation of human rights values at the international level.

## Regulating Terrorism *through* International Law

The resort to law has been a marked feature of the international response to September 11 2001 (9/11) and its aftermath. While there was already an extensive body of international law addressing terrorism before then, there has been a surge of law-making internationally and regionally since that time. At the United Nations (UN) level, the completion of conventions on terrorist bombing and nuclear terrorism followed quickly upon the attacks on New York and Washington, adding these two new conventions to the 11 existing UN anti-terrorism conventions.[5] The numbers of states parties to the terrorism conventions increased rapidly, and work on the drafting of a comprehensive anti-terrorism convention was given additional stimulus (though this process has continued to move slowly toward a conclusion, bedevilled by the difficulties of defining terrorism and solving political issues largely mired in the situation in the Middle East).[6] Regional conventions have been adopted by the Organisation of American States and by the Council of Europe, and specialised agencies and other bodies have adopted a range of measures to minimise the risk of terrorism and to enhance efforts to identify, disrupt and bring to justice persons engaged in terrorist activities.

---

[5] See the list of the (now) 13 counter-terrorism conventions and other details of the United Nations' responses to terrorism at UN Action Against Terrorism <http://www.un.org/terrorism>.
[6] Report of the Ad Hoc Committee established by GA Res 51/210 of 17 December 1996, 10th session (27 February-3 March 2006), UN Doc A/61/37 (2006); Report of the Ad Hoc Committee established by General Assembly Resolution 51/210 of 17 December 1996, 11th session, (5, 6 and 15 February 2007), UN Doc A/62/37 (2007). See A Byrnes, 'United Nations Reform and Human Rights' in M Smith (ed), *Human Rights 2005 – The Year in Review* (Melbourne: Castan Centre for Human Rights, 2006) 31, available at <http://www.law.monash.edu.au/castancentre/events/2005/byrnes-paper.html>.

These instruments represent the traditional broadly-based form of international law-making that involves participation of a large number of states in the legislative process, the absence of any obligation to join the resulting treaty regime, and an instrument containing substantive obligations that often reflect the least common denominator. However, an equally — indeed, perhaps more — important form of law-making has come to prominence post-9/11 in relation to terrorist issues, namely the use of 'executive', 'Great Power' law-making, through the UN Security Council.

In a series of resolutions adopted under Chapter VII of the *UN Charter* (and thus formally binding all member states as a matter of international law), the Security Council has legislated wide-ranging obligations for states in relation to terrorism. In significant respects, these obligations extended well beyond the obligations that many states had individually or collectively accepted under existing treaties. In addition, the establishment of supervisory institutions by the Council to monitor the implementation of these measures has meant that the decisions have become much more than powerful political exhortations.

The development of this 'legislative' function by the Council — largely driven by the efforts of the US to use the authority of the Council to advance an energetic agenda against terrorism — is controversial for various reasons, including that it is seen as pushing a predominantly US/Western agenda and endeavouring to impose it on the rest of the world.[7]

The adoption of new international law in the form of a treaty or other programmatic instruments does not necessarily bring with it the institutional structure to drive the implementation of obligations accepted or political undertakings given by states parties or the states which have supported the adoption of the instrument. Even if institutions are established, they may be under-resourced or limited in their functions and powers.

However, the recent Security Council resolutions, which form the centrepiece of the Council's response to terrorism are an exception,[8] since each of them established a committee of the Council to monitor its implementation.

The most important of these has been the Counter-Terrorism Committee (CTC), established under the far-reaching Resolution 1373, adopted on 28 September 2001. The role of that Committee is to monitor the implementation by states of the extensive obligations imposed on member states by the Council in Resolution

---

[7] See A Bianchi, 'Security Council's Anti-terror Resolutions and their Implementation by Member States: An Overview' (2006) 4 *Journal of International Criminal Justice* 1044, 1059-70; A Conte, *Counter-Terrorism and Human Rights in New Zealand* (Wellington: New Zealand Law Foundation, 2007) 37-49; E Rosand, 'Security Council Resolution 1373, the Counter-Terrorism Committee, and the Fight against Terrorism' (2003) 97 *American Journal of International Law* 333; Gross and Ní Aoláin, above n 4, 404.

[8] SC Res 1267 (1999) (Al Qaida and Taliban Sanctions Committee); SC Res 1373 (2001), establishing the Counter-Terrorism Committee (CTC); and SC Res 1540 (2004) (Weapons of Mass Destruction and Non-State Actors).

1373. The Committee initially received significant resources to support its work, and has continued to benefit from such support.

Since its establishment in 2001, the Committee has been able to persuade all member states to report at least once (and many more than once) on the steps they have taken to implement Resolution 1373; these reports have been reviewed by the Committee through its sub-committees. Expert advisers assist the Committee; in its evaluation of the reports, the Committee offers comments, recommends that states obtain technical assistance to assist the implementation of their obligations, and facilitates that process; and the Committee also carries out visits to member states.

The CTC is now well-established and has entered that stage of institutional development during which a body ensures that it will continue to exist by the identification of constantly shifting or emerging new needs that it is able to fulfil. With the CTC this evolution seems well underway: in 2004 the Committee sought permission to 'revitalise' itself, something which involved the establishment of a substantial Counter-Terrorism Executive Directorate (CTED). That 'revitalisation' took place in late 2005, and it is clear that the CTC and CTED will be with us for the long-haul. The CTC's tasks include putting pressure on states to report, analysing reasons for states' non-reporting, carrying out technical needs assessment, visiting states, and providing them with guidance on implementation.

The role of human rights in the mandate and practice of the CTC has been the subject of analysis by a number of commentators.[9] In the resolution establishing the CTC, there was only limited reference to the relevance of human rights to the work of the Committee,[10] and there seemed initially to be little interest in making human rights scrutiny a significant part of the supervisory and support work of the CTC.

The scope of the mandate and the assumptions of CTC members at an early stage in the Committee's work about the relevance of human rights are exemplified by a statement made on 18 January 2002 to the Security Council by Sir Jeremy Greenstock, at the time United Kingdom Permanent Representative to the UN and the first chair of the CTC:

---

[9] R Foot, 'The United Nations, Counter Terrorism and Human Rights: Institutional Adaptation and Embedded Ideas' (2007) 29 *Human Rights Quarterly* 489; E J Flynn, 'The Security Council's Counter-Terrorism Committee and Human Rights' (2007) 7 *Human Rights Law Review* 371; Conte, above n 7, 37-49, 144-49; Bianchi, above n 7; P Mathew, 'Resolution 1373 — a Call to Preempt Asylum Seekers? (or, "Osama the Asylum Seeker")', in J McAdam (ed), *Forced Migration, Human Rights and Security* (Oxford: Hart Publishing, 2008) 19.

[10] Operative para 3(f) of resolution 1373 contains the only specific reference to human rights: '[The Security Council] [c]alls upon all States to ... (f) Take appropriate measures in conformity with the relevant provisions of national and international law, including international standards of human rights, before granting refugee status, for the purpose of ensuring that the asylum seeker has not planned, facilitated or participated in the commission of terrorist acts.'

the Counter-Terrorism Committee is mandated to monitor the implementation of resolution 1373 (2001). Monitoring performance against other international conventions, including human rights law, is outside the scope of the Counter-Terrorism Committee's mandate. But we will remain aware of human rights concerns, and we will keep ourselves briefed as appropriate. It is, of course, open to other organizations to study States' reports and take up their content in other forums ... I would encourage them to do so.[11]

Early on in the international response to 9/11, a number of international human rights bodies and non-government organisations (NGOs) saw clearly the danger posed to human rights by the possibility of excessive reactions to those events, and sought to remind international organisations and national governments of the importance of complying with human rights in designing their responses to terrorism. The Security Council, in particular its counter-terrorism committees, was seen as an especially important forum to engage with.

Among the important interventions[12] were the actions taken by the then UN High Commissioner for Human Rights, Mary Robinson, who shortly after the adoption of Resolution 1373 expressed concern about the potential impact of the resolution on human rights, and in September 2002 presented the CTC with material on the human rights issues relevant to counter-terrorism measures, including a proposal to supplement the guidance already given to states as to what they should include in their reports to the CTC.[13] As Human Rights Watch

---

[11] Security Council, 4453rd meeting, 18 January 2002, UN Doc S/PV.4453, 5. The Chair also noted that the Committee had 'established the practice of acting with maximum transparency': ibid 4. In a similar speech delivered in June 2002, he reiterated that human rights monitoring fell outside the Counter-Terrorism Committee's mandate, but that the Committee would remain aware of the concerns through its contacts with the OHCHR and would 'welcome parallel monitoring of observance of human rights obligations', and that 'the CTC is also operating transparently and openly so that NGOs with concerns can bring them to our attention or follow up with the established human rights machinery': Ambassador Greenstock, then Chairman of the CTC (Speech delivered at the Symposium 'Combating International Terrorism: The Contribution of the United Nations', Vienna, 3-4 June 2002 <http://www.un.org/Docs/sc/committees/1373/ViennaNotes.htm>. The position outlined by the Ambassador Greenstock still appears as current on the CTC's website: <http://www.un.org/sc/ctc/humanrights.shtml>.

[12] See generally, on the range of interventions, Foot, above n 9, 501-7; Flynn, above n 9, 376-8, 382-4.

[13] Office of the High Commissioner for Human Rights, *Note to the Chair of the Counter-Terrorism Committee: A Human Rights Perspective On Counter-Terrorist Measures* (23 September 2002) <http://www.un.org/Docs/sc/committees/1373/ohchr1.htm>; *Proposals for 'Further Guidance' for the submission of reports pursuant to paragraph 6 of Security Council Resolution 1373 (2001) (intended to supplement the Guidance of 26 October 2001)* (23 September 2002) <http://www.un.org/Docs/sc/committees/1373/ohchr2.htm>. See also the Joint statement by Mary Robinson, UN High Commissioner for Human Rights, Walter Schwimmer, Secretary General of the Council of Europe, and Ambassador Gérard Stoudmann, Director of the OSCE Office for Democratic Institutions and Human Rights (29 November 2001) <http://www.unhchr.ch/huricane/huricane.nsf/view01/4E59333FFC5341A7C1256B13004C58F5>.

points out, while the document was posted on the CTC's website, the Committee was not prepared to circulate it as an official document to member states.[14]

In January 2002 Amnesty International also called on the CTC to appoint human rights experts to its staff and to incorporate human rights standards into its guidance.[15] Robinson's successor as Human Rights Commissioner, Sergio Vieira de Mello, addressed the CTC in October 2002 calling on the Committee to incorporate a human rights approach in its work.[16] In June 2003 Sir Nigel Rodley, Vice-Chair of the Human Rights Committee and former Special Rapporteur on Torture, also appeared before the Committee to urge the CTC to assume responsibility for ensuring that counter-terrorism measures complied with human rights and to question states on the human rights dimensions of their anti-terrorism measures.[17] In the same year the Office of the High Commissioner for Human Rights (OHCHR) released its digest of jurisprudence of human rights norms relevant to counter-terrorism activities.[18] Louise Arbour, de Mello's successor, has also spoken out consistently on the need for counter-terrorism measures to fully respect human rights. The Special Rapporteur on the protection of human rights and fundamental freedoms while countering terrorism, Martin Scheinin, appointed in 2005, has also engaged with the Committee, through meetings and in his reports. Various states, such as Mexico, Chile and Germany, have also consistently supported the need for the CTC to take into account human rights standards as part of its work.[19]

This sustained pressure from a variety of sources appears to have had an impact on the work of the CTC, at least in formal terms. The relevance of human rights norms to the implementation of Resolution 1373 and the work of the CTC was partly clarified in early 2003 by Resolution 1456, which stated that counter-terrorist measures should comply with international human rights law,[20] although Flynn suggests that 'there remained ambiguity as to whether it gave

---

[14] Human Rights Watch, *The Security Council's Counter-Terrorism Effort* (10 August 2004) 2, <www.hrw.org/backgrounder/un/2004/un0804/2.htm>.
[15] Flynn, above n 9, 376.
[16] Sergio Vieira de Mello, High Commissioner for Human Rights (Address to the Counter-Terrorism Committee of the Security Council, 21 October 2002)
<http://www.un.org/Docs/sc/committees/1373/HC.htm>.
[17] 'Human Rights and Counter-Terrorism Measures', Security Council Counter-Terrorism Committee UN Headquarters, 19 June 2003, Briefing by Sir Nigel Rodley, Vice-Chairperson Human Rights Committee <http://www.unhchr.ch/huricane/huricane.nsf/0/EE1AC683F3B6385EC1256E4C00313DF5?opendocument>.
[18] OHCHR, *A Digest of Jurisprudence of the United Nations and Regional Organizations on the Protection of Human Rights While Countering Terrorism* (2003)
<http://www.ohchr.org/english/about/publications/docs/digest.doc>.
[19] See Foot, above n 9, 507-10.
[20] Operative para 6 of SC Res 1456 provided: 'States must ensure that any measure taken to combat terrorism comply with all their obligations under international law, and should adopt such measures in accordance with international law, in particular international human rights, refugee, and humanitarian law'.

the Committee a firm basis to inquire into human rights-related matters'.[21] That ambiguity he sees as put beyond doubt by Resolution 1624, adopted on 14 September 2005 following the London bombings of July 2005. Under the Resolution, the Council stressed that states should ensure that any measures they take to implement the resolution 'comply with all of their obligations under international law, in particular international human rights law, refugee law, and humanitarian law' and directed the CTC to '[i]nclude in its dialogue with Member States their efforts to implement this resolution'.[22]

Internally, it had also been suggested in 2004 as part of the proposed 'revitalisation' of the CTC that there would be close cooperation with the OHCHR and the creation of a specific human rights position in the CTED.

In his report to the 62nd session of the Commission on Human Rights, submitted in late 2005, the Special Rapporteur on the promotion and protection of human rights and fundamental freedoms while countering terrorism,[23] Martin Scheinin, set out his analysis of the roughly 640 reports, which had been submitted to the CTC by member states under Resolution 1373 by the time he submitted his report.[24] The purpose of the examination was 'to assess the role of the CTC in promoting methods of counter-terrorism that are in conformity with human rights, insensitive to human rights or, in the worst case, hostile to human rights'.[25] The examination of the impact of the CTC's scrutiny was not based on the CTC's questions or comments — despite the CTC's stated commitment to transparency and openness, these are not publicly available — but on the responses of states in their reports. Scheinin noted four categories of responses from states relevant to human rights issues:

- cases in which the CTC had explicitly promoted responses to terrorism that were in conformity with human rights ('few in number ... but a promising sign that the CTC is willing to give recognition to and promote response to terrorism that respect human rights');[26]
- cases where the implementation of CTC recommendations had been 'met with human rights-based criticism or resistance at the domestic level';[27]
- 'perhaps the most problematic category': cases in which 'subsequent reports by a State suggested that the CTC's questions and recommendations to the

---

[21] Flynn, above n 9, 380.
[22] SC Res 1624 (2005) [4], [6(a)].
[23] The office of the Special Rapporteur on the promotion and protection of human rights while countering terrorism was established by CHR Res 2005/80 for three years from 2005. For the various reports submitted by the Special Rapporteur, Martin Scheinin of Finland, see <http://www.ohchr.org/english/issues/terrorism/rapporteur/srchr.htm>.
[24] UN Doc E/CN.4/2006/98, [57]-[63].
[25] Ibid [57].
[26] Ibid [58].
[27] Ibid [59].

State in question might have been insensitive to human rights', particularly where the CTC appeared to be urging the adoption of a wide range of criminal investigation techniques that may have serious human rights implications, but without any reference to those limitations;[28] and

- cases in which reports to the CTC showed that the CTC 'has shown little, if any, interest in the definition of terrorism at the national level', something which Scheinin considered problematic because of the vagueness of some definitions and the potential for misuse of the term terrorism to outlaw political opposition, repress religious groups and permit or provide cover for other abuses.[29]

Scheinin remained concerned that 'the CTC has not always been sufficiently clear in respect of the duty to respect human rights while countering terrorism' and that '[some] States may even have understood the CTC as promoting measures of counter-terrorism irrespective of their adverse consequences for human rights'.[30]

Following the Council's approval of the 'revitalisation' of the CTC at the end of 2005, the Committee adopted guidance on incorporating human rights in its work, and a human rights expert has been appointed to the staff of the CTED. The relevant document reiterates the need for states to ensure that counter-terrorism measures comply with human rights law, and also requires the CTED to provide the CTC with advice on how to ensure that states do this, to liaise with the OHCHR, and to include human rights into their communications strategy.[31]

It is too early yet to tell whether the specific incorporation of human rights within the overall mandate of the Committee and the practice and personnel of the CTED will have a significant impact in terms of ensuring appropriate human rights scrutiny of states' actions by the Committee, or more importantly the observance of human rights by states in their counter-terrorism measures. It seems that some significant progress has been made in the institutional design, but it will take some time before the effects of those changes can be seen.[32] On 20 December 2006, the outgoing Chair of the CTC, Ambassador Ellen Margrethe Løj from Denmark, told the Security Council that '[it] has now become routine to include human rights aspects of States' implementation of resolution 1373

---

[28] Ibid [60]-[61].
[29] Ibid [62].
[30] Ibid [63].
[31] 25 May 2006, UN Doc S/AC.40/2006/PG.2 <http://www.un.org/sc/ctc/pg25may06.html>.
[32] Flynn above n 9: 'While there have been tangible gains, the Committee's activities are to a large extent invisible to the public and the impact of heightened attention to human rights concerns is difficult to gauge': at 384.

(2001) in the work of the Committee'.[33] While there is a standard description of the relevance of human rights to the work of the CTC and CTED in the CTC's 2006 report to the Security Council,[34] there is little detail of exactly how these considerations have been built into the work of the CTC and CTED.

Nevertheless, it is clear that the advances made from the original Resolution 1373, and early attitude of the CTC to the relevance of human rights to its work, has been significantly moved along through a process of mainstreaming. This has been the result of interventions by a wide range of actors: human rights bodies and individual experts, NGOs, and governments committed to ensuring that counter-terrorism priorities did not simply displace human rights values. Since the CTC and related bodies are politically important and well-resourced actors in the counter-terrorism realm, it has been important to seek to insert human rights values in their normative framework and practices. Close scrutiny at international and national levels will be needed to ensure that these changes have a significant effect, and to continue to urge the full respect for human rights while supporting effective counter-terrorist measures. The broader lesson to be drawn from this is the importance of ensuring that human rights standards and expertise are mainstreamed into those bodies whose primary mission is counter-terrorism.

## Regulating Terrorism *Despite* Law and While Engaging with Human Rights Law

The response of human rights institutions to counter-terrorism measures has been far more extensive than efforts to mainstream human rights standards and expertise into the work of specific counter-terrorism initiatives and law enforcement operations, such as the CTC. A variety of human rights actors (such as the UN human rights treaty bodies and the UN thematic mechanisms of the Human Rights Council) have sought to engage with states, both on an ad hoc basis and as part of their regular activities, on counter-terrorism issues.

In this context, one can identify another way in which some leading governments use law to bolster the legitimacy of their counter-terrorism measures. They claim not only that their actions are effective counter-terrorism measures, but at the same time they do not violate human rights and, indeed, promote the enjoyment

---

[33] Security Council, 5601st meeting, 20 December 2006, UN Doc S/PV.5601, 4; quoted in Flynn, above n 9, 383.
[34] Report of the Counter-Terrorism Committee to the Security Council for its consideration as part of its comprehensive review of the Counter-Terrorism Committee Executive Directorate, UN Doc S/2006/989, [26]; Semi-Annual Comprehensive Report on the Work of the Counter-Terrorism Committee Executive Directorate for the Period 1 January to 30 June 2006, UN Doc S/2006/989, Appendix I, 24; Semi-Annual Comprehensive Report on the Work of the Counter-Terrorism Committee Executive Directorate for the Period 1 July 2006 to 31 December 2006, UN Doc S/2006/989, Appendix II, 51.

of the human rights of the community.[35] A related stratagem by some states has been to seek to remove themselves from external scrutiny by maintaining that a treaty has no application to particular activities, with the consequence in some cases that the external body seeking to scrutinise that behaviour is argued to have no jurisdiction to do so. These positions are characterised by the adoption of interpretations of the law, which are simply wrong, which are so extreme that they cannot be justified on any reasonable interpretive account, or which are accepted by few or no other members of the international community and other interpreters.

This section examines the controversies over a number of critical issues of human rights law and the manner in which the US in particular has sought to put forward extreme or distorted interpretations of human rights law to argue that its actions are not inconsistent with human rights law, and fall outside the remit of human rights bodies seeking to scrutinise those actions. The responses of the UN Working Group on Arbitrary Detention, the Inter-American Commission on Human Rights, and the UN Human Rights Committee and Committee against Torture (CAT) are examined.

Among the issues which have been critical to determining the international legality of the actions of the US and others are the following (my discussion focuses on the first two):

- the applicability of human rights law to situations of armed conflict to which international humanitarian law also applies;
- the applicability of obligations under UN human rights treaties to actions of the state party that take place outside the territory of the state party;
- the extent of the obligations with respect to torture and other forms of cruel, inhuman or degrading treatment or punishment under international treaties (CAT and the International Covenant on Civil and Political Rights (ICCPR));[36] and
- the acceptability of diplomatic assurances in the context of treaty obligations relating to *non-refoulement*.

In relation to nearly all of these issues, there is an overwhelming preponderance of legal opinion about the meaning of the relevant obligations. Yet the US and some other countries have sought to justify their actions as consistent with human rights or to avoid scrutiny of them by relying on constructions of the relevant obligations, which distort the meaning of the relevant obligations and fall outside the range of acceptable international legal interpretation, even in the face of highly authoritative pronouncements to the contrary. While some of

---

[35] See, eg, the analysis of the Australian Attorney-General's approach in G Carne, 'Reconstituting "Human Security" in a New Security Environment: One Australian, Two Canadians and Article 3 of the Universal Declaration of Human Rights' (2006) 25 *Australian Year Book of International Law* 1.

[36] *International Covenant on Civil and Political Rights*, 999 UNTS 171 (entered into force 23 March 1976).

these issues have arisen directly as a result of the measures taken to address terrorism post-9/11, many of the disputes of interpretation are continuing ones, which predate the latest 'war on terror'.

The controversies over these specific issues have taken place against the broader canvas of how one characterises the post-9/11 world and the nature of the dangers that the international community (or certain sectors of it) now face. The US has tended to argue that the 'world changed forever' on 9/11 because of the nature and extent of the terrorist threats illustrated by the events of that day, and that the ongoing emergency justifies extraordinary measures. Others have argued that, while 9/11 was a significant event, it does not represent a seismic shift in world affairs, at least so far as the need for an entirely new legal approach to responding to emergencies or threats is concerned: terrorism and violence have been prevalent in many other countries for many decades, and the current situation does not require us to abandon older models of emergency and law to ensure a reasonable level of community safety.

There has been much rhetoric, as well as serious debate, over whether the events of 9/11 and the non-state terrorist threats they manifest represent an epochal shift in the threats to security that confront our world. There is something to be said for the argument that the threat of decentralised, and loosely coordinated terrorist networks prepared to engage in violence against civilian targets with scant regard for traditional forms of warfare, poses new challenges and threats, and that failure to address this threat may well result in considerable loss of life or injury if terrorist attacks are successfully launched.

But whether these developments represent an epochal change is another matter entirely. Such a view is ahistorical, as well as myopic, and is a largely US-centric viewpoint, given the recent and enduring experience of insurgencies, conflict between state and non-state actors, and terrorist activity in many parts of the world over the last decades. For example, it fails to recall the atmosphere of fear that was widespread just over 30 years ago during the period of significant terrorist activity in the 1960s and 1970s.[37] There are no doubt differences — every new form of violence has its distinctive motivations and forms — but the critical point is that asymmetric non-state violence directed at times against civilians is not without parallel in recent times. States have had to deal with it, and have done so in ways that have been of varying success and involving various levels of compliance with human rights standards.

It has frequently been remarked that the risk to life and limb from terrorism in Western countries is far less than the risk of death from other avoidable

---

[37] Anthony Aust notes that in 1968 and 1969 there were 122 aircraft hijackings – one a week: A Aust, 'Comment on the Presentation by Volker Röben' in C Walter (ed), *Terrorism as a Challenge for National and International Law: Security Versus Liberty* (Berlin: Springer, 2004) 824.

activities.[38] Even in non-Western countries where the toll from terrorist incidents has been far higher consistently over recent decades than in Western countries, the major risks to life and health come from other causes: poverty, disease (including HIV/AIDS, malaria and other avoidable or treatable disease), maternal mortality, vulnerability to flooding, earthquakes and tsunamis, and rising sea levels.[39]

In any case, even if the world has not fundamentally changed, the widespread perception that it may have (leading to actions based on that assumption), has added a new dimension to argumentation over appropriate responses to perceived threats of terrorism.

One of the argumentative strategies adopted by a number of the human rights bodies is to place current threats of terrorism in an historical context, and to assert the normality (or commonality, at any rate) of terrorism, and the need for a principled approach to such emergencies. The point is made that the relevant bodies of law, including human rights law, contain adequate provision for responding to crises in a principled, measured and effective way. Law's role is thus to define the existence of an emergency or exceptional situation and to regulate it through rules (albeit general and flexible) developed for such situations, rather than simply to define the existence of such a situation and step back from any attempt to regulate what takes place within that context.

## United Nations Working Group on Arbitrary Detention

One body that has adopted this analysis is the UN Working Group on Arbitrary Detention, one of the thematic mechanisms of the former UN Commission on Human Rights,[40] established in 1991.[41] Comprising five independent experts, its mandate empowers it to investigate complaints by individuals that they have been detained arbitrarily or in a manner inconsistent with the Universal Declaration of Human Rights (UDHR)[42] or other relevant legal instruments. The Working Group has also adopted an urgent action procedure, and may visit a state at the invitation of its government. The Working Group adopts Opinions

---

[38] See, eg, in relation to developed countries, N Wilson and G Thomson, 'Deaths from International Terrorism Compared to Road Crash Deaths in OECD Countries' (2005) 11 *Injury Prevention* 332, 332-3; 'The Epidemiology of International Terrorism Involving Fatal Outcomes in Developed Countries (1994-2003)' (2005) 20 *European Journal of Epidemiology* 375; 'Policy Lessons from Comparing Mortality from Two Global Forces: International Terrorism and Tobacco' (2005) 1 *Global Health* 18.
[39] See also World Health Organisation, 'Causes of Death', December 2004, <http://www.who.int/healthinfo/statistics/bodgbddeathdalyestimates.xls>.
[40] See generally and in relation to the Working Group on Arbitrary Detention, J Gutter, *Thematic Procedures of the United Nations Commission on Human Rights and International Law: In Search of a Sense of Community* (Antwerp: Intersentia, 2006); B Rudolf, *Die thematischne Berichterstatter und Arbeitsgruppen der UN-Menschenrechskommission – Ihr Beitrag zur Fortentwicklung des internationalen Menschenrechtsschutzes* (Berlin: Springer, 2000) 199-334.
[41] Commission on Human Rights Resolution 1991/42 of 5 March 1991. The Working Group now comes under the aegis of the UN Human Rights Council.
[42] GA Res 217A(III), UN Doc A/810 (1948).

in individual cases after seeking information from the government concerned and other relevant parties. It also adopts Deliberations, its reflections 'on matters of a general nature involving a position of principle in order to develop a consistent set of precedents and assist States, for purposes of prevention, to guard against the practice of arbitrary deprivation of liberty'.[43] In recent years, it has also adopted formal Legal Opinions on a number of matters, including issues relating to counter-terrorism measures and arbitrary detention.

The Working Group has grappled with issues resulting from the vigorous pursuit of the 'war on terror' since 2001, including in relation to allegations made against the US and its close allies in the pursuit, capture and interrogation of terrorist suspects. The arguments put to the Working Group in individual cases reflect a number of the issues, which have arisen in other contexts, and the Working Group's responses in those cases and in two Legal Opinions illustrate how a number of UN human rights bodies have dealt with them.

The Working Group has engaged with the argument that the circumstances facing the world post-9/11 represent a changed world, in which the nature and extent of the threat require and justify responses that might not have been seen as acceptable in the pre-9/11 world. It has also contested the attempts by some governments to avoid accountability for their actions by limiting external review of their actions (a result achieved by taking advantage of physical remoteness of detention facilities and their invisibility — secret detention centres), rejecting the applicability of certain bodies of law and the jurisdiction of responsible international bodies, and governments' refusal to provide any details of the intelligence that is often relied on to justify administrative detention. The Working Group has also set out what it considers to be the rights that are of primary importance in the fight against terrorism and the approach that should be taken when it is proposed to limit those rights.[44]

The Working Group has gone to some trouble to challenge government claims that the threat faced in the post-9/11 world is completely unprecedented. It has underlined the fact that it has itself been addressing issues of arbitrary detention in the context of counter-terrorist measures since its inception. In its 2004 report, for example, the Working Group observed that it had confronted issues relating to detention in the context of the fight against terrorism well before 9/11, noting that in its experience 'when action is taken and/or legislation is adopted to combat what States rightly or wrongly qualify as terrorism, subversive activities or attacks against State security, there is an increase in human rights violations'.[45] The report continued:

---

[43] OHCHR, Working Group on Arbitrary Detention, *Fact Sheet No 26* <http://www.ohchr.org/english/about/publications/docs/fs26.htm#note>.
[44] Report of the Working Group on Arbitrary Detention, UN Doc E/CN.4/2004/3, [50]-[71].
[45] UN Doc E/CN.4/2003/3, [55] (referring to its 1995 report, UN Doc E/CN.4/1995/31, [25(d)]).

> Its experience from the outset has been that the main causes of arbitrary deprivation of liberty are the abuse of states of emergency, the exercise of the powers specific to a state of emergency without a formal declaration, recourse to military, special or emergency courts, non-observance of the principle of proportionality between the gravity of the measures taken and the situation concerned, and loose definitions of offences that are often described as infringements of State security.[46]

Throughout its report the Working Group refers to the situation both before and after 9/11,[47] thereby seeking to portray the normality (or at least frequency) of emergency situations and terrorist threats. By doing this, it is challenging the myopic view of the US. More importantly, it is at the same time arguing that existing international law provides for emergency situations in ways that allow states to take the measures necessary to address the problem of terrorism while still working within a human rights framework. This framework, in the Working Group's view, should form part of the tools that need to be used in developing counter-terrorism strategies and laws, rather than the adoption of laws and policies that reject existing constraints and interpretations.

In 2002 the Inter-American Commission on Human Rights articulated a similar approach to how emergencies should be approached. It noted that the Commission had dealt with issues of terrorism by state and non-state actors for decades, that terrorism continued to be a serious threat to the protection of human rights, and that the events of 9/11 'suggest that the nature of the terrorist threat faced by the global community has expanded both quantitatively and qualitatively, to encompass private groups having a multinational presence and the capacity to inflict armed attacks against states'.[48]

This approach — while recognising that there are significant new elements in patterns of international non-state terrorism that may ultimately give rise to new international law — nevertheless posits that the existing framework under human rights law for dealing with terrorist activities and threats is, on the whole, adequate and that there is considerable experience in the region on which to draw.[49]

## The Applicability of International Human Rights Law in Situations of Armed Conflict

One of the issues over which there has been contention between certain states (in particular the US) and international and regional human rights bodies, is the

---

[46] UN Doc E/CN.4/2003/3, [59] (referring to its 1995 report, UN Doc E/CN.4/1995/31, [14]).
[47] See UN Doc E/CN.4/2003/3, [58], [59], [64], [67].
[48] Inter-American Commission on Human Rights, Report on Terrorism and Human Rights, OEA/Ser.L/V/II.116 Doc 5 rev. 1 corr, [1]-[3] (2002).
[49] It appears to correspond in large measure to the 'Business as Usual' model of responding to emergency situations articulated by Gross and Ní Aoláin, above n 4.

extent to which human rights law, and in particular specific treaty obligations, apply in situations of armed conflict. While it is clear that international humanitarian law (IHL) will apply in situations of armed conflict once the relevant threshold is reached, there has been much discussion of whether and how human rights law can operate contemporaneously. The US in particular has maintained in a number of international fora that those detained as a result of its prosecution of the 'war on terror' have been detained in the course of an armed conflict, that IHL provides the *lex specialis* in that context, and therefore human rights law has no application.

This position is contentious for a number of reasons. The first is that many of the detainees in question were not detained anywhere near any of the relevant battlefields (for example, Afghanistan), so they could hardly have been detained as part of an armed conflict. Second, the notion that, apart from clear cases involving armed conflict such as Afghanistan and Iraq, loosely organised terrorist networks are engaged in an armed conflict more generally with the US, seems to go well beyond the accepted position under IHL of what constitutes an 'armed conflict', the existence of which is a precondition for the application of IHL.[50] Even in relation to those persons captured on the battlefield or clearly involved in an armed conflict, the argument that human rights law has no application is contentious.

The US has argued for the non-applicability of human rights law for at least two reasons. The first is that it saw IHL as offering it greater freedom to detain and to interrogate detainees than if human rights law applies as the governing regime (since in an armed conflict, it is permissible to detain belligerents from the other side until the end of the conflict without needing to charge them with criminal offences or to otherwise justify their detention).[51] The second reason is a

---

[50] 'International humanitarian law recognises two categories of armed conflict – international and non-international. Generally, when a state resorts to force against another state (eg, when the 'war on terror' involves such use of force, as in the recent US and allied invasion of Afghanistan) the international law of international armed conflict applies. When the 'war on terror' amounts to the use of armed force within a state, between that state and a rebel group, or between rebel groups within the state, the situation may amount to non-international armed conflict a) if hostilities rise to a certain level and/or are protracted beyond what is known as mere internal disturbances or sporadic riots, b) if parties can be defined and identified, c) if the territorial bounds of the conflict can be identified and defined, and d) if the beginning and end of the conflict can be defined and identified. Absent these defining characteristics of either international or non-international armed conflict, humanitarian law is not applicable.' G Rona (Legal Adviser, ICRC), 'When is a War Not a War? – The Proper Role of the Law of Armed Conflict in the 'Global War on Terror' (Workshop on the Protection of Human Rights While Countering Terrorism, Copenhagen, 15-16 March 2004) <http://www.icrc.org/web/eng/siteeng0.nsf/html/5XCMN>. See generally H Duffy, *The 'War on Terror' and the Framework of International Law* (Cambridge; Cambridge University Press, 2005), 217-228.

[51] This approach can be seen from the account given by John Yoo, who served as Deputy Assistant Attorney-General in the Office Legal Counsel in the Justice Department and was closely involved in the drafting of the so-called 'torture memos'. See J Yoo, *War By Other Means* (New York: Atlantic Monthly Press, 2006) 171-2 ('The harder question was what interrogation methods fell short of the torture ban and could be used against Al-Qaeda leaders ... Legally, we are not required to treat captured terrorists engaged in a war against us as if they were suspects held at an American police station'). To

jurisdictional one: in contrast to the IHL regime, which does not have specialised bodies for the receipt and adjudication of alleged violations — human rights law does have such bodies and the US is subject to the jurisdiction of a number of them under a variety of procedures. The corollary of the argument that human rights law does not apply to persons detained in the 'war on terror' is that human rights bodies that seek to review the actions taken by the US have no jurisdiction to do so, since their mandate is to review observance with specific human rights standards, not with IHL standards.

The argument is not a new one, yet the international consensus on the interrelation of human rights law and IHL has been clear in principle for some years now: IHL and human rights law can both apply in situations of armed conflict, although the interpretations given to human rights guarantees will necessarily be informed by IHL as the *lex specialis*.[52] This position has been confirmed by the International Court of Justice (ICJ),[53] the European Court of Human Rights, the Inter-American Commission[54] and Court of Human Rights, and a number of UN human rights treaty bodies.[55]

Yet the US has persisted in making the jurisdictional argument, including in cases which have been brought to the Working Group on Arbitrary Detention and the Inter-American Commission on Human Rights against the US on behalf of persons detained by the US and other countries as part of counter-terrorist operations.

While the Working Group on Arbitrary Detention has taken the view that its mandate extends to the review of alleged arbitrary detention in situations of armed conflict, it does not generally deal with complaints relating to situations of international armed conflict where the International Committee of the Red Cross (ICRC) has a role to play.[56] However, where persons caught up in

---

similar effect, J Goldsmith (who followed Yoo in the OLC), *The Terror Presidency: Law and Judgment Inside the Bush Administration* (New York and London: W W Norton & Co, 2007), 102-15.

[52] The many discussions include F Hampson and I Salama, 'Working Paper on the Relationship Between Human Rights Law and International Humanitarian Law', UN Doc E/CN.4/Sub.2/2005/14; N Lubell, 'Challenges in Applying Human Rights Law to Armed Conflict' (2005) 87 *International Review of the Red Cross* 860, 737-54.

[53] See International Court of Justice, 'Legality of the Threat or Use of Nuclear Weapons', Advisory Opinion of 8 July 1996; International Court of Justice, 'Legal Consequences of the Construction of a Wall in the Occupied Palestinian Territory', Advisory Opinion of 9 July 2004 [Wall Advisory Opinion], [66]-[100], [102]-[13] (holding that the ICCPR, ICESCR, and CRC applied in the Israeli Occupied Territories). See also the Separate Opinion of Judge Simma in Armed Activities on the Territory of the Congo (*Democratic Republic of the Congo v Uganda*), International Court of Justice, Judgment of 19 December 2005, [30]-[31].

[54] See generally the Commission's Report on Terrorism and Human Rights, above n 48, [61]-[62]. See also the discussion below.

[55] See, eg, Human Rights Committee, General Comment No 31 (2004), [11].

[56] See the Working Group's Revised Methods of Work, in OHCHR, Fact Sheet No 26, above n 43, Annex IV, [16]. See, eg, the Working Group's refusal to a consider complaint by former Iraqi Prime Minister Tariq Aziz and former President Saddam Hussein during the period of international armed conflict resulting from the invasion of Iraq in 2003: *Tariq Aziz v Iraq and the United States of America*, Opinion

international armed conflict do not in fact enjoy the protections of IHL, it has been prepared to examine complaints of arbitrary detention.[57]

In *Ayub Ali Khan and Azmath Jaweed v United States of America* [58] the Working Group considered a complaint from two persons who had been arrested in the US in connection with the events of 9/11 and had been detained 'for more than 14 months, apparently in solitary confinement, without having officially been informed of any charge, without being able to communicate with their families and without a court being asked to rule on the lawfulness of their detention'.[59] The Working Group found the detention arbitrary. The Working Group also considered the position of a number of persons detained in Guantánamo Bay at the same time, indicating its view that the appropriate legal framework was either the Third Geneva Convention[60] or the ICCPR.[61] Subsequently, the US government indicated its disagreement with the Legal Opinion of the Working Group, arguing that as the Detaining Power under the law of armed conflict it was 'not obliged to prosecute detained enemy combatants or release them prior to the end of the conflict', and that it was important not to conflate international human rights law and humanitarian law.[62]

In *Mourad Benchellali et al v United States of America* [63] a number of persons detained in Guantánamo Bay who had been captured or arrested in Afghanistan or Pakistan complained that they had been held without charge or access to legal assistance, and had not been brought before a court. The Working Group concluded that the detention was arbitrary, in violation of Article 9 of the UDHR and Article 9 of the ICCPR.[64] Although the US authorities provided no

---

No 45/2005, 30 November 2007, A/HRC/4/40/Add 1, [27], [23], [34]; and *Saddam Hussein al-Tikriti v Iraq and United States of America*, Opinion No 46/2005, 30 November 2005, A/HRC/4/40/Add 1, 34, [26], [40].

[57] *Abdul Jaber al-Kubaisi v Iraq and United States of America*, Opinion No 44/2005, 30 November 2005, A/HRC/4/40/Add 1, [14]. In such cases the Working Group has examined the extent of compliance with the specific protections prescribed by IHL (eg, the limitations under art 78 of the *Fourth Geneva Convention* on administrative detention of civilians in occupied territories) and related them to the more general standards set out in the ICCPR. (Al Kubaisi, [15]-[18]). Other examples are *Bdurahman Nacer Adullah al-Dahmane al-Chehri et al v Saudi Arabia*, Opinion No 12/2006, 11 May 2006, A/HRC/4/40/Add.1, 63 (detention by Saudi authorities in Riyadh for the purposes of interrogation in relation to his brother-in-law who was detained in Guantánamo Bay — no charge, no court appearance, and no access to legal assistance — held to be arbitrary); *Walid Mohammed Shahir Muhammed al-Qadasi et al v Yemen*, Opinion No 47/2005, 30 November 2005, A/HRC/4/40/Add.1, 41.

[58] Opinion No 21/2002, 3 December 2002, UN Doc E/CN.4/2004/3/Add.1, 20.

[59] Ibid [15].

[60] *Convention Relative to the Treatment of Prisoners of War*, 75 UNTS 135 (entered into force 21 October 1950).

[61] 'Legal Opinion Regarding the Deprivation of Liberty of Persons Detained in Guantanamo Bay', Report of the Working Group on Arbitrary Detention, UN Doc E/CN.4/2003/8, [61]-[64].

[62] Report of the Working Group on Arbitrary Detention, UN Doc E/CN.4/2004/3, [17]-[18].

[63] Opinion No 5/2003, 8 May 2003, UN Doc E/CN.4/2004/3/Add.1, 33.

[64] Opinion No 5/2003, 8 May 2003, UN Doc E/CN.4/2004/3/Add.1, [12].

information in response to the original request from the Working Group, following the adoption of the Opinion, they responded in detail.[65]

In its response the US restated its position that the mandate of the Working Group was confined to issues of human rights law and '[did] not include competence to address the Geneva Conventions of 1949 or matters arising under the law of armed conflict', which was the applicable law in this context; the Working Group had simply misunderstood the constraints permissible under the law of armed conflict and mistakenly conflated the two bodies of law.[66] At the same time, although it rejected the jurisdictional competence of the Working Group, the response nevertheless did engage with many of the substantive issues raised about the extent to which the guarantees of IHL had been observed. Indeed, this has been a feature of a number of the US government responses to human rights bodies: while rejecting the jurisdiction, they have addressed many of the substantive issues raised by those bodies.

In a later communication brought against both Iraq and the US in relation to the detention (possibly in Camp Cropper) of Abdul Jaber al-Kubaisi,[67] a newspaper owner and political activist opposed to the US-led military occupation of Iraq, the Working Group rejected the restated US position that persons held in Iraq were held by the multinational force in Iraq under the authority of IHL and Security Council Resolution 1546, and therefore fell outside the mandate of the Working Group.[68] The Working Group asserted once again that the two bodies of law were not mutually exclusive and, that where there was a conflict, then IHL as *lex specialis* would normally be applied.[69]

Apart from these cases, the Working Group has also expressed its views on other aspects of the fight against terrorism. For example, in its 2005 report the Working Group articulated its concerns about the increasing resort by states to administrative detention and to emergency legislation limiting review rights, broad definitions of terrorism, and the misuse of terrorism legislation to silence political opponents and other groups challenging government authority.[70]

Attempts to limit the application of human rights law in armed conflict and thereby avoid international scrutiny by ousting the jurisdiction of an external

---

[65] *U.S. Response to Opinion No. 5/2003 of May 8, 2003 and the Communication of January 8, 2003 of the Working Group on Arbitrary Detention, UNHRC* (August 2003) <http://www.state.gov/s/l/2003/44335.htm>.
[66] Ibid.
[67] *Abdul Jaber al-Kubaisi v Iraq and United States of America*, Opinion No 44/2005, 30 November 2005, A/HRC/4/40/Add 1, at 24 (2007).
[68] Ibid [10], [13].
[69] The Working Group had asserted the applicability of its mandate to situations of armed conflict before 9/11: see, eg, 'Legal Opinion Regarding Detention at El-Khiam Prison, Report of the Working Group on Arbitrary Detention', UN Doc E/CN.4/2000/4, [11]-[18] (relating to detention by forces of the South Lebanon Army).
[70] Report of the Working Group on Arbitrary Detention, UN Doc E/CN.4/2005/6, [61]-[65].

body have also been seen in other contexts. For example, in a case involving a request for precautionary measures in relation to detainees at Guantánamo Bay, the Inter-American Commission on Human Rights has consistently asserted its jurisdiction and requested the US to take appropriate action.[71] In response, the US has continued both to articulate its view that IHL governs the situation and that therefore the Commission has no jurisdiction, and also to contest in detail the accuracy of the alleged violations of humanitarian or human rights law.[72]

The US has also met with criticism from other human rights bodies in relation to its position on the same issues.[73] In response to these findings the US has reiterated the position that it is IHL, which is the governing body of law relating to detention in Guantánamo Bay.[74] The UN Human Rights Committee has also criticised the US for its unwillingness to concede that the ICCPR may apply in situations of armed conflict,[75] as has the Committee against Torture in relation to the Convention against Torture.[76]

---

[71] For the orders of the Commission, see Inter-American Commission on Human Rights, 'Pertinent Parts of July 23, 2002 Reiteration of Precautionary Measures regarding Detainees in Guantanamo Bay, Cuba' (2006) 45(3) *International Legal Materials* 667; 'Pertinent Parts of March 18, 2003 Reiteration of Precautionary Measures and Request for Additional Information (Detainees In Guantanamo Bay, Cuba)' (2006) 45(3) *International Legal Materials* 669; 'Pertinent Parts of July 29, 2004 Reiteration and Amplification of Precautionary Measures and Request for Additional Information: (Detainees In Guantanamo Bay, Cuba)' (2006) 45(3) *International Legal Materials* 671; 'Pertinent Parts of October 28, 2005 Reiteration and further Amplification of Precautionary Measures (Detainees In Guantanamo Bay, Cuba)' (2006) 45(3) *International Legal Materials* 673. The full text of the documents is available at <http://www.ccr-ny.org/v2/legal/september_11th/sept11Article.asp?ObjID=7lt0qaX9CP&Content=134>.

[72] Response of the United States to Request for Precautionary Measures – Detainees in Guantánamo Bay, Cuba, (12 April 2002) <http://www.ccr-ny.org/v2/legal/september_11th/docs/4-15-02GovernmentResponse.pdf>; Response of the Government of the United States of America to Inter-American Commission on Human Rights Detainees in Guantánamo Bay, Cuba, Precautionary Measures No 259 (2004) <http://www.ccr-ny.org/v2/legal/september_11th/docs/IACHR_goveresponsePM.pdf>; Response of the Government of the United States of America to Inter-American Commission on Human Rights Detainees in Guantánamo Bay, Cuba, Precautionary Measures No 259 (October 19, 2005) <http://www.ccr-ny.org/v2/legal/september_11th/docs/IACHR_Govts101905response.pdf>.

[73] See the 2005 report by five mandate-holders of the UN Human Rights Commission: Report of the Chairperson-Rapporteur of the Working Group on Arbitrary Detention, Leila Zerrougui; the Special Rapporteur on the independence of judges and lawyers, Leandro Despouy; the Special Rapporteur on torture and other cruel, inhuman or degrading treatment or punishment, Manfred Nowak; the Special Rapporteur on freedom of religion or belief, Asma Jahangir; and the Special Rapporteur on the right of everyone to the enjoyment of the highest attainable standard of physical and mental health, Paul Hunt, UN Doc E/CN.4/120 (2005), discussed in Mathew Chapter 9 this volume.

[74] See Reply of the Government of the United States of America to the Report of the Five UNCHR Special Rapporteurs on Detainees in Guantanamo Bay, Cuba (March 10, 2006) <http://www.asil.org/pdfs/ilib0603212.pdf> and (2006) 45(3) *International Legal Materials* 742; Response of the United States of America dated October 21, 2005 to Inquiry of The UNCHR Special Rapporteurs dated August 8, 2005 Pertaining to Detainees at Guantanamo Bay, Cuba, 2-4 <http://www.asil.org/pdfs/ilib0603211.pdf> and (2006) 45(3) *International Legal Materials* 769.

[75] Human Rights Committee, 'Concluding Observations on the Second and Third Periodic Reports of the United States of America' (2006) CCPR/C/USA/CO/3/Rev.1, [10].

[76] *Convention against Torture and Other Cruel, Inhuman or Degrading Treatment or Punishment*, 1465 UNTS 85 (entered into force 26 June 1987). Committee against Torture, 'Concluding Observations on the Second Report of the United States of America', A/61/44, [37(14)], [37(15)] (affirming applicability of the Convention in time of armed conflict in all territories under State party's jurisdiction). The

## Resistance to the Extraterritorial Applicability of Human Rights Norms

Another argument advanced by the US to attempt to rebuff scrutiny of its actions by human rights bodies has been the claim that certain of its treaty obligations do not apply to its actions in territory that does not form part of the sovereign territory of the state. The argument has been that the ICCPR in particular has no application to its actions in Guantánamo *ratione loci*.

This argument — the non-applicability of a state party's obligations to actions of its organs in territory that is not part of its sovereign territory[77] — has been firmly rebuffed by a number of international bodies, including human rights bodies.[78] In the context of the ICCPR, the issue was addressed generally by the Human Rights Committee in its General Comment No 31 (adopted in March 2004), in which it made clear that the ICCPR applies to the actions of a state in territory that is not part of its sovereign territory but is under its jurisdiction on a long-term basis (such as the long-term administration of Guantánamo Bay by the US) or if in effective control of territory or persons in a situation of armed conflict or occupation. In that General Comment — in which it responded indirectly to some of the jurisdictional issues raised by the arguments of the US in relation to the applicability of the ICCPR to Guantánamo Bay — the Committee stated:

> States Parties are required by article 2, paragraph 1, to respect and to ensure the Covenant rights to all persons who may be within their territory and to all persons subject to their jurisdiction. This means that a State party must respect and ensure the rights laid down in the Covenant to anyone within the power or effective control of that State Party, even if not situated within the territory of the State Party ... This principle also applies to those within the power or effective control of the forces of a State Party acting outside its territory, regardless of the circumstances in which such power or effective control was obtained, such as forces constituting a national contingent of a State Party assigned to an international peace-keeping or peace-enforcement operation.[79]

Both the Human Rights Committee and the ICJ have taken a similar view in relation to the application of the ICCPR (the Court also with regard to the

---

Committee against Torture has also reached the same conclusion in relation to Israel's obligations under the Torture Convention applied in the Occupied Territories.

[77] See generally F Coomans and M Kamminga (eds), *Extraterritorial Application of Human Rights Treaties* (Antwerp: Intersentia, 2004).

[78] The assertion by the US of this position is not the only recent instance of the claim: Israel has maintained that certain of its treaty obligations do not extend to the Occupied Territories, in part because it has delegated control over those areas to the Palestinian Authority. This argument was decisively rejected by the ICJ in its Advisory Opinion on the Wall, and has been rejected by the various UN human rights treaty bodies. See the sources referred to in the Wall Advisory Opinion, above n 53, [102]-[113].

[79] Human Rights Committee, General Comment No 31 (Nature of the General Legal Obligation imposed on State Parties to the Covenant), [10], HRI/GEN/1/Rev.8, at 233 (2006).

International Covenant on Economic, Social and Cultural Rights (ICESCR)[80] and the CRC) to the actions of Israeli authorities in the West Bank and Gaza.[81]

In its 2005 report to the Human Rights Committee, the US reasserted at length its position that Article 2 of the Covenant made it clear that the treaty imposed obligations only in relation to persons 'within the territory and subject to the jurisdiction' of the state party, and did not apply outside its territory.[82] The Committee addressed this issue with some attention in the dialogue with the US delegation in July 2006,[83] during which the US maintained its position[84] though nevertheless provided relevant information to the Committee 'as a courtesy'.[85] In its concluding observations the Committee called on the US 'to review its approach and interpret the Covenant in good faith, in accordance with the ordinary meaning to be given to its terms in their context, including subsequent practice, and in the light of its object and purpose' and to 'acknowledge the applicability of the Covenant with respect to individuals under its jurisdiction but outside its territory, as well as its applicability in time of war', and 'to consider in good faith the interpretation of the Covenant provided by the Committee pursuant to its mandate'.[86] The unusual, and double, reference to the concept of good faith in treaty interpretation may be a sign of the exasperation felt by the Committee in the face of the US intransigence on this issue.

There has been a similar interpretive tussle between the Committee against Torture and the US in relation to the scope of the Convention against Torture.[87] The US has asserted that those provisions of the Convention, which include the phrase 'territory under the State's party's jurisdiction', are limited in their operation to the sovereign territory of the state, and that further the obligation

---

[80] 993 UNTS 3 (entered into force 3 January 1976).
[81] See Human Rights Committee, Concluding Observations on the Second Periodic Report of Israel (2003) CCPR/CO/78/ISR, [11]; Wall Advisory Opinion, above n 53, [103]-[113]. The CEDAW Committee has taken the same view with respect to the provisions of the CEDAW Convention: CEDAW/C/SR.685 (2005) and Concluding Comments on the Third Periodic Report of Israel (2005) A/60/38, [243]-[244]. See *Convention on the Elimination of All Forms of Discrimination against Women*, 1249 UNTS 513 (entry into force 3 September 1981).
[82] Third periodic report of the United States of America under the ICCPR (2005) CCPR/C/USA/3, [130].
[83] See List of issues to be taken up in connection with the consideration of the second and third periodic reports of the United States of America (2007) CCPR/C/Q/3, [4]-[5] <http://www.ohchr.org/english/bodies/hrc/hrcs87.htm>.
[84] One member of the Committee, Sir Nigel Rodley noted that 'some of the delegation's responses had been dogged reaffirmations of positions already stated in the report and the written responses to the list of issues. He hoped that any requests for a review of those positions in the Committee's concluding observations would not be met with the same dogged rejection': (2007) CCPR/C/SR.2380, [64].
[85] Third periodic report of the United States of America under the ICCPR (2005) CCPR/C/USA/3, [130].
[86] (2006) CCPR/USA/CO/3/Rev.1, [10].
[87] Art 2(1) of the Convention provides: 'Each State Party shall take effective legislative, administrative, judicial or other measures to prevent acts of torture in any territory under its jurisdiction'.

of *non-refoulement* under Article 3 of the Convention[88] is similarly limited to the sovereign territory of the state party. This interpretation has had particular relevance in relation to transfers of persons who have come into the custody of the US and who have then been sent to third countries where there is at least an expectation that they will be subject to torture and, some claim, where it is intended that they will be subject to interrogation by national authorities in ways that would not be permissible in US custody. The Committee against Torture has emphatically rejected these views,[89] in which the US persists.

In these examples we see the importance of the engagement by human rights bodies in the interpretive struggle. The views that have been advanced by the US and some other states are, to put it at its highest, minority views, which find little support among states parties, or in the practice and jurisprudence of the treaty bodies, or of international courts. Yet the privileged position of the state under international law and the lack of a formally binding interpretation of the disputed provisions permit the state to continue to assert an untenable position, and to base its policies on that when it wishes. The human rights bodies have energetically and persistently engaged with these interpretations and challenged the states concerned over them — not with a lot of obvious success at this stage (though the passage of time may tell a different story) — but in doing so they have also engaged the states in substantive discussion of the implementation of the disputed standards in the territories where the alleged violations are occurring.

## Regulating Terrorism *outside* International Law

A third strategy in the struggle against terrorism has been regulation *outside* the law: the adoption of counter-terrorism measures that simply ignore international legal prescriptions and are undertaken covertly and with the deliberate purpose of avoiding international scrutiny or accountability. The practices of extraordinary rendition and secret detention centres are two major examples.

From very early on in the military and counter-terrorist measures that were taken after 9/11, concerns began to emerge about the manner in which persons captured on the battlefield or elsewhere were being processed. There were a number of dimensions of this problem: an awareness that there were specific detention facilities in places such as Guantánamo Bay but little knowledge of the identities of persons who were being held in those facilities. Second, there

---

[88] Art 3(1) of the Convention provides: 'No State Party shall expel, return ("refouler") or extradite a person to another State where there are substantial grounds for believing that he would be in danger of being subjected to torture'.
[89] Concluding observations on the second report of the United States of America, A/61/44, [37(20)] (*non-refoulement* applies outside the state party's sovereign territory). See also Draft General Comment No 2 (2007) CAT/C/GC2/CRP.1/Rev.2, [6], [16] (affirming the application of the Convention to all territories or persons under the *de iure* or de facto control of the state party).

was concern that there were secret detention centres in certain countries in which detainees were being held by the US for the purposes of interrogation in a deliberate effort to remove them from the legal protections of the country in which they were located, the US legal system, and international scrutiny, whether by the ICRC under IHL or by other bodies. Third, there was concern that persons were being 'rendered' or returned by the US or other states outside any formal legal process to third countries, where there was a substantial risk that they might be subject to torture and/or in the expectation that the intelligence agencies of that country would use whatever methods were necessary to extract intelligence that would be of assistance to the anti-terrorist struggle. The disappearance of many individuals, their incommunicado detention, and the categorical denials that there were any such places, made it extremely difficult to ascertain the extent to which rights were being respected. It must have been clear to the officials involved, whether American or other, that what was involved in this type of behaviour was clearly inconsistent with international human rights standards and other international and national norms.

The attempt to assert human rights values in the face of determined action by governments to avoid public knowledge of what was going on has been an important aspect of the work of a number of human rights actors since 2001. Non-governmental organisations played an important role, going to considerable lengths to attempt to identify persons who had disappeared and who, it was suspected, were being held in secret detention locations, and seeking to hold governments accountable by publicising that information and engaging with human rights institutions to assist them in taking these matters up with governments.

Where governments devote themselves to hiding their activities and refusing to confirm or deny claimed facts (or simply lying) in order to avoid public scrutiny, particular challenges are presented to civil society institutions. A critical component of a human rights response to such behaviour has to be the grinding work of fact-finding, piecing together individual items of information to form a larger mosaic, and then using this material to challenge both government secrecy and unlawful behaviour. NGOs, the media, public bodies at the national level (such as parliamentary committees, human rights commissions or courts) and international human rights bodies all potentially have a role to play in putting together the pieces of the puzzle. It is a difficult task, and one in which government holds most of the cards. While it seems likely that much of the information will eventually emerge, this may take years, by which stage most of the damage will have been done.

The most prominent example of this in the context of the 'war against terror' has been the human rights community's response to secret detentions and so-called 'extraordinary renditions'. Despite denials of secret detentions outside the US (until President Bush's open admission of such a program in September 2006),[90] the US had held 'high-value detainees' ('HVD') in detention facilities in undisclosed locations in a number of countries in Europe and elsewhere. It is also now clear that in a significant number of cases, persons were transferred from US custody to countries where it was clear that there was a substantial risk of torture — and in some cases those returnees were indeed tortured after their return.[91]

The uncovering of this story involved many actors at the international and national level, but various organs of the Council of Europe played an important role. Spurred on and assisted by NGOs and the media, they determinedly employed the public power of an international organisation and the political weapon of publicity to draw attention to what was going on, in an attempt to hold accountable at least some of the governments involved.

The primary arena of activity was the Committee on Legal Affairs and Human Rights of the Parliamentary Assembly of the Council of Europe (the Committee), whose Chair and Rapporteur on this issue, Swiss Senator Dick Marty,[92] played a critical role, describing his efforts to uncover what had gone on with very limited resources as pitting 'Mountainbike against Ferrari'.[93]

The work spearheaded by Marty through the Committee was one of a number of responses by different parts of the Council of Europe to the media and NGO claims of secret detention centres, illegal transfers, and torture and other ill treatment. These suggested that these activities may have taken place on the territory of some member states of the Council of Europe (as well as elsewhere), with the complicity of those states. In particular, there were claims that secret detention centres had been run by the US on the territory of at least two member states, and that other member states may have permitted their territory and airspace to be used by Central Intelligence Agency (CIA) flights to carry out its program of 'extraordinary renditions'.

The Committee took up the issue in late 2005,[94] and appointed Marty as its Rappporteur on the issue.[95] Around the same time, on 21 November 2005, the

---

[90] G Bush, 'Remarks by the President on the Global War on Terror' (War against terrorism is a struggle for freedom and liberty, Bush says), (Speech delivered in the East Room of the White House, 6 September 2006).
[91] See generally M Satterthwaite, 'Rendered Meaningless: Extraordinary Rendition and the Rule of Law' (2006) *NYU Public Law and Legal Theory Working Papers* 43.
[92] On the lead-up to the commencement of the Marty investigation, see Committee on Legal Affairs and Human Rights, 'Alleged Secret Detentions in Council of Europe Member States, Information Memorandum II' (2006) AS/Jur 03 rev, 22 January 2006, [1]-[16] [Marty January 2006 Report].
[93] 'Alle gegen Marty' <http://www.dickmarty.ch/>.
[94] See Committee on Legal Affairs and Human Rights of the Parliamentary Assembly of the Council of Europe, 'Alleged Secret Detention Centres in Council of Europe Member States, Information Memorandum (Revised)' (2005) AS/Jur (2005) 52 rev 2, 22 November 2005, [Marty November 2005 Report].
[95] Marty January 2006 Report, above n 92, [15]-[16].

Secretary-General of the Council of Europe made use of his power under Article 52 of the European Convention on Human Rights[96] to request an explanation from member states as to how their laws and practices provided protection against unacknowledged detention (including at the instigation of a foreign state) and details of any instances which had occurred since early 2002.[97] This was by no means the Committee's or the Council's first post-9/11 engagement with the general human rights issues arising from the 'war on terror', nor with the specific actions of the US in relation to transfer and detention of persons claimed to be involved in terrorist activities (or suspected of this).[98]

The Committee approached its work on a number of fronts. First, Marty sought a legal opinion from the European Commission for Democracy through Law (the Venice Commission) on the legality of secret detentions in the light of Council of Europe member states' international obligations.[99] The Commission is a body of the Council of Europe with considerable legal expertise and standing and the purpose of the request was to obtain an authoritative general statement of the relevant international legal issues; the Commission provided its opinion in March 2006.[100] Second, Marty sought information from a number of European agencies (including the EU Satellite Centre and Eurocontrol) that held information about flights and certain sites. He also sought information from various governmental delegations to the Council and certain parliamentary delegations, and subsequently held interviews with NGOs, journalists, persons who claimed they had been detained in secret centres or clandestinely transported, and also with persons currently or previously employed in relevant governmental agencies (including intelligence agencies), among others.

---

[96] *European Convention for the Protection of Human Rights and Fundamental Freedoms* (ECHR) 213 UNTS 222 (entered into force 3 September 1953).
[97] Ibid, Appendix IV.
[98] On 11 July 2002 the Committee of Ministers of the Council of Europe had already issued Guidelines on human rights and the fight against terrorism, <http://www.coe.int/t/f/droits_de_l'homme/Guidelines.asp>. The Committee on Legal Affairs and Human Rights had already prepared a report on the legality of the Guantánamo Bay detentions: Committee on Legal Affairs and Human Rights, Lawfulness of detentions by the United States in Guantánamo Bay, Doc 10497, 8 April 2005, <http://assembly.coe.int//Main.asp?link=http://assembly.coe.int/Documents/WorkingDocs/Doc05/EDOC10497.htm>, which led to the adoption by the Parliamentary Assembly of the Council of Europe of Resolution 1433 (2005) on the Lawfulness of detentions by the United States in Guantánamo Bay, <http://assembly.coe.int/Main.asp?link=http://assembly.coe.int/Documents/AdoptedText/ta05/ERES1433.htm>.
[99] Marty January 2006 Report, above n 92, Appendix III.
[100] European Commission for Democracy through Law, 'Opinion on the International Legal Obligations of Council of Europe Member States in Respect of Secret Detention Facilities and Inter-State Transport of Prisoners Adopted by the Venice Commission at its 66th Plenary Session' (17-18 March 2006), Opinion No 363/2005, CDL-AD(2006)009. See M Hakimi, 'The Council of Europe Addresses CIA Rendition and Detention Program' (2007) 101 *American Journal of International Law* 442.

Over the next 18 months, by piecing together the information from these sources, Marty presented three reports[101] providing an account of the activities of governments, which showed in his view that there had been widespread violations of human rights in which member states of the Council of Europe had been complicit. In his June 2006 report, focusing on the alleged CIA rendition program relating to the transport and detention of high-value detainees and others and based on information from air traffic control authorities, and other sources, Marty concluded that:[102]

> 5. ... [A]cross the world, the United States has progressively woven a clandestine 'spider's web' of disappearances, secret detentions and unlawful inter-state transfers, often encompassing countries notorious for their use of torture. Hundreds of persons have become entrapped in this web, in some cases merely suspected of sympathising with a presumed terrorist organisation.
>
> 6. The 'spider's web' has been spun out with the collaboration or tolerance of many countries, including several Council of Europe member States. This co-operation, which took place in secret and without any democratic legitimacy, has spawned a system that is utterly incompatible with the fundamental principles of the Council of Europe.
>
> 7. The facts and information gathered to date, along with new factual patterns in the process of being uncovered, indicate that the key elements of this 'spider's web' have notably included: a world-wide network of secret detentions on CIA 'black sites' and in military or naval installations; the CIA's programme of 'renditions', under which terrorist suspects are flown between States on civilian aircraft, outside of the scope of any legal protections, often to be handed over to States who customarily resort to degrading treatment and torture; and the use of military airbases and aircraft to transport detainees as human cargo to Guantánamo Bay in Cuba or to other detention centres.
>
> ...
>
> 9. Some Council of Europe member States have knowingly colluded with the United States to carry out these unlawful operations; some others have tolerated

---

[101] Marty January 2006 Report, above n 92; Committee on Legal Affairs and Human Rights of the Parliamentary Assembly of the Council of Europe, 'Alleged Secret Detentions and Unlawful Inter-State Transfers Involving Council of Europe Member States', Draft report – Part II (explanatory memorandum), Doc 10957, 12 June 2006 [Marty June 2006 Report]; and Committee on Legal Affairs and Human Rights of the Parliamentary Assembly of the Council of Europe, 'Secret Detentions and Unlawful Inter-State Transfers Involving Council of Europe Member States', Second report, Doc 11302 rev, 11 June 2007 [Marty 2007 Report].

[102] Draft Resolution, [5]-[7], [9], Marty June 2006 Report, above n 101, 2 (summarising the findings of the report). See also Amnesty International, 'Off the Record: U.S. Responsibility for Enforced Disappearances in the "War on Terror"', June 2007, AI Index: AMR 51/093/2007, 5-6; J Margulies, *Guantánamo and the Abuse of Presidential Power* (New York: Simon & Schuster, 2006) 18-200; T Paglen and A C Thompson, *Torture Taxi: On the Trail of the CIA's Rendition Flights* (Hoboken, NJ: Melville House, 2006); S Grey, *Ghost Plane: the True Story of the CIA Torture Program* (New York: St Martin's Press, 2006).

them or simply turned a blind eye. They have also gone to great lengths to ensure that such operations remain secret and protected from effective national or international scrutiny.

By the time that Marty presented his next substantial report to the Committee and the Parliamentary Assembly in mid-2007, he considered that his earlier conclusions had received further support and that there was extensive and reliable evidence of systematic violations in which Council of Europe states had been actively or passively involved. He concluded that two secret detention centres (in Poland and Romania) had been part of the CIA operations as part of the HVD program, and that the program had been set up with the cooperation of European officials and kept secret under North Atlantic Treaty Organization (NATO) confidentiality rules. Marty also concluded that detainees were subjected to 'inhuman and degrading treatment, sometimes protracted' and that 'certain "enhanced" interrogation methods used' violated the prohibitions against torture and other ill treatment under European and UN human rights treaties.[103]

The Marty reports provide a compelling account of the manner in which the arrangements between the US and various countries (including ones outside Europe) were reached, and the procedures for transferring detainees between various countries and the purposes for which this was undertaken. A number of the countries involved have denied the accuracy of the findings,[104] while other critics have argued that the evidence supporting the conclusions is based on media reports or is unreliable. Marty has defended his findings, noting that all his findings were based on a variety of different sources, and all findings were corroborated from different sources.

While it is certainly true that for some of his information, Marty relied on (or at least started with) media and NGO reports, the use of air traffic control data supplied by various national and international authorities, the interviews with victims and present and former government officers, and the various statements by government officials on which he also relied, belie the criticism that the report has no solid evidential basis. Marty noted that the Committee was 'not an investigating authority: we have neither the powers nor the resources … our task is … to assess, as far as possible, allegations of serious violations of human rights committed on the territory of Council of Europe member states'.[105] While he plainly considered that the evidence was strong enough to reach firm factual conclusions, the primary responsibility lay with states to carry out proper investigations into the violations alleged to have taken place on their territory, and they had failed to fulfil that responsibility.

---

[103] Draft Resolution, [2]-[7], Marty 2007 Report, above n 101, 2 (summarising the findings of the report).
[104] See in particular the strong denials by Poland and Romania in Marty 2007 Report, above n 101, Appendix, Doc 11302 Addendum (19 June 2007).
[105] Marty 2007 Report, above n 101, [9].

Marty also documented the unwillingness or refusal of many states to provide relevant information.[106] He also notes that in some cases, states had issued flat denials of particular practices, yet subsequently incontrovertible evidence of them had emerged. Perhaps the most striking is the admission by President Bush on 6 September 2006 that indeed the CIA had been running an HVD program, which had involved detention of suspects in undisclosed locations. Marty also notes the ready resort by states to the invocation of national security grounds to justify the refusal to provide relevant information, not just to his inquiry, but also in proceedings brought before national courts by persons who alleged that they had been the victims of serious human rights violations at the hands of the governments concerned.

Although the story that emerges from Marty's reports is the deliberate and systematic disregard of fundamental international human rights norms by the governments involved, there is also another dimension of these events, which reveals a different use of law and legal structures. Marty finds that some of the arrangements for the secret detention centres and illegal renditions were entered into under the framework of NATO cooperation arrangements, as well as by a series of bilateral agreements between various governments (generally at the agency level).[107] Furthermore, he draws attention to what appears to have been an attempt by President Bush to confer the mantle of domestic legality on the CIA's program by the signature on 17 September 2001 of a classified Presidential Finding, which granted the CIA significant new powers in relation to its covert activities directed against terrorism.[108] These patterns of behaviour suggest that the intelligence agencies involved were not totally oblivious to the utility of law, but that theirs was a partial view, which saw a practical and political importance in using established or ad hoc international arrangements to pursue their goals and relying on domestic authorisations to protect themselves against liability under US law,[109] while showing complete disregard for fundamental human rights standards. The only law that really appears to have mattered was domestic law — whether or not it was in flagrant violation of international law[110] — and also the rules of the intelligence and military communities in the context of NATO and bilateral cooperative arrangements between intelligence agencies.

---

[106] Ibid, Summary.
[107] Ibid [9].
[108] Ibid [58]-[60].
[109] This approach was also seen in relation to the notorious 'torture memos' that emerged from the US Department of Justice, which argued for legal positions the effect of which was to minimise the exposure of US military and intelligence officials to any criminal liability under US laws in relation to the use of 'enhanced interrogation techniques' (aka 'torture or cruel, inhuman or degrading treatment or punishment').
[110] The primacy of domestic law emerges from the account given of the Bush administration's response to the events of 9/11 by two of the principal legal players in the first Bush administration, John Yoo, and one of his successors, Jack Goldsmith: see Yoo, above n 51; Goldsmith, above n 51, 129-34.

The work carried out by the Council of Europe and many other parties in uncovering the conduct of the government agencies involved in the secret detentions and illegal renditions demonstrates the significant challenges that face civil society and public institutions in holding governments accountable for human rights violations of this sort. The governments involved were determined to undertake secret operations in clear violation of international standards, and went to great efforts to conceal these from the public and our political institutions, to deceive the public when questions were raised, and to resist disclosure of information on national security grounds when persons affected sought to hold them to account through judicial or other proceedings. The resources available to uncover such conduct are often limited when compared with the resources governments devote to their concealment. It is only through concerted efforts by and collaboration among various public institutions at the international and national level, the media, NGOs and others — as seen in the Council of Europe inquiries — that the story can emerge, and trigger or reinforce further exercises in accountability in different forms at the national level.

## Conclusion

In this chapter I have sought to explore a number of ways in which states have drawn on law or operated outside the international human rights legal framework, in their attempts to address what they perceive as the serious threat of terrorism. The discussion above shows that law has been a central part of that response at the international level and that there have been different forms of regulatory response drawing on law, described as regulation through law, despite the law, and outside the law. The proponents of strong counter-terrorism measures have enlisted the power and legitimacy of international law and legal institutions to legitimate the many new measures adopted, while in other cases they have chosen to disregard the applicability of the law or to deny its relevance or inhibiting effect.

All these types of regulatory activity have drawn ameliorative responses from a range of institutions and organisations whose mandates or missions involve the promotion and protection of human rights at international and national levels. The institutions with a primary responsibility within the international system for the protection of human rights have sought both to arrest the excesses and to reassert the importance of human rights norms and the values they represent. In a very real sense the rule of law and human rights has been fighting back on various fronts, more slowly than the breathless pace of the development of new counter-terrorism laws, policies and programs, but painstakingly reaffirming the importance of human rights standards as goals and means. In this task, NGOs, the media, and parliamentary institutions at the international and national level have been indispensable collaborators in the process.

The strategies adopted by international human rights institutions in responding to the direct and serious encroachments on established human rights norms in the struggle against terrorism have been diverse. Three of them have been the focus of this chapter: mainstreaming, critical engagement and disputation over authoritative interpretation of norms, and fact-finding as a form of ensuring public accountability. The strategies have involved arguing for normative inclusion and the availability of human rights expertise in the specialised counter-terrorism bodies, the reaffirmation of accepted principles of human rights law to the familiar and new situations presented by the phenomenon of terrorism in the modern world, and the use of fact-finding methods to reveal the nature and extent of infringements states have engaged in and to institute forms of accountability for those actions.

The specific measures adopted have included efforts to ensure the insertion or incorporation of human rights standards and perspectives in the mandates and procedures of the specialised counter-terrorism bodies; the establishment of new mechanisms to engage directly with the counter-terrorism bodies, states and other actors, and to provide political and normative scrutiny of the work of those bodies; and the use of existing bodies and procedures to focus on the human rights implications of states' legislative and other actions.

In terms of substantive argumentation, one can see at least two fundamental features of the manner in which counter-terrorism measures and the modes for their implementation have been justified and implemented. The first is the construction of the emergency, the crisis, the world that changed forever on 9/11, and the corresponding need to take exceptional measures that would neither be needed nor justified in 'normal' times. The second is a mode of implementation that is based on lack of transparency, secrecy, invisibility and very limited opportunity for an external and independent review.

To each of these features, the riposte has come from human rights institutions that the need to confront crises and emergencies is in fact not so unusual and does not require major departures from established principles and approaches. Second, the importance of transparency and accountability have been rearticulated, and the need for them in identifying and remedying violations of international and national law has been vividly underlined by the vigorous efforts of human rights bodies to tear away the veil of secrecy behind which states have sought to conceal them.

# Chapter Nine

# Black Holes, White Holes and Worm Holes: Pre-emptive Detention in the 'War on Terror'

## Penelope Mathew[*]

## I. Introduction

This chapter explores the use of detention as a response to terrorism in the United States (US), United Kingdom (UK) and Australia. I have chosen to focus on these three countries because it is clear that Australia has taken some leads from the US and UK in this area as a result of its close connections with them. The three countries have obvious cultural connections and they were all members of the 'coalition of the willing' that invaded Iraq in 2003. It is apparent that detention has become a favoured preventative measure in the 'fight against terror' in all three countries, and that the rules that would generally govern and constrain detention have altered dramatically. Indeed, the rules are so different, subject to so many ongoing changes, and based on such flimsy rationales that they lack legitimacy.

In this chapter, I also comment on the relationship between detention and torture. Places of detention are often places of torture, which is one reason for human rights safeguards surrounding detention such as the right to come before a judge. The interrogation techniques used by the US in Guantánamo Bay have been denounced as torture by international non-government organisations, as well as bodies within the United Nations human rights system.[1] Meanwhile, the UK has sought to deport people whom it would otherwise wish to keep in detention on the basis of 'diplomatic assurances' that torture will not occur once the person is returned to their home country, assurances that should carry little, if any, weight.

---

[*] Reader in Law, ANU College of Law, The Australian National University. From August 2008, Visiting Professor and Interim Director, Program in Refugee Law and Asylum, University of Michigan Law School, Ann Arbor, USA. This research was funded by an Australian Research Council grant '*Terrorism and the Non-State Actor After September 11: The Role of Law in the Search for Security*' (DP0451473 awarded for 2004-2007).

[1] See, eg, Amnesty International, 'Close Guantánamo. Guantánamo – Torture and other ill-treatment' AMR 51/189/2006. The findings of various parts of the UN human rights system are examined below in part II.B.

Various argumentative strategies used by governments to support the use of detention and to circumvent the prohibition on torture, the flaws in these strategies, and possible long-term ramifications for core human rights norms such as the prohibitions on arbitrary detention and against torture are examined. I will focus on two principal arguments put by governments, which are sometimes interrelated. One is to deny that a person is truly a person entitled to all human rights — for example, by attempting to differentiate between aliens and citizens, or lawful and unlawful combatants. The other is to put the person in a legal 'black hole', to use Lord Steyn's terminology,[2] whether by removing the person from a state's territory, or creating executive-controlled detention — for example, by depriving courts of jurisdiction. A third argument will also be noted along the way. This is the 'balancing' argument, namely that human rights need to be balanced against national security, which is another route to the same result — denial of a person's rights as a fellow human being, or a justification for putting them into a legal black hole.

A common theme underlying these arguments is that there exists an emergency that permits extraordinary measures. The emergency may be characterised as a 'war', or a 'threat to the life of the nation', which justifies derogation from rights,[3] or a situation in which the executive is able to limit rights without invoking the need to derogate from rights. As the title of the chapter suggests, the argumentative strategies employed by the governments concerned are as dangerous as space travel, and as improbable as some science fiction.

## II. The Black Hole of Guantánamo Bay

The analogy of the black hole was first employed as a description of Guantánamo Bay by Lord Steyn in the Twenty-Seventh F A Mann Lecture[4] in order to describe the right-less vacuum into which the US sought to place the detainees in Guantánamo Bay.[5] The analogy also warns that by denying the detainees'

---

[2] Lord Johan Steyn, 'Guantánamo Bay: The Legal Black Hole' (2004) 53 *International and Comparative Law Quarterly* 1.
[3] See the language of the 'derogation clause' in art 4, *International Covenant on Civil and Political Rights*, 999 UNTS 171 (entered into force 23 March 1976) (ICCPR).
[4] Above n 2.
[5] According to Steyn, 'the purpose of holding the prisoners at Guantánamo Bay was and is to put them beyond the rule of law, beyond the protection of any courts, and at the mercy of the victors.' Ibid 8.

status as rights-holders, US society itself — not just the detainees, who are usually, but not always, foreigners[6] — may be sucked into the vortex.[7]

Four years after Lord Steyn gave his speech, US policy in relation to Guantánamo Bay remains largely unchanged, although there have been some important victories in US courts and some strong denunciations of US policy at the international level. The US government has tried to shield its policies from scrutiny with variations on the theme of the black hole, such as attempting to deprive US courts of jurisdiction or denying that treaties that prohibit torture extend to Guantánamo. I turn first to examine the extent to which US courts have confronted and dismissed the strategies outlined above.

## A. Staring into the Abyss? Confronting Jurisdictional Limits before US Courts

US courts have granted the detainees some recognition of their rights, resulting in changes to the legislative regime governing the treatment of the detainees. In *Hamdi v Rumsfield*,[8] the Court found that detainees had the right to challenge their classification as an enemy combatant before a neutral decision-maker. Combatant Status Review Tribunals were then established for the purposes of this task.

In *Hamdan v Rumsfeld*, the Court held that the military commissions established to try Guantánamo detainees were not validly constituted, because, among other things, they violated common Article 3 of the Geneva Conventions.[9] Article 3 requires detainees to be tried by a 'regularly constituted court affording all the judicial guarantees which are recognized as indispensable by civilized peoples.'[10] This phrase incorporates the customary international legal requirements for a fair trial, including the right of accused persons both to be present at their trial and to see the evidence against them.[11]

So long as the US government regulates the treatment of the detainees, through the establishment of military commissions and so on, any attempt to keep questions regarding the detentions completely out of the courts may be doomed

---

[6] A recent decision from the US Supreme Court concerns a US national arrested at O'Hare airport in Chicago after returning from Pakistan: *Padilla v Hanft*, 547 U.S. 1062 (2006). The Supreme Court declined to hear the case because Padilla's case is now being heard by the civilian justice system instead of the controversial military commissions and he is entitled to the full protection of the ordinary criminal law, including the right to a speedy trial. In their explanation of their vote to deny *certiarari*, Chief Justice Roberts and Justices Kennedy and Stevens concluded that 'Padilla's current custody is part of the relief he sought, and ... its lawfulness is uncontested'. Ibid 4.
[7] '[D]enial of justice to foreigners was bound to erode the civil liberties of citizens in the United States.' Lord Steyn, above n 2, 12.
[8] *Hamdi v Rumsfield*, 543 US 507 (2004).
[9] *Hamdan v Rumsfeld*, 126 S Ct 2749 (2006), (Stevens J), 2797.
[10] See eg, art 3(1)(d), *Geneva Convention relative to the Treatment of Prisoners of War*, 75 UNTS 135 (entered into force 21 October 1950).
[11] *Hamdan*, above n 9, 2798.

to failure. The very act of regulation contradicts the concept of the black hole, and opens the US government up to scrutiny on the basis of standards that are not of the executive's making. In the latest of the Guantánamo detainees' victories against the US government, the US Court of Appeals (DC Circuit) held that in order for the courts to fulfil their role in 'determining the validity' of a Combatant Status Review Tribunal's determination under the *Detainee Treatment Act 2005* (USA),

> the court must be able to view the Government Information with the aid of counsel for both parties; [and] a detainee's counsel who has seen only the subset of the Government Information presented to the Tribunal is in no position to aid the court. There is simply no other way for the counsel to present an argument that the Recorder withheld exculpatory evidence from the Tribunal in violation of the specified procedures.[12]

The US government has, however, attempted to keep at bay what is perhaps the most fundamental question concerning US courts' jurisdiction — the constitutional right of detainees to petition the court for *habeas corpus* — using the device of 'jurisdiction stripping'[13] (or what Australians call a 'privative clause'). The first round of jurisdiction-stripping came in the wake of *Hamdi*[14] and *Rasul v Bush*,[15] in which the Supreme Court held that the statutory right to claim *habeas corpus* applied to the Guantánamo detainees. The *Detainee Treatment Act 2005* attempted to remove the right to claim *habeas corpus* retrospectively. However, in *Hamdan*,[16] the Supreme Court found, on the basis of ordinary principles of statutory construction, that the courts had not been deprived of their jurisdiction. The question of whether Congress could achieve its aim with a clearer statute was left open. Subsequently, the *Military Commissions Act 2006* (USA) was enacted, and its privative clause has so far been upheld, both as in accordance with principles of statutory interpretation and as constitutional by the US Court of Appeals (DC Circuit).[17]

---

[12] *Bismullah v Gates*, 501 F.3d 178, 196 (D.C. Cir. 2007), 2007 WL 2067938, 6. It should also be noted that in two cases, the Military Commissions have refused to proceed with cases on the basis that the Combatant Status Review Tribunals had not determined that the detainees concerned were enemy alien combatants as required for the purposes of the *Military Commissions Act 2006* (US), only that they were enemy combatants. See *United States of America v Omar Ahmed Khadr*, 4 June 2007 <http://www.nimj.com/documents/Khadr%20Order%20on%20Jurisdiction.pdf>, and *United States of America v Salim Ahmed Hamdan*, 4 June 2007.

[13] See generally G Shay and J Kalb, 'More Stories of Jurisdiction-Stripping and Executive Power: Interpreting the Prison Litigation Reform Act (PLRA)' (2007) (29)(1) *Cardozo Law Review* 291.

[14] Above n 8.

[15] *Rasul v Bush*, 542 U.S. 466 (2004).

[16] Above n 9.

[17] *Boumedienne v Bush*, 476 F 3d 981 (DC Cir 2007). Interestingly, in *Boumedienne v Bush*, the D C Circuit disagreed with the Supreme Court's reading of the common law right to *habeas corpus* in *Rasul*, holding that under the common law in 1789 (when the US Constitution came into force), *habeas corpus* 'would not have been available to aliens ... without presence or property within the United States.' *Boumedienne*, ibid 990. It will be interesting to see whether the Supreme Court continues to follow its own reading

## B. Exposing the Black Hole to the Light of Human Rights: the US Confronts the UN Human Rights System

The US has also sought to rely on the black hole conceit at the international level. In its dealings with the UN Human Rights system, the US has denied that the human rights treaties to which it is party apply in Guantánamo. The US relies on the fact that Guantánamo is not fully 'sovereign' US territory (as opposed to being completely within US jurisdiction). The US has also relied on strained readings of the terms of the treaties as well as US reservations to them. The report by five of the UN Commission on Human Rights mandate-holders[18] and the official US response[19] provides us with a good illustration of the US's argumentative strategy.

In their report, the five mandate-holders made several damning conclusions. First, they concluded that the detention is, or rather the *detentions* are, governed by general international human rights law, despite the US's insistence that they are governed solely by the law of armed conflict. From this starting point, they went on to find that the detentions and military commissions are in breach of Article 9 of the *International Covenant on Civil and Political Rights* (ICCPR) — the right to liberty — as well as Article 14 which guarantees the right to a fair trial.[20]

The finding that general human rights law governs the situation is made after the mandate-holders draw attention to several important factual variations in the detention of particular detainees. These concern:

1. The context in which persons were initially detained — whether on the battle-field in Afghanistan or, rather, off the battle-field in a distinctly civilian context as in the case of six Algerians arrested in Bosnia-Herzegovina (a factor which was also important to the Supreme Court in *Hamdan* when it found the military commissions to be invalidly constituted);[21]
2. The purpose for which the persons are detained — whether they are 'combatants' detained for the duration of the armed conflict or persons

---

once Justice Roberts (formerly of the D C Circuit Court) is able to sit. Justice Roberts abstained from the decision in *Hamdan* because he had ruled on the decision of the DC Circuit Court which was being appealed. See *Hamdan v Rumsfeld*, 415 F 3d 33 (DC Cir 2005).

[18] 'Situation of detainees at Guantánamo Bay', Report of the Chairperson of the Working Group on Arbitrary Detention, Ms Leila Zerrougui; the Special Rapporteur on the independence of judges and lawyers, Mr Leandro Despouy; the Special Rapporteur on torture and other cruel, inhuman or degrading treatment or punishment, Mr Manfred Nowak; the Special Rapporteur on freedom of religion or belief, Ms Asma Jahangir and the Special Rapporteur on the right of everyone to the enjoyment of the highest attainable standard of physical and mental health, Mr Paul Hunt, 15 February 2006, UN Doc E/CN.4/2006/120 ('the five mandate-holders' report').

[19] Letter dated 31 January 2006, addressed to the Office of the High Commissioner for Human Rights, by the Permanent Representative of the United States of America to the United Nations and Other International Organizations in Geneva, ibid, Annex 2, 43-4.

[20] Above n 18, [84] and [85].

[21] Above n 9, (Stevens J), 2777-8.

detained for criminal prosecution as a result of activities that took place during such conflict, or, by contrast, persons detained for the illegitimate purpose of intelligence-gathering; and

3. The prevailing context of the detentions, namely whether the United States was or continued to be currently engaged in an international armed conflict between two parties to the Third and Fourth Geneva Conventions.[22]

The mandate-holders said that the US was not, at the time of their investigation, engaged in an international armed conflict.[23] Accordingly, it was not permissible for the US to read down the guarantees associated with the protection against arbitrary detention in Article 9 of the ICCPR so that they cohere with the *lex specialis* prevailing during a time of international armed conflict.[24] The mandate-holders noted that the US is a party to the ICCPR and that Article 2 of the ICCPR applies to persons within the effective control of the state party, whether or not they are within the physical territory of the state party.[25]

The US response to this finding was as follows:

> The United States ... is engaged in a continuing armed conflict against Al Qaida ... the law of war applies to the conduct of that war and ... related detention operations, and ... the International Covenant on Civil and Political Rights, by its express terms, applies only to "individuals within its territory and subject to its jurisdiction." ... The Report's legal analysis rests on [a] flawed position ... [which] leads to a manifestly absurd result; that is, during an ongoing armed conflict, unlawful combatants receive more procedural rights than would lawful combatants under the Geneva Conventions.[26]

There are several problems with this response. The main one lies in the US argument that the global 'war on terror' is an armed conflict, rather than a struggle against various groups committing criminal acts. It is to be expected that all persons receive more procedural rights than lawful combatants under the Geneva Conventions when there is no armed conflict. On the other hand, the Supreme Court accepted that Hamdan had been detained during the course of a non-international armed conflict in Afghanistan, in which case some of the laws of war are applicable.[27] However, the Supreme Court did acknowledge

---

[22] *Geneva Convention relative to the Treatment of Prisoners of War*, above n 10 ('Third Geneva Convention'); *Geneva Convention relative to the Protection of Civilian Persons in Time of War*, 75 UNTS 287 (entered into force 21 October 1950) ('Fourth Geneva Convention').

[23] Above n 18, [24]. The US Supreme Court found that common art 3 of the Geneva Conventions was applicable precisely because the conflict between Al Qa'ida and the US should be considered a 'conflict not of an international character' ie, one that does not involve conflict between two states. Above n 9, (Stevens J), 2796.

[24] Above n 18, [24].

[25] Ibid [11].

[26] Above n 19, 54.

[27] Above n 9, (Stevens J), 2796.

problems with using military commissions with respect to particular detainees where they had not been detained within the theatre of war and when the charges against them did not relate to well-established war crimes.[28] The report of the mandate-holders and the decision of the Supreme Court in *Hamdan* both demonstrate that while there may be some aspects of the 'war on terror' that really do involve armed conflict and require the invocation of the laws of war, the attempt to categorise every governmental action against every detainee as part of a 'war' is ridiculous.

As for the distinction between unlawful combatants and lawful combatants — terminology that is not contained in any international instrument dealing with international humanitarian law — that distinction means that those designated as unlawful combatants forfeit possible status as prisoners of war. However, this does not leave them in a rights vacuum. They cannot be tortured, they are still entitled to a fair trial and they may not be arbitrarily detained.[29] There are fundamental linkages between these three aspects of the detainees' treatment in Guantánamo Bay as it is clear that the prolonged detention and other forms of ill-treatment occurring there will impact on any prospect of a fair trial at the end of the day.

Finally, the interpretation adopted by the Human Rights Committee in relation to the language of Article 2 of the ICCPR,[30] upon which the five mandate-holders draw, is preferable to that adopted by the US. Article 2 requires a state party 'to respect and to ensure to all individuals within its territory and subject to its jurisdiction the rights recognized in the present Covenant.' The word 'and' in Article 2 is read disjunctively, rather than as imposing cumulative prerequisites for legal responsibility. The Committee has recently pointedly reaffirmed its interpretation in its concluding observations on the US periodic report under

---

[28] Above n 9, (Stevens J), 2777-8 (relating to when and where persons were apprehended); 2779-86 (concerning the need for a well-established war crime).

[29] The prohibition on torture is a well-accepted norm of *jus cogens*. According to the Human Rights Committee, the rights to a fair trial and the prohibition on arbitrary detention, while not listed as non-derogable rights in art 4 of the ICCPR, are also *jus cogens* and may never be derogated from. Human Rights Committee, General Comment No 29, UN Doc CCPR/C/21/Rev.1/Add.11, 31 August 2001. Even a more cautious reading of *jus cogens* norms to include *prolonged*, arbitrary detention would pose a challenge to the detentions at Guantánamo Bay. Academic writing has also pointed out that it doesn't matter what labels are used, some model of rights will still be applicable. Tom Farer points out that the military commissions model shares many of the same fair trial deficits of the military trials for civilians conducted in Latin America when he was a member of the Inter-American Commission on Human Rights. T J Farer, 'The Two Faces of Terror' (2007) 101 *American Journal of International Law* 363. Tom Franck, who appears to accept that new norms may be required for the post-September 11 world still requires that a minimum rule of law model has to apply. T M Franck, 'Criminals, Combatants, or What? An Examination of the Role of Law in Responding to the Threat of Terror' (2004) 98 *American Journal of International Law* 686. See also the point that the rights of 'protected civilians' may be applicable in L Vierucci, 'Prisoners of War or Protected Persons qua Unlawful Combatants? The Judicial Safeguards to which Guantanamo Bay Detainees are entitled' (2003) 1 *Journal of International Criminal Justice* 284.

[30] Human Rights Committee, General Comment No 31, The Nature of the General Legal Obligation Imposed on States Parties to the Covenant, CCPR/C/21/Rev.1/Add. 13, [10].

Article 40 of the ICCPR.[31] The Human Rights Committee's reading is one of the alternatives open on the ordinary meaning of the text and it is the one that coheres with the object and purpose of the treaty and the intentions of the framers.[32] The language of Article 2 was designed to avoid responsibility in situations where another sovereign was responsible — for example, in the case of occupying troops.[33] The US, on the other hand, seeks to achieve the opposite (and manifestly absurd) result in relation to Guantánamo Bay, namely to do what it would not be allowed to do on US soil in a geographical region that is technically not part of the US but that is nevertheless subject to its physical and legal jurisdiction as a result of its lease agreement with Cuba.

## C. The Terrorists Unmasked

The mandate-holders made a second very important finding, namely that the US is in violation of the prohibitions on torture enshrined in the *Convention against Torture and Cruel, Inhuman or Degrading Treatment of Punishment* ('Convention against Torture') and the ICCPR. Des Manderson, in this volume,[34] attacks the philosophical basis for arguments that torture may sometimes be justified. In this chapter, I offer a more limited, legal discussion of the issues as they arose in the context of the exchange between the mandate-holders and the US, and in the context of subsequent consideration by the Human Rights Committee of the US' second and third periodic reports under the ICCPR.

There are four main aspects of the treatment of the Guantánamo detainees that raise allegations of torture. They are the interrogation techniques; the overall conditions of detention; excessive force during transportation; and force-feeding of detainees on hunger strike. The five mandate-holders' report found that the conditions of detention,

> in particular the uncertainty about the length of detention and prolonged solitary confinement, amount to inhuman treatment and to a violation of the right to health as well as a violation of the right of detainees under Article 10(1) of the ICCPR to be treated with humanity and with respect for the inherent dignity of the human person.[35]

The excessive violence and force-feeding were found to constitute torture — the latter finding evoking an expression of 'bewilderment' by the US given that

---

[31] Human Rights Committee, Concluding Observations, United States of America, CCPR/C/USA/CO3, 15 September 2006, [10].
[32] This is consistent with the usual rules of treaty interpretation, as codified in art 31 of the *Vienna Convention on the Law of Treaties*, 115 UNTS 331 (entered into force 27 January 1980).
[33] See the discussion in M Nowak, *UN Covenant on Civil and Political Rights: CCPR Commentary*, 1st ed, (Strasbourg: NP Engel, 1993) 41-3.
[34] See Chapter 3.
[35] Above n 18, [88].

the purpose of force-feeding is to save lives.[36] Interesting as this aspect of the treatment of detainees is, I will focus on the issue of the interrogation techniques, which have attracted so much attention in the media.

As described by the mandate-holders' report, the interrogation techniques authorised at the time of writing the report were as follows:

- B. Incentive/Removal of Incentive ie, comfort items;
- S. Change of Scenery Down might include exposure to extreme temperatures and deprivation of light and auditory stimuli;
- U. Environmental Manipulation: Altering the environment to create moderate discomfort (eg, adjusting temperature or introducing an unpleasant smell).
- V. Sleep Adjustment; Adjusting the sleeping times of the detainee (eg, reversing sleep cycles from night to day). This technique is not sleep deprivation.
- X. Isolation: Isolating the detainee from other detainees while still complying with basic standards of treatment.[37]

The US has defended these techniques with various arguments, the first of which is a narrow reading of the definition of torture. In a notorious advice from J S Bybee, then Assistant Attorney-General, to Alberto Gonzales, then Counsel advising the President, torture was defined as follows:

> [W]e conclude that torture as defined in and proscribed by Sections 2340-2340A [of title 18 of the United States Code], covers only extreme acts. Severe pain is generally of the kind difficult for the victim to endure. Where the pain is physical, it must be of an intensity akin to that which accompanies serious physical injury such as death or organ failure. Severe mental pain requires suffering not just at the moment of infliction but it also requires lasting psychological harm, such as seen in mental disorders like posttraumatic stress disorder. ... Because the acts inflicting torture are extreme, there is a significant range of acts that though they might constitute cruel, inhuman, or degrading treatment or punishment fail to rise to the level of torture. ... Finally, even if an interrogation method might violate Section 2340A, necessity or self-defense could provide justifications that would eliminate any criminal liability.[38]

---

[36] Above n 19, 53.
[37] 'Counter Resistance Techniques in the War on Terror', Secretary of Defence memorandum for the commander, US Southern command, 16 April 2005, 1, see above n 18, [50].
[38] See Memorandum for Alberto R Gonzales Counsel to the President, from Jay S Bybee, Assistant Attorney-General, US Department of Justice, Re Standards of Conduct for Interrogation under 18 USC, ('Bybee-Gonzales memorandum') in K J Greenberg and J L Dratel, *The Torture Papers: the road to Abu Ghraib* (Cambridge: Cambridge University Press, 2005) 172, 213-4.

The advice makes clear that the relevant sections of the US Code are designed to implement the US' reservations and understandings to the ICCPR and CAT[39] (the Convention against Torture).[40]

This memorandum has been overtaken by the memorandum from former Acting Assistant Attorney-General, Daniel Levin, to James B Comey, then Deputy Attorney-General.[41] Nevertheless, it seems plain from the US' response to the five mandate-holders' report that the US still seeks to rely on the arguments put forward in the original advice. In its response to the report, the US coyly, cryptically and in my view, largely mischievously, asserted that the mandate-holders,

> have relied on international human rights instruments ... without serious analysis of whether the instruments by their terms apply extraterritorially; whether the United States is a State Party — or has filed reservations or understandings — to the instrument; whether the instrument ... is legally binding or not; or whether the provisions cited have the meaning ascribed to them in the Unedited Report.[42]

The argument concerning extra-territoriality has already been dealt with.[43] The next question is whether the reservations — another kind of 'black hole' — provide an excuse for the US.

The US has entered reservations to Article 7 of the ICCPR and Article 16 of the Convention against Torture stipulating that the US is bound by the provisions concerning cruel, inhuman or degrading treatment or punishment 'only insofar as the term ... means the cruel, unusual and inhumane treatment or punishment prohibited by the Fifth, Eighth, and/or Fourteenth Amendments to the Constitution of the United States.'[44] The US has also entered a 'declaration of understanding' to Article 1 of the Convention against Torture. Article 1 contains the definition of torture. The US 'understanding' is as follows:

> The United States understands that, in order to constitute torture, an act must be specifically intended to inflict severe physical or mental pain or suffering and that mental pain or suffering refers to prolonged mental harm caused by

---

[39] Bybee-Gonzales memorandum, ibid 172 and 183.
[40] *Convention Against Torture and Other Cruel, Inhuman or Degrading Treatment or Punishment* 1465 UNTS 85 (entered into force 26 June 1987).
[41] Memorandum for James B Comey Deputy Attorney-General, from Daniel Levin Acting Assistant Attorney-General, US Department of Justice, Re Legal Standards Applicable Under 18 USC §§ 2340-2340A. The second memorandum specifically replaces the earlier memo in its entirety in response to a request that the earlier memo be rescinded.
[42] Above n 19, 54.
[43] See above n 30 and accompanying text.
[44] See the reservations and declarations in the Multilateral Treaties Deposited with the Secretary-General in the UN Treaty Collection:
<http://untreaty.un.org/ENGLISH/bible/englishinternetbible/partI/chapterIV/treaty6.asp> (ICCPR)
<http://untreaty.un.org/ENGLISH/bible/englishinternetbible/partI/chapterIV/treaty14.asp> (CAT).

or resulting from (1) the intentional infliction or threatened infliction of severe physical pain or suffering; (2) the administration or application, or threatened administration or application, of mind altering substances or other procedures calculated to disrupt profoundly the senses or the personality; (3) the threat of imminent death; or (4) the threat that another person will imminently be subjected to death, severe physical pain or suffering, or the administration or application of mind altering substances or other procedures calculated to disrupt profoundly the senses or personality.[45]

Interestingly, the US did not enter a similar reservation to the ICCPR, which, although it does not define torture, does prohibit it. This raises an arcane question. Given that the Convention against Torture definition is read into Article 7 of the ICCPR, could the US rely on its reservation to the Convention against Torture with respect to its obligations under the ICCPR? The answer has to be no. The Human Rights Committee did not consider such an argument when it expressed concerns about the interrogation techniques in its concluding observations on the US periodic report under Article 40 of the ICCPR.[46] This is undoubtedly because the US is required to enter appropriate reservations to all treaties to which it becomes party if it wishes to narrow its obligations.

In any event, I doubt that the reservation or the understanding is helpful to the US. To begin with there is the question of validity. The mandate-holders note the view taken by the Human Rights Committee that the reservation to the ICCPR is invalid.[47] Of course the decision by the Human Rights Committee that it has the power of determination in relation to reservations and may therefore sever the reservation[48] is controversial. However, if it is accepted that, as the mandate-holders say, the prohibition on torture is a norm of *jus cogens*, then it

---

[45] See the US reservations and declarations to the Convention Against Torture, ibid.

[46] Concluding Observations of the Human Rights Committee, UN Doc CCPR/C/USA/CO/3/Rev 1, 18 December 2006, [13].

[47] Above n 18, [45]. In General Comment No 24, the Human Rights Committee states that: 'Reservations that offend peremptory norms would not be compatible with the object and purpose of the Covenant. Although treaties that are mere exchanges of obligations between States allow them to reserve *inter se* application of rules of general international law, it is otherwise in human rights treaties, which are for the benefit of persons within their jurisdiction. Accordingly, provisions in the Covenant that represent customary international law (and *a fortiori* when they have the character of peremptory norms) may not be the subject of reservations. Accordingly, a State may not reserve the right to engage in slavery, to torture, to subject persons to cruel, inhuman or degrading treatment or punishment, to arbitrarily deprive persons of their lives, to arbitrarily arrest and detain persons, to deny freedom of thought, conscience and religion, to presume a person guilty unless he proves his innocence, to execute pregnant women or children, to permit the advocacy of national, racial or religious hatred, to deny to persons of marriageable age the right to marry, or to deny to minorities the right to enjoy their own culture, profess their own religion, or use their own language. And while reservations to particular clauses of article 14 may be acceptable, a general reservation to the right to a fair trial would not be.' Human Rights Committee, General Comment No 24, Issues relating to reservations made upon ratification or accession to the Covenant or the Optional Protocols thereto, or in relation to declarations under art 41 of the Covenant, UN Doc CCPR/C/21/Rev.1/Add.6, 11 April, 1994.

[48] General Comment No 24, ibid [18].

is arguable that no reservations to the definition of torture are permitted. The International Law Commission's work on reservations to treaties has avoided drawing this conclusion owing to the theoretical debate between those who think certain reservations are simply impermissible and invalid and those who think that the key issue is acceptance or rejection of reservations by other states (the question of 'opposability' of reservations to other states). However, the ILC has provisionally adopted a guideline which states that '[a] reservation cannot exclude or modify the legal effect of a treaty in a manner contrary to a peremptory norm of general international law'.[49] In other words, the US reservations cannot have the effect of permitting the US to practise torture on the basis of a definition of torture that does not accord with the internationally accepted definition. It should also be said that the norm prohibiting torture binds the United States as a matter of customary international law, regardless of the impact of reservations to treaties.[50]

These propositions also stand true for the 'understanding' that might well be a disguised reservation,[51] and which, in any event, could only provide an acceptable interpretation of the treaty if it was consistent with the broader international community's interpretation of torture. This, however, is not the case. In its concluding observations concerning the US' initial report, the Committee against Torture expressed its concern about the US' 'failure to enact a federal crime of torture in terms consistent with article 1 of the Convention', and '[t]he reservation lodged to article 16, in violation of the Convention, the effect of which is to limit the application of the Convention'.[52] The Committee recommended that the US 'withdraw its reservations, interpretations and understandings relating to the Convention'.[53] More recently, in its concluding observations on the US' second report, the Committee reiterated this recommendation as well as making the following, very specific one:

> The State party should ensure that acts of psychological torture, prohibited by the Convention, are not limited to 'prolonged mental harm' as set out in the State party's understandings lodged at the time of ratification of the Convention, but constitute a wider category of acts, which cause severe mental suffering, irrespective of their prolongation or its duration.[54]

---

[49] See Guideline 3.1.9. Reservations contrary to a rule of *jus cogens*. International Law Commission, Report on the Work of its Fifty-Ninth Session, UN Doc. A/62/10, 2007, chapter IV, 65. For the explanation for the compromise, see the commentary to the guideline, ibid 99-104.

[50] In my view, a norm of *jus cogens* must, by definition, form part of customary or general international law. The test for a norm of *jus cogens* set out in art 53 of the Vienna Convention on the Law of Treaties speaks of its acceptance by the international community as a whole.

[51] It is accepted that an understanding that attempts to alter the sense of treaty words is in fact a reservation: *Belilos v Switzerland* (10328183) [1988] ECHR 4 (29 April 1988).

[52] Report of the Committee against Torture, UN GAOR Supp. No 44 (A/55/44) (2000), [175][180], [179].

[53] Ibid [180].

[54] Concluding Observations of the Committee against Torture, UN Doc. CAT/C/USA/CO/2, 25 July 2006, [13].

These responses from the Committee against Torture, along with the typically few, but principled objections to the US' reservations and understandings by other states parties,[55] show that the US' right to make the reservations and understandings in question is not accepted.

Having dismissed the contentions concerning extra-territoriality and reservations, the remaining arguments are the definitional question and the argument concerning necessity, which appears as an afterthought in case the definitional arguments are unsustainable and it is necessary to contend that 'anything goes' in wartime. The argument based on necessity should be put to rest first. Simon Bronitt's chapter in this volume[56] refutes the necessity argument on the basis that 'balancing' is an inappropriate framework for dealing with terrorism and human rights, given that its effect is to trade away human rights in the name of 'security'. Similarly, Manderson in Chapter 3 this volume, puts paid to the idea that torture — a consciously manipulative process that seeks to gain a particular end and is used by the *state* — could ever be viewed as an act of self-defence. Action in self-defence is an immediate response by a person directly under threat. Moreover, it should be noted that although the Bybee-Gonzales memo is discussing domestic US law, as a matter of international law, the US' contention is also unsound. It has already been shown that the laws of war do not oust general human rights law, so any argument concerning 'military necessity' as part of the laws of war may rest on a shaky foundation. The fact that torture is prohibited by the laws of war and is a war crime[57] makes a nonsense of any such argument in any event. It is also highly questionable whether one can mount a case based on a more general defence of necessity that lies outside the parameters of the exceptions established by the governing human rights instruments. As noted by the International Court of Justice in the opinion on the *Legal Consequences of the Construction of a Wall in the Occupied Palestinian Territory*, '[s]ince those treaties already address considerations of this kind within their own provisions, it might be asked whether a state of necessity as recognized in customary international law could be invoked with regard to those treaties as a ground for precluding the wrongfulness of the measures or decisions being

---

[55] Of the three objections received, two noted that the understanding had no effect. Only three states lodged objections to the US' reservations and understandings: Finland, the Netherlands and Sweden. The Netherlands stated that '[t]he Government of the Kingdom of the Netherlands considers the following understandings to have no impact on the obligations of the United States of America under the Convention: II.1 a [the understanding concerning the definition in Article 1 of the Convention] [t]his understanding appears to restrict the scope of the definition of torture under article 1 of the Convention.' Sweden stated that '[i]t is the view of the Government of Sweden that the understandings expressed by the United States of America do not relieve the United States of America as a party to the Convention from the responsibility to fulfil the obligations undertaken therein.'

[56] See Chapter 5.

[57] Common art 3 of the *Geneva Conventions* prohibits torture. Torture is also defined as one of the 'grave breaches' that can result in prosecutions. See, eg, art 130 of the Third Geneva Convention, above n 10.

challenged.'[58] In any event, as the prohibition on torture is a norm of *jus cogens*, no derogation is permitted on any basis whatsoever.

All that is left, then, is the definitional question. Article 1 of the Convention against Torture defines torture as an act that inflicts 'severe pain or suffering, whether physical or mental'.[59] It also requires participation or acquiescence of a public official and the pain has to be inflicted for particular purposes, such as gaining a confession from a person. The Bybee-Gonzales memo imposes additional requirements to the international definition of torture that do not comport with the ordinary meaning of the words of the Convention, read in the light of their context and the object and purpose of the Convention.[60] Internationally, the weight of opinion is against the US. The report of the five mandate-holders concluded that some of the techniques, particularly if used simultaneously, amount to torture.[61]

Having dismissed all the US' legal arguments, a more intriguing question arises. The true puzzle is not whether or not the interrogation techniques constitute torture. Rather, it is why, given that they clearly constitute cruel, inhuman or degrading treatment in any event[62] and the Human Rights Committee and the Committee against Torture have both indicated that this is the case,[63] the US seeks to utilise such techniques. Evidence gained from torture is unreliable, and those who have argued to the contrary have met with sound rebuttals.[64] Do US officials think that the evidence gained from cruel, inhuman or degrading

---

[58] *Legal Consequences of the Construction of a Wall in the Occupied Palestinian Territory*, International Court of Justice, 9 July 2004, [2004] ICJ Rep 136, [140]. The Court did not have to decide the question given that it held that the construction of the wall was not the 'only means to safeguard the interests of Israel against the peril which it has invoked as justification for that construction': ibid.

[59] Above n 40.

[60] This reading is required by the ordinary rules of treaty interpretation under art 31 of the *Vienna Convention on the Law of Treaties* above, n 32. For a critique of the ethics of the memo see R B Bilder and D F Vagts, 'Speaking Law to Power: Lawyers and Torture' (2004) 98 *American Journal of International Law* 689.

[61] Above n 18, [87]. The mandate-holders' conclusion was based, among other things, on the interviews with former detainees undertaken by the Special Rapporteur on Torture, which yielded the information that detainees perceived the techniques to cause severe suffering: ibid [52]. The remaining elements of the prohibition on torture are clearly met, as stated in the report, ibid [51]. We should note here that the US did not want any interviews to take place. Three of the mandate-holders were offered a one-day visit to Guantánamo Bay by the US government. However, the visit was to be subject to the proviso that no private interviews could be carried out with detainees. The offer was therefore refused as being inconsistent with the work of the special procedures of the UN Commission on Human Rights and interviews were undertaken with former detainees instead. Yet the US castigated the mandate-holders for not basing their conclusions 'clearly in the facts': ibid 53.

[62] See generally M E O'Connell, 'Affirming the Ban on Harsh Interrogation' (2005) 66 *Ohio State Law Journal* 1231.

[63] See the Concluding Observations of the Human Rights Committee, UN Doc. CCPR/C/USA/CO/3/Rev 1, 18 December 2006, [13], and the Concluding Observations of the Committee against Torture, n 54 above, [13], [19], [22], [24].

[64] See, eg, the rejoinder to the arguments in favour of torture put by Mirko Bagaric and Julie Clarke in P N S Rumney, 'Is Coercive Interrogation of Terrorist Suspects Effective? A response to Bagaric and Clarke' (2006) 40 *University of San Francisco Law Review* 479.

treatment or punishment is reliable? If not, are the detention and interrogation themselves a form of punishment of the individuals concerned? This is really what torture is about — the transformation of a person, the very self, with that person's body used as a means to effect this transformation.[65] As the Secretary-General of the UN has noted, torture is a form of terror.[66] The black hole has swallowed its creators.

## III. A Black Hole or a White Hole: Does Belmarsh Prison have Only Three Walls?

In December 2004, the House of Lords handed down its decision in *A and Others v Secretary of State for the Home Department, X and another v Secretary of State for the Home Department*.[67] The case concerned foreign terror suspects detained in Belmarsh prison. As is well-known, the Court determined that the detention was discriminatory and disproportionate as nationals suspected of terrorism were not also detained.[68]

As a result, the relevant provisions of the *Anti-Terrorism, Crime and Security Act 2001* (UK) were repealed — demonstrating that the declarations of incompatibility that the judiciary are empowered to issue under the *Human Rights Act 1998* (UK)[69] are not toothless. 'Control orders' that impose severe restrictions and that are applicable to all nationals were instituted instead,[70] however. Thus, along with Chris Michaelsen, Chapter 7 in this volume, we may ask whether the Court should have gone further in its decision and questioned the characterisation of the terrorist threat as an emergency that permits such intrusions. In doing so, we note that, as Colm O'Cinneide, Chapter 15 this volume relates, control orders have also been subjected to searching review by the courts. The present chapter looks at the way in which detention was characterised in the context of Belmarsh — as a semi-black hole into which only foreigners could fall and from which they could potentially escape, provided they were willing to run the risk of any consequences when they were returned home.

---

[65] See the analysis in R Copelon, 'Intimate Terror: Understanding Domestic Violence as Torture' in R J Cook (ed), *Human Rights of Women* (Pennsylvania: University of Pennsylvania Press, 1994); P Dubois, *Torture and Truth* (New York: Routledge, 1991).
[66] UN Secretary-General, Press Release, 'Torture, Instrument of Terror, Can Never Be Used to Fight Terror', SG/SM/10257 HR/4877 OBV/533, <http://www.un.org/News/Press/docs/2005/sgsm10257.doc.htm>.
[67] *Belmarsh* [2005] 2 AC 68.
[68] Ibid (Lord Bingham) (lead judgment) [68]; (Lord Nicholls) [83]; (Lord Hope) [132]-[139]; (Lord Scott) [155]-[160]; (Lord Rodger) [189]-[190]; (Baroness Hale) [228]-[239]; and (Lord Carswell) [240].
[69] *Human Rights Act 1998* (UK), s 4.
[70] *Prevention of Terrorism Act 2005* (UK), ch 2.

## A. The Belmarsh Detainees: Caught between Liberty and Torture

Detention in Belmarsh prison shared some characteristics with the black hole of Guantánamo, but there were some crucial differences in the way in which the UK tried to justify the detention. The UK's arguments have a decidedly more legal character than the simple and rather rhetorical characterisation by the US of the struggle against terrorism as a 'war'. The UK has attempted to characterise terrorism as a threat to the life of the nation that permits derogation from certain rights.[71] This is, in fact, a questionable characterisation, although Lord Hoffmann was the only judge in the Belmarsh detainees' case willing to take on the executive on this issue.[72] However, it is less extreme than the stand taken by the US.

Moreover, unlike the US, which is determined to hold persons in Guantánamo indefinitely, until such time as the 'war on terror' is over, apparently the UK was and remains keen to get rid of the Belmarsh detainees. Detention was to be indefinite only if the detainees could not be ejected. The obstacle in the path of the UK acting as it wished and deporting foreign suspects, was that the suspects feared they would be tortured upon return. The guarantees against *refoulement* in Article 3 of the Convention against Torture,[73] and implicit in Article 3 of the European Convention on Human Rights[74] and Article 7 of the ICCPR prevented the UK from returning them. And yet, these suspects had no legal right to be in the UK, thus detention was — as the government saw it — the only option, unless the suspects volunteered to return, or the UK was able to rely on diplomatic assurances to the effect that the person would not be tortured. It was argued before the House of Lords that Belmarsh prison had only three walls, since foreigners could purportedly elect to go home, whereas for nationals the prison would most definitely have four walls.[75]

Since the 'choice' for the individuals concerned is really no choice at all, and the diplomatic assurances on which the UK seeks to rely have been said to have

---

[71] Art 4 ICCPR. Note that art 9 is not listed as a non-derogable right, however, the Human Rights Committee has stated that art 9, paras (3) and (4) are also non-derogable as they underpin rights that are listed as non-derogable. 'In order to protect non-derogable rights, the right to take proceedings before a court to enable the court to decide without delay on the lawfulness of detention, must not be diminished by a State party's decision to derogate from the Covenant.' Human Rights Committee, General Comment No 29 above n 29, [16] and fn 9.
[72] *Belmarsh* [2005] 2 AC 68, (Lord Hoffmann), [91]-[97].
[73] Above n 59.
[74] *European Convention for the Protection of Human Rights and Fundamental Freedoms*, 213 UNTS 222 (entered into force 3 September 1953, amended by the various protocols).
[75] *Belmarsh* [2005] 2 AC 68, (Lord Nicholls) [81].

no legal worth[76] (although they have been accepted in some UK decisions),[77] the detention was really just like the black hole of Guantánamo. Taking the space analogy a little further, we might say that the alternative of deportation pursuant to a diplomatic assurance is like a white hole. Unlike the black hole that sucks in all matter, the white hole is never reached as it pushes all matter away.[78] Exit from Belmarsh prison was impossible in many senses. Deportation would often not be effected despite the UK government's best efforts. There is also no real guarantee that torture will not occur. Finally, deportation is ineffective as a tool against terrorism.

On the question of effectiveness, some of the Law Lords (one of them a Lady) commented on the unlikely utility of deportation.[79] As Baroness Hale asked, '[w]hat sense does it make to consider a person such a threat to the life of the nation that he must be locked up without trial, but allow him to leave, as has happened, for France where he was released almost immediately?'[80]

Yet it appears that the UK is hell-bent on pursuing the expulsion of the Belmarsh detainees and others like them. Indeed, the UK is so determined, that one senses a ritual purge is taking place. The state, as in Foucault's description of the scaffold, displays its power,[81] even though the effectiveness of the measure in deterring or preventing future crime is highly questionable.

## B. Great Britain: Caught between Life and Torture?

It is tempting to see the UK as simply reckless as to whether torture will eventuate — that it regards expulsion to a possible place of torture as an appropriate

---

[76] The Special Rapporteur on the question of torture is particularly clear on this point. In his first report to the UN Commission on Human Rights, the Special Rapporteur, Manfred Nowak, gave a summary of his presentation at a meeting of experts discussing possible guidelines for diplomatic assurances. In addition to the fact that the principle of *non-refoulement* is non-derogable, he included the following concern. 'Diplomatic assurances are sought from countries with a proven record of systematic torture, i.e., the very fact that such diplomatic assurances are sought is an acknowledgement that the requested State, in the opinion of the requesting State, is practising torture. In most cases, those individuals in relation to whom diplomatic assurances are being sought belong to a high-risk group ('Islamic fundamentalists').' Further, he says, '[d]iplomatic assurances are not legally binding. It is therefore unclear why States that violate binding obligations under treaty and customary international law should comply with non-binding assurances.' He concludes by saying 'diplomatic assurances with regard to torture are nothing but attempts to circumvent the absolute prohibition on torture and refoulement ...' Report of the Special Rapporteur on the question of torture, Manfred Nowak, E/CN.4/2006/6, [31]-[32].
[77] See the discussion in O'Cinneide's chapter in this volume (Chapter 15).
[78] The author takes no responsibility for accuracy of the scientific explanations underlying the conceits that link the various species of detention examined in this chapter. For a basic description of the science, see <http://www.crystalinks.com/wormholes.html>.
[79] *Belmarsh* [2005] 2 AC 68, (Lord Bingham) [43] approving the appellant's 'central complaint' that 'the choice of an immigration measure to address a security problem had the inevitable result of failing adequately to address that problem' (by allowing non-UK suspected terrorists to leave the country with impunity and leaving British suspected terrorists at large).
[80] Ibid (Baroness Hale), [230].
[81] M Foucault, *Discipline and Punish: the Birth of the Prison* (trans A Sheridan) 48-65 (NY: Pantheon Books, 1977).

punishment. Certainly, the UK's latest attempt to secure its objective suggests that the UK government believes that, given the perceived risk to the UK community, the risk to the individual terror suspect should be downplayed. The UK has led the intervention in the case of *Ramzy v the Netherlands* before the European Court of Human Rights.[82] The intervening governments argue that the Court should read down the absolute prohibition on torture and related *non-refoulement* obligation so that it is no longer absolute, but is consonant with the narrower obligation of *non-refoulement* set out in the *1951 Convention Relating to the Status of Refugees* ('Refugee Convention').[83] The governments point out that *non-refoulement* has been read into Article 3 of the European Convention on Human Rights, whereas the Refugee Convention expressly denies refugee status to persons who act contrary to the principles and the purposes of the UN.[84] (And of course, according to the UN Security Council, terrorism is now considered to be contrary to these principles and purposes.[85]) The intervening governments argue that '[i]n those circumstances, it is difficult to see how those who negotiated and agreed upon both Conventions can have intended that that position under the 1951 Convention should effectively be reversed by interpretation of Article 3 of the Convention.'[86]

This argument is seriously misguided. The submission seeks to pull a dynamic interpretation of provisions that are silent on the question of *refoulement* back to the notion that there are some people 'unworthy' of protection. Article 5 of the Refugee Convention preserves the more extensive rights that refugees may have under other instruments, and international law has moved on since 1951. The Convention against Torture now expressly prohibits *refoulement* to a place of torture, on the basis that notions of worthiness are anathema to human rights law. The older and newer law are not incompatible. It is perfectly consistent with the Refugee Convention to exclude someone from refugee status, but to refuse to return such persons to a place of torture because of a recognition of common humanity. The underlying rationale for each position is actually the same. Refugee status is about avoiding complicity in persecution and it is therefore wrong to give 'safe haven', in the sense of giving a persecutor the particular rights that attend refugee status, or to deny a request for extradition in the case of someone accused of a crime. It is equally necessary to avoid

---

[82] See *Observations of the Governments of Lithuania, Portugal, Slovakia and the United Kingdom Intervening in Application No 25424/05 Ramzy v the Netherlands* (available at the International Commission of Jurists' site <http://www.icj.org/IMG/pdf/UK_observations_Ramzy_case.pdf>).
[83] *Convention Relating to the Status of Refugees*, 606 UNTS 267, (entered into force 22 April 1954).
[84] Art 1F(c) Refugee Convention, ibid.
[85] SC Res 1373, UN Doc S/RES/1373 (2001), [5].
[86] Above n 82, [8]-[9.3].

complicity in the erasure of humanity that torture inflicts.[87] The best solution is to prosecute or extradite for the purposes of a prosecution.[88]

In a further attempt to counter the absolute nature of the prohibition on *refoulement* to a place of torture, the intervening governments make arguments about the standard of proof. They point out that the wording of Article 3 of the Convention against Torture, 'substantial grounds for believing that [a person] would be in danger of being subject to torture,' is open to interpretation, while the standard of proof in a prosecution — beyond reasonable doubt — is high.[89] The governments then argue that they have also to be concerned about the risk to the lives of persons in the community. Thus, it is argued, they need to undertake a balancing act between the rights of citizens and others living in the community, on the one hand, and alien terrorist suspects on the other.[90] In this balancing act, the active duty to protect the right to life of the people in Britain prevails over duties of non-complicity in relation to the prohibition on torture.[91]

This strategy is deeply concerning. Indeed, it may be more concerning than the US' attempt to justify torture by US officials. Essentially, the UK's intervention seeks to subvert the entire philosophy underlying human rights — that rights are universal, indivisible, interdependent and inter-related.

## IV. A Parallel Universe — Preventative Detention Down-Under

It is not surprising that when the country in which the writ of *habeas corpus* was developed attempts to resile from it, its former colonies follow suit. So it is with preventative detention in Australia. The model of preventative detention adopted in this country was based on the UK model under the *Terrorism Act 2000*,[92] and the apparent trigger was the London bombings of 7 July 2005. Nothing had occurred in Australia that would have indicated that the legislation was necessary.

---

[87] See P Mathew, 'Resolution 1373 – a Call to Preempt Asylum Seekers? (or 'Osama the Asylum Seeker')' in J McAdam (ed), *Forced Migration, Human Rights and Security* (Oxford: Hart Publishing 2008) 19, 45-6.
[88] The Convention against Torture is one of the building blocks allowing prosecution to occur, as art 5 establishes a semi-universal jurisdictional basis for prosecution of torturers, and the establishment of the International Criminal Court is perhaps the cap-stone in the architecture of international prosecutions.
[89] Above n 82, [17]-[26].
[90] Ibid [5] as compared with [8].
[91] Ibid [10].
[92] Preventative detention is permitted in the UK under s 41 and sch 8 of the *Terrorism Act 2000* (UK). Section 41(1) provides that '[a] constable may arrest without a warrant a person whom he reasonably suspects to be a terrorist.' This includes persons who have been 'concerned in the commission, *preparation or instigation* of acts of terrorism': s 40(1)(b) [emphasis added]. The initial period of detention under s 41 lasts for 48 hours. After that, detention may be authorised by a 'judicial authority' for up to 28 days. (The original period of seven days was lengthened to 14 by the *Criminal Justice Act 2003* (UK), and then to 28 by the *Terrorism Act 2006* (UK) (see ss 23 and 24)).

In 2005, two anti-terrorism bills were introduced into the Commonwealth Parliament. That legislation sought to introduce preventative detention in cases where it was sought to prevent an imminent terrorist attack or to preserve evidence relating to a recent attack, create a control order regime and update sedition offences, among other things. I will focus here on the provisions concerning preventative detention.

## A. The Legislative Scheme for Preventative Detention Orders

Under division 105 of the *Criminal Code Act*, an initial preventative detention order may be sought for up to 24 hours[93] by a member of the Australian Federal Police (AFP) and made by a senior member of the AFP.[94] If detaining someone in connection with an imminent attack — one that will take place within 14 days[95] — the AFP has to be 'satisfied' that:

a.  there are reasonable grounds to suspect that the subject:
    i.   will engage in a terrorist act; or
    ii.  possesses a thing that is connected with the preparation for, or the engagement of a person in, a terrorist act; or
    iii. has done an act in preparation for, or planning, a terrorist act; and
b.  making the order would substantially assist in preventing a terrorist act occurring; and
c.  detaining the subject for the period for which the person is to be detained under the order is reasonably necessary for the purpose referred to in paragraph (b).[96]

If detaining someone in connection with a recent attack — one that has taken place within the last 28 days[97] — the AFP has to be 'satisfied' that:

a.  a terrorist act has occurred within the last 28 days; and
b.  it is necessary to detain the subject to preserve evidence of, or relating to, the terrorist act; and
c.  detaining the subject for the period for which the person is to be detained under the order is reasonably necessary for the purpose referred to in paragraph (b).[98]

The initial preventative detention order may be extended and further extended, so long as the total period of detention does not exceed 24 hours.[99]

---

[93] *Criminal Code Act 1995* (Cth) ('Criminal Code'), s 105.8(5).
[94] See the definition of issuing authority, Criminal Code s 100.1(1).
[95] Criminal Code s 105.4(5).
[96] Criminal Code s 105.4.
[97] Criminal Code s 105.4(6)(a).
[98] Criminal Code s 105.4(6).
[99] Criminal Code s 105.10.

A continuing preventative detention order[100] may then be issued by a Federal Judge or Magistrate, a State or Territory Supreme Court Judge, a retired Judge, or the President or Deputy President of the Administrative Appeals Tribunal (provided the latter two persons are lawyers)[101] sitting in a personal capacity.[102] The entire period of detention under the initial and continuing preventative detention order is a maximum of 48 hours.[103]

The reason for the short period of time is that this is federal legislation and there is some concern that any longer period of detention could breach the constitutionally embedded separation of powers doctrine.[104] Deprivation of liberty for the purposes of punishment is accepted as a core feature of judicial power and unduly long detention could transform the detention from non-punitive, preventative detention to impermissible punitive detention ordered by the executive. The States and Territories were to enact their own legislation to provide for detention for up to 14 days, effectively taking over from the Commonwealth if it is thought necessary to detain a person for longer than 48 hours.[105]

Under the Commonwealth legislation, there is no court hearing and the proceedings are purposefully *ex parte*. Although the Act spells out that a remedy (which is not defined) may be sought from a federal court,[106] it appears that in many cases there will be no basis upon which the court could order a remedy such as *habeas corpus* because the legislation authorises this sort of administrative detention. The jurisdiction of State and Territory supreme courts is specifically ousted with respect to a Commonwealth preventative detention order while that order is on foot.[107] State and Territory supreme courts may, however, review the Commonwealth order on the same grounds on which review is provided for by the relevant legislation in relation to state orders,[108] once a person has been detained under a state order. Also after the detention pursuant to a Commonwealth order is over, the Administrative Appeals Tribunal may determine that the decision to issue the preventative detention order is void and that compensation should be paid.[109]

---

[100] Criminal Code ss 105.11 and 105.12.
[101] Criminal Code s 105.2.
[102] Criminal Code s 105.18(2).
[103] Criminal Code s 105.12(5).
[104] See speech by the President of the Australian Human Rights and Equal Opportunity Commission, Justice Von Doussa, 'Are We Crossing the Line? Forum on National Security and Human Rights', Canberra 31 October 2005. Section 71 of the *Australian Constitution* entrenches the separation of judicial power.
[105] See, eg, the *Terrorism (Extraordinary Temporary Powers) Act 2006* (ACT).
[106] Criminal Code s 105.51(1).
[107] Criminal Code s 105.51(2).
[108] Criminal Code s 105.52.
[109] Criminal Code s 105.51(5).

Quite apart from issues of jurisdiction, it may prove difficult for any detainee to bring proceedings given the problems in securing adequate reasons concerning the order. The detainee must be informed about 'the fact that the preventative detention order has been made in relation to the person',[110] but this does not deal with the reasons for which the order was made. A summary of the grounds on which the order is made must also be supplied,[111] but it is unclear how far this summary might go beyond, say, information that the order was imposed to prevent an imminent attack or to preserve evidence of a past attack. Moreover, some information may not be included if it is 'likely to prejudice national security (within the meaning of the *National Security Information (Criminal and Civil Proceedings) Act 2004* (Cth)).'[112]

## B. Enter the Worm Hole: Is this Executive-controlled Detention Legal?

Having set out the scheme of preventative detention under the Commonwealth legislation, it is now possible to examine whether it is legal under international human rights law. Unlike the jurisprudence of the European Court of Human Rights (which may have led the UK formally to derogate from its obligations under the European Convention in November 2001, although it is notable that the UK has also derogated from its obligations under the ICCPR), preventative detention has received an ambiguous acceptance in the jurisprudence of the Human Rights Committee. In *Lawless v Republic of Ireland*, the European Court of Human Rights clearly stated that it was not permissible to detain a person without intending to bring the person before a court unless the State concerned was derogating from the right to liberty set out in Article 5 of the European Convention on Human Rights.[113] The Human Rights Committee, which has not yet had to consider the precise issue of preventative detention occurring in the context of terrorism in an individual communication,[114] has stated somewhat

---

[110] Criminal Code s 105.28(2)(a).
[111] As soon as practicable after being taken into custody, the detainee must be given a copy of the preventative detention order: Criminal Code s 105.32. The order contains a summary of the grounds on which it is given: see in relation to initial preventative detention orders, s 105.8(6)(c); in relation to continuing preventative detention orders, s 105.12(6)(d).
[112] Criminal Code s 105.8(6A) (initial preventative detention orders); s 105.12(6A) (continuing preventative detention orders).
[113] '[T]he said clause [art. 5(c)] permits deprivation of liberty only when such deprivation is effected for the purpose of bringing the person arrested or detained before the competent judicial authority, irrespective of whether such person is a person who is reasonably suspected of having committed an offence, or a person whom it reasonably considered necessary to restrain from committing an offence, or a person whom it reasonably considered necessary to restrain from absconding after having committed an offence.' *Lawless v Republic of Ireland* (No 3), [1961] ECHR 2 (1 July 1961), [14].
[114] Preventative detention has been endorsed in the quite different case of convicted sex offenders where the period of detention had been extended owing to the likelihood of the prisoner re-offending: See *Rameka v New Zealand*, CCPR/C/79/D/1090/2002.

cryptically in General Comment Number 8 that if preventative detention is imposed, it must comply with the provisions set out in Article 9 of the ICCPR.[115]

Under Article 9, three requirements must be met. First, the detention must not be arbitrary (art 9(1)). Second, arrested persons must be informed of the reasons for arrest (art 9(2)). Third, proceedings may be taken before a court in order that the court may decide 'without delay' on the lawfulness of the detention (art 9(4)) — lawfulness, according to the jurisprudence of the Committee, meaning that the courts may determine whether or not the detention is arbitrary as a matter of *international* law.[116]

It may not be surprising that this apparent legal loophole has been exploited so assiduously, when we consider that Mr Philip Ruddock has until recently been Attorney-General. As Minister for Immigration, Mr Ruddock proved a past master at exploiting the many frustrating silences in the Refugee Convention. However, the Howard government may have misread the relevant international law and placed the bar too low. In relation to Commonwealth preventative detention orders, it appears that there is *no* meaningful court control as required by Article 9(4) of the ICCPR. Apparently, it is thought that the duration of the detention is so short that meaningful judicial control is not necessary, or that a (most probably) post hoc remedy for detention that is wrongful under Australian law is all that is required. After all, the rule of thumb for bringing an ordinary criminal suspect before a judge appears to be around 48 hours. In the context of pre-trial detention, the Human Rights Committee has suggested guidelines of a couple of days in relation to bringing someone 'promptly' before a court for the purposes of Article 9(3) (which is specific to criminal cases), while a few weeks has been suggested as a guideline for a 'decision without delay' by a court for the purposes of Article 9(4).[117]

But, if this is what the Commonwealth seeks to rely on, then the Howard government took the outer limits of what is *permissible* (giving governments some leeway) and effectively made it *impermissible*, or at least virtually meaningless, for a person to complain within that period. Therefore, even if we view General Comment 8 as endorsing the idea of preventative detention, it may be that Parliament has failed to enact a scheme that would satisfy the requirements of Article 9 of the ICCPR because it has effectively created a parallel universe of detention — one that is almost entirely within executive control.

---

[115] For the text of General Comment No 9, see <http://www2.ohchr.org/english/bodies/hrc/comments.htm>.
[116] *A v Australia*, UN Doc. CCPR/C/59/D/560/1993, [9.5].
[117] See the discussion of the Human Rights Committee's jurisprudence in M Nowak, *UN Covenant on Civil and Political Rights* (1st ed, 1993) 176, 179. See also S Joseph, J Schultz and M Castan, *The International Covenant on Civil and Political Rights, Cases and Commentary* (2nd ed, 2004) 325.

In any event, the idea that the presumption of liberty enshrined in Article 9(3) has been overturned when it is not contemplated that a full and fair trial will follow, on the basis there will be some remedy if, in fact, the executive got it wrong, should be at least mildly discomforting. An executive-controlled power to detain even for very short periods may be enough to terrorise those persons who experience it.

Australia's legislation underscores the fundamentally problematic nature of preventative detention highlighted by the European Court of Human Rights in *Lawless*. In *Lawless*, the Court concluded that its interpretation — that detention could only be *for the purposes of bringing someone before a judge*, unless the state concerned was derogating from the right to liberty — had to be correct. It warned of the consequences of the alternative interpretation:

> anyone suspected of harbouring an intent to commit an offence could be arrested and detained for an unlimited period on the strength merely of an executive decision without its [sic] being possible to regard his arrest or detention as a breach of the Convention; whereas such an assumption, with all its implications of arbitrary power, would lead to conclusions repugnant to the fundamental principles of the Convention.[118]

Moreover, while the Human Rights Committee's general comment seems to permit preventative detention to some degree, the Committee has also said that it is not possible simply to escape the protections due in ordinary criminal and civil proceedings pursuant to Article 14 of the ICCPR. Article 14(1) states that:

> All persons shall be equal before the courts and tribunals. In the determination of any criminal charge against him, or of his rights and obligations in a suit at law, everyone shall be entitled to a fair and public hearing by a competent, independent and impartial tribunal established by law.

The Committee's 'concluding observations' in relation to India's third periodic report under the ICCPR with respect to India's use of preventative detention in connection with national security are instructive:[119]

> 24. ... The Committee is ... of the view that preventive detention is a restriction of liberty imposed as a response to the conduct of the individual concerned, that the decision as to continued detention must be considered as a determination falling within the meaning of article 14, paragraph 1, of the Covenant, and that proceedings to decide the continuation of detention must, therefore, comply with that provision. Therefore:

---

[118] *Lawless Case*, above n 113. For similar analysis, see J Fitzpatrick, *Human Rights in Crisis: the International System for Protecting Rights During States of Emergency* (Philadelphia: University of Pennsylvania Press, 1994) 38.

[119] It should be said that the periods of detention in India were often very lengthy indeed.

> ... *The question of continued detention should be determined by an independent and impartial tribunal* constituted and operating in accordance with article 14, paragraph 1, of the Covenant. [emphasis added][120]

In the attempt to avoid judicial scrutiny, the detention regime in Australia shares some similarity with the black hole of Guantánamo Bay. One of the Constitutional heads of power upon which the Commonwealth has relied in order to defend the enactment of the legislation that introduced preventative detention orders is the defence power (s 51(vi) *Australian Constitution*). A majority of the High Court has accepted that characterisation in a case concerning a challenge to the provisions relating to control orders.[121] Only Justice Kirby dissented on that point,[122] expressing the view that,

> [a]s drafted, Div 104 proceeds outside the proper concerns of s 51(vi) and into areas of ordinary civil government.[123]

However, it appears that the Australian government views preventative detention orders as consistent with the right to liberty protected by Article 9 ICCPR, and unlike the UK, it certainly has not sought to derogate from its obligations under Article 9. Perhaps, then, rather than being a black hole, a more appropriate comparison is that preventative detention in Australia is like a 'worm hole'. A worm hole is a short cut through time and space. Just as a worm eats its way through the apple from one point to another, instead of wriggling across the apple's surface, it is sometimes suggested that a worm hole may allow us to travel from one parallel universe to another. The Australian legislation is rather like a worm hole as it seeks to place detainees quickly and temporarily into a parallel universe of executive detention that is almost entirely free of judicial scrutiny. And, like the worm hole, *legal* preventative detention may not exist. At least, the detention may not be legal if there is no possibility of meaningful court control, even, perhaps, if this is for only a brief period of time as under the Commonwealth legislation.[124]

The existence or adequacy of court control of the Commonwealth order is not the only point at which Australia may fail to comply with Article 9 of the ICCPR. The question of court control intersects with questions as to whether arbitrary detention could result in any particular case from the AFP being 'satisfied' that

---

[120] UN Doc CCPR A/52/40 (1997) at [439].
[121] *Thomas v Mowbray* [2007] HCA 33 (2 August 2007), (Gleeson CJ) [6]; (Gummow and Crennan JJ), [132]-[148]; (Hayne J) [444]; (Callinan J) [582]-[589]; (Heydon J) [611]-[649].
[122] Justice Hayne dissented but not on the grounds relating to the defence power.
[123] *Thomas v Mowbray*, [2007] HCA33 (2 August 2007), (Kirby J) [264].
[124] These concerns would be magnified had the States and Territories essentially tracked the Commonwealth model for the lengthier period of 14 days' detention, however, most of them have written in some form of court control. In the ACT, for example, the Supreme Court must issue an order. In the Northern Territory, although an issuing authority is a judge sitting in a personal capacity, there is provision for review of the order by the Supreme Court. Queensland's model is probably closest to the Commonwealth model, although it does provide for the involvement of the Public Interest Monitor.

there are 'reasonable grounds to suspect' that the prerequisites for the detention are present. The thresholds for detention are low.[125] I think it is arguable that detention pursuant to the provisions concerning preservation of evidence will almost by definition be arbitrary. And while some element of proportionality has been incorporated, there is no explicit consideration as to whether there are less restrictive measures that may be imposed.[126] The existence of remedies against wrongful detention under *Australian* law is not an adequate safeguard from detention that is arbitrary as a matter of international law. It is also worth reiterating the point that the short duration of the detention does not assuage the concern that the presumption of liberty has been displaced and on so *slim* a basis.

Finally, there are the questions about the timing and quality of the reasons given to the detainee.[127] The Human Rights Committee has specifically dealt with the situation where the only information given to the detainee was that a person was arrested 'under prompt security measures without any indication of the substance' and the Committee determined that Article 9(2) was violated.[128] The Australian model appears to go beyond this, but it may be questionable how much information detainees receive. So there are many points at which a human rights lawyer should be critical of the legislation.

## C. Liberty *or* Security of the Person?

As in the US and the UK, there has been an attempt to shift thinking concerning human rights in Australia.[129] The former Australian Attorney-General sought to justify all anti-terrorism legislation with the language of human security. In a speech delivered at the Australian National University, he said:

> there is growing support for the view that national security and human rights are not mutually exclusive. This analysis is based on the concept of human security and it builds upon Article 3 of the Universal Declaration of Human Rights which states that 'everyone has the right to life, liberty and security of person'. In broad terms, 'human security' argues that people will only be able to reach their full potential if they live in a secure environment where their fundamental human rights can be realised. Based on this premise, there is not a massive dichotomy between security legislation and human rights. Indeed, the extent to which we can continue to enjoy our civil liberties rests upon the effectiveness of our counter-terrorism laws. I am not suggesting that

---

[125] See above n 96 and accompanying text.
[126] The legislation in the ACT incorporates the test that detention must be the 'least restrictive' means. See sub-s 18(4)(c) and 18(6)(c), *Terrorism (Extraordinary Temporary Powers) Act 2006* (ACT).
[127] See above n 111.
[128] *Drescher Caldas v Uruguay*, UN GAOR Supp. No. 40 (A/38/40) at 192 (1983), [13.2].
[129] It should be said that Australians have until fairly recently been 'reluctant' to adopt bills of rights. See H Charlesworth, 'The Australian Reluctance about Rights' (1993) 30 *Osgoode Hall Law Journal* 195.

counter-terrorism legislation should not be scrutinised to ensure that limitations on human rights are minimised. But we must recognise that national security can in fact promote civil liberties by preserving a society in which rights and freedoms can be exercised.[130]

Essentially,[131] the argument posits that in order to secure the right to life or human security for some, the right to liberty of others must be sacrificed. Although the legislation itself is facially neutral, in practice, these others will often be Muslims. The legislation ignores the fact that by creating a sense of insecurity for these Australian citizens and residents, a sense of grievance that provides fertile ground for extremism may well be created or maintained. This misunderstands the idea of human security — it is not a trade whereby a sense of security is created for some (and a false sense at that) by generating real insecurity for others.

That this insecurity is real is demonstrated by the case of Dr Haneef. Mohamed Haneef was arrested at Brisbane airport on 2 July 2007 on the basis of a suspicion that he was involved in the failed car bombings at Glasgow airport. Dr Haneef was not detained under a preventative detention order, but under a different provision allowing the police to hold a person without charge for an extended interrogation. Under s 23CA of the *Crimes Act 1914* (Cth), a recently created provision for terrorist investigations, a person may generally be arrested for investigation for up to four hours.[132] An extension of the period for another 20 hours may be sought under s 23DA of the *Crimes Act*. Dr Haneef was held for 12 days before being charged, as a result of provisions that stop the clock from running when, for example, the detainee is communicating with his or her lawyer or resting.[133] His 'crime' was that he was a cousin of one of the bombers and had lived with this cousin, and he had also 'recklessly' given this cousin his mobile phone SIM card. Originally, it was reported that the card was found in the burnt out car at Glasgow airport, but events subsequently transpired to show that the SIM card was found hundreds of miles away in Liverpool, at the flat which Dr Haneef had shared with his cousin. Eventually charged with providing support for an organisation being reckless as to whether the organisation is a terrorist organisation,[134] Dr Haneef was granted bail, only to have his visa cancelled by then Immigration Minister, Mr Kevin Andrews, on

---

[130] P Ruddock, 'International and Public Law: Challenges for the Attorney-General' (Speech at the Australian National University, Tuesday June 2004).
[131] For a far more nuanced and detailed critique of the Attorney's reading of human security, readers may look to G Carne, 'Reconstituting "Human Security" in a New Security Environment: One Australian, Two Canadians and Article 3 of the Universal Declaration of Human Rights' (2006) 25 *Australian Year Book of International Law* 1. This paper was also presented at the workshop on which this book is based.
[132] In the case of a person who is or appears to be under 18 years of age or who is an Aborigine or Torres Strait Islander, the limit is two hours.
[133] Sub-s 23CA(8).
[134] Criminal Code s 102.7.

the grounds of 'bad character' pursuant to s 501 of the *Migration Act 1958* (Cth). This permitted Dr Haneef to be placed in immigration detention. Ultimately, in a highly embarrassing series of events, the charges were dropped, and Dr Haneef was permitted to leave for India, which he had been trying to reach 24 days earlier, in order to meet his new-born baby girl.[135] In addition, the Federal Court determined that the cancellation of Dr Haneef's visa was invalid.[136]

A little caution may be required when commenting on Dr Haneef's case given that not all of the evidence known by the police is in the public domain. However, one may hope that the Kafka-esque nature of Dr Haneef's ordeal may have alerted the Australian public to the false hierarchy established by the Australian government, in which human rights are actually traded away in the name of a false sense of security. On the other hand, perhaps the silent majority feels the same way as one member of the public who, after watching the tabloid-style television current affairs program '60 Minutes', expressed sympathy with Dr Haneef but opined that it was the 'price we have to pay' if we want to combat terrorism successfully. It is perhaps unnecessary to point out that 'we' are not paying — only Dr Haneef has paid the immediate price — and that the long-term cost to Australians also needs to be considered.

## V. Conclusion

The three countries whose laws and practices have been examined in this chapter exist in a shared universe in which one cosmic event has ramifications for other entities in the universe. The US and the UK have attacked the prohibition on torture which was, until now, thought to be absolute and beyond attack in principle (although the practice never conformed to that principle). The results are sadly evident in the appalling pictures of torture that emanated from Abu Ghraib. Torture becomes routine and it degrades the torturer as well as its victims. Victims become terrorists.

The detention practices of each state attempt by various devices to erect a shield against legal scrutiny. None of these attempts may be successful in the end, with Australia's being, perhaps, the most reasonable — a seemingly plausible attempt to milk the legal ambiguity surrounding the concept of preventative detention. However, each of them is fraught with danger from a human rights perspective.

Perhaps the most dangerous of these developments are those in the UK — in many respects a country that could be seen as the Big Bang of human rights. The intervention in the *Ramzy Case* comes close to a full-frontal attack on the fundamentals of international human rights law, that is, that rights are universal, indivisible, interdependent, and inter-related. The UK's argument may be shown

---

[135] For some of the details concerning the saga, see H Thomas and P Walters, 'Liberty for Haneef', *The Australian* (Sydney), 28 July 2007.
[136] *Haneef v Minister for Immigration and Citizenship* [2007] FCA 1273 (21 August 2007).

to be spurious or misguided, however, in many ways it is fairly honest and perhaps, therefore, when compared with the language of 'war' used by the US, a more formidable argument that could reshape international human rights law.

I hope not. Human rights have long been criticised for their absolute nature and hidden assumptions that are said to belie their purported universalism.[137] I am, in many respects, a fellow-traveller with these critics.[138] Clearly, however, in the case of the 'fight against terrorism', it would be even worse if human rights failed to remain absolutist at this point, transparently bending to the will of the powerful. In the 'fight against terror', the road to hell is paved with 'balanced' arguments.

---

[137] For an example of such criticism in this volume, see Pue, Chapter 4.

[138] Indeed, at a launch of a number of books, including a text for students written by myself and others, my fellow authors and I were challenged by a High Court judge for espousing postmodern views. We had presented a number of critical perspectives on the law, such as feminist perspectives, in order to assist students in criticising laws that entrench an unjust status quo. We did this, because we all heartily wished that more of our teachers had done the same for us. We felt that this would have allowed us the space to be critical of laws that, for example, denied Aboriginal people property rights in the land they had occupied for time immemorial.

# Chapter Ten

# Forgiving Terrorism: Trading Justice for Peace, or Imperiling the Peace?

## Ben Saul[*]

## Introduction

Despite the unflinching public policy of some states never to negotiate with terrorists, realpolitik sometimes forces states to adopt a less strenuous path. Negotiating with terrorists is sometimes thought necessary to peacefully or humanely end particular terrorist incidents. One example is the *Achille Lauro* cruise ship hijacking in 1986, where Egypt and Italy attempted to negotiate an end to the crisis (and save the lives of the hostages), while the United States (US) used military force and declared itself 'completely averse to … any form of negotiation'.[1] In contrast, in 1986, US President Reagan secretly agreed to sell arms to Iran in return for promises to seek the release of US hostages.[2] It is a perennial humanitarian dilemma of governments whether to pay ransom to save hostages,[3] in light of fears that negotiation may encourage others to resort to political violence to secure a seat at the bargaining table. Since 11 September 2001 (9/11), there have been frequent abductions of journalists, humanitarian workers, employees of international reconstruction efforts, and military personnel by terrorist organisations in Afghanistan, Pakistan, Iraq and Palestine, often accompanied by political demands on the hostages' national governments — for example, to withdraw from occupied territories or Muslim lands.

---

[*] Senior Lecturer and Director of the Sydney Centre for International Law, Faculty of Law, University of Sydney, Australia.
[1] A Cassese, *Terrorism, Politics, and Law* (Cambridge: Polity, 1989) 127. See also G Gooding, 'Fighting Terrorism in the 1980s: The Interception of the Achille Lauro Hijackers' (1987) 12 *Yale Journal of International Law* 158. Paradoxically, Abu Abbas, organiser of the Achille Lauro action, was apprehended in Iraq in 2003 and died in US custody in 2004, even though the US had earlier revoked his international arrest warrant, and Israel had granted him immunity from prosecution in 1999: R Tait, 'Hijacking Mastermind Dies in Iraq', *The Guardian* (UK), 10 March 2004; J Risen and D Johnston, ''85 Hijacker is captured in Baghdad', *New York Times* (New York), 16 April 2003.
[2] E McWhinney, *Aerial Piracy and International Terrorism* (Dordrecht, Boston: M Nijhoff, 1987) 171.
[3] See G Sacerdoti, 'States' Agreements with Terrorists in Order to Save Hostages: Non-Binding, Void or Justified by Necessity?' in N Ronzitti (ed), *Maritime Terrorism and International Law* (1990) 25; J Hooper, 'Italians Ready to Pay Ransom for Release of Hostages Held in Iraq', *The Guardian* (UK), 21 April 2004; M Baker and C Banham, 'Arroyo Pulls Out Troops to Save a Life', *Sydney Morning Herald* (Sydney), 15 July 2004; J Miller, 'US Plans to Act More Rigorously in Hostage Cases', *New York Times* (New York), 18 February 2002; J Forero, 'Colombia President Ready for Hostage Talks' *New York Times* (New York), 15 December 2005.

Negotiating with terrorists is also sometimes judged necessary by governments to resolve longstanding terrorist campaigns, beyond specific negotiations to end particular terrorist acts. Three iconic figures — Yasser Arafat (of the Palestine Liberation Organisation), Gerry Adams (of the Irish Republican Army (IRA)) and Nelson Mandela (of the African National Congress) — were at some point arguably responsible for or complicit in 'terrorism' by their organisations. Although there is still no internationally accepted definition of terrorism,[4] the deliberate, instrumental killing of civilians by at least some of the groups represented by these leaders as a means of political struggle counts as terrorism on even the narrowest definitions of the term. While the degree of responsibility of each of these figures differs (particularly in organisations with ostensibly separate political and military wings), it is startling how persons once regarded as terrorists were later embraced as legitimate representatives of political movements, entitled to a share of state power, entry into the world of international diplomacy, and even Nobel Prizes (Arafat in 1994, and Mandela in 1993). All were absolved of, or immunised from criminal responsibility for terrorism, as a necessary condition of full participation in political settlements.

In Northern Ireland, under the 1998 *Good Friday Agreement*, over 500 political prisoners were released by Britain and Ireland by July 2001,[5] while amnesties were conferred for the decommissioning of armaments. Ahead of the IRA's renunciation of armed struggle in July 2005, Britain released the convicted 'Shankill Road bomber', Sean Kelly, although the broader question of amnesties remains controversial,[6] as it does in Spain following a unilateral ceasefire by the Basque separatist group Euskadi Ta Askatasuna in March 2006.[7] In contrast, the leader of the Liberation Tigers of Tamil Eelam (LTTE), Velupillai Prabhakaran, was sentenced to 200 years in prison, *in absentia*, while simultaneously negotiating a Norwegian-brokered peace settlement with the Sri Lankan government.[8] Some foreign governments continue to treat the LTTE as a terrorist organisation,[9] despite its position as a party to a non-international armed conflict under international humanitarian law. Even so, the ceasefire agreement between Sri Lanka and the LTTE suspends search operations and arrests under the

---

[4] See B Saul, *Defining Terrorism in International Law* (Oxford: Oxford University Press, 2006).
[5] UK and Irish Governments, *Good Friday (Belfast) Agreement*, 10 April 1998, 'Prisoners', [1]-[5]; UK and Irish Governments, 'Achievements in Implementation of the Good Friday Agreement', 14 July 2001.
[6] 'IRA's Shankill Bomber Released From Prison', *Sydney Morning Herald* (Sydney), 28 July 2005; J Button, 'Barricades Fall as British Troops Pull Back', *Sydney Morning Herald* (Sydney), 30-31 July 2005, 13; A Chrisafis, 'After 35 Years of Bombs and Blood the IRA Ends its War', *Guardian Weekly* (UK), 5-11 August 2005, 1. Amnesties were included in the 1962 *Evian Agreements* settling the conflict between France and Algeria.
[7] 'Basque Ceasefire Brings Hope to Spain', *Sydney Morning Herald* (Sydney), 24 March 2006.
[8] A Waldman, 'Rebel Leader Sentenced to 200 Years' Jail as Talks Start', *Sydney Morning Herald* (Sydney), 2 November 2002.
[9] 'EU Terrorism Ban Will Shake Peace Process, Warn Rebels', *Sydney Morning Herald* (Sydney), 31 March 2006.

*Prevention of Terrorism Act*,[10] in a pragmatic recognition that concessions of this kind may be necessary. In another mixed example, on the thirtieth anniversary in 2007 of the 'German Autumn', some convicted members of the Red Army Faction (or Baader-Meinhof Gang) received pardons from the German President for serious terrorist acts committed in the 1970s, while others have been refused clemency.[11]

As these brief examples indicate, there has been considerable ambivalence in the response of the international community and different national governments towards the problem of how to respond to individual terrorist acts and sustained campaigns of terrorist violence. Responses vacillate between a desire to punish and deter terrorists through the strict application of the criminal law, and counter impulses to temper or even suspend the application of the law to mitigate the potential harm from exceptional threats of extreme violence. This chapter first outlines how international law has responded to the question of amnesties for serious international crimes, before extracting and elaborating some basic guidelines for their use. It then specifically examines whether terrorist acts raise similar or different considerations in relation to amnesties than other serious international crimes, before focusing on the impacts of terrorism amnesties on international security and justice issues.

## The Lawfulness of Amnesties for International Crimes

While domestic legal systems are infused with discretionary political concepts such as immunities, amnesties and pardons, the availability of (domestic or international) amnesties for *international* crimes is an unsettled question.[12] The issue is not directly addressed in the 1998 *Rome Statute* [13] in relation to international crimes within the jurisdiction of the International Criminal Court (ICC).[14] State practice on the availability and conditions of amnesties is variable,

---

[10] Agreement on a Ceasefire Between the Government of the Democratic Socialist Republic of Sri Lanka and the Liberation Tigers of Tamil Eelam, February 2002, cl 2.12.
[11] 'Red Army Faction Guerrilla to Stay in Jail, German's President Decides', *The Guardian* (UK), 8 May 2007.
[12] See generally, R Slye, 'The Legitimacy of Amnesties under International Law and General Principles of Anglo-American Law: Is a Legitimate Amnesty Possible?' (2003) 43 *Vanderbilt Journal of International Law* 173; D Cassel, 'Lessons From the Americas: Guidelines for International Response to Amnesties for Atrocities' (1996) 59 *Law and Contemporary Problems* 197; K Henrard, 'The Viability of National Amnesties in View of the Increasing Recognition of Individual Criminal Responsibility at International Law' (1987) 8 *Michigan Yearbook of International Legal Studies* 595; A Cassese, *International Criminal Law* (Oxford: Oxford University Press, 2003) 312-16; C Stahn, 'United Nations Peace-Building, Amnesties and Alternative Justice: A Change in Practice?' (2002) 845 *International Review of the Red Cross* 193; J Dugard, 'Dealing with Crimes of a Past Regime: Is Amnesty still an Option?' (2000) 12 *Leiden Journal of International Law* 1001; W Burke-White, 'Reframing Impunity: Applying Liberal International Law Theory to an Analysis of Amnesty Legislation' (2001) 42 *Harvard International Law Journal* 467.
[13] *Rome Statute of the International Criminal Court*, open for signature 17 July 1998, 2187 UNTS 90 (entered into force 1 July 2002).
[14] On amnesties in the ICC, see C Stahn, 'Complementarity, Amnesties and Alternative Forms of Justice: Some Interpretative Guidelines for the International Criminal Court' (2005) 3 *Journal of International*

while international organisations have similarly rejected and endorsed amnesties in different contexts.[15] There is no explicit customary rule against amnesties.[16] Amnesties have also featured prominently in peace agreements (including those brokered by the United Nations (UN))[17] for ending protracted non-international armed conflicts and terrorist campaigns, as a mechanism helping to bring peace and to restore or aid the transition to democracy.

International human rights law does not expressly preclude amnesties, although they may be incompatible with human rights law where they result in impunity for serious rights violations.[18] Of course, criminal prosecution is not the only means of avoiding impunity for serious rights violations, and a variety of methods outside the criminal justice system may effectively remedy such violations. In addition, in exceptional cases, amnesties that would confer impunity (where there are no alternative means of accountability) may still be lawful where, for instance, other branches of international law (such as the enforcement powers of the UN Security Council under Chapter VII of the *UN Charter*) provide a basis for suspending human rights to secure international peace and security.[19]

There is, however, a trend in practice towards the restriction of amnesties for serious international crimes. In the *Lomé Amnesty Case* the Special Court for Sierra Leone suggested that there is a 'crystallizing international norm that a government cannot grant amnesty for serious violations of crimes under international law'.[20] For example, in 2005, Argentina's Supreme Court declared unconstitutional two laws of 1986-87, which effectively conferred amnesties on

---

*Criminal Justice* 695; J Gavron, 'Amnesties in the Light of Developments in International Law and the Establishment of the International Criminal Court' (2002) 51 *International and Comparative Law Quarterly* 91; D Majzub, 'Peace or Justice: Amnesties and the International Criminal Court' (2002) 3 *Melbourne Journal of International Law* 247.

[15] Cassese, above n 12, 312-16.

[16] *Prosecutor v Morris Kallon and Brima Buzzy Kamara (Jurisdiction)* (*Lomé Amnesty Case*), SCSL-2004-15-AR72(E) and SCSL-2004-16-AR72(E), Appeals Chamber, 13 March 2004, [82]; Cassese, above n 12, 315. Some writers suggest that there is a trend and presumption against national amnesties: Gavron, above n 14, 116-17.

[17] R O'Brien, 'Amnesty and International Law' (2005) 74 *Nordic Journal of International Law* 261, 264, 270.

[18] See, eg, *Chumbipuma Aguirre et al v Peru* (*Barrios Altos*) (2001) Series C, No 75, [41]-[44]. In particular, self-amnesty laws were found to violate arts 1(1) and 2 (general obligations to guarantee rights), 8 (right to a fair trial) and 25 (right to an effective remedy) of the Inter-American Convention on Human Rights; see also the concurring opinions of Judge Trindade, [10]-[11] and Judge García-Ramírez, [9]-[17]; *Barrios Altos (Interpretation of Merits Judgment)*, IACHR (3 September 2001); *Castillo Páez (Reparations) Case* (27 November 1998) Ser C, No 43, [103]-[108] and concurring opinion of Judge García-Ramírez, [6]-[9]; see also UN Human Rights Committee, General Comment No 20 (1994).

[19] Pursuant to art 103 of the *UN Charter*, states' obligations arising under the *Charter* including enforcement measures imposed by the Security Council take precedence over other international obligations, including those arising under human rights conventions. A recent example is the English case of *R (Al-Jedda) v Secretary of State for Defence* [2006] EWCA Civ 327, where it was accepted that a Security Council resolution authorising the detention of terrorist suspects by a multinational force in Iraq lawfully suspended the procedural guarantees in detention provided for under the European Convention on Human Rights.

[20] *Lomé Amnesty Case*, above n 16.

those responsible for violating human rights in Argentina's 'Dirty War' of 1976-83.[21] The Court reasoned that amnesty laws conferred by alleged human rights violators upon themselves while still in government violated both international human rights law as well as the duty to prosecute serious international crimes under international law.

Similarly, while the 1999 *Lomé Peace Agreement* in Sierra Leone conferred an 'absolute and free pardon and reprieve to all combatants and collaborators in respect of anything done by them in pursuit of their objectives' between 1991 and 1999, the Statute of the Special Court for Sierra Leone precludes amnesties for crimes within its jurisdiction.[22] In the *Lomé Amnesty Case*, the Special Court for Sierra Leone found that while the conferral of amnesties is within the sovereign discretion of states, a state cannot exercise that power to deprive other states of universal jurisdiction over international crimes.[23] Thus, an amnesty conferred in one jurisdiction (in that case, by a peace agreement that was held not to comprise an international treaty) may not necessarily hold in other jurisdictions, particularly when the tribunal examining the amnesty is an international or a hybrid tribunal and is thus invested with an international mandate on behalf of the international community, rather than merely reflecting the criminal justice interests of one state.

Some recent instruments to prosecute mass violence have expressly excluded the possibility of amnesties. The Agreement between the UN and Cambodia to establish Extraordinary Chambers to prosecute the Khmer Rouge's abuses forbids the Cambodian government from requesting 'an amnesty or pardon for any persons who may be investigated for or convicted of crimes'.[24] However, the Agreement leaves to the Extraordinary Chamber the question of the scope of the one pardon already granted in 1996 for a genocide conviction in 1979. While UN negotiators have sometimes endorsed amnesties in the past, the UN recently signalled a shift away from supporting amnesties for any serious international crimes.[25]

---

[21] *Simón Case*, Argentine Supreme Court, causa No 17.768 (14 June 2005) S.1767.XXXVIII. The decision upheld the findings of lower courts on this issue and confirmed that Argentina's Congress had validly annulled the amnesty laws in 2003; see C Bakker, 'A Full Stop to Amnesty in Argentina' (2005) 3 *Journal of International Criminal Justice* 1106.
[22] *Peace Agreement between the Government of Sierra Leone and the Revolutionary United Front of Sierra Leone*, 7 July 1999, Lomé, UN Doc S/1999/777, art 9 (and a freedom from any 'official or judicial action'); Statute of the Special Court for Sierra Leone, art 10.
[23] *Lomé Amnesty Case*, above n 16, [66]-[74]; see also S Meisenberg, 'Legality of Amnesties in International Humanitarian Law: The Lomé Amnesty Decision of the Special Court for Sierra Leone' (2004) 856 *International Review of the Red Cross* 837.
[24] *Agreement Between the United Nations and the Royal Government of Cambodia Concerning the Prosecution under Cambodian Law of Crimes Committed During the Period of Democratic Kampuchea*, Signed at Phnom Penh, 6 June 2003, article 11 (Amnesty), available at
<http://www.cambodia.gov.kh/krt/pdfs/Agreement%20between%20UN%20and%20RGC.pdf>.
[25] UN Secretary-General's Report on Transitional Justice and the Rule of Law in Conflict and Post-Conflict Societies, tabled in the UN Security Council, 6 October 2004, UN Doc CCPR/C/56/D/540/1993, [10]-[11];

## Amnesties and International Policy Considerations

Policy objections to amnesties include that they conflict with obligations to prosecute international crimes; thwart victims' rights to a remedy; and undermine the rule of law.[26] In some cases, far from promoting peace or reconciliation, amnesties may counter-productively foster perceptions of injustice and accentuate grievances, destabilising efforts to re-establish order or democracy in the aftermath of violence. In part, this is why some amnesties have later been overturned, often many years later (as in Latin America) where short-term gains are gradually overshadowed by the long-term implications of failing to remedy structural violence across society. On one view, prosecutions can be validly suspended in the short-term to ensure security, as long as there is the prospect of accountability at some point, and as long as the exceptional suspension of justice does not destroy the rule in favour of prosecution.[27]

In a recent example, in 2006 former Liberian President Charles Taylor was apprehended fleeing Nigeria, where he had earlier been granted asylum in an agreement to end 14 years of vicious civil war in Liberia. While his surrender to the Special Court for Sierra Leone for prosecution (including on terrorism charges) can be viewed as a victory for his victims, a prospective danger of not honouring amnesties is that strongmen may never agree to surrender power. Insistence on criminal justice over all else may carry a price in many more lives lost in the perpetuation of conflict.

Amnesties need not be a capitulation to power politics, but can be, depending on their form and mode of adoption, a necessary, pragmatic and principled concession to the political realities that bound the operation of law. Their importance lies not only in inducing the immediate end of conflict, but in establishing the conditions for a lasting peace. In some situations, promoting (if not necessarily achieving) 'a forgetting, an oblivion, so that thoughts of revenge or reprisal would not reopen the conflict'[28] may be preferable to criminal justice.

Indeed, a criminal justice model, with its emphasis on punishment and retribution, is not always the most appropriate way of dealing with international crimes or serious human rights abuses, including for cultural reasons in some circumstances. Alternative forms of truth-telling, such as reconciliation processes combined with amnesties, may contribute more effectively to peace building.[29] Even where prosecutions are necessary, they may carry other costs which ought to be recognised. The individualisation of guilt may also fail to capture the

---

UN Principles for the Protection and Promotion of Human Rights through Action to Combat Impunity, February 2005, UN Doc E/CN.4/2005/102 (18 February 2005).

[26] Slye, above n 12, 182-201.

[27] See, eg, D Orentlicher, 'Settling Accounts' Revisited: Reconciling Global Norms with Local Agency' (2007) 1 *International Journal of Transitional Justice* 10.

[28] O'Brien, above n 17, 264.

[29] For a useful analysis of some of the key developments in the area, see Orentlicher, above n 27.

structural nature of violence across society. While a failure to individualise may create a culture of personal impunity, conversely too much individualisation of guilt can atomise responsibility in a way which fails to explain why violence occurred and how it might best be prevented from reoccurring.

At a pragmatic level, criminal justice systems may simply be unable to cope with systemic, large-scale violence, where individual prosecutions would overwhelm the capacity of regular courts — as in Rwanda, where 100,000 suspected *genocidaires* languished for many years in pre-trial detention, without realistic prospects of coming to trial, until the *gacaca* system of village-based justice (adapted from local dispute resolution techniques) was brought into play (which itself raises distinctive questions of procedural fairness). In addition, societies recovering from conflict may have other priorities: reconstruction, development, rehabilitation, administrative and governmental reform and so on, which may have to be balanced against the availability of resources for investment in individual criminal trials.

## Conditions of the Legitimacy of Amnesties

Any amnesty process must, however, satisfy minimum conditions if it is to carry and maintain its legitimacy. First, conferring amnesties or immunities, or exercising a discretion not to prosecute or extradite,[30] must be necessary as a last resort, to secure fundamental objectives such as the preservation of a fragile peace agreement or the survival of a transitional government,[31] national reconciliation, or to save lives. Allowing prosecution in such circumstances would imperil vital countervailing public interests. A corollary of this first condition is that if the preconditions for the grant of amnesties have disappeared — for example, where a party in a civil war resumes the use of violence — then agreement on amnesties must also dissolve.[32] The cost of these approaches is that criminal justice — including punishment, retribution, deterrence, and satisfaction for victims — is rationally traded for, or weighed against, other more pressing public goods.

Second, amnesties tailored to the specific circumstances of particular individuals following a fair and transparent determination procedure (such as a national reconciliation process) are more acceptable than blanket amnesties that immunise

---

[30] Historically, selectivity in international prosecutions has been based on unstated or opaque reasons, undermining perceptions of legitimacy: D Zolo, 'Peace through Criminal Law?' (2004) 2 *Journal of International Criminal Justice* 727, 730; A Garapon, 'Three Challenges for International Criminal Justice' (2004) 2 *Journal of International Criminal Justice* 716, 717.
[31] Y Naqvi, 'Amnesty for War Crimes: Defining the Limits of International Recognition' (2003) 85 *International Review of the Red Cross* 583, 624; R McCarthy, S Goldenberg and N Watt, 'Amnesty for Iraqi Insurgents', *The Guardian* (UK), 5 July 2004; 'Putin Sets Chechnya Amnesty in Train', *The Guardian* (UK), 15 May 2003.
[32] See, eg, *Prosecutor v Kondewa* SCSL-2004-14-AR72(E) (25 May 2004) (concurring opinion of Judge Robertson); see also O'Brien, above n 17, 276.

whole classes of people, irrespective of their individual responsibility.[33] There should also be alternative forms of accountability for perpetrators and redress for victims, for example, through civil claims, compensation schemes and rehabilitation programs, and broader efforts to prevent violence through disarmament, social integration of ex-combatants, and institutional restructuring.[34]

Further, amnesty processes are more legitimate where they do not foreclose the prosecution of the most serious crimes, whether for offenders who fail to fully disclose their crimes (as in post-apartheid South Africa) or for more serious crimes (as in independent East Timor).[35] This was the approach in Iraq in 2006, when the Iraqi Prime Minister offered amnesties to insurgents who had not targeted civilians or committed war crimes.[36] By 2007, however, Iraq's (Shi'ite) Prime Minister was deeply opposed to amnesties being offered to Sunni insurgents by the US military commander in Iraq (in exchange for those insurgent groups ceasing hostilities against US forces) due to concerns about their potential impact on sectarian violence in Iraq.

An amnesty offer by Indonesia to members of the Free Aceh Movement (GAM) in 2005, along with the release of more than 1500 prisoners, was similarly limited in scope, by encompassing only political offences (such as rebellion) and excluding ordinary criminal offences such as rape, murder and arson. The agreement between Indonesia and GAM provides for the Aceh Monitoring Mission to decide on amnesty disputes,[37] which is essential given that it is unclear whether some offences, such as the illegal possession of weapons, will be classed as political or non-political. Amnesties are also connected with the establishment of a Commission for Truth and Reconciliation and are conditional in that the continuing use of weapons by GAM members disqualifies them from amnesties. Limiting amnesties to purely political offences (such as treason or sedition), and not extending them to 'blood' crimes, was advocated by the

---

[33] Cassese, above n 12, 316.
[34] O'Brien, above n 17, 276.
[35] R Goldstone, 'Past Human Rights Violations: Truth Commissions and Amnesties or Prosecutions' (2000) 51 *Northern Ireland Legal Quarterly* 164; see, eg, *Promotion of National Unity and Reconciliation Act 1995* (South Africa), ss 3(1)(b), 4(c), 16-22; UN Transitional Administration in East Timor, Regulation 2001/10 on the Establishment of a Commission on Reception, Truth and Reconciliation in East Timor (13 July 2001); note that the Report of the East Timorese Reception, Truth and Reconciliation Commission recommended prosecuting perpetrators of rights violations during the Indonesian occupation prior to 1999, but then President Xanana Gusmao recommended suppressing it in the public interest: J Aglionby, 'Timorese Truth May Stay Hidden', *Sydney Morning Herald* (Sydney), 30 November 2005. A constitutional challenge to the South African amnesty laws was dismissed in *Azanian People's Organization & Others v The President of the Republic of South Africa and Others*, Constitutional Court Case No CCT17/96.
[36] 'Iraq Reconciliation Deal Unveiled', *The Australian* (Sydney), 26 June 2006; 'US Furious at Pardon Plan for Insurgents', *Sydney Morning Herald* (Sydney), 27 June 2006.
[37] Memorandum of Understanding Between Indonesia and the Free Aceh Movement, Helsinki, 15 August 2005.

International Bar Association in relation to Fiji,[38] although it may not be practical in higher intensity armed conflicts, particularly where violence by combatants generally complies with humanitarian law.

Third, amnesties granted by democratic parliamentary processes (as in Angola in 2002), or through consultative processes that engage victims and the community, are more likely to produce more appropriate amnesties than those conferred by national leaders upon themselves prior to leaving office. As Judge García-Ramírez found in the Inter-American Court of Human Rights case of *Castillo Páez (Reparations)*:

> a distinction must be made between the so-called "self-amnesty laws" promulgated by and for those in power, and amnesties that are the result of a peace process, with a democratic base and reasonable in scope, that preclude prosecution for acts or behaviors of members of rival factions but leave open the possibility of punishment for [these] kind of very egregious acts ...[39]

Claims to democratic legitimacy underlying amnesty offers must, however, be carefully scrutinised. In February 2007, ostensibly to promote reconciliation, the Afghan Parliament passed legislation giving legal and judicial immunity to '[a]ll political parties and belligerent groups who fought each other during the past two and a half decades'.[40] The legislation expressly doubted the credibility of reports by Human Rights Watch about atrocities committed by senior jihad and national leaders. Afghan politicians were free to pursue this approach because the Bonn Peace Accord of December 2001 did not address transitional justice issues or establish mechanisms for dealing with them, not least because 'all parties to the peace agreement were involved in serious human rights abuses during the course of the conflict' there.[41] Indeed, the UN Secretary-General's Special Representative, Lakhdar Brahimi, seemingly promoted peace over justice in the immediate political stabilisation of Afghanistan, paradoxically undermining peace and security by encouraging further violence by regional warlords and allowing serious rights violators to take up positions in the government and the judiciary.[42] A number of suspected war criminals hold positions in the Afghan government and military, with the support — purportedly in the interests of stability — of some foreign governments involved in the multinational force stabilising Afghanistan.[43]

---

[38] International Bar Association, Comments on Fiji's Promotion of Reconciliation, Tolerance and Unity Bill, 2005, 13.
[39] *Castillo Páez (Reparations) Case* (27 November 1998) Ser C, No 43, [7] (Concurring Opinion of Judge García-Ramírez), [9].
[40] P McGeough, 'Atrocity Survivors Still Wait for Justice', *Sydney Morning Herald* (Sydney), 24-25 February 2007, 13.
[41] A N Nadery, 'Peace or Justice? Transitional Justice in Afghanistan' (2007) 1 *International Journal of Transitional Justice* 173, 174.
[42] Ibid 174-75.
[43] P McGeough, above n 40.

In response to the legislation, the Afghanistan Independent Human Rights Commission complained that the legislation 'will only promote impunity and leave those with serious human rights violations unpunished'.[44] The legislation is incompatible with principles in the Afghan government's own 'Action Plan for Peace, Reconciliation and Justice in Afghanistan', which states that the commission of international crimes 'does not fall into the scope of amnesty on the basis of the principles of the sacred religion of Islam and internationally accepted standards'.[45] The Action Plan itself had been based on widespread consultation with Afghans throughout the country. Moreover, a survey of 6000 Afghans by the Afghanistan Independent Human Rights Commission found that 90 per cent of respondents wanted human rights violators removed from office, and 40 per cent wanted them prosecuted, indicating popular unease about forgiving violations.

Further, amnesties conferred by one group that benefited from the crimes of others should be precluded for bias as in the case of self-amnesties. For example, the Reconciliation, Tolerance and Unity Bill 2005 (Fiji) proposed amnesties following full disclosure of crimes by those involved in a racialised coup by indigenous Fijians against a democratic, ethnic-Indian-led government in 2000.[46] The Bill was sponsored by an indigenous-led government, which came to power as a result of the coup. The International Bar Association has criticised the proposal for being unilateral rather than negotiated; for immunising acts aimed at overthrowing a democratic government; and for encouraging impunity and a coup culture, not least because amnesties following an earlier coup in 1987 did not prevent the next coup.[47]

In a different example, in Palestine, Irgun leaders such as Menachim Begin, a future Israeli Prime Minister, were never brought to justice for 'terrorist' crimes committed during the violent struggle to establish Israel. Underlying the exclusion of self-amnesties or the beneficiaries of others' violations is a concern for non-discrimination, that is, that if amnesties are part of a reconciliation process, they should be extended equally to all participants in a conflict, without distinction.

Fourth, in most situations, since international crimes are matters of international concern, no single state should be permitted to decide unilaterally whether to confer amnesties. Although the views of the affected state should be accorded significant weight, they are not the exclusive consideration. It may not be

---

[44] Said Nader Nadery, Afghan Commissioner for Transitional Justice, 1 February 2007.
[45] Action Plan of the Government of the Islamic Republic of Afghanistan: Peace, Reconciliation and Justice in Afghanistan.
[46] 'Fiji's Indigenous Leaders Back Release of Coup Plotters', *Sydney Morning Herald* (Sydney), 30-31 July 2005, 15. The new State of Israel also gave amnesties to 'Stern Gang' members who assassinated the UN mediator in Palestine in 1948.
[47] International Bar Association, above n 38.

acceptable to the international community, for example, for Afghanistan to offer an amnesty to insurgents fighting against the Afghan government and US forces where they extend to those suspected of serious crimes such as Taliban leader Mullah Mohammad Omar and sectarian 'warlord' Gulbuddin Hekmatyar.[48]

In a different example, Britain's willingness to secretly negotiate with Hamas and Hizballah in 2005 was questioned by Israel, the US and others, although that case is more complex because of the success of those organisations in democratic elections in the West Bank, Gaza and Lebanon in May and December of 2005 and January 2006.[49] While electing terrorists may be democratic in the thinnest popular sense of democracy, the better normative view is that democracies founded on human rights principles ought to be constrained by rights-based limits precluding terrorism. While human rights law is not pacifist — tolerating the taking of human life in some circumstances (as in self-defence, or under humanitarian law in armed conflict) — it does not permit the instrumental killing of innocent civilians for political purposes,[50] which is the essence of terrorist action.

## Amnesties for Terrorism: Special Considerations?

In light of these general principles, it is important to note that amnesties for terrorism may raise different issues than those applying to existing international crimes. To begin with, there is not yet any general international crime of terrorism, so that acts of terrorism do not automatically trigger the same kind of legal analysis as war crimes, crimes against humanity or genocide, which have well-developed international legal frameworks and institutional responses (including the ICC, which does not, by contrast, have jurisdiction over terrorism).

Certain manifestations of terrorism have, however, been addressed by 13 sectoral anti-terrorism treaties, prohibiting and often criminalising physical acts such as hijacking, hostage-taking, bombings or the misuse of nuclear material. Those transnational criminal law treaties typically establish 'prosecute or extradite' regimes for the relevant offences, but fall short of creating customary international law crimes attracting universal jurisdiction under general international law (with the possible exception of the most well-established sectoral offences of hostage-taking and hijacking, which exist as parallel customary law prohibitions).

---

[48] C Gall, 'Amnesty May Include Taliban Leaders', *Sydney Morning Herald* (Sydney), 11 May 2005.
[49] E MacAskill, 'UK Ponders Talking with Hamas and Hizbullah: Militants' Gains at Polls Persuade Foreign Office to Rethink Policy', *The Guardian* (UK), 20 May 2005; C McGreal, 'Israelis Pressure Straw Over UK Contacts with Hamas', *The Guardian* (UK), 8 June 2005; C McGreal, 'Hamas Election Victory Sets New Middle East Challenge', *Guardian Weekly* (UK), 3-9 February 2006, 1; see International Crisis Group, 'Enter Hamas: The Challenges of Political Negotiation', Middle East Report No 49, Amman/Brussels, 18 January 2006.
[50] Saul, above n 4, 79.

Since 9/11, the international community has increasingly regulated 'terrorism' directly through the enforcement powers of the UN Security Council, which has required all states to criminalise terrorism in domestic law.[51] Terrorism is, therefore, of significant concern to the international community, and so the question of amnesties for terrorism arguably now attracts the interest of international law and cannot be left to domestic jurisdiction alone. At the same time, isolated or low-level terrorist acts of a purely domestic character may raise different considerations than high-intensity acts of international terrorism, and the latter will inevitably engage more issues of international law and policy than the former.

In many cases, war crimes or crimes against humanity will be typically more widespread and affect larger sections of the population than terrorism, and so amnesties for terrorism may not be justifiable as necessary to achieve national reconciliation or to restore harmony between rival ethnic or religious groups in the community. Indeed, prosecuting terrorism is often necessary precisely because terrorists attack the institutions of the state and the community that the state protects. State practice confirms that the international community considers terrorism wrongful precisely because it undermines the stability of political structures within which the life of the community may take place.[52] It may be questioned, for example, whether it was proper in 2005 for the King of Morocco to pardon seven Islamists convicted of involvement in the May 2003 terrorist attacks in Casablanca, which killed 45 people.[53]

On the other hand, amnesties for terrorism may be appropriate where conflict is sectarian and affects significant parts of the population, or in specific cases where life is at imminent risk. In an effort to defuse a violent and widespread Islamist insurgency, in 1999 Algeria passed a Law on Civil Concord, which offered immunity from prosecution for insurgents who demilitarised. Immunity was not available for those who participated in collective massacres, rapes, or public bombings. Claimants were assessed by a three-member panel of judges and officials, and received housing and integration assistance if successful. The law was overwhelmingly approved by 98 per cent of Algerian voters.[54] As a result, 4500 insurgents laid down their weapons.

By 2005, Algeria estimated that around 1000 insurgents remained. To entice them to demilitarise, the government put a *Charter on Peace and National Reconciliation* to referendum in September 2005, which was endorsed by 97 per

---

[51] UN SC Res 1373 (2001).
[52] Saul, above n 4, 35-45.
[53] Aljazeera, *Morocco Islamists Get Royal Pardon* (20 August 2005) <http://english.aljazeera.net/English/archive/archive?ArchiveId=14430>.
[54] On a voter turn-out of 85 per cent: Algerian Embassy (Washington DC), *Algeria Today*, 30 September 2005.

cent of voters.[55] The *Charter on Peace and National Reconciliation* pardons those convicted or imprisoned for armed violence or support of terrorism. It also offers amnesties to those who renounce violence and disarm; those who were involved in networks of support for terrorism and who declare their activities to the authorities; and those sought in Algeria or abroad who present themselves to the authorities. Pardons and amnesties are not available to those involved in collective massacres, rapes, or public bombings. While human rights organisations have been critical of the *Charter on Peace and National Reconciliation*,[56] the real concern is not so much its text as the apparent failure of Algeria to seriously attempt to bring to justice those suspected of committing the serious crimes exempt from pardon or amnesty.

International terrorism affecting multiple states may require different analysis than predominantly domestic terrorism of the kind experienced in Algeria. Where terrorist acts affect multiple states, waiving prosecution or extradition should 'only be exercised in agreement between the nation and the states whose citizens and property are the object of the terrorists' acts'.[57] Illegitimate reasons for failing to bring terrorists to justice might include appeasement, fear of reprisals, or the protection of commercial interests.[58] The more serious the terrorist acts involved, the stronger the justification must be for waiving prosecution or extradition. Such decisions should not be taken arbitrarily or unilaterally, but should be based on a careful balancing of vital community interests, such as humanitarian needs, justice for victims, long-term peace, or sustainable political solutions.

## Amnesties for Terrorism: a Role for the Security Council

Where terrorism threatens *international* peace and security, the Security Council is the natural body in which to consider claims of amnesty or immunity. The historical precedent, a 1937 League of Nations Convention to establish an international criminal court to prosecute international terrorism, did not maintain centralised control over amnesty decisions concerning international terrorism, but instead endowed the state responsible for enforcing the penalty against an offender with a right of pardon, to be exercised after mere consultation with the president of the court.[59] The drafters of the Convention rejected an

---

[55] On a voter turn-out of 80 per cent: ibid; see Algerian Ministry of Foreign Affairs, 'Projet de charte pour la paix et la reconciliation nationale', 6 September 2005.
[56] ICJ, 'Algeria: Amnesty Law Risks Legalizing Impunity for Crimes Against Humanity', Joint Press Statement, 14 April 2005; Amnesty International, 'Algeria: President Calls for Referendum to Obliterate Crimes of the Past', Public Statement, 22 August 2005, AI Index: MDE 28/010/2005.
[57] T Franck and D Niedermeyer, 'Accommodating Terrorism: An Offence against the Law of Nations' (1989) 19 *Israeli Yearbook on Human Rights* 75, 128.
[58] S Rosen and R Frank, 'Measures against International Terrorism', in D Carlton and C Schaerf (eds), *International Terrorism and World Security* (1975) 60, 63.
[59] 1937 Convention for the Creation of an International Criminal Court, opened for signature at Geneva, 16 November 1937, art 42.

alternative proposal to give the League Council the right of pardon, to be exercised on the motion of the state in which the sentence was to be carried out, the state against which the terrorism was directed, or the state of which the offender was a national.[60]

Under the modern law since 1945, the *UN Charter* posits peace and security as higher values than justice, given its comparatively fleeting references to human rights in Article 1(3) (in contrast to detailed provisions on collective security enforcement under Chapter VII), the extensive preservation of domestic jurisdiction and national sovereignty, and the absence of explicit provisions on humanitarian intervention. *Charter* obligations prevail over other treaty obligations,[61] and the certainty of treaty responses to terrorism may need to yield to exceptional security interests. For example, at the provisional measures phase in the Lockerbie incident, the International Court of Justice (ICJ) accepted that Libya's rights under an anti-terrorism treaty (to prosecute rather than extradite a national) would likely impair the rights enjoyed by the UK and US under Security Council Resolution 748 (which demanded the surrender of the suspects to those countries).[62] It is clear that the drafters of the *Charter* anticipated exceptional circumstances where the maintenance of peace and security might conflict with efforts to remedy serious violations of human rights, including through international criminal justice processes. While it might be hoped, as former UN Secretary-General Kofi Annan writes, that '[j]ustice and peace are not contradictory forces' but forces that 'promote and sustain one another',[63] it cannot be ruled out that exceptions to that rule will arise.

In relation to ICC prosecutions of potential terrorism offences, Article 16 of the *Rome Statute* explicitly recognises the Security Council's competence in security matters by providing that the Council may postpone the investigation or prosecution of an international crime for a renewable 12-month period.[64] The Council has relied on this provision to preclude temporarily the investigation or prosecution of ICC crimes by personnel from states not party to the *Rome Statute* engaged in UN operations.[65] While this particular measure has been

---

[60] League of Nations Committee on the International Repression of Terrorism, Synopsis of Proposals and Suggestions Contained in the Replies from Governments, Doc CRT 6, Geneva, 1 May 1935, League Archives Geneva Doc R3759/3A/17702/5237.
[61] *Charter of the United Nations* (26 June 1945) [1945] ATS 1, art 103.
[62] *Case Concerning Questions of Interpretation and Application of the 1971 Montreal Convention Arising from the Aerial Incident at Lockerbie* (*Libyan Arab Jamahiriya v United Kingdom, Libyan Arab Jamahiriya v United States of America*), [1992] ICJ Rep 3; [1992] ICJ Rep 114 [39]-[41]. See discussion in text below at n 67 and also n 69.
[63] Report of the UN Secretary-General Kofi Annan, 'The Rule of Law and Transitional Justice in Post-Conflict Societies', UN Doc S/2004/616 (2004).
[64] However, under art 103 of the *UN Charter*, the Council may impose obligations overriding states' commitments under any other treaty, which may trump art 16's 12-month limitation period.
[65] UN SC Res 1422 (2002), [1].

criticised on a number of legal grounds,[66] it illustrates that a practical mechanism for managing the potentially competing interests of international justice and international security has been built into the ICC. The use of that mechanism may be perceived as legitimate where there is specific justification of the need to postpone the investigation or prosecution of a particular case to meet demonstrated security needs, in contrast to the foregoing example where the Council has given blanket immunity to a whole class of people without an individualised assessment of the relative interests of justice and security at stake.

Council interference with treaty frameworks is not to be lightly presumed, and the discontinuance of the *Lockerbie* case in the ICJ ensured that the question of the availability and conditions of review of Council measures that conflict with other treaty obligations remain undecided. Like political decisions to grant pardons or amnesties generally, Council decisions of this kind are not outside the realm of law; indeed: '[a] discretion can only exist within the law'.[67] If a duty to prosecute terrorism, or not to confer amnesties for serious crimes, were to emerge as a norm of *jus cogens*, then the Council may be prohibited from conferring amnesties,[68] if it is accepted that the Council cannot lawfully override norms of *jus cogens*.[69] Respect for *jus cogens* norms is arguably an outermost limit on the Council's security powers, even in its efforts to confront the serious threat of international terrorism.

The International Criminal Tribunal for the former Yugoslavia has specifically suggested that the *jus cogens* character of the international crime of torture would not permit a national amnesty to preclude an international or foreign prosecution,[70] although whether it would also displace a Security Council amnesty is less clear, given that the question of conflict of a *jus cogens* norm and a Chapter VII Security Council measure has not been definitively settled by any

---

[66] These grounds include failure to first determine a threat under art 39 of the Charter, exceeding the scope of art 16 of the *Rome Statute*, violation of *jus cogens*, inconsistency with UN purposes and principles, and unlawful interference in treaty regimes. See Amnesty International, 'International Criminal Court: The Unlawful Attempt by the Security Council to Give US Citizens Permanent Impunity From International Justice', May 2003, AI Index: IOR 40/006/2003, 42-75.

[67] I Brownlie, 'The Decisions of the Political Organs of the United Nations and the Rule of Law', in R St J MacDonald (ed), *Essays in Honour of Wang Tieya* (Dordrecht, Boston: Martinus Nijhoff, 1993) 91, 95-96.

[68] Cassese, above n 12, 316 (referring to international crimes generally).

[69] *Bosnia Case* [1993] ICJ Rep 440 (Lauterpacht J); A Reinisch, 'Developing Human Rights and Humanitarian Law Accountability of the Security Council for the Imposition of Economic Sanctions' (2001) 95 *American Journal of International Law* 851, 859; K Doehring, 'Unlawful Resolutions of the Security Council and their Legal Consequences' (1997) 1 *Max Planck Yearbook of United Nations Law* 91, 99. Concerning *Lockerbie* itself, it has been argued that the Council's actions implicitly supported a breach of *jus cogens* by those states (Britain and the US) that unlawfully threatened force against Libya (contrary to art 2(4) of the Charter and the customary law prohibition on the use of force) if it did not comply with their demands. A Orakhelashvili, 'The Impact of Peremptory Norms on the Interpretation and Application of United Nations Security Council Resolutions' (2005) 16 *European Journal of International Law* 59, 71.

[70] *Prosecutor v Furundzija* IT-95-17/1-T (10 December 1998).

superior international court. State participation in anti-terrorism treaties may also be less attractive if they do not offer certainty and predictability, due to vulnerability to Council interference. There is the further danger that powerful states may attempt to circumvent treaty regimes by pursuing Council measures. At the same time, the Council's broad discretion under the Charter cannot be unduly fettered in dealing with serious terrorist threats to security, and criminal law responses may not always be the appropriate solution.

## Amnesties for Terrorism: the Role of Prosecutorial Discretion

In addition to the Council's role with respect to amnesties in light of its powers concerning international peace and security, the ICC prosecutor has a discretion not to investigate where, '[t]aking into account the gravity of the crime and the interests of victims, there are nonetheless substantial reasons to believe that investigation would not serve the interests of justice'.[71] It is plausible to argue that the existence of a legitimate national amnesty, or amnesty under an international peace agreement, accompanied by alternative forms of justice[72] could supply a legitimate reason not to prosecute, though much may depend on the degree of latitude accorded to states by the prosecutor. Certainly, in national legal systems, the existence of a (foreign) amnesty may be a relevant factor in the ordinary exercise of prosecutorial discretion.[73]

Further, the ICC must determine that a case is inadmissible where a state with jurisdiction has decided not to prosecute and the decision does not result from an unwillingness of the state to genuinely prosecute (art 17(1)(b) of the *Rome Statute*).[74] Acceptance by a national court or prosecutorial authority of a legitimate amnesty arguably does not amount to an unwillingness genuinely to prosecute. However, the ICC will consider whether the national proceedings or decision not to prosecute 'was made for the purpose of shielding the person concerned from criminal responsibility for crimes within the jurisdiction of the court', and whether any proceedings were conducted in a manner 'inconsistent with an intent to bring the person concerned to justice' (art 17(2)(a) and (b) respectively).[75] While a person may be brought to justice by means outside the criminal justice system, an amnesty does shield a person from criminal responsibility, notwithstanding any benevolent intention to effect justice by other means. The potential contradiction within these provisions may require

---

[71] Art 53(1)(c).
[72] W Schabas, *An Introduction to the International Criminal Court* (Cambridge: Cambridge University Press, 2002) 69; O'Brien, above n 17, 271.
[73] O'Brien, above n 17, 266.
[74] Above n 13.
[75] Ibid.

creative interpretation to reconcile them. The Court may also consider amnesties in its inherent judicial discretion to control abuse of process.

The ICC may have to grapple with these issues in the near future. The Lord's Resistance Army (LRA) has entered into negotiations, brokered by Sudan, with the Ugandan government to end the 20-year civil conflict in northern Uganda, and Ugandan President Yoweri Museveni has offered immunity to LRA leader Joseph Kony and to the rebels as a whole.[76] This is despite Uganda's earlier request to the ICC that the LRA be investigated for war crimes and crimes against humanity, which resulted in the ICC issuing arrest warrants for Kony and others in 2005.[77] Subsequent pleas by Uganda for the ICC to abandon the case have not been favourably received, despite Uganda's view that this is necessary to stabilise the truce after August 2006. In principle, it may be correct to regard amnesties for ICC crimes as incompatible with the *Rome Statute* other than in exceptional cases where amnesties are conditional and alternative forms of justice are available.[78] The Ugandan example would not seem to satisfy these principles, but it is nonetheless an extremely hard case; the price of prosecuting the LRA could well be the disintegration of a fragile truce and a return to the vicious and unrestrained attacks on civilians by the LRA.

## Conclusion

The Ugandan case is yet another example of the dilemma at the heart of the international community's ambivalence towards amnesties for serious crimes over many years. It may be that no strict legal rules can be formulated to encompass the myriad and complex factors that must be considered in evaluating the propriety of an amnesty in a particular case. Perhaps the best that can be done is to apply a series of guiding principles, such as those outlined earlier, which may assist in balancing the competing interests and in reaching a legitimate result that serves the ends of both justice and security as far as is possible in the circumstances.

These principles include: the existence of a sufficiently important end that amnesties are designed to realise; an individualised amnesty process (where possible); a democratic, participatory or consultative process for determining transitional justice mechanisms; the availability of alternative justice or accountability mechanisms, to prevent impunity and lack of redress for victims; the exclusion of self-interested amnesties; international or multinational participation in amnesty decision-making (where appropriate); and the

---

[76] R Dowden, 'African Rebel Cult Offers to Talk Truce', *The Australian* (Sydney), 19 May 2006; 'Uganda: Locals Want Rebel Leader Forgiven', *IRIN*, 1 August 2006.
[77] See, eg, Warrant of Arrest for Joseph Kony issued on 8 July 2005 as amended on 27 September 2005, ICC-02/04-01/05-53, available at http://www.icc-cpi.int/library/cases/ICC-02-04-01-05-53_English.pdf.
[78] C Stahn, 'Complementarity, Amnesties and Alternative Forms of Justice: Some Interpretative Guidelines for the International Criminal Court' (2005) 3 *Journal of International Criminal Justice* 695.

preservation of a prosecution option for the most serious international crimes (where possible).

Amnesties are sometimes necessary to extricate a society from protracted conflict and to facilitate the immediate transition to peace and the establishment or restoration of democracy. While amnesties may offer immediate gains, the way they are framed and structured has a critical effect on whether immediate gains translate into enduring ones. The wrong kind of amnesties counterproductively destabilise peace and democracy in the longer term, as communal relief at the cessation of hostilities or terrorist violence simmers over, with the lapse of time, into dissatisfaction about impunity and the absence of genuine justice for victims. Even the best practice example of amnesty processes, South Africa, remains controversial. On the one hand, the South African Amnesty Committee concluded that

> the amnesty process made a meaningful contribution to a better understanding of the causes, nature and extent of the conflicts and divisions of the past. It did so by uncovering many aspects of our past that have been hidden from view, and by giving us a unique insight into the perspective and motives of those who committed gross violations of human rights and the context in which these events took place.[79]

On the other hand, critics observed that the process failed to secure the convictions of high-ranking perpetrators; most amnesty applicants only revealed what was already known to investigators; and senior leaders did not disclose their involvement in structural violence because amnesties were only available for specific acts, rather than structural participation in organisations.[80]

Some of these defects could be cured by reforming the structure of amnesty processes, and certainly careful attention must be given to formulating the procedures and powers of amnesty and truth commissions.[81] Local agency in the design of processes that are appropriate to cultural and resource conditions is vital,[82] though not necessarily an exclusive determinant of legitimacy. Ultimately, amnesties should be understood as an outcome of a reconciliation process, rather than merely the vehicle for it — and they cannot be isolated from deeper institutional and structural reforms designed to redress and prevent violence.[83] Of necessity, this includes efforts to address the underlying causes that precipitate at least some terrorist violence.

---

[79] Amnesty Committee, Truth and Reconciliation Commission of South Africa, 'Some Reflections on the Amnesty Process' *Report* vol 6, s 1, ch 5 (2003) 90.
[80] J Klaaren and H Varney, 'A Second Bite at the Amnesty Cherry? Constitutional and Policy Issues around Legislation for a Second Amnesty' (2000) 117 *South African Law Journal* 572.
[81] Dugard, above n 12.
[82] Orentlicher, above n 27, 22.
[83] International Bar Association, above n 38, 16.

# PART FOUR

Reports from Two Theatres of War:
Legislation, Sanctions and Prosecutions
in Europe and Australia

# Chapter Eleven

# The European Union as a Collective Actor in the Fight against Post-9/11 Terrorism: Progress and Problems of a Primarily Cooperative Approach

Jörg Monar[*]

## Introduction

Protecting the security of their citizens is one of the core functions and reasons of being of the modern nation state. In a system like the European Union (EU), where the constituent member states retain full national sovereignty over matters of internal security, the role of EU common institutions in this critical domain is far from obvious. When terrorism first afflicted the European Community member states in the 1970s they responded in 1975 by setting up a loose intergovernmental cooperation framework outside of the partly supranational legal and institutional framework of the European Communities (EC) of the time. This so-called TREVI[1] framework remained outside of the EC treaty framework; had no legal base, permanent structures, legislative powers or budget. Nevertheless TREVI was seen at the time as quite successful in that it allowed for information exchange and occasional cross-border coordination of measures. In 1993, as a result of the *Maastricht Treaty* (the *Treaty on European Union* or TEU),[2] TREVI was incorporated into the EU as part of the provision on Justice and Home Affairs (JHA) cooperation in the context of the new third pillar, Title VI of the TEU. Inclusion of TREVI in the third pillar brought cooperation against terrorism for the first time within the ambit of the EU Treaties and institutions. Yet the absence of any defined objectives and of any external action competence, the inadequate legal instruments provided for by the *Maastricht Treaty*, and institutional provisions that retained much of the intergovernmental nature of

---

[*] Professor, Marie Curie Chair of Excellence, Université Robert Schuman de Strasbourg, Strasbourg, France, and Director of the European Union-funded SECURINT project on EU internal security governance.
[1] TREVI stood officially for *Terrorisme, Radicalisme, Extrémisme et Violence Internationale*, but its real background seems to have been a word game linked to the Dutch Minister Fonteijn (in Dutch, 'fountain') who chaired the meeting that established TREVI and a dinner the ministers had close to the Trevi Fountain in Rome.
[2] *Treaty on European Union*, opened for signature 7 February 1992, OJ C 191, (entered into force 1 November 1993) (*Maastricht Treaty*, hereinafter cited as TEU).

the previous TREVI cooperation made the third pillar an only marginally more effective framework for anti-terrorism cooperation.

The situation changed substantially with the reforms introduced by the *Treaty of Amsterdam* [3] in 1999. Under the overarching fundamental treaty objective of maintaining and developing the Union as an 'area of freedom, security and justice'[4] ('AFSJ') the EU was for the first time vested with an explicit internal security mandate: Article 29 TEU establishes the objective of providing citizens with a 'high level of safety' within the AFSJ and Article 61(e) of the *Treaty Establishing the European Community* (TEC)[5] links police and judicial cooperation in criminal matters to the aim of 'a high level of security by preventing and combating crime within the European Union'. Related to the new objectives were a number of other important reforms such as:

- the introduction of more appropriate legal instruments for the third pillar;[6]
- the incorporation of the until then 'exiled' Schengen system[7] with its considerable array of law enforcement cooperation mechanisms;
- the 'communitarisation', that is, transfer into the more supranational part of the Treaties, of part of the JHA areas in the context of a new Title IV TEC (which includes border controls as one area of obvious relevance to the fight against terrorism); and
- the creation of an external treaty-making competence of the EU/EC in the JHA domain.[8]

To these reforms one has to add a changed political context at the end of the 1990s. While still asserting their full sovereignty in matters of internal security, member states were at least willing to fill the notion of the AFSJ with some substance through a deepening of their cooperation on a broad range of internal

---

[3] *Treaty of Amsterdam amending the Treaty on European Union, the Treaties establishing the European Communities and certain related acts*, opened for signature 2 October 1997, OJ C 340, (entered into force 1 May 1999) (*Treaty of Amsterdam*).

[4] TEU, above n 2, art 2.

[5] Originally the *Treaty Establishing the European Economic Community*, renamed by the TEU to *Treaty Establishing the European Community*, opened for signature 25 March 1957, 298 UNTS 11 (entered into force 1 January 1958) (hereinafter cited as TEC), consolidated version published OJ C 321E.

[6] Framework Decisions and Decisions were added as legislative instruments of the Council, in order to provide alternatives to the cumbersome Conventions subject to national ratification procedures.

[7] Established in 1985 outside of the EC framework by initially only five EC member states through the Schengen Agreement, which provided for the abolition of controls on persons at internal borders and hence forced the countries involved to adopt a whole range of 'compensatory measures' to offset potential internal security risks stemming from this step.

[8] TEU art 38 in conjunction with art 24 for the matters of the remaining third pillar (police and judicial cooperation in criminal matters). In the domains of internal Community competence the Community enjoys in accordance with the doctrine of parallelism between the internal and the external competences developed by the European Court of Justice (ECJ) an implied power to act externally as far as such action is necessary for achieving objectives under the TEC. As a result the Community has gained 'automatically' external action capabilities in the JHA areas communitarised as a result of the 1999 reforms.

security-related matters. This political will is demonstrated by the Conclusions of the Tampere European Council of October 1999 with, inter alia, their emphasis on developing judicial cooperation in criminal matters and the decision to establish the cross-border prosecution unit Eurojust.

When the attacks of 11 September 2001 (9/11) brutally inaugurated a new phase of terrorism, the EU was therefore in a better position than ever before to develop a common response to the challenge. Since then the Madrid attacks of March 2004 and the London attacks of July 2005 (as well as foiled major attacks in several member states) have brought this threat much closer to home. The question is therefore how, and how well, the EU has used its improved potential to emerge as an actor in the fight against terrorism. This chapter will try to provide an answer to this question and to bring out both the progress and the problems connected with the Union's role in this sensitive field.

## The European Union's Response: an Evolving Threat Definition and Multidimensional Action

### The Evolution of the Threat Definition: 'Internalisation' and Differentiation

Whatever means the potential victim — be it a state, a company or even a group of individuals — has at its disposal to counter any threat, the first thing it must do is actually define and identify the nature of that threat. The EU is obviously no exception to this requirement. If one looks at the host of declarations adopted by the EU institutions since 9/11 one can discern a quite substantial evolution of threat definition post-9/11. Three phases can be distinguished.

In the immediate aftermath of the 9/11 attacks, EU statements were focused on the threat posed to the United States (US) as part of a more general global threat to 'open' and 'democratic' societies.[9] While cross-border intelligence and law enforcement cooperation was immediately stepped up in order to identify and dismantle terrorist networks in the EU, such networks were treated as part of a global threat posed to Western societies by Al Qa'ida. In that sense, EU terrorist networks were seen as posing an 'external' threat. This 'global' definition also prevailed in the first more substantial legislative act in the fight against terrorism, the *Framework Decision on Combating Terrorism* of 13 June 2002. The Decision started with a strongly worded preamble that identified terrorism as 'one of the most serious violations' of the 'universal values' (human dignity, liberty, equality, solidarity, respect for human rights and fundamental freedoms) and 'principles' (rule of law and democracy) on which the EU is founded. Terrorism was also referred to as a global threat to democracy, human rights and economic and

---

[9] See the Conclusions of the extraordinary European Council meeting of 21 September 2001, which also defined terrorism, rather philosophically, as 'a challenge to the conscience of every human being' (EU Council Document No SN 140/01).

social development in line with the *La Gomera Declaration* that the European Council adopted in 1995.[10] The main emphasis in this first common EU post-9/11 terrorist threat definition was clearly on a broad and rather undifferentiated threat of a global nature to the political, constitutional and socio-economic foundations of the EU and its member states. This emphasis was also reflected in the common definition of terrorist acts as this included the aim of terrorists seriously to destabilise or destroy 'the fundamental political, constitutional, economic and social structures of a country'.[11]

The rather undifferentiated global threat definition showed its limitations in the light of the growing evidence of the terrorist potential within some of the member states when logistical bases and cells in the United Kingdom (UK), Italy, Germany, Spain and Belgium were uncovered during 2002 and 2003. The adoption of the *European Security Strategy*[12] in 2003 formally marked the passage to a new phase with a more 'internalised' and differentiated threat perception. The *Security Strategy* not only identifies terrorism as the first of the 'key threats' the Union was facing in the security domain but also describes it as a threat having both an internal and an external dimension. The *Security Strategy* emphasises that terrorism not only endangers lives and causes huge costs but that it also 'seeks to undermine the openness and tolerance of our societies'. Although maintaining the global nature of the threat, there is recognition also of an internal threat with a significant risk of 'home grown' terrorism. The *Security Strategy* also links terrorism with other international threats, in particular, the proliferation of weapons of mass destruction, 'state failure' (a concept not further defined in the EU texts) and organised crime, seeing terrorism as part of a differentiated set of interrelated internal and external security threats rather than an individual and isolated one.

The third, and current, phase started after the London attacks of July 2005 brought to the fore the full scale of home grown terrorism. This third phase found its full expression when the European Council, partly in response to the London attacks of July 2005, adopted the *EU Counter-Terrorism Strategy* on 15-16 December 2005.[13] The *Counter-Terrorism Strategy* broadly reaffirms the earlier threat assessment, but places an even stronger emphasis on the threat posed by 'home grown' terrorism through radicalisation and terrorist recruitment within the EU[14] — an obvious reaction to the background of the Madrid and London attacks. The *Strategy* adds a further element to the common definition that deals more specifically with the EU's particular vulnerability to terrorist

---

[10] [2002] OJ L 164/3, [1]-[2].
[11] Ibid, art 1.
[12] Council of the European Union, *A Secure Europe in a Better World. European Security Strategy* (Paris: Institute for Security Studies, 2003).
[13] EU Council Document No 14469/4/05 REV 4 of 30 November 2005.
[14] Ibid [6]-[12].

activities. After re-emphasising the threat posed by terrorism to the EU's security, values and rights and freedoms, the text continues:

> The European Union is an area of increasing openness, in which the internal and external aspects of security are intimately linked. It is an area of increasing interdependence, allowing for free movement of people, ideas, technology and resources. This is an environment which terrorists abuse to pursue their objectives.[15]

This addition provides a new element to the threat definition as the threat is presented as being, at least partially, due to the Union's specific 'openness': terrorists may abuse the free movement of people across borders and the freedoms of the Internal Market. Accordingly, the threat is even more 'internalised' and more justification is provided — as the *Strategy* emphasises in the same paragraph — for 'concerted and collective European action'. Finally, a further distinctive feature of this most recent stage of the EU's threat definition is its diversification: The *Counter-Terrorism Strategy* no longer focuses almost exclusively on Al Qa'ida as did some of the earlier texts; it refers to Al Qa'ida only once, and even then only as an example.[16] The *European Union Strategy for Combating Radicalisation and Recruitment to Terrorism* of November 2005, which is an integral part of the *Counter-Terrorism Strategy*, defines the terrorism perpetrated by Al Qa'ida 'and extremists inspired by' it as the main terrorist threat to the Union. Although 'other types of terrorism ... continue to pose a serious threat to EU citizens' the Union's response is going to focus on this main threat.[17]

It is important to note that a considerable effort has also been made to avoid anything in the official definition of the threat that could make Islam or the Muslim world appear as the 'threat' or 'enemy'. While Europol's TE-SAT Report liberally uses the term 'Islamist terrorism' and 'Islamist terrorist propaganda',[18] the EU's *Counter-Terrorism Strategy* consistently employs very neutral language. The term 'Islam' appears only once and then only for the purpose of rejecting the claim of 'a clash between the West and Islam'.[19] Equally, in the *Strategy for Combating Radicalization and Recruitment to Terrorism*, two entire paragraphs are dedicated to the need to avoid linking Islam to terrorism and, in close cooperation with Muslim communities, to reject distorted views of Islam.[20]

Compared with the initial focus on a largely 'external' global threat posed by Al Qa'ida the common EU threat definition has clearly evolved to encompass

---

[15] Ibid [2].
[16] Ibid [6] ('terrorist groups such as Al Qa'ida').
[17] EU Council Document No 14781/1/05 of 24 November 2005, [3].
[18] Europol, *EU Terrorism Situation and Trend Report (TESAT) 2007* (The Hague: Europol, 2007) 10, 18-26.
[19] EU Council Document No 14469/4/05 REV 4 of 30 November 2005, [10].
[20] EU Council Document No 14781/1/05 of 24 November 2005, [10]-[11].

the concept of an 'internal' threat. It also reveals an appreciation of post-9/11 terrorism as a more differentiated and complex phenomenon, both inside and outside of the EU, than the activities of Al Qa'ida. As far as the new emphasis on the particular vulnerability of the EU is concerned, there is little doubt that terrorists can potentially benefit from the 'openness' of the EU's internal borders and the provisions on free movement.[21] A further positive element is that the threat definition clearly tries to avoid any simplified or simplistic identification of the post-9/11 terrorist threat with Islamist activities and the Muslim world.

## The Terrorist Threat as a Multidimensional Law Enforcement Challenge

The growing 'internalisation' of the threat definition in line with the realisation of a potential for internal radicalisation and recruitment has enhanced the perception of the post-9/11 terrorist threat as primarily a law enforcement challenge. In contrast to the US concept of the 'war on terror', for the EU the fight against terrorism has in fact remained a challenge to be met primarily by the use of law enforcement instruments. The reasons for that are partly historical and partly systemic.

Historically, one has to remember that several of today's member states, especially the United Kingdom, Germany, Italy and Spain, have had to tackle serious terrorist threats since the 1970s. Although the countries concerned responded to the terrorist challenge with a range of measures that had serious implications for civil liberties, they did so primarily by adapting and toughening law enforcement instruments. Wherever significant suspensions of civil liberties and the use of military force was resorted to — such as by the British government in Northern Ireland — this was generally seen as a response *in extremis* and of doubtful effectiveness. In several member states, such as Germany, Italy and, more recently, France,[22] the experiences with a strong law enforcement response to the challenge of terrorism were on the whole regarded as positive, with terrorist threats eventually receding again or at least being contained. The European experience with a law enforcement-focused approach has therefore been not only a long one but also, at least in some cases, an effective one. It has also received some qualified endorsement through the case law of the European Court of Human Rights, which has more or less systematically accepted the right of European countries to criminalise violent political behaviour.[23] Although there has also been a growing perception in Europe that the post-9/11 terrorism

---

[21] The flight of Osman Hussain, one of the suspected July 2005 London terrorists, from London to Rome might otherwise have been more difficult.
[22] France suffered a series of major attacks in 1985-86 (by Hizballah-linked terrorists) and 1995 (by Algerian terrorists).
[23] C Warbrick, 'The European Response to Terrorism in an Age of Human Rights' (2004) 15 *European Journal of International Law* 989.

challenge is qualitatively different from the more 'traditional' forms of earlier decades,[24] many policy-makers in Europe continue to be influenced by their experiences with 'old' terrorism and the relative successes achieved by a law enforcement centred approach.[25]

There is also a 'systemic' disposition of the EU towards a law enforcement response. Terrorism is mentioned in the Treaties only once, as one of the forms of crime that should be targeted 'in particular' in the context of the internal security mandate of Article 29 TEU (focusing on police and judicial cooperation in criminal matters). The security mandate of the Common Foreign and Security Policy (CFSP) to 'strengthen the security of the Union in all ways'[26] may be broad enough to include international action against security threats posed by global terrorism within the remit of the CFSP and the European Security and Defence Policy (ESDP) elements it comprises, and the latter include tasks of rescue, peacekeeping, crisis management and peacemaking (the so-called 'Petersberg tasks'), which could obviously be of relevance to the fight against terrorism. Yet there is no explicit mention of the fight against terrorism as an objective of the CFSP, nor have any of the CFSP Petersberg tasks been linked to combating terrorist activity. Indeed, it seems far from certain that the EU could claim any legal competence to engage in a military operation abroad in order to prevent a terrorist attack on the EU, let alone to retaliate militarily against any such attack. Even if such a legal competence to act does exist, it seems highly improbable that, given the serious doubts in many EU capitals about both the legality and the effectiveness of military interventions abroad, the necessary unanimity in the Council for using ESDP instruments could be achieved. This contrasts rather strikingly with the US strategic culture and capability, which relies heavily on the use of 'hard power'[27] and must be counted among the contributory factors to the EU's reliance on a law enforcement approach.

Yet the focus on law enforcement by the EU does not limit internal police and judicial cooperation measures. As indicated above the internal and external nature of the terrorist challenge is a core element of the EU threat definition, so that the response must necessarily be both an internal and an external one. Because of the complex and multifaceted nature of the identified challenge, the response must also be a multidimensional one involving, as the *European Union Security Strategy* of 2003 emphasised, a 'mixture' of means beyond policing and enhanced judicial cooperation.[28]

---

[24] T Delpech, *International Terrorism and Europe* (2002), Chaillot Paper No 56, Paris: Institute for Security Studies.
[25] J Stevenson, 'How Europe and America Defend Themselves' (2003) 82 *Foreign Affairs* 75.
[26] TEU art 11(1).
[27] W Rees, *Transatlantic-Counter Terrorism Cooperation: The New Imperative* (Abingdon/New York: Routledge, 2006) 69-73.
[28] *A Secure Europe in a Better World*, above n 12.

This multidimensional approach forms the basis of the *Counter-Terrorism Strategy* of December 2005. It defines the strategic objectives of EU action in countering the terrorist threat. These objectives and the main measures to be taken are regrouped under the four headings of 'PREVENT' (radicalisation and recruitment), 'PROTECT' (citizens and infrastructure), 'PURSUE' (terrorists across borders) and 'RESPOND' (to the consequences of terrorist attacks). The *Counter-Terrorism Strategy* has the merit of providing a broad structure for the variety of EU measures, a list of priorities and a justifying narrative. Yet in terms of the substance of the action planned or taken, the key document remains the EU *Action Plan* against terrorism, which has been frequently revised and added to since September 2001.[29] Together the *Counter-Terrorism Strategy* and the *Action Plan*, which currently comprises well over 200 individual measures, allow us to identify four key elements of the EU's response to post-9/11 terrorism which will be dealt with in turn.

## The Combination of Legislative and Operational Measures

The EU has adopted a considerable number of legislative instruments to enhance cross-border law enforcement capabilities within the EU. The most important of these has been the already mentioned *Framework Decision on Combating Terrorism* of 13 June 2002.[30] This provides not only for a common minimum definition of terrorist acts, focused on a specific intent to commit such an act and its actual or potential consequences for a country or an international organisation, but also for common minimum/maximum custodial penalties for directing (15 years) or participating in (eight years) a terrorist group. The common definition contains some vague and subjective elements,[31] it does not regulate all aspects of the definition of terrorist acts as an offence, and its minimum/maximum penalty levels leave wide margins of discretion to the member states. Nevertheless, the common definition is substantial enough to provide a common platform for the comprehensive criminalisation and prosecution of terrorist offences throughout the Union.[32] This platform is all the more important as several member states did not have specific provisions on terrorism as a criminal act in their criminal legislation or codes before the adoption of the *Framework Decision*. It is also worth noting that in its list of proscribed acts, the *Framework Decision* goes beyond the conventional *acquis* of the United Nations.[33]

---

[29] Latest version: *Revised EU Action Plan on Terrorism*, EU Council Document No 7233/07 of 9 March 2007.
[30] [2002] OJ L 164.
[31] See E Symeonidou-Kastanidou, 'Defining Terrorism' (2004) 12 *European Journal of Crime, Criminal Law and Criminal Justice* 14.
[32] See E Dumitriu, 'The E.U.'s Definition of Terrorism: The Council Framework Decision on Combating Terrorism' (2004) 5 *German Law Journal* 585.
[33] See S Peers, 'EU Responses to Terrorism' (2003) 51 *International and Comparative Law Quarterly* 227.

Much legislative activity has been focused on the financing of terrorism. In addition to measures freezing funds and property of certain presumed terrorists and terrorist groupings on the basis of Council Regulation (EC) 881/2002,[34] there are other major instruments such as the *Council Framework Decision on the Execution of Orders Freezing Property or Evidence* of 22 July 2003,[35] the *Council Framework Decision on the Confiscation of Crime-Related Proceeds, Instrumentalities and Property* of 24 February 2005,[36] and the *Directive on the Prevention of the use of the Financial System for the Purpose of Money Laundering and Terrorist Financing* (the so-called 'Third Money Laundering Directive') of 26 October 2005.[37]

Although not solely directed at terrorists, the adoption of the *Framework Decision on the European Arrest Warrant* of 13 June 2002[38] was much accelerated because of anti-terrorism objectives, thereby generating one of the most advanced cross-border law enforcement instruments of the Union.[39] The European Arrest Warrant, which provides for the arrest and transfer of wanted persons by the police and judicial authorities of one member state on demand from the authorities of another member state, can also be regarded as an instrument of cross-border operational cooperation between national authorities in the fight against terrorism.

As a further counter-terrorism measure, the Commission introduced in 2003 a proposal for a *Framework Decision on a European Evidence Warrant*, on which political agreement was reached in the Council in June 2007.[40] Similarly to the European Arrest Warrant, the Evidence Warrant constitutes an application of the principle of mutual recognition to a judicial decision in the form of a European Warrant, in this case for the purpose of obtaining from the authorities of other member state's objects, documents and data for use in proceedings in criminal matters. The adoption on 15 March 2006 of *Directive 2006/24/EC on the Retention of Telecommunication Data* [41] was also motivated, at least in part, by counter-terrorism objectives. The Directive obliges telecommunication service providers to retain personal data such as the calling number, name and address of the subscriber and the identity of a user of an Internet Protocol address for a period of between six months and two years to ensure their availability for

---

[34] [2002] OJ L 139.
[35] [2003] OJ L 196.
[36] [2005] OJ L 68.
[37] [2005] OJ L 309.
[38] [2002] OJ L 190.
[39] For a comprehensive analysis see R Blekxtoon and W van Ballegooij (eds), *Handbook on the European Arrest Warrant* (The Hague: TMC Asser Press, 2005); J Spencer, 'The European Arrest Warrant' (2005) 6 *The Cambridge Yearbook of European Legal Studies* 201.
[40] Provisional text: EU Council Document No 9913/07 of 25 May 2007. This text is still subject to national parliamentary scrutiny.
[41] [2006] OJ L 105.

the purpose of the investigation, detection and prosecution of terrorism and other serious crimes.

In parallel to these legislative counter-terrorism measures in relation to criminal law, financial and data-retention issues, the EU has placed right from the beginning an emphasis on enhancing the operational interaction between the national law enforcement and criminal justice systems of member states. A host of measures have been taken or are under negotiation to increase multinational investigations and the supply of information to Europol; to enhance the common threat analysis capacity through Europol and the Situation Centre (SitCen) in the Council; and to improve the exchange of relevant data — such as crime registry data on convictions and lost and stolen passports. Key instruments adopted for primarily operational purposes include the *Framework Decision on Joint Investigation Teams* of 13 June 2002,[42] the *Council Decision on the Implementation of Specific Measures for Police and Judicial Cooperation to Combat Terrorism* of 19 December 2002,[43] the *Council Decision on the Exchange of Information and Cooperation Concerning Terrorist Offences* of 20 September 2005,[44] the *Council Decision on the Exchange of Information Extracted from the Criminal Record* of 21 November 2005[45] and the *Framework Decision on Simplifying Exchange of Information and Intelligence Between Law Enforcement Agencies* of 18 December 2006.

The most recent step concerns progress with the so-called 'principle of availability', aimed at granting law enforcement officers access to all relevant law enforcement information available anywhere in the EU. In 2005, seven member states went ahead with the implementation of this principle by signing the so-called Prüm Convention.[46] On 12 June, the JHA Council reached political agreement on a Draft Decision in relation to the stepping up of cross-border cooperation, particularly in combating terrorism and cross-border crime, which incorporates many aspects of the original Prüm Convention into the EU.[47] It establishes, inter alia, the conditions and procedures for the automated transfer of DNA profiles, dactyloscopic data and certain national vehicle registration data as well as the conditions for the supply of information on terrorist suspects, even if not requested, in order to prevent terrorist offences. It also seeks to improve cross-border police cooperation through various measures, including joint operations.

---

[42] Its provisions are now part of the *Convention on Mutual Assistance in Criminal Matters* which entered into force on 23 August 2005 ([2000] OJ C 197).
[43] [2003] OJ L 16.
[44] [2005] OJ L 253.
[45] [2005] OJ L 322.
[46] Text: EU Council Doc No 10900/05 of 7 July 2007. For a critical assessment see, T Balzaq, D Bigo, S Carerra and E Guild, *Security and the Two-Level Game: The Treaty of Prüm, the EU and the Management of Threats* (CEPS Working Paper No 234, Centre for European Policy Studies, Brussels, 2006).
[47] EU Council Document No 10232/07 of 5 June 2007.

All these measures are aimed at reducing obstacles to cross-border movements of law enforcement officers and/or law enforcement intelligence for operational purposes. Legislative mutual recognition and law enforcement instruments have therefore been complemented by action aimed at enhancing operational capabilities, although no operational powers have been transferred to EU structures as such (see below). This corresponds not only to the internal security dimension of the EU's common threat definition, but also to the realisation that a variety of instruments are needed and that the EU is particularly vulnerable because of the abolition of controls at internal borders.

## The Combination of Internal and External Measures

In parallel with the above developments, the Union has made extensive use of its external relations instruments to pursue counter-terrorism objectives. There has in fact been a 'mainstreaming' of the fight against terrorism in EU external relations.

Two elements should be distinguished here. One is the fact that the EU has, to a significant extent, developed its external action in the domain of law enforcement cooperation with third countries — the most notable example being cooperation with the US. This has not only led to the conclusion of two agreements of Europol with the US government on data-exchange[48] and two EU-US agreements on extradition and mutual legal assistance,[49] but also to the exchange of liaison officers and invitations to US officials to participate in relevant EU Council working party meetings.[50] This development should be regarded as quite significant, as EU external relations in the third pillar domain were rather poorly developed before the 9/11 attacks pushed them much higher up on the EU's agenda. While US interests and pressures have had only a limited impact on internal EU approaches to the post 9/11 threat, they certainly greatly contributed to this 'externalisation' of the EU's anti-terrorism action, pushing the EU in certain cases — such as the EU-US agreement on the processing and transfer of Passenger Name Records (PNR) data[51] — to a rather controversial extension of its external counter-terrorism measures. Specific forms of EU anti-terrorism cooperation, though at a much less intensive level, have since also

---

[48] Agreement between the US and the European Police Force (Europol), 6 December 2001, <http://www.europol.eu.int/legal/agreements/Agreements/16268-2.pdf> allowing for the exchange of strategic data, and Supplemental Agreement between the Europol Police Office and the United States of America on the Exchange of Personal Data and Related Information, 20 December 2002, <http://www.europol.eu.int/legal/agreements/Agreements/16268-1.pdf> allowing for the exchange of personal data.
[49] EU Council Doc No 9153/03 of 3 June 2003.
[50] On the various aspects of EU cooperation with the US in the internal security field after the 9/11 attacks see Rees, above n 27.
[51] The agreement was originally signed in May 2004, then annulled in May 2006 by the ECJ on application by the European Parliament eventually to be put provisionally into force pending ratification in October 2006. Text of the agreement: EU Council Do No 13216/06 of 11 October 2006.

been developed with other major international partners, such as the Russian Federation.[52]

The second element of the mainstreaming process has been a significant 'cross-pillarisation' of anti-terrorism objectives that have spread to external relations in the second pillar (common foreign and security policy ('CFSP') and its military ancillary, the European Security and Defence Policy (ESDP)) and external economic relations (common commercial policy). Examples in CFSP include the systematic use of 'political dialogues' with third countries (such as China and India) or with groups of third countries (such as EUROMED, the Asian countries in the Asia-Europe-Meetings (ASEM) and the countries of the Gulf Cooperation Council). A further example is the very active role taken by the EU at the UN (such as EU participation in the UN Counter-Terrorism Executive Directorate (CTED) assessment missions to Morocco, Kenya, Albania, Macedonia and Tanzania in 2005).[53] Examples in the first pillar context are the use of economic and financial aid and trade instruments of the EC to shore up the international coalition against terrorism and to support moderate reformers in countries with a high terrorist recruitment potential. Pakistan, for instance, has been granted preferential trade quotas in recognition of its contribution to the fight against terrorism.[54]

Since September 2001, the EU has also been systematically negotiating the insertion of clauses on cooperation against terrorism and terrorist financing into trade and cooperation agreements. Other examples are the technical assistance measures provided to Algeria and Morocco for upgrading maritime, air and border security in the fight against terrorism and the support for upgrading Morocco's counter-terrorism capabilities in fields like the combat against radicalisation in prisons.[55] The EU is also contributing to the anti-terrorism programs of the Jakarta Centre for Law Enforcement — and similar support for the African Union Counter-Terrorism Centre in Algiers is currently under negotiation.[56] Overall this quite comprehensive use of external instruments across the different pillars in parallel with internal measures reflects the link between the internal and external side of the EU's threat definition.

## The Combination of Repressive and Preventative Measures

Most of the above-mentioned internal legislative and operational measures are essentially aimed at improving law enforcement and are in that sense repressive in nature. More recently, especially since the Madrid and London terrorist attacks

---

[52] EU Council Doc No 7233/07 of 9 March 2007, 38.
[53] For these other examples: EU Council Doc No 10043/06 of 31 May 2006, 28-32.
[54] See O Brown, *EU Trade Policy and Conflict* (Winnipeg: International Institute for Sustainable Development, 2005) 7.
[55] EU Council Doc No 7233/07 of 9 March 2007, 5-6, 16, 29.
[56] EU Council Doc No 9666/07 of 21 May 2007, 12.

demonstrated the 'home grown' dimension of the terrorist threat, the EU has moved towards complementing its repressive measures by enhancing its preventative measures. The principal result so far is the adoption in November 2005 of the already mentioned *European Union Strategy for Combating Radicalisation and Recruitment to Terrorism*.[57] This Strategy is focused on disrupting the activities of networks and individuals that draw people into terrorism — through, inter alia, an increased monitoring of the internet (involving Europol), coordination of national measures against terrorist incitement as well as action programs both to encourage engagement with moderate Muslim organisations and to enhance language and other training for foreign Imams in Europe. The Strategy is marked by a strong emphasis on improving long-term integration and the dialogue with Muslim communities and religious authorities.[58] Measures implementing the 2005 Strategy include:

- the creation of an expert group on violent radicalisation;
- a (classified) report on recruitment to terrorism in the EU (and the adoption of a coordinated long-term strategy based upon it);
- a report by the EU Monitoring Centre on Racism and Xenophobia in Vienna[59] on the impact of the London terrorist attacks on Muslim communities in the EU;
- the establishment of a high-level group on minorities;
- the organisation of special journalist training programs; and
- a substantial investment in research on radicalisation phenomena.[60]

Further measures with a particular focus on the 'Islamist' side of the threat include common monitoring and evaluation mechanisms of Islamist websites; encouraging Muslim communities not to rely on foreign Imams; and research on inter-faith dialogues in the 6th and 7th Research Framework Programs of the EU.[61] External prevention measures have included the provision of training for police forces to reduce radicalisation potential in the Balkans; support for the build-up of an interfaith dialogue in Indonesia and the Mediterranean; and EU assistance to Algeria and Morocco on the identification of radicalisation patterns and preventative measures.[62] This greater effort to understand and address the roots of 'home grown' terrorism reflects both the strong internal side of the EU's threat definition and an appreciation of the complexity of the causes of terrorism.

---

[57] EU Council Doc No 14781/1/05 of 24 November 2005.
[58] Ibid, in particular [11], [13], [15].
[59] Since 1 March 2007 the EU Agency for Fundamental Rights.
[60] European Commission Memo/06/269 of 6 July 2006: Commission activities in the fight against terrorism, and part 1 of EU Council Doc No 7233/07 of 9 March 2007.
[61] EU Council Docs No 9666/07 of 21 May 2007, 4; No 10043/06 of 31 May 2006, 4; and No 7233/07 of 9 March 2007, 7.
[62] For these and other examples, see part 1 of EU Council Doc No 7233/07 of 9 March 2007.

## The Strengthening of European Union Institutional Capacity

Since 9/11 the mandate and actual role of the European police organisation Europol and of the cross-border prosecution unit Eurojust have been strengthened several times in terms of both their analysis functions and the support they receive for cross-border investigations and prosecutions.[63] The information flow from national authorities to these agencies has also been enhanced. Both institutions play a significant role in counter-terrorism both by providing cross-border assessments of anti-terrorism cases and by bringing national authorities together to work more effectively on such cases.[64] In addition, the tasks of some existing structures, such as the SitCen in the Council and the Police Chiefs Task Force (PCTF), have been redefined or reoriented to allow for a new focus on terrorism. The SitCen, for example, has been enabled to receive and process information from national intelligence services. The PCTF, although a non-permanent body with ill-defined powers, has been effectively mandated to play a role in the implementation of a common crime intelligence model and the identification and transfer of best counter-terrorism practices in local policing.[65] Newly created institutional structures, such as the European Police College (CEPOL) and the new EU external border management agency FRONTEX have also been immediately assigned tasks in the fight against terrorism.[66] The European Commission has undertaken a partial reorganisation to enhance its administrative capacity in the anti-terrorism field[67] and has reallocated funding instruments for research into terrorist issues.[68]

All this is clearly aimed at equipping the Union with a minimum of common response capacity, in addition to coordinated national capacities, to the defined common terrorist threat. Last but not least, with the creation of the Office of the EU's *Anti-Terrorism Coordinator*, a completely new senior office with a small supporting staff has been set up in the General Secretariat of Council in 2003 to monitor the implementation of the EU *Action Plan* and help coordinating EU and national counter-terrorism efforts.

---

[63] Of particular importance has been the entry into force on 18 April 2007 of the third amending protocol to the Europol Convention (opened for signature 27 November 2003, OJ C 2). This increases the capacity of Europol to support the member states in the fight against terrorism and other forms of serious cross-border crime. As a result of the Protocol, Europol officers can now make information from ongoing Europol analysis files directly available to the joint investigation team. It has also become possible for Europol to receive directly and process relevant information from the joint investigation team. In addition, Europol has also been given the possibility to request individual member states to institute criminal investigations.

[64] See the elucidating examples in the latest Eurojust Annual Report, Eurojust, *Annual Report 2006*, Eurojust, The Hague 2007, 31-4, 43-4.

[65] EU Council Doc No 7233/07 of 9 March 2007, 21.

[66] A typical example is the inclusion of terrorism in the risk analysis function of FRONTEX as regards the EU's external borders (EU Council Doc No 10043/06 of 31 May 2006, point 2.5.8).

[67] Reformed unit D/1 in the Directorate General Justice Freedom and Security.

[68] See European Commission Press Release No IP/05/1031 of 2 August 2005. Much more substantial funding allocations to the fight against terrorism have been allocated for the financial period 2007-2013.

## The Limitations of and Problems with the European Union's Response

### A Response Based on Cooperation Rather than Integration

With its broad range of measures in each of the contexts discussed above — legal and operational, internal and external, repressive, preventative and institutional — the EU's response to the post-9/11 terrorist threat appears substantially in line with its current threat definition. Further, that response is also quite substantial by the EU's own standards. For an actor like the EU, which has to struggle with particular obstacles of legal and institutional complexity, such as the pillar structure, and has to bring together 27 member states that remain fully sovereign in most matters of counter-terrorism, the agreement on such a comprehensive common response action plan is surely no minor achievement. Yet the very nature of the EU response given imposes certain limitations on the Union's capacities as an actor in the anti-terrorism field. This response has so far been based largely on cooperation between, rather than integration[69] of, the national systems.

The member states have so far clearly preferred to use instruments that are aimed at facilitating and supporting cooperation and coordination between their national counter-terrorism structures and capabilities. They have not transferred any competences to the EU in the field of anti-terrorism, and have abstained from creating any legal framework and structures at EU level that could form a basis for a legal and structural integration of their capabilities. This tendency is clearly shown in the legislative field by a preference for only minimal(ist) harmonisation of national criminal law (an example is the agreement on only minimum maximum penalties for terrorist offenders in the *Framework Decision on Combating Terrorism*) as well as mutual recognition (a key example is the *European Arrest Warrant*) instead of comprehensive harmonisation of relevant criminal law. In the operational field, the same tendency can be discerned. There is, for example, a persistent refusal to transfer any operational powers to the EU law enforcement agencies such as Europol, which in spite of its now nearly 600 staff must still content itself with supporting information exchange and analysis functions. Even the EU's Anti-terrorism 'Coordinator' office — which is currently in limbo as its first office-holder decided at the beginning of 2007 not to seek a renewal of his appointment[70] — has no actual powers to coordinate, but rather the office can simply monitor how the member states implement common measures and suggest improvements.

---

[69] The term of 'integration' is used here — along the lines of the definition of economic integration developed in B Balassa, 'Towards a Theory of Economic Integration' (1961) 14(1) *Kyklos* 1, 1-17 — with the very basic meaning of a process leading to the creation of single new system through the merging of several separately existing ones as opposed to 'cooperation' as a process where these systems interact but remain essentially separate.

[70] L Kubosova, 'EU in No Hurry to Appoint a New Anti-Terror Chief', *EU Observer*, 9 July 2007.

The main reasons for this preference for cooperation rather than integration in the anti-terrorism domain are not difficult to identify. Security, both internal and external, is a very sensitive issue from the point of view of national sovereignty, as well as being highly topical in domestic politics. Accordingly, national governments are wary of subjecting themselves and their national anti-terrorist capabilities to supranational decision-making, more extensive common legal rules and European operational command structures. Another factor is the absence of a real common (ie, largely identical) threat perception of the member states behind their common threat definition.[71] The terrorist threat assessments of EU governments are in fact still largely national assessments. Although a considerable effort has been made at the EU level to improve the 'common' analysis of terrorist threats, especially through the reports drawn up by Europol and the assessments provided by the SitCen, member states continue to assess these threats primarily from a national perspective. They are seen as threats to national structures, within national boundaries that require a specific national response. An example is the UK's counter-terrorism strategy of July 2006.[72] The sections of the strategy document dealing with threat assessment do not contain any reference to a European dimension of the terrorist threat. Rather what is referred to is essentially a threat to British institutions and territory.[73] The prevalence of national threat assessments has also, to some extent, been identified as a problem by Europol. In the TESAT report published in May 2006, Europol pointed out that the 'assessment of the threat level' posed by fundamentalist jihadist terrorism 'varies depending on the Member States, some of which still consider that they are under no direct threat'.[74] Inevitably, therefore, the national sense of urgency, national priority definitions and national resources committed to anti-terrorism measures vary considerably from one member state to another, reducing the willingness to engage in a more 'integrated' response.

As a result the EU has, five years after the 9/11 attacks, still no harmonised legal framework and no operational capabilities of its own as regards the fight against terrorism. While a harmonised legal framework and strong central operational agencies are no guarantee of maximum efficiency in the fight against terrorism, as the US example has shown, it is also clear that there is a price to be paid for not making any effort to integrate the national legal systems and structures. Their continuing difference and autonomy not only means that a huge continuous coordination effort is needed — the proliferation of agencies, working parties

---

[71] See on this point J Monar, 'Common Threat and Common Response? The European Union's Counter-Terrorism Strategy and Its Problems' (2007) 42(3) *Government and Opposition* 292.
[72] HM Government, *Countering International Terrorism: The United Kingdom's Strategy: July 2006*, HMSO, London, 2006.
[73] Ibid [3]-[4], [25]-[40].
[74] Europol, *Terrorist Activity in the European Union: Terrorism Situation and Trend Report (TESAT) 2004-2005* (The Hague: Europol, 2006) 19.

and expert groups is a testimony to that — but also that frequent friction and the partial failure of common efforts are inevitable. One example in this respect is the judgments rendered by the constitutional courts of Germany, Finland, Poland and Cyprus in 2005 and 2006 with respect to the compatibility of national provisions transposing the *Framework Decision on the European Arrest Warrant*. At least in the case of the judgment of the German *Bundesverfassungsgericht*,[75] the decision signalled a marked 'constitutional distrust' in the systems of the other member states that might not in all procedural aspects be similar to German standards and, as a result, also of a certain measure of distrust in the principle of mutual recognition as long as procedural standards are not harmonised, ideally in line with the German standards.[76] Another example is provided by Europol's continuing difficulties in obtaining the information it needs from national authorities[77] — which are often not as cooperative as they should be.

## The Implementation Deficit

Linked to the 'costs' of an essentially cooperative rather than integrative approach are the problems of implementation of EU anti-terrorism measures. The member states are much better at agreeing on comprehensive packages of measures than at implementing them in an effective manner. The half-yearly progress reports on the implementation of the *Counter-Terrorism Strategy* and the *Action Plan* abound with examples of agreed measures not being implemented on time or being only partially implemented.[78] Part of the implementation problems are due to the requirement of unanimity in the Council. The hugely delayed *Framework Decision on the European Evidence Warrant* (originally planned for 2004, still not adopted at the beginning of 2008) and the *Framework Decision on the organisation and content of the exchange of information extracted from criminal records between Member States on the content of the exchange of information from criminal records* (proposed by the Commission as early as 2005, but so far only the object of a 'general approach' agreed on in the Council) are just two of many examples where planned EU measures of obvious relevance for the fight against terrorism have not been implemented on time.

The latest progress report describes the process of decision-making in relation to implementation in the Council as 'slow and uncertain'.[79] This is a rather

---

[75] Judgment of 18 July 2005, BVerfG, 2 BvR 2236/04.
[76] For an analysis see F Geyer, 'The European Arrest Warrant in Germany: Constitutional Mistrust Towards the Concept of Mutual Trust' in E Guild (ed), *Constitutional Challenges to the European Arrest Warrant* (Nijmegen: Wolf Publishers, 2006) 101.
[77] On Europol's information problems see the summary of the Chairman of the Council's art 36 Committee of the High Level Conference on the Future of Europol of 23/24 February 2006 (Council Doc No 7868/06 of 29 March 2006).
[78] These reports were formerly provided by the Anti-terrorism Coordinator, Gijs de Vries, and since his departure in March 2007 by unit DG H 2 of the General Secretariat of the Council.
[79] EU Council Doc No 9666/07 of 21 May 2007, 3.

carefully worded characterisation for a situation that is marked by a serious gap between the often rapidly agreed upon declaratory common objectives and the actual political will of the member states to quickly and effectively achieve them. Yet it would be wrong to reduce this problem to one of voting requirements in the Council. It has also to do with the aforementioned absence of either a real common threat perception or of its corollary: a common sense of urgency. In addition, officials in the Council working parties are often much more inflexible on details than their ministers in the JHA Council on political programming and there is undoubted complexity in compromise-building in the (over-)extended EU of 27.

The gap between declared objectives and actual implementation appears even wider if one looks at legislative implementation at the national level. By May 2007, the 2002 *Framework Decision on Combating Terrorism*, arguably the most important legislative measure of EU action in the field, had still not been fully implemented by five member states. As at the same date, the May 2000 Convention on mutual legal assistance, essential for effective judicial cooperation, had still not been fully implemented by seven member states and the *Framework Decision on the execution of orders freezing property or evidence* of 22 July 2003 had not been implemented at all by 14 member states. These deficits were in spite of repeated deadlines set by the Council.[80] Part of the problem is that the Commission cannot put much pressure on non-fulfilling member states because of its limited powers in the domain of the third pillar. Of particular importance in this context is the absence of 'normal' treaty infringement procedures as enshrined in Articles 226 to 228 TEC, the possibilities of infringement actions against member states under Article 35(7) TEU being very limited.[81] Yet the core of the problem is that when it comes to implementation in the anti-terrorism domain, the EU still has to struggle with 27 largely autonomous and different systems with their own political priorities, domestic politics, institutional structures and parliamentary procedures. The absence of a tight implementation discipline can also affect the operational side of the measures to be implemented, as Europol's aforementioned problems in obtaining all relevant information from national police authorities demonstrate.

## The Legitimacy Deficit and Fundamental Rights Protection Issues

The last few years have again shown, at a global level, that anti-terrorism measures, especially in the spheres of policing and criminal justice, are among

---

[80] On these and other missed implementation deadlines see Council Doc No 9666/07 ADD 1 REV 2 of 4 June 2007.
[81] The European Commission placed a major emphasis on the absence of effective infringement procedures before the ECJ under Title VI TEU in its major June 2006 initiative to use the art 42 TEU 'passerelle' procedure for a 'communitarisation' of police and judicial cooperation in criminal matters. See COM (2006) 331 of 28 June 2006, 12.

the most invasive forms of action states are willing to use against individuals, with a corresponding negative impact on civil liberties and human rights. The absence of any law enforcement powers or of a criminal justice system at the EU level 'protects' the Union in a certain sense against the risk of infringing, via its own institutions and agencies, civil liberties and human rights. Yet the EU is an increasingly important provider of framework legislation on cross-border anti-terrorism matters, whose definition (or non-definition) of standards of protection can have an impact on how individuals are treated in cross-border police operations and judicial proceedings. The EU has been setting up more and more data-exchange and analysis instruments and procedures that also deal with personal data, and it serves, mainly on the basis of EC competences, as a framework for the implementation of UN Security Council Resolutions regarding financial sanctions against suspected terrorists. There is also a risk that major anti-terrorism objectives are agreed upon by the member states in the Council (in the form of program documents or even framework legislation), which can thereafter be used for sanctioning more controversial restrictive measures at the national level. National governments can use the argument of an existing broad European consensus to push through more invasive measures at the domestic level, and there have indeed been serious questions about the real need for some of the invasive measures agreed upon in the Council.[82] It would therefore seem all the more important that decisions in the counter-terrorism field are vested with the necessary legitimacy. Yet this legitimacy cannot be taken as a given as long as the European Parliament has no co-decision powers on relevant legislation on police and judicial cooperation in criminal matters.[83] National parliaments cannot really compensate for the absence of democratic control and scrutiny at the European level as they are not in a position to control the collective element of decision-making in the Council and are more often than not presented with a *fait accompli* by their national governments as regards the outcome of negotiations on anti-terrorism measures.

Effective judicial control of anti-terrorism measures, especially with regard to the protection of fundamental rights, is surely another crucial condition for their

---

[82] Some examples are given — from a very critical perspective — in the 'Statewatch Scoreboard on Post-Madrid Counter-Terrorism Plans' (March 2004). <http://www.statewatch.org/news/2004/mar/swscoreboard.pdf#search=%22Statewatch%20EU%20action%20plan%20terrorism%22>.

[83] The Parliament needs only to be consulted on such legislation — which gives it no power of amendment or rejection — and the ECJ's jurisdiction is limited by several member states not accepting preliminary rulings in this domain and by a more extensive public security exemption (TEU art 35). See, on this issue, European Parliament Policy Unit, 'Citizens' Rights and Constitutional Affairs: The fight against terrorism: How to improve effectiveness with due regard for fundamental rights', note prepared for the Joint Parliamentary Meeting between the European Parliament and the National Parliaments on 2/3 October 2006 in Brussels (EP Doc No NT\630666EN.doc).

legitimacy in any system firmly based on the principle of the rule of law.[84] The Union currently fulfils this condition at best partially. The current treaty provisions still impose important limitations on the role of the European Court of Justice (ECJ) in terms of fundamental rights protection. On issues of police and judicial cooperation in criminal matters under Title VI TEU, the Court may by virtue of Article 35(2) TEU receive requests for preliminary ruling only from the jurisdictions of member states that have made a declaration to that effect.[85] Unlike the situation under the TEC, these requests cannot concern the interpretation of primary law but only Framework Decisions, Decisions and Conventions. Other acts of the Council such as 'common positions' are excluded. As regards annulment proceedings, pursuant to Art 35(6) TEU these can only be introduced by a member state or the Commission, not by individuals. All these are serious limitations; particularly in light of the important role preliminary rulings have played in the development of fundamental rights protection under the TEC and the importance of annulment in cases of EU anti-terrorism measures directed against individuals. A further restriction is the absence of any possible action for damages under Title VI TEU.

In a number of cases, the Court has given a restrictive interpretation of these limitations, affirming its general judicial control functions on the basis of rule of law and legal coherence considerations. After an earlier general affirmation by the ECJ in Case C-170/96[86] of its right to interpret the third pillar provisions with implications for the EC framework, even if such a competence was not explicitly provided for by the Treaties, the Court of First Instance (CFI) even went a step further in asserting its judicial control powers in Case T-228/02 *Modjahedines*.[87] This case, coming after a range of cases dealing with challenges to the placing of suspected individuals and entities on the so-called 'terrorist lists' for the purpose of financial and other property sanctions (see below), concerned the financial sanctions adopted by the Council against the alleged terrorist organisation *Modjahedines du peuple d'Iran* on the basis of EC Regulation 2580/2001.[88] That EC Regulation, in turn, implemented a common position adopted on the basis of Articles 15 TEU (CFSP) and 34 TEU (AFSJ)[89] which was the initial EU decision to freeze funds. While stating that scrutiny of the common

---

[84] This point is also emphasised in E Guild and S Carrera, 'No Constitutional Treaty? Implications for the Area of Freedom, Security and Justice' (CEPS Working Document No 231, Centre for European Policy Studies, Brussels, 2005) 4.
[85] According to information provided by the General Secretariat of the Council, only 15 of the 27 member states had made a declaration to that effect on 30 June 2007.
[86] Case C-170/96, *Commission v Council* [1998] ECR I-2763.
[87] Case T-228/02, *Modjahedines* [2006] ECR II-4665.
[88] Council Regulation (EC) No 2580/2001 of 27 December 2001 on specific restrictive measures directed against certain persons and entities with a view to combating terrorism, OJ L 344/70 of 28 December 2001.
[89] *Council Common Position 2001/931/CFSP on the application of specific measures to combat terrorism*, [2001] OJ L 344/93.

position was, in principle, outside its jurisdiction, the Court nevertheless asserted that it had jurisdiction to hear an action for annulment 'to the extent that, in support of such an action, the applicant alleges an infringement of the Community's competences'.[90] As a result the Court felt in a position to annul the EC Decision to implement the second and third pillar measures and freeze the Modjahedines' assets on the grounds that it did not contain a sufficient statement of reasons and did not observe the right to a fair hearing.[91]

With its judgment in the *Modjahedines Case*, the CFI not only reaffirmed the Court's power to review any third pillar measures with regard to their implications for the first pillar domain, but also its general role in safeguarding the application of the rule of law across the pillar divide. The rule of law approach to 'bridge' that divide has been further developed in two recent judgments of the ECJ in appeal proceedings against dismissal orders issued by the CFI — Cases C-354/04 P *Gestoras pro Amnisia* and C-355/04 P *Segi*. Those dismissal orders had declared inadmissible actions for damages by two groups that had been the object of financial sanctions decisions as alleged terrorist groups by virtue of an EU common position.[92] While recognising that the provisions under Title VI TEU did not provide for any action for damages, and recommending a corresponding reform of the EU legal framework,[93] the Court held that because pursuant to Article 6 TEU, the Union is based on the rule of law and the respect of fundamental rights: 'the institutions are subject to review of the conformity of their acts with the treaties and the general principles of law, just like the Member States when they implement the law of the Union'.[94] The Court thereby affirmed that all measures adopted by EU institutions that directly affect individual rights, independently from the pillar under which they are adopted, can be made subject to judicial review by the ECJ under the preliminary rulings procedure. The Court extended this position to include Title VI TEU 'common positions'[95] although these are not listed in Article 35(1) TEU as acts on which a preliminary ruling can be requested.

While the Court has clearly affirmed its own judicial control function of anti-terrorism measures on the grounds of rule of law principles, it has until now not given much content to that protection. It is true that in the aforementioned *Modjahedines Case*, the CFI annulled the EC Decision to freeze the Modjahedines' assets on grounds of not containing a sufficient statement of reasons and non-observation of the right to a fair hearing. Yet the annulment only concerned an EC implementing decision, and not the common positions on

---

[90] Case T-228/02, *Modjahedines* [2006] ECR II-4665, [56].
[91] Ibid [173].
[92] Cases C-354/04 P, *Gestoras pro Amnestia* [2007] ECR I-1579 and C-355/04 P, *Segi* [2007] ECR I-1657.
[93] Ibid [50].
[94] Ibid [51].
[95] Ibid [54].

which it was based. In its ruling, the CFI emphasised that the non-observation of the above-mentioned legal guarantees provided a ground of annulment only because the UN Security Council Resolution 1373(2001)[96] at the origin of the common position had in fact left discretion to the Council as regards the individualisation of the sanctions concerned. As a result, the Council was bound to observe all applicable legal guarantees under EC law.[97] The Court explicitly recognised in this context the 'broad discretion' of the Council in deciding on the imposition of the sanctions. It declared that 'the Community Courts may not, in particular, substitute their assessment of the evidence, facts and circumstances justifying the adoption of such measures for that of the Council', so that its judicial review role would need to be limited to the respect of procedural rules and the exclusion of a manifest error of judgement or abuse of power.[98] This is not the only instance of the Court showing reluctance to review the substantive grounds of the Council for imposing sanctions on individuals in the fight against terrorism. In two of the earlier 'terrorist lists' cases — Case T-306/01 *Yusuf* and T-315/01 *Kadi*[99] — the CFI had even refused to enter into the merits of the case by adopting the position that the UN Security Council Resolutions at the origin of the sanctions imposed enjoyed supremacy over EC/EU law, a reasoning that has attracted vigorous criticisms.[100] In the two subsequent 'terrorist lists' cases — Case T-253/02 *Ayadi*[101] and Case T-49/04 *Hassan*[102] — the CFI also rejected the applications for annulment against the sanctions. This time it did so essentially on the grounds of the responsibility of the member states to ensure in the given case adequate protection of the rights of the individuals within their jurisdiction, including the rights of those individuals to seek a 'de-listing' of their names by the UN Sanctions Committee. The existence of this responsibility was strongly affirmed by the Court.

As far as the protection of personal data in the context of anti-terrorism measures is concerned, the Court has so far avoided any substantive decision. In its 2004 application for annulment of the controversial EU-US agreement on the processing and transfer of PNR data, the European Parliament had sought the termination of the agreement because of both its concerns about adequate protection of personal data and the aim to assert its co-decision rights. In its judgment of 30 May 2006, the ECJ in fact annulled the Council decision to conclude the

---

[96] UN SC Res 1373 (2001) of 28 September 2001.
[97] Case T-228/02, *Modjahedines* [2006] ECR II-4665, [107].
[98] Ibid [159].
[99] Case T-306/01 *Yusuf* [2005] ECR, II-3533 and T-315/01 *Kadi* [2005] ECR, II-3649.
[100] See, inter alia, D Simon and F Mariatte, 'Le Tribunal de première instance des Communautés: Professeur de droit international' (2005) *Europe* 12, 6-12; H Labayle, 'Architecte ou Spectatrice, la Cour de Justice de l'Union dans l'espace de Liberté, Sécurité et Justice, à Paraître' (2006) *Revue trimestrielle de Droit Européen* 1, 38-45.
[101] Case T-253/02 *Ayadi v Council* [2006] ECR II-2139, under appeal.
[102] Case T-49/04 *Hassan v Council* [2006] ECR II-52, under appeal.

agreement, but did so only on the grounds that the first pillar legal basis (art 95 TEC) of the agreement was inappropriate. The ECJ did not enter into the substance of the data protection arguments put forward by the Parliament.[103] In this case, as well as in a range of the 'terrorist lists' cases, the Court therefore showed a considerable degree of 'judicial restraint'. While the principle of judicial review of Council measures in the fight against terrorism has certainly been affirmed by the Court in recent years, the content and extent of this review currently appears relatively thin.

Finally, it should also be mentioned that the Council has not been in any hurry to adopt legislation aimed at counterbalancing the growth of repressive measures in the form of texts ensuring an EU-wide protection of the rights of individuals caught by those measures. The *Framework Decision on procedural rights in judicial proceedings*, proposed by the Commission in April 2004[104] and originally due to be adopted at the end of 2005, is still on the Council's negotiating table. This seems all the more regrettable from a fundamental rights protection point of view as the judicial rights provided for by the *EU Charter of Fundamental Rights* continue, along with the Charter, not to have any binding status.

## Conclusion

At the outset I raised the question of how, and how well, the EU has used its improved potential after the *Treaty of Amsterdam* to emerge as an actor in the fight against terrorism. There can be no doubt that the Union has indeed emerged as an actor in its own right in this field, both at an internal and at an international level. Today the fight against terrorism is no longer, as it was a decade ago, within the exclusive domain of the member states. Those states may still have a largely national perception of terrorist threats and of their domestic priorities in responding to them, but when it comes to cooperating across borders, and the post-9/11 challenge is essentially a cross-border challenge, then the EU is now the uncontested primary framework for doing so: even for pursuing common approaches towards third countries.

When it comes to assessing the way in which the EU's potential has been realised so far, the obvious overall conclusion is that its role in the 'war on terror' has evolved through cooperation rather than through integration. Member states continue to be highly protective of national sovereignty and their position as primary providers of internal security. They do not necessarily share either a perception of threat or a corresponding sense of urgency in matters of counter-terrorism. As a result, they want to maintain a significant degree of autonomy and to limit as far as possible any necessity to adapt their national legislation, structures and capabilities to common objectives and requirements.

---

[103] Joined Cases C-317/04 and C-318/04, *European Parliament v Council* [2006] ECR I-4721.
[104] COM(2004) 328 of 28 April 2004.

Instruments of cooperation rather than integration, such as mutual recognition of judicial decisions, enhanced data-exchange and common structures supporting cross-border cooperation, are therefore the preferred method of proceeding. Most of the progress achieved since 9/11 is indeed due to such instruments.

The answer to the question of how well the EU has used its potential as an actor in this field must be a more nuanced one. On the one hand, it has to be said that there is no other example in the world of a group of countries agreeing on a comprehensive common strategy and action plan similar to that of the EU. As security, both in its internal and external dimension, arguably remains the area in which the European integration process has made least progress, this must be regarded as a major achievement in itself. It can also not be denied that the EU has managed to arrive at a reasonably specific common threat definition that avoids any simplistic reductions to an 'Islamic threat', and a response that is sufficiently multidimensional to address the different aspects — internal and external, legislative and operational, repressive and preventative as well as institutional — of this threat. There is today a common platform of legislation, operational mechanisms and institutional structures that, whatever its limitations, nevertheless provides clear added value as far as the interaction between the national systems in the fight against terrorism is concerned.

Yet the almost purely cooperative approach has major limitations. These include the absence of real common operational capabilities, a continuing significant diversity of national legislation and structures (which create friction and require a huge coordination effort) and serious problems regarding the effective implementation of objectives and measures agreed upon at the EU level. The preference for cooperation rather than integration also contributes to the legitimacy deficit of the Union in the anti-terrorism domain: the restrictions imposed on the roles of both the European Parliament and the Court of Justice reflect the reluctance of at least some member states to subject themselves in the sensitive internal security domain to 'supranational' parliamentary control and judicial review procedures. This justifies some concern over the level of protection of the rights of individuals in relation to EU anti-terrorism measures. Although the ECJ has strongly asserted its right to judicially review such measures, it has on substantive issues followed a line of judicial restraint. Such restraint corresponds all too well to the political climate. Member states want to exclude as far as possible any judicial interference with their preferred form of cooperation that continues to be based very much on the principles of sovereignty and territoriality.

The EU as a system may have many deficits in terms of effectiveness and legitimacy. Nevertheless it is definitely more dynamic than most national systems. The agreement reached at the June 2007 European Council on a framework for the new Reform Treaty,[105] planned to be negotiated in Autumn 2007 and to enter into force in 2009, also offers some development perspectives for the EU's role in the anti-terrorism domain. Various predicted reforms, including the abolition of the pillar structure, enhanced competences in the criminal justice field (especially as regards criminal procedure) and an extended use of qualified majority voting could strengthen the EU's effectiveness as an actor in the sphere of counter-terrorism. The anticipated removal of most of the restrictions on the role of the ECJ, the extension of the European Parliament's co-decision rights to most of the current Title VI TEU matters as well as the legal codification of the *Charter of Fundamental Rights* could further strengthen its legitimacy. If all these reforms are implemented, the Union will remain a collective actor in the fight against terrorism — but it will be a stronger and more legitimate one.

---

[105] See EU Council Document No 11177/07 of 23 June 2007 (Presidency Conclusions), Annex I: *Draft IGC Mandate*.

# Chapter Twelve

# The European Union, Counter-Terrorism Sanctions against Individuals and Human Rights Protection

### Gabriele Porretto[*]

## I. Introduction

Since 1999, action by the European Union (the EU) as well as by the European Community (the Community or the EC) has been necessary to implement United Nations Security Council resolutions adopted under Chapter VII of the UN Charter, which impose economic measures against 'blacklisted' persons and corporate entities, in the framework of the so-called 'war on terror'.[1] A list of

---

[*] Formerly Research Associate and Sparke Helmore Lecturer, ANU College of Law, The Australian National University, Canberra, Australia. This research was funded by an Australian Research Council grant 'Terrorism and the Non-State Actor After September 11: The Role of Law in the Search for Security' (DP0451473 awarded for 2004-2007). My thanks go to Dr Pene Mathew, Ms Miriam Gani and Professor Andrew Byrnes for their editing work and comments on this article. I am also grateful to Professor Simon Bronitt and Dr Mark Nolan for reading early drafts of this article. Finally, I am indebted to Ms Helen Bermingham, a graduate of the ANU College of Law, for her invaluable research work on many sources I used in this article. All mistakes remain mine. The chapter is updated to January 2007.

[1] On UN Security Council sanctions in general, and for a discussion, from the perspective of human rights protection, of the sanctions regimes currently in place, see V Gowlland-Debbas (ed), *United Nations Sanctions and International Law* (The Netherlands: Kluwer Law International, 2001); A Reinisch, 'Developing Human Rights and Humanitarian Law Accountability of the Security Council for the Imposition of Economic Sanctions' (2001) 95 *American Journal of International Law* 851; M E O'Connell, 'Debating the Law of Sanctions' (2002) 13 *European Journal of International Law* 63; B Fassbender, 'Targeted Sanctions and Due Process' (2006) Humboldt-Universität zu Berlin and United Nations Office of Legal Affairs, Office of the Legal Counsel <www.un.org/law/counsel/Fassbender_study.pdf>; I Cameron, 'The European Convention on Human Rights, Due Process and United Nations Security Council Counter-Terrorism Sanctions' (2006) Council of Europe
<http://www.coe.int/t/e/legal_affairs/legal_co-operation/public_international_law/ Texts_&_Documents/2006/I.%20Cameron%20Report%2006.pdf>; A Bianchi, 'Assessing the Effectiveness of the UN Security Council's Anti-Terrorism Measures: The Quest for Legitimacy and Cohesion' (2006) 17 *European Journal of International Law* 881; A Bianchi, 'Security Council's Anti-terror Resolutions and their Implementation by Member States' (2006) 4 *Journal of International Criminal Justice* 1044. For a discussion of the work of the different sanctions committees, see the report by T Biersteker and S Eckert, *Strengthening Targeted Sanctions Through Fair and Clear Procedures* (2006) The Watson Institute for International Studies, <http://watsoninstitute.org/pub/Strengthening_Targeted_Sanctions.pdf>; J Farrall, *United Nations Sanctions and the Rule of Law* (Cambridge: Cambridge University Press, 2007). Scholarly contributions analysing the EU (and EC) implementation of Security Council sanctions include: S Bohr, 'Sanctions by the UN Security Council and the EC' (1993) 4 *European Journal of International Law* 256; I Canor, 'Can Two Walk Together, except they Be Agreed? The Relationship between International Law and European Law: The Incorporation of UN Sanctions against Yugoslavia into European Community Law through the Perspective of the ECJ' (1998) 35 *Common Market Law Review*

persons and entities having ties with the Taliban, Osama bin Laden, Al Qa'ida, or their associates, is managed and updated by a Security Council committee set up, inter alia, to monitor states' efforts to implement the sanctions imposed with Resolution 1267 (1999), and known as the '1267 Committee' or the 'Taliban Sanctions Committee'.[2] A separate committee, called the 'Counter-Terrorism Committee' (CTC) was set up by the Security Council in order to supervise states' compliance with Resolution 1373 (2001),[3] most notably with the measures providing for the freezing of assets and other economic and financial resources of those who commit acts of terrorism, or attempt to commit them, or who take part in them. The 1267 Committee's list of terrorist individuals and entities is 'based on information provided by states and regional organisations'.[4] The CTC, unlike the 1267 Committee, does not draw up or impose any such lists.

The implementation of UN counter-terrorism sanctions by the EU is in many aspects a good test of the efficacy of the UN strategy to combat terrorism, through the imposition of specific obligations on states and of sanctions on non-state actors.[5] According to several commentators, one of the most controversial aspects

---

137; N Vennemann, 'Country Report on the European Union' in C Walter et al (ed), *Terrorism as a Challenge for National and International Law: Security versus Liberty?* (Berlin, London, New York: Springer, 2004) 217; A Reinisch, 'The Action of the European Union to Combat International Terrorism' in A Bianchi (ed), *Enforcing International Law Norms against Terrorism* (Oxford: Hart Publishing, 2004) 119-62; R Pavoni, 'UN Sanctions in EU and National Law: The Centro-Com Case' (1999) 48 *International and Comparative Law Quarterly* 582. Pavoni correctly notes that 'a very interesting and unprecedented (but now established) practice has emerged in the EC/EU context with respect to the implementation of UN embargoes of the 1990s and a particular institutional machinery ... has been set up for that purpose' (at 583).

[2] In para 6 of Resolution 1267 (1999), the Security Council established a committee composed of all the Council's members. The committee is responsible most notably for ensuring that states implement the measures imposed by para 4 of the said resolution, and for designating the funds or other financial resources referred to in this paragraph. Initially established to monitor states' sanctions on Taliban-controlled territory, the 1267 Committee has progressively seen its scope of activity extended to all measures against individuals and entities associated with the Taliban, Osama bin Laden and Al Qa'ida. See E Rosand, 'The Security Council's Efforts to Monitor the Implementation of Al-Qaida/Taliban Sanctions', (2004) 98 *American Journal of International Law* 745.

[3] On the work of the CTC see, inter alia, E Rosand, 'Security Council Resolution 1373, the Counter-Terrorism Committee, and the Fight against Terrorism' (2003) 97 *American Journal of International Law* 333; E J Flynn, 'The Security Council's Counter-Terrorism Committee and Human Rights' (2007) 7 *Human Rights Law Review* 371.

[4] S/RES/1333 (2000) [16b].

[5] On the EU implementation of counter-terrorism sanctions, see generally I Cameron, 'European Union Anti-Terrorist Blacklisting' (2003) 3 *Human Rights Law Review* 225, who examines various aspects of the implementation and the legal effects of EU sanctions (most notably through the case study of Sweden) and of the legal remedies available to the blacklisted individuals, especially before the ECrtHR. He correctly highlights that 'while the ECrtHR is a better body than the CFI or ECJ to check the compatibility of EU measures with human rights, it is easy to forget that the ECHR standards are designed to be subsidiary, or supplementary to the national constitutional standards, which form the first, and most important, line of defence of the Rechtstaat' (255). See also the contributions of C Warbrick, 'The European Response to Terrorism in an Age of Human Rights' (2004) 15 *European Journal of International Law* 989; B Bowring and D Korff, 'Terrorist Designation with Regard to European and International Law: The Case of the PMOI', (Paper presented at the International Conference of Jurists in Paris, 10 November 2004) 30 (2005) *Statewatch* <http://www.statewatch.org/news/2005/feb/bb-dk-joint-paper.pdf>; I Tappeiner, 'The Fight against

of the sanctions regimes is the risk that such measures, under the pretext of the 'war on terror', may encourage and legitimise violations of some fundamental human rights at the UN level,[6] at the regional level (eg the EU), as well as at the domestic level. Most notably, the procedure through which individuals and entities associated with the Taliban, Osama bin Laden and Al Qa'ida are labelled as 'terrorists' and put into a list has been the object of extensive criticism.

In this chapter I focus on the case law of the European Court of Justice (ECJ) originating from lawsuits filed by individuals and entities targeted by the sanctions adopted by EU and EC institutions when implementing the UN sanctions.[7] Such complaints are always dealt with initially by the Court of First Instance (CFI) and its judgments may be appealed to the ECJ. The thrust of the plaintiffs' complaints is the alleged invalidity of certain Community acts under which they are listed. They argue that they are prevented from living normal lives and conducting their financial activities normally, as a consequence of being listed by the EU and having their assets and funds frozen, and because of damage to their personal and professional reputation. Violations of several human rights which are guaranteed under international law, Community law and constitutional traditions common to the EC member states,[8] are thus alleged, including the right to use property, the right to a fair hearing and the right to effective judicial review.

Judicial review of counter-terrorism sanctions listing individuals and entities is not available at the suit of individuals through the principal judicial organ of the UN, the International Court of Justice (ICJ). Nor has the Security Council manifested any intention to set up any subsidiary body empowered to examine

---

Terrorism. The List and the Gaps' (2005) 1 *Utrecht Law Review* 97; N Lavranos, 'Judicial Review of UN Sanctions by the Court of First Instance' (2006) 11 *European Foreign Affairs Review* 471; R A Wessel, 'Regulation beyond the State: Accountability of International Organizations in a Multilevel Legal Order', (Paper presented at the Annual Ius Commune Conference, Edinburgh, 1-2 December 2005); W Vlcek, 'Acts to Combat the Financing of Terrorism: Common Foreign and Security Policy at the European Court of Justice' (2006) 11 *European Foreign Affairs Review* 491; C Lehnardt, 'European Court Rules on UN and EU Terrorist Suspect Blacklists' (2007) 11 *ASIL Insight* < http://www.asil.org/insights/2007/01/insights070131.html>. Monar's Chapter 11 in this volume, provides a general background on the EU response to international terrorism, including most notably the recent 'Terrorism Framework Decision' and the 'European Arrest Warrant Framework Decision'.

[6] The issues relating to the lack, or to a belated and partial incorporation, of a human rights framework in the procedural and substantive aspects of the CTC are analysed with respect to the treatment of asylum-seekers by P Mathew, 'Resolution 1373 — a Call to Preempt Asylum Seekers? (or, "Osama the Asylum Seeker")', in J McAdam (ed), *Forced Migration, Human Rights and Security* (Oxford: Hart Publishing, 2008) 19.

[7] The relevant acts must be adopted by the European Council ('the Council') also on the basis of the EC treaty, because action of the Community is always necessary to implement certain aspects of 'common positions' adopted in the EU framework: it would then be appropriate to refer each time to 'EU/EC' sanctions and 'EU/EC' counter-terrorism action — see also below n 19. However, throughout the paper I will be referring mostly to 'EU sanctions' or 'EU action' for simplicity's sake.

[8] For more discussion on the sources of human rights protection in the EU system, see below, section III.

individuals' claims.[9] As for the remedies offered by international courts and bodies supervising the implementation of international human rights instruments, they are an option only once domestic remedies have been exhausted: this is, for instance, the case for the jurisdiction *ratione materiae* of the European Court of Human Rights (ECrtHR), under Article 35 (1) of the *European Convention on Human Rights and Fundamental Freedoms* (ECHR).[10] However, it is not clear how this prerequisite may be satisfied where UN sanctions are implemented through acts adopted at the EU level rather than by states.[11] So, even though some commentators have argued that, as a matter of principle, national courts may legally afford judicial review of mandatory resolutions adopted by international organisations (and of international treaties),[12] this does not seem an option in the cases examined here. As the remainder of this paper will show, the ECJ is sometimes the first and the only avenue of relief available to concerned individuals and entities.[13] But is the ECJ willing and able to play its role in such cases?

The Court has previously been confronted, in the mid-1990s, with the issue of the legality of sanctions of a different kind, most notably comprehensive diplomatic, economic and trade sanctions (eg, general trade embargoes), imposed on either states or non-state actors, or both, involved in armed conflicts. For instance, in the *Bosphorus Case* the Court examined the question as to whether restrictions of property rights and of the right to exercise economic activities may be justified in the framework of the implementation at Community level of UN sanctions adopted against the former Federal Republic of Yugoslavia.[14]

---

[9] Interestingly, a reference to this possibility (in particular, to an 'independent international court') was made by the CFI in two judgments handed down on 21 September 2005: *Yusuf and Al Barakaat International Foundation v Council and Commission* (T-306/01) [2005] ECR II-3533 [340] (hereafter *Yusuf*) and *Yassin Abdullah Kadi v Council and Commission* (T-315/01) [2005] ECR II-3649 [285] (hereafter *Kadi*). Both cases are discussed below, section III, subparagraphs A and B.

[10] *European Convention for the Protection of Human Rights and Fundamental Freedoms*, 213 UNTS 222 (entered into force 3 September 1953). According to art 35 (1) '[t]he Court may only deal with the matter after all domestic remedies have been exhausted, according to the generally recognised rules of international law, and within a period of six months from the date on which the final decision was taken.'

[11] On the right to effective access to the ECrtHR, see Cameron, above n 5, 248-50.

[12] This point is developed, inter alia, by Benedetto Conforti in the report he submitted to the Institute of International Law (*Institut de droit international*), 'The Activities of National Judges and the International Relations of their State' (1993) 65 *Annuaire de l'Institut de droit international* I-65, 347-51, 389-91; see also B Conforti, 'Decisioni del Consiglio di sicurezza e diritti fondamentali in una bizzarra sentenza del Tribunale comunitario di primo grado' (2006) 11 *Il Diritto dell'Unione Europea* 333, 344; E de Wet and A Nollkaemper, 'Review of Security Council Resolutions by National Courts' (2002) 45 *German Yearbook of International Law* 166, 184-202.

[13] Bowring and Korff, above n 5. For a discussion of the ECJ jurisdiction in such cases, see below, section III.

[14] This is still the leading case in this area (*Bosphorus Hava Yollari Turizm ve Ticaret AS v Minister for Transport, Energy and Communications, Ireland and the Attorney General* (C-84/95) [1996] ECR I-3953). Bosphorus Airways was a Turkish charter airline which leased a Yugoslav State-owned plane, subsequently seized by the Irish authorities under the sanctions regime decided by the UN Security Council against the Federal Republic of Yugoslavia (FRY), and implemented through an EC Regulation

However, the case law of the ECJ offers no precedent exactly in the area of counter-terrorism sanctions of the kind examined here, that is, measures targeting designated non-state actors suspected of being involved in terrorist activities or associated with terrorist organisations.[15]

Recently confronted with claims against these measures, the CFI has held that it could not review them.[16] I will analyse from the perspective of the protection of human rights some of the most controversial issues emerging from representative cases before the CFI, in order to show the extent to which there has been an evolution in the Court's approach to the review of European counter-terrorism sanctions. As I will show, with respect to the EU sanctions implementing Security Council Resolution 1267 (1999) the Court maintains that review of the relevant Community acts would necessarily entail review of the UN Resolution itself, which would be clearly beyond its jurisdiction. However, the Court reserves to itself the power to review Security Council resolutions at

---

(*Council Regulation No 990/93 of 26 April 1993, concerning trade between the EC and the Federal Republic of Yugoslavia (Serbia and Montenegro)*, [1993] OJ L 102/14). Bosphorus Airways challenged the seizure before the Irish courts, arguing that the EC sanctions were not susceptible to being applied against an undertaking not incorporated (and not operating) in the FRY. The Irish Supreme Court eventually referred the case to the ECJ for a preliminary ruling (under art 234 of the EC Treaty), given that Ireland was implementing the EC sanctions adopted to implement, in turn, the UN-mandated economic sanctions. The ECJ stated that the aim to stop the armed conflict in the FRY had to be given precedence over the rights invoked by Bosphorus Airways; the latter, according to the Court, are not absolute rights and may thus be sacrificed for the objectives of general interest pursued by the Community, that is, ending the conflict. Thus, the seizure of the aircraft required by the EC regulation constituted no violation of the property right of Bosphorus. The applicant then decided to institute proceedings before the European Court of Human Rights: see below n 71 and accompanying text. The CFI subsequently upheld the *Bosphorus* judgment in *Dorsch Consult Ingenieurgesellschaft mbH v Council and Commission* ((C-184/95) [1998] ECR I-1443), where the applicant, a German-based engineering consulting company, asked the Court to order the Council and the Commission to compensate it for damage suffered as a result of Regulation (EC) No 2340/90, on the embargo on trade with Iraq and Kuwait. The application was dismissed by the CFI, because the contested EC regulation was adopted in order to implement Security Council Resolution 661 (1990), and therefore as part of the action towards the maintenance of international peace and security in the area. In the Court's opinion, negative consequences for some operators (essentially, limitations to the freedom to trade) were justified also because the economic risk in doing business in Iraq had not been exceeded. See the note on the *Dorsch Consult Case* by J Kokott and R Schlölch in International Decisions (1999) 93 *American Journal of International Law* 668.

[15] These measures are sometimes referred to as 'smart sanctions'. Such is the terminology adopted, for instance, by the CFI in the *Yusuf* and *Kadi* judgments of 21 September 2005. The Court said that such sanctions, being targeted and selective, 'reduce the suffering endured by the civilian population of the country concerned, while none the less imposing genuine sanctions on the targeted regime and those in charge of it' (*Yusuf* (T-306/01) [2005] ECR II-3533 [113], [122] and *Kadi* (T-315/01) [2005] ECR II-3649 [90]). The Court was clearly trying to show the distinction between these sanctions and other kinds of sanctions adopted by the Security Council under Chapter VII of the UN Charter, already mentioned in the text, and which are not examined any further in this paper. Fassbender (above n 1, 4), correctly points out that the regime instituted under SC Resolution 1267 (1999) differs from all the other UN sanctions regimes 'in that, after the Taliban were removed from power in Afghanistan, there is no particular link between the targeted individuals and entities and a specific country'.

[16] According to a note prepared by *Statewatch* in January 2007, the CFI judgment of December 2006 in the *OMPI Case* (see below n 139) 'represents the first successful legal challenge to the EU proscription regime: 13 previous challenges have been dismissed (seven cases have been appealed to the ECJ, another seven cases are pending)' (Statewatch News Online, *Successful Challenge to EU "Terrorist" list by PMOI* (2007) *Statewatch* <http://www.statewatch.org/news/2007/jan/04ecj-pmoi.htm>).

least where violations of human rights protected by *jus cogens* norms are alleged. This line of reasoning, which has failed to convince several commentators, will then be analysed.[17] In contrast, the Court has fully scrutinised and declared invalid an EC regulation implementing UN Security Council Resolution 1373 (2001) because of the different features of the sanctions regime established under that resolution.[18] My analysis will also illustrate how the potential concurrent jurisdiction of different judicial bodies may in some cases produce the result that only very limited judicial review of EU counter-terrorism sanctions is offered when human rights violations are alleged.

## II. Enforcing United Nations Counter-Terrorism Sanctions in the European Community/European Union System

In order to provide some background information for the analysis to follow, it is appropriate first to outline briefly the main features of the two sanctions regimes set up by the UN Security Council as part of its counter-terrorism strategy, and then the implementing measures ('common positions' and regulations) adopted within the EU framework.[19]

---

[17] These points are further developed later in this chapter, see below section III, subparagraphs A and B.

[18] See the discussion below at section III, subpara D.

[19] Generally speaking, UN sanctions of an economic and financial nature must be implemented by the EC rather than by its member states because, under art 133 EC Treaty, the Community has an exclusive competence in the area of external trade. Action by the Community, under art 301 and art 60 EC Treaty, depends in these cases on previous action by the EU pursuant to the EU Treaty provisions in the field of the common foreign and security policy (CFSP, see below n 23), that is, by the agreement of a common position or a joint action. As to the acts adopted, they are usually regulations and 'common positions', respectively. Council regulations are normative acts adopted by the EC and identified by their general and direct applicability in the Community legal order, as well as by their binding character in their entirety. In other words, regulations produce direct effects, and thus confer rights and duties, in the domestic orders of all member states, even in the absence of measures for domestic implementation (see, for instance, J Steiner, L Woods and C Twigg-Flesner, *EU Law* (Oxford: Oxford University Press, 9th ed, 2006) 93-4; S Bronitt, F Burns and D Kinley, *Principles of European Community Law* (New South Wales, Australia: Law Book Company, 1995) 102; or the EU official website, <http://europa.eu/scadplus/constitution/legislation_en.htm>). On the other hand, EU 'common positions' are not acts of a Community nature and must be defined within the framework of two procedures of the EU law-making process, that is, the cooperation procedure and the co-decision procedure: see arts 251 and 252 of the EC Treaty, formerly arts 189b and 189c respectively, the full text of which, together with the rules of procedures of the European Parliament relating to common positions, can be read at <http://www.europarl.europa.eu/commonpositions/default_en.htm> (for insights on the EU law making process, see *ex multis* Bronitt, Burns and Kinley, 86-91). In other words, common positions are adopted by the Council but not on the basis of the EC Treaty. For instance, common positions may be adopted by the Council, composed of representatives of the governments of member states, in the field of Justice and Home Affairs (JHA, or the third pillar of the EU, see below n 23) under Title VI, art 34 of the EU Treaty, as well as in the field of Common Foreign and Security Policy (CFSP, or second pillar of the EU, see Bronitt, Burns and Kinley, 86-91) under Title V, art 15 of the EU Treaty. The most relevant element, for our analysis, is the fact that common positions are not subject to review of their lawfulness before the CFI/ECJ.

Prior to 11 September 2001 (9/11), the EU institutions had put in place a common response to international terrorism[20] in order to implement Security Council resolutions 1267 (1999)[21] and 1333 (2000).[22] They were acting on the basis of both the *Treaty on the European Union* (in particular, the so-called second and third pillars of the EU, respectively the CFSP and the JHA)[23] and the European Community Treaty (the so-called first pillar).[24] The European Council adopted implementing acts as early as November 1999, and then regularly adopted updates in order to follow the 1267 Committee's updates.[25] The European measures include the freezing of funds and of other financial assets of Osama bin Laden and individuals and entities associated with him, as designated by the 1267 Committee. UN sanctions were further implemented by the European Council with *Regulation* (EC) No 467/2001, which prohibited the export of certain goods

---

[20] A detailed review of all the acts adopted by the EU institutions to implement UN sanctions is provided by Tappeiner, above n 5, 102-10, as well as by Vennemann, above n 1, 219-29.

[21] Under Resolution 1267, adopted on 15 October 1999, the Security Council required that the Taliban hand over Osama bin Laden to the appropriate authorities. To this end, para 4(b) of this resolution required that all the states 'freeze funds and other financial resources, including funds derived or generated from property owned or controlled directly or indirectly by the Taliban, or by any undertaking owned or controlled by the Taliban, as designated by the [1267 Sanctions] Committee', established by para 6 of the same resolution. The Council further imposed on states an obligation to ensure that neither the said funds 'nor any other funds or financial resources so designated are made available, by their nationals or by any persons within their territory, to or for the benefit of the Taliban or any undertaking owned or controlled, directly or indirectly, by the Taliban, except as may be authorised by the Committee on a case-by-case basis on the grounds of humanitarian need'.

[22] In para 8 (c) of this resolution the Council asked all states to freeze without delay funds and other financial assets of Osama bin Laden, as well as individuals and entities associated with him, and to ensure that funds of financial resources be made available, directly or indirectly, for the benefit of Osama bin Laden, his associates or any entities owned or controlled, directly or indirectly, by Osama bin Laden or individuals and entities associated with him, including the Al Qa'ida organisation. Furthermore, the Security Council instructed the Sanctions Committee to maintain an updated list, based on information provided by the states and regional organisations, of the individuals and entities designated as associated with Osama bin Laden, including those in the Al Qa'ida organisation. In para 17, the Security Council called upon all states and all international and regional organisations, including the UN and its specialised agencies, to act strictly in accordance with the provisions of the resolution, notwithstanding the existence of any rights or obligations conferred or imposed by any international agreement. The measures adopted were established for 12 months and it was for the Security Council to decide, at the end of that period, whether to extend them for a further period on the same conditions.

[23] CFSP is the acronym for 'Common Foreign and Security Policy', indicating pillar two of the EU, whereas 'Justice and Home Affairs' (JHA) constitutes the third pillar. They are regulated under arts 11-28 of the EU Treaty (Title V) and arts 29-42 (Title VI), respectively. It must be noted that the second and third pillars share the same institutions of the EC, but all decisions must be made unanimously, for instance, the common positions. See Steiner, Woods and Twigg-Flesner, above n 19, 9. The said pillars are entirely based on inter-governmental cooperation among the member states, and therefore acts of a Community nature may never be adopted in these fields (see the synopsis on 'The Union's founding principles' in the EU official website, <http://europa.eu/scadplus/constitution/legislation_en.htm>).

[24] The first pillar of the EU has absorbed the European Communities and their traditional fields of activity and competence.

[25] In order to impose the sanctions established under SC Resolution 1267, the Council adopted on 15 November 1999 Common Position 1999/727/CFSP, concerning restrictive measures against the Taliban. The measures were subsequently defined by the Council in Regulation (EC) No 337/2000 concerning a flight ban and the freezing of funds and other financial resources in respect of the Taliban of Afghanistan. In February 2001, the Council adopted Common Position 2001/154/CFSP, which implemented UN Security Council Resolution 1333 (2000).

and services to Afghanistan, strengthened the flight ban and extended the freezing of funds and other financial resources in respect of the Taliban of Afghanistan.[26]

On 27 May 2002, in order to implement Security Council Resolution 1390 (2002)[27] the European Council adopted *Common Position* 2002/402/CFSP, concerning restrictive measures against Osama bin Laden, members of the Al Qa'ida organisation, the Taliban and other individuals, groups, undertakings and entities associated with them.[28] On the same day, the European Council adopted *Regulation* (EC) No 881/2002, repealing its previous regulations on the subject.[29]

A separate path was followed by the Security Council with the adoption of Resolution 1373 (2001) immediately after the attacks of 9/11.[30] The new regime of sanctions thereby created was implemented by the European Council through two common positions adopted on 27 December 2001 (the most relevant being

---

[26] *Council Regulation (EC) No 467/2001 of 6 March 2001 prohibiting the export of certain goods and services to Afghanistan, strengthening the flight ban and extending the freeze of funds and other financial resources in respect of the Taliban of Afghanistan, and repealing Regulation (EC) No 337/200* [2001] OJ L 67/1. It was not until 8 March 2001 that the 1267 Committee published the first consolidated list of the entities and the persons to be subjected to the freezing of funds, pursuant to Security Council resolutions 1267 (1999) and 1333 (2000). This list has since been amended and supplemented several times, so the Commission adopted various regulations pursuant to art 10 of Regulation No 467/2001 in order to amend Annex 1.

[27] Resolution 1390 (2002) laid down new measures to be directed against Osama bin Laden, members of the Al Qa'ida network and the Taliban and other associated individuals, groups, undertakings and entities.

[28] *Council Common Position 2002/402/CFSP of 29 May 2002 concerning restrictive measures against Osama bin Laden, members of the Al-Qaida organisation and the Taliban and other individuals, groups, undertakings and entities associated with them and repealing Common Positions 96/746/CFSP, 1999/727/CFSP, 2001/154/CFSP and 2001/771/CFSP* [2002] OJ L 139/4. Art 3 of the common position prescribed the continuation of the freezing of the funds and other financial assets or economic resources of the individuals, groups, undertakings and entities referred to in the list drawn up by the Sanctions Committee in accordance with Security Council resolutions 1267 (1999) and 1333 (2000). In accordance with para 3 of Resolution 1390 (2002), the measures adopted must be maintained and then reviewed by the Security Council 12 months after their adoption, at the end of which period the Council must either allow those measures to continue or decide to improve them.

[29] *Council Regulation (EC) No 881/2002 of 27 May 2002 imposing certain specific restrictive measures directed against certain persons and entities associated with Usama bin Laden, the Al-Qaida network and the Taliban, and repealing Council Regulation No 467/2001 prohibiting the export of certain goods and services to Afghanistan, strengthening the flight ban and extending the freeze of funds and other financial resources in respect of the Taliban of Afghanistan* [2002] OJ L 139/9.

[30] Resolution 1373 (2001) obliges states to freeze all assets and other economic and financial resources of those who commit acts of terrorism or attempt to commit them, or who take part in them or who facilitate the carrying out of these acts. Furthermore, states have to take steps that forbid assets and other economic and financial resources, as well as other financial and allied services, from being made available to these persons.

*Common Position* 2000/931),[31] as well as through *Regulation* (EC) No 2580/2001.[32] Under this regime, the procedure leading to a measure to freeze funds takes place first at the national level and then at the Community level. Whereas in the first phase a 'competent national authority', which in principle must be judicial, takes a decision to include a certain party in the list, in the second phase the European Council must decide on the actual inclusion, on the basis of precise information or material in the relevant file transmitted by the national authority.[33]

As soon as the two UN sanctions regimes entered into operation, it became manifest that the listing and de-listing procedures lacked transparency and failed to safeguard what may be called due process rights. Even though a de-listing procedure is set up under the sanctions regime, individuals and entities are not allowed to petition the committees for de-listing, nor are they granted a hearing.[34] Petitions for de-listing may be submitted only to governments, which may in turn bring the issue to the attention of the committee. However, any decision concerning de-listing would still be left to the discretion of the committee or of the Security Council.[35] The 1267 Committee therefore adopted, in November 2002, written guidelines for inclusion in and removal from the list.[36] Shortly thereafter, the Security Council adopted Resolution 1452 (2002), which provided for a number of derogations from, and exceptions to, the freezing of funds and economic resources imposed by its previous resolutions. Such derogations and exceptions were to be decided by member states on 'humanitarian grounds' and with the Sanctions Committee's consent.[37] Just as in the previous phases, the

---

[31] *Council Common Position of 27 December 2001 on the application of specific measures to combat terrorism (2001/931/CFSP)* [2001] OJ L 344/93. This common position includes an Annex with a list to be 'drawn up on the basis of precise information or material in the relevant file which indicates that a decision has been taken by a competent authority in respect of the person, groups and entities concerned, irrespective of whether it concerns the instigation of investigations or prosecution for a terrorist act, an attempt to perpetrate, participate in or facilitate such an act based on serious and credible evidence or clues, or condemnation for such deeds' (art 1 (4)).

[32] *Council Regulation (EC) No 2580/2001 of 27 December 2001 on specific restrictive measures directed against certain persons and entities with a view to combating terrorism* [2001] OJ L 344/70.

[33] See, most notably, arts 1 (4) ('the initial decision to freeze funds') and 1 (6) ('subsequent decisions to freeze funds') of Common Position 2001/931, as well as art 2 (3) of Council Regulation (EC) No 2580/2001.

[34] See, generally, Bierstecker and Eckert, above n 1, 34-7; as to the 1267 Committee, see also Fassbender, above n 1, 4.

[35] Ibid.

[36] Security Council Committee established pursuant to Resolution 1267 (1999) Concerning Al-Qaida and the Taliban and Associated Individuals and Entities, *Guidelines of the Committee for the Conduct of its Work (as amended on 29 November 2006)* (2002) United Nations <www.un.org/Docs/sc/committees/1267/1267_guidelines.pdf>. The guidelines provide, inter alia, that submission of names should, to the extent possible, include a statement of the basis for the designation, generally focusing on the connection between the individual and Al Qa'ida, the Taliban, or Osama bin Laden, together with identifying information for use by the national authorities who must implement the sanctions.

[37] On this point, see G Burci, 'Interpreting the Humanitarian Exceptions through the Sanctions Committees' in Gowlland-Debbas (ed), above n 1, 143; E de Wet, 'Human Rights Limitations to Economic Enforcement Measures Under Article 41 of the United Nations Charter and the Iraqi Sanctions Regime'

implementation of further Security Council resolutions involved the adoption by the European Council of a new *Common Position* (2003/140/CFSP) and of further amendments to *Regulation* (EC) No 881/2002, thus introducing a system of exceptions to the restrictive measures previously imposed.[38]

*Regulation* (EC) No 881/2002 and its consolidated list,[39] which are part of the 1267 sanctions regime against the Taliban, Osama bin Laden and Al Qa'ida, are the object of most of the lawsuits discussed in this paper. Other complaints were filed against *Regulation* (EC) No 2580/2001, and are therefore within the framework of the 1373 sanctions regime. As the remainder of this paper will show, the Court has dealt with the two different sanctions regimes in very different ways in terms of the judicial review which it is prepared to offer to individuals and entities targeted by the measures.

## III. Challenging the European Union Sanctions before the Court of First Instance/European Court of Justice

Since 2001, the legality of the counter-terrorism sanctions adopted under the different EU pillars has, on several occasions, been challenged before the CFI. The plaintiffs are individuals resident, or entities incorporated, in both EU and non-EU states, such as Sweden, the United Kingdom (UK) and Saudi Arabia, and whose names were included in Annex 1 of *Council Regulation* (EC) No 881/2002, or in *Regulation* (EC) No 2580/2001.[40] In all the cases considered, applicants have not only challenged the Community's competence to adopt the contested regulations, but they have also asked the Court to declare these acts invalid, alleging violations of fundamental human rights, as protected by Community law. This paper aims to cover some of the legal issues concerning the protection of the applicant's human rights.

As to the jurisdictional questions, for the purposes of my analysis I will only note that most of the relevant cases arise from 'annulment actions' brought by individuals (natural or legal persons) under Article 230 of the EC Treaty. An individual may only challenge a decision addressed to him/herself or a decision

---

(2001) 14 *Leiden Journal of International Law* 277, 281-4; and more recently, Bierstecker and Eckert, above n 1, 31-3.

[38] *Regulation (EC) No 881/2002 imposing certain specific restrictive measures directed against certain persons and entities associated with Usama Bin Laden, the Al-Qaida network and the Taliban* [2003] OJ L 81/1.

[39] By the end of 2006, the regulation and the attached list had been amended more than 60 times, both by the Council and by the Commission.

[40] See, respectively, above nn 38 and 32. When analysing EU counter-terrorism sanctions, some commentators have highlighted the distinction between European (or 'EU internal') terrorists and non-European (or 'EU external') terrorists, especially in light of Common Position 2001/931. According to this argument, whereas the Council Decisions of June 2002, implementing Regulation 2580/2001, only list 'EU external' terrorists, the list annexed to Common Position 2001/931 include both internal and external terrorists (see, for instance, Reinisch, above n 1, 130). However, this dichotomy is far from being clear-cut, as shown by Tappeiner, above n 5, 109-10.

'which, although in the form of a regulation or a decision addressed to another person, is of *direct* and *individual* concern to the former'.[41] The other form of individual direct action before the ECJ against Community institutions is action seeking compensation for any damage that may have been caused by a Community act.[42] However, in a couple of cases the CFI rejected applications for compensation, lodged by organisations (*Segi and Others* and *Gestoras Pro-Aministía*, respectively) blacklisted by the European Council when implementing Security Council Resolution 1373 (2001).[43] The Court concluded that it could not afford judicial review to the applicants, because it lacks jurisdiction to examine complaints against acts adopted under Title VI of the EU Treaty (JHA or third pillar).[44]

As to the merits of individuals' actions for annulment, the applicants usually claim that the EU decisions to freeze their funds, and all related subsequent decisions, are never communicated to them in advance. Also, the decisions never mention the specific information allegedly provided by a competent national authority in order to justify the inclusion of individuals and organisations in the disputed list, therefore the right to a fair hearing does not seem to be protected. Persons affected by decisions of public authorities must be given the right to put their case, in particular with respect to the correctness and the relevance of the facts and the circumstances alleged as well as to the evidence adduced. The principle of due process of law, which encompasses both the right to be heard and the right to effective judicial protection, presupposes the existence of courts and tribunals, which are impartial and independent of the executive power.[45]

---

[41] Art 230 (4) EC Treaty [emphasis added].

[42] This is regulated under art 288 EC Treaty.

[43] The two organisations filed two distinct applications for damages as compensation for damage allegedly suffered as a result of their inclusion in the list attached to Common Position 2001/931 (referred to above, n 31) as well as to other acts applying specific measures to combat terrorism (*Action brought on 31 October 2002 by the Gestoras Pro Amnistía association, Juan Mari Olano Olano and Julen Zelarain Errasti against Council of the European Union* (T-333/02) [2003] OJ C 19/36; *Action brought on 13 November 2002 by the SEGI association, Araitz Zubimnedi Izaga and Aritza Galarraga against Council of the European Union* (T-338/02) [2003] OJ C 7/24).

[44] Even though Common Position 2001/931 was adopted under the CFSP heading, the Court found in an Order of 7 June 2004 that the applicants were only affected by its art 4, which entails measures falling within the area of police and judicial cooperation in criminal matters (JHA) (*Segi and Others v Council of the European Union*, (T-338/02) [2004] II-1647 [33]). Since the Community legal system is based on the principle of conferred powers (see art 5 EU Treaty) and the ECJ powers are listed exhaustively under art 46 EU Treaty, the Court concluded that no judicial remedy for compensation is available in the context of Title VI of the EU Treaty (JHA) [34]. On the other hand, '[t]he Community courts have jurisdiction over the present action for damages in so far as the applicants allege failure to observe the powers of the Community' [41]. See, in the same sense, the order delivered on the same date in the case *Gestoras Pro Amnistía and Others v Council of the European Union* (T-333/02) (unreported; a summary of the order is available in [2004] OJ C 228/40).

[45] Fassbender, above n 1, 6. Although these rights were first developed in the context of criminal justice, where the principle of fairness of the legal process is of particular relevance, they are nowadays seen as relevant each time fundamental human rights are at stake. On these aspects, it is appropriate to refer to the reasoning of the ECrtHR in the seminal judgment delivered in the *Golder Case* (1975) 18 Eur

As is well known, the case law of the ECJ gradually built up a framework for human rights protection, in the absence of any general provision in the EC Treaty on the protection of fundamental rights.[46] Only with the Maastricht Treaty were the constitutional traditions and the international human rights obligations of member states formally integrated into the legal order of the EU itself.[47] According to Article 6 (1) of the EU Treaty, the Union is founded on the principles of liberty, democracy, respect for human rights and fundamental freedoms, and the rule of law. Under Article 6 (2), the Union is bound to respect fundamental rights as guaranteed by the *European Convention on Human Rights* and as they derive from the constitutional traditions common to the member states, as general principles of Community law. General principles of Community law are 'unwritten principles used by the Court to supplement the Treaties and acts of the institutions' and to ensure that 'Community law reflects and is firmly rooted in the basic legal values of the Member States'.[48] It has correctly been noted that, although no human rights treaty is directly binding upon the EU and its institutions, the CFI and the ECJ normally rely on the ECHR when reconstructing general principles in the field.[49]

The principle of respect for fundamental human rights is the measure of legality of EU anti-terrorist sanctions relevant for the purposes of this chapter.[50] In

---

Court HR (ser A) 4, 12-8. See also the recent analysis by Cameron, above n 1, 7-10, on aspects of due process in criminal matters, civil matters and with respect to blacklisting in general. He correctly highlights that 'UN blacklisting does not fit into this more traditional pattern of due process. It bears a superficial similarity to interim seizure of assets pending a trial, but it is in fact entirely different. ... at the UN level, the freezing measures are alternatives to criminal investigations, not adjuncts'.

[46] See, *ex multis*, F G Jacobs, 'European Community Law and the European Convention on Human Rights' in D Curtin and T Heukels (eds), *Institutional Dynamics of European Integration (Essays in Honour of Henry G. Schermers)* (Dordrecht, Boston: M Nijhoff, 1994), 561; A Arnull, *The European Union and its Court of Justice* (Oxford: Oxford University Press, 2nd ed 2006) 337-66. Notwithstanding the absence of provisions of a general scope on the protection of fundamental human rights, the EC Treaty of 1957 specifically prohibited discriminatory practices based on grounds of nationality or gender.

[47] A discussion of the hierarchy of sources in the EU system is clearly beyond the scope of this paper. May I just refer to the following passage by Giorgio Gaja, 'The Protection of Human Rights under the Maastricht Treaty', in D Curtin and T Heukels (eds), above n 46, 549, 551-52: 'the constant characterization by the [ECJ] of fundamental rights as "an integral part of the general principles of law" appears to locate the protection of human rights at a level which is higher than Community secondary legislation, but lower that the Treaty establishing the Communities' [footnotes omitted].

[48] Arnull, above n 46, 335.

[49] T Ahmed and I de Jesús Butler, 'The European Union and Human Rights: An International Law Perspective' (2006) *European Journal of International Law* 771, 774-5, 780.

[50] More recently, the constitutional traditions common to the member states and the standards of the ECHR as interpreted by the ECrtHR and by the Community courts have been drawn on in the Charter of Fundamental Rights of the European Union (hereafter, the EU Charter, the full text of which is published in [2000] OJ C 364/1), an instrument signed by all member states but not yet ratified. I will note that, according to art II-112 of the EU Treaty, '[i]nsofar as this Charter contains rights which correspond to rights guaranteed by the [European] Convention for the Protection of Human Rights and Fundamental Freedoms, the meaning and scope of those rights shall be the same as those laid down by the said Convention.' The relevant part for our analysis is Chapter VI (art 47-50), under the heading of 'Justice'. Most notably, art 47 codifies the right to an effective remedy and to a fair trial, whereas art 48 deals with the presumption of innocence and the right of defence.

particular, the right to a fair hearing and the right to access to courts as set out in Articles 6 and 13 of the ECHR are indisputably part of the general principles of Community law.[51]

However, the CFI has shown a certain reluctance to exercise judicial review. As early as December 2001, two actions under Article 230 EC were brought by different applicants (to whom I will refer as *Yusuf* and *Kadi*, respectively) against the European Council, asking the Court to annul *Regulation* (EC) No 881/2002, whose Annex 1 listed the applicants as targets of restrictive measures.[52] Most notably, *Yusuf* and *Kadi* alleged the infringement of their right to use property, of their right to a fair hearing and of their right to an effective judicial remedy.[53]

---

[51] See, for instance, *Yusuf* (T-306/01) [2005] ECR II-3533 [192]. For further discussion see, inter alia, C Harlow, 'Access to Justice as a Human Right: The European Convention and the European Union' in P Alston (ed), *The EU and Human Rights* (Oxford, New York: Oxford University Press, 1999) 187. Art 6 of the ECHR reads, in the relevant parts:

1. 'In the determination of his civil rights and obligations or of any criminal charge against him, everyone is entitled to a fair and public hearing within a reasonable time by an independent and impartial tribunal established by law ...
2. Everyone charged with a criminal offence shall be presumed innocent until proved guilty according to law.
3. Everyone charged with a criminal offence has the following minimum rights:
   a. to be informed promptly, in a language which he understands and in detail, of the nature and cause of the accusation against him;
   b. to have adequate time and facilities in the preparation of his defence;
   c. to defend himself in person or through the legal assistance of his own choosing or, if he has not sufficient means to pay for legal assistance, to be given it free when the interests of justice so require;
   d. to examine or have examined witnesses against him and to obtain the attendance and examination of witnesses on his behalf under the same conditions as witnesses against him;
   e. to have the free assistance of an interpreter if he cannot understand or speak the language used in court.'

Under art 13 of the ECHR: 'Everyone whose rights and freedoms as set forth in this Convention are violated shall have an effective remedy before a national authority notwithstanding that the violation has been committed by persons acting in an official capacity.'

Summing up, the main aspects of the due process rights protected by the ECHR are (i) the right to procedural fairness, (ii) the presumption of innocence in criminal proceedings, (iii) specific rights for persons accused of criminal offences, including the right to be informed of the charge and the right to be tried within a reasonable time and (iv) the right to be free from retrospective criminal law (art 7 ECHR). These rights must be read in conjunction with other corollaries of the principle of fair trial, most notably: the right not to be deprived of liberty unless in accordance with a procedure described by law (art 5 (1) ECHR); the right of appeal in criminal matters (7$^{th}$ Protocol to the ECHR, art 2); the right to compensation for wrongful conviction (7$^{th}$ Protocol to the ECHR, art 3); the right not to be tried twice for the same offence (7$^{th}$ Protocol to the ECHR, art 4).

[52] *Action brought on 10 December 2001 by Abdirisak Aden and Others against the Council of the European Union and the Commission of the European Communities* and *Action brought on 18 December 2001 by Yassin Abdullah Kadi against the Council of the European Union and the Commission of the European Communities* [2002] OJ C 56/16. The applications were originally brought against both the Commission and the Council; however, the CFI ruled that, on account of the repeal of some acts adopted by the Commission, the action had to be regarded as being brought against the Council alone (*Yusuf* (T-306/01) [2005] ECR II-3533 [71]-[77]; *Kadi* (T-315/01) [2005] ECR II-3649 [52]-[8]).

[53] Infringements of the right to property are also the object of most of the lawsuits considered in this chapter. Both the domestic legislation of most European states and customary international law require that interferences with individual property be in principle grounded on judicial findings and not on

In two nearly identical judgments handed down on 21 September 2005, the CFI held that it lacked jurisdiction to review EC sanctions implementing Security Council Resolution 1267 (1999), because it had no jurisdiction to review the legality of the latter; it thus rejected all the pleas.[54]

Only the pleas concerning the breach of the applicants' fundamental rights will be dealt with in this chapter. In light of *Yusuf* and *Kadi* and subsequent cases, I will now assess the way in which the Court interpreted its power to review the legality of the contested EC regulation (A). I will then analyse the alleged breach of the applicants' right to a fair hearing and to an effective judicial remedy, when 1267 sanctions are implemented at the EU level (B). Interestingly, the Court has concluded, in a more recent case, that an essential guarantee for the protection of the applicants' rights is their right to diplomatic protection (C). Lastly, I will turn to a case relating to the protection of human rights with respect to the implementation of the 1373 sanctions regime (D).

## A. The Court's Jurisdiction, the Primacy of the United Nations Legal Order and the Role of *Jus Cogens* in the Protection of Human Rights

The *Kadi* and *Yusuf* cases presented the CFI with the opportunity to discuss several issues of EU law and international law, including: the legal basis for counter-terrorism measures in EU and EC law;[55] the obligations of the EU and of its member states resulting from the UN Charter and Security Council

---

administrative procedures, such as the procedures of the 1267 Committee. Violations of the right to privacy and to the protection of personal information of the targeted individuals and organisations may also be considered when analysing the judicial review of EU counter-terrorism measures. See Bianchi, 'Security Council's Anti-terror Resolutions and their Implementation by Member States', above n 1, 1064-9.

[54] *Yusuf* (T-306/01) [2005] ECR II-3533 and *Kadi* (T-315/01) [2005] ECR II-3649. For comments on various aspects of the two judgments see, inter alia, Steve Peers, 'First EU Court Ruling on Terrorist Lists' (2005) *Statewatch* <http://www.statewatch.org/news/2005/sep/10terrorlists.htm>; C Tomuschat, 'Ahmed Ali Yusuf and Al Barakaat International Foundation v. Council and Commission: Case Note' (2006) 43 *Common Market Law Review* 537; B Conforti, above n 12, 333; A Gianelli, 'Il rapporto tra diritto internazionale e diritto comunitario secondo il Tribunale di primo grado delle Comunità Europee' (2006) 89 *Rivista di diritto internazionale* 131; L Pech, 'Trying to Have it Both Ways: On the First Judgments of the Court of First Instance Concerning EC Acts Adopted in the Fight against International Terrorism' (2007) 1 *Irish Human Rights Law Review* 1 (available on the SSRN database: <http://ssrn.com/abstract=915386>).

[55] The first ground of annulment put forward by the applicants was the Council's incompetence to adopt the contested regulation. The position of the CFI on this point may be summarised as follows (*Yusuf* (T-306/01) [2005] ECR II-3533 [108]-[66]). Whereas arts 60 and 301 EC Treaty constitute in themselves a sufficient basis for the adoption of restrictive measures against the rulers of a third state (ie, the Taliban of Afghanistan), and thus the measures laid down by Regulation No 467/2001 come within the power of the Community; the legal basis for the parts of the same regulation that impose economic and financial sanctions on individuals not presenting a link with a third state may not be found in the said articles if taken in isolation, because the powers to adopt economic sanctions do not encompass the interruption of economic relations with third states. It is thus necessary to read these articles together with art 308 EC Treaty (on residual powers of the Community), in order to have an appropriate joint legal basis, notwithstanding the fact that the adoption of 'smart sanctions' against individuals or entities is not part of any power expressly attributed to the Community.

resolutions; the Court's power to review the lawfulness of UN sanctions; the scope of the applicants' right to a hearing and of the right to judicial review. With regard to the breach of the right to a hearing, the applicants' submission was that the European Council never examined the reasons for their listing, first by the states and then by the Sanctions Committee.[56] The plaintiffs alleged that '[t]he entire procedure leading to the addition of the applicants to the list in Annex 1 to the contested regulation is ... stamped with the seal of secrecy.'[57]

The challenges to the EU sanctions were rejected in light of the Court's interpretation of the relationship between the UN Charter and Community law. According to the CFI, although it is undisputed that the Community is based on the rule of law and that all acts of its institutions may be reviewed by the Court, member states' obligations under the UN Charter and Security Council's resolutions must nevertheless prevail over all other conventional obligations, including obligations under the EC Treaty and under the ECHR.[58] In other words, the principle of primacy of the UN legal order and of the Charter's obligations, as expressed by Article 103 of the Charter, sets the scene for the Court's analysis of its power to entertain the claims. The Court's line of reasoning implies, first, that the Community itself, although not a UN Member, is bound by obligations stemming from UN Security Council's resolutions, to the extent that the Community's member states are bound by such resolutions and must comply with them also in their dealings with the Community.[59] This means that the Community, in exercising its powers, is required to adopt all necessary provisions to allow its member states to fulfil their obligations, including the obligation to implement UN counter-terrorism sanctions.[60]

The second limb of the CFI's reasoning stems from the circumstance that the European Council, when adopting the contested EC regulation, was acting 'under circumscribed powers [and] had no autonomous discretion'.[61] Thus, the Court considers that:

> [a]ny review of the internal lawfulness of the contested regulation, ... would ... imply that the Court is to consider, indirectly, the lawfulness of [Security

---

[56] *Yusuf* (T-306/01) [2005] ECR II-3533 [191] (Yusuf and Al Barakaat International Foundation, during argument); *Kadi* (T-315/01) [2005] ECR II-3649 [141]-[5].
[57] *Yusuf* (T-306/01) [2005] ECR II-3533 [191]. It must be noted that EC regulations No 467/2001 and No 881/2002 do not make clear, unlike Common Position 2001/931 and Regulation 2580/2001, that 'competent authority' for blacklisting individuals and entities 'shall mean a *judicial* authority, or, where judicial authorities have no competence in the area covered by this paragraph, an *equivalent* competent authority in that area' [emphasis added].
[58] Ibid [231]-[34]; *Kadi* (T-315/01) [2005] ECR II-3649 [181]-[84].
[59] States' obligations discussed here stem from arts 25, 48 and 103 of the UN Charter.
[60] *Yusuf* (T-306/01) [2005] ECR II-3533 [254]; *Kadi* (T-315/01) [2005] ECR II-3649 [204]. Several scholars have commented upon this extension of the monist idea of hierarchy between the Community legal system and member states' legal systems to the relationship between UN law and Community law. See, for instance, Tomuschat, above n 54, 540; Lavranos, above n 5, 475.
[61] *Yusuf* (T-306/01) [2005] ECR II-3533 [265]; *Kadi* (T-315/01) [2005] ECR II-3649 [214].

Council] resolutions [given that] the origin of the illegality alleged by the applicant would have to be sought not in the adoption of the contested regulation but in the resolutions of the Security Council which imposed the sanctions.[62]

As a consequence, the Court saw no other option than to refrain from exercising any judicial review of the Community measures, as it lacks power to review judicially the underlying Security Council's resolutions,[63] and thus rejected the applicants' claims.[64]

The third limb of the CFI reasoning further complicates an already disputable argument, since the Court notes that the (indirect) exercise of judicial review of the Security Council's resolution would still be an option in all cases of alleged violations of fundamental rights guaranteed by peremptory norms of international law (*jus cogens*).[65]

One is left with the impression that some of the elements of the test outlined by the Court were not really necessary. Indeed, the Court had simply been asked to examine the compatibility of a regulation, implementing UN sanctions, with primary Community law, which includes the EC Treaty and fundamental rights as protected by the constitutional traditions common to member states and by the ECHR. Thus, it does not seem that the Court had any truly persuasive reason not to exercise judicial control of the observance of Community law by Community institutions, under Article 220 EC Treaty.[66] It is difficult to see what would have really prevented the Court from invalidating the contested regulation with respect to the applicants, had such regulation been found to violate procedural and substantive rights guaranteed under Community law, without adjudicating on the legality of Security Council Resolution 1267 (1999). As we will see, the Court has moved towards this approach in the more recent *OMPI Case*.[67]

A different outcome would have been welcome especially as the Court itself notes the lack of other avenues of judicial review open to the applicants.[68] One wonders where else targeted individuals and entities might seek legal protection. The Court's reasoning seems to be in conflict with the principle that 'access to justice is one of the constitutive elements of a Community based on the rule of law and is guaranteed in the legal order based on the EC Treaty'.[69]

---

[62] *Yusuf* (T-306/01) [2005] ECR II-3533 [266]; *Kadi* (T-315/01) [2005] ECR II-3649 [215].
[63] *Yusuf* (T-306/01) [2005] ECR II-3533 [276]; *Kadi* (T-315/01) [2005] ECR II-3649 [224].
[64] *Yusuf* (T-306/01) [2005] ECR II-3533 [346]; *Kadi* (T-315/01) [2005] ECR II-3649 [291].
[65] *Yusuf* (T-306/01) [2005] ECR II-3533 [277]; *Kadi* (T-315/01) [2005] ECR II-3649 [226].
[66] See Lavranos, above n 5, 474-9.
[67] Analysed below, subparagraph D.
[68] *Yusuf* (T-306/01) [2005] ECR II-3533 [339]-[40] and *Kadi* (T-315/01) [2005] ECR II-3649 [284]-[5].
[69] See *Philip Morris International v Commission* (T-377/00) [2003] ECR II-1 [121].

It is true that invoking the primacy of UN law in order to exclude any judicial review of Community acts by the CFI seems in line with the *Bosphorus Case*, where the ECJ affirmed that the exercise of fundamental rights may be subject to restrictions justified by objectives of general interest pursued by the Community, for instance the effective implementation of UN sanctions.[70] However, the consolidation of this jurisprudence is a source of concern if one considers that the ECrtHR, in its more recent cases, has concluded that in future cases it would exercise its jurisdiction *only* where the protection of fundamental rights within the EC is 'manifestly deficient'.[71] One commentator has labelled this reluctance of both the ECJ and the ECrtHR to exercise jurisdiction in such cases as a 'common hands-off approach'.[72]

Another problematic aspect of the *ratio decidendi* in the cases at hand is that the threshold triggering the CFI's powers of (indirect) judicial review of UN resolutions is a violation of *jus cogens* rules.[73] However, not all fundamental rights are the subject of protection by peremptory rules of international law.[74] The jurisprudence of the ICJ does not offer clear guidance on this point.[75] The

---

[70] Above n 14, [22]-[6].

[71] *Bosphorus v Ireland* [2005] 42 E.H.R.R. 1 [156]. After the ECJ delivered its judgment in this case (*Bosphorus*, above n 14), the applicants brought the case before the ECrtHR and instituted proceedings against Ireland, alleging a violation of the right to property, as guaranteed under art 1 of Protocol I to the ECHR. See the case note by Steve Peers, 'Limited responsibility of European Union member States for actions within the scope of Community Law' (2006) 2 *European Constitutional Law Review* 443.

[72] Lavranos, above n 5, 475.

[73] E de Wet, 'Holding the UN Security Council Accountable for Human Rights Violations: A Role for Domestic and Regional Courts?', (Paper presented at the Workshop on *Connecting the Public with the International: Law's Potential*, The Australian National University, Canberra, 2-4 July, on file with author).

[74] See Pech, above n 5, [9], who argues that the notion of *jus cogens* 'does not seems warranted and is certainly rather perilous in practice'.

[75] With the exception of the recent judgment handed down on 3 February 2006 in the dispute opposing the DRC and Rwanda (*Armed Activities on the Territory of the Congo (New Application 2002) (Democratic Republic of the Congo v Rwanda)*, [2006] [74], available at <http://www.icj-cij.org/docket/files/126/10435.pdf>), the ICJ has never expressly mentioned *jus cogens* in its case law. The exact scope of *jus cogens* norms at international law cannot be determined precisely, although there is a general consensus that the notion encompasses norms protecting fundamental interests of the international community, eg, the norms prohibiting aggression, slavery, genocide, apartheid, torture, the use or threat of force, as well as most norms of international humanitarian law, in particular those prohibiting war crimes and crimes against humanity (see A Cassese, *International Law* (Oxford: Oxford University Press, 2nd ed, 2005) 202-3). This being said, there is certainly an argument in favour of the CFI's choice of the *jus cogens* test, because in the legal doctrine there seems to be a broad agreement to the effect that *jus cogens* does indeed limit the authority of the Security Council, most notably when the protection of fundamental human rights is at stake: see, generally, the recent study of A Orakhelashvili, 'The Impact of Peremptory Norms on the Interpretation and Application of United Nations Security Council Resolutions' (2005) 16 *European Journal of International Law* 59. In the Bosnia case, Judge Lauterpacht rightly emphasised in his separate opinion that the UN Security Council is bound by peremptory norms of international law and that 'it is not to be contemplated that the Security Council would ever deliberately adopt a resolution clearly and deliberately flouting a rule of *jus cogens* or requiring a violation of human rights' (*Application of the Convention on the Prevention and Punishment of the Crime of Genocide (Bosnia and Herzegovina v Serbia and Montenegro) (Order of 16 September 1993)* [1993] ICJ Rep 440-1).

CFI simply defines *jus cogens* as 'a body of higher rules of public international law binding on all subjects of international law, including the bodies of the United Nations, and from which no derogation is possible'.[76] One may, on the one hand, welcome the CFI's message to the Security Council, defining the limits within which the Court would unconditionally accept the exercise by the latter of its powers in the counter-terrorism field.[77] However, an element of uncertainty is thereby introduced, because the standard of *jus cogens* is not a well-established feature of the case law of the ECJ in the field of human rights protection.[78] It is not clear how applicants may be able to prove before the CFI whether *jus cogens* norms are at stake or not in a given case.[79]

## B. Assessing the Alleged Human Rights Violations: Inconsistencies in the *Jus Cogens* Test

It is now time to discuss in more depth the way in which the *jus cogens* test is applied by the Court, in order to assess (and dismiss) the applicants' claims against the EC regulations. It is where the ECJ deals with the rights allegedly violated by the EC regulation that the *jus cogens* test reveals its weaknesses. For instance, the Court finds that the right to property may be regarded as protected by *jus cogens* when arbitrary deprivations are involved.[80] The Court thereby broadens the scope of peremptory norms, which do not traditionally seem to cover the right to property.[81] The discussion of *jus cogens* appears even less convincing with reference to the right to a fair hearing and the right to an effective judicial remedy, to which I now turn.

### 1. Right to a Fair Hearing

The authority provided by the Court when analysing the right to a fair hearing is quite scant. The Court makes passing reference to the 'complete system of legal remedies and procedures designed to enable the Court of Justice to review

---

[76] *Yusuf* (T-306/01) [2005] ECR II-3533 [277] and *Kadi* (T-315/01) [2005] ECR II-3649 [226].

[77] See Lavranos, above n 5, 485. Pech, above n 54, [17], quoting other commentators, argues that the two cases discussed here apply by analogy the line of reasoning of the German Federal Constitutional Court in 1974 in the *Solange I* judgment (*Internationale Handelsgesellschaft mbH v Einfuhr-und Vorratsstelle für Getreide und Futtermittel*, reported in (1974) 2 *Common Market Law Review* 540). The German Constitutional Court reserved for itself the power of reviewing and setting aside EC secondary legislation, where this would be found to violate fundamental rights protected in the German legal system. In the same vein, so Pech's arguments runs, the CFI may be sending a message to the Security Council expressing its intention to offer judicial review each time that fundamental rights protected under EU and EC law are sacrificed by the Security Council to other interests. Gianelli, above n 54, 139, argues that the *Kadi* and *Yusuf* judgments may play a significant role, hopefully, in inducing the ICJ to deal with *jus cogens* in a bolder way.

[78] According to Peers, above n 54 '[t]his is believed to be the first time that an EU Court has even referred to the principle of 'jus cogens', never mind applied it to a specific case.'

[79] For instance, Lavranos, above n 5, 476, argues that such an element would be impossible to prove before the ECJ.

[80] *Yusuf* (T-306/01) [2005] ECR II-3533 [293].

[81] See for instance de Wet, above n 73.

the legality of acts of the institutions', based on its own case law and on the ECHR;[82] it also clarifies that observance of the right to a fair hearing is today a fundamental principle of Community law, as it emerges from the Court's case law.[83] However, despite lengthy discussion of other matters, the Court does not address the content of the right to a fair hearing as *jus cogens*,[84] because at each passage of its reasoning it emphasises the exception rather than the rule, thereby restricting the procedural right in the present cases.[85]

The Court's main point is that for cases of counter-terrorism sanctions the right to a hearing must be weighed against the consideration that an advance warning to targeted individuals and entities would help the latter to relocate their funds and thus nullify the 'surprise effect'.[86] In the Court's view, this limitation is admissible because 'it appears that no mandatory rule of public international law requires a prior hearing for the persons concerned in circumstances such as those of this case',[87] that is, counter-terrorism sanctions adopted by the Security Council under Chapter VII. The Court emphasises that there are still safeguards, offered in the first place by the periodical re-examination of the contested decision by the issuing authority,[88] and then by the (additional) possibility of petitioning the Sanctions Committee through the applicants' respective state of residence or citizenship.[89] Although this is a restriction of the right to be heard (because the applicants were not heard before the adoption of the Security

---

[82] *Yusuf* (T-306/01) [2005] ECR II-3533 [260]-[1]; 'As the Court has repeatedly held ... "judicial control ... reflects a general principle of law which underlies the constitutional traditions common to the Member States ... and which is also laid down in Articles 6 and 13 of the [ECHR]".'
[83] Ibid [325].
[84] The lack of a clear position of the Court on this point has been interpreted in completely opposite ways by the doctrine. To give just two examples, whereas Tomuschat, above n 54, 549, says that 'the Court does not even make an attempt to show that [the right to a hearing] might have the nature of *jus cogens*'; Ahmed and de Jesús Butler, above n 49, 780, have no doubt that '[p]erhaps overgenerously, the Court of First Instance (CFI) recently appeared to consider all human rights [including the right to a hearing] to have attained the status of *jus cogens* in international law.'
[85] It is generally acknowledged that art 6 ECHR 'is concerned, not with substantive, but with procedural due process', which implies that the ECrtHR 'may not substitute its own assessment of the facts for that of domestic courts. Its task is to "ascertain whether the proceedings in their entirety, including the way evidence was taken, were fair".' (Leonard Leigh, 'The Right to a Fair Trial and the European Convention on Human Rights' in D Weissbrodt and R Wolfrum (eds), *The Right to a Fair Trial* (Berlin, New York: Springer, 1997) 645, 646-7, quoting the ECrtHR judgment in *Edwards v United Kingdom* (1992)).
[86] '[A prior hearing would] jeopardise the effectiveness of the sanctions and would [be] incompatible with the public interest objective pursued' (*Yusuf* (T-306/01) [2005] ECR II-3533 [308]).
[87] Ibid [307].
[88] The Court refers here to the circumstance that Resolution 1390 (2002) provides that measures such as the freezing of funds, imposed by the previous resolutions, must be reviewed by the Security Council 12 months after their adoption. The options following such review include the decision to allow those measures to continue, or to improve them (see para 3 of the resolution). The same system of review of the sanctions after 12 months is adopted under Resolution 1455 (2003), adopted one year later (see para 2 of the resolution).
[89] *Yusuf* (T-306/01) [2005] ECR II-3533 [309]-[11], 345]; *Kadi* (T-315/01) [2005] ECR II-3649 [263]-[64], [290].

Council sanctions and of the EC regulations),[90] such *restriction*, in the Court's view, is not 'to be deemed improper in the light of the mandatory prescriptions of international law'.[91]

The decisive element leading the Court to dismiss the alleged violation of the right to a hearing is the circumstance that, according to the Court's settled case law, the exercise by the Community of a power of appraisal is the prerequisite for the obligation to respect the procedural rights guaranteed by the Community legal order, including the right to a hearing.[92] Since the European Council does not enjoy any powers of investigation and inquiry when transposing the Security Council's decision into an EC sanction, a hearing before the enactment of the contested regulations would be pointless:

> [T]he Community institutions were required to transpose into the Community legal order resolutions of the Security Council and the decisions of the Sanctions Committee in no way authorised [the Community institutions], at the time of actual implementation, to provide for any Community mechanism whatsoever for the examination or re-examination of individual situations, since both the substance of the measures in question and the mechanisms for re-examination … fell wholly within the purview of the Security Council and its Sanctions Committee. As a result, the Community institutions had no power of investigation, no opportunity to check the matters taken to be facts by the Security Council and the Sanctions Committee, no discretion with regard to those matters and no discretion either as to whether it was appropriate to adopt sanctions vis-à-vis the applicants. The principle of Community law relating to the right to be heard cannot apply in such circumstances, *where to hear the person concerned could not in any case lead the institutions to review its position*.[93]

## 2. The Right to an Effective Judicial Remedy

The Court then turns to a discussion of the claim concerning the appellants' right to an effective judicial remedy and applies the *jus cogens* test in an

---

[90] In the Court's words, '[t]he fact remains that any opportunity for the applicants effectively to make known their views on the correctness and the relevance of the facts in consideration of which their funds have been frozen and on the evidence adduced against them appears to be definitely excluded. Those facts and that evidence, once classified as confidential or secret by the State which made the Sanctions Committee aware of them, are not, obviously, communicated to them, any more than they are to the Member States of the United Nations to which the Security Council's resolutions are addressed.' Ibid [319].

[91] *Yusuf* (T-306/01) [2005] ECR II-3533 [315] [emphasis added].

[92] Ibid [327].

[93] *Yusuf* (T-306/01) [2005] ECR II-3533 [328] [emphasis added]. The Court followed, on this point, the European Council's submission, based on the need to give effect to Chapter VII resolutions of the UN Security Council. In the European Council's view, doing otherwise would constitute an infringement of member states' international obligations. Furthermore, the lack of any autonomous discretion of the European Council would preclude any unlawful conduct on its part. See Ibid [205]-[17] (the European Council, during argument); *Kadi* (T-315/01) [2005] ECR II-3649 [160] and comments by Pech, above n 54, [15].

unconvincing way. The argument based on the need to respect the Security Council's prerogatives under Chapter VII of the Charter seems to be the decisive one here. The judges limit themselves to noting that, even though there is no other judicial remedy available to the applicants, 'any such lacuna in judicial protection is not in itself contrary to *jus cogens*',[94] because the limitation is justified by the nature and the objective of Security Council decisions.[95] In other words, the Court argues that the *jus cogens* norm on the right to an effective judicial remedy does contain in itself a limitation to the enjoyment of such a right, that is, the exercise by the Security Council of Chapter VII powers.[96] It seems that the Court is not following coherently the *jus cogens* test as originally outlined.[97] In this case, the Court would probably do better to re-frame the test and conclude that it simply cannot offer any judicial review, under any circumstance whatsoever, of EC decisions implementing Chapter VII sanctions.

## 3. Critique

The Court's holdings on these points are hardly persuasive, particularly as it generally appears inaccurate in its discussion of several international law points. Two elements may be highlighted in this respect.

First, the two judgments would have benefited from a more thorough analysis of some fundamental aspects of the universal and regional systems of human rights protection.[98] For instance, the CFI argues that proof that the right to access to the courts is not absolute is provided on the one hand by the possibility to derogate from it under Article 4 (1) of the *International Covenant on Civil and Political Rights* (ICCPR),[99] at a time of public emergency that threatens the life of the nation, and on the other hand by certain restrictions inherent in the right itself.[100] The Court's reasoning seems to be based on insufficient analysis of the

---

[94] *Yusuf* (T-306/01) [2005] ECR II-3533 [340]-[41].
[95] Ibid [270].
[96] 'In this instance, the Court considers that the limitation of the applicants' right to access to a court, as a result of the immunity from jurisdiction enjoyed as a rule, in the domestic legal order of the Member States of the United Nations, by resolution of the Security Council adopted under Chapter VII of the Charter of the United Nations, in accordance with the relevant principles of international law (in particular Articles 25 and 103 of the Charter), is inherent in that right as it is guaranteed by *jus cogens*.' (*Yusuf* (T-306/01) [2005] ECR II-3533 [343]).
[97] See above n 65.
[98] For instance, on the basis of art 6 of the ECHR there was no reason why the judges might not have analysed the right of audience and the right to judicial review as two sides of the same coin, instead of analysing them separately, as they did. See the text of art 6, above n 51.
[99] *International Covenant on Civil and Political Rights*, 999 UNTS 171 (entered into force 23 March 1976).
[100] *Yusuf*, (T-306/01) [2005] ECR II-3533 [342]. Art 4 of the ICCPR reads, in the relevant parts:
'4. In time of emergency which threatens the life of the nation and the existence of which is officially proclaimed, the States Parties to the present Covenant may take measures derogating from their obligations under the present Covenant to the extent strictly required by the exigencies of the situation, provided that such measures are not inconsistent with their other obligations under international law and do not involve discrimination solely on the ground of race, colour, sex, language, religion or social origin;

international rules on derogation from protected rights, or on limitations thereto. To begin with, the Court's assertion as to derogations from the right of access to the courts (including the right to a hearing) differs with the position expressed by the Human Rights Committee in General Comment No 29:

> States parties may in no circumstances invoke article 4 of the [ICCPR] as justification for acting in violation of humanitarian law or *peremptory norms of international law*, for instance ... by deviating *from fundamental principles of fair trial*, including the presumption of innocence.[101]

Since *jus cogens* norms may still be subject to restrictions or exceptions in the sense of *limitations*, the issue here is whether there is a permissible limitation on the right of access to courts. The Court resorts to a 'balance of interests' argument, according to which the applicants' interest in having a court hear their case on its merits is not enough to outweigh the essential public interest in the maintenance of international peace and security in the face of a threat clearly identified by the Security Council.[102]

Some commentators have persuasively contended that 'the balance metaphor is inappropriate to describe the process of reconciling respect for civil liberties and human rights with the (alleged) imperatives of ... security.'[103] In particular,

---

5. No derogation from Articles 6, 7, 8 (paragraphs 1 and 2), 11, 15, 16 and 18 may be made under this provision.'

[101] Human Rights' Committee General Comment no. 29: States of Emergency (art 4), 31 August 2001, UN Doc CCPR/C/21/Rev.1/Add.11 [11] [emphasis added]. Even though the ECJ invokes the maintenance of international peace and security as an 'essential public interest', this would not be enough to meet the requirements of a 'public emergency', as defined by the ECrtHR when interpreting art 15 of the ECHR, as well as by the Human Rights Committee with reference to art 4 ICCPR. See, inter alia, R Ergec, *Les droits de l'homme à l'épreuve des circonstances exceptionnelles: étude sur l'article 15 de la Convention européenne des droits de l'homme* (Brussels: Editions de lÚniversite libre de Bruxelles, 1987) 123-236 ; A Svensson-MacCarthy, *The International Law of Human Rights and States of Exception: With Special Reference to the "Travaux Préparatoires" and Case Law of the International Monitoring Organs* (The Hague, Boston: M. Nijhoff, 1998), *passim*; C Michaelsen, 'International Human Rights on Trial – The United Kingdom's and Australia's Legal Response to 9/11' (2003) 25 *Sydney Law Review* 275, 288-92; O Gross and F Ní Aoláin, *Law in Times of Crisis* (Cambridge, UK, New York: Cambridge University Press, 2006) 247-325. Most notably, while the case law of the ECrtHR leaves a considerable amount of discretion to a state that is trying to derogate from the conventional regime, under the 'margin of appreciation' doctrine (on this point, and in particular on the progressive broadening of the notion in the case law of the ECrtHR, see O Gross and F Ní Aoláin, 'From Discretion to Scrutiny: Revisiting the Application of the Margin of Appreciation Doctrine in the Context of Article 15 of the European Convention of Human Rights' (2001) 23 *Human Rights Quarterly* 625), it has been shown that 'an overwhelming majority of Council of Europe States have not regarded the actual terrorist threat to be of sufficient gravity to meet the "public emergency" criteria' of art 15 ECHR (Michaelsen, 293). According to art 15 of the ECHR, derogation is only permissible to the extent 'strictly required by the exigencies of the situation'. It would be difficult to argue that the measures adopted by the Security Council under Resolutions 1267 (1999) and 1390 (2002) satisfy such conditions, especially because of the lack of a system of independent supervision.

[102] *Yusuf*, (T-306/01) [2005] ECR II-3533 [344]; *Kadi*, (T-315/01) [2005] ECR II-3649 [289].

[103] See the debate as analysed by C Michaelsen, 'Balancing Civil Liberties against National Security? A Critique of Counterterrorism Rhetoric' (2006) 29 *University of New South Wales Law Journal* 1, 19; for a similar conclusion from a criminal law perspective and with reference to the 'war on drugs', see S

Michaelsen has suggested replacing this metaphor with the proportionality test, which is more consistent with the spirit and the letter of international human rights instruments,[104] so that each time derogating measures must be assessed against particular emergencies.[105] The test of proportionality is, of course, more rigorous than the one of the balance of interests, because it is based on requirements such as suitability, necessity and appropriateness.[106]

The right of access to courts as enunciated by Article 6 ECHR is not absolute and may be subject to limitations, which must be legitimate and proportionate.[107] Whether the gravity of the threat posed by international terrorism is enough to justify limitations of access to courts as outlined by the CFI is a matter for debate. However, there is at least a serious concern that such limitations restrict access to courts 'in such a way or to such an extent that the very essence of the right is impaired'.[108] Indeed, affected individuals and entities are never put in a position to bring potential claims to court to prove their innocence; they may only petition their respective national states. A review mechanism resting essentially on a government's choice to trigger the de-listing procedure before the Sanctions Committee, and in which the affected individuals are not granted any standing,[109] cannot constitute an appropriate solution to enforce the victims' rights.[110] In particular, the de-listing procedure cannot generally satisfy the terms required by Article 6 (1) ECHR, which, in the words of the ECrtHR, embodies the 'right to a court', meaning 'the right to have any claim relating to [one's] civil rights and obligations brought before a court or a tribunal'.[111]

---

Bronitt, 'Constitutional Rhetoric versus Criminal Justice Realities: Unbalanced Responses to Terrorism?' (2003) 14 *Public Law Review* 76.
[104] Michaelsen, above n 103, 20.
[105] Michaelsen, above n 101, 291.
[106] Michaelsen, above n 103, 20.
[107] *Osman v the United Kingdom* (1998) VIII Eur Court HR 3169 [147]. Most notably, the ECrtHR clarifies that limitations 'are permitted by implication since the right of access by its very nature calls for regulation by the State' (ibid). For a discussion on the doctrine of inherent limitations in the system of the ECHR, see P Van Dijk et al (ed), *Theory and Practice of the European Convention on Human Rights* (Deventer, London: Kluwer Law and Taxation, 4$^{th}$ ed, 2006) 343-50.
[108] Ibid.
[109] 'Admittedly, the procedure described above confers no right directly on the persons concerned themselves to be heard by the Sanctions Committee, the only authority competent to give a decision, on a State's petition, on the re-examination of their case. Those persons are thus dependent, essentially, on the diplomatic protection afforded by the States to their nationals' (*Yusuf*, (T-306/01) [2005] ECR II-3533 [314]).
[110] I do not think that this conclusion should be reconsidered in light of the Court's consideration that a wrongful refusal by the competent domestic authority to bring a case before the 1267 Committee may always constitute the basis for an individual action for judicial review before domestic judges; such action, in the Court's view, may also be directed against the contested EC regulation and the Security Council resolutions themselves. The point was presented by the UK at the hearing and was cursorily mentioned by the Court in both *Yusuf* (T-306/01) [2005] ECR II-3533 [317] and *Kadi* (T-315/01) [2005] ECR II-3649 [270]. It was subsequently developed in the *Ayadi* and *Hassan* cases (see below, nn 114-115 and accompanying text).
[111] *Waite and Kennedy v Germany* (1999) I Eur Court HR 393 [50].

Summing up, there does not seem to be a relationship of proportionality between the means employed and the (legitimate) aims pursued.

One might conclude that an effective and independent procedure to protect human rights within the framework of the Security Council counter-terrorism resolutions does not exist or is, at best, seriously ill-equipped to deal with individual grievances, if the only means available to individuals to challenge the sanctions is a mere inter-governmental mechanism before the Security Council itself, not offering any guarantees of independence and transparency.[112] The ECJ should never decline to afford judicial review when no other avenues are available to the plaintiffs. In the cases under examination, the Court should have invalidated the EC regulation at least with respect to the plaintiffs, purely because of the failure of the Community institutions to include in the regulation an appropriate mechanism for independent judicial review of complaints by affected individuals and entities.[113]

## C. A 'Right' to Diplomatic Protection under European Union Law and its Enforcement

In two subsequent cases on the implementation of the 1267 sanctions regime, decided on 12 July 2006, *Ayadi*[114] and *Hassan*,[115] the CFI substantially upheld the main line of argument and findings of the *Kadi* and *Yusuf* judgments, but then developed a few aspects further, perhaps in order to address, at least partially, the perplexity and scepticism with which the earlier judgments had generally been received by scholars.

Ayadi, a Tunisian national resident in Dublin and designated by the Sanctions Committee as a person associated with Osama bin Laden, asked the CFI to annul Article 2 of Regulation (EC) No 881/2002, with respect to his position.[116] The plea in law relevant for my analysis is the alleged infringement of the fundamental principle of respect for human rights, in particular Ayadi's right to access to his

---

[112] See for instance de Wet, above n 73. I also agree with Conforti, above n 12, 343, on the point that the CFI's argument according to which the applicants were able to bring an action for annulment before the Court itself under art 230 EC Treaty (*Yusuf* (T-306/01) [2005] ECR II-3533 [333]-[7]) sounds almost like a mockery, given that the applicant's plea referred to the lack of judicial remedies within the UN sanctions regime.
[113] As suggested also by Lavranos, above n 5, 480-3.
[114] *Ayadi v Council* (T-253/02) [2006] ECR II-2139 (hereafter *Ayadi*).
[115] *Hassan v Council* (T-49/04) [2006] ECR II-52 (hereafter *Hassan*).
[116] Art 2 of Regulation No 881/2002 provides:

1. All funds and economic resources belonging to, or owned or held by, a natural or legal person, group or entity designated by the Sanctions Committee and listed in Annex 1 shall be frozen;
2. No funds shall be made available, directly or indirectly, to, or for the benefit of, a natural or legal person, group or entity designated by the Sanctions Committee and listed in Annex 1;
3. No economic resources shall be made available, directly or indirectly, to, or for the benefit of, a natural or legal person, group or entity designated by the Sanctions Committee and listed in Annex 1, so as to enable that person, group or entity to obtain funds, goods or services'.

property and the right to a judicial remedy under Article 6 ECHR.[117] Hassan, a Libyan national, was detained in the UK while awaiting the outcome of extradition proceedings brought at the request of the Italian authorities, on terrorism charges. Hassan maintained that Regulation 881/2002 infringes fundamental rights and general principles of Community law, most notably the right to property, the right to respect for private and family life, the right to be heard and the right to an effective judicial remedy. He lamented he had not been given any opportunity to put his case forward with respect to his listing in the contested regulation.[118] Most notably, he pointed out that he was not given any information with respect to the basis for his inclusion in the Sanctions Committee's list nor with respect to the state that requested such inclusion.[119] In this respect, he claimed that if prior hearing was not appropriate when dealing with counter-terrorism sanctions, he still ought 'to have been given the right to be heard subsequently, so that he might have his name removed from the list at issue'.[120] He furthermore submitted that the de-listing procedure 'does not provide for access to an independent or impartial tribunal to challenge on the merits the refusal of the State concerned to petition the Sanctions Committee for removal or the Committee's decision to reject such a petition'.[121]

The Court relies extensively on *Kadi* and *Yusuf*, because during the hearing, the applicants acknowledged 'the exhaustive answers to the arguments, in essence identical, put forward in those cases by the parties in their written pleadings'.[122] One of the arguments relied upon by the applicants concerned the Court's previous conclusion that the lacuna found to exist in the judicial protection of the persons targeted by sanctions was still to be seen as compatible with *jus cogens*.[123] The CFI develops its previous position in at least two directions.[124]

First, it upholds the point made in *Yusuf* and *Kadi* according to which the de-listing procedure does not confer upon individuals any right to be heard before the 1267 Committee, the whole mechanism being based on the traditional

---

[117] *Ayadi* (T-253/02) [2006] ECR II-2139 [92]-[102]. Most notably, *Ayadi* claimed that 'there is no effective mechanism for reviewing the individual measures freezing funds adopted by the Security Council, with the result that the danger is that his property will remain frozen for the rest of his life. On his head the applicant has argued that he had endeavoured in vain to persuade the Security Council to alter its stance in relation to him. So, he wrote twice to the Irish authorities, on 5 February 2004 and 19 May 2004, seeking their assistance in having him removed from the Sanctions Committee list. By letter of 10 October 2005 those authorities informed him that his file was still being considered, but did not give him to understand that they would take any steps to his advantage' [102].
[118] *Hassan* (T-49/04) [2006] ECR II-52 [74]-[6].
[119] Ibid [83].
[120] Ibid [81].
[121] Ibid [83].
[122] *Ayadi* (T-253/02) [2006] ECR II-2139 [117]; *Hassan* (T-49/04) [2006] ECR II-52 [93].
[123] *Ayadi* (T-253/02) [2006] ECR II-2139 [118]; *Hassan* (T-49/04) [2006] ECR II-52 [95].
[124] *Ayadi* (T-253/02) [2006] ECR II-2139 [134]; *Hassan* (T-49/04) [2006] ECR II-52 [104].

notion of diplomatic protection afforded by a state to its own nationals.[125] However, the Court describes the possibility of presenting a request of re-examination to one's own government as a *'right* guaranteed not only by [the Guidelines of the Committee for the Conduct of its Work] but also by the Community legal order'.[126] This right corresponds to an obligation for each EU member state to protect fundamental human rights, spelled out by the Court in such a way that it is clear the Court is not following *Yusuf* and *Kadi*:[127]

> [an obligation] in accordance with Article 6 EU, to respect the fundamental rights of the persons involved, as guaranteed by the ECHR and as they result from the constitutional traditions common to the Member States, as general principles of Community law, given that the respect of those fundamental rights *does not appear capable of preventing the proper performance of their obligations* under the Charter of the United Nations.[128]

In other words, there can be no conflict between human rights and other obligations under the UN Charter. EU member states must ensure that affected persons and entities are able to present their cases before the respective domestic authorities. Also, they must 'act promptly to ensure that such ... cases are presented without delay and fairly and impartially to the Committee,[129] with a view to their re-examination, if that appears to be justified in light of the relevant information supplied'.[130] While the Court must be commended for this effort towards a more effective protection of human rights, the obligation that it derives from EU law, most notably from Article 6 of the Treaty, has no equivalent under current customary international law, given that there is no general obligation for states to exercise diplomatic protection.[131] Also, some commentators have

---

[125] *Ayadi* (T-253/02) [2006] ECR II-2139 [141]; *Hassan* (T-49/04) [2006] ECR II-52 [111]. In this sense, the Guidelines of the Committee for the Conduct of its Work, above n 36, offer to states guidance on how to address the 1267 Committee, in order to start a re-examination procedure.

[126] *Ayadi* (T-253/02) [2006] ECR II-2139 [145]; *Hassan* (T-49/04) [2006] ECR II-52 [115] [emphasis added].

[127] It is probably appropriate to reiterate here that in the previous cases the Court concluded that, under both customary international law and the EC Treaty, EC member states had an obligation to leave unapplied any Community law provision that would impede the proper performance of their obligations under the UN Charter and Security Council resolutions (*Yusuf* (T-306/01) [2005] ECR II-3533 [240] and *Kadi*, (T-315/01) [2005] ECR II-3649 [190]).

[128] *Ayadi* (T-253/02) [2006] ECR II-2139 [146]; *Hassan* (T-49/04) [2006] ECR II-52 [116] [emphasis added].

[129] The Court inferred from the different resolutions adopted by the Security Council an obligation for states to cooperate fully with the Sanctions Committee and to act in good faith during the re-examination procedure (*Ayadi* (T-253/02) [2006] ECR II-2139 [142]; *Hassan* (T-49/04) [2006] ECR II-52 [112]).

[130] *Ayadi* (T-253/02) [2006] ECR II-2139 [147], [149]; *Hassan* (T-49/04) [2006] ECR II-52 [117], [119]. This means that states must not refuse to initiate a re-examination procedure where requested in accordance with the Guidelines, even if the affected subjects are not able to provide all relevant information for the complaint (*Ayadi* (T-253/02) [2006] ECR II-2139 [148] *Hassan* (T-49/04) [2006] ECR II-52 [118]).

[131] Diplomatic protection is a topic currently under consideration by the International Law Commission. Some draft articles have been provisionally adopted. See for instance draft articles 1 ('Definition and Scope') and 2 ('Right to Exercise Diplomatic Protection') provisionally adopted by the ILC at its fifty-fourth session in 2002 (*Report of the International Law Commission*, 55th sess, UN GAOR, 58th sess, Supp. 10, UN Doc A/58/10 (2003) 81). For a more recent analysis of these issues, see S Touzé, *La Protection*

shown a fair degree of scepticism towards inferring such a right from the Guidelines or the Community legal order.[132] It remains to be seen whether the Court's innovative position will encourage further developments in the international practice, in cases involving counter-terrorism sanctions.[133]

A second aspect of the *Ayadi* and *Hassan* cases deserves attention here. The Court clarifies that the right individuals have to diplomatic protection before the Sanctions Committee is enforceable before the domestic courts of the state in question. The role of the domestic judges this time appears to be grounded on a clearer and firmer basis in Community law, first of all because we now know that there is an individual 'right' to diplomatic protection, but also because the interaction between the different levels (EC and domestic) of enforcement of the said right is explained. The Court draws on a jurisprudential Community principle that is now part of its settled case-law, and according to which '*in the absence of Community provisions*, it is for the domestic legal system of each Member State to determine the detailed procedural rules governing actions at law intended to safeguard *the rights which individuals derive from the direct effect of Community law*'.[134] This principle is applicable in the cases under review, each time a right to diplomatic protection, derived from EC law, is violated by the competent national authorities through their refusal to submit a de-listing request to the 1267 Committee. The Court also clarifies that the domestic procedural rules to be applied in such cases cannot be less favourable than those governing rights originating in domestic law, nor can they render the exercise of the right to diplomatic protection virtually impossible or excessively difficult.[135] However, in instances of conflict between the domestic rules and the raison d'être and objective of the contested EC act, the latter must prevail over the application of the former.[136]

---

*des Droits des Nationaux à l'Étranger – Recherches sur la Protection Diplomatique*, PhD thesis, University of Paris II Panthéon-Assas (2006) 307-450.

[132] See Lavranos, above n 5, 483; de Wet, above n 73.

[133] J Dugard, 'Diplomatic Protection and Human Rights: The Draft Articles of the International Law Commission' (2005) 24 *Australian Year Book of International Law* 75, analyses international judicial practice demonstrating the emergence of a duty of the state to provide diplomatic protection when certain conditions are met. In particular, he focuses on the recent decision of the South African Constitutional Court in *Kaunda and others v President of the Republic of South Africa* (CCT 23/04) [2004] ZACC 5 (4 August 2004), although the majority argument on the existence of some form of a state's (a government's) obligation to offer diplomatic protection to its nationals abroad was based on the 1996 South African Constitution (82-3).

[134] *Ayadi* (T-253/02) [2006] ECR II-2139 [151]; *Hassan* (T-49/04) [2006] ECR II-52 [121] [emphasis added]. The principle was spelled out by the ECJ in the *Leffler* judgment (*Götz Leffler v Berlin Chemie AG*, Case C-443/03, Grand Chamber, Decision of 8 November 2005, ECR 2005-1, 9611), and quoted in Dugard, above n 133.

[135] This results from an application of the Community law principles of equivalence and effectiveness (see *Ayadi*, (T-253/02) [2006] ECR II-2139 [152]; *Hassan* (T-49/04) [2006] ECR II-52 [122]).

[136] Ibid.

To sum up, the cases reviewed in this section contribute to giving the protection of fundamental human rights a higher rank in the hierarchy of international law obligations. However, the mechanism 'invented' by the CFI for the protection of fundamental human rights of blacklisted individuals and entities does not actually challenge in any meaningful way the supremacy of UN law over both Community and domestic law. Indeed, the Court makes it clear that the states' possible lack of cooperation with concerned individuals, even when it is made the object of a judicial finding by domestic judges, 'in no way means that the [UN's] procedure for removal from the list is in itself ineffective'.[137] One is thus left with the impression that responses coming from the 'lower' levels — the Community and the domestic levels — apart from inter-governmental action in the framework of the 1267 Committee, do not have any real impact on what seems to be a rather human rights-resistant[138] UN sanctions regime.

## D. New Developments for European Community/European Union Sanctions Adopted Pursuant to Security Council Resolution 1373 (2001)

A partially new approach emerges from a judgment handed down by the Court on 12 December 2006, with respect to an action brought against an EC decision in the framework of *Community Regulation* No 2580/2001 and of *Common Position* 2001/931/CFSP,[139] both implementing Security Council Resolution 1373 (2001). In 2002, the France-based *Organisation des Modjahedines du peuple d'Iran* (hereafter OMPI), which appeared in the list annexed to the above-mentioned acts, filed a lawsuit with the CFI for the partial annulment of the above-mentioned common positions and of a Council decision implementing the above-mentioned regulations.[140] The OMPI claimed that the contested decision, by imposing sanctions on it without giving the possibility to express its views, infringed its right to a fair hearing, as guaranteed in particular by Article 6 (2) EU Treaty and Article 6 ECHR. The OMPI also claimed that it was not even aware of the identity of the national authority that took the decision to put it on the list for the purposes of the contested EU/EC acts, nor was it aware of the evidence and

---

[137] *Ayadi* (T-253/02) [2006] ECR II-2139 [154]; *Hassan* (T-49/04) [2006] ECR II-52 [124].

[138] I am quoting here from the title of Pene Mathew's presentation at the ANZSIL Annual Meeting 2005 ('Anti-terrorist = rights-resistant? The Work of the Counter-Terrorism Committee' Australian and New Zealand Society of International Law Thirteenth Annual Meeting, The Australian National University, Canberra, 16-18 June 2005, on file with the author).

[139] See above n 31.

[140] *Organisation des Modjahedines du peuple d'Iran v. Council of the European Union* (T-228/02) [2006] (unreported, available at <http://curia.europa.eu/jurisp/cgi-bin/form.pl?lang=en&Submit=Rechercher&alldocs=alldocs&docj=docj&docop=docop&docor=docor&docjo=docjo&numaff=T-228/02&datefs=&datefe=&nomusuel=&domaine=&mots=&resmax=100>), hereafter *OMPI*.

information on the basis of which such a decision was taken.[141] It thus alleged that its inclusion in the disputed list was decided 'apparently solely only on the basis of documents produced by the Tehran regime'.[142] Inclusion in the list without a previous hearing and without the slightest indication of the factual and legal grounds providing legal justification also constituted, in the applicant's view, an infringement of the obligation to state reasons provided for in Article 253 EC Treaty and of the right to effective judicial protection.[143]

The Court, while dismissing the action as in part inadmissible and in part unfounded in so far as it sought annulment of a Council Common Position,[144] on the other hand annulled a Council Decision, in so far as it concerned the applicant, on specific restrictive counter-terrorism measures.[145] The decision of the Court is ground-breaking, because it sets aside some of the obstacles, which in the previous cases, barred the appellants' right to judicial review.

It is essential to note that this is the first decision on the merits of a complaint challenging a sanctions regime different from the one discussed in the previous cases, and indeed the Court clarifies that its conclusion is determined by the different features of the 1373 sanctions regime, which the contested EU acts were implementing.[146] Member states are required not only to identify suspected persons (meaning persons other than those already covered by Resolution 1267), but also to put in place their own procedure for the freezing of funds. It is therefore for the member states, and for the Community in some particular cases, to identify specifically the persons, groups and entities whose funds are to be frozen, in accordance with the rules in their own legal orders. Then the European Council, deliberating on the basis of 'precise information or material which indicates that a decision has been taken by a competent [national] authority',[147] unanimously decides to set up a list of persons to whom sanctions apply under the 1373 regime.[148] Thus, the CFI holds that, under this sanctions regime, the

---

[141] Art 1 (4) of *Common Position* 2001/931 spells out the criteria to establish the list of persons, groups and entities involved in terrorist acts. These criteria were then listed under art 2 (3) of Regulation No 2580/2001.
[142] *OMPI* (T-228/02) [2006] [64], [167].
[143] Ibid [65]. I will not consider here the further pleas presented by the applicant and relating, respectively, to a manifest error of assessment and to the violation of the presumption of innocence (ibid [66]-[7]).
[144] Ibid [60]. The act contested is *Council Common Position 2005/936/CFSP of 21 December 2005, updating Common Position 2001/931/CFSP on the application of specific measures to combat terrorism and repealing Common Position 2005/847/CFSP* [2005] OJ L 340/80. As mentioned at above n 19, the Court cannot review EU common positions.
[145] *Council Decision of 21 December 2005 implementing Article 2 (3) of Regulation (EC) No 2580/2001 on specific restrictive measures directed against certain persons and entities with a view to combating terrorism and repealing Decision 2005/848/EC* [2005] OJ L 340/64.
[146] *OMPI* (T-228/02) [2006] [99]-[108].
[147] This is the language of art 2 (3) EC Reg 2580/2001 and art 1 (4) Common Position 2001/931.
[148] The initial decision is regulated by art 1 (4) of Common Position 2001/931, which spells out the criteria to establish the list of persons, groups and entities involved in terrorist acts. The subsequent decisions to freeze funds are regulated under art 1 (6) of the same common position, under which the

fundamental human rights and safeguards allegedly infringed are fully applicable to cases such as *OMPI*, because the relationship between the UN and the Community level does not limit the action of the latter to the exercise of circumscribed powers, but rather requires the exercise of its discretionary powers and appreciation in the establishment and the maintenance of the terrorists' list.[149] Even if this means that the Court will probably decide to uphold the previous cases when assessing future lawsuits filed against sanctions implementing the 1267 regime, rather than the 1373 regime, one may still argue that some elements in the *OMPI* judgment may lead the Court to reconsider its position even with respect to the latter regime, at least partially and on a case-by-case basis.

For instance, the Court does not use the *jus cogens* argument here and brings the discussion on the right to a fair hearing back to the terms of the case-law of the ECJ and of the ECrtHR. The main point is now that even when the disclosure of confidential material in counter-terrorism sanctions may affect national security, individuals must still be heard before measures adversely affecting them are taken.[150] In all cases where the right to full disclosure of evidence to the concerned parties is subject to exceptions,[151] the Court concludes that the right to judicial review is the ultimate guarantee for affected individuals. These points deserve further explanation.

In the first place, the Court gives the right to a fair hearing at the Community level a very limited scope.[152] According to *Common Position* 2001/931, the decision to list individuals and entities at the national level is normally taken by a competent *judicial* authority,[153] which should ensure adequate protection of the right to a fair hearing at the domestic level.[154] The Court concludes that 'observance of the right to a fair hearing has a relatively limited purpose in respect of the Community procedure for freezing funds'.[155] Indeed, as a general

---

names of persons and entities in the list are to be reviewed at regular intervals, and at least once every six months to ensure that there are grounds for keeping them in the list. The relevant rules are also laid down in art 2 (3) of Regulation No 2580/2001, according to which the Council is to establish, review and amend the list of persons, groups and entities to which that regulation applies, in accordance with the said Common Position. At the time of writing, the most recent updates are included in Common Position 2006/380, of 30 May 2006.

[149] *OMPI* (T-228/02) [2006] [102]-[3]. One may note the difference with the ratio decidendi in the *Yusuf* and *Kadi* cases, reproduced above, n 93 and accompanying text.

[150] *OMPI* (T-228/02) [2006] [114]-[37].

[151] In the Court's words, 'the general principle of observance of the right to a fair hearing requires, *unless precluded by overriding considerations concerning the security of the Community or its member States, or the conduct of their international relations,* that the evidence adduced against the party concerned ... should be notified to it, in so far as possible, either concomitantly with or as soon as possible after the adoption of the initial decision to freeze funds' (ibid [137] emphasis added).

[152] Ibid [118].

[153] See above n 33.

[154] *OMPI* (T-228/02) [2006] [120].

[155] Ibid [126].

rule the European Council must defer as far as possible to the assessment made by the competent domestic authority, and only when the evidence on which the national decision is based are not assessed by the said authority, a notification and a hearing at the Community level will be required.[156]

On the one hand, the Court highlights how different factors may tend to restrict the scope of the right to a fair hearing.[157] The Court resorts to one of the main arguments used in the *Yusuf* and *Kadi* cases: the need for a 'surprise effect' for counter-terrorism sanctions. Notification to the OMPI of the evidence adduced by the relevant domestic authority and the granting of a hearing prior to the decision to freeze funds 'would thus be incompatible with the public interest objective pursued by the Community pursuant to Security Council Resolution 1373 (2001)'.[158] Drawing on the case law of the ECrtHR, most notably on the *Chahal* and *Jasper* cases,[159] the CFI concludes that:

> in circumstances such as those in this case, where what is at issue is a temporary protective measure restricting the availability of the property of certain persons, groups and entities in connection with combating terrorism, overriding considerations concerning the security of the Community and its Member States, or the conduct of their international relations, may preclude the communication to the parties concerned of certain evidence adduced against them, and, in consequence, the hearing of those parties with regard to such evidence, during the administrative procedure.[160]

---

[156] Ibid [124]-[5]. Most notably, the Court is aware that, on the basis of the principle of 'sincere cooperation' between member states and the Community institutions, the European Council has an 'obligation to defer as far as possible to the assessment conducted by the competent national authority, at least where it is a judicial authority.' (This is a general principle of Community law, postulating the reciprocal duty to cooperate in good faith; however, it is also binding in the area of pillar three, JHA (see Ibid [122]-[4])).

[157] Ibid [127].

[158] Ibid [128], [136]. Given the need for a surprise effect, the overriding considerations concerning the security of the Community and of its member states may never be invoked with respect to a *subsequent* decision *to maintain* a person or entity on the disputed list, as distinct from the initial decision to list such person or entity [131].

[159] *Chahal v United Kingdom* (1996) 23 ECR 1996-V 1831; *Jasper v United Kingdom* (2000), unreported [51]-[3]. Mr Chahal was a Sikh separatist leader, who had been detained in custody in the UK for deportation purposes since August 1990, when his application for asylum was refused and the UK Home Secretary decided that he was a threat to national security. Mr Chahal filed a lawsuit before the ECrtHR, alleging that his deportation to India would expose him to a real risk of torture or inhuman or degrading treatment. Also, he complained that his detention pending deportation had been too long, and that he had no legal remedy for his convention claims because of the national security element in his case. The complaint was brought under arts 3, 5 and 13 of the ECHR. Mr Jasper was a British national who filed a lawsuit to obtain a decision as to whether the facts of the case disclosed a breach by the UK of its obligations under art 6 of the Convention. With respect to some criminal proceedings before the Crown Court and the Court of Appeal, taken together, the applicant submitted that any failure to disclose relevant evidence undermined the right to a fair trial, as protected under arts 6 (1) and 3(b) and (d) of the Convention. Most notably, he contended that *ex parte* hearings before the judge violated art 6, because no safeguard against judicial bias or error was afforded, nor was there any opportunity to put arguments on behalf of the accused.

[160] *OMPI* T-228/02 [2006] [133].

This being said, under the ECrtHR case law restrictions on the rights of the defence, justified by public interest in non-disclosure, should nevertheless be strictly proportionate and counterbalanced by adequate procedural safeguards followed by the judicial authorities.[161] The CFI accordingly finds that there is a need to notify to the parties concerned the evidence adduced against them in so far as this is reasonably possible, 'either concomitantly with or as soon as possible after the adoption of the initial decision to freeze funds', to ensure that they are able to defend their rights effectively.[162] Each time a party is not given the opportunity to be heard before the adoption of one initial decision to freeze funds, then the obligation to state reasons is the necessary 'surrogate' to allow the affected subjects to challenge the lawfulness of that decision.[163]

It is against this background that the Court highlights the importance of the right to effective judicial protection, especially where 'it constitutes the only procedural safeguard ensuring that a fair balance is struck between the need to combat international terrorism and the protection of fundamental rights'.[164] Judicial review of the lawfulness of a decision to freeze funds may be provided by the Court upon an action for annulment (Article 230 EC Treaty) brought by affected individuals. The CFI finds in the case under review that the contested decision to include OMPI in the list does not contain a sufficient statement of reasons and thus it violates the applicant's right to a fair hearing. Since the Court

---

[161] See the case of *Chahal*, above n 159 [131], [135], where the ECrtHR found that in cases concerning national security and terrorism certain restrictions on the right to a fair hearing may be envisaged, especially concerning disclosure of evidence adduced or terms of access to the file, but then added: 'This does not mean, however, that the national authorities can be free from effective control by domestic courts whenever they choose to assert that national security and terrorism are involved'. In *Jasper v the UK*, above n 159 [52]-[3], the same principle implied the need to ensure that the decision-making procedure, as far as possible, 'complied with the requirements to provide adversarial proceedings and equality of arms and incorporated adequate safeguards to protect the interests of the accused'. In particular, *Jasper* agreed with the UK Government and the European Human Rights Commission that the right to full disclosure was not absolute and could, in pursuit of a legitimate aim such as the protection of national security or of vulnerable witnesses or sources of information, be subject to limitations. However, in the Court's opinion, any such restriction on the rights of the defence should be strictly proportionate and counterbalanced by procedural safeguards adequate to compensate for the handicap imposed on the defence. The views of the ECrtHR were subsequently codified by the Committee of Ministers of the Council of Europe in the *Guidelines on Human Rights and the Fight against Terrorism* (2002) Council of Europe
<http://www.coe.int/t/e/legal_affairs/legal_co-operation/fight_against_terrorism/2_adopted_texts/Guidelines%20HR%202005%20E.pdf>. Art IX, under the heading of 'Legal proceedings', affirms that 'a person accused of terrorist activities has the right to a fair hearing, within a reasonable time, by an independent, impartial tribunal established by law' (para 1). The restrictions to the right of defence mentioned under para 3 include the arrangements for access to and contacts with counsel, the arrangements for access to the case-file and the use of anonymous testimony. Para 4 clarifies that the said restrictions to the right of defence 'must be strictly proportionate to their purpose, and compensatory measures to protect the interests of the accused must be taken so as to maintain the fairness of the proceedings and to ensure that procedural rights are not drained of their substance'.
[162] *OMPI* T-228/02 [2006] [129].
[163] Ibid [141].
[164] Ibid [155].

is not in a position to review the lawfulness of the decision contested by the OMPI, it annuls the said act in so far as it concerns the applicant.[165]

The persuasiveness of the Court's argument rests on the departure from the *jus cogens* test and from the heavy reliance on the 'state of emergency' paradigm. The way in which the Court resorts in *OMPI* to the 'balance metaphor' — which is the test to check that the concerns about the confidentiality of intelligence information in counter-terrorism are weighed against the procedural justice standards that must at all times be accorded to individuals — seems more in line with the jurisprudence of the ECrtHR concerning proportionality of limitations, as well as with the constitutional traditions common to the member states.[166]

In conclusion, the *OMPI* judgment must be welcomed not only for the findings as to the applicability *in abstracto* of the right to a fair hearing, but also for its reasoning as to the safeguards available to enforce this fundamental right.

## IV. Concluding Remarks

This chapter has reviewed some of the cases brought before the CFI (ECJ) by individuals and entities seeking judicial review of EU counter-terrorism sanctions, implementing Security Council Resolution 1267 (1999) (and its successor instruments) and Security Council Resolution 1373 (2001). In the first judgments handed down in these cases, the CFI pays (probably) excessive deference to a monist vision of the relationship between the United Nations order and the EU law, postulating an undisputable supremacy of Security Council resolutions adopted under Chapter VII over the EU legal order. The Court thus declines to review the lawfulness not only of Security Council's counter-terrorism sanctions but also of the implementing acts adopted by the European Council under the EC Treaty. The CFI position is not in line with the current picture of the EU system, where as a result of a long work of judicial construction, the protection of fundamental human rights is well entrenched in the EU Treaty.

It is not clear at this stage whether the ECJ may be ready to uphold the more encouraging *OMPI* judgment in future cases arising from the 1267 Sanctions regime. The *OMPI Case* may not, then, constitute the charting of a new direction, nor would it provide an answer to the general question of the *designation* of individuals and entities as 'terrorists'.[167] The CFI's acceptance of a serious lacuna in the EU human rights framework is all the more worrying if one considers the

---

[165] Ibid [160]-[74].

[166] The Court makes it clear that only restrictions to the right to a fair hearing, which are admissible under domestic law, may be admissible in the case before it. It satisfies itself that restrictions to the right to be heard in the course of an administrative procedure are permitted in many member states on grounds of public interest, public policy or the maintenance of international relations, or where the purpose of the decision to be taken is or could be jeopardised if the said right is observed (ibid [133]-[4]).

[167] The information note published by *Statewatch* on the *OMPI* judgment (see above n 16) correctly highlights that 'the ruling is limited to the decision to freeze the OMPI's assets, rather than the broader issuer of its designation as "terrorist"'.

lack of alternative avenues of redress open to individuals affected by counter-terrorism measures. Not only must one exclude any significant role for domestic judges when dealing with judicial review of EC measures (with the possible exception of preliminary ruling procedures, which would anyway bring the ball back to the ECJ's court),[168] but also the ECrtHR, in the recent *Bosphorus* judgment,[169] appears inclined to exercise judicial review only when fundamental human rights are not otherwise protected in a manner that is equivalent to the protection afforded by the ECHR. However, this outcome is difficult to reconcile with the established case law of the ECrtHR, according to which 'the Convention is intended to guarantee not rights that are theoretical or illusory but rights that are practical and effective'.[170]

---

[168] 'To help safeguard the uniform application of Community law, Article 234 (ex 177) EC therefore lays down a procedure which enables national courts to refer to the Court of Justice questions of Community law that they have to decide before giving judgment' (Arnull, above n 46, 95).
[169] Above n 71.
[170] *Artico v Italy* (1980) 37 Eur Court HR (ser A) [33].

# Chapter Thirteen

# How Does it End? Reflections on Completed Prosecutions under Australia's Anti-Terrorism Legislation

## Miriam Gani[*]

## Introduction

Much has been written, both in this collection of essays and elsewhere, about the overbreadth of the terrorism offences contained in Part 5.3[1] of the *Criminal Code Act 1995* (Cth) ('Criminal Code').[2] Likewise, the unwieldy nature and conceptual complexity of the definition of 'terrorist act' upon which most of the terrorism offences depend has received significant criticism.[3] Whilst academic commentary based on the text of both the offences and the definition has abounded, given the few actual prosecutions in this country,[4] there has

---

[*] Senior Lecturer, ANU College of Law, The Australian National University, Canberra, Australia. This research has been supported by a Commonwealth grant from the Australian Research Council: 'Terrorism and the Non-State Actor After September 11: The Role of Law in the Search for Security' (DP0451473).

[1] Part 5.3 in its original form was inserted into the *Criminal Code Act 1995* (Cth) ('Criminal Code') as a result of the *Security Legislation Amendment (Terrorism) Act 2002* (Cth). The Act came into force on 6 July 2002.

[2] For examples outside this collection see: M Gani and G Urbas, 'Alert or Alarmed? Recent Legislative Reforms Directed at Terrorist Organisations and Persons Supporting or Assisting Terrorist Acts' (2004) 8(1) *Newcastle Law Review* 23, 49-50; S Bronitt and B McSherry, *Principles of Criminal Law* (Sydney: Lawbook Co, 2nd ed, 2005) 894-6; B McSherry, 'Terrorism Offences in the Criminal Code: Broadening the Boundaries of Australian Criminal Laws' (2004) 27(2) *University of New South Wales Law Journal* 354, 364-9; A Lynch and G Williams, *What Price Security? Taking Stock of Australia's Anti-Terror Laws* (Sydney: UNSW Press, 2006) 14-28.

[3] Such criticisms have come from a variety of sources and perspectives and have been made in respect of a range of aspects of the definition. For example, in its submission to the Sheller Committee (the Security Legislation Review Committee) in 2006, the Commonwealth Director of Public Prosecutions (DPP) argued for the definition to be simplified by removing some of its requirements in order to facilitate prosecutions: Parliamentary Joint Committee on Intelligence and Security, *Review of Security and Counter Terrorism Legislation* (December 2006) [5.12]. Other critics argue that the current definition incorporates inherently vague concepts: McSherry, above n 2, 362 — or is overbroad in some respect(s): see, eg, K Roach, 'A Comparison of Australian and Canadian Anti-Terrorism Laws' (2007) 30(1) *University of New South Wales Law Journal* 53, 56 in relation to 'serious damage to property'. The Sheller Committee itself found that inclusion of a 'threat of action' in the definition increased the 'complexity of the definition of "terrorist act"'. Sheller Committee, *Report of the Security Legislation Review Committee* (June 2006) [6.10] and recommended that this aspect of the definition be removed and become the basis for a separate offence: [6.14] and [6.15].

[4] The completed prosecutions are the subject of this chapter. At the time of writing there are over 25 people who have been committed to stand trial on charges under Part 5.3 of the Criminal Code. They will be referred to in the context of the particular offences with which they have been charged.

necessarily been less scrutiny of how those offences have been dealt with in specific cases.

As at the beginning of 2008, there have been three prosecutions under Part 5.3 of the Criminal Code that have proceeded through to verdict and sentence: the prosecutions of Zak Mallah (aka Zeky Mullah), Jack Thomas and Faheem Lodhi. There are some clear differences between the cases — the most obvious being that Lodhi and Mallah were charged with 'terrorist act' offences, while Thomas' prosecution related to 'terrorist organisation' charges.[5] Nevertheless, these three prosecutions have several things in common. Each of them involved (to a greater or lesser degree) the jury grappling with the complexities of the Criminal Code definition of 'terrorist act'[6] in the course of its consideration of whether particular terrorist offences had been committed by the accused. Each of these three prosecutions also required the jury to consider that definition in the context of a 'simple' case, in the sense that the motivation for the terrorist act alleged by the prosecution coincided with the motivation of the accused.[7] Accordingly, at least in the context of such 'simple' cases, the outcome of each prosecution sheds interesting light on both the theoretical scope and the practical function of that definition.

The central argument of this chapter can be summed up very briefly: the outcomes of these three cases suggest that whilst both the terrorism offences and the definition of 'terrorist act' are indeed broadly drafted, the intricacy of that definition may have had the perverse effect of confining the ambit of those offences that rely upon it. In short, the current definition of 'terrorist act' is so dense and multi-layered that offences that incorporate it will be difficult to prove except in the more obvious or blameworthy cases.[8] Flowing from this first argument is a second one: that broadly drafted offences that do not incorporate the definition of 'terrorist act' are not similarly confined or constrained in their application. In this regard, 'terrorist organisation' offences where executive proscription is the method by which an organisation has been designated as 'terrorist', are particularly worrying in their breadth and scope. The same overbreadth may also apply to 'difficult' terrorist act cases, where the accused does not share the motivations of those involved in a terrorist act with which he or she is connected.

In drawing out the arguments set out in the previous paragraph, this chapter will be divided into two parts. Part I will briefly address the offences in Part

---

[5] See the discussion below on the significance of this difference.
[6] Contained in s 100.1 of the Criminal Code. See discussion below.
[7] See below for discussion of the concept of 'simple' and 'difficult' cases in the context of motivation for the terrorist act alleged.
[8] Note that the current definition of 'terrorist act' is highly problematic in a number of important ways, in particular, in how it deals with 'motive' (see discussion in McSherry, above n 2, 359-64). This aspect of the definition is beyond the scope of this chapter.

5.3 of the Criminal Code in order to provide the context for the discussion of the prosecutions of Mallah, Thomas and Lodhi. It will also explain the concept, as I use it in this chapter, of 'simple' as opposed to 'difficult' terrorist act cases. Part II will consider the details of the prosecutions as well as the implications of their outcomes.

## I. Brief Overview of Part 5.3

The terrorism provisions in the Criminal Code prohibit a range of activities connected with 'terrorist acts'; 'terrorist organisations'; and 'financing terrorism'. Offences in each of these areas were first inserted into the Code in mid-2002,[9] but a series of amending acts have both added new offence provisions[10] and increased the scope of original and new offences.[11] The following section briefly summarises the anti-terrorism offences contained in Part 5.3 of the Criminal Code as well as analysing some of their important features.

## A. Terrorist Act Offences

The original range of 'terrorist act' offences has not been extended by amending legislation. In relation to 'terrorist acts', ss 101.1 to 101.6 of the Criminal Code prohibit the following conduct:

- 101.1 Engaging in a terrorist act (penalty: life imprisonment).
- 101.2 Providing or receiving training connected with terrorist acts where the person either knows that the training is connected with preparation for, engagement in or assistance in a terrorist act (penalty: 25 years) or is reckless as to the existence of that connection (penalty: 15 years).
- 101.4 Possessing things connected with a terrorist act where the person knows of the connection (penalty: 15 years) or is reckless as to its existence (penalty: 10 years).
- 101.5 collecting or making a document where the document is connected with a terrorist act and the person knows of that connection (penalty: 15 years) or is reckless as to the existence of that connection (penalty: 10 years).[12] There is no offence if the collection or making of the document

---

[9] For an analysis of the 'terrorist act' and 'terrorist organisation' offences as originally passed in 2002, see Gani and Urbas, above n 2.

[10] See *Anti-terrorism Act (No 2) 2004* (Cth) which inserted a new offence relating to association with members of a terrorist organisation; *Anti-Terrorism Act (No 2) 2005* (Cth) which added the offence of financing a terrorist.

[11] See *Anti-terrorism Act 2004* (Cth) which amended terrorist organisation membership offences; and offences of providing training to or receiving training from a terrorist organisation; *Anti-Terrorism Act (No 1) 2005* (Cth) which provided that no specific terrorist act need be identified under the terrorist act offences (see discussion below); and *Anti-Terrorism Act (No 2) 2005* (Cth) which extended the grounds upon which a terrorist organisation could be proscribed to include those organisations that advocated the doing of a terrorist act.

[12] Belal Khazaal has been committed to stand trial in relation to a charge under this offence (making a document — a book — in connection with the engagement of a person in a terrorist act, knowing of that connection). He is also charged with inciting the commission by others of an offence of engaging

was not intended to facilitate preparation for, the engagement of a person in, or assistance in a terrorist act.

- 101.6 doing any act in preparation for or planning a terrorist act (penalty: life imprisonment).[13]

There are several important aspects of these 'terrorist act' provisions relating to fault elements (or mental states), preventative function and jurisdiction that should be noted.

### 1. Fault Elements

Different penalties apply depending on whether the accused knows or is reckless as to whether their conduct is connected with terrorist acts. The Criminal Code defines each of these mental states — 'knowledge' and 'recklessness' (as well as the concept of 'intention' which is central to the definition of 'terrorist act') — in its Chapter 2.[14]

### 2. Preventative Function

#### (a) Original 'Terrorist Act' Offences

With the exception of s 101.1, under each of these provisions as they existed before the *Anti-Terrorism Act (No 1) 2005* (Cth) came into effect in November 2005 (see discussion below), an offence may be committed 'even if the terrorist act does not occur'.[15] In addition, s 101.6 specifically prohibits acts done in preparation for or planning of terrorist acts. Accordingly, a significant function of the offences as they were originally conceptualised was prevention — to allow for the arrest and punishment of planners of terrorist acts well before those acts had occurred.[16] In particular, s 101.6 sought to deal with potential terrorist activity at its very earliest stage (even before the inchoate forms of these offences — attempts, conspiracy and incitement — are considered).[17] The original s

---

in a terrorist act, contrary to ss 11.4 and 101.1 of the Criminal Code. Pre-trial hearings began on 12 November 2007 and are listed to recommence in February 2008.

[13] See n 17 below for details of current prosecutions under this offence.

[14] Chapter 2 of the Criminal Code sets out General Principles of Criminal Responsibility and all federal offences must be interpreted by reference to those principles (see s 2.1 of the Criminal Code). For a discussion of interpretive issues relating to the Code, see M Gani, 'Codifying the Criminal Law: Issues of Interpretation' in S Bottomley and S Corcoran, *Interpreting Statutes* (Sydney: Federation Press, 2005) 197; I Leader-Elliott, 'Elements of Liability in the Commonwealth Criminal Code' (2002) 26 *Criminal Law Journal* 28.

[15] See original ss 101.2(3), 101.4(3), 101.5(3) and 101.6(2).

[16] The centrality of the preventative function of the legislation was emphasised by the Attorney-General's Department in its submission to the Senate Legal and Constitutional Legislation Committee in relation to the Security Legislation Amendment (Terrorism) Bill 2002 [No 2] (Cth). See *Submission 383A*, 1-3.

[17] Clearly, inchoate forms of these broadly drafted preparation offences extend liability to very preliminary conduct. On 25 February 2008, the trial of Mirsad Mulahalilovic, Abdul Rakib Hasan, Khaled Cheikho, Moustafa Cheikho, Mohamed Ali Elomar, Mazen Touma, Khaled Sharrouf, Omar Baladjam and Mohammad Omar Jamal commenced. The accused were arrested in November and December 2005 as part of Operation Pendennis in Sydney. They are charged with conspiring to do an act in

101.6 covered 'any act' (that is any conduct whatsoever) done in preparation for or planning of a terrorist act even if that terrorist act does not occur. It was with this last offence (s 101.6) that Zak Mallah was charged in December 2003 — the first terrorism charge laid in Australia under the new anti-terrorism legislation.

## (b) 'Terrorist Act' Offences as a Result of the Anti-Terrorism Act (No 1) 2005 (Cth)

Whilst no new 'terrorist act' offences have been added to Part 5.3 by the numerous Anti-Terrorism Acts referred to above, it is arguable that the ambit of those offences has been enlarged as a consequence of amendments contained in the *Anti-Terrorism Act (No 1) 2005* (Cth). Those amendments spell out that liability for 'terrorist act' offences can be established even if the prosecution cannot identify any specific terrorist act with which the accused's behaviour is connected. Liability for prohibited conduct rests in the connection of that conduct with 'a' terrorist act even if 'the' particular terrorist act cannot be ascertained.[18]

It should be noted here that the amendments effected by *Anti-Terrorism Act (No 1) 2005* post-date the commencement (and, in the case of Mallah, the conclusion) of the three prosecutions that are the subject of this chapter. Whilst the amendments have retrospective effect as a result of s 106.3 of the Criminal Code,[19] the NSW Court of Criminal Appeal held, in relation to Faheem Lodhi, that s 106.3 could not apply retrospectively where criminal prosecutions had already commenced.[20] It is interesting to observe that the full court of the NSW Court of Criminal Appeal suggests in the same judgment that the amendment itself may not have been necessary.[21] That Court held that the original formulation (discussed above) already demonstrated that the Parliament intended it to apply to conduct connected to a non-specific terrorist act and, further, that

---

preparation for a terrorist act contrary to ss 11.5 and 101.6 of the Criminal Code. No time or place in relation to the act is specified.

[18] The formula adopted by the legislation is to set out, in relation to each 'terrorist act' offence barring s 101.1, that an offence may be committed even if:

(a) a terrorist act does not occur;

(b) the prohibited activity or thing is not connected with a specific terrorist act; or

(c) it is connected with more than one terrorist act.

See the discussion of both the circumstances and the significance of these amendments in A Lynch, 'Legislating with Urgency — the Enactment of the *Anti-Terrorism Act [No 1] 2005*' (2006) 30 *Melbourne University Law Review* 747.

[19] Section 106.3 was inserted into the Criminal Code by Item 22 of Schedule 1 to the *Anti-Terrorism Act (No 2) 2005* (Cth) and was proclaimed on 15 February 2006.

[20] *Lodhi v The Queen* (2006) 199 FLR 303, [22]-[56]. The judgment was delivered by Spigelman CJ with McClellan CJ at CL and Sully J agreeing.

[21] As Andrew Lynch has done in Lynch, above n 18, 765-7.

'the clear intention of Parliament [was] to create offences where an offender has not decided precisely what he or she intends to do'.[22]

### 3. Jurisdiction

The most extreme form of extended jurisdiction under the Criminal Code (Category D jurisdiction) applies to each offence.[23] This is also the case for the terrorist organisation and financing terrorism offences discussed below.[24] Under Category D, an offence can be committed whether or not either the conduct constituting that offence or the effects of that conduct occurs in Australia.[25] So, at least technically, any person of any nationality, anywhere in the world, could be pursued under this legislation. Of course, such a prosecution is unlikely in any but the most extraordinary of cases.[26] What is noteworthy, in this context, is the attempt by the Commonwealth to assert universal jurisdiction over terrorism-related offences, which it clearly regards as an archetype of trans-national crime.[27]

## B. Definition of Terrorist Act

Given the discussion above, the definition of 'terrorist act' under s 100.1 of the legislation is crucial to understanding the operation of these offences. In summary, that section provides that a terrorist act is an action or threat of action done or made with two intentions present: the intention of advancing a political, religious or ideological cause; **and** the intention of coercing, or influencing by intimidation a government (including that of a foreign country) or intimidating the public or a section of the public.

---

[22] *Lodhi v The Queen* (2006) 199 FLR 303, [66]. For the full discussion see [63]-[70] where Spigelman CJ broadly endorses the analysis of Whealy J at first instance in *R v Lodhi* (2005) 199 FLR 236, [43], [52]; *R v Lodhi* [2006] NSWSC 584 (Unreported, Whealy J, 14 February 2006) [65]-[69], [76].
[23] By virtue of ss 101.1(2), 101.2(4), 101.4(4), 101.5(4), 101.6(3) of the Criminal Code.
[24] See ss 102.9 and 103.3.
[25] Section 15.4 Extended geographical jurisdiction — category D

If a law of the Commonwealth provides that this section applies to a particular offence, the offence applies:

(a) whether or not the conduct constituting the alleged offence occurs in Australia; and

(b) whether or not a result of the conduct constituting the alleged offence occurs in Australia.

Note: The expression *offence* is given an extended meaning by ss 11.2(1), 11.3, 11.6(1).

[26] See the discussion of extended geographical jurisdiction in Gani and Urbas, above n 2, 27-8; and in B McSherry, 'The Introduction of Terrorism-Related Offences in Australia: Comfort or Concern?' (2005) 12(2) *Psychiatry, Psychology and Law* 279, 282.
[27] Explanatory Memorandum, Security Legislation Amendment (Terrorism) Bill 2002 [No 2] (Cth), 17: 'This jurisdiction is appropriate due to the transnational nature of terrorist activities, to ensure that a person cannot escape prosecution or punishment based on a jurisdictional loophole.'

Under s 100.1(2), to constitute a terrorist act, the action must also do one (or more)[28] of the following:

a. cause serious physical harm to a person other than the offender
b. cause serious damage to property
c. cause death
d. endanger another's life
e. create a serious risk to the health or safety of the public
f. seriously interfere with, disrupt or destroy an electronic system (including, but not limited to, an information system; a telecommunications system; a financial system; a system used for the delivery of essential government services; a system used for, or by, an essential public utility; or a system used for, or by, a transport system).

Under s 100.1(3), action that is advocacy, protest, dissent or industrial action falls outside the definition of terrorist act provided that it is not intended to bring about serious physical harm or death, or to endanger the life of a person, or to create a serious risk to the health or safety of the public or a section thereof.

## Observations on the 'Terrorist Act' Definition and its Implications for 'Simple' and 'Difficult' Cases

The definition of 'terrorist act', as outlined above, demonstrates obvious complexities as well as a parliamentary intention to achieve an expansive scope.[29] The definition is undoubtedly drafted very broadly in a number of respects: it covers both an action and a threat of action; it encompasses an intention to coerce a government (including the government of another country), the public or a section of the public; it takes in actions that do cause and threats of action that would cause a wide variety of harm (and not just fatal harm) and potentially extends even to a mere threat of action that would, if carried out, seriously interfere with certain types of electronic systems. Nevertheless, despite this breadth of drafting, the prosecution has a high hurdle to clear in that it must show, beyond reasonable doubt, two levels of 'intention'[30] in relation to the terrorist act — that there was an intention to advance a political, religious or ideological cause by the action or threat of action and, further, that there was an intention to coerce or intimidate a government or to intimidate the public.

---

[28] Justice Whealy made this clear in *R v Lodhi* [2006] NSWSC 584 (Unreported, Whealy J, 14 February 2006) [98]. The NSW Court of Criminal Appeal agreed with Whealy J's analysis: *Lodhi v The Queen* (2006) 199 FLR 303, [74].
[29] Justice Whealy has remarked that 'it will be seen that the definition of "terrorist act" postulates an action or threat of action of the widest possible kind': *R v Lodhi* [2006] NSWSC 584 (Unreported, Whealy J, 14 February 2006) [75].
[30] Defined in s 5.2 of the Criminal Code. See discussion below in n 37.

It has now been made clear in the judgment of the New South Wales Court of Criminal Appeal in *Lodhi* [31] that the intentions in relation to advancement and coercion attach to the terrorist act itself and not to the state of mind of the accused as he or she was engaging in the conduct that constitutes the offence. Accordingly, the Court explained, these intentions are physical elements that characterise the action or threat of action that constitutes the 'terrorist act'[32] and are not fault elements applying to the accused themselves (although the accused may indeed hold such intentions).[33] This dimension adds a further degree of conceptual difficulty to the 'terrorist act' definition that must be understood and applied by a jury. It also, potentially, has the undesirable effect of lowering the prosecutorial hurdles posed by the dual inquiry into 'intention' in what I will call 'difficult' cases. By 'difficult' cases, I mean the prosecution of very peripheral or marginal players in terrorist acts (who *themselves* do not intend the advancement or coercion required by the definition but who are knowingly or recklessly connected with a plan where such motivations are clearly present in others).[34]

As has already been noted, none of the three cases that are the subject of this chapter represents a 'difficult' case of the kind described above. In *Mallah* and *Lodhi*, the person argued to have held the intentions referred to in the terrorist act definition was the accused himself.[35] Indeed, the sentencing remarks in the case of *Mallah* [36] suggest that the prosecution addressed the issue of intention by reference to the state of mind of the accused as he engaged in the alleged terrorist act (that is by reference to what Mallah meant to do or accomplish[37] by his plan of action). In Thomas' case, the accused was argued to have shared

---

[31] *Lodhi v The Queen* (2006) 199 FLR 303 (Spigelman CJ with McClellan CJ at CL and Sully J agreeing).
[32] The Court suggests at [90] that the intentions identifying the character of a terrorist act are 'circumstances' within the meaning of s 4.1(1)(c) of the Criminal Code. The prosecution is not required to particularise the person who has the relevant 'intention' because that person may not be known.
[33] The Court quoted extensively at [80] and endorsed at [90] Whealy J's judgment of 14 February 2006 — *R v Lodhi* [2006] NSWSC 584 (Unreported, Whealy J, 14 February 2006) [83], [103].
[34] Such a difficult case is posed by Gani and Urbas, above n 2, where the hypothetical accused is a humanitarian aid worker tending to the physical injuries of Tamil Tigers.
[35] In relation to Lodhi's case on this point, see *R v Lodhi* (2006) 199 FLR 354, [28]. The situation in Thomas' case is somewhat different. Thomas was charged with terrorist organisation offences in relation to Al Qa'ida (a proscribed organisation since 2002). However, as will be seen in the discussion below, the offence for which he was acquitted, s 102.7, incorporates the definition of 'terrorist act'. For Mallah, see below.
[36] *R v Mallah* [2005] NSWSC 317 (Unreported, Wood CJ at CL, 21 April 2005).
[37] See *R v Mallah* [2005] NSWSC 317 (Unreported, Wood CJ at CL, 21 April 2005) [22]. The definition of 'intention' in relation to conduct is contained in s 5.2(1) of the Criminal Code. A person intends conduct if he or she 'means to' engage in it. It appears from the sentencing remarks in this case that it was Mallah's intention in relation to his conduct that was argued. However, as has already been noted, in the later case of *Lodhi* both Whealy J and the NSWCCA discussed the two references to intention in the terrorist act definition as circumstances identifying the character of the action or threat of action as terrorist. Under s 5.2(2), a 'person has intention with respect to a circumstance if he or she believes that it exists or will exist'. Arguably, then, conceptualising the intention requirements of the terrorist act definition as in respect of circumstance would make the prosecutor's task easier.

the philosophies and motivations of Al Qa'ida.[38] Accordingly, the prosecutions of Mallah, Thomas and Lodhi were 'simple' cases, in that, in each, the relevant terrorist act motivations were argued either to have been held solely by the accused or to have been shared by the accused with others.

The discussion of the case law that follows will focus particularly on the issue of whether the enquiry into intention in these 'simple' cases has tempered the effects of both overbroad offence provisions and an overexpansive definition of 'terrorist act'.

## C. Terrorist Organisation Offences

The second category of offences set out in Part 5.3 of the Criminal Code is those involving 'terrorist organisations'. Unlike the 'terrorist act' offences discussed above, the original list of terrorist organisation offences enacted in 2002[39] has been augmented by a variety of subsequent Anti-Terrorism Acts.[40] Current offences relating to terrorist organisations are:

- 102.2 — intentionally directing the activities of a terrorist organisation, knowing that it is a terrorist organisation (penalty: 25 years) or being reckless as to whether it is such an organisation (penalty: 15 years);
- 102.3 — intentionally being a member of a terrorist organisation where the person knows the organisation is a terrorist organisation (penalty: 10 years).[41] Under subsection 2, an accused may escape liability if he/she proves that he/she took all reasonable steps to cease to be a member of the organisation as soon as practicable after learning that this was a terrorist organisation.[42]
- 102.4 — intentionally recruiting a person to join or participate in the activities of a terrorist organisation, knowing that it is a terrorist organisation

---

[38] In relation to the second of the two s 102.7 counts against him (discussed below), Thomas was alleged to be a 'sleeper' in Australia who could be activated by Al Qa'ida to undertake a terrorist act. See the discussion of such prosecution allegations by the Chief Magistrate attached as Appendix B to Teague J's decision in relation to bail: *DPP (Cth) v Thomas* [2005] VSC 85 (31 March 2005).

[39] For the original terrorist organisation offences, see Gani and Urbas, above n 2, 34-5.

[40] See above nn 10 and 11 for a brief description of these amending Acts.

[41] Following police operations and arrests in November and December 2005 in Melbourne, the trial of 12 men for terrorist organisation offences began in the Supreme Court of Victoria on 13 February 2008. The charges mainly relate to the membership offence, but charges against some accused also include making funds available to a terrorist organisation (a s 102.6 offence). The accused are Abdul Nacer Benbrika (who is also charged with directing the activities of a terrorist organisation under s 102.2), Amer Haddara, Aimen Joud, Shane Kent, Abdullah Merhi, Ahmed Raad, Ezzit Raad, Fadal Sayadi, Hany Taha, Shoue Hammoud, Majed Raad and Bassam Raad. On 14 December 2007 Aruran Vinayagamoorthy, Sivarajah Yathavan and Arumugan Rajeevan were committed to stand trial for this offence and also for offences under s 102.6 in relation to their alleged membership and funding of the Liberation Tamil Tigers of Eelam (LTTE). Vinayagamoorthy and Yathavan are also charged under s 102.7 with providing support or resources to LTTE.

[42] This offence was originally confined to membership of terrorist organisations that were listed under the Act. The amended provision was introduced by the *Anti-Terrorism Act 2004* (Cth), which came into effect on 1 July 2004.

(penalty: 25 years) or being reckless as to whether it is such an organisation (penalty: 15 years).[43]

- 102.5 — intentionally providing training to or receiving training from a terrorist organisation being reckless as to whether it is a terrorist organisation (penalty: 25 years) or where the organisation is a proscribed terrorist organisation (penalty: 25 years).[44]
- 102.6 — intentionally receiving funds from or making funds available to or collecting funds for a terrorist organisation (whether directly or indirectly), knowing the organisation is a terrorist organisation (penalty: 25 years) or being reckless as to whether it is such an organisation (penalty: 15 years). There is an exception for funds received solely for the purpose of providing legal representation for a person in proceedings related to terrorist offences or for assisting the organisation to comply with the law.
- 102.7 — intentionally providing to a terrorist organisation support or resources that would help the organisation engage (directly or indirectly) in preparing, planning, assisting in or fostering the doing of a terrorist act (whether or not a terrorist act occurs), knowing that the organisation is a terrorist organisation (penalty: 25 years) or being reckless as to whether it is such an organisation (penalty: 15 years).[45]
- 102.8 — intentionally associating,[46] on two or more occasions, with another person who is a member of a terrorist organisation or who promotes or directs the activities of such an organisation where that intentional association provides support to the terrorist organisation. To be guilty of this offence, the person would have to know both that the organisation involved was a terrorist organisation and that the person with whom they were associating was a member of, or a promoter or director of the activities of the organisation. Additionally, he or she would have to intend that the support provided by the association with that member assist the organisation to expand or to continue to exist. (Penalty: 3 years.) Exceptions apply to family members, providers of humanitarian aid, persons providing legal advice or

---

[43] Lodhi was originally charged with this offence on 22 April 2004. It was alleged that he attempted to recruit medical student Izhar ul-Haque to participate in Lashkar-e-Tayyiba (LeT) activities (relating to periods before that organisation was listed as a proscribed organisation). The charges in relation to this offence were later dropped.

[44] This offence is another that has been amended since its original enactment. See Gani and Urbas, above n 2, 35 for its original form. Amongst other changes, the new offence increases the penalty where an accused is reckless as to whether an organisation is terrorist from 15 to 25 years. The offence was amended by the *Anti-Terrorism Act 2004* (Cth) sch 1 para 20. Izhar ul-Haque was charged with receiving training from a terrorist organisation (LeT) under the original offence in April 2004. After some delay, due to a 2006 application to the High Court in relation to the constitutionality of the legislation, his trial began in the NSW Supreme Court in October 2007. On 12 November, the charge against ul-Haque was dropped, following a decision by Adams J that ruled certain records of interview inadmissable as evidence: *R v ul-Haque* [2007] NSWSC 1251 (Unreported, Adams J, 5 November 2007).

[45] Thomas was acquitted of two counts of this offence. See discussion below.

[46] Under s 102.1(1) associating means meeting or communicating with another person. This offence was inserted into the Criminal Code as a result of the *Anti-Terrorism Act (No 2) 2004* (Cth).

representation and to association which takes place in the course of practising a religion and in a place of religious worship.

## 1. Observations on s 102.8: a Workable Provision?

This last provision, associating with a terrorist organisation, has several features in common with the definition of 'terrorist act' that has been discussed above. Like that definition, s 102.8 is very broadly drafted (so much so that it needs explicitly to exempt family members from its scope). But, I would argue that because of its multiple layers and complexity, the offence is probably very narrow in its application. Like the definition of 'terrorist act', this provision casts its net widely in a number of respects: it covers any form of meeting or communication with a member of a terrorist organisation (including an informal member)[47] or simply a person who 'promotes'[48] the activities of a terrorist organisation on two or more occasions. Nevertheless, it requires multiple physical and fault elements to be in place (including the provision of support, knowledge that the organisation is a terrorist one and the intention to assist the organisation through the support provided by the association). In practical terms, the offence is likely to be difficult to prove beyond reasonable doubt to a jury except in the most blameworthy cases. In any event, in such egregious cases, the behaviour it seeks to sanction is clearly dealt with by other offences.

## 2. Implications of Broadly Drafted 'Terrorist Organisation' Offences

The implications of overbreadth in relation to terrorist organisation offences are even more troubling than those in relation to terrorist act offences in a number of respects. First, these are arguably serious 'status offences' whereby individuals are liable for lengthy jail sentences because of their status (for example, as 'members' of a terrorist organisation), type or associations rather than because of their actual conduct. The issues and problems associated with 'status offences' such as the terrorist organisation offences have been addressed by a number of authors since the introduction of Part 5.3[49] and I will not go into them further here. Second, given the serious consequences that may flow to an individual through association of various kinds with a 'terrorist organisation', the process by which an organisation is designated as 'terrorist' requires the closest scrutiny.

---

[47] Under s 102.1(1) a member of an organisation includes:

(a) a person who is an informal member of the organisation; and

(b) a person who has taken steps to become a member of the organisation; and

(c) in the case of an organisation that is a body corporate — a director or an officer of the body corporate.

[48] This term is not defined in the legislation and is likely to be interpreted by reference to its normal or dictionary meaning.

[49] See, eg, Gani and Urbas, above n 2, 33; Bronitt and McSherry, above n 2, 779; McSherry, above n 2, 364-6, McSherry, above n 26, 282-3.

Particularly problematic in this regard is the method by which the executive can proscribe an organisation as terrorist, under the current arrangements.[50]

As will be seen below, the definition of 'terrorist act' plays an important part in the prosecution of 'terrorist organisation' offences, particularly in relation to their characterisation as such.

## D. Definition of Terrorist Organisation

The definition of a terrorist organisation under s 102.1(1) of the Criminal Code is lengthy and complex — running to 18 subsections and nearly 800 words. The original 2002 definition was controversially amended in 2004[51] to allow for executive proscription of organisations.

Under that first definition, there were two methods by which an organisation could be a 'terrorist organisation' for the purposes of prosecution of an individual under Part 5.3 of the Criminal Code. First, a jury could determine that an organisation was a terrorist one in the course of a prosecution by application of limb (a) of the definition: that is, by deciding that the organisation in question was one 'that is directly or indirectly engaged in, preparing, planning, assisting in or fostering the doing of a terrorist act (whether or not a terrorist act occurs)'. Second, under limb (b) an organisation could be listed under regulations (which itself could only occur if it had first been listed by the Security Council of the United Nations) so that the issue of whether an organisation with which an individual was allegedly associated was terrorist was settled before any prosecution of that individual. A further alternative that was used prior to the 2004 amendments (in order to circumvent the requirement for prior Security Council listing under limb (b)) was to pass legislation to list a specific organisation as terrorist. This legislative option was followed in order to list Hizballah, Hamas and Lashkar-e-Tayyiba.[52]

Under the current mechanism, the original limb (a) remains in place, but, under limb (b), terrorist organisations can be specified in regulations by executive action independent of Security Council listing.[53] Under s 102.1(2), before the Governor-General can make such a regulation, the Minister (the Attorney-General) must be:

> satisfied on reasonable grounds that the organisation:

---

[50] See Hogg's Chapter 14 in this volume.
[51] This was as a result of the *Criminal Code Amendment (Terrorist Organisations) Act 2004* (Cth) which was enacted in March 2004. The political history of that Act, which allowed for executive proscription of terrorist organisations, and the way it eventually became law is discussed in both Gani and Urbas, above n 2, 48-9 and in M Gani, 'Upping the Ante in the "War on Terror"' in P Fawkner (ed), *A Fair Go in an Age of Terror* (Victoria: David Lovell Publishing, 2004) 97-8.
[52] See the *Criminal Code Amendment (Hizballah) Act 2003* (Cth) and the *Criminal Code Amendment (Hamas And Lashkar-E-Tayyiba) Act 2003* (Cth).
[53] Limb (b) of the s 102.1(1) definition now reads: (b) an organisation that is specified by the regulations for the purposes of this paragraph (see sub-sections (2), (3) and (4)).

(a) is directly or indirectly engaged in, preparing, planning, assisting in or fostering the doing of a terrorist act (whether or not a terrorist act has occurred or will occur); or

(b) advocates the doing of a terrorist act (whether or not a terrorist act has occurred or will occur).[54]

Section 102.1(2A) requires that the Leader of the Opposition be briefed (though no more) before an organisation is listed under this procedure. There is a de-listing mechanism contained in s 102.1(4) and reviews by the Parliamentary Joint Committee on the Australian Security Intelligence Organisation (ASIO), the Australian Secret Intelligence Service (ASIS) and the Defence Signals Directorate (DSD)[55] are provided for by s 102.1A.

Clearly then, the definition of 'terrorist act' is central to decision-making about whether an organisation is 'terrorist', whether that decision is made by a jury during a trial or by the Attorney-General outside of the context of a prosecution. Under limb (a) of the definition, a jury must decide, in the course of an individual's prosecution for a 'terrorist organisation' offence whether or not the organisation involved was directly or indirectly engaged in, preparing, planning, assisting in or fostering the doing of a terrorist act (regardless of whether any terrorist act has actually occurred). Under limb (b) an organisation can only be listed as terrorist if the Attorney-General is satisfied (on reasonable grounds) that the organisation is so involved or that it advocates the doing of a terrorist act.

Again, limb (a) is very broadly drafted. Involvement by an organisation in a terrorist act need not be direct: engagement can be indirect and extends beyond planning and assisting to 'fostering'[56] a terrorist act even if it does not occur. Nevertheless, it is at least arguable that the same issues of complexity discussed above in relation to the 'terrorist act' definition, may, in practice, incline a jury towards caution in finding that an organisation is 'terrorist' under limb (a). This is especially so where a jury might wonder why a particular organisation has

---

[54] Under s 102.1(1A) the definition of advocates is as follows:

(1A) In this Division, an organisation *advocates* the doing of a terrorist act if:

(a) the organisation directly or indirectly counsels or urges the doing of a terrorist act; or

(b) the organisation directly or indirectly provides instruction on the doing of a terrorist act; or

(c) the organisation directly praises the doing of a terrorist act in circumstances where there is a risk that such praise might have the effect of leading a person (regardless of his or her age or any mental impairment (within the meaning of section 7.3) that the person might suffer) to engage in a terrorist act.

[55] Now known as the Parliamentary Joint Committee on Intelligence and Security.

[56] 'Fostering' is another undefined term.

not already been listed by the Attorney-General under his broad proscription powers if it is, indeed, terrorist.[57]

Those proscription powers are, undeniably, sweeping. Whilst the Minister must be satisfied of the relevant matters 'on reasonable grounds', the broad drafting of s 102.1(2)(a) and the inclusion of mere 'advocating' in paragraph (b) — which itself extends both to indirect urging and to direct praising of an act in circumstances where there is *a risk* that a person *might* be led to engage in a terrorist act[58] — make the Attorney-General's listing powers expansive.[59]

Accordingly, regardless of any difference of approach or understanding that the Attorney-General on the one hand and a jury, on the other, might bring to the legal definition of 'terrorist act', that definition is unlikely to play the same kind of tempering role in the Minister's decision-making as it is in the context of a jury deliberating whether an organisation is terrorist under limb (a) of the s 102.1(1) definition. If the bar is set so low as to allow the Minister to proscribe an organisation on the basis that it praises an act in circumstances where there is a risk that such praise might have the effect of 'leading a person (regardless of his or her age or any mental impairment) ... to engage in a terrorist act',[60] then that bar barely constitutes a hurdle at all.

Again, there has been, and continues to be, significant academic and political criticism of the executive proscription method.[61]

---

[57] The Sheller Committee, above n 3, 11, recommends (at Recommendation 10) that limb (a) of the definition of terrorist organisation be removed if the process of proscription is reformed to meet the requirements of administrative law (see the discussion in n 59 below).

[58] The Sheller Committee, above n 3, 11 also recommended (at Recommendation 9) that paragraph (c) of s 102.1(1A) (the definition of 'advocates' set out above in n 54), be removed.

[59] The Sheller Committee did recommend a change to the proscription process either: 1. by retaining executive proscription but building into that process a notification method or, 2. by replacing the executive proscription process with a judicial one. In relation to 1. the Committee recommended the adoption of: 'a method for providing a person, or organisation affected, with notification, if it is practicable, that it is proposed to proscribe the organisation and with the right to be heard in opposition. An advisory committee, established by statute, should be appointed to advise the Attorney-General on the case that has been submitted for proscription of an organisation. The Committee would consist of people who are independent of the process, such as those with expertise or experience in security analysis, public affairs, public administration and legal practice. The role of the committee should be publicized, and it should be open to the committee to consult publicly and to receive submissions from members of the public.'

In relation to 2, the judicial proscription process recommended was one made 'on application by the Attorney-General to the Federal Court with media advertisement, service of the application on affected persons and a hearing in open court': Sheller Committee, above n 3, Recommendation 4, 9-10. However, the Parliamentary Joint Committee on Intelligence and Security explicitly stated that it did not look at proscription issues for its December 2006 Report because the Committee itself had general oversight of this matter under the legislation and would be enquiring into it in early 2007: Parliamentary Joint Committee on Intelligence and Security, above n 3, [1.7].

[60] See paragraph (c) of the s 102.1(1A) definition in n 54 above.

[61] See, as just a few examples, the Gani and Urbas, above n 2, 48-9; Gani, above n 51, 97-8; J Hocking, *Terror Laws: ASIO, Counter-Terrorism and the Threat to Democracy* (Sydney: UNSW Press, 2004) 204-11; Commonwealth, *Parliamentary Debates*, House of Representatives, 3 June 2003, 15774 (Simon Crean, Leader of the Opposition); Sheller Committee, above n 3, Ch 9; and Hogg Chapter 14 in this volume.

## E. Financing Terrorism Offences

There are two financing terrorism offences in Division 103 of Part 5.3 of the Criminal Code. Again, this is a Division that has been amended since 2002, particularly as a result of the *Anti-Terrorism Act (No 2) 2005* (Cth), which added the second offence below. The financing terrorism offences are:

- 103.1 — intentionally providing or collecting funds being reckless as to whether the funds will be used to facilitate or engage in a terrorist act (penalty: life imprisonment); and
- 103.2 — intentionally making available to or collecting funds for or on behalf of another person (whether directly or indirectly) being reckless as to whether the other person will use the funds to facilitate or engage in a terrorist act (penalty: life imprisonment).

Once again, the definition of 'terrorist act', as understood and applied by a jury, plays a central part in these offences. As yet, there have been no prosecutions for financing terrorism under this legislation.

## II. The Cases of Zak Mallah, Jack Thomas and Faheem Lodhi

As mentioned above, Mallah and Lodhi were charged with 'terrorist act' offences whilst Thomas was prosecuted under two 'terrorist organisation' provisions. In addition to the terrorism offences, Mallah and Thomas were each charged with another, non-terrorist offence: Mallah pleaded guilty to threatening to cause harm to a Commonwealth public official; and Thomas was found guilty of having in his possession a falsified Australian passport.

The coupling of terrorist charges with other lesser offences is a phenomenon that was warned against by early critics of the terrorist offences contained in Part 5.3 of the Criminal Code. It was argued that the existence of these broadly drafted terrorism offences would fulfil a symbolic as well as a somewhat insidious practical role: with a terrorism offence in their back pocket, prosecutors could secure pleas to lesser, more traditional criminal law offences.[62] In the context of the central thesis of this chapter, it is at least arguable that the difficulties experienced by jury members in conceptualising the terrorist act definition and applying it to the offences that contain it, may also encourage then to convict on the more traditional 'fall-back' charge.

Each of the cases of Mallah, Thomas and Lodhi is analysed in turn.

---

[62] See, eg, the submission by Justice John Dowd on the original Bill in 2002 on behalf of the International Commission of Jurists in the Report of the Senate Legal and Constitutional Legislation Committee, Parliament of the Commonwealth of Australia, *Consideration of Legislation Referred to the Committee: Security Legislation Amendment (Terrorism) Bill 2002 [No 2]* (2002) 38.

## A. Zak Mallah

The first prosecution under the 'terrorist act' offences was that of Zak Mallah who was arrested and charged in December 2003. The charges he eventually faced involved two counts under s 101.6 — doing an act in preparation for or planning a terrorist act (which carries a penalty of life imprisonment)[63] and threatening to cause harm to a Commonwealth public official under s 147.2 of the Criminal Code (which carries a penalty of two years' imprisonment).[64] He

---

[63] The provision as it read at the time that Mallah was charged (note the discussion of the subsequent changes to sub-s (2), above in the text at n 18) is as follows:

Section 101.6 Other acts done in preparation for, or planning, terrorist acts

(1) A person commits an offence if the person does any act in preparation for, or planning, a terrorist act.

Penalty: Imprisonment for life.

(2) A person commits an offence under subsection (1) even if the terrorist act does not occur.

(3) Section 15.4 (extended geographical jurisdiction—category D) applies to an offence against subsection (1).

[64] Section 147.2(2) Threatening to cause harm

(2) A person (the *first person*) is guilty of an offence if:

(a) the first person makes to another person (the *second person*) a threat to cause harm to the second person or to a third person; and

(b) the second person or the third person is a public official; and

(c) the first person:

(i) intends the second person to fear that the threat will be carried out; or

(ii) is reckless as to causing the second person to fear that the threat will be carried out; and

(d) the first person makes the threat because of:

(i) the official's status as a public official; or

(ii) any conduct engaged in by the official in the official's capacity as a public official; and

(e) the official is a Commonwealth public official; and

(f) if subparagraph (d)(i) applies—the status mentioned in that subparagraph was status as a Commonwealth public official; and

(g) if subparagraph (d)(ii) applies—the conduct mentioned in that subparagraph was engaged in by the official in the official's capacity as a Commonwealth public official.

Penalty: Imprisonment for 2 years

(2A) Absolute liability applies to the paragraphs (2)(e), (f) and (g) elements of the offence.

The charge as set out in the ruling of Wood CJ at CL (on pre-trial issues relating to the admissibility of evidence) in *R v Mallah* [2005] NSWSC 358 (Unreported, 11 February 2005) [1] was that the accused: 'Between about 28 November 2003 and 3 December 2003 at Sydney in the State of New South Wales:

(a) made to another person, namely, to undercover officer using an assumed name 'Greg' (the second person) a threat to cause serious harm to a third person, namely, he threatened to kill unidentified officers of the Department of Foreign Affairs and Trade or the Australian Security Intelligence Organisation; and

(b) the third person is a public official; and

(c) he was reckless as to causing the second person to fear that the threat will be carried out; and

(d) he made the threat because of the official's status as a public official; and

(e) the official is a Commonwealth public official.'

was acquitted on both counts of the terrorist act offence and pleaded guilty to the non-terrorism offence (see below). The terrorist act alleged in relation to both the s 101.6 counts (and also the threat alleged under s 147.2) was that Mallah threatened to kill officers of ASIO or the Department of Foreign Affairs and Trade (DFAT). The particular acts charged as the preparatory or planning acts for the purposes of s 101.6 were buying a rifle and selling a videotape, photographs and a three-page typed statement to an undercover police officer.

## 1. Facts of the Case

The facts of the case are relatively straightforward.[65] Mallah had been refused an Australian passport on the grounds that he was likely to engage in conduct that might prejudice the security of Australia or of a foreign country (he was interviewed by ASIO officers and during that interview he told those officers that he could not rule out joining a jihad). He was very upset as a result of his application being refused and began behaving erratically and appearing on television and radio making provocative statements. He purchased a rifle and ammunition and the police became aware of this. They executed a search warrant and:

> The rifle and ammunition were found along with a number of documents, including a handwritten will, a printed document 'How can I prepare myself for Jihad', a handwritten letter which appears to have been a message to ASIO, and a typed manifesto setting out his grievances and identifying ASIO as his target, as well as a copy of a job application and supporting documents which he had sent to ASIO.[66]

Mallah was arrested and charged with firearms offences for which he was fined. The trial attracted more media attention and he appeared on various television shows and was also interviewed by various newspapers (including *The Australian*). In the course of these numerous interviews he

> showed, or sold, to the journalists copies of some of the documents which police had earlier seized, as well as some photographs of himself in dramatic poses, holding a knife, and wearing the kind of garb which, it seems, he considered appropriate for a would-be terrorist or suicide bomber. It is also evident that he made it known that he had made a videotape which, amongst other things, included recitations from the Koran, images of himself, and a recitation of what purportedly was to be his last message to the world.[67]

As a result of this behaviour, New South Wales Counter-Terrorist Coordination Command undertook an undercover operation to see if Mallah was in fact

---

[65] The facts are set out in *R v Mallah* [2005] NSWSC 317 (Unreported, Wood CJ at CL, 21 April 2005) [3]-[27].
[66] Ibid [11].
[67] Ibid [14].

planning a terrorist related offence. An operative 'Greg' posed as a freelance journalist who wanted to write a story on Mallah. He made phone contact and met several times with Mallah over a period of days. They negotiated a price of $3000 for the videotape and photos and other items that related to a seige he said he was planning of an ASIO or DFAT building during which he planned to take and kill hostages. It appears that Mallah also expected to be shot and killed by police during the seige.

At trial, Mallah pleaded guilty to the s 147.2 offence (which had been an offence under the Criminal Code since well before the enactment of the terrorism provisions).[68] The jury acquitted him of both counts of the s 101.6 offence. Mallah was sentenced to two years six months with release to be subject to entering a good behaviour bond with conditions attached.[69]

## 2. Case Analysis

The jury's acquittal of Mallah in relation to the terrorism offences means, of course, that the prosecution did not prove beyond reasonable doubt all the elements of the offence in relation to either s 101.6 count. The defence had argued that there was no genuine plan for a terrorist act — Mallah was not in fact planning to kill ASIO or DFAT officers but was just talking nonsense and stringing 'Greg' along in order to make money and get some publicity. In relation to the intentions that must be shown for there to be a 'terrorist act', the issue was whether, if Mallah did have such a plan to kill government officers, he meant to advance a political, religious or ideological cause in pursuing it 'as distinct from some purely personal cause either to secure a passport, or to exact revenge on ASIO or DFAT for obstructing its issue, or to gain publicity for himself'.[70] Additionally, the defence argument was that, if there was a genuine plan to kill, Mallah did not mean by its implementation to coerce or influence by intimidation the government of the Commonwealth to alter its policies or to do something that it would not otherwise have done. Again, his motivation was merely to pursue a personal vendetta against ASIO and/or DFAT.

Effectively, in order to show the physical and fault elements of the offence,[71] the prosecution needed to establish that Mallah meant to do an act as part of a genuine plan to commit a terrorist act. The jury did not accept this.

---

[68] The offence was inserted into the Criminal Code as a result of the *Criminal Code Amendment (Theft, Fraud, Bribery and Related Offences) Act 2000* (Cth).

[69] *R v Mallah* [2005] NSWSC 317 (Unreported, Wood CJ at CL, 21 April 2005) [88]-[90]. Mallah was, in fact, released in October 2005 — his sentence effectively being increased by six weeks after he assaulted a prison officer in May 2005.

[70] Ibid [22].

[71] The fault element of s 101.6, by virtue of the default fault element provision of the Criminal Code (s 5.6), is that the accused *intentionally* engaged in the prohibited conduct (here 'doing any act in preparation for or planning a terrorist act'. Under s 5.2(1) a person has intention with respect to conduct if he or she 'means to engage in that conduct'.

In response to Mallah's acquittal on the terrorism offence, the Attorney-General expressed disappointment and stated, through a spokeswoman, that he would see whether the verdict 'exposed any technical difficulties in the law'.[72] The Anti-Terrorism Acts of 2005 (particularly Act No 1) contained measures that were designed to 'clarify' (effectively broaden the ambit of) the terrorism offences.[73] Crucially, though, there was no revisiting of the actual definition of 'terrorist act' contained in s 100.1 of the Criminal Code.

## B. Jack Thomas

Jack Thomas was arrested in November 2004 and, like Mallah, was charged with both terrorism and non-terrorism related offences.[74] In the former category, he was charged under s 102.6(1)[75] of the Criminal Code with intentionally receiving funds from a terrorist organisation (Al Qa'ida — which has been a proscribed organisation since 2002) knowing it was a terrorist organisation. He was also charged under s 102.7(1)[76] of the Code with two counts of intentionally providing resources (himself) to a terrorist organisation that would help it engage in preparing or planning a terrorist act (count one in relation to preparing for a terrorist act overseas and count two in relation to preparing for such an act in Australia) knowing that the organisation to which he was providing resources was a terrorist organisation. In the category of non-terrorism-related offences,

---

[72] Quoted in N Wallace and J Kerr, 'Not a Terrorist, Just an Angry Loner Starved of Attention', *Sydney Morning Herald* (Sydney), 7 April 2005, 1.
[73] Former Prime Minister of Australia, John Howard, Joint Press Conference with the then Attorney-General, Philip Ruddock, Parliament House, 8 September 2005.
[74] The charges and facts of the case are clearly set out in *DPP v Thomas* [2006] VSC 120 (Unreported, Cummins J, 31 March 2006) [1]-[5].
[75] That subsection reads:

Section 102.6 Getting funds to or from a terrorist organisation

(1) A person commits an offence if:

(a) the person intentionally receives funds from, or makes funds available to, an organisation (whether directly or indirectly); and

(b) the organisation is a terrorist organisation; and

(c) the person knows the organisation is a terrorist organisation.

Penalty: Imprisonment for 25 years.

[76] Section 102.7(1) provides:

(1) A person commits an offence if:

(a) the person intentionally provides to an organisation support or resources that would help the organisation engage in an activity described in paragraph (a) of the definition of *terrorist organisation* in this Division; and

(b) the organisation is a terrorist organisation; and

(c) the person knows the organisation is a terrorist organisation.

Penalty: Imprisonment for 25 years.

Paragraph (a) of the definition of terrorist organisation provides:

**Terrorist organisation** means (a) an organisation that is directly or indirectly engaged in, preparing, planning, assisting in or fostering the doing of a terrorist act (whether or not a terrorist act occurs).

Thomas was charged under s 9A(1)(e) of the *Passports Act 1938* (Cth) with possessing a falsified passport.

Thomas contested all charges but was ultimately found guilty of the receiving funds and the false passport offences. However, significantly from the point of view of the central thesis of this chapter, he was acquitted by the jury in relation to both counts of providing resources to a terrorist organisation. In March 2006, Thomas was sentenced to five years for receiving funds from Al Qa'ida and one year for the passport offence (sentences to be served concurrently). The non-parole period was set at two years.[77] Given that the maximum penalty for the s 102.6 offence is imprisonment for 25 years, the sentence was very much at the lower end of those available.

Thomas' case and its aftermath are extraordinary in a number of respects and his story continues to be played out both in the courts and in the public arena. In August 2006, the Supreme Court of Victoria Court of Appeal overturned Thomas' conviction on both the counts set out above on the basis that self-inculpatory statements made by Thomas in the course of interviews with Australian Federal Police (AFP) officers in Pakistan were not voluntarily made and, accordingly, should not have been admitted as evidence in his trial.[78] Nine days after Thomas' acquittal, he became the first Australian to be made subject to an interim control order,[79] that set significant limits on Thomas' movements, communications and other freedoms. Thomas has since unsuccessfully attempted to have the control order quashed on the grounds that Division 104 of the Criminal Code is wholly invalid under the *Australian Constitution*.[80] In addition, criminal proceedings are pending against Thomas in the Victorian Supreme Court. This is as a result of the Supreme Court of Victoria Court of Appeal ordering his retrial in December 2006.[81] The basis for the Court's decision was that admissions by Thomas in a *Four Corners* program on ABC television and in *The Age* newspaper were both voluntarily made and capable of supporting a conviction and, further, that in the circumstances of the case, it would not be unjust to order a retrial.[82]

## 1. Facts of the Case

Jack Thomas trained with Al Qa'ida at the Al Farooq training camp in Afghanistan for a period of three months from March to July 2001 (that is before the events of September 11 2001). After a period in Kabul, Thomas went to Pakistan and

---

[77] See the sentencing remarks of Cummins J in *DPP v Thomas* [2006] VSC 120 (Unreported, Cummins J, 31 March 2006) [18]-[21].
[78] *R v Thomas* (2006) 14 VR 475, [94] (Maxwell P, Buchanan and Vincent JJA).
[79] Under pt 5.3, div 104, sub-div B, s 104.4 of the Criminal Code.
[80] See the decision of the High Court in *Thomas v Mowbray* [2007] HCA 33 (2 August 2007).
[81] The re-trial was listed to commence in February 2008.
[82] *R v Thomas* (No 3) (2006) 14 VR 512.

stayed in Al Qa'ida safe houses until he received, from a senior Al Qa'ida operative (Khaled Bin Attash), funds of $3500, an airline ticket to Australia and a passport that had been falsified (in order that his stay in Pakistan would appear to have been much shorter than it, in fact, was).

Shortly after this, Thomas was arrested by Pakistani authorities and remained in custody in Pakistan (during which he was interrogated by Pakistani and United States (US) operatives and subjected to threats and some physical violence by them)[83] until 6 June 2003 when he returned to Australia. Whilst in Pakistani custody, he was also interviewed by officers both of ASIO and the AFP. It was evidence that he gave during an interview with AFP officers in March 2003 that was the subject of the appeal described above.

## 2. Case Analysis

With respect to the two s 102.7 offences (of which the jury found Thomas not guilty) the prosecution had alleged that Thomas was trusted by Al Qa'ida operatives who saw him as being a believer in their cause. Further, it alleged that he took the money and plane ticket (as well as a phone number and email address through which he could communicate with the organisation when he got back to Australia) because he had agreed to operate as a sleeper cell for Al Qa'ida in Australia. Thomas had argued that he had never pledged allegiance to the organisation, had never offered himself as a resource and had only accepted the ticket and money in order to get home to his family.

Thomas' acquittal on these charges demonstrates that the jury was not convinced beyond a reasonable doubt that Thomas was providing resources (in this case his services as a 'sleeper cell' in Australia) to Al Qa'ida that would help that organisation engage in preparing a terrorist act in Australia or elsewhere.

Once again, it is arguable that the complexities of the definition of 'terrorist act' (which is incorporated into the s 102.7 offence) played a part in his acquittal. In particular, it is arguable that the breadth given to the offence by the tenuous nature of the connection required between the provision of support or resources to a terrorist organisation and the complex concept of a 'terrorist act' gave the jury pause. All that is required for an accused to be liable under this provision is that he or she intentionally[84] provide to a terrorist organisation support or resources that *would* [85] (not does) help it engage (*directly or indirectly*) in

---

[83] In his 'Reasons for Ruling Number 3', the trial judge, Cummins J detailed Thomas' description of treatment he had received in custody at the hands of Pakistani and two US operatives and generally accepted its accuracy at [41]. See *DPP v Thomas* [2006] VSC 243 (Unreported, Cummins J, 7 April 2006) [36]-[40].
[84] This requirement is part of the offence as a result of s 5.6 of the Criminal Code. See above n 71 for an explanation of this provision and a definition of intention.
[85] It is arguable that this constitutes a circumstance associated with conduct, which would, as a result of s 5.6, require the prosecution to prove that the accused was 'reckless' as to whether their provision

preparing, planning, assisting in or fostering the doing of a terrorist act[86] (*whether or not a terrorist act occurs*) in the knowledge that the organisation in question is a terrorist one. The doctor who patches up an injured Al Qa'ida operative, knowing who she is dealing with might be caught by this provision and subject to up to 25 years' imprisonment if successfully prosecuted.[87] Whilst Thomas' situation is clearly more blameworthy than that of any such hypothetical doctor, discomfort with the tenuousness of the link required by the offence, in conjunction with the difficulties of working with the terrorist act definition might incline the jury to require a great deal from the prosecution if it is to convict on this offence. This is especially so when it is returning guilty verdicts in relation to other offences.

## C. Faheem Lodhi

At the time of writing, Faheem Lodhi is the only person who has been convicted of a 'terrorist act' offence under the Commonwealth Criminal Code.[88] Lodhi is currently serving a 20-year sentence (with a minimum non-parole period of 15 years)[89] in New South Wales as an AA classified inmate (a classification applying to inmates who represent a special risk to national security).[90] He was originally charged in April 2004 with a variety of 'terrorist act' offences with the prosecution eventually settling on the following:

---

of support or resources would help the organisation to engage in preparing a terrorist act. Recklessness with respect to circumstances is defined in s 5.4 of the Criminal Code as:

(1) A person is reckless with respect to a circumstance if:

(a) he or she is aware of a substantial risk that the circumstance exists or will exist; and

(b) having regard to the circumstances known to him or her, it is unjustifiable to take the risk.

Alternatively, if this is characterised as part of the prohibited conduct, the default fault provision of intention might be argued to extend to whether the accused meant to provide support or resources of a kind that would help the terrorist organisation prepare for a terrorist act: see Gani and Urbas, above n 2, 43.

[86] As defined in s 100.1(2).
[87] See the hypothetical scenario referred to above in n 34.
[88] Lodhi's appeal against both his conviction and sentence was dismissed by the NSW Court of Criminal Appeal in December 2007: *Faheem Khalid Lodhi v R* [2007] NSWCCA 360 (Unreported, Spigelman CJ, Barr and Price JJ, 20 December 2007). Lodhi has filed an application for special leave to appeal to the High Court.
[89] Section 19AG of the *Crimes Act 1914* (Cth) (inserted into that Act as a result of Item 1B of Schedule 1 of the *Anti-Terrorism Act 2004* (Cth)) requires a judge sentencing for terrorism offences to set the single non-parole period at a percentage of at least three-quarters of the sentence. See the sentencing remarks of Whealy J in *R v Lodhi* (2006) 199 FLR 364, [105].
[90] See Regulation 22 of the *Crimes (Administration of Sentences) Regulation 2001* (NSW) under which AA classified inmates must 'at all times be confined in special facilities within a secure physical barrier that includes towers or electronic surveillance equipment'. Justice Whealy discusses the conditions in which Lodhi had been and was likely to be held, including (effective) 'solitary confinement', in his sentencing remarks in *R v Lodhi* (2006) 199 FLR 364, [79]-[82].

- one count of s 101.4(1) — possessing a thing (in this case a document about how to make bombs) connected with a terrorist act, knowing of such a connection;[91]
- two counts of s 101.5(1) — collecting or making documents (collecting maps of the electricity supply system and making aerial photos of Australian Defence Force establishments) connected with terrorist acts, knowing of such a connection;[92] and
- one count of s 101.6 — doing an act (seeking information about the availability of materials that could be used to make bombs) in preparation or planning a terrorist act.[93]

Lodhi was found guilty of three of the four charges (he was acquitted by the jury of the second count under s 101.5, in relation to the aerial photos) and was sentenced to 20 years' imprisonment in relation to the most serious offence (s 101.6) and ten years' imprisonment for each of the other offences, with the sentences to be served concurrently.

The prosecution of Lodhi was a lengthy and complex affair raising questions relating to a range of issues, including the form of the indictments, the constitutional validity of the *National Security Information (Criminal & Civil Proceedings) Act 2004* (Cth), the taking of evidence in Pakistan and the retrospective application of s 106.3 of the Criminal Code.[94] As a result, there were multiple rulings by both the trial judge and the NSW Court of Criminal Appeal. The discussion in the first part of this chapter has already analysed some of these judgments, most importantly the significance of the rulings of both Whealy J and the three judges of the NSW Court of Criminal Appeal in relation to the definition of 'terrorist act'. Both Courts ruled that the 'intention' requirements in the definition of terrorist act (in relation to both advancing a

---

[91] The relevant provision is: s 101.4 Possessing things connected with terrorist acts:

(1) A person commits an offence if:

(a) the person possesses a thing; and

(b) the thing is connected with preparation for, the engagement of a person in, or assistance in a terrorist act; and

(c) the person mentioned in paragraph (a) knows of the connection described in paragraph (b).

Penalty: Imprisonment for 15 years.

[92] The relevant provision is: 101.5 Collecting or making documents likely to facilitate terrorist acts

(1) A person commits an offence if:

(a) the person collects or makes a document; and

(b) the document is connected with preparation for, the engagement of a person in, or assistance in a terrorist act; and

(c) the person mentioned in paragraph (a) knows of the connection described in paragraph (b).

Penalty: Imprisonment for 15 years.

[93] See above n 63 in relation to Mallah for the full text of the offence.

[94] See the text at n 20 above in relation to this issue.

religious, political or ideological cause and coercing or intimidating a government) did not relate to the state of mind of the accused, but rather constituted circumstances attaching to the terrorist act itself. Accordingly, it was not necessary for the prosecution to show that the accused himself held such intentions.[95] Lodhi's situation was, however, a 'simple' case in this regard, as the discussion below highlights.

## 1. Facts of the Case

Lodhi worked at a firm of architects in Sydney.[96] He became involved with Willie Brigitte (a French citizen who had trained with Lashkar-e-Tayyiba[97] in Pakistan in 2001) when Brigitte came to Australia in May 2003. Lodhi claimed that he had been asked to look after Brigitte by a common acquaintance of the two men: Sajid Mir, whom Lodhi had met at a mosque in Pakistan in 2002 and 2003. The trial judge, Whealy J, found that this association was 'not an innocent one' and that the two men were meeting 'so that, in general terms, the prospect of terrorist actions in Australia could be explored'.[98] In October 2003, Brigitte was deported back to France after French authorities contacted Australian Intelligence agencies reporting that he had 'substantial links' to terrorism.[99] Shortly before Brigitte's detention and subsequent deportation, Lodhi obtained a desk map and a wall map of the Australian electricity supply system from Energy Supply giving a false name and contact details. On execution of a search warrant at the firm where Lodhi worked police found a 15-page document in Urdu in Lodhi's handwriting that was described by the prosecution as 'a terrorism manual for the manufacture of homemade poisons, explosives, detonators and incendiary devices'.[100] The document referred to a particular explosive device containing an explosive called urea nitrate. The day after Brigitte was detained, Lodhi sent a fax under the name and address of a fictitious company to a chemical firm and obtained, in response, a price list for various chemicals including urea and nitric acid (the components of urea nitrate).

## 2. Case Analysis

The trial judge's remarks, at sentencing, reveal several interesting points. First, the evidence against Lodhi demonstrated that his planning of a terrorist act was at a very early stage. As Whealy J states:

---

[95] See the text at nn 31-33 above.
[96] The facts of the case are set out in full by Whealy J in his sentencing remarks: *R v Lodhi* (2006) 199 FLR 364.
[97] Now a proscribed terrorist organisation under the Criminal Code.
[98] See the sentencing remarks of Whealy J in *R v Lodhi* (2006) 199 FLR 364, [10].
[99] Brigitte and Mir have since been convicted of terrorism related offences in France (Mir in absentia).
[100] *R v Lodhi* (2006) 199 FLR 364, [24].

> I am perfectly satisfied that the proposal had not reached the stage where the identity of a bomber, the precise area to be bombed or the manner in which the bombing would take place, had been worked out.[101]

Nevertheless, the offences with which Lodhi was charged target precisely the type of preparatory behaviour undertaken at a very early stage in the planning of a terrorist act. The fault element of knowledge[102] of a connection with a terrorist act (present in both s 101.4(1) and s 101.5(1)) does not require awareness at the time of the prohibited conduct of either a specific or a general terrorist act, nor of a specific target.[103] Second, Whealy J, emphasised that this was, in fact, what I term a 'simple' case in relation to the definition of 'terrorist act' in the sense that evidence was presented that Lodhi himself held the necessary intentions to advance a religious cause and to coerce the government. Whealy J describes the evidence going to prove such an intention as follows:

> There was also found in his possession a significant amount of material which threw considerable light on his intentions in relation to these offences. The material included a CD-Rom which was described, throughout the trial, as the 'jihadi CD'. This was a virtual library containing exhortations to violent jihad, justifications for suicide bombings (called 'martyrdom' in the text of the material), and which extolled the virtues of those who had given their lives to the murder of innocent civilians and others in the name of extremist Islam. Much of the material exhorted the reader or listener to follow, or at least support violent jihad. In addition to this CD, there were two volumes of the Lion of Allah, other material and [a] Chechnyan videocassette glorifying those who had given their lives in the fight between Chechnya and Russia.[104]

He further found that:

> all this material makes it clear that the offender is a person who has, in recent years, been essentially informed by the concept of violent jihad and the glorification of Muslim heroes who have fought and died for jihad, either in a local or broader context. The material is eloquent as to the ideas and emotions that must have been foremost in the offender's mind throughout October 2003 and later, at least until the time of his arrest.[105]

Such evidence together with evidence of Lodhi's association with Brigitte and Mir was clearly sufficient to convince the jury that Lodhi's conduct was undertaken with the intention to advance the cause of violent jihad and to coerce

---

[101] Ibid [26].
[102] Under s 5.3 of the Criminal Code a person has knowledge of a circumstance or a result if he or she is aware that it exists or will exist in the ordinary course of events.
[103] *R v Lodhi* [2006] NSWSC 584 (Unreported, Whealy J, 14 February 2006) [82]-[83].
[104] *R v Lodhi* (2006) 199 FLR 364, [18].
[105] Ibid [20].

the Australian government and/or intimidate the public.[106] If the complexity of the definition of 'terrorist act' serves as a break on convictions in relation to less blameworthy cases, as I argue, nevertheless in 'simple' cases, where evidence going to the state of mind of the accused is powerful, a jury will infer intention in relation to the 'terrorist act' definition even when the offence relates to very preparatory behaviour.

## III. Conclusion

It is indisputable that the definition of 'terrorist act' in Part 5.3 of the Criminal Code plays a crucial role in the operation of anti-terrorism offences in Australia. Indeed, this fact was the subject of specific comment in the 2006 Review of Security and Counter Terrorism Legislation:

> The Sheller Committee recognised that the definition of a 'terrorist act' is pivotal within this overall scheme. Any change to the definition will influence the scope of offences and powers afforded to the Commonwealth law enforcement and intelligence agencies.[107]

The influence of the definition on the scope of these offences has been the subject of this chapter. My central argument has been that whilst the definition of 'terrorist act' in the Criminal Code is complex, unwieldy and apparently very expansive, it may, in what I have called 'simple' cases, have the somewhat perverse effect of confining the operation of broadly-drafted offences. The definition has not yet been tested by a 'difficult' case — although the judgment in *R v Lodhi* foreshadows that it may not play the same moderating role where a very peripheral player is linked to a clear case of terrorism.

By contrast, where prosecutions do not rely on a jury working with the 'terrorist act' definition, convictions will be easier to secure. In particular, this will be the case where the charges relate to terrorist organisation offences and the organisation has already been proscribed by the Attorney-General (as opposed to being found to be a terrorist organisation in the course of a trial). Accordingly, the least defensible form of terrorist offences (status offences in relation to executively proscribed organisations) may become the primary basis for prosecutions. This would be a worrying development. Reform of the proscription process,[108] is urgently required.

Re-working of the 'terrorist act' definition is a more delicate prospect. As has been demonstrated, any change to that definition would have widespread consequences for the operation of all the offences into which it is incorporated.

---

[106] See Whealy J's further remarks in *R v Lodhi* (2006) 199 FLR 364, [33].
[107] Parliamentary Joint Committee on Intelligence and Security, above n 3, [5.11].
[108] The Sheller Committee recommends a series of reforms of the proscription process to meet the requirements of administrative law in the *Report of the Security Legislation Review Committee*, above n 3, 9ff, ch 9.

Indeed, whilst its simplification is desirable, the preservation of its tempering effects must be ensured. What is even more important, however, is that the substantive offences relating to terrorist acts, including their capacity to encompass (and disproportionately punish) marginal players and inchoate or very preparatory conduct be re-visited.

# Chapter Fourteen

# Executive Proscription of Terrorist Organisations in Australia: Exploring the Shifting Border between Crime and Politics

### Russell Hogg[*]

## Introduction

A core feature of anti-terror laws enacted throughout the world after the events of 11 September 2001 (9/11) has been the provision for executive proscription of terrorist organisations.[1] This chapter examines the Australian provisions and their use since their enactment in 2002.

It begins in Part I with a brief account of the background to the legislation. Part II examines in detail the legislative scheme governing the listing of terrorist organisations, including the concept of a 'terrorist act', the statutory criteria for listing organisations, the definition of an 'organisation', the listing procedure and the range of terrorist organisation offences. Part III focuses on the provisions in action, including the range of organisations currently listed, the reviews of listings undertaken by the Parliamentary Joint Committee on Intelligence and Security and controversies relating to the listing criteria and listing procedures. Part IV considers some of the actual and potential impacts of listing particular organisations. An important theme woven through the entire analysis is the play between two essential elements of terrorist legal discourse: the criminal and the political. Part V is devoted to an explicit consideration of this issue. I argue that in addition to endangering established legal principles, proscription laws distract from the need for political initiatives to address effectively the roots of violent political conflicts. Ironically, whilst enhancing the coercive powers of the executive they may inhibit recourse to the more flexible political and policy

---

[*] Associate Professor of Law, School of Law, University of New England, Armidale, NSW, Australia. This research was funded by the ARC Discovery Project DP0451473 'Terrorism and the Non-State Actor: the Role of Law in the Search for Security'.

[1] For a useful overview of the anti-terror laws of several countries see UK Foreign and Commonwealth Office, *Counter-Terrorism Legislation and Practice: a Survey of Selected Countries* (2005). Also see V Ramraj, M Hor and K Roach (eds), *Global Anti-Terrorism Law and Policy* (Cambridge, New York: Cambridge University Press, 2005).

instruments (diplomacy, aid, trade) needed to safeguard national security interests.

In liberal democratic societies, use of the criminal law to ban political organisations and to punish individuals for a connection with a banned organisation, thus dispensing with the need to prove any element of harmful conduct or intent, is inevitably controversial. Where the banning power is placed in the hands of the executive it is even more so. Reviewing the first major package of anti-terror legislation, which contained the proscription provisions in their initial form, the Senate Legal and Constitutional Committee of the Australian Parliament noted that executive proscription 'was clearly one of the most significant issues of concern during this inquiry and aroused the most vehement opposition'.[2]

Critics object that executive proscription threatens the rule of law, violating its core requirements like the principle of individual responsibility and eroding the role of the courts in judging criminal liability. They also point to the manner in which the law offends fundamental freedoms, such as freedoms of association and expression. Some invoke Justice Dixon's warning from the *Communist Party Case*, in which the High Court struck down the most famous attempt by an Australian government to ban a political organisation: 'History and not only ancient history, shows that in countries where democratic institutions have been unconstitutionally superseded, it has been done not seldom by those holding the executive power.'[3]

Defenders of the new laws respond that the threat we face from global terrorism driven by violent, fundamentalist Islamic ideology is unprecedented. It necessitates a response that reflects both the global character of the threat and the imperative of preventing potentially catastrophic attacks. Banning organisations is required to disrupt terrorist activities and stem actual and potential sources of terrorist support.[4]

## I. Executive Proscription: Background to the Legislation

Executive proscription powers were contained in the first major package of Australian anti-terrorism legislation passed by the Australian Parliament

---

[2] Senate Legal and Constitutional Legislation Committee, Parliament of the Commonwealth of Australia, *Consideration of Legislation Referred to the Committee: Security Legislation (Terrorism) Bill 2002 [No2]; Suppression of the Financing of Terrorism Bill 2002; Criminal Code Amendment (Suppression of Terrorist Bombings) Bill 2002; Border Security Legislation Amendment Bill 2002; Telecommunications Interception Legislation Amendment Bill 2002* (2002) [3.155].

[3] *Australian Communist Party v Commonwealth* (1951) 83 CLR 1, [178].

[4] Australian Government: Department of Foreign Affairs and Trade, *Transnational Terrorism: the Threat to Australia* (Canberra: Commonwealth of Australia). The former Commonwealth Attorney-General more recently argued that '[t]errorism is arguably the greatest threat this nation has faced in many decades, and perhaps the most insidious and complex threat we have ever faced': P Ruddock, 'A Safe and Secure Australia: An Update on Counter-Terrorism' (Speech delivered at Manly Pacific Hotel, 21 January 2006).

following 9/11.[5] In its original form, the Security Legislation Amendment (Terrorism) Bill 2002 would have empowered the Attorney-General to proscribe an organisation by declaration. It provided very broad grounds for proscription.[6]

The Bill also created broadly defined strict liability offences carrying serious penalties. It permitted no merits review of proscription decisions and no revocation mechanism was provided. The provisions attracted concerted criticism and issues of constitutionality were also raised.[7]

In its review of the Bill, the Senate Legal and Constitutional Committee expressed particular concern over the potential reach of the proscription regime:

> The Committee raised with the Department the concerns expressed by witnesses and in submissions about support by Australians for pro-independence or other similar movements in other countries, but was not persuaded by the Department's response. The Committee considers that any review of the proscription provisions must ensure that such organisations would not be caught by the provisions.[8]

The Committee recommended against enactment of the Bill and that the Attorney-General develop an alternative procedure.

In the regime that passed into law in the *Security Legislation Amendment (Terrorism) Act 2002* (Cth), the power to proscribe by declaration was replaced by a power allowing the making of a regulation specifying an organisation as a terrorist organisation. The grounds for proscription were restricted by linking them to United Nations Security Council decisions and resolutions. In 2003, each of the states passed legislation referring constitutional powers to the Commonwealth in an endeavour to guarantee the constitutionality of executive proscription.[9]

---

[5] Senate Legal and Constitutional Legislation Committee, above n 2.
[6] Under the proposed s 102.2 the Attorney-General could declare an organisation to be a terrorist organisation if satisfied on reasonable grounds that:

- the organisation, or a member of the organisation, has committed or is committing a terrorism offence, whether or not the organisation or member has been charged with, or convicted of, the offence;
- the declaration is reasonably appropriate to give effect to a decision of the UN Security Council that the organisation is an international terrorist organisation;
- or the organisation has endangered or is likely to endanger the security or integrity of the Commonwealth or another country.

[7] Reference was made to the striking down by the High Court of the Menzies government's legislation to dissolve the Australian Communist Party in the Communist Party Case: *Australian Communist Party v Commonwealth* (1951) 83 CLR 1: Senate Legal and Constitutional Legislation Committee, above n 2, [3.107]-[3.109].
[8] Senate Legal and Constitutional Legislation Committee, above n 2, [3.115].
[9] *Criminal Code Amendment (Terrorism) Act 2003* (Cth). There nevertheless remain unresolved constitutional questions that will not be further discussed here. They relate not to the subject of legislative power under which the laws were passed, as that is resolved by the state referral of power under s 51 (xxxvii) of the *Australian Constitution*, but to possible infringements of implied freedoms of political speech and association protected by the Constitution and the separation of the judicial power. For a full

In 2003, legislation was used to ban particular organisations on the basis that the required link to UN Security Council decisions and resolutions imposed undue restriction on the ability to deal with specific threats within Australia.[10] Subsequently, the requirement for a link to UN Security Council resolutions and decisions was dropped.[11] The criteria for listing an organisation were linked to the concept of a 'terrorist act' (see below), restoring the Attorney-General's broad listing power subject to the Parliament's disallowance power in relation to any listing regulation. The amendments also provided that the Parliamentary Joint Committee on the Australian Security Intelligence Organisation (ASIO), Australian Secret Intelligence Service (ASIS) and Defence Signals Directorate (DSD) (since re-named the Parliamentary Joint Committee on Intelligence and Security (PJC)) can review each regulation and report its findings and recommendations to the Parliament before the expiry of a disallowance period of 15 sitting days.[12] Decisions to list are also subject to judicial review restricted to testing the legality of the decision.

The only merits review is that which may be conducted by the PJC. In its first report the PJC stated its intention to undertake reviews of all listings both as to merits and process. It dismissed the advice of the then Attorney-General and ASIO that it restrict its role to reviewing the appropriateness of the process adopted for listing an organisation and deciding whether the Attorney-General's supporting statement provided sufficient grounds for the listing.[13] I will return to a more detailed examination of the PJC reviews later.

A regulation specifying an organisation as a terrorist organisation has effect for a period of two years.[14] In the intervening period, the regulation may be repealed or cease to have effect upon a declaration by the Attorney-General that s/he is no longer satisfied that the organisation is a terrorist organisation.[15] An organisation may be re-listed before, at or after the expiry of the two-year period.[16] There is also provision for application to the Attorney-General to de-list a listed organisation.[17] The PJC has adopted a policy of fully reviewing

---

discussion see J Tham, 'Possible Constitutional Objections to the Powers to Ban "Terrorist" Organisations' (2004) 27(2) *University of New South Wales Law Journal* 482, 509-22.

[10] *Criminal Code Amendment (Hizballah) Act 2003* (Cth); *Criminal Code Amendment (Hamas and Lashkar-e-Tayyiba) Act 2003* (Cth).

[11] *Criminal Code Amendment (Terrorist Organisations) Act 2004* (Cth).

[12] *Criminal Code Act 1995* (Cth) s 102.1A ('Criminal Code').

[13] Parliamentary Joint Committee on Intelligence and Security, Parliament of the Commonwealth of Australia, *Review of the listing of the Palestinian Islamic Jihad PIJ* (2004) [2.2]-[2.9].

[14] Criminal Code s 102.1(3).

[15] Criminal Code s 102.1(4).

[16] Criminal Code s 102.1(5).

[17] Criminal Code s 102.1(17).

the re-listing of organisations, reflecting its view that the two-year sunset clause should be taken seriously.[18]

## II. Listing Terrorist Organisations

### A. Concept of a 'Terrorist Act'

The criteria for listing a terrorist organisation revolve around the concept of a 'terrorist act'. 'Terrorist act' is defined as an action *or threat* of action where the action:

- causes serious harm that is physical harm to a person;
- causes serious damage to property;
- causes a person's death;
- endangers a person's life, other than the life of the person taking the action;
- creates a serious risk to the health or safety of the public or a section of the public; or
- seriously interferes with, seriously disrupts, or destroys, an electronic system.[19]

Such conduct is already covered by the general criminal law. What gives this conduct its terrorist character is the additional requirement that the action is taken or threat is made with the dual intent of advancing a political, religious or ideological cause *and* coercing or intimidating a government or intimidating the public or a section of the public.[20]

Action that is advocacy, protest, dissent or industrial action is exempted from the definition of 'terrorist act' if it is not intended to cause serious physical harm to a person, cause a person's death, endanger the life of a person (other than the person taking the action), or create a serious risk to the health or safety of the public or a section of the public.[21] The onus of proof is on an accused to bring him or her self within the exemption.

The definition of 'terrorist act' is broad, complex and uncertain. In *R v Lodhi* Justice Whealy observed that the provision 'postulates an action or threat of action of the widest possible kind' as long as it is accompanied by the double intent of advancing a political, religious or ideological cause and coercing or intimidating a government or the public or a section of the public.[22] It includes

---

[18] Parliamentary Joint Committee on Intelligence and Security, Parliament of the Commonwealth of Australia, *Review of the relisting of Al Qa'ida and Jemaah Islamiyah as Terrorist Organisations under the Criminal Code Act 1995* (2006) [1.15]-[1.17]; Parliamentary Joint Committee on Intelligence and Security, Parliament of the Commonwealth of Australia, *Review of the Listing of Four Terrorist Organisations* (2005) [2.8].
[19] Criminal Code s 100.1(2).
[20] Criminal Code s 100.1(1).
[21] Criminal Code s 100.1(3).
[22] *R v Lodhi* [2005] NSWSC 1377 (Unreported, Whealy J, 23 December 2005) [52].

a wide range of actions beyond those conforming to the image of terrorism as involving acts that cause or threaten death or serious injury to persons. Threats of these other types of action are also included.

The commission of a terrorist act (which includes making threats to engage in one of the relevant types of action) is a crime punishable by life imprisonment.[23] Ancillary offences criminalise an ill-defined range of additional behaviour antecedent to the commission of a terrorist act. These include: providing or receiving training connected with a terrorist act,[24] possessing things connected with a terrorist act,[25] collecting or making documents likely to facilitate the commission of a terrorist act,[26] other acts done in preparation for, or planning, a terrorist act.[27] In each case there is no requirement to prove that a terrorist act occurred or the connection with a specific intended terrorist act. The offences carry penalties ranging from ten years to life imprisonment.

Terrorist activity attracts particular condemnation because it targets civilians. This definition is not so confined, but extends to conduct aimed directly at coercing or intimidating governments as well. The equation of government and citizenry for this purpose might not generate great concern in contemporary Australia, but the definition is not restricted to Australia or to governments in Australia. The provisions also have extended geographical jurisdiction.[28] In the words of Justice Bell in *R v Ul-Haque*, they create offences 'that may be committed by a foreigner against a foreigner in a foreign country remote geographically from, and of no particular interest to, Australia'.[29] Broadly defined actions of the relevant kind are included in the definition of terrorism regardless of the character of the government or political regime against which they are directed. All forms of national independence struggle, from the American and French revolutions to the anti-colonial struggles of the recent past, would constitute terrorism, as would many lesser forms of political and industrial activism.

## B. Criteria for Listing a Terrorist Organisation

Based on this broad concept of a 'terrorist act', the executive proscription regime extends the scope of criminal liability even further by creating a range of terrorist organisation offences. Before considering these (in section E below) it is necessary to outline the statutory criteria for listing terrorist organisations. The Attorney-General may make a regulation specifying that an organisation is a

---

[23] Criminal Code s 101.1.
[24] Criminal Code s 101.2.
[25] Criminal Code s 101.4.
[26] Criminal Code s 101.5.
[27] Criminal Code s 101.6.
[28] Criminal Code s 100.1(4).
[29] *R v Ul-Haque* (Unreported, NSW Supreme Court, Bell J, 8 February 2006) [32].

terrorist organisation if satisfied on reasonable grounds that the organisation is directly or indirectly engaged in, preparing, planning, assisting in or fostering the doing of a terrorist act or advocates the doing of a terrorist act, whether or not in each case a terrorist act has occurred or will occur.[30]

The advocacy provision is a recent addition to the *Criminal Code Act 1995* (Cth) ('Criminal Code'). It is defined in broad terms. An organisation advocates the doing of a terrorist act if it directly or indirectly counsels or urges the doing of a terrorist act, directly or indirectly provides instruction on the doing of a terrorist act, or directly praises the doing of a terrorist act in circumstances where there is a risk that such praise might have the effect of leading a person to engage in a terrorist act.[31]

The advocacy provision, in particular, is of uncertain scope[32] although it clearly takes in organisations far removed from participation in violent activity, especially via its third limb concerning 'praise' for terrorist acts. Statements by an organisation in Australia that condemned Israel's invasion of Lebanon in 2006 and expressed support for the resistance led by Hizballah could well be defined as advocacy justifying proscription of the organisation as a terrorist organisation. The definition invades what many would conceive as the realm of open, pluralistic, democratic discourse concerning events of international significance.

It is important to note that in addition to proscription by the executive an organisation may be determined to be a terrorist organisation by a court.[33] If an individual is charged with an offence relating to an alleged terrorist organisation, being an unlisted organisation, proof of the offence requires proof that the organisation in question is in fact a terrorist organisation. That would in turn require proof of the necessary connection to a 'terrorist act' (see Gani Chapter 13 this volume).

## C. What is an 'Organisation'?

The concept of terrorism has received a great deal of attention but it is salient to ask also what constitutes an 'organisation' under the legislation. In its submissions in *R v Ul-Haque* the Crown stressed the breadth of the definition of 'organisation' under s 100.1(1) of the Criminal Code, which defined 'organisation' to mean 'a body corporate or an unincorporated association':

> In considering the meaning of 'terrorist organisation', it is first to be noted that the legislation is referring to an organisation, that is, a standing body of people

---

[30] Criminal Code s 102.1.
[31] Criminal Code s 102.1(1A).
[32] Eg, it is not clear what links are required between an organisation and statements amounting to advocacy to justify proscription of the organisation. Do the statements have to be endorsed as the policy of the organisation? Will it be enough that they are statements by a leader of the organisation? Would statements by any member on behalf of the organisation suffice?
[33] Under para (a) of the definition of 'terrorist organisation' in Criminal Code s 102.1(1).

with a particular purpose; not a transient group of conspirators who may come together for a single discrete criminal purpose. The requirement for an 'organisation' is consistent with the provision for an entity with an ongoing purpose of committing a number of terrorist acts with the intention of advancing the same political, religious or ideological purpose.[34]

It is widely agreed that the principal threat and target of laws passed after 9/11 is the organisation held responsible for that atrocity, Al Qa'ida, and those it inspires. However, it is the ideological influence of Al Qa'ida rather than its organisational form or power that is central in this assessment.[35] Many expert commentators argue that Al Qa'ida can be more accurately conceived as an idea rather than an organisation.[36] This tends to be confirmed by events like the Madrid and London bombings, which suggest that the major threat stems from local, self-starter individuals and groupings who are inspired by a combination of extremist Islamic ideology and outrage at what they perceive to be the injustices inflicted on the Arab and Muslim world by the West. Such attacks require little by way of structured organisation or finance.[37] What is needed in the way of motivation, training, technical knowledge and support is available in the constant, global flow of information delivered by new communications media: the internet, satellite television and so on. Thus even the broad definition of 'organisation' offered in *R v Ul-Haque* may fail to capture the extremely fluid and elusive forms of organisational activity involved in contemporary global terrorism. The effect of invoking the word 'organisation' may therefore be mostly symbolic, to provide illusory comfort by imposing a familiar shape on a formless threat.

## D. Listing Procedure

Listing an organisation involves a number of steps. An unclassified statement of reasons is prepared by ASIO that details the case for the listing. This is submitted to the Attorney-General who signs the statement confirming that the criteria for listing the organisation are satisfied, signs a regulation with respect to the organisation and sets in train the other formalities required to make the regulation. Prior to making a regulation the Attorney-General is required by

---

[34] *R v Ul-Haque* (Unreported, NSW Supreme Court, Bell J, 8 February, 2006) [51].

[35] P Varghese (Director-General of the Office of National Assessments), 'Islamist Terrorism: The International Context' (Speech delivered at the Security in Government Conference, Canberra, 11 May 2006); Dame E Manningham-Buller (Director General of the UK Security Service), 'The International Terrorist Threat to the UK' (Speech delivered at Queen Mary's College, London, 9 November, 2006).

[36] J Burke, *Al-Qaeda — the True Story of Radical Islam* (London: Penguin, 2004) 1-21; K Greenberg (ed), *Al Qaeda Now — Understanding Today's Terrorists* (Cambridge: Cambridge University Press, 2005) 9-12.

[37] United Kingdom, Report of the Official Account of the Bombings in London on 7$^{th}$ July 2005 (2006); D Benjamin and S Simon, *The Next Attack — the Globalization of Jihad* (UK: Hodder and Stoughton, 2005) 5-16.

law to brief the Leader of the Opposition.[38] The Commonwealth also agreed under the Inter-Governmental Agreement on Counter-Terrorism to consult the State and Territory leaders prior to each listing and not to proceed with any listing if objected to by a majority. Having fulfilled these requirements the Attorney-General notifies the chair of the PJC of the decision to list an organisation and provides the statement of reasons. A press release is issued announcing the listing and providing the reasons. A regulation takes effect immediately it is made, but is subject to disallowance by the Parliament.

## E. Terrorist Organisation Offences

Listing an organisation as a terrorist organisation is a momentous decision for a number of reasons. Its immediate legal effect is to bring into play a range of serious criminal offences relating to those with a connection to the listed organisation (see Gani Chapter 13 this volume). Strictly speaking the listing does not directly ban or dissolve the organisation. Proscription is achieved by the effect of these offences. The offences are:

- directing the activities of a terrorist organisation;[39]
- membership of a terrorist organisation;[40]
- recruiting for a terrorist organisation;[41]
- training a terrorist organisation or receiving training from a terrorist organisation;[42]
- getting funds to, from or for, a terrorist organisation;[43]
- providing support to a terrorist organisation;[44] and
- associating with a terrorist organisation.[45]

Aside from the association offence (punishable by three years imprisonment) the other offences carry penalties of between ten and 25 years imprisonment. These are serious crimes, therefore, although they require proof of no element of violent conduct or intent on the part of the individual, only the specified connection with the listed organisation. We have seen that the concept of a 'terrorist act' is very broadly defined and encompasses virtually any form of politically motivated violence. Political entities of all kinds (including states, armies, police forces as well as national liberation movements) use violence for political ends. In most cases the violence is a means to an end, not an end in itself. It is the objective that commands popular allegiance and support (the

---

[38] Criminal Code s 102.1(2A).
[39] Criminal Code s 102.2.
[40] Criminal Code s 102.3.
[41] Criminal Code s 102.4.
[42] Criminal Code s 102.5.
[43] Criminal Code s 102.6.
[44] Criminal Code s 102.7.
[45] Criminal Code s 102.8.

maintenance of the peace by a legitimate government, the achievement of a national homeland, the overthrow of a despotic regime). Thus individuals join, support, fund and participate in political organisations for reasons entirely unrelated to the violent means that those organisations may adopt on occasions.

If the qualifying adjective 'terrorist' is momentarily bracketed out it will be seen therefore that these offences criminalise a broad range of conventional activities constitutive of any political movement or organisation. If then we recall the breadth of the definition of terrorist organisation, a definition that does not differentiate according to the contexts and causes of political conflict, the potential reach of the proscription regime will be seen to be both very extensive and uncertain. The uncertainty offends a basic principle of the rule of law: that the law should afford a guide to conduct. Citizens should be able to ascertain with some certainty the boundary demarcating acceptable and unacceptable conduct. When the conduct in question is political in character, uncertainty may also have a chilling impact on democratic institutions and discourse.

It has also been regarded as fundamental to the concept of the rule of law that punitive consequences should attach to conduct, not to the status or social type of the offender.[46] In reality, status offences have been far from uncommon in the criminal laws of liberal states. Laws relating to vagrancy, 'common prostitutes' and consorting afford examples. But such offences have overwhelmingly fallen at the less serious end of the spectrum of crimes.

The terrorist organisation offences are a fundamental departure insofar as they attach severe penalties to proof of the relevant status. Key terms, like 'member' and 'support', are not defined and none of the offences require proof of a link between the prohibited status or activity and the commission or intention to commit a terrorist act. Thus, a person who is a member (including an 'informal member') of an organisation designated as terrorist by a regulation made by the Attorney-General may be sentenced to ten years imprisonment for what others in the organisation have done or are preparing, planning, assisting, fostering or advocating regardless of the person's knowledge, intent or attitude with respect to these activities.

The terrorist organisation offences have an extended geographical jurisdiction.[47] Organisations may be proscribed that are involved in violent political conflicts far removed from Australian territory or interests and without reference to the conditions (of state autocracy, repression, discrimination and so on) that may be driving such conflicts. Members and supporters of these organisations are

---

[46] For a classic normative liberal account of the conduct requirement in criminal law see H Packer, *The Limits of the Criminal Sanction* (Stanford, Cal: Stanford University Press, 1968) ch 5.

[47] Criminal Code s 102.9 provides that extended geographical jurisdiction category D applies to these offences. Under s 15.4, jurisdiction applies whether or not the conduct constituting the offence occurred in Australia and whether or not a result of that conduct occurred in Australia.

liable to punishment under Australian law. The laws are practically unenforceable against most of the people involved with such organisations because they are not resident in Australia and major issues of national sovereignty and the comity of nations would be raised by any attempt at apprehension or extradition.[48] However, the laws directly affect those persons with an organisational connection who are resident in Australia. They are liable to prosecution under the proscription regime although they may be law-abiding Australian citizens or residents with no grievance against Australia, its government or people.

## III. The Listing Provisions in Action

### A. Listed Organisations

Nineteen organisations have been and remain listed under the proscription provisions.[49] Many of these organisations have been re-listed on one or more occasions. No organisation has been de-listed and no organisation has had its status as a terrorist organisation lapse after the two-year sunset period. All the organisations are self-declared Islamic organisations with one exception, the Kurdistan Workers Party (PKK). The PKK is the most recent organisation to be listed for the first time.[50]

Of the 18 other organisations most are acknowledged by the Government to have no links to organisations or activities in Australia. A few have notoriety in Australia and globally, like Al Qa'ida and Jemaah Islamiyah. Most operate within the confines of specific geo-political conflicts, their Islamic ideology being merged in struggles over territory, political power and national rights. The most prominent of these are the Palestinian organisations, the military wing of Hamas (known as Izz al-Din al-Qassam Brigades) and Palestinian Islamic Jihad (PIJ)), and the alleged external wing of the Lebanese organisation, Hizballah (known as Hizballah External Security Organisation).[51] Other groups variously operate in Algeria, Iraq, the Philippines and Kashmir.

Aside from their recourse to politically inspired violence, a trait shared with many organisations and governments around the world, it is not clear why these organisations have been singled out for proscription, other than that (with the exception of the PKK) they are all Islamic revivalist (or fundamentalist) organisations. Quite apart from differences in geo-political focus, some are Sunni

---

[48] See the discussion in Parliamentary Joint Committee on ASIO, ASIS and DSD, Parliament of the Commonwealth of Australia, *Review of the Listing of Six Terrorist Organisations* (2005) [2.28].
[49] A complete list of proscribed organisations is provided on the National Security website of the Attorney-General's Department: <http://www.nationalsecurity.gov.au/agd/www/nationalsecurity.nsf/AllDocs/95FB057CA3DECF30CA256FAB001F7FBD?OpenDocument>.
[50] Listed on 17 December, 2005: <http://www.nationalsecurity.gov.au/agd/www/nationalsecurity.nsf/AllDocs/28B052FC3CCE4009CA2570DF000FB458?OpenDocument>.
[51] Hamas and Hizballah were originally proscribed by legislation at a time when the statutory listing criteria were linked to UN Security Council decisions: see above n 10.

and others Shia. It is acknowledged in many instances that they have no direct links with each other or with Al Qa'ida. In fact, the predominant focus of organisations like Hamas and Hizballah on national rights and their participation in local and national elections are anathema to Al Qa'ida.[52]

Hamas and Hizballah are mass political organisations. Hizballah represents the largest (and poorest) ethno-religious group in Lebanon (the Shi'ites) and constitutes a significant bloc in the Lebanese Parliament. Its popular standing within Lebanon (outside as well as within the Shi'ite community) derives from its role in resisting the Israeli occupation of southern Lebanon between 1982 and 2000, a conflict that was renewed in the second half of 2006.[53] It has supporters within the Lebanese community in Australia as evidenced by calls from respected community leaders during the 2006 Israel/Lebanon war for the organisation to be de-listed.[54] Hamas (a Sunni organisation) won a landslide victory in the January 2006 Palestinian Authority elections, eclipsing the older secular Fatah organisation.

Both organisations have been engaged in long-term territorial and political conflicts with the state of Israel. Both have engaged in suicide bombings within their immediate region. They have also observed ceasefires at different times. It is not their recourse to violence that explains their popular following but, amongst other things, their reputation for honesty and the effective delivery of a range of social, educational and health services to beleaguered local populations in Lebanon and the Palestinian Occupied Territories.[55]

Acts of violence against civilians on both sides of these conflicts deserve condemnation. To define the violence of one side only as 'terrorist', however, serves tacitly to justify the violence of the other. It also obscures the causes of violent conflict and hinders the search for effective political responses to it.

The proscription of Hamas and Hizballah suggests a tendency to assimilate many different forms of political Islam to Al Qa'ida and see it as part of a monolithic

---

[52] K Hroub, *Hamas — A Beginner's Guide* (London: Pluto Press, 2006) 99-103; A Crooke, 'The Rise of Hamas', *Prospect* (UK), February 2006; L Deeb, 'Hizballah: A Primer', *Middle East Report Online*, 31 July 2006.
[53] Deeb, ibid.
[54] R Kerbaj, 'PM Can't Be Swayed on Hezbollah', *The Australian* (Sydney), 4 August 2006, 8.
[55] Hroub, above n 52; P McGeough, 'Between Hezbollah and Hell', *Sydney Morning Herald* (Sydney), 29-30 July 2006, 29.

global conspiracy against Western values and interests.[56] This is simplistic.[57] It is also dangerous. It contributes to the perception that anti-terror laws are a proxy for official anti-Islamism without regard for the particularities of any conflict involving Islamic groups and the justice or otherwise of their cause.

Whilst not recommending disallowance of any listing, the PJC has expressed scepticism regarding several of the listings.

## B. Reviews of the Parliamentary Joint Committee on Intelligence and Security

The PJC reviews all decisions to list and re-list terrorist organisations and reports to Parliament with comments and recommendations with respect to each, including a recommendation as to whether the regulation should be disallowed. Its reviews are concerned with the merits of each listing and the adequacy of the process adopted by the executive in each case. The reviews are the major source of information concerning the administration of the executive proscription regime. They are relevant to an empirical assessment of the merits of each listing, the integrity, quality and fairness of the procedures adopted to list organisations and the attitude of the executive to the exercise of the listing powers.

The PJC is a distinctive parliamentary committee. Because it is concerned with national security it adopts a self-consciously conservative and executive-oriented approach to its responsibilities.[58] Independents and minor parties have not been represented. During the Howard government, members of the Opposition were, if possible, selected from former ministers. It seeks to avoid dividing on party lines.[59] Unsurprisingly, the PJC has on no occasion recommended disallowance

---

[56] This is the way the problem of terrorism is constructed in the government's 2004 White Paper: Australian Government, above n 4, 2. The analysis in the White Paper concentrates on Islamic extremist groups and sees the source of the threat in what it depicts as their underlying religious ideology and goals: 'an ideology that is inaccessible to reason … with objectives that cannot be negotiated'. The then Australian Foreign Minister described it in his press club launch of the White Paper as 'a terrorist project of limitless ambition, merciless methods and reckless zealotry which is almost incomprehensible to the modern mind': A Downer, 'Transnational Terrorism: the Threat to Australia' (Speech delivered to the National Press Club, Canberra, 15 July 2004). The 'main reason' Australia is a target, we are told in an information sheet produced by DFAT is 'the terrorists feel threatened by us and by our example as a conspicuously successful modern society'. They simply hate our freedoms and want 'to destroy our way of life and, where possible, to destroy us': Department of Foreign Affairs and Trade, *Transnational Terrorism: Why Australia is a Terrorist Target* (2004) <http://.dfat.gov.au/publications/terrorism/is2.html>.

[57] See, eg, the special report, 'Forty Shades of Green', *The Economist* (London), 4 February 2006, 22-4. It describes the very different ideologies, goals and methods of Islamic political organisations with their roots in the tradition of the Muslim Brotherhood (eg, Hamas) compared with those of Al Qa'ida. In particular there is a fundamental divergence of view on the use of violence, the former seeing it as justified only in exceptional circumstances like self defence or foreign occupation.

[58] It has declared its 'cautious approach' on several occasions. See Parliament of the Commonwealth of Australia, *Review of the Listing of Six Terrorist Organisations* (2005) [3.47]; Parliament of the Commonwealth of Australia, *Review of the Re-Listing of ASG, JuA, GIA and GSPC* (2007) [2.49].

[59] Parliament of the Commonwealth of Australia, *Review of the listing of the Kurdistan Workers' Party (PKK)* (2006) Minority Report [1.1].

of a listing regulation. It has, however, expressed misgivings about some of the listings[60] and been relentlessly critical of the approach and procedures adopted by the Howard government in the listing process. This may seem to expose the limitations, and perhaps inadequacy, of parliamentary review as a mechanism of accountability in relation to proscription. To be fair to the PJC the 'war on terror' creates a difficult political climate for parliamentary scrutiny of executive action and its effectiveness should not be judged by immediate impact. One of the most striking impressions left by the reports of the PJC is of a major tension between the Parliament and the executive on the issue of the proscription regime. This is reflected more concretely in some of the recurrent themes, criticisms and recommendations in the reports of the PJC.

## 1. The Question of Listing Criteria

Two themes related to the criteria for listing organisations recur in the PJC reports. First, the PJC has frequently observed that the definition of a terrorist organisation in the Criminal Code is so broad as to permit a countless number of organisations throughout the world to be proscribed.[61] It has repeatedly requested that the Attorney-General articulate, and apply, a clear and meaningful set of criteria for listing an organisation.[62] As it was baldly put in one report: 'The question remains: how and why are some organisations selected for proscription by Australia?'.[63]

In several reports, the PJC observed that the listed organisation had no known links to Australia, nor presented an apparent threat to Australian interests. It expressed concern that the Attorney-General did not regard these as critical considerations in the decision to list. The Attorney-General's Department responded by pointing to the breadth of the statutory criteria, reminding the PJC that 'the Criminal Code does not require that an organisation have a link to Australia before it can be listed' and stressing that the rationale of the legislation was 'proactive' and preventative.[64] The PJC countered that this was only 'superficially logical', 'vague' and afforded no explanation of how proscription in Australia of an organisation with no connections to Australia contributed to

---

[60] Above n 58, *Review of the Listing of Six Terrorist Organisations* (2005) [3.48]-[3.49]. The recommendations of the majority on the listing of the PKK were also qualified: above n 59.
[61] See, eg, Parliament of the Commonwealth of Australia, *Review of the Listing of Six Terrorist Organisations* (2005) [2.14].
[62] The issue has been raised, and the request has been made formally or informally, in all or most of the PJC reports. See, eg, Parliament of the Commonwealth of Australia, *Review of the listing of the Palestinian Islamic Jihad (PIJ)* (2004) [3.5] and the comments and formal recommendation in a recent report noting that there has been no response to previous requests, and renewing them: Parliament of the Commonwealth of Australia, *Review of the Re-Listing of Al Qa'ida and Jemaah Islamiyah as Terrorist Organisations* (2006) [1.20] and Recommendation 1.
[63] Parliament of the Commonwealth of Australia, *Review of the Listing of Six Terrorist Organisations* (2005) [2.22].
[64] Ibid [2.18].

the prevention of terrorist violence.[65] The PJC argued that the listing of organisations that have no Australian links is mere 'symbolism', 'with little practical effect' and is 'costly in time and effort and possibly distracting for Australia's anti-terrorism efforts'.[66]

ASIO provided a list of criteria used by it to assess organisations, which included links with Australia,[67] although the manner in which these criteria are applied has not been clarified.[68] However, it frequently acknowledged that no link existed or claimed a vague or indirect link. In one instance the only link consisted of the claim that some individuals in Australia shared the 'ideology' of the listed organisation.[69] Sometimes Australian interests were subsumed within an amorphous conception of 'Western interests'. The PJC described ASIO's view as being that 'Australian interests should be considered at threat if they are part of a generalised threat from any organisation which clearly targets Western or foreign interests in a given country or region'.[70] Elsewhere ASIO claimed that proscription was justified because Australians travelling overseas may fall victim to an indiscriminate attack perpetrated by the organisation, the example given being that 'there is always the possibility that an Australian or Australians visiting Israel will be involved in an attack'.[71] This invites the riposte that if the same Australians travelled to the Palestinian territories they may be at equal risk of being unlawfully killed by Israeli armed forces, as British citizens have been recently.[72]

A second theme running through the PJC reports repeats the concerns expressed by the Senate Legal and Constitutional Committee in its report on the original Bill: that there was a need to distinguish terrorism from violence associated with national independence struggles, civil conflicts and similar movements where peace processes should be pursued:

---

[65] Ibid [2.19]-[2.20].
[66] Parliament of the Commonwealth of Australia, *Review of the Listing of Six Terrorist Organisations* (2005) [3.50]; *Review of the Re-Listing of ASG, JuA, GIA and GSPC* (2007) [2.48].
[67] Parliament of the Commonwealth of Australia, *Review of the Listing of Six Terrorist Organisations* (2005) [2.24].
[68] Parliament of the Commonwealth of Australia, *Review of the Re-Listing of ASG, JuA, GIA and GSPC* (2007) [1.26].
[69] Parliament of the Commonwealth of Australia, *Review of the listing of the Palestinian Islamic Jihad (PIJ)* (2004) [3.15].
[70] Parliament of the Commonwealth of Australia, *Review of the Listing of Four Terrorist Organisations* (2005) [3.82].
[71] Ibid [3.34].
[72] 'Jury Rules Israeli Soldier Murdered British Journalist', *Sydney Morning Herald* (Sydney), 8-9 April 2006, 19; T Judd, 'Activist was Unlawfully Killed in Israel, Says Inquest Jury', *The Independent* (London), 11 April 2006. The story refers to the intentional shooting by an Israeli soldier of 22-year-old British peace activist Tom Hurndell whilst he was sheltering Palestinian children from Israeli military fire in Gaza in April 2003. Hurndell was one of three British civilians killed in a seven-month period by Israeli soldiers. British inquests have found in each case that the shooting was intentional.

> [T]he Committee would also note there are circumstances where groups are involved in armed conflict and where their activities are confined to that armed conflict, when designations of terrorism might not be the most applicable or useful way of approaching the problem. Under these circumstances — within an armed conflict — the targeting of civilians should be condemned, and strongly condemned, as violations of the Law of Armed Conflict and the Geneva Conventions. The distinction is important. All parties to an armed conflict are subject to this stricture. Moreover, these circumstances usually denote the breakdown of democratic processes and, with that, the impossibility of settling grievances by democratic means. Armed conflicts must be settled by peace processes. To this end, the banning of organisations by and in third countries may not be useful, unless financial and/or personnel support, which will prolong the conflict, is being provided from the third country. ASIO acknowledged this point to the Committee: "[When] there is a peace process ... you can unintentionally make things worse if you do not think through the implications of the listing."[73]

It is significant that ASIO has acknowledged that proscription may on occasions not only be ineffective but actually 'make things worse'. It can undermine peace efforts, exacerbate violence and further entrench and broaden conflict. This is a salutary reminder that the listing provisions carry risks to security, and not only to legal and political freedoms. The statutory criteria do not protect against such risks. As ASIO acknowledged it is necessary to 'think through the implications of the listing'.

## 2. The Executive and the Listing Process

It was maintained by the Howard government that this responsibility is most effectively undertaken by the executive in conjunction with the Parliament. The Howard government rejected arguments that favour replacing executive proscription with a judicial or quasi-judicial procedure.[74]

> [T]he listing of organisations is a process that does not just involve the executive: it also involves the Parliament, as it is Parliament that has the power to disallow a regulation that prescribes an organisation as a terrorist organisation. It is appropriate that the executive and the Parliament play a role in determining the nature of the organisation taking into account the expert advice of those with an extensive knowledge of the security environment. The expertise of

---

[73] Parliament of the Commonwealth of Australia, *Review of the Listing of the Palestinian Islamic Jihad (PIJ)* (2004) [3.21], also quoted by the Committee in its conclusion to its review of the listing of four organisations, including Hamas and Hizballah, Parliament of the Commonwealth of Australia, *Review of the Listing of Four Terrorist Organisations* (2005) [3.87].
[74] A recommendation made by some members of the Security Legislation Review Committee, *Report of the Security Legislation Review Committee* (2006) [9.8]-[9.19].

members of the executive, who have contact with senior members of the Governments and agencies of other countries, cannot be understated.[75]

The argument that the executive is better placed than a court to consult widely, to draw on relevant expertise and to do so in a timely fashion is persuasive, but whether or not it does so is an empirical question. Far from providing empirical confirmation of the then government's claims, the PJC reviews have been consistently critical of the performance of the executive in relation to the listing process.

Notwithstanding rhetorical affirmations of the important role of the Parliament, the former government on occasions failed to even provide appropriate warning of impending listings to the PJC so that it could effectively meet its responsibilities.[76] The PJC has repeatedly complained of a failure to provide comprehensive, accurate and balanced information to support listings and validate the process. Information supplied to the Committee and/or published by the then Attorney-General in a press release to support a listing proved on at least two occasions to be inaccurate and was subsequently corrected in private hearings with the Committee.[77] Some listings have been supported by ASIO assessments that are contradicted by other authoritative sources.[78] Generally the impression is of a highly formulaic approach to the statement of reasons supporting listings. The re-listing of organisations, in particular, is treated as a mechanical process, with little if any effort to provide updated information.[79]

Within the executive decision-making framework favoured by the former government it would be expected that the broader political implications and foreign policy context of particular listings would be treated as of central importance. Yet the PJC has commented adversely on the frequent abdication of any meaningful role in the process by the Department of Foreign Affairs and

---

[75] Joint Submission of the Attorney-General's Department, Commonwealth Director of Public Prosecutions and ASIO to the Parliamentary Joint Committee on Intelligence and Security, Parliament of the Commonwealth of Australia, *Review of the Listing Provisions of the Criminal Code Act 1995* (2007) [9.5].
[76] Parliament of the Commonwealth of Australia, *Review of the Listing of Six Terrorist Organisations* (2005) [2.2]-[2.3].
[77] Parliament of the Commonwealth of Australia, *Review of the Listing of Four Terrorist Organisations* (2005) [3.13], [3.39]-[3.40].
[78] Parliament of the Commonwealth of Australia, *Review of the Listing of Six Terrorist Organisations* (2005) [3.32].
[79] In its reports on re-listing the PJC has repeatedly called for up-to-date information rather than a mere rehearsal of the original statement of reasons for listing the organisation: Parliament of the Commonwealth of Australia *Review of the Listing of Four Terrorist Organisations* (2005) [2.7]-[2.8]; Parliament of the Commonwealth of Australia, *Review of the Re-Listing of Al Qa'ida and Jemaah Islamiyah as Terrorist Organisations* (2006) [1.16]-[1.17]; Parliament of the Commonwealth of Australia, *Review of the Re-Listing of ASG, JuA, GIA and GSPC* (2007) [1.17]-[1.18]. In the last of these reports the PJC requested as one of its formal recommendations that the Attorney-General and ASIO provide the PJC with a set of criteria indicating the circumstances in which an organisation will *not* be re-listed: [1.28] and Recommendation 1.

Trade (DFAT). The sum total of its contribution in some cases was a one line email endorsement of the decision to list,[80] a decision apparently already taken by the then Attorney-General without consultation.[81]

A further recurrent theme is the failure of the Howard government to undertake a community consultation and information program notifying the public of impending listings and according a right to be heard to interested parties.[82] To publicise a listing the Attorney-General's Department has done no more than issue a press release and post information on the National Security website. This is a grave departure from the principles of administrative law, especially given the serious consequences of listing an organisation.[83] No effort is made to ensure affected persons know of their vulnerability to serious criminal charges.

The government at the time responded to some of the criticisms and recommendations relating to the listing process, but it steadfastly ignored the most important of them, those relating to the quality of the information provided in support of listings and community consultation and notification. In sum, the PJC reports point to an abysmal record on the part of the then government so far as its cooperation with and responsiveness to parliamentary processes was concerned. This was in keeping with its dismissive attitude towards all criticism of its anti-terror laws.

The former government also summarily dismissed the major recommendations of the independent external committee appointed by it to review the legislation. The Security Legislation Review Committee (the Sheller Committee) made recommendations for greater accountability and transparency in the listing process, including: provision for notification of affected parties and an opportunity to be heard prior to listing; consideration of a judicial mechanism for proscription in place of executive proscription; amendment of the legal criteria for listing to restrict the meaning of advocacy in the definition of a 'terrorist organisation'; repeal of the offence of associating with a terrorist organisation; and a narrowing of the definition of some of the other terrorist organisation offences to ensure the need to prove a link to an actual or planned

---

[80] Parliament of the Commonwealth of Australia, *Review of the Listing of Six Terrorist Organisations* (2005) [2.5]-[2.7]; Parliament of the Commonwealth of Australia, *Review of the Listing of Four Terrorist Organisations* (2005) [2.9]-[2.16].

[81] The PJC has listed the factors that should be covered by DFAT advice on proposed listings: Parliament of the Commonwealth of Australia, *Review of the Listing of the Kurdistan Workers' Party (PKK)* (2006) [1.18].

[82] Parliament of the Commonwealth of Australia, *Review of the Listing of Six Terrorist Organisations* (2005) [2.38]-[2.40]; Parliament of the Commonwealth of Australia, *Review of the Listing of Seven Terrorist Organisations* (2005) [2.15]-[2.17]; Parliament of the Commonwealth of Australia, *Review of the Listing of Four Terrorist Organisations* (2005) [2.17]-[2.21]; Parliament of the Commonwealth of Australia, *Review of the Listing of the Kurdistan Workers' Party (PKK)* (2006) [1.20]-[1.23].

[83] *Kioa v West* (1985) 159 CLR 550.

terrorist act.[84] Tabling the report in Parliament the then Attorney-General simultaneously issued a press release in which he stated:

> The Government believes the current listing process contains sufficient safeguards, including judicial review and parliamentary oversight, and that it is more appropriate for the proscription power to be vested with the executive.[85]

Following the Security Legislation Review Committee the PJC conducted its own general review of the anti-terror legislation and made similar recommendations to restrict the scope of the terrorist organisation offences.[86] These recommendations appear destined to gather dust along with the others, a worrying sign of executive intransigence in the face of all criticism no matter the source or weight.

## IV. The Impact of the Listing Provisions

## A. Enforcement

Given the breadth of the proscription regime, comfort could be taken from the fact there have been no prosecutions relating to listed organisations. In one sense this is not surprising given most of the listed organisations are not active in Australia. However, given the global movement patterns that characterise the contemporary world, and settler societies like Australia in particular, significant numbers of immigrants and refugees from many regions of conflict have settled in communities in Australia. As noted earlier, the reach of the terrorist organisation offences are such that members of these communities are at risk of prosecution for connections with listed organisations, although they may be law-abiding citizens or residents of Australia who have no political grievance with the Australian government or people. The listing of organisations may even create a dragnet effect in relation to some ethno-religious communities in Australia (eg, Kurds, Lebanese Shia), with the threat of prosecution hanging over many of their members.

That there have been no prosecutions also does not mean that there has been no relevant enforcement of the laws. A stated rationale of new counter-terrorist measures is to gather intelligence and disrupt terrorist activity. The former Director-General of ASIO described the approach as follows:

> it is essential there be a seamlessness in our intelligence and law enforcement counter-terrorism efforts ... When those known to be involved in terrorism are

---

[84] *Report of the Security Legislation Review Committee* (2006) [8.10], [9.1], [10.41], [10.42], [10.54], [10.56]-[10.78].
[85] Attorney-General Media Release 111/2006, 15 June 2006.
[86] Parliament of the Commonwealth of Australia, *Review of Security and Counter Terrorism Legislation* (2006), Recommendations 14-19. The PJC also conducted a review of the listing provisions. Its report was published too late for consideration in this paper. See Parliament of the Commonwealth of Australia, *Inquiry into the proscription of 'terrorist organisations' under the Australian Criminal Code* (2007).

taken into custody, is the community best served by an immediate application of law enforcement processes, or is it best served through seeking to obtain, through lawful means, information concerning plans and intentions, and the location of others involved in terrorism?[87]

The question is of course rhetorical and the new laws, with their broad and vaguely defined offences, reflect the priority he stressed. They do not seek to guide citizen conduct but to empower officials, often enabling the threat of prosecution to be used to compel cooperation that escapes legal scrutiny. Listing also supports the use or threat of other less-visible sanctions carrying fewer safeguards. Refusing or cancelling passports can have even more onerous effects on individuals, families and communities than a criminal prosecution. We simply do not know the extent, nature and impact of this type of enforcement activity, but it would be a mistake to assume it is not occurring and occurring in the shadow of the proscription regime.

## B. Refugee and Immigration Law

It is a well-established principle of law that politically inspired violence against a foreign government may be justified in a claim for refugee status in Australia or in resisting an extradition order by an Australian court to face criminal charges in another country. The courts have said that the violence needs to be judged by reference to the political context in which it occurred rather than against abstract universal standards of behaviour.[88]

The executive proscription regime contravenes this principle, but it also goes much further insofar as the net cast by listing captures persons and activities with a connection to a listed organisation but no connection to violence. The problem is illustrated by a decision of the Refugee Review Tribunal involving an application for refugee status by a Turkish Kurd. The summary of the decision provided by the Tribunal states:

> The Tribunal noted independent evidence to the effect that the security forces continued to torture, beat and otherwise abuse people, particularly Kurds regarded as 'activists'. It found that the applicant's records would show that he had been identified as a Kurd who had admitted to supporting the PKK. The Tribunal accepted that the authorities continued to be highly motivated to identify any Kurd who wanted a separate state for Kurds, or was a supporter of the PKK. It found that laws to protect individual rights existed, but were not properly implemented in practice. The Tribunal accepted that persons merely

---

[87] C Richardson (then ASIO Director-General) (Address to the LawAsia Conference, Gold Coast, 23 March 2005).
[88] *Minister for Immigration and Multicultural Affairs v Singh* (2002) 209 CLR 533; *T v Home Secretary* [1996] AC 742.

suspected of membership of an illegal organisation were handed over to the Anti-Terror Branch of the police where torture was practised systematically.[89]

As a consequence of proscription, legitimate claims for asylum under the Refugee Convention,[90] like this one, may be prevented for fear that evidence justifying the claim will provide grounds for laying a serious criminal charge under Australian anti-terrorism laws. The effect is to erode seriously refugee law protections. More profoundly, there is the question of who now are the persecutors. The PKK having been proscribed in Australia the applicant in the above case could be handed over to Australia's 'Anti-Terror' police. His reasons, according to an Australian Tribunal, for having a well-founded fear of persecution in Turkey may now be reasons for him to fear prosecution (persecution?) under Australian criminal laws.

## C. Putting Australia's Criminal Laws at the Disposal of Foreign Governments

A problem with the current listing process is that it cannot allay the suspicion that decisions may be unduly influenced by foreign governments engaged in long-running civil conflicts with minority populations seeking recognition of their national, political and civil rights. Examples are not hard to find: the Turkish government's conflict with its Kurdish population, Sri Lanka and the Tamils, and Israel and the Palestinians. The Turkish, Sri Lankan and Israeli governments have a manifest political interest in labelling organisations representing these peoples as terrorist and in white-washing their own repressive policies against them.

In late 2005, police raided a Melbourne Tamil group (the Tamils Rehabilitation Organisation) after a Sri Lankan government warning to the Australian government that charity donations to the group for tsunami relief may have been used to fund the Liberation Tigers of Tamil Eelam ('Tamil Tigers'), a political movement engaged in a lengthy and bloody war to establish a separate homeland in northern Sri Lanka. The Tamil Tigers are not currently listed as a terrorist organisation in Australia, but there must be a serious possibility that they will be listed in the future and the raid illustrates the plight of organisations and persons in Australia who have a connection with civil and political conflicts in other countries. The director of the Tamils Rehabilitation Organisation in Australia, a Melbourne doctor, pointed out that it was impossible to avoid cooperating with the Tigers in directing charitable support to those parts of the country effectively controlled by them. He also indicated his support for the

---

[89] N04/49229 decision of the Refugee Review Tribunal, 30 September 2004. The summary is taken from the *Refugee Review Tribunal Bulletin* 2/2005, 12.
[90] *Convention Relating to the Status of Refugees*, 189 UNTS 150 (*entered into force* 22 April 1954).

political cause of national self-determination for the Tamils, although not necessarily the methods of the Tamil Tigers.[91]

There were suggestions that the decision to list the PKK was taken in response to overtures by the Turkish government, a suspicion bolstered by the timing of the proscription to coincide with a visit by the Turkish Prime Minister to Australia in December 2005. The PJC concluded that there was no evidence that the listing had been influenced by an approach from the Turkish government. Yet DFAT acknowledged that such an approach was made in April 2005, coinciding with a visit by then Prime Minister Howard to Turkey. Despite discrepancies in the evidence given by DFAT and ASIO to the PJC it appears that the process leading to proscription did not begin prior to that time. The coincidences hardly dispel suspicions that Turkish representations exercised an influence.[92]

This illustrates some of the problems with proscription by the executive. Whilst the executive can consult widely and access expertise relevant to a decision to list (much of which may be inaccessible to a court or tribunal, for example), the process lacks transparency. The executive can pick and choose who and what it wants to hear before making a decision to list. Consultations may be broad-ranging and balanced, but equally they may be excessively narrow and characterised by tunnel vision. Any closed executive process lends itself to these problems. Principles of natural justice are designed not only to ensure fairness and protect rights, but to improve decision-making by increasing the range of interests and information represented in the process. Confidence in the outcome is also increased. Listing may cloak a process driven more by political considerations than Australian security interests. Even where this is not the case, the process may often fail to remove the perception that it is.

In other words, the listing provisions may quite understandably be perceived in some minority communities as in effect an agent of foreign governments, extending the arm of authoritarian rule so that it reaches them in Australia, the place to which they have come seeking refuge from it. Ironically, given the preventative rationale of the law, this carries a risk over time of fostering community tensions in Australia and transplanting violence *to* Australia.

## V. Crime and Politics: the Antimonies of Executive Proscription

Although under Australian law it is proof of a political, ideological or religious motive that distinguishes terrorism from ordinary crime, governments, and some

---

[91] C Stewart and N Robinson, 'Tamil Tigers in Tsunami Funds Row', *The Australian* (Sydney), 25 November 2005, 7.
[92] Parliament of the Commonwealth of Australia, *Review of the Listing of the Kurdistan Workers' Party (PKK)* (2006) [1.24]-[1.29].

commentators alike, argue that groups like Al Qa'ida 'cannot be engaged politically and must instead be defeated militarily' or presumably by other coercive means, including those provided by the criminal law.[93]

If actually confined to Osama bin Laden and his confederates the argument may be sound. Even here it would be imprudent to allow a concern to understand the precise character of Al Qa'ida and its political strategy and objectives to be overwhelmed by emotional and moral reactions to extreme acts of terrorist violence.[94] As regards terrorism generally, history reveals many instances where governments publicly condemned and criminalised groups as terrorists whilst privately negotiating with them.[95] This merely illustrates that, on occasion, use of the criminal law and the criminal label is (like war)[96] the continuation of politics by other means.

The concept of 'terrorism' carries heavy moral and emotional freight. In isolating the focus on means — the use of violence — it efficiently closes off any question of the particular political causes, claims, antecedents or contexts surrounding the uses of violence. It also creates a fundamental political and moral asymmetry between perpetrators and victims. The accent on the innocence, ordinariness and essential goodness of civilian victims of terrorist violence (often narrated over and over in highly personalised terms by the media) permits only one judgment on the actions and motives of terrorists: they are monstrous, evil, lacking any possible justification or mitigation. And thus they must be crushed.

This also positions governments to depict themselves as merely reacting to terrorist actions and threats when they adopt repressive methods, like military campaigns, missile attacks, torture, rendition, extra-judicial killings and indefinite detention.[97] In representations of terrorism, political ends are extinguished by the focus on violence and its human consequences. In counter-terrorist discourse the means/ends relationship is inverted. The cause being just, it dictates the necessity and legitimacy of the means adopted, whose character and effects are pushed into the background. That, like terrorism, this involves killing innocent people is obscured by technical rational language: 'pre-emption', 'counter-measures', 'collateral damage'. The victims not only disappear in a corporeal sense; unlike the victims of terrorism, they also tend to be anonymous,

---

[93] M Ignatieff, *The Lesser Evil — Political Ethics in an Age of Terror*, (Edinburgh: Edinburgh University Press, 2005) 99; also see Australian Government, above n 56.
[94] M Doran, 'Somebody Else's Civil War' (2002) 81(1) *Foreign Affairs* 22; B Lawrence, *Messages to the World — the Statements of Osama bin Laden* (US: Verso, 2005) xxii; Parliamentary Joint Committee on Intelligence and Security, Parliament of the Commonwealth of Australia, *Review of the Re-Listing of Al Qa'ida and Jemaah Islamiyah as Terrorist Organisations* (2006) [2.7].
[95] P Neumann, 'Negotiating with Terrorists' (2007) 86(1) *Foreign Affairs* 128.
[96] C Von Clausewitz, *On War* (UK: Penguin Classics, first published 1832, 1982) 119.
[97] L Donohue 'Terrorism and Counter-Terrorist Discourse' in V Ramraj, M Hor and K Roach (eds), *Global Anti-Terrorism Law and Policy* (Cambridge, New York: Cambridge University Press, 2005) 13.

divested of individual, moral and cultural identity. Moral sensibilities and psychological inhibitions against the infliction of suffering are thereby blunted.

These considerations underline the fact that the terrorist label is a potent and flexible ideological instrument. Its use can rarely if ever be seen as disinterested or without a crucial subjective element.[98] This is not altered in any significant way by new laws centred on the concept that have been enacted since 9/11. That is, the crux of the problem remains the definitional issue, or more to the point, as Jenny Hocking has asked, 'How does this discourse of terrorism operate?'[99]

Of central importance is the way the executive proscription regime redraws the 'frontiers of criminal law'.[100] There are two aspects to this. One is literal: the abrogation of any requirement for a territorial nexus with Australia or Australian interests.[101] Aside from a handful of crimes of universal jurisdiction (piracy, crimes against humanity), criminal law has been local and territorial in character. Its legitimacy has depended upon the relationship it maintains with the values of the community and polity it is designed to protect and serve. Now we are warned the threat of terrorism is global and our laws therefore must have an extended geographical jurisdiction. But this does not mean that standards of political behaviour and the boundaries of acceptable and unacceptable political violence can validly and usefully be drawn for all the world by law-makers in Canberra, without reference to the political cultures, regimes and conditions pertaining in particular states and regions to which in principle they apply. This is manifestly absurd as well as being contrary to well-established principles within our own legal traditions.

A second related aspect involves redrawing the boundary separating crime and politics. The net of criminality is cast so wide as to capture a range of political activities remote in time, space or character from the use of violence. In 1990, Gearty traced the expansionary tendencies in the definitions of terrorism over the 1970s and 1980s: a 'drift from terror to terrorism', from a narrow focus on indiscriminate violence to much looser conceptions encompassing all or most forms of political insurgency.[102] During this time terrorist discourse in its expanded form also migrated from the liberal democracies to places where recourse to political violence presented more difficult ethical questions, as autocratic governments (in Latin America, apartheid South Africa, the Middle

---

[98] Ibid; J Hocking, *Terror Laws — ASIO, Counter-terrorism and the Threat to Democracy* (Sydney: University of New South Wales Press, 2004) 2.
[99] Hocking, ibid 5.
[100] I Loveland (ed), *Frontiers of Criminality* (London: Sweet & Maxwell, 1995).
[101] B McSherry, 'Terrorism Offences in the *Criminal Code*: Broadening the Boundaries of Australian Criminal Laws' (2004) 27(2) *University of New South Wales Law Journal* 354.
[102] C Gearty, *Terror* (UK: Faber & Faber, 1990) 13.

East and elsewhere) embraced counter-terrorist measures to repress political movements struggling to advance popular national and democratic rights.

These developments saw a further expansionary manoeuvre whereby:

> [a]ll the activities of the groups engaged in acts of terror are automatically classed as terrorist, even when many of those activities, such as fund-raising and political campaigning, are conducted in a peaceful manner. In *extreme cases* those who merely share the political goals of subversive groups may find themselves described as terrorists.[103]

Gearty's 'extreme cases' no longer appear so extreme. And the migration has been the other way. These cases now find expression in the contemporary anti-terrorist laws of Australia and other liberal democracies. The precise stratagems Gearty describes can even be detected in the statements of reasons provided by the Australian government to justify listing organisations. Suppressed is any sense that there might be two (often equally brutal) sides to the conflicts in which listed organisations are engaged. Shorn of history and context, we are presented with a solitary image of violence without reason. In the case of organisations like Hamas and Hizballah, for example, there is no reference to the political and historical circumstances conditioning their resort to violence, to their mass following and success in elections, to their recourse to truces and ceasefires, or to the illegal occupation of Lebanon (between 1982 and 2000) and the Palestinian territories by their principal adversary (the state of Israel). Where reference is made to their other political, welfare and fund-raising activities, it is represented through the prism of terrorism: welfare services are undertaken to recruit terrorists, funding is 'channelled into ... terrorist infrastructure' and so on.[104] Rather than being one dimension, one tactic, in a multi-faceted political movement, recourse to political violence appears as their defining characteristic, the sole reason for their existence.

It follows also that these laws, in their extra-territorial effect, endorse the authority of foreign governments without regard to their own policies and methods (killing civilians, use of torture and so on). This is dangerous because it directly aligns Australia with those regimes in the international community. It can also visit the impact of that allegiance on domestic Australian law and politics by placing law-abiding Australian citizens and residents at risk of criminal prosecution for some vaguely specified connection with a listed foreign political organisation regardless of the justice and popular legitimacy of its cause.

---

[103] Ibid 3 [emphasis added].
[104] See Australian Attorney-General's Department, National Security Website, Listed Organisations — Hamas's Izz al-Din al-Qassam Brigades
<http://www.nationalsecurity.gov.au/agd/www/nationalsecurity.nsf/
AllDocs/CADAB9AC4723C526CA256FCD001BA892?OpenDocument>.

In seeking to more directly wield the criminal law as an instrument of executive power, governments cloak political decisions in a veneer of legalism. They thereby risk damaging both the legal *and* political capacities of the state to address problems of political conflict and violence. Much criticism has been levelled at the manner in which anti-terror laws violate established legal principle and threaten the legitimacy of the law. Less attention has been accorded to their distorting effects on politics and on the policy instruments available to mitigate or resolve violent political conflicts, like peace initiatives, diplomacy, aid and trade.[105]

## VI. Conclusion

A major obstacle to a more clear-sighted debate and response on anti-terrorist law and policy stems from the rhetorical power of the term 'terrorist' itself. It was partly by relying on this that the Howard government was able to disdain the reports and recommendations of the PJC and deflect calls for meaningful listing criteria and processes of consultation and deliberation. The PJC reports expose grave inadequacies in the administration of the listing provisions and it is only self-declared deference to the executive on matters of national security that appear to have prevented outright rejection of the case for listing in many instances. In the political and popular climate created by the 'war on terror' the listing of an organisation by the government has inevitably carried its own politically-driven momentum to confirmation and, in practice a strong, perhaps irresistible, presumption against disallowance.

Existing safeguards cannot protect against this but they do offer some advantages compared with executive proscription in other countries. Decisions to list are based on open source materials and the PJC reviews the process in relation to each listing and re-listing. The two-year sunset clause on each listing ensures that there are regular reviews if an organisation is to continue to be listed. Parliamentary processes may be of limited utility once an executive decision has been taken to list an organisation, but the cumulative impact may be more positive, producing benefits over time to the quality of public debate and the policy process. This can affect the political climate so as to encourage more cautious use of the listing power.

The problems exposed by the PJC are a major, legitimate source of concern given the serious implications proscription powers have for individual rights and democratic freedoms. Of equal concern, however, is whether the exercise of these powers has been governed by a coherent conception of Australia's security interests. There is little evidence of it in the reviews of the PJC. The much

---

[105] R Cooper, *The Breaking of Nations — Order and Chaos in the Twenty First Century* (London: Atlantic, 2004).

vaunted trade-off, or 'balance',[106] between security and freedom, therefore, may be no such thing. Australia's proscription laws and their administration may be putting both in jeopardy. It remains to be seen whether the new government will adopt a different approach to the proscription power.

---

[106] S Bronitt, 'Constitutional Rhetoric v Criminal Justice Realities: Unbalanced Responses to Terrorism?' (2003) 14 *Public Law Review* 69.

# PART FIVE

## Calling a Halt:
## The Role of Bills of Rights

# Chapter Fifteen

# Strapped to the Mast: The Siren Song of Dreadful Necessity, the United Kingdom Human Rights Act and the Terrorist Threat

Colm O'Cinneide[*]

## Introduction

The United Kingdom (UK) has a long and complex history of engagement with terrorism and other forms of violence directed at achieving political aims.[1] Acts that might be characterised as 'terrorism' in contemporary political and media analysis have taken place in the UK as far back as the Fenian bombings of the 1860s. Similar acts occurred during the anarchist scares of the 1890s and 1900s and the repeated Irish Republican Army (IRA) bombing campaigns in Northern Ireland and mainland Britain from the 1950s to the 1990s. Now, the 11 September 2001 (9/11) terrorist attacks on New York and Washington DC and the London tube and bus bombs in July 2005 have resulted in the threat presented by fundamentalist Islamist groups coming to the forefront of public and political concern.

These different waves or spasms of political violence have stemmed from different controversies and ideologies. The tactics, targets and *modus operandi* of the different terrorist groups have varied greatly over time. Nevertheless, the responses that have been adopted by the UK legislative, executive and law enforcement authorities to these threats have tended to conform to a distinct pattern. Acts of political violence make governments determined to show they are ready to take strong action to ensure the safety of the public. This instinctive response is often reinforced by the demands of security services, police and

---

[*] Senior Lecturer in Law, Faculty of Laws, University College London, London, UK.
[1] The important debate as to what constitutes 'terrorism' and whether it serves any meaningful purpose to apply that particular label is not addressed here: for excellent analysis on this issue, see B Golder and G Williams, 'What is "Terrorism"? Problems of Legal Definition' (2004) 27 *University of New South Wales Law Journal* 270; C A Gearty, *Terror* (London: Faber and Faber, 1991); C A Gearty, 'Terrorism and Morality' [2003] *European Human Rights Law Review* 377; J Waldron, 'Terrorism and the Use of Terror' (2004) 8(1) *Journal of Ethics* 5. For a comprehensive discussion of the definition of the term 'terrorism' in international law, see B Saul, *Defining Terrorism in International Law* (Oxford: Oxford University Press, 2006). The definition of 'terrorism' in the UK legislation is, however, problematic and a source of controversy: see below.

other civil authorities for a freer hand to deal with the threat in question. Often, 'panic' measures are rushed through Parliament, with scant debate.[2] Subsequent terrorist atrocities (or threats of such atrocities) serve to ratchet up the ensuing sense of threat and panic. These lead in turn to tougher security measures, greater pressure on governments to stand firm and further departures from conventional criminal and public law norms. A cycle of trigger and response is established, where calm, reasoned analysis can be notable for its absence.[3]

The measures taken to repress the terrorist threat are justified time and again as required by the 'strict necessity' of the circumstances and the need to counter the very real violence caused by terrorist acts.[4] The emphasis switches from treating violent acts as breaches of the 'ordinary' criminal law to a 'security' model of response, where the executive is conferred with sweeping powers often untrammelled by the normal constitutional checks and constraints.[5] The threat of imminent disaster serves as a trump card, permitting the suspension of conventional civil liberties, the enhancement of police powers, and the targeting of particular minority groups associated with terrorist groups for special surveillance. This tends to generate resentment amongst these minorities, which in its turn can result in even greater resentment, alienation and radicalisation. A cycle of terror, repression and response is established that can take decades to break.

Further, counter-terrorism measures are usually presented as temporary deviations from the normal constitutional state of affairs. The problem is that these 'temporary' special measures tend to leave a permanent residue. As the threat from particular groups rarely ends at a clear and defined point in time, and new threats from other groups invariably emerge, some elements of emergency legislation become embedded in the conventional criminal law framework. This can result in a gradual and often unchallenged expansion in the coercive power of the state, which again can generate fear, resentment and radicalisation amongst those most exposed and vulnerable to the exercise of this power.

---

[2] For comparative discussion of this tendency for legislation to be introduced with speed in 'panic' situations, see J H Marks, '9/11+3/11+7/7=? What Counts in Counterterrorism?' (2006) 37 *Columbia Human Rights Law Review* 559; E A Posner and A Vermeule, 'Emergencies and Democratic Failure' (2006) 92 *Virginia Law Review* 1091.
[3] For an analysis of how a similar process of rushed responses to crises resulted in the overly enthusiastic suppression of freedom of expression in the United States during the Second World War, see G R Stone, 'Free Speech in World War II: "When Are You Going to Indict the Seditionists?"' (2004) 2 *International Journal of Constitutional Law* 334.
[4] Loader and Walker have referred to this as a cycle of 'terror, fear and repression': see I Loader and N Walker, *Civilising Security* (Cambridge: Cambridge University Press, 2007) 89.
[5] See Loader and Walker, *Civilising Security*, ibid; see also C A Gearty, 'Human Rights in an Age of Counter-Terrorism: Injurious, Irrelevant or Indispensable?' (2005) 58 *Current Legal Problems* 25; L Zedner, 'Seeking Security by Eroding Rights: The Side-Stepping of Due Process' in B Goold and L Lazarus (eds), *Security and Human Rights* (Oxford: Hart Publishing, 2007).

This general pattern of terror, repression and response has recurred over and over in UK responses to political violence, from as far back as the 1790s (see below) through to the long years of the Northern Ireland conflict. Since 9/11, this cycle has predictably been put into motion once again. In some jurisdictions, the new era of emergency powers and counter-terrorism panic may be experienced as a rupture, an abrupt departure from previous standards and norms. In the UK, it has been greeted to some extent with weary resignation and a sense of 'here we go again'.

However, there are some new dimensions to the current crisis that are worth noting. The scale and savagery of 9/11, the subsequent terrorist attacks in London and elsewhere, and the use of suicide bombers (unfamiliar in the UK even with its long history of political violence) has generated a sense that the current crisis is different and more serious than previous outbreaks of terrorist activity. In addition, the rhetoric of the 'War on Terror', with its eschatological language of 'clash of civilisations', 'good and evil' and 'life and death struggle', has provided new impetus to the sense of crisis. As with other Western countries, a new conception of 'militant democracy' has emerged,[6] best encapsulated by the warning issued by the then Prime Minister, Tony Blair, soon after the London bombings: '[l]et no one be in any doubt, the rules of the game are changing.'[7] This has fed and been fuelled in turn by fears of the Muslim 'Other', ensuring a steady political, media and security focus on the UK's large Muslim communities. It has also stirred up populist agitation for greater border control, exclusionary immigration polices and a shift away from the UK's previous fumbling, tentative yet largely well-meaning embrace of multicultural policies towards a new emphasis on cultural integration.[8] The global dimensions of the current counter-terrorism frenzy also add a new and sinister dimension. There is evidence of some limited UK involvement in the new and opaque transnational mechanisms such as 'extraordinary rendition' that are designed to evade scrutiny in the handling of terrorist suspects.[9]

---

[6] C Walker, 'The Treatment of Foreign Terror Suspects' (2007) 70(3) *Modern Law Review* 427, 427, citing A Sajo (ed), *Militant Democracy* (Amsterdam: Eleven International Publishing, 2004).
[7] *The Times* (London), 6 August 2005, 1.
[8] See T Modood, 'Muslims and the Politics of Difference' (2003) 74(1) *Political Quarterly* 100; B Hepple, 'Race and Law in Fortress Europe' (2004) 67(1) *Modern Law Review* 1; S Brighton, 'British Muslims, Multiculturalism and UK Foreign Policy: "Integration" and "Cohesion" in and beyond the State' (2007) 83(1) *International Affairs* 1.
[9] See the findings by the Council of Europe Parliamentary Assembly, *Alleged Secret Detentions and Unlawful Inter-State Transfers of Detainees Involving Council of Europe Member States* (the 'Marty Report') Doc 10957, 12 June 2006 (Strasbourg: Council of Europe, 2006), available at <http://assembly.coe.int/Documents/WorkingDocs/doc06/edoc10957.pdf>; see also P Sands, 'The International Rule of Law: Extraordinary Rendition, Complicity and its Consequences' (2006) 4 *European Human Rights Law Review* 408. See also L Arbour, 'In Our Name and on Our Behalf' (2006) 4 *European Human Rights Law Review* 371 for an analysis of the implications and nature of this transnational dimension.

However, the abuses and failures of the past have resulted in some lessons being learnt. In particular, the use and periodic abuse of counter-terrorism measures in Northern Ireland have shown those willing to learn from the past what can go wrong with the over-enthusiastic application of such powers. There have been strong dissenting voices in the UK debates on counter-terrorism since 9/11: media, legal and political debates have raged on the question of how to respond to terrorist threats, and activists such as Shami Chakrabati (director of Liberty, a leading UK human rights non-governmental organisation (NGO)) have been prominent in challenging the government's constant attempts to secure new and expanded powers.

In addition, new constitutional mechanisms recently introduced as part of the New Labour constitutional reform agenda have come into play this time around. In particular, the *Human Rights Act 1998* (UK) (HRA), which incorporates the European Convention on Human Rights (ECHR)[10] into UK law, has made the courts a battleground where the legitimacy of counter-terrorist powers has come under sustained (if not always successful) challenge. Parliamentary mechanisms, such as the Joint Select Committee on Human Rights (JCHR), which was established in late 2001 to provide a parliamentary vehicle for consideration of the human rights implications of legislation and government policy,[11] have also played an important role in questioning the inherent logic of the counter-terrorism cycle. The ever-growing case law of the European Court of Human Rights (ECrtHR) has also had a considerable influence in shaping and constraining the routes available to the government in securing its objectives.

Perhaps to an unexpected degree, these mechanisms have played some role in impeding the apparently inevitable unfolding of the counter-terrorism cycle and the unthinking adoption of the security model of response. If the use of a somewhat extended and florid metaphor can be permitted, they have played some role in restraining the ship of state from wholly coming under the influence of the 'siren song' of the impulses that generate the counter-terrorism cycle of repression and response: however, the helmsmen of the ship are not securely bound to the mast, and the struggle to control the direction taken in the post-9/11 climate continues.

## The Lessons of History

One can trace the outlines of the counter-terrorism cycle of terror and repression in action as far back as the early 1790s, when the radicalism and violence of the French Revolution triggered panic about similar 'subversion' occurring in the

---

[10] *European Convention for the Protection of Human Rights and Fundamental Freedoms*, 213 UNTS 222 (entered into force 3 September 1953).
[11] On the JCHR and the comparison between it and its Australian equivalent, see C Evans, 'Legislative Scrutiny Committees and Parliamentary Conceptions of Human Rights' (2006) *Public Law* 785.

UK.[12] This resulted in aggressive measures taken by the executive and Parliament against 'sedition', with many of the civil liberties that had been won over the preceding period of political activism being rolled back by the tide of reaction. This period is often neglected in contemporary debates about emergency powers and terrorism. Nevertheless, all the key ingredients of the cycle of reaction and response discussed above are present in the panic and clampdown that followed the 'Terror' of the 1789 Revolution.

However, the use of special emergency powers first became widely established in the colonial territories of the British Empire, where in periods of crisis (often involving challenges to British rule) normal common law and legislative provisions could be suspended and a regime of emergency powers introduced. The exercise of these powers very often involved the suspension of *habeas corpus*, detention without trial and the use of military tribunals.[13] The normative standards of the common law and the British ideology of the rule of law, often held out as justifications for the colonial enterprise, were frequently sidelined during these periods of emergency.[14]

In a much less morally equivocal context, similar emergency powers were utilised during both World Wars, with the executive given sweeping powers to detain individuals suspected of enemy sympathies and to take necessary measures to safeguard the security of the threatened state. The Second World War case of *Liversidge v Anderson*[15] saw the majority of the House of Lords take the position that the conventional approach to statutory interpretation, whereby legislation affecting the liberty of the subject should be read in favour of the individual, should not be applied to regulations introduced to protect the state in times of 'public danger'. Despite Lord Atkin's famous and eloquent dissenting opinion in this case (see below), *Liversidge* established that the executive was entitled to considerable freedom of action when Parliament had conferred emergency powers upon it.

In Northern Ireland, special powers legislation had been periodically utilised in response to spasms of political violence since partition of the island in 1922.[16] With the modern outbreak of the 'Troubles' in 1969, these special powers provisions were triggered anew. However, as the communal violence escalated, these powers were quickly enhanced and supplanted by the *Northern Ireland*

---

[12] See C Emsley, 'Repression, "Terror" and the Rule of Law in England during the Decade of the French Revolution' (1985) 100 *English Historical Review* 801.

[13] See N Hussein, *The Jurisprudence of Emergency: Colonialism and the Rule of Law* (Ann Arbor, MA: University of Michigan Press, 2003).

[14] It should be noted that these colonial special powers provisions, which were incorporated into the legislative framework of the different colonial territories, have subsequently been used with enthusiasm by the newly independent post-colonial states, including Singapore and Malaysia.

[15] [1942] AC 206.

[16] See L K Donohue, 'Regulating Northern Ireland: The Special Powers Acts, 1922-1972' (1998) 41(4) *Historical Journal* 1089.

*(Emergency Provisions) Acts 1973-96* (UK). In Britain, an IRA bombing campaign in 1939 had resulted in the introduction of the *Prevention of Violence (Temporary Provisions) Act 1939* (PVA), which introduced special powers of expulsion, prohibition, arrest and detention. Originally intended to be an interim statute, it remained in force until 1953 and was only repealed in 1973. However, following the outbreak of the IRA bombing campaign in Britain in 1974, new special powers legislation was introduced in the form of the *Prevention of Terrorism (Temporary Provisions) Act 1974* (PTA).[17] The PTA, likewise intended to be a short-term measure, was repeatedly renewed and became bedded-down as a semi-permanent feature of British law.[18]

These successive waves of counter-terrorism legislation, often enacted rapidly in response to spiralling patterns of violence in Ulster and atrocities in Britain, introduced an array of measures including: new powers of search, arrest and seizure; suspended jury trial in Northern Ireland for certain types of offences linked to paramilitary activity; and extended detention periods before charge. They also made some erosion into the right to silence and other traditional constraints in the criminal process, introduced a series of new offences and extended police and army powers. Some of these measures, in particular the suspension of jury trial, were necessary responses to the desperate situation in which Northern Ireland found itself for much of the 1970s. Others were excessively far-reaching in nature and were implemented ineffectively and often unfairly, often as a result of their introduction as rushed responses to the pressure of events.

In particular, internment without trial was introduced in August 1971. This was an old tool of state response to political violence, used previously with considerable success both in Northern Ireland and in the Republic of Ireland, but its implementation in 1971 was both notoriously unsuccessful and poorly handled. The introduction of internment and the manner of its implementation triggered a violent backlash.[19] The use of this internment power by the security forces ceased in 1975. However, controversy about the use of the other special search, arrest and interrogation powers became a recurring feature of the Northern Irish political landscape,[20] generating enormous resentment and anger

---

[17] The PTA went through Parliament in a matter of days in 1974: see C Walker, *The Prevention of Terrorism in British Law* (2nd ed) (Manchester: Manchester University Press, 1992) ch 4.

[18] See L K Donohue, *Emergency Powers and Counter-Terrorist Law in the United Kingdom 1922-2000* (Dublin: Irish Academic Press, 2000) for a comprehensive account of the Northern Irish and UK legislation.

[19] R J Spjut, 'Internment and Detention without Trial in Northern Ireland 1971-1975: Ministerial Policy and Practice' (1986) 49(6) *Modern Law Review* 712; K McEvoy, *Paramilitary Imprisonment in Northern Ireland: Resistance, Management, and Release* (Oxford: Oxford University Press, 2001); F Davis, 'Internment Without Trial; The Lessons from the United States, Northern Ireland & Israel' (August 2004), available at <http://ssrn.com/abstract=575481>.

[20] See G Hogan and C Walker, *Political Violence and the Law in Ireland* (Manchester: Manchester University Press, 1989); D Walsh, *The Use and Abuse of Emergency Legislation in Northern Ireland* (London: Cobden Trust, 1983); K Boyle, T Hadden and P Hillyard, *Ten Years On in Northern Ireland:*

among the Catholic/Nationalist minority community in Northern Ireland in particular.[21]

In 1978, the ECrtHR found in *Ireland v UK*[22] that certain interrogation practices used in detention centres in Northern Ireland, including hooding of prisoners, sleep deprivation and subjection to noise, constituted inhuman and degrading treatment in breach of Article 3 of the ECHR. Subsequent decisions of the Strasbourg Court found that other aspects of UK counter-terrorist practice had violated the Convention,[23] requiring the UK to derogate from certain provisions of the ECHR.[24] Additional legal and political pressure, combined with a growing realisation of the backlash triggered by the excessive application of the counter-terrorist powers, resulted in a shift of approach on the part of the UK government. This involved a change to a 'criminalisation' strategy, whereby the ordinary mechanism of the criminal law would be used to respond to 'terrorist' acts in preference to the counter-terrorist special powers.[25]

The strategy met with mixed success. Whilst controversy continued to haunt security operations in Northern Ireland, Campbell and Connolly have suggested that the 'dampening' of the excesses of the 1970s counter-terrorist strategy and the move towards 'formal rationality' (rather than overt repression) played a role in 're-framing' and calming the Northern Irish conflict from the mid-1980s onwards.[26] There has certainly been wide acceptance that serious errors were committed in the initial flush of emergency in Northern Ireland. However, despite extensive repentance in leisure for these errors, it appears as if these lessons of history have not been adequately learnt.

---

*The Legal Control of Political Violence* (London: Cobden Trust, 1980); F Ní Aoláin, *The Politics of Force: Conflict Management and State Violence in Northern Ireland* (Belfast: Blackstaff Press, 2000).

[21] See K McEvoy, 'Paramilitary Imprisonment in Northern Ireland', above n 19, 214; M O'Connor and C Rumann, 'Into the Fire: How to Avoid Getting Burned by the Same Mistakes Made Fighting Terrorism in Northern Ireland' (2003) 24 *Cardozo Law Review* 1657. Whether Nationalist anger at the use of these powers was always justified is open to debate. However, there is no doubt that abuse of these powers occurred and much of the ensuing resentment was genuine and deeply-felt.

[22] (1978) 2 EHRR 25. See K O'Boyle, 'Torture and Emergency Powers under the ECHR: Ireland v. the United Kingdom' (1977) 71(4) *American Journal of International Law* 674.

[23] See eg *McCann v UK* (1995) 21 EHRR 97; *Brogan v UK* (1989) 11 EHRR 117 — but see *Donnelly and Others v UK*, Application 5577, 5583/73, Decision of the Commission, 5 April 1973.

[24] For the effect of the derogation, which permitted the UK to detain individuals for longer than the ECrtHR had previously in the *Brogan Case* (ibid) held was compatible with the right to liberty in art 5 of the Convention, see *Brannigan and McBride v UK* (1994) 17 EHRR 539; see also K Cavanaugh, 'Policing the Margins: Rights Protection and the European Court of Human Rights' (2006) 4 *European Human Rights Law Review* 422.

[25] See B O'Leary and J McGarry, *The Politics of Antagonism: Understanding Northern Ireland* (London: Athlone Press, 1997).

[26] C Campbell and I Connolly, 'Making War on Terror? Global Lessons from Northern Ireland' (2006) 69(6) *Modern Law Review* 935, 953-55.

## The *Terrorism Act 2000* and the Post-9/11 Legislation

Despite this change in strategy, many of the special counter-terrorism provisions became permanently embedded in UK law. These powers proved useful tools not only against Irish-linked terrorism but also against animal rights extremists and other groups. As a result, the PTA was at first renewed annually: then, these powers were permanently institutionalised in the *Terrorism Act 2000* (UK). Note the date: this legislation made provision for a separate and permanent 'code' of anti-terrorist legislation before the events of 11 September 2001.[27] This codification and extension of the counter-terrorism laws, carried out in 2000 even without the spur of a recent atrocity, shows how the logic of 'security' thrives even when the cycle of terror and repression is not in motion. Once opened, the Pandora's Box of special powers is almost impossible to close again.[28]

Despite the controversial and far-reaching provisions of the 2000 Act, the events of 9/11 triggered the counter-terrorism cycle afresh. A month after the attacks on New York and Washington DC, the *Anti-Terrorism, Crime and Security Act 2001* was rushed through Parliament. This legislation made provision for extra powers to compel the forfeiture of property and to freeze funds held by individuals linked to terrorist activity. It also extended police powers in areas such as fingerprinting in order to identify terrorist suspects. Most controversially, it permitted the detention without trial of certain categories of non-nationals who, but for the decision of the ECrtHR in *Chahal v UK*,[29] would be subject to deportation for reasons of national security. That case prohibited the deportation of non-nationals to countries where there was a 'real risk' that they might face torture or inhuman and degrading treatment: the Act now permitted such individuals to be detained on an indefinite basis if they were deemed to constitute a threat to national security.[30]

## The *Belmarsh* Decision and Detention without Trial

It is notable that this provision for detention without trial in Part 4 of the Act attracted comparatively little parliamentary debate or media criticism during its rapid progress through Parliament. This lack of debate was all the more striking given that the power of detention without trial required the UK to derogate from the right to personal liberty guaranteed by Article 5 of the ECHR, as the Convention requires that detained individuals must be charged and brought to

---

[27] Now, to teach students what the London police can do by way of search and arrest under the general codifying police powers legislation, without mentioning the separate and very wide range of permanent anti-terrorist police powers, would be a highly misleading exercise.

[28] See C Gearty, 'Terrorism and Human Rights: A Case Study in Impending Legal Realities' (1999) 19 *Legal Studies* 367.

[29] (1997) 23 EHRR 413.

[30] See H Fenwick, 'The Anti-Terrorism, Crime and Security Act 2001: A Proportionate Response to September 11?' (2002) 65 *Modern Law Review* 724.

trial as soon as possible.[31] Derogations from the Convention under Article 15 require the existence of a war or 'public emergency threatening the life of the nation'. The UK was therefore effectively declaring the existence of a national emergency, as it had done previously in Northern Ireland, and suspending the protection of some of the Convention rights. The UK government promptly moved to detain a number of individuals using this new power in the months after the passage of the legislation.[32]

However, this detention power subsequently became a major legal and political battleground between government and civil liberties groups, the detainees and their lawyers.[33] In the dramatic *Belmarsh* decision of the House of Lords,[34] the Court was prepared to accept that a 'public emergency threatening the life of the nation' existed so as to justify derogation from the ECHR (with Lord Hoffmann dissenting on this point, arguing that no such emergency existed).[35] However, the detention power itself was found to be outside the permissible scope of derogation from the Convention provided for by Article 15 of the ECHR, which also requires derogating measures to satisfy a test of objective justification. The applicability of the detention power to non-nationals alone was held by a majority of eight to one of the Law Lords (sitting unusually as a nine-judge bench in light of the importance of the case) to constitute discriminatory treatment that could not be shown to be proportionate, given the absence of any clear justification as to why non-nationals were being singled out for special treatment. The Law Lords therefore issued a declaration of incompatibility under the HRA. Such a declaration has no binding legal force and the UK government can, in theory, choose to disregard it.[36] However, after initial threats to disregard the *Belmarsh* decision, the government agreed to end the use of the detention power in its current form.[37]

---

[31] See C Walker, 'Prisoners of "War All the Time"' (2005) *European Human Rights Law Review* 50.

[32] Seventeen detention orders were issued under Part IV, over half of which commenced in December 2001: see C Walker, 'Keeping Control of Terrorists Without Losing Control of Constitutionalism' (2007) 59 *Stanford Law Review* 1395, 1406.

[33] A panel of Privy Counsellors established to report on the detention procedure was highly critical and recommended its repeal: see Privy Counsellor Review Committee, *Anti-Terrorism, Crime and Security Act 2001 Review Report*, Session 2003-4, HC 100 (London: Stationery Office, 2004) ('the Newton Report'). For the official Home Office response, see UK Home Office, *Counter-Terrorism Powers: Reconciling Security and Liberty in an Open Society*, Cm. 6147 (London: Home Office, 2004). For the Home Secretary's unofficial response, see R Ford and D McGrory, 'Blunkett Fury as Privy Councillors Attack Terror Laws', *The Times* (London) 19 December 2003, 4.

[34] *A v Secretary of State for the Home Department* [2005] 2 AC 68 (commonly known as the '*Belmarsh* decision' after the prison in which the detainees were being held).

[35] On this point, see the contrasting views of T R Hickman, 'Between Human Rights and the Rule of Law: Indefinite Detention and the Derogation Model of Constitutionalism' (2005) 68 *Modern Law Review* 655 and S Tierney, 'Determining the State of Exception: What Role for Parliament and the Courts?' (2005) 68 *Modern Law Review* 668.

[36] See *Human Rights Act 1998* (UK) s 4.

[37] For a comprehensive analysis of the background and impact of the *Belmarsh* decision, see Gearty, above n 5. See also A Tomkins, 'Readings of *A v Secretary of State for the Home Department*' [2005] *Public Law* 259.

## Circumventing *Belmarsh* — Control Orders and Detention Pending Deportation

In the wake of the *Belmarsh* decision, new legislative proposals in the form of the Prevention of Terrorism Bill 2005 were quickly brought before Parliament. This bill made provision for the UK Home Secretary to impose 'control orders' (substantive restraints on liberty in the form of quasi-civil injunctions) on nationals and non-nationals, where the Home Secretary had 'reasonable suspicion' that the individual in question is or has been involved in terrorism-related activity.[38] Under the Bill, such orders could come in two forms: 'non-derogating' orders that fell within the permitted extent of restrictions on individual liberty permitted by Article 5 of the ECHR, and 'derogating' orders that went beyond this permissible limit and would have to be imposed by a court, as well as requiring a new derogation from the Convention. The making of the 'non-derogating' orders would be subject to automatic judicial supervision, but the scope of such review was limited to ascertaining whether the Home Secretary had 'reasonable grounds' for making an order.[39] Confidential or sensitive intelligence evidence that supported the making of an order would not be subject to examination by the lawyers instructed by those subject to the orders, but instead would be reviewed by 'special advocates': barristers with special security clearance who would 'stand in' for the appellant's lawyers but who were not allowed to share the evidence with them.[40]

This proposed new power to issue control orders was rapidly cobbled together by government lawyers in response to the *Belmarsh* decision: it was intended to allow the UK government to continue to target those who had been detained in Belmarsh, as well as to allow UK nationals (who had been exempt from the

---

[38] PTA 2005, above n 17, s 2(1)(a).

[39] See Walker, above n 32, 1395-463 for a detailed analysis of the control order mechanism.

[40] This 'special advocate' procedure was introduced by the *Special Immigration Appeals Commission Act 1997* (UK) in respect of immigration appeals against decisions to deport based on national security concerns, where sensitive intelligence information was at issue. It was based to an extent on a Canadian model, but its introduction was prompted by the *Chahal* decision of the ECrtHR, which found a breach of the applicant's right to liberty under art 5(4) of the Convention on the basis that although judicial review was available to challenge decisions by the Home Secretary to deport an individual on the grounds of national security, the effective determination of the actual risk to national security was made by an internal Home Office advisory panel (the 'Three Wise Men') on the basis of sensitive intelligence material, which the deportee had no opportunity to challenge or question. The 2001 Act extended the function of the special advocates to detention cases under Part Four, and the 2005 Act did the same for control orders. The House of Lords has approved the use of the procedure in *Secretary of State for the Home Department v Rehman* [2001] UKHL 47, [2003] 1 AC 153, 159, and accepted that the use of the special advocate procedure is compatible with the ECHR and may be a necessary mechanism: see *Roberts v Parole* Board [2005] UKHL 45. The ECrtHR has remained relatively non-committal as yet about the procedure: see *Al-Nashif v Bulgaria* [2002] 36 EHRR 655, 20 June 2002. The Constitutional Affairs Select Committee of the House of Commons has expressed serious reservations about how the special advocate procedure was working in practice: see 7th Report, Session 2004-05, Constitutional Affairs Select Committee, *The Operation of the Special Immigration Appeals Commission (SIAC) and the Use of Special Advocates*, HC 323-I (London: The Stationery Office, 2005). See also the concerns expressed by special advocates themselves in *Abu Qatada v SSHD*, SC/15/2005, 26 February 2007, [528]-[537].

detention powers in the 2001 Act) to be subject to similar controls. Gearty has identified the elements of the proposed control orders that constitute significant departures from normal standards:

> The proposed orders will not be criminal; nor (unless there has been a need to derogate) will they be imposed by a court. They will not depend on proof of wrongdoing or even imminent wrongdoing of any sort. The evidence on which they are based will not be exposed to adversarial scrutiny. And yet their effect will be more severe on individuals, perhaps also on their families, dependants and friends, than many criminal sanctions. [41]

Other leading commentators have made similar attacks on the scope and nature of control orders, with Zedner describing them as a form of 'preventative justice' and as departing 'so radically from established legal norms that the mere fact of their legal existence poses a challenge to the rule of law that demands our close attention'.[42] While not precluding the possibility that some form of preventative detention mechanism may have a role in combating terrorism, serious concerns about the nature and scope of control orders have also been expressed by the JCHR[43] and the Council of Europe's Commissioner for Human Rights,[44] as well as by leading non-governmental organisations (NGOs).[45]

Nevertheless, the Bill establishing this far-reaching new power was once again propelled rapidly through Parliament and faced little sustained political or media attack. With a general election looming, the government raised the spectre of the Belmarsh detainees walking free.[46] This pressure allowed the government to rush the Bill through Parliament in under two weeks — a speed that left Opposition MPs 'absolutely incredulous'.[47] The one concession to Opposition

---

[41] Gearty, above n 37, 43 [footnote omitted].
[42] L Zedner, 'Preventive Justice or Pre-Punishment? The Case of Control Orders' (2007) *Current Legal Problems* 174. See also L Zedner, 'Seeking Security by Eroding Rights: The Side-Stepping of Due Process' in B Goold and L Lazarus (eds) *Security and Human Rights* (Oxford: Hart Publishing, 2007); D Bonner, 'Checking the Executive? Detention without Trial, Control Orders, Due Process and Human Rights' (2006) 12 *European Public Law* 45.
[43] Joint Select Committee on Human Rights, 10th Report, Session 2004-05, *Prevention of Terrorism Bill*, HL68/HC334 (London: The Stationery Office, 2005); 9th Report, Session 2004-05, *Prevention of Terrorism Bill: Preliminary Report*, HL61/HC389 (London: The Stationery Office, 2005).
[44] A Gil-Robles, *Report by Mr Alvaro Gil-Robles, Commissioner for Human Rights on his visit to the United Kingdom* Comm DH (2005) 6 (Strasbourg: Council of Europe, 2004) 9.
[45] See, eg, Liberty, *Renewing the PTA 2005: Submission to the JCHR*, February 2006, available at <http://www.liberty-human-rights.org.uk/pdfs/policy06/pta-renewal-for-jchr-.PDF>.
[46] *The Times* political commentator reported the government pressure placed on its own backbench MPs, the Opposition and the House of Lords as follows: 'They are basically saying to the House of Lords: if you don't pass this by March 14, the Belmarsh boys walk free'. See *Times Online*, 21 February 2005. See also G P Phillipson, 'Deference, Discretion and Democracy in the Human Rights Act Era' (2007) 60 *Current Legal Problems* 40.
[47] Phillipson, ibid.

concerns following an intense debate in the (unelected) House of Lords was the insertion of a 'sunset clause' in respect of the control orders power.[48]

Subsequent to the introduction of this power, the Home Secretary issued a variety of control orders. The orders imposed a series of far-reaching restrictions upon those persons subject to this new regime of executive supervision (which have included many of the Belmarsh detainees and, for the first time, UK nationals). These control orders included the following provisions, as noted by the JCHR:

> an 18 hour curfew, electronic tagging, a ban on use of the garden, requirements to report to a monitoring company twice a day, a ban on visitors and meetings with people anywhere other than those approved in advance by the Home Office, requirements to allow police to enter the house at any time and search and remove any item, and to allow the installation of monitoring equipment, prohibitions on phones, mobile phones and internet access, and restrictions on movement to within a defined area. [49]

At first glance, the sweeping nature of these restrictions would appear to violate the right to personal liberty guaranteed by Article 5 ECHR, which in general can only be restricted via the normal processes of the criminal law. However, the control order scheme was carefully designed to take advantage of a series of ECrtHR decisions concerning the imposition by Italy of extensive restrictions on the personal liberty of Mafia suspects: in these cases, the Strasbourg court had distinguished between the total deprivation of liberty (which under Article 5 was required to be based upon a criminal conviction in the ordinary course of law) and restrictions on freedom of movement and residence, which depending on their nature and extent would not necessarily constitute a violation of Article 5 if imposed outside of the ordinary criminal process.[50] The ECrtHR has emphasised that this distinction is a matter of degree: nevertheless, the UK government maintained that the control order scheme in general, and the specific orders that it imposed on the suspect individuals, fell on the acceptable side of this distinction.

In addition, the executive also continued to make use of its extensive detention powers under the immigration control legislation, which permit non-nationals deemed by the executive to pose a threat to national security to be detained

---

[48] Ibid. Zedner notes that when the control orders provision was renewed a year later, only 13 MPs were in the House of Commons for the debate: see Zedner, 'Preventive Justice or Pre-Punishment? The Case of Control Orders' , above n 42. Subsequent renewal debates have however attracted greater interest and controversy.
[49] 12th Report, Joint Select Committee on Human Rights (2005-06) [34].
[50] See *Guzzardi v Italy* (1980) 3 EHRR 533; *Raimondo v Italy* (1994) 18 EHRR 237; *Ciancimino v Italy* (1991) 70 DR 103.

pending deportation.[51] Judicial oversight of decisions to detain pending deportation is available in the form of the Special Immigration Appeals Commission (SIAC). However, in the immediate aftermath of 9/11, the House of Lords in *R v Secretary of State for the Home Department, ex p Rehman* [52] took the position that SIAC should give considerable deference to executive views as to whether a non-national constituted a threat to national security and therefore was a suitable case for deportation. In addition, detention pending deportation has been deemed to be compliant with the ECHR, if maintained for a fixed period of relatively short- to medium-term duration and periodically reviewed.[53]

The leeway thus given to the use of the immigration detention powers was exploited by the UK government to ensure the continued detention of many of the Belmarsh suspects. However, many of these individuals could only be deported back to countries where they faced a real risk of being tortured, which again would fall foul of the European Court of Human Rights decision in *Chahal*.[54] As the immigration control legislation only permitted detention pending deportation, the UK government therefore set diplomatic processes in train with a view to reaching 'no-torture' agreements with some of the potential 'destination' countries (such as Jordan, Algeria and Libya): these agreements were supposed to provide sufficient safeguards against torture to enable the detainees to be returned without breaching *Chahal*. These diplomatic negotiations proved to be a difficult and long-drawn out process: however, in the interim, the UK government has been able to continue detaining a small group of non-nationals.

The use of control orders and the power to detain pending deportation has therefore allowed the UK government to circumvent to some degree the impact of the *Belmarsh* decision.[55] These devious legal strategies have provided mechanisms for constraining the liberty of a small group of suspect individuals: the control order and immigration detention regimes have also served as a useful way of pressuring the non-nationals within that group to return to their home countries. At least two individuals appear to have returned 'voluntarily' to

---

[51] The *Immigration Act 1971* (UK) permits a form of home detention 'pending deportation'. The government's strategy has been furthered by recent changes to immigration rules and guidelines that widen the permissible grounds of deportation: see Home Office, *Exclusion or Deportation from the UK on Non-Conducive Grounds* (London, 2005); Home Office, *Asylum Policy Instructions on the 'Cessation, Cancellation and Revocation of Refugee Status* (London, 2005); and Walker, above n 6, 434.
[52] [2001] UKHL 47, [2003] 1 AC 153.
[53] See *R (Q) v Secretary of State for the Home Department* [2006] EWHC (Admin) 2690; *Saadi v United Kingdom*, App. No. 13229/03 (Eur Court HR 2006).
[54] States party to the ECHR cannot derogate from art 3 of the Convention, which guarantees the right to freedom from torture and inhuman and degrading treatment and which was the right at stake in *Chahal*.
[55] See the comprehensive and excellent analysis in Walker, above n 6.

Algeria.[56] This twin-track strategy has been carefully designed to take advantage of ambiguities and weaknesses in European and domestic human rights protection: whereas more blunt tools may have been used in Northern Ireland and elsewhere, the 'human rights era' is now apparently marked by the deployment of more subtle tools that nevertheless appear at times to be capable of achieving somewhat similar results.

## The Partial Malfunctioning of the Control Order and Deportation Strategy

However, it would be very premature to write off the ability of human rights controls to provide serious obstacles to the exercise of unconstrained executive power in the counter-terrorism context. While initially successful, the use of the twin-track control order/detention pending deportation strategy has over time again mired the UK government in a morass of political and legal controversy. At the political level, the JCHR, along with many civil liberties groups, have expressed consistently strong criticism of the use of the control orders power.[57] Lord Carlile of Berriew QC, the Independent Reviewer of the legislation, also expressed substantial concerns about both the terms of certain specific orders and how they were being enforced, describing them as verging on 'house arrest'.[58] The language of human rights has been effectively deployed by campaigners to challenge the government's twin-track strategy.

However, with little political mileage to be extracted from campaigning for the rights of a tiny group of unpopular individuals, the real obstacles to the use of control orders have been generated through legal processes. Several court decisions have applied the HRA so as to restrict the scope of the restraints that can be imposed on individuals by control orders and enhanced the ability of detainees under both the control order and immigration control regimes to challenge the justification for their detention. (The UK has not as yet derogated from the Convention, which would permit the Home Secretary to make use of 'derogating' control orders and therefore to evade judicial scrutiny under the HRA.)

---

[56] Press Association, 'Terror Suspect Deported Voluntarily', *The Guardian* (London), 16 June 2006; P Donovan, 'Out of Control Orders', *New Statesman*, 17 April 2008.

[57] Joint Select Committee on Human Rights, 12th Report, Session 2005-2006, *Counter-Terrorism Policy and Human Rights: Draft Prevention of Terrorism Act 2005 (Continuance in force of sections 1 to 9) Order 2006*, HL122/HC915 (London: The Stationery Office, 2006); 8th Report, Session 2006-2007, *Counter-Terrorism Policy and Human Rights: Draft Prevention of Terrorism Act 2005 (Continuance in force of sections 1 to 9) Order 2007*, HL60/HC365 (London: The Stationery Office, 2006); Joint Select Committee on Human Rights, 10th Report, Session 2007-2008, *Counter-Terrorism Policy and Human Rights: Annual Renewal of Control Orders Legislation 2008*, HL 57/HC 356 (London: The Stationery Office, 2008).

[58] See *Second Report of the Independent Reviewer pursuant to section 14(3) of the Prevention of Terrorism Act 2005* (19 February 2007), available at
<http://security.homeoffice.gov.uk/news-publications/publication-search/independent-reviews/lordcarlile-ann-report.pdf>. The Independent Reviewer comments on the operation of the UK's anti-terrorism legislation in regular reports (see below).

In *Re MB*,[59] the first real legal challenge to a control order, Sullivan J accepted that the control orders were civil proceedings and not criminal: this meant that the individuals affected were only entitled to the lower standard of procedural fairness guaranteed in civil proceedings by virtue of the right to fair trial contained in Article 6 ECHR. However, he went on to conclude that the judicial supervisory role within the control orders mechanism was 'very limited indeed', that the standard of proof to be applied by the Home Secretary in deciding to impose an order was too low, and, in the particular case in front of him, that there was substantial reliance on closed material to which the applicant had no access. He therefore considered that the right to fair trial in civil proceedings provided for in Article 6 of the Convention had been violated. On appeal, the Court of Appeal disagreed that Article 6 had been violated: the Court considered that the supervisory role given to SIAC in control order cases was adequate to secure a fair trial. However, this judgment was based upon a finding by the Court that the terms of the Prevention of Terrorism Act 2005 required the Home Secretary to satisfy a more rigorous standard of proof before a control order would be confirmed than Sullivan J had assumed was necessary.[60] In other words, the Court of Appeal interpreted the 2005 Act as permitting more intensive judicial scrutiny of the grounds for making a control order.

Applying this marginally more intensive standard of review, the Court of Appeal in *Re JJ*[61] subsequently approved another decision by Sullivan J to the effect that the extent of the restraints on the individual's freedom of movement and liberty imposed by the specific control order at issue in that case constituted a violation of Article 5(1) of the ECHR.[62] Beatson J in *Secretary of State for the Home Department v E*[63] subsequently found another control order to have violated Article 5(1). However, the Court of Appeal reversed the decision in *E*, finding that the requirements of the order in question were not sufficiently intrusive upon the individual's personal liberty so as to violate the Convention.

All of these decisions subsequently were appealed to the House of Lords. In *Secretary of State for the Home Department v JJ*,[64] the House of Lords applied the ECHR jurisprudence on Article 5 discussed above and took the view that control orders that imposed very substantial restrictions on liberty (such as the control order at stake in the *JJ Case* itself, which required the individual subject

---

[59] [2006] EWHC (Admin) 1000. It is worth noting that the person subject to the control order in this case was apparently attempting to leave the UK to fight against the Coalition troops in Iraq.
[60] *Secretary of State of the Home Department v MB* [2006] EWCA (Civ) 1140.
[61] [2006] EWCA Civ 1141; [2007] QB 446.
[62] Whether a civil order requiring detention will comply with art 5 ECHR will depend on the extent of the restrictions imposed on liberty: see *Guzzardi v Italy*, App. No 7367/76, SerA 39, ECHR; *Raimondo v Italy*, App 12954/87, SerA 281-A, ECHR; *R (Saadi) v Secretary of State for the Home Department* [2001] EWCA Admin 670, [41].
[63] [2007] EWHC (Admin) 233.
[64] [2007] UKHL 45; [2007] 3 WLR 643.

to the order to remain at home for 18 hours in a day) would fall foul of Article 5 ECHR, as they would effectively constitute a total deprivation of liberty. However, the judgments in *JJ* left a considerable degree of ambiguity as to where the distinction should be drawn between total deprivation of liberty and less serious restrictions on freedom of movement, essentially leaving it to the lower courts to consider the application of Article 5 ECHR on a case-by-case basis, taking into account the 'cumulative impact' of the specific orders in question.[65]

In the two other judgments, *Secretary of State for the Home Department v MB*[66] and *Secretary of State for the Home Department v E and S*,[67] the House of Lords upheld the position of the Court of Appeal that the lower civil standard of protection under Article 6 ECHR applied in the context of control orders. However, their Lordships also agreed with the Court of Appeal that the Home Secretary was under a duty to consider the possibility of a prosecution in place of using the control order mechanisms and to facilitate regular reviews of the necessity of control orders. In addition, the majority of their Lordships (with Lord Hoffmann dissenting on this point) also took the view that Article 6 ECHR required that the 'accused' in control order proceedings have access to the key evidence against him: in the views of the majority, this requirement meant that the use of the 'special advocate' procedure (discussed above) had to be modified to permit the accused and their lawyers to have access to this evidence where this was necessary to ensure compliance with Article 6. Once again, how this very general guidance was to be interpreted was left to the lower courts.[68]

The approach adopted by the House of Lords in these cases is a muddy compromise: the inherent validity of the control order scheme was accepted, but substantial constraints were nevertheless imposed on the extent and scope of control orders and new procedural rights were introduced into the process. Nevertheless, the overall impact of this sequence of cases has been a greater judicial readiness to strike down or modify the terms of control orders.[69] The extra procedural safeguards introduced by the House of Lords into the control order procedure, widely seen in the immediate aftermath of the judgment as largely tokenistic, have also been interpreted as requiring greater disclosure of key evidence directly to the accused than was available hitherto.[70] As the endless process of appeal and counter-appeal proceeds, it is apparent that the control

---

[65] For further analysis, see D Feldman, 'Deprivation of Liberty in Anti-Terrorism Law' (2008) 67(1) *Cambridge Law Journal* 4.
[66] [2007] UKHL 46; [2007] 3 WLR 681.
[67] [2007] UKHL 47; [2007] 3 WLR 720.
[68] See C. Forsyth, 'Control Orders, Conditions Precedent and Compliance with Article 6(1)' (2008) 67(1) *Cambridge Law Journal* 1.
[69] See *SSHD v Rideh and J* [2007] EWCA Civ 804; *SSHD v AF* [2007] EWHC 651 (both of which pre-dated the decisions of the House of Lords in *JJ*, *MB* and *E*): *SSHD v Bullivant* [2008] EWHC B2 (Admin), which post-dated those decisions.
[70] See *Re Bullivant* [2007] EWHC 2938 (Admin).

order scheme is facing increased judicial resistance. Cerie Bullivant in January 2008 became the first person to be completely liberated from the control order regime, following a decision by Collins J to quash the relevant control order.[71]

At a wider political level, there are also clear signs of a growing sense of public concern about the control order process. Several persons subject to control orders have managed to abscond and evade surveillance, exposing the Government to ridicule.[72] A jury subsequently refused to convict one of these individuals (Cerie Bullivant, once again) for failing to comply with the terms of his control order.[73] Politicians have begun to wash their hands of the control order scheme, while blaming the courts for necessitating the introduction of this mechanism in the first place.[74] The control order strategy therefore appears to be partially unraveling. However, the basic mechanism remains alive and still imposes substantial constraints on certain individuals.

The UK government's 'detention pending deportation' strategy has also run into some trouble. In *A v Secretary of State for the Home Department (No 2)*,[75] the House of Lords held that evidence obtained through torture could not be admissible in UK court proceedings. Controversially, the majority of the Law Lords however also held that the onus to make an arguable case that evidence was linked to torture rested on the defendant, a burden that may be difficult to discharge in practice. Nevertheless, this means that when courts and SIAC consider control or detention orders, evidence that supports the making of such orders must be discounted if the defendant can make a good arguable case that this evidence was obtained via the use of torture in another jurisdiction. This has resulted in particular evidence being withdrawn by government lawyers in at least one control order case.[76] In addition, SIAC has released several detainees on the basis that they posed no immediate risk to national security.[77]

The UK government's attempt to circumvent *Chahal* by obtaining reassurances from 'destination' countries that deportees would not be tortured on their return has also run into trouble. The government had some initial success in convincing SIAC that the return of individual detainees to Jordan and Algeria would not

---

[71] *SSHD v Bullivant* [2008] EWHC B2 (Admin).
[72] A Travis and A Kumi, 'Manhunt as Terror Suspect Escapes Control Order: Man Absconds Four Days After Restrictions Imposed: British Citizen Wanted to Go Abroad "For Terrorism"', *The Guardian* (London), 17 January 2007, 6; S Tendler, 'Terror Suspect on Run After Breaking Out of Mental Unit', *The Times* (London), 17 October 2006, 2; *BBC Online*, 'Three on Control Orders Abscond', 23 May 2007; *BBC Online*, 'Control Orders Flawed, Says Reid', 24 May 2007.
[73] See *BBC Online*, 'Court Clears Control Order Nurse', 13 December 2007. The fact that this headline refers to the accused as a 'control order nurse', instead of identifying him as a 'terrorist suspect' as has previously been more likely to have been the case, is in itself indicative of the changing public attitude.
[74] T Blair MP, 'Shackled in War on Terror', *Sunday Times* (London), 27 May 2007.
[75] [2005] UKHL 71 [2005] All ER (D) 124 (Dec); [2006] 1 All ER 575.
[76] See *Rideh*, above n 69.
[77] See *BBC Online*, 'Terror Suspect Cannot Be Deported', 14 May 2007; see also *G V SSHD* [2004] EWCA Civ 265, SIAC.

violate Article 3 of the ECHR. However, it has had much greater difficulty in doing the same in respect of Libya.[78] Subsequently, the Court of Appeal have taken the view that there was a real risk of treatment in violation of Article 3 if the individuals in question were returned to Libya, Jordan and Algeria, effectively throwing the government's strategy into chaos.[79] In addition, the European Court of Human Rights in *Saadi v Italy* [80] has recently decisively reaffirmed its ruling in *Chahal*, despite an invitation to reconsider its earlier judgment presented by Italy and the UK, which intervened in this case in a (predictably) vain attempt to shift the position of the Strasbourg court.[81]

As a consequence, the use of both control orders and deportation powers is running into difficulties. The short-term rushed strategy of detention of key suspects, which was initiated in 2001 and which has continued ever since, looks badly flawed. However, it is worth noting that those suspects caught up in the process have been detained or kept under effective house arrest for the best part of six years, often under psychologically distressing and uncertain conditions.[82] Many remain subject to considerable restrictions, which effectively make it impossible for them to live normal lives: at least one detainee has been hospitalised in a mental health institution.[83]

## The Other Problematic Dimensions of the Counter-Terrorism Legislation: The Definition of 'Terrorism', Stop and Search Powers and Ninety-Day Detention

There are additional by-products of the cycle of response and counter-response. The wide definition of 'terrorism' used in s 1 of the *Terrorism Act 2000* generates significant problems, as it potentially encompasses a very broad range of activity and activism. It includes: 'the use or threat of action' where it endangers life, or poses a serious risk to health or to property, and is 'designed to influence the government [or international governmental organisation] or to intimidate the public or a section of the public', and where 'the use or threat is made for the purpose of advancing a political, religious or ideological cause'. Crucially, the

---

[78] See, for the decision on Algeria, *Y v SSHD*, SC/36/2005, 24 August 2006. For the Jordan decision *Abu Qatada v SSHD* SC/15/2005, 26 February 2007; for the Libya decision, see *DD and AS v SSHD*, SC/42 and 50/2005, 27 April 2007, available at <http://www.justice.org.uk/images/pdfs/DD%20AND%20AS%20OPEN%20JUDGMENT%2020%20APRIL%202007.pdf>.

[79] *AS & DD (Libya) v Secretary of State for the Home Department* [2008] EWCA Civ 289; *Othman (Jordan) v Secretary of State for the Home Department* [2008] EWCA Civ 290. See also *MT (Algeria) v Secretary of State for the Home Department* [2007] EWCA Civ 808.

[80] Application No. 37201/06, Decision of 28 February 2008, Grand Chamber.

[81] The European Court of Human Rights in *Saadi* also made clear that the existence of any agreement with a 'destination' state not to torture would not preclude it from assessing whether a real risk to the deportee nevertheless still existed: ibid [148].

[82] See the facts established in *SSHD v Rideh and J* [2007] EWCA Civ 804; see also I Robert et al, 'Psychiatric Problems of Detainees under the Anti-Terrorism Crime and Security Act 2001' (2005) 29 *Psychiatric Bulletin* 407.

[83] See Robert, ibid.

definition extends to action outside the UK.[84] As financially supporting terrorist activities or organisations, or 'encouraging' terrorism, are now offences, the effect of the broad definition is that expressing support for proscribed 'terrorist' organisations such as Hizballah or advocating attacks against coalition forces in Iraq can potentially leave one as exposed to the application of the counter-terrorism powers as a supporter of internal terrorism within the UK. As this definition triggers many of the special powers provided for in the legislation, as well as opening the door for the imposition of criminal liability, its potential width is a real problem.[85]

Stop and search powers under the 2000 Act continue to be applied with enthusiasm. In *R (Gillan) v Commissioner of Police for the Metropolis*,[86] the Law Lords upheld a decision by police officers to apply these stop-and-search powers to protestors outside an arms fair in East London. The Lords felt that the courts should not intervene to second-guess decisions by senior police personnel as to what might constitute a terrorist target. However, it appears that the police are making very intensive use of stop-and-search powers. Under the powers provided for in s 44 of the 2000 Act, 29,407 stop and searches were conducted from October 2003 to September 2004 alone.[87] There have also been some very questionable instances of the application of other counter-terrorist powers. For example, the use of powers conferred under the 2000 Act to eject protesters from party political conferences has attracted media controversy.[88]

Furthermore, the cycle of response and counter-response continues to roll on, generating new offences, new legal problems and new pressure on the groups most exposed to the application of the legislation. The London bombs in July 2005, with their terrible loss of life, were followed by what, in the context of UK counter-terrorism policy, was an unusual period of calm and restraint.[89] However, the UK government subsequently unveiled yet more new counter-terrorist powers, accompanying them with a drumbeat of rhetoric about the need for tough measures to fight the terrorist threat. The upshot of this was the introduction of the *Terrorism Act 2006*, which provided for new offences of a potentially very broad and uncertain nature. These include the prohibition of

---

[84] See s 1(4)(a) of the 2000 Act.
[85] See C Walker, 'The Legal Definition of "Terrorism" in United Kingdom Law and Beyond' [2007] *Public Law* 331; Joint Select Committee on Human Rights, 3rd Report, Session 2005-06, *Counter-Terrorism Policy and Human Rights: Terrorism Bill and Related Matters*, HL75/HC 561, (London: Stationery Office, 2005) [12]-[13]; Lord Carlile, *The Definition of Terrorism: A Report*, Cm 7052 (London: Home Office, 2007).
[86] [2006] UKHL 12.
[87] See C Fraser, 'Are The Police Misusing Stop and Search?' *BBC Online*, 23 October 2005.
[88] See, eg, BBC News, 'Labour Issues Apology to Heckler', 28 September 2005. In this particular case, an 82-year-old man who had fled from Nazi Germany in 1937 was ejected from the Labour Party Conference for heckling a senior minister and was prevented from re-entering the venue under the 2000 Terrorism Act.
[89] See Walker, above n 6, 427.

behaviour that might 'glorify' or 'encourage' terrorism, as well as acts 'preparatory' to terrorism.[90] (Note however that the Court of Appeal in *R v Zafar* [91] has recently adopted a restrictive interpretation of the definition of what will constitute possession of material for a 'purpose connected with the commission, preparation or instigation of an act of terrorism', which is prohibited by s 57 of the *Terrorism Act 2000*. If a similar approach is applied to the new offences introduced by the 2006 Act, this may limit their potential scope of application.)

The 2006 Act also widened the grounds on which organisations can be proscribed and extended the permissible period of detention without charge upon arrest from 14 days to 28 days.[92] The Government originally sought to extend the detention period to a maximum of 90 days,[93] but this proposal was defeated following a backbench revolt in the House of Commons.[94] The debate on the 90-day detention proposal was notable for the failure of the government to present solid reasons for the need to use such an extended detention period.[95] Nevertheless, the temptation to be seen to be responding to the July 2005 atrocity and to deliver every conceivable tool that might be of use to the police and security services still appears to be overwhelming. The government at the time of writing is seeking Parliamentary approval of a maximum period of 45-day detention subject to some limited judicial controls.[96] This persistence is all the more striking given the previous rejection of the attempt to introduce 90-day detention in 2006, the availability of alternative detention methods (including the government's own control order scheme) and the widespread opposition from police officers, the media and other political parties that this proposal has attracted. It also appears very likely to be contrary to the ECHR, but the UK Government appears willing to take this risk.[97] In addition, press leaks in May

---

[90] See ss 1 and 5 of the 2006 Act. For criticism of these new offences, see Joint Select Committee on Human Rights, 3rd Report, Session 2005-06, *Counter-Terrorism Policy and Human Rights: Terrorism Bill and Related Matters*, HL75/HC 561, (London: Stationery Office, 2005) [18]-[25]. See also D Barnum, 'Indirect Incitement and Freedom of Speech in Anglo-American Law' [2006] *European Human Rights Law Review* 258.
[91] [2008] EWCA Crim 184.
[92] The period had been originally increased from seven days by s 306 of the *Criminal Justice Act 2003* (UK), an extension that was again justified on the grounds of the need to combat terrorism.
[93] See Terrorism Bill 2005-06, HC No. 55, cl 23.
[94] Even the shorter 28 day period has been criticised as disproportionately long by the JCHR: see Joint Select Committee on Human Rights, *Counter-Terrorism Policy and Human Rights: The Terrorism Bill and Related Matters*, 2005-06, HL 75, HC 561, [92].
[95] See the analysis of the Joint Select Committee on Human Rights, 3rd Report, Session 2005-06, *Counter-Terrorism Policy and Human Rights: Terrorism Bill and Related Matters*, HL75/HC 561, (London: Stationery Office, 2005) [64]-[103].
[96] 'Undesirable and Unproven', *The Independent* (London), 21 November 2006, at <http://comment.independent.co.uk/leading_articles/article2001493.ece>.
[97] See the analysis of the Joint Select Committee on Human Rights, 3rd Report, Session 2005-06, *Counter-Terrorism Policy and Human Rights: Terrorism Bill and Related Matters*, HL75/HC 561, (London: Stationery Office, 2005) [64]-[103], and the response by the government, Joint Select Committee on

2007 indicated that the Government was contemplating introducing legislation to extend stop and question powers, despite the apparent bemusement of senior police officers, who see little need for the new proposal.[98]

## The Siren Song of Necessity: Why the UK Government is Addicted to Devising More and More Emergency Counter-Terrorist Powers

Stepping back from this narrative, it is possible to draw some conclusions about the legal, political and institutional factors that appear in the UK context to drive this apparently unrelenting counter-terrorism cycle. The UK government is obviously attached to the use of sweeping emergency powers, even despite the difficulties it has faced since *Belmarsh* in having its own way in this area. As Gearty has argued, the rhetoric of the 'War on Terror' seems to have resulted in a loss of historical perspective on the causes and nature of political violence.[99] Despite increasing political and media restiveness about the use of the emergency powers, the Government appears committed to its course. Senior ministers have called for unspecified modifications to the UK and European human rights frameworks.[100]

The general stance of the UK government in recent years is well illustrated by a recent comment piece written by Tony Blair MP:

> Over the past five or six years, we have decided as a country that except in the most limited of ways, the threat to our public safety does not justify changing radically the legal basis on which we confront this extremism ... [The] right to traditional civil liberties comes first. I believe this is a dangerous misjudgment. This extremism, operating the world over, is not like anything we have faced before. It needs to be confronted with every means at our disposal. Tougher laws in themselves help, but just as crucial is the signal they send out: that Britain is an inhospitable place to practise this extremism.[101]

In this piece, the then Prime Minister directly indicated his fundamental disagreement with Lord Hoffmann's opinion in the *Belmarsh* decision that the UK was not threatened by a serious state of emergency. In his view, the nature of the current terrorist threat has been seriously underestimated by civil libertarians and the judiciary.

---

Human Rights, 10th Report, Session 2005-06, *Government Response to the Committee's Third Report of this Session: Counter-Terrorism Policy and Human Rights: Terrorism Bill and Related Matters* HL 114/HC 888, (London: Stationery Office, 2005).
[98] M White, V Dodd and D Pallister, 'Minister's Plan for New Stop-and-Question Powers Takes Senior Officers by Surprise', *The Guardian* (London), 28 May 2007.
[99] C Gearty, 'Rethinking Civil Liberties in a Counter-Terrorism World' (2007) 2 *European Human Rights Law Review* 111.
[100] *BBC Online*, 'Reid Urges Human Rights Shake-Up', 12 May 2007.
[101] Blair, above n 74.

Following the replacement of Tony Blair by Gordon Brown MP as Prime Minister, there has been a tendency for ministers to adopt a softer and more nuanced tone. This was particularly noticeable in the wake of the attempted bombings in London and Glasgow in June 2007, where both the new Prime Minister and the newly appointed Home Secretary refrained from calling for fresh new powers in their moderate response to the attempted attacks.[102] However, it appears as if the policy of the UK government on issues such as extending the time for which terrorist suspects can be detained has not altered significantly, despite the change of leadership and tone.

This enthusiasm for introducing more and more new counter-terrorism legislation may seem unwarranted. Civil libertarian groups are fond of calling the effectiveness of counter-terrorism powers into question. As Crenshaw has pointed out, there is little evidence of their unqualified success.[103] However, it is also important to appreciate the driving forces behind the UK government's attachment to emergency action. The executive is expected by the public to defend the state: as a consequence, politicians feel the need to be seen to do something.[104] Government ministers see the intelligence reports and phone intercept transcripts and are naturally influenced by this material. Concerns about the toll that can be exacted by suicide bombing add a new dimension to these motivational factors: the possible consequences of inaction appear very grave.

In addition, there exists a clear perception in government, the police and the security services that counter-terrorism powers are effective. While they may not generate many successful prosecutions in themselves, they are seen as vital tools to enable police surveillance of suspect groups and to reassure an anxious public.[105] There also exists the belief that desperate times require desperate measures, and that the pressing necessity to combat extremism justifies strong action. As the historical pattern repeats itself, yet again the siren song of necessity demonstrates its attractiveness. Governments feel compelled to act, and the consequences of the application of emergency powers are readily dismissed as collateral damage. This tendency to reach repeatedly for emergency powers, appears to be structural, the product of institutional and political expectations about how governments should act in times of terrorist threat.

---

[102] P Wintour, 'Ministers Step Up Muslim Hearts and Minds Campaign', *The Guardian* (London), 3 July 2007.
[103] M Crenshaw, 'The Psychology of Terrorism: An Agenda for the 21st Century' (2000) 21 *Political Psychology* 405.
[104] A point well made by Gearty, above n 37.
[105] See Donohue, above n 18.

## The Damaging Impact of Counter-Terrorism Powers

The problem with this powerful lure is that the immediate imperatives of responding to the necessity of the moment can blind policy-makers to the long-term consequences of their actions. The development of law through legislation, case law or constitutional principles is usually the product of a long drawn out process of trial and error, experimentation and cumulative experience. However, the demands of necessity, when expressed in the context of counter-terrorism, tend to short-circuit all of this carefully installed hard-wiring. This can result in bad law that is disjointed and alien to the norms and expectations of the system.

For example, the criminal law as developed over time attempts to provide clarity, certainty and proportionate responses: counter-terrorism laws frequently cut through this careful organic growth, and establish parallel systems of control and repression that can contradict the values of the 'mainstream' legal code. Control orders and the massive expansion of police powers under the 2000 Act are both recent examples of this phenomenon. The language of necessity, with its emphasis on short-term response, also often serves to camouflage the reality that temporary counter-terrorism measures have a bad habit of becoming permanent parts of legal systems. As they become embedded in national law, these repressive measures leave a permanent residue that rubs against the grain of the prevailing norms of the system.[106]

In addition, the demands of necessity often serve as a cloak for utilitarian approaches to complex social issues. Emergency measures inevitably confer greater powers on organs of state security, including the police. Occasionally, these powers are abused, or used in a procedurally correct manner that nevertheless generates an unjust outcome. The use of such powers has a tendency to generate certain distinct negative consequences: a) they are often *over-inclusive* in impact, targeting (and thereby radicalising) a much wider segment of the 'suspect' minority than necessary, and b) they are often perceived to be *over-severe* in impact, often resulting in serious deprivations of fundamental rights that again alienate the 'target communities'.

Radicalisation also flows from the abuses and mistakes committed by state security and the media hysteria that accompanies the emergency. The result is the enhancement of siege mentalities among the affected communities. This in turn can breed more violence, perpetuating the cycle of terror, repression and response. Once again, there seem to be structural factors built into the operation

---

[106] See C Walker, 'Terrorism and Criminal Justice: Past, Present and Future' [2004] *Criminal Law Review* 311, 325-26. The gradual expansion of the use of the special advocate system discussed above at n 40 could serve as an example of this. See the discussion in *Roberts v Parole Board* [2005] UKHL 45, especially the concerns expressed by Lord Bingham, dissenting, [26]-[30].

and design of counter-terrorism powers that perpetuates this apparently inescapable cycle.

Campbell and Connolly in their insightful work on how law both impacts upon and is affected by the counter-terrorism cycle have described this cycle as involving a 'symbiosis ... of repression and mobilisation'.[107] The law is used as a tool of repression: this repression can trigger mobilisation and resistance in the targeted communities, which in turn can feed greater repression, or at least expose these communities to greater targeting. Campbell and Connolly use qualitative research from Northern Ireland to illustrate how this symbiotic process functioned in the 1970s with respect to the increasingly radicalised Catholic/Nationalist community.[108]

This process seems to some extent to be repeating itself again in how counter-terrorism powers are impacting upon the UK Muslim population. The overwhelming majority of Muslims in the UK reject political violence, however, the use of counter-terrorism powers is increasingly seen as impacting to an excessive and unfair extent upon Muslim communities. Specific incidents have tended to reinforce this belief. For example, a high-profile police raid in Forest Gate in East London in June 2006 resulted in the shooting and wounding of a Muslim man and arrests that received considerable media coverage, only for the police to admit subsequently that they lacked any real evidence of wrong-doing.[109] Other anti-terrorist raids have generated much media coverage, but have resulted in a limited number of successful convictions.[110] The counter-terrorism cycle is seen as generating repressive and unfair outcomes, which in turn is threatening to delegitimise the state in the eyes of many in the Muslim community.

## 'Dampening': How Legal Mechanisms Can Offer a Partial Respite from the Counter-Terrorism Cycle

This 'symbiotic' relationship between counter-terrorism measures and political violence, and the apparently inevitable negative impact of the use of emergency

---

[107] See Campbell and Connolly, above n 26, 955.
[108] Ibid. See also O'Connor and Rumann, above n 21.
[109] *The Times* (London), 3 June 2006, 1; 10 June 2006, 2. On 13 February 2007, the Independent Police Complaints Commission (IPCC) released a report on its inquiry into the raid, which concluded that Scotland Yard should apologise to the families affected: see *IPCC Independent Investigations into Complaints Made Following the Forest Gate Counter-Terrorist Operation on 2 June 2006* (London: IPCC, 2007), available at <http://www.ipcc.gov.uk/forest_gate_2_3report.pdf>. See also M Wainwright, 'Kurds and Police Meet Over "Old Trafford Plot": Community angry at raids that led to no terror charges', *The Guardian* (London), 8 May 2004.
[110] Following the acquittal of most of the accused in the 'ricin' case of April 2005 (which involved allegations of an attempt to prepare a form of nerve gas from castor beans), several of those acquitted were subsequently detained pending deportation, to the public horror of several jurors in the original criminal trial. See R Verkaik, 'Jurors Attack Deportation of Cleared "Ricin Plot" Suspect', *The Independent* (London), 25 August 2006.

powers upon 'target' communities, would indicate that it makes sense to be very cautious in the use of such powers. However, the impact on individuals and 'target' communities can be too easily disregarded when set against the apparent demands of the greater good. Justice Jackson's famous quote in *Terminiello v Chicago* [111] that the United States Bill of Rights should not be turned into a 'suicide pact' has considerable resonance in times of crisis, and often is used as a catch-all response to the 'bleatings' of civil libertarians.[112] The structural factors discussed above that appear to drive the response of successive UK governments to terrorist acts seem to invariably result in a depressing repetition of mistakes.

However, certain legal processes appear to have some capacity to slow down the excesses of the counter-terrorism cycle. What is becoming apparent in the UK context since 9/11 is that there are factors at play this time round that were not in play in the early years of the Northern Irish crisis. A series of parliamentary, judicial and transnational mechanisms are now in place that appear to have some moderate 'dampening' effect on the application of emergency powers.

This phrase 'dampening' is borrowed from Campbell and Connolly, who have recently suggested that law can play a 'dampening' role on the progression of the counter-terrorism cycle before it reaches its end. Legal processes can provide an avenue of political opportunity and mobilisation in their own right, whereby the 'relatively autonomous' framework of a legal system can be used to moderate the impact of the cycle of repression and backlash. They also suggest that this 'dampening' effect can 're-frame' conflicts in a manner that shifts perceptions about the need for the use of violence or extreme state repression.[113] State responses that have been subject to this dampening effect may have more legitimacy and generate less repression: the need for mobilisation in response may therefore also be diluted.

Campbell and Connolly suggest that such 'dampening' in the form of greater caution in the use of counter-terrorist powers, and a move towards relying upon ordinary criminal law instead of emergency powers, played a role in re-framing the Northern Irish conflict from the mid 1980s.[114] If this analysis is correct, and it appears convincing, it suggests that even where the repeated pattern of attack, repression and response has begun, legal processes may open up avenues for nudging the use of emergency powers towards greater conformity with normal criminal law and human rights standards. The key question, is whether law is

---

[111] 337 US 1 (1949).
[112] See R Posner, *Not a Suicide Pact: The Constitution in Times of Emergency* (New York: Oxford University Press, 2006).
[113] Campbell and Connolly, above n 26, 942-45, 955.
[114] Ibid 953-55.

capable of playing such a 'dampening' role at present in the UK. Also, Campbell and Connolly concentrate their analysis upon the potential 'dampening' effect of legal processes: however, other 'relatively autonomous' processes could doubtless have a similar effect. Do such alternative processes exist?

## The Inevitable Limits of Parliamentary Control over Counter-Terrorism Powers

In line with the 'political constitution' of the UK, the validity or otherwise of the deployment of counter-terrorism measures has historically been seen as a matter solely for parliamentary debate and determination, a presumption confirmed by the *Liversidge* decision.[115] However, the mistakes arising out of the application of emergency powers in Northern Ireland made it clear that reliance on parliamentary mechanisms alone might be not enough, especially when the political situation of the day ensured that no real political opposition to the use of such powers existed within Westminster.[116] The same concerns exist today. An additional problem is that it is easy for Parliament to pass counter-terrorism measures with the best of intentions, but no really effective parliamentary mechanism exists to monitor the application of these measures in practice.[117]

The cycle of terror, panic and repression can itself cow parliamentary opposition to such measures. The UK experience has been that substantial parliamentary opposition to counter-terrorism measures often only begins to stir well after the initial legislation has been rushed through, and often only in response to challenges to the legislation elsewhere. As Gearty has argued, the *Belmarsh* decision of the House of Lords was probably influenced to a significant extent by NGO campaigning and a growing sense of something awry in the application of the counter-terrorism legislation.[118] However, it was only in the wake of the *Belmarsh* decision that parliamentary opposition became really emboldened and ready to challenge the logic of the government's counter-terrorism response, culminating in the decision to reject 90-day detention in 2006.

When Parliament does take action to reduce the impact of counter-terrorism measures, such steps obviously benefit immensely from the seal of democratic validity. Court decisions lack the *imprimatur* of parliamentary votes, and can, in any case, usually be reversed or circumvented with reasonable ease. However, the track record of parliamentary intervention to dampen down the consequences

---

[115] See above n 15.
[116] See Donohue, above n 18, for an analysis of the political position in respect of counter-terrorism legislation in Northern Ireland from the early 1970s to 2000.
[117] See M Tushnet, 'Controlling Executive Power in the War on Terrorism' (2005) 118 *Harvard Law Review* 2673 for an excellent critique in the US context of the inability of the legislature to control the use of executive use of emergency powers.
[118] Gearty, above n 37.

of the counter-terrorism cycle is poor. The political process is insufficiently insulated against the chill wind of panic that accompanies the repeated pattern of terror and repression. Also, executive concerns too readily set the agenda. This is a particular problem in the UK with the executive's usual iron de facto grip on its parliamentary majority.

## The Independent Reviewer

This leaves open the question of whether other institutional structures can play an active role in 'dampening' the use of counter-terrorism powers. Some element of non-political consideration of the impact of counter-terrorist measures was introduced in the 1990s by means of the independent reviewer mechanism, whereby an appointed legal expert would report on the operation and implementation of the anti-terrorism legislation, recommending changes if necessary. Lord Lloyd, acting as independent reviewer, produced a significant analysis of the flaws of the existing legislation in 1996.[119] The use of this mechanism was extended with the codification of counter-terrorism law in the 2000 Act, with Lord Carlile QC being given a watching brief to report on the operation of this legislation and that of the subsequent 2001, 2005 and 2006 Acts. The Newton Committee of Privy Counsellors was also established to report on the detention power under the 2001 Act.

The independent reviewer is a valuable and useful innovation, as is the use of the Newton Committee. However, no independent reviewer has yet been appointed who disagrees with the government policy of the day when it comes to the fundamental issues: Lord Carlile is widely respected, but has nevertheless been subject to sharp criticism from Liberty for his stance on control orders.[120] The opinions of independent reviewers can in any case be disregarded by the Government and its parliamentary majority, as was the recommendation by the Newton Committee in favour of repeal of the detention powers provided for in the 2001 Act. It took the *Belmarsh* decision to provoke a change in the law. In other words, the institutional mechanism that has provided the most effective 'dampening' effect upon the use of emergency powers in recent experience has been the legal process of court-enforced domestic and transnational human rights guarantees. It is therefore worth having a closer look at how effective this process might be in reining in the use of counter-terrorist powers.

## The Potential of Human Rights

The most significant constitutional shift since the years of the Northern Irish emergency has been the incorporation of the ECHR into UK law via the *Human*

---

[119] Lord Lloyd, *Inquiry into Legislation against Terrorism*, Cm. 3420 (London: Stationery Office, 1996).
[120] See Liberty, Press Release, 'Independent Reviewer Calls to Renew Prevention of Terrorism Act 2005', 2 February 2006, available at <http://www.liberty-human-rights.org.uk/news-and-events/1-press-releases/2006/carlile-calls-for-renew-of-pta.shtml>.

*Rights Act 1998*, and the growing salience of human rights ideology in NGO activity, public debate and legal argumentation. Human rights approaches can be viewed as attempts to steer or 'orientate' legal systems away from the easy discounting of individual rights:[121] they obviously therefore have some potential to act as a brake on the cycle of counter-terrorism responses. The JCHR has been established in Parliament to ensure that the language and perspectives of rights ideology are fed into the parliamentary process. The UK courts have new authority under the HRA to interpret legislation in a manner compatible with the ECHR where possible and to strike down secondary legislation that does not satisfy the Convention, while the Strasbourg Court retains a watching brief over the UK at the regional level.

However, applying human rights approaches in the counter-terrorism context can be a double-edged sword. Gearty has warned that the security approach to counter-terrorism can readily adopt the language and clothes of human rights. Protecting the rights of many can become the justification for severely restricting the rights of the few.[122] In addition, counter-terrorist measures can readily be designed to be formally 'Convention-compliant'. Once this exercise in legal design is completed, such measures can benefit from their purported 'human rights friendly' status, while the cycle of repression continues. The architecture of the 'non-derogating' control orders introduced by the 2006 Act (see above) is a classic example of this: government lawyers designed a legal avenue to effectively place individuals under house arrest, while straining to remain within the substantial scope apparently afforded by the Strasbourg Court to similar types of restraint.[123]

Further potential problems exist. The Convention mechanisms, as is common among constitutional and international rights instruments, build in the possibility of derogation, offering a ready escape hatch for governments facing terrorist attacks.[124] Also, the academic literature is replete with critiques of the stance

---

[121] For this concept of 'orientation' and how it plays out in the UK context, see C O'Cinneide, 'Democracy and Rights: New Directions in the Human Rights Era' [2004] 57 *Current Legal Problems* 175.
[122] See C Gearty, *Can Human Rights Survive?* (Cambridge: Cambridge University Press, 2006) ch 5, and in particular his criticism of Michael Ignatieff's views at 132-35.
[123] It should be noted that the relevant Strasbourg jurisprudence mainly concerned the very different context of injunctions sought by the Italian authorities to restrain the movement of individuals allegedly involved with the Mafia or similar organisations: see *Guzzardi v Italy*, App. No 7367/76, SerA 39, ECHR; *Raimondo v Italy*, App 12954/87, SerA 281-A, ECHR. It remains to be seen what the ECrtHR will think of control orders: the UK government is perhaps too confident that they would survive a challenge in Strasbourg.
[124] Gearty, above n 37, 40. He also uses at p 31 the nice phrase 'confetti at a funeral' to describe the sprinkling of the language of rights over the hard reality of counter-terrorist strategies. See also L Zedner, 'Securing Liberty in the Face of Terror: Reflections from Criminal Justice' (2005) 32 *Journal of Law and Society* 507, 525-9.

of the judiciary in times of emergency.[125] In any case, it may inevitably be unwise to place responsibility for invalidating emergency measures on unelected individual judges, who, often conscious of being deprived of the intelligence information available to the executive, have a tendency to defer to expert opinion,[126] and who are unable to indulge in the luxury of comment without immediate impact that is available to academics and NGOs. As has been argued by Jackson, judges live in the 'same universe of fear' as the rest of the menaced population. It may be unreasonable and even inappropriate for them to take a more active role.[127] Tushnet has also made the point that judicial mechanisms for upholding rights claims are very slow: witness the considerable time delays in the endless litigation surrounding the original Belmarsh detainees and the ability of the government thus far to circumvent the judgments in which it has been defeated.[128]

These considerations all raise legitimate concerns about the capability of human rights frameworks to act as a check or brake on the counter-terrorism cycle. These concerns have been emphasised by critical scholarship and 'civil libertarian pessimists', who are sceptical in general about the ability of rights frameworks to constrain state power although strongly committed to the importance of civil liberties.[129] This scepticism has underpinned the recent interest in Carl Schmitt's contention that executive control of the emergency power constitutes the real 'effective' power in the liberal state order.[130] For Schmitt, as well as for Agamben and others, the pretensions of the liberal state to tolerance and adherence to the rule of law dissolve when emergency powers are triggered.[131] In Kelsen's phrase, the mask slips, the 'Gorgon' of state power is exposed, and those subject to the chill blast of counter-terrorism powers become the *homo sacer* or sacred man of Agamben's analysis, cut loose and cast adrift from the *polis* and deprived of the

---

[125] See, eg, M Tushnet, 'Defending Korematsu?: Reflections on Civil Liberties in Wartime' (2003) *Wisconsin Law Review* 273; Tushnet, above n 117; K D Ewing, 'The Futility of the Human Rights Act' [2004] *Public Law* 829.

[126] See, eg, the considerable degree of weight given to the opinion of a Foreign Office diplomat in *Abu Qatada v SSHD* SC/15/2005, 26 February 2007, [339]-[343].

[127] V C Jackson, 'Proconstitutional Behaviour, Political Actors and Independent Courts: A Comment on Geoffrey Stone's Paper' (2004) 2 *International Journal of Constitutional Law* 368, 369.

[128] See M Tushnet, 'The Political Constitution of Emergency Powers: Parliamentary and Separation of Powers Regulation' (2007) 3 *International Journal of Law in Context* 275.

[129] See P A J Waddington, 'Slippery Slopes and Civil Libertarian Pessimism' (2005) 15(3) *Policing and Society* 353, for a critical analysis of the views of 'civil libertarian pessimists'.

[130] See, eg, O Gross, 'The Normless And Exceptionless Exception: Carl Schmitt's Theory Of Emergency Powers and The "Norm-Exception" Dichotomy' (2000) 21 *Cardozo Law Review* 1825; J P McCormick, 'The Dilemmas of Dictatorship: Carl Schmitt and Constitutional Emergency Powers', in D Dyzenhaus (ed), *Law as Politics: Carl Schmitt's Critique of Liberalism* (Durham, NC: Duke University Press, 1997) 217-51.

[131] See the excellent analysis of this strain of thought in W E Scheuerman, 'Survey Article: Emergency Powers and the Rule of Law After 9/11' (2006) 14(1) *Journal of Political Philosophy* 61; see also, eg, C Schmitt, *Legality and Legitimacy* [1932], trans Jeffrey Seitzer (Durham, NC: Duke University Press, 2003).

shelter of the law.[132] This line of analysis certainly resonates to a degree with the UK experience since 9/11. The Belmarsh detainees resemble living embodiments of Agamben's *homo sacer*, existing as exiles outside the law. The experience of the Muslim community at times does call into question the promises of tolerance and fidelity to the rule of law values that the UK constitutional order is supposed to embody.

If any sort of limited 'dampening' effect is to be generated in any way other than merely waiting for the executive to soften its counter-terrorism strategies, then the application of human rights principles within the UK's legal system needs to rise to the challenge. Actors working with rights principles, whether judges, activists or lawyers, need to be wary about unduly accommodating emergency powers, and to require counter-terrorism responses to respect rights and conform more closely to the standard modes of criminal law.[133] The civil libertarian pessimists may doubt the ability of human rights principles to achieve this. However, as Gearty has suggested, this may be the only realistic aspiration to hope for at present:

> the 'alien codes' generated by the cycle of terror and repression may be transformed into something which much more closely resembles ordinary criminal law than it does at present. Given that it is unlikely that the terrorism laws are going to disappear anytime soon, this is certainly a goal worth working towards.[134]

Interestingly, there are distinct signs of this step occurring in the UK: the historical predictions about the propensity of human rights frameworks to do little more than accommodate the counter-terrorism cycle appear to be a little over-deterministic in their approach and assumptions. A 'dampening' effect has been generated through the *Human Rights Act* and other legal processes. This has ensured that some pressure now exists upon the UK executive to make more use of conventional criminal law processes and less use of its sweeping counter-terrorism powers. Perhaps unexpectedly, it has been the willingness of the judiciary to engage with the ECHR standards and apply them to the executive's use of emergency powers that has made a substantial contribution towards the generation of this dampening effect.

## The Dampening Effect of Human Rights Norms

Admittedly, the UK courts over the last few decades have instinctively adhered to the position established in *Liversidge*, where the majority followed an earlier

---

[132] G Agamben, *State of Exception*, trans Kevin Attell (Chicago: University of Chicago Press, 2005).
[133] For similar arguments, see B Dickson, 'Law Versus Terrorism: Can Law Win?' [2005] *European Human Rights Law Review* 11; Walker, above n 32.
[134] Gearty, above n 99, 126.

decision by the House of Lords in the First World War case of *R v Halliday* [135] and adopted a highly deferential approach to the executive's use of emergency powers.[136] As Dyzenhaus notes, Lord Atkin's famous dissenting opinion in *Liversidge*, to the effect that 'amid the clash of arms, the laws are not silent', has been enthusiastically embraced and quoted with approval throughout English administrative law, but quietly sidelined in the national security context.[137] Post-9/11, a similar approach appeared to be inevitable. In *Secretary of State for the Home Department v Rehman*,[138] the Law Lords adopted a very deferential stance towards the executive's views on what constituted a threat to national security, with Lord Hoffmann adding an extraordinary postscript to his judgment explicitly linking the need for this deference to the events of 9/11.[139]

However, the *Belmarsh* decision marked a dramatic change in direction. While the judgment itself changed little, especially for the individuals caught up in the government's detention/control order/deportation strategy, it was remarkable for the rejection by eight of the nine Law Lords of the appropriateness of deferring to the executive in assessing the proportionality of measures taken under the cloak of national security.[140] (In contrast, the majority showed considerable deference on the issue of whether a national emergency existed, which arguably was the correct decision, based on the ECHR jurisprudence and the UK constitutional framework.)[141] While the subsequent stop and search case of *Gillan* [142] saw a less robust approach taken by the Law Lords, the *Belmarsh* decision has opened the door for lower courts to apply a stricter proportionality analysis in other counter-terrorism cases, including those involving control orders.[143]

More significantly, perhaps, *Belmarsh* has opened up the political and legal debate about the necessity of adhering to the logic of the cycle of terror and repression. In particular, the decision served to embolden campaigning NGOs

---

[135] [1917] AC 260.
[136] [1942] AC 206.
[137] See D Dyzenhaus, 'Intimations of Legality Amid the Clash of Arms' (2004) 2(2) *International Journal of Comparative Constitutional Law* 244, 250-253. See also Lord Denning's opinion in *R v Secretary of State ex parte Hosenball* [1977] 1 WLR 776, at 778 that '[t]here is a conflict between the interests of national security on the one hand and the freedom of the individual on the other. The balance between these two is not for a court of law. It is for the Home Secretary. He is the person entrusted by Parliament with the task.'
[138] [2002] 1 All ER 122.
[139] Ibid 142, [49].
[140] For a robust defence of this approach, see D Feldman, 'Human Rights, Terrorism and Risk: The Roles of Politicians and Judges' (2006) *Public Law* 364.
[141] See S Tierney, 'Determining the State of Exception: What Role for Parliament and the Courts?' (2005) 68(4) *Modern Law Review* 668, 668-72.
[142] Above n 86.
[143] Gearty, usually a sceptic about the efficacy, likelihood or desirability of judicial activism, has suggested the judiciary have for the most part joined much of the UK's legal community in being 'civil libertarians now' above n 99, 112.

and political opposition to the legislation, by confounding the automatic assumption that counter-terrorism measures were untouchable. A climate of resistance has developed to the executive's adherence to the logic of the counter-terrorism cycle. This has led to increasing pressure from NGOs, commentators and some politicians for a shift away from the 'security' emergency powers paradigm to a more restrained approach, based around the use of the normal avenues of the criminal law to deal with the terrorist threat, and adherence to conventional human rights norms.

For example, the JCHR has indicated in a recent report its strong preference for normal criminal law routes to be used to deal with terrorist suspects rather than the counter-terrorism legislation.[144] Pressure upon the government has also been growing to permit intercept evidence obtained by the intelligence services to be admissible as evidence in ordinary criminal trials. The current automatic exclusion in UK law of such evidence is based on a desire to protect the sources of intelligence information: however, its exclusion is often also used to justify government reluctance to bring prosecutions against terrorist suspects and instead to reach for the cudgel of control orders. Liberty, the JCHR and others have called for this exclusion rule to be repealed and for terrorist suspects to be prosecuted under ordinary criminal law and procedure.[145] In addition, the High Court has begun to take the reasonableness of a ministerial decision not to seek an 'ordinary' criminal prosecution into account when assessing the legitimacy of control orders made against an individual.[146]

Not all of this pressure for a return to a more conventional 'criminalisation' approach has its origins in the *Belmarsh* decision. Much of it originally stems from the persuasive arguments made by academics and NGOs. However, these criticisms and the recent judicial decisions mutually reinforce each other, and generate more political and legal pressure on the Government. This is reinforced by public outrage about the behavior of Coalition troops in Iraq and Guantánamo Bay, where again attempts to use the legal process to compel adherence to rights standards and an increasingly concerned public opinion have combined to put pressure on the executive for a change of policy.[147]

In addition, it is worth emphasising the ongoing constraints imposed on government action by the Strasbourg jurisprudence. The ECrtHR has the

---

[144] Joint Select Committee on Human Rights, 24th Report, *Counter-Terrorism Policy and Human Rights: Prosecution and Pre-Charge Detention*, HL 240/HC 1576 (London: Stationery Office, 2006).
[145] Ibid.
[146] See, eg, *SSHD v E* [2007] EWHC (Admin) 233.
[147] Members of the judiciary have been forthright in condemning the 'legal black hole' of Guantánamo Bay, with Lord Steyn commenting that it would be 'forever be a historical reference point for our time', a 'stain on American justice', 'utterly indefensible' and 'reminiscent of the worst actions of totalitarian states'. Lord Steyn, 'Democracy, the Rule of Law and the Role of Judges' (2006) 3 *European Human Rights Law Review* 243, 253; see also Lord Steyn, 'Guantanamo Bay: the Legal Black Hole' (2004) 53 *International and Comparative Law Quarterly* 1.

advantage of being abstracted from the domestic situations in the Convention's states parties, which has historically given it a degree of insulation from prevailing political pressures. Its case law on the use of emergency powers is mixed: it has tended to show considerable deference to states asserting the existence of states of emergency,[148] but has been more assertive in assessing the proportionality of what states have done, an approach now reflected in the *Belmarsh* decision.[149] The Strasbourg Court has also held fast thus far to its jurisprudence on the right to life and freedom from torture and inhuman and degrading treatment. This has meant that decisions such as *Chahal* and *Ireland v UK* still substantially constrain what the UK government is capable of doing while remaining within the Convention.

This umbilical cord to European standards continues to act as a significant 'dampening' factor on the counter-terrorism cycle.[150] The UK government can try to work around these limitations, but it remains hemmed in to some extent, both by the Convention and by the HRA incorporating those standards internally. Taken together, the impact of the ECHR/HRA with the shift in approach in the *Belmarsh* decision has created a 'push back' factor, which, along with other factors, is generating some resistance to the counter-terrorism cycle.

It appears that, as Scheuerman has noted, it is too easy to assume that the liberal constitutional order is incapable of generating meaningful internal resistance to the unfolding counter-terrorism cycle.[151] The 'relative autonomy' of national and transnational legal processes from prevailing political winds opens up these processes as an avenue for activists to challenge the use of emergency powers and the apparently inevitable unfolding of the counter-terrorism cycle. This is not to underestimate the potency of the symbiosis between terror, repression and backlash. Nor is it to downplay the way in which the rhetoric of emergency and the distorting impact of counter-terrorism strategies can continue to dominate the government response to the terrorist threat. The views of the 'civil libertarian pessimists' as to the inevitable limits of the protection that legal processes can offer are not unfounded, being rooted in both history and contemporary events. They may however underestimate to some extent the ability of the new regime of human rights protection to generate some sort of 'dampening' effect.[152]

---

[148] *Lawless v Ireland* (1960) 1 EHRR 1; *Brannigan and McBride v UK* (1993) 17 EHRR 539; Cavanaugh, above n 24; S Marks, 'Civil Liberties at the Margin: The UK Derogation and the ECHR' (1995) 15 *Oxford Journal of Legal Studies* 69; O Gross, '"Once More Unto the Breach": The Systematic Failure of Applying the European Convention on Human Rights to Entrenched Emergencies' (1998) *Yale Journal of International Law* 437.
[149] See, eg, *Aksoy v Turkey* (1996) 23 EHRR 553.
[150] See J Fitzpatrick, 'Speaking Law to Power: The War Against Terrorism and Human Rights' (2003) 14 *European Journal of International Law* 241.
[151] See Scheuerman, above n 131. See also Dyzenhaus, above n 137.
[152] For more on this, see C O'Cinneide, 'Controlling the "Gorgon" of State Power in the State of Exception: A Reply to Professor Tushnet' (2008) 3(4) *International Journal of Law in Context* 15. For a similar argument in the US context, see D Cole, 'Judging the Next Emergency: Judicial Review and Individual

## Conclusion

Over time, the UK experience has been that the counter-terrorism cycle of terror, panic and repression recurs again and again, with consequent negative results for civil liberties, the integrity of the law and suspect minorities. Interestingly, however, and perhaps contrary to some academic expectations, the HRA and ECHR have in the wake of 9/11 played a role in disrupting the repetition of the usual cycle of responses to terrorism. First, the existence of the HRA has very much restricted what the UK government has attempted to achieve using new anti-terrorist powers. It has forced the government to use 'Convention-compliant' routes. While these routes can readily be used to evade the requirements of the Convention, some real obstacles still remain in the path of the cycle. Second, the greater salience given to human rights discourse since the incorporation of the HRA, and in particular the symbolic impact of the *Belmarsh* decision, has galvanised political and media scepticism about the deployment of anti-terrorist powers.

It would be erroneous to argue that the HRA has fundamentally changed the political landscape. The UK government is still constantly pushing at the boundaries of what it can achieve within the constraints of the ECHR/HRA. Dorling has drawn an interesting contrast between Spain, the European country to suffer the worst terrorist attack since 9/11, and the UK. She notes that Spanish political office-holders remain committed to adhering to conventional human rights norms and the use of ordinary criminal law, while the UK government has in general been dismissive of human rights norms and attached to using its panoply of ever-expanding counter-terrorism powers.[153] However, the UK experience since 9/11 shows that the constraints imposed by legal processes that build in some commitment to human rights do have some teeth, even in 'states of exception'. Legally-enforceable rights mechanisms are perhaps more durable than has been feared. Human rights may not prevent the siren song of 'strict necessity' from setting the course of state policy, but can play some role in impeding its traditional bulldozing progress.

---

Rights in Time of Crisis' (2003) 101 *Michigan Law Review* 2565; see also by the same author 'The Priority of Morality: The Emergency Constitution's Blind Spot' (2004) 113 *Yale Law Journal* 1753.

[153] K Dorling, 'An Exceptional Situation? A Comparative Assessment of Anti-Terrorism Arrest and Detention Powers in the UK and Spain and of their Compliance with the European Convention on Human Rights' (2007) 4(1) *Essex Human Rights Review* 1.

# Chapter Sixteen

# The ACT *Human Rights Act 2004* and the Commonwealth *Anti-Terrorism Act (No 2) 2005*: A Triumph for Federalism or a Federal Triumph?

Andrew Byrnes[*] and Gabrielle McKinnon[**]

## Introduction

In 2004 the Legislative Assembly of the Australian Capital Territory (ACT) enacted the first modern bill of rights adopted by any jurisdiction in Australia. The *Human Rights Act 2004* (ACT) (HRA) which entered into operation on 1 July 2004, is a modest endeavour by comparison with many overseas models.[1] The ACT HRA is a statutory bill of rights closely modelled on the United Kingdom's *Human Rights Act 1998* and is thus not entrenched as a constitutional charter; it incorporates a limited range of human rights (the classic civil and political rights contained in the *International Covenant on Civil and Political Rights*[2] (ICCPR)); it is primarily an interpretive instrument; and it does not explicitly provide for remedies for violations of the HRA[3] (although it does empower the Supreme Court to make a declaration of incompatibility in cases where the Court is unable to construe a statute in accordance with the human rights guaranteed by the Act). The HRA is intended to promote a dialogue on human rights between the various arms of government, but preserves the final say on disputes over the extent of and limitations on rights to democratically elected politicians, and

---

[*] Professor of International Law, Faculty of Law and Australian Human Rights Centre, The University of New South Wales, Sydney, Australia.
[**] Research Associate, Regulatory Institutions Network, Centre for International Governance and Justice, The Australian National University, Canberra, Australia.

This chapter forms part of two ARC-funded projects: ARC Linkage Project LP0455490 'Australia's First Bill of Rights: Assessing the Impact of the Australian Capital Territory's *Human Rights Act 2004*' (with the ACT Department of Justice and Community Safety); and ARC Discovery Project DP0451473 'Terrorism and the Non-State Actor: The Role of Law in the Search for Security'.

[1] For references to primary and secondary materials on the ACT HRA, see the website of the ACT Human Rights Act Research Project <http://acthra.anu.edu.au/>.
[2] *International Covenant on Civil and Political Rights*, 999 UNTS 171 (entered into force 23 March 1976).
[3] However, a new remedy for contravention of human rights by public authorities was introduced by the *Human Rights Amendment Act* 2008 (ACT), which will come into force on 1 January 2009.

envisages that the most important way for the HRA to have an impact is to bring about cultural change in government.[4]

Much of the debate around this Bill of Rights, like that about bills of rights in other countries, focused on the implications for the traditional distribution of powers among the organs of the State: to what extent would it disturb the traditional assignment of roles between the legislature, the executive and the courts and, in particular, would it give inordinate power to unelected judges to second-guess and override the decisions of democratically elected legislators? There was less attention given to the impact that the HRA might have on federal law and on the law of other States, though it was hoped that the HRA would break the logjam on the enactment of bills of rights in Australia by showing that it was politically possible to enact a bill of rights and that the sky would not fall in on traditional arrangements if one did so. This hope appears to have been borne out, with the passage of the *Victorian Charter of Rights and Responsibilities* in 2006,[5] and the consideration of proposals for bills of rights in Western Australia[6] and Tasmania.[7]

In this paper we explore the impact of the ACT HRA in one of the recent debates about Australia's anti-terrorism legislation, namely the measures introduced by the former federal government in late 2005 as part of a package agreed with the State and Territory Premiers and Chief Ministers in the aftermath of the London bombings of July 2005. The package contained, among other measures, a legislative regime for preventative detention and control orders, and a revision of existing sedition laws. These proposals were eventually enacted as the *Anti-Terrorism Act (No 2) 2005* (Cth),[8] and as a series of State and Territory enactments giving effect to the agreement between the Commonwealth and the States/Territories, with some variation among the various jurisdictions.

We first outline the role that a federal division of powers may play in providing protection for human rights though its diffusion of political power, and the limitations of this protection in a context of cooperative federalism. We then

---

[4] See J Stanhope, 'The Human Rights Act 2004 (ACT): Making a Stand in the ACT' (2005) 30 *Alternative Law Journal* 54; C Evans, 'Responsibility for Rights: the ACT Human Rights Act' (2004) 32 *Federal Law Review* 291; H Charlesworth and G McKinnon, 'Australia's First Bill of Rights: The Australian Capital Territory's Human Rights Act' *Centre for International and Public Law, Law & Policy Paper No 28* (Sydney: Federation Press, 2006).
[5] See G Williams, 'The Victorian Charter of Rights and Responsibilities: Origins and Scope' (2007) 26 *Melbourne University Law Review* 880.
[6] See *A WA Human Rights Act: Statement of Intent by the Western Australian Government* (May 2007) <http://www.humanrights.wa.gov.au/>, together with a consultation paper and draft Bill for public consultation on the same website.
[7] See Tasmanian Law Reform Institute, *A Charter of Rights for Tasmania*, Issues Paper No 11 (August 2006); Tasmanian Law Reform Institute, *A Charter of Rights for Tasmania*, Report No 10 (October 2007).
[8] See generally the 'The Anti-Terrorism Bill (No 2) 2005', *Human Rights Defender* (2005 Special Issue); A Lynch and G Williams, *What Price Security? Taking Stock of Australia's Anti-Terrorism Laws* (Sydney: UNSW Press, 2006) 41-58.

describe the process of the agreement and debates, which led to the enactment of the Commonwealth's *Anti-Terrorism Act (No 2) Act 2005*, and the process involved in drafting its ACT counterpart, the *Terrorism (Extraordinary Temporary Powers) Act 2006*. By comparing the content of critical provisions of the draft laws and their final versions, we seek to identify the impact that the express invocation of human rights standards may have had on the process. Finally, we seek to put this analysis in a broader political context, noting the other factors that influenced the debate, and assessing whether the impact of the HRA has been significant in terms of substance either on the federal legislation or in differentiating the human-rights-informed ACT legislation from the federal legislation.

## Federalism, Diffusion of Power and Protection of Human Rights

One of the benefits sometimes claimed for a federal system is that its distribution of power among different governments provides some institutional protection against the abuses of power that can easily arise when it is concentrated in a unitary government. Federal compacts generally embody a bargain over a range of issues between the political communities coming together in a federation. Such agreements are often primarily concerned with the broader interests of those entities and their communities (in the Australian context, trade interests were of particular importance), rather than seeking to protect individuals from the exercise of governmental power that infringes on human rights. Accordingly, protection of the rights of individuals is often a by-product or a subordinate feature of such arrangements. Nevertheless, the potential exists for a demarcation of powers to provide limits on what one government may do to those under its jurisdiction. The extent of protection that this actually provides will depend not just on the formal legal and constitutional arrangements, but also on the political alignment of the different governments and the extent to which they agree upon appropriate policies or the need for cooperative federalism reflected in uniform national legislation and schemes.

The trend towards the greater concentration of power in the central government in countries such as Australia — reflected in the expansive reading of Commonwealth legislative powers since Federation and the de facto power that comes from significant control over the finances of the nation[9] — also means that a federal distribution of powers may present less of an impediment to a Commonwealth government intent on pursuing particular policies than it once did. Commonwealth governments on both sides of politics have not scrupled to

---

[9] For a recent overview, see M McHugh, 'The Impact of High Court Decisions on the Governance of Australia' (Speech delivered at the Hal Wootten Lecture 2007, University of New South Wales, 23 August 2007).

use such dominance when their political and policy preferences led them in that direction.

At the same time, the federal system has also shown its potential for high levels of cooperation, in different fields and at different times — something which depends as well on the configuration of governments at national, State and Territory levels. Efforts to work towards uniform or at least consistent schemes of regulation across the country in many areas reflect the increasing integration of the national economy, and constitutional limitations on the power of the Commonwealth and the States mean that in some cases the two levels of government must work closely together to achieve the goals they share. This cooperation may take the form of uniform national legislation, a combined legislative scheme where federal legislation is supplemented by State legislation that mirrors or complements the federal legislation, or referral to the Commonwealth by the States of particular subjects of legislative power.

It has become more common for States to refer aspects of their legislative powers to the Commonwealth to allow for Australia-wide regimes in areas where Commonwealth power is piecemeal. In recent years referrals have been negotiated in relation to corporations, child custody, de facto relationships and the first raft of counter-terrorism laws. Although the Territories derive their powers of self-government from the Commonwealth rather than the Constitution (and the Commonwealth retains the power to legislate for the Territories without need for referral of powers), they have been included in the cooperative process.

There are a number of bodies in which this formal collaboration between the Commonwealth and State/Territory governments take place. Of particular importance for legal developments are the Council of Australian Governments (COAG) and the Standing Committee of Attorneys-General (SCAG). But the collaboration and debate over policy coordination takes place at many other levels as well.

This chapter looks at one particular instance of Commonwealth-State collaboration, namely the effort to enact wide-ranging amendments to anti-terrorism law, which were initiated by the Commonwealth government during 2005. The measures, which included preventative detention and control order regimes, relied upon the continuation of the referral of State powers in relation to terrorism to the Commonwealth, and the enactment of complementary State and Territory legislation. Such legislation was necessary first to apply the new provisions to State and Territory law enforcement agencies and, second, to overcome perceived constitutional limitations on the Commonwealth in relation to certain aspects of the preventative detention regime (in particular the extension of the administrative detention of a person for more than 48 hours up to a maximum of 14 days).[10] Quite apart from these legal reasons, both federal and State leaders faced the political imperative of being seen to act decisively and, when the Commonwealth was able to argue that there were credible threats that needed to be addressed, State and Territory leaders had little option but to go along with the general thrust of the proposals, since none of them could afford to be left out.

## The ACT *Human Rights Act 2004*

When the ACT *Human Rights Act* was enacted in 2004, some commentators saw it as an illustration of another advantage of a federal system, namely the opportunity for experimentation that allows the effect of an initiative to be explored in one jurisdiction without adopting it across the nation (which would in this case not have been possible in any event, due to the opposition of the former federal government to a bill of rights): a successful initiative in one jurisdiction might be taken up by other jurisdictions and, ultimately, at a national level.[11] Supporters of bills of rights also hoped that the ACT initiative would break the psychological barrier that seemed to lie in the way of efforts to adopt bills of rights in Australia; recent developments suggest that this may indeed be the case, at least insofar as the ACT legislation has provided encouragement to other States to consider adopting similar models.

Most of the discussion of the ACT HRA proposals concentrated on their likely effect on the distribution of powers among the various arms of government in the ACT, and there was relatively little discussion of the potential impact of a HRA on federal law and the law of other jurisdictions.[12] However, there was speculation that the HRA might influence federal law and the law of other States and Territories through the institutions of cooperative federalism, in particular COAG and SCAG. If the ACT Government was required to certify that any legislation it enacted as part of a cooperative scheme was compatible with the HRA, it was thought that in uniform scheme negotiations ACT representatives might be able to persuade their federal and State colleagues to adopt an explicit human rights analysis in examining any proposals and that the HRA might provide a point of leverage to ensure that cooperative schemes and legislation were more consistent with human rights standards.[13]

---

[10] See A Lynch and A Reilly, 'The Constitutional Validity of Terrorism Orders of Control and Preventative Detention' (2007) 10 *Flinders Journal of Law Reform* 105.

[11] See, eg, A Byrnes, 'The ACT Bill of Rights: its Relevance and Potential Effectiveness' (Paper presented at the State Legal Convention, Adelaide, 22-23 July 2004).

[12] See the discussion by J Stellios in 'Federal Dimensions to the ACT Human Rights Act' (2005) 47 *AIAL Forum* 33 (noting the potential impact of the HRA on various cooperative arrangements between the Commonwealth and ACT governments).

[13] In fact it does not appear that this has been the case to any great extent. For example, the negotiation of uniform defamation laws by the Standing Committee of Attorneys-General did not appear to reflect the influence of the ACT HRA. In fact in the explanatory statement to the Civil Law (Wrongs) Amendment Bill 2005 (No 2) (ACT), which introduced the new model provisions, some limitations on human rights

The process leading to the enactment of the federal *Anti-Terrorism Act (No 2) 2005* and its State and Territory counterparts provides an interesting case study of the role that federalism — cooperative or otherwise — and the existence of a bill of rights in one Australian jurisdiction can play in moderating the excesses of Commonwealth legislative proposals that make serious inroads into traditional human rights protections. The next section outlines the background to the Commonwealth's legislative proposals and the response by the ACT Government to those proposals. We then examine the way in which the explicit human rights standards contained in the ACT HRA were invoked in an effort to moderate the more excessive provisions proposed by the Commonwealth.

## The New Measures

On 8 September 2005, in the wake of the London bombings of July 2005, the former Prime Minister announced his government's intention to introduce additional anti-terrorism measures[14] and released details of the proposals for new legislation in anticipation of the coming meeting of COAG later that month.[15] At the meeting of State and Territory Premiers and Chief Ministers with the then Prime Minister, held on 27 September 2005, the participants adopted a communiqué setting out their consensus on a number of issues relating to efforts to combat terrorism. The day-long meeting included a briefing by the Directors-General of the Office of National Assessments and the Australian Security Intelligence Organisation, which appears to have had a persuasive effect on the leaders. The leaders agreed to a number of proposals to strengthen existing counter-terrorism laws, including the introduction of control orders, as well as a system of preventative detention.[16] For reasons that reflected constitutional concerns as well as the politics of cooperative federalism, it was necessary for the States to enact complementary legislation, which in some respects simply tracked the Commonwealth legislation, but in other respects would supplement it. It was also necessary for the Commonwealth to secure the consent of at least four States, and the majority of all States and Territories, to amend provisions of the *Criminal Code Act 1995* (Cth) (Criminal Code) relating to terrorism that relied in part upon a referral of powers from the States.[17]

---

are justified by reference to the federal nature of Australian government and the legitimate purpose of promoting uniform laws: 4. See further the discussion in the ACT Scrutiny Committee, *Scrutiny Report No 21* (2006) 6-19 and the ACT, *Parliamentary Debates*, Legislative Assembly, 14 February 2006, 7ff.

[14] For an overview of the background to the enactment of the *Anti-Terrorism (No 2) Act 2005* (Cth), see *Bills Digest*, No 64 2005-06, 'Anti-Terrorism (No 2) Bill 2005'.

[15] J Howard, 'Counter-Terrorism Laws Strengthened' (Press Release, 8 September 2005).

[16] Council of Australian Governments', *Communiqué, Special Meeting on Counter-Terrorism*, (27 September 2005) <http://www.coag.gov.au/meetings/270905/coag270905.pdf>.

[17] *Criminal Code Act 1995* (Cth) div 100.8.

## The Federal Anti-Terrorism Legislation

Although the State and Territory leaders were all publicly in agreement with each other at the conclusion of the meeting, it seems that the hothouse environment in which it was held may have pressured some Premiers and Chief Ministers into agreeing to broad-brush proposals to which they might not have consented if they had had further time to consider the issues. At the very least, some State and Territory leaders appeared a little discomfited (or affected to be so in the light of public criticism) when the Commonwealth provided them with the draft federal legislation, which it claimed was giving effect to the COAG agreement; others began to give the proposals more critical scrutiny once public debate took place and criticism of them began to emerge.

Following the COAG meeting, the Commonwealth provided the States and Territories with a draft of the federal legislation on a confidential basis; its intention was, it seems, to introduce a Bill into Parliament that had been cleared by the State leaders and to ensure that the Commonwealth had the numbers to pass amendments to the Criminal Code. The Commonwealth anticipated introducing the Bill into Parliament in early November, and proposed to have it enacted before Christmas, a schedule that allowed very little time for substantive review by the relevant Parliamentary Committee (the Senate Legal and Constitutional Legislation Committee).[18] It was not clear why the Commonwealth felt that there was no need for broad public consultation on the draft legislation, given its scope and the lengthy and detailed nature of the draft Bill.

The Commonwealth was frustrated in its attempt to minimise public scrutiny of the Bill by the ACT Chief Minister, Jon Stanhope. Stanhope took the view that it was important for there to be adequate public scrutiny of the Bill and earned the ire of the former Prime Minister by releasing the draft Bill[19] on his own website on 14 October 2005.[20] He also commissioned legal opinions on the consistency of the proposed Bill with Australia's international human rights obligations and with the provisions of the ACT HRA.[21]

Stanhope's motivations for the release of the Commonwealth draft doubtless included a genuine concern that legislation of this significance should receive broad-ranging public scrutiny. The decision also needs to be seen in light of what may have been his surprise at the draconian content of the draft legislation and a feeling that it had gone beyond what he understood to have been approved

---

[18] See Senate Legal and Constitutional Legislation Committee, *Report on the Provisions of the Anti-Terrorism (No 2) Bill 2005* (2005).
[19] Then known as the Anti-Terrorism Bill 2005 (Cth). Version 28 of the Bill (dated 7 October 2005) may be found at <>http://www.chiefminister.act.gov.au/docs/B05PG201_v281.pdf>.
[20] 'Howard on Attack Over Draft Bill Release', *Sydney Morning Herald* (Sydney), 15 October 2005.
[21] See the materials at <http://acthra.anu.edu.au/terrorism/index.html>.

by COAG (or that where things had been left unclear by COAG, extreme provisions were being proposed). The broader context is also important — Stanhope was one of the eight State and Territory Labor leaders opposed to a Liberal government at the federal level. Stanhope had also been critical of a number of aspects of the Howard government's human rights record.[22] The Howard government had also expressed its hostility to a number of the ACT government's human rights initiatives, even suggesting on various occasions that, notwithstanding the system of self-government given to the ACT in 1988,[23] the Commonwealth might use its plenary legislative power of the Territories under section 122 of the *Commonwealth Constitution* to override ACT legislation which it considered inappropriate (including the HRA itself),[24] something that it did do in relation to the *Civil Unions Act 2006* (ACT).[25]

Immediately after the COAG meeting, Stanhope explained the basis on which he had approached the meeting and had agreed to the Commonwealth proposals:

> I had publicly indicated and released the eight critical human rights safeguards and legal safeguards that the ACT would be seeking to achieve today, particularly in relation to preventative detention. They were a requirement that preventative detention only be applied to people reasonably suspected of having committed or being likely to commit a terrorist offence and where immediate detention was necessary to protect public safety; the Commonwealth has responded positively to that. Effective judicial oversight including the right of detainees to know the reasons for their detention and the right to appeal their detention; that's to be incorporated in the legislation. The principle that detention should be kept to the minimum period consistent with public safety; the period of detention will be determined by a judge and will be a period of

---

[22] The Stanhope government has consistently criticised aspects of the human rights record of the former Howard government, and has contrasted this with the protection of rights in the ACT under the HRA. The treatment of asylum seekers, and of Australian detainees in Guantánamo Bay were often the subject of comment in the ACT Legislative Assembly. On some issues, such as the abolition of the Aboriginal and Torres Straight Islander Commission, the Chief Minister has made specific claims that federal government actions breach the ACT HRA (see Debates of the ACT Legislative Assembly, Week 10, 23 August 2005, 3069). Such statements are, of course, rhetorical, as the *Human Rights Act* (ACT), being an ordinary statute of the ACT, has no direct application to federal laws on Indigenous issues, or on immigration or external affairs.

[23] See the *Australian Capital Territory (Self-Government) Act 1988* (Cth).

[24] In a letter to Chief Minister Jon Stanhope dated 30 January 2004, then Prime Minister John Howard stated that it was 'inherently undesirable that a Territory should act unilaterally' by adopting a bill of rights, and noted that his government would 'consider' the Human Rights Bill 2003 (ACT), together with the Sexuality Discrimination Legislation Amendment Bill 2003 (ACT) and the Parentage Bill 2003 (ACT). The Chief Minister commented that '[t]his was in reality a very thinly veiled threat to use the Commonwealth's power to interfere with the affairs of the Territory': J Stanhope, 'Stanhope Rejects Call for Federal Intervention' (Press Release, 17 February 2004).

[25] In June 2006, the federal government overrode the *Civil Unions Act 2006* (ACT), passed in May 2006, by advising the Governor-General to exercise his power to disallow ACT legislation under sub-section 35(2) of the *Australian Capital Territory (Self-Government) Act 1988* (Cth): *Commonwealth Special Gazette 2006*, No S93, 14 June 2006. See J Stanhope, 'Ruddock's Attacks on ACT Laws Hurt Us All', *Canberra Times* (Canberra), 25 July 2006.

24 hours up to 14 days. And I'm satisfied with that response. That detainees have access to their lawyer of choice; that will be incorporated in the legislation. That detainees have the right to contact their family and their employers and where relevant, their consulate; those rights will be included within the legislation. The right to humane treatment preferably in accordance with published protocols; the ICCPR and subject to independent monitoring, those are features of the legislation and the [former] Prime Minister has indicated today that the legislation will be monitored by the Ombudsman; there will be a right of appeal to the Ombudsman in relation to the decisions taken and there will be annual parliamentary oversight of the operation of the scheme.

The right to a fair trial in the event that charges are ultimately laid indicating that questioning and the continuation of a criminal investigation through questioning or interrogation would not apply during a period of detention; and that will be the case. And finally I expressed the desire for a sunset clause and that too has been agreed. From the ACT Government's point of view I did come here with significant concerns around preventative detention and whether or not it was proportionate response [sic] to the issue we faced. The Commonwealth has responded to every issue that the ACT Government put on the table and the ACT Government is supporting willingly this new approach to national counter-terrorism.[26]

The effect of Stanhope's release of the draft Bill was to initiate a vigorous public discussion of the Bill, in particular its consistency with human rights norms.[27] Stanhope took the position that, because the ACT mirror-legislation contemplated under the COAG agreement would need to be consistent with the ACT HRA, it was important for the federal legislation to be consistent with those same standards. That in itself seems unexceptionable, given that the HRA gives effect to international human rights guarantees binding on Australia by virtue of its ratification of the ICCPR and the Howard government had consistently stated its position that counter-terrorism legislation should be (and was) consistent with Australia's international obligations: though the assertion has not always been persuasive in particular cases.

Stanhope also took the opportunity to seek, and make public, advice from a number of external advisers on the human rights and constitutional implications of the Commonwealth draft Bill both before and after he publicly released the Commonwealth draft.[28] The opinions provided by a number of human rights

---

[26] COAG Joint Press Conference, Parliament House, Canberra, 27 September 2005 <http://www.pm.gov.au/media/Interview/2005/Interview1588.cfm>.
[27] See M Grattan, 'Stanhope Fires Up Debate Over Secretive Terror Laws', *Sydney Morning Herald* (Sydney), 16 October 2005.
[28] These included the ACT Human Rights Commissioner. The Chief Minister had also previously sought the advice of the ACT Human Rights Commissioner, Dr Helen Watchirs, on the human rights implications

and constitutional experts (including the present authors)[29] pointed to a number of inconsistencies between the draft Bill, and the provisions of international human rights treaties and the ACT HRA.

This initial debate — in which many others joined to voice their criticisms of the human rights impact of the Bill — was followed by a review of the Bill as introduced into the Parliament. This Bill contained significant improvements over the draft which was released by Stanhope, with new provisions allowing for merits review of preventative detention by the Administrative Appeals Tribunal, and giving persons subject to interim control orders the right to attend a court hearing to determine whether a final order should be granted, rather than the process taking place in their absence. Nevertheless, the Bill remained draconian in many aspects. The Senate inquiry received submissions and evidence from many participants, many of whom underlined human rights concerns that had already been ventilated in the earlier debate. While some amendments were made to the Bill following the inquiry, a number of provisions of the legislation as enacted still raise considerable concern on human rights grounds.

While there seems little doubt that many of the human rights concerns (based on our common law traditions and the applicable international human rights norms) would have been raised before the Senate Committee when the matter was eventually referred to it, the effect of the Stanhope release — and his invocation of the need to comply with the ACT HRA in agreeing to uniform legislation to be enacted at the Territory level — played a role in focusing attention on these issues earlier than would otherwise have been the case and gave critics of the Bill the opportunity to analyse its provisions in more depth. Since the time originally planned to be given to the legislation was very short and the actual time given was not much greater, the extra time that Stanhope's actions provided for scrutiny appears to have been valuable.[30]

What we see in this case is the use by an individual Chief Minister of the COAG process and the desire to achieve a reasonable degree of uniformity across jurisdictions, to invoke the standards of his jurisdiction in an attempt to lever up the standards of the common scheme. (This presumably occurs in other cases in cooperative federal legislative schemes.) Admittedly, the result was a piece of legislation that had been modified somewhat, but which still gave rise to a number of serious human rights concerns.

---

of the proposals announced by the Prime Minister on 8 September 2005. Copies of the opinions provided may be found at <http://acthra.anu.edu.au/terrorism/index.html>.

[29] A Byrnes, H Charlesworth and G McKinnon, 'Human Rights Implications of the Anti-Terrorism Bill 2005' (18 October 2005) <http://acthra.anu.edu.au/media/Advice%2018%20oct.pdf>.

[30] For references to public comment on the Bill, see Parliamentary Library, 'Proposals to Further Strengthen Australia's Counter-Terrorism Laws', *E-Brief* issued 6 October 2005 updated 25 November 2005 <http://www.aph.gov.au/library/intguide/LAW/TerrorismLaws.htm>.

The strategy of the Commonwealth Government involved presenting a proposal for federal legislation, which was extreme in its potential inroads on human rights, and allowing only a limited public consultation and parliamentary process in which the proponents of human rights bore the political onus of demonstrating the excesses of the draft and persuading those in positions of political power to modify them. Although the actions of Jon Stanhope undermined this strategy to some extent, the control by the Howard government of both houses of Parliament meant that once the State Premiers had agreed to the regime, the opportunity to achieve changes to the legislation through the consultation process was restricted. Nevertheless, the early debate generated by the release of the draft Bill may have given more impetus to internal critics within the Liberal-National coalition who were able to bring about some amendments through the discussions within the coalition.

## The ACT Legislation

When it came to the drafting of the ACT mirror-legislation agreed to in the COAG Agreement, the influence of the ACT HRA standards (and the prior political debate) is quite striking. The very title of the draft legislation — the Terrorism (Extraordinary Temporary Powers) Bill 2006 (ACT) — reflected the difference of approach the ACT Government wished to take, one which saw the draconian measures involved as a temporary response to an emergency situation, rather than a statute for all time.

The ACT proposals were first released as an exposure draft in late 2005,[31] underlining the Commonwealth's earlier failure to do the same with its proposals. The content of the legislation was heavily influenced by an attempt to ensure as high a level of consistency with the standards of the HRA/ICCPR as seemed possible, given that the legislation had to start with the basic scheme agreed to at COAG and reflected in the Commonwealth legislation (which had been enacted before the ACT consultation draft was released).

The ACT exposure draft introduced a much higher level of judicial involvement in and scrutiny of the procedures for making preventative detention orders ('PDOs'), for example, by providing that:

- only the Supreme Court could make PDOs, whereas the Commonwealth legislation provided that senior Australian Federal Police members could make interim PDOs;
- a statement of reasons for the making of a PDO had to be provided to the person affected (the Commonwealth legislation required a summary of the grounds for the order to be provided to the person, but this was weakened

---

[31] See <http://www.chiefminister.act.gov.au/docs/TerrorExtraTempPowers-V08%20Final.pdf>.

by an exception allowing the exclusion of information on the basis of national security concerns);
- a PDO could only be made if it were 'the least restrictive means to prevent a terrorist act or the only effective way to preserve evidence' (whereas the Commonwealth test was that it would 'substantially assist in preventing a terrorist act, or is necessary to preserve evidence');
- persons under 18 could not be subject to PDOs (in the Commonwealth legislation children 16 and over could be subject to PDOs);
- limitations on the monitoring of legal communications (there is no such restriction in the Commonwealth legislation);
- an explicit requirement for legal representation to be provided by Legal Aid (the Commonwealth legislation made no mention of this);
- a detainee would be able to tell his or her family of the fact and place of detention (under the Commonwealth legislation he or she is only able to inform family that he/she is 'safe' but 'not able to be contacted for the time being');
- there were no 'disclosure' offences concerning telling another person that someone is detained under a preventative detention order (maximum of five years' imprisonment under Commonwealth legislation); and
- the Public Interest Monitor would represent the public interest at a hearing for a PDO or prohibited contact order (Commonwealth legislation requires only that the Ombudsman be notified when a PDO or prohibited contact order is made).

Many of these changes were among those proposed by the human rights experts whom the Chief Minister had consulted during the process.[32] However, the exposure draft was not the final step in the process of seeking to ensure human rights compliance. The Chief Minister sought further advice on the question of whether the exposure draft was fully compliant with the provisions of the ACT HRA,[33] and on 15 December 2005, the exposure draft was referred to the Standing Committee on Legal Affairs of the ACT Legislative Assembly.[34]

The Standing Committee, chaired by ACT Shadow Attorney-General Bill Stefaniak, conducted an examination of the exposure draft, in the course of which it received 20 written submissions and held three days of public hearings in January and February 2006.[35] Although many witnesses gave evidence about the importance of complying with human rights, media attention focused almost exclusively on the comments of Australian Federal Police Commissioner, Mick

---

[32] See ACT, *Parliamentary Debates*, Legislative Assembly, 15 December 2006, 4932.
[33] Ibid 4932; ACT, *Parliamentary Debates*, Legislative Assembly, 30 March 2006, 826.
[34] *Parliamentary Debates*, above n 32, 4934.
[35] Standing Committee on Legal Affairs, *Report on Terrorism (Extraordinary Temporary Powers) Bill 2005 – Exposure Draft* (2006) Report 3
<http://www.legassembly.act.gov.au/downloads/reports/03AntiTerrorismReport.pdf>.

Keelty, who warned the Committee that inconsistencies between the ACT draft legislation and the federal and State legislation would place the ACT at risk of being targeted by terrorists.[36]

The Committee Report,[37] which was tabled on 28 February 2006, reflected a somewhat uneasy compromise between the diverse positions of its members. These included those of the Chair, Mr Stefaniak, who strongly endorsed the comments of Commissioner Keelty, and would have preferred that the ACT laws simply follow the New South Wales (NSW) model,[38] as well as those of Dr Deb Foskey, the Greens MLA, who did not agree that a persuasive case had been made to justify the introduction of PDOs in any form.[39] Overall, the Committee recommended several changes to the laws to bring them more closely into line with other jurisdictions, and to rectify some perceived anomalies within the Bill. One recommendation of the Committee was to lower the age at which young people could be subject to preventative detention orders, from 18 to 16 years. Surprisingly, Dr Foskey agreed with this recommendation, but on the basis that otherwise children would simply be dealt with under the harsher Commonwealth and NSW regimes.[40]

The ACT Government accepted a number of the proposed changes, although very few of those that might be regarded as regressive in human rights terms (it rejected the recommendation in relation to children) and introduced a revised Bill on 30 March 2006.[41] This was passed by the Assembly at its next sitting, on 11 May 2006, after three more days of vigorous debate.[42] The *Terrorism (Extraordinary Temporary Powers) Act 2006* commenced operation on 19 May 2006.

## Did the *Human Rights Act 2004* (ACT) Make a Difference?

There are a number of levels at which the ACT HRA as deployed by the ACT Chief Minister might have had an impact on legislative processes, in particular:

- in relation to the debate around and content of the Commonwealth proposals which were finally enacted as the *Anti-Terrorism Act (No 2) 2005;*

---

[36] See, eg, 'Canberra is Target for Terror; Soft Laws to Blame: Keelty', *Canberra Times* (Canberra), 1 February 2006.
[37] Standing Committee on Legal Affairs, above n 35.
[38] Indeed, on 29 March 2006, the day before the government introduced the Terrorism (Extraordinary Temporary Powers) Bill 2006 (Cth), Mr Stefaniak introduced his own private member's Bill, the Terrorism (Preventative Detention) Bill 2006 (ACT), which he described as essentially identical to the NSW legislation on preventative detention (the *Terrorism (Police Powers) Amendment (Preventative Detention) Act 2005* (NSW)): ACT, *Parliamentary Debates*, Legislative Assembly, 29 March 2006, 725.
[39] Standing Committee on Legal Affairs, above n 35, Additional and Dissenting Comments of Dr Deb Foskey, 121.
[40] Ibid 126.
[41] Terrorism (Extraordinary Temporary Powers) Bill 2006 (ACT).
[42] See ACT, *Parliamentary Debates*, Legislative Assembly, 9, 10, 11 May 2006.

- by influencing State legislation — in particular the NSW legislation — to diverge from the more draconian provisions of the Commonwealth proposals; and
- by influencing the content of both the ACT exposure draft of December 2005 and the Bill as finally introduced into the Legislative Assembly in 2006.

Attempting to identify the particular contribution of the ACT intervention and legislative framework to the content of the Commonwealth legislation poses methodological problems. Many of the criticisms raised in the public debate over the Anti-Terrorism Bill (No 2) 2005 (Cth) and in the submissions to and report of the Senate Legal and Constitutional Legislation Committee were similar to those made by commentators analysing the proposals in light of the ACT HRA, and it seems likely that many of those criticisms would in any event have been directed against the Commonwealth legislative proposals. This is hardly surprising, given the coincidence of the guarantees in the HRA and the international human rights instruments to which Australia is a party, and which thus are regularly invoked in human rights analyses of federal government bills and policies.

But one tangible contribution of the invocation of the imperatives of the ACT HRA was certainly the additional time that was available for the debate as a result of Jon Stanhope's decision to publish the Commonwealth's draft legislation. Given the relatively short time planned by the Government for public debate and the still short time that was eventually permitted, the additional weeks and the focus that was brought to the proposals by the opinions requested by the Chief Minister made a more intensive scrutiny of the Bill possible. This focus appears to have prompted the changes incorporated into later versions of the Bill, even if it was not reflected in the acceptance by the former federal government of the recommendations of the Senate Committee, which were informed by these human rights criticisms.

So far as the effect on the legislation of other States is concerned, it is equally difficult to identify a particular influence of the ACT intervention or the ACT HRA. What is clear is that the general discussion around the human rights implications of the Commonwealth Bill had an impact on the legislation of at least some States. For example, the NSW legislation enacted in pursuance of the COAG Agreement, the *Terrorism (Police Powers) Amendment (Preventative Detention) Act 2005* (NSW) contained a number of provisions not in the Commonwealth legislation that clearly responded to human rights concerns — although it contained others such as the extension of preventative detention from 48 hours to 14 days, which cut the other way.[43] Once again, the period of

---

[43] See the Second Reading Speech to the Terrorism (Police Powers) Amendment (Preventative Detention) Bill 2005 (NSW): NSW, *Parliamentary Debates*, Legislative Assembly 7 November 2005, 20008 (Mr Milton Orkopoulos, Minister for Aboriginal Affairs, and Minister Assisting the Premier on Citizenship).

debate generated by Stanhope's actions may have provided an opportunity for refinement of the NSW proposals, but in the absence of a detailed report on the NSW draft by a Parliamentary Committee, a more direct impact is difficult to trace.

It is in relation to the provisions of the ACT's own draft legislation that the impact of the HRA and its use by the ACT Government can be most clearly seen.[44] The ACT exposure draft of December 2005 had already taken into account a number of the criticisms from a human rights perspective made of the draft and final Commonwealth proposals and the Senate Committee's report on the Commonwealth Bill, as well as the provisions of legislation enacted by some of the other States (in particular NSW).[45] Although the Standing Committee process in some ways served as a vehicle for the then federal government and its agencies to exert pressure on the ACT to conform to the regimes of the Commonwealth and other States, very few of these recommendations were accepted by the Government in the final 2006 Bill when it was introduced into the Assembly.[46]

The ACT exposure and final draft Bills thus departed significantly from the draft and enacted Commonwealth proposals, in ways that sought to align the ACT proposals with the standards of the ACT HRA. The NSW legislation also sought to alleviate some of the problems with the federal legislation, for example, by providing that the process of granting preventative detention orders was a judicial one at all stages. However, the final ACT Bill went further than the NSW improvements, in an effort to further strengthen the human rights consistency of the ACT Bill.

## Assessment

It is clear that the existence of the ACT HRA played a significant role in the debate over the 2005-2006 anti-terrorism legislative measures. However, the mere existence of a law on the statute books does not of itself generate a particular result, and it seems that a number of factors contributed to the manner in which the process has unfolded. These include:

---

[44] A comparison of the provisions of the Commonwealth Act and the ACT Bill shows that there were a number of differences of substance between the two pieces of legislation. See the table prepared by the ACT Department of Justice and Community Service, which appears in the report of the Committee: 'Appendix 3 — Anti-Terrorism Legislation Comparative Provisions', in Standing Committee on Legal Affairs, above n 35, 132-40.

[45] The Chief Minister stated: 'The provisions in the exposure draft that relate to preventative detention have been modelled on the parts of the State bills that are considered the best in terms of human rights compatibility, constitutionality and adherence to established principles of justice. Additional safeguards, including some contained in the legislation of the other States, have also been incorporated in the exposure draft to ensure that the ACT has the best and most human rights compatible legislation. Making the bill compatible with Australia's international human rights obligations has not altered the effectiveness of the law or limited its reach. It remains consistent with the COAG agreement.' ACT, *Parliamentary Debates*, Legislative Assembly, 15 December 2006, 4932.

[46] ACT, *Parliamentary Debates*, Legislative Assembly, 30 March 2006, 822.

- the personal commitment by the ACT Chief Minister to the promotion of fundamental human rights principles and the ACT HRA in particular;
- concern about the desirability of enacting wide-ranging anti-terrorism legislation;
- the political oppositional stance of the ACT government on issues of human rights, including the bills of rights issue and the need for extraordinary anti-terrorism powers, and the political advantage that might be gained from putting the federal government under pressure on the issue;
- the requirement imposed by the ACT HRA for a 'compatibility statement' in relation to all new ACT legislation; and
- the impact of the external debate and critique of the various legislative proposals.

Although the ACT HRA appeared to have only an indirect influence on the federal legislation enacted as part of this cooperative regime, this may partly reflect the status of the ACT as a Territory. Had such human rights objections been raised by a State, the Commonwealth may have been forced to make further concessions in order to rely upon a referral of powers from the States in relation to terrorism. Under s 100.8 of the Criminal Code, the agreement of at least four States was required before the Commonwealth could make amendments to Part 5.3 of the Code (terrorism-related offences), but it would also have been open to a State to withdraw its referral of powers: a move that may have created some difficulty for the validity of the Commonwealth legislation within that State.[47] The momentum that seems to be gathering among the States towards the acceptance of bills of rights, following the example of the ACT and now Victoria, may mean that much greater pressure for human rights compliance will be brought to bear in such cooperative arrangements in the future.

At the end of the day, the ACT, like the other jurisdictions, did not escape a system of preventative detention, and its residents can be subjected to Commonwealth control orders and sedition laws, amongst other provisions. Concerns about the possibility of overreaching in exercise of the powers granted under the new legislation have been confirmed in the public mind by the handling of investigations such as that into the connections of Dr Mohamed Haneef with persons suspected to have been involved in the terrorist incidents in London and at Glasgow airport in June 2007.[48] However, the ACT HRA did lead the Territory to develop an anti-terrorism regime that offers far greater protection for human rights than its State and federal counterparts, while still

---

[47] The decision of the High Court in *Thomas v Mowbray* [2007] HCA 33 suggests that the doubts about the extent of the Commonwealth's constitutional power (at least in relation to the control order regime challenged in that case) were unfounded. The majority of the Court in that case upheld the validity of the control order regime under two heads of power, namely the powers to legislate with respect to defence and with respect to external affairs.

[48] See *Haneef v Minister for Immigration and Citizenship* [2007] FCA 1273 (21 August 2007).

apparently meeting the goals agreed by COAG. The ACT legislation thus stands as a challenge to the rhetoric of the Commonwealth that individual human rights must inevitably be sacrificed in such unusual times, to ensure the security of the community.

# Bibliography
## Books / Book Chapters

**Agamben G**, *Homo Sacer: Sovereign Power and Bare Life* (D Heller-Roasen trans of *Homo sacer: Il potere sovrano e la nuda vita*, (first published Turin: Einaudi, 1995) Stanford: Stanford University Press, 1998).

**Agamben G**, *State of Exception* (K Attell trans of *Stato di eccezione*, (first published Turin: Bollati Boringhieri, 2003) Chicago: University of Chicago Press, 2005).

**Al-Azmeh A**, *Islams and Modernities* (London: Verso, 1993).

**Aldridge A O**, *Voltaire and the Century of Light* (Princeton, NJ: Princeton University Press, 1975).

**Ali T**, *Bush in Babylon: the Recolonisation of Iraq* (London: Verso, 2004).

**Alston P** (ed), *The EU and Human Rights* (Oxford, New York: Oxford University Press, 1999).

**Andreopoulos G**, *Genocide: Conceptual and Historical Dimensions* (Philadelphia: University of Pennsylvania Press, 1994).

**Ariès P**, *The Hour of Our Death* (H Weaver trans of *L'homme devant la mort* (first published 1981) New York: Knopf: distributed by Random House, 1981).

**Arnull A**, *The European Union and its Court of Justice* (Oxford: Oxford University Press, 2nd ed 2006).

**Aust A**, 'Comment on the Presentation by Volker Röben' in C Walter (ed), *Terrorism as a Challenge for National and International Law: Security Versus Liberty* (Berlin: Springer, 2004).

**Bakan J**, *Just Words: Constitutional Rights and Social Wrongs* (Toronto: University of Toronto Press, 1997).

**Baker R W**, *Islam Without Fear: Egypt and the New Islamists* (Cambridge Massachusetts, London: Harvard University Press, 2003).

**Bar-Tal D**, 'The Masada Syndrome: A Case of Central Belief' in N Milgram (ed), *Stress and Coping in Time of War* (New York: Brunnor/Mazel, 1986).

**Benjamin D** and **Simon S**, *The Next Attack — the Globalization of Jihad* (UK: Hodder and Stoughton, 2005).

**Bergen P**, *Holy Terror, Inc.: Inside the Secret World of Osama bin Laden* (New York, Simon & Schuster, 2001).

**Besterman T**, *Voltaire* (London: Longmans, 1969).

**Bianchi A** (ed), *Enforcing International Law Norms against Terrorism* (Oxford: Hart Publishing, 2004).

**Blekxtoon R** and **van Ballegooij W** (eds), *Handbook on the European Arrest Warrant* (The Hague: TMC Asser Press, 2005).

**Bottomley S** and **Bronitt S**, *Law in Context* (Sydney: Federation Press, 3$^{rd}$ ed, 2006).

**Bottomley S** and **Corcoran S**, *Interpreting Statutes* (Sydney: Federation Press, 2005).

**Boyle K**, **Hadden T** and **Hillyard P**, *Ten Years On in Northern Ireland: The Legal Control of Political Violence* (London: Cobden Trust, 1980).

**Braithwaite J**, *Crime, Shame, and Reintegration* (Cambridge, UK; New York: Cambridge University Press, 1989).

**Bronitt S** and **McSherry B**, *Principles of Criminal Law* (Sydney: LawBook Co, 2$^{nd}$ ed, 2005).

**Bronitt S**, **Burns F** and **Kinley D**, *Principles of European Community Law* (New South Wales, Australia: Law Book Company, 1995).

**Brown O**, *EU Trade Policy and Conflict* (Winnipeg: International Institute for Sustainable Development, 2005).

**Brownlie I**, 'The Decisions of the Political Organs of the United Nations and the Rule of Law', in R St J Macdonald (ed), *Essays in Honour of Wang Tieya* (Dordrecht, Boston: Martinus Nijhoff, 1993).

**Buergenthal T**, 'To Respect and Ensure: State Obligations and Permissible Derogations' in L Henkin (ed), *The International Bill of Rights: The Covenant on Civil and Political Rights* (New York: Columbia University Press, 1981).

**Burke J**, *Al-Qaeda — the True Story of Radical Islam* (London: Penguin, 2004).

**Burke J**, *Al-Qaeda: Casting a Shadow of Terror* (London: I B Tauris, 2003).

**Butler C** (ed), *Guantanamo Bay and the Judicial–Moral Treatment of the Other* (West Lafayette, Ind: Purdue University Press: Published in cooperation with the Institute for Human Rights, Indiana University-Purdue University Fort Wayne, 2007).

**Campbell T**, **Goldsworthy J** and **Stone A** (eds), *Protecting Human Rights: Instruments and Institutions* (Oxford: Oxford University Press, 2003).

**Carlton D** and **Schaerf C** (eds), *International Terrorism and World Security* (1975).

**Cassell E J**, 'Pain and Suffering' in W T Reich (ed), *Encyclopedia of Bioethics* vol 4 (New York: Macmillan Library References USA, 1994).

**Cassell E**, *The Nature of Suffering and the Goals of Medicine* (New York: Oxford University Press, 1991).

**Cassese A**, *International Criminal Law* (Oxford: Oxford University Press, 2003).

**Cassese A**, *Terrorism, Politics, and Law* (Cambridge: Polity, 1989).

**Charlesworth H** and **McKinnon G**, 'Australia's First Bill of Rights: The Australian Capital Territory's Human Rights Act' *Centre for International and Public Law, Law & Policy Paper No 28* (Sydney: Federation Press, 2006).

**Chermak S**, **Bailey F Y** and **Brown M** (eds), *Media Images of September 11* (Westport and London: Praeger, 2003).

**Cohen N**, *What's Left? How Liberals Lost Their Way* (London: Fourth Estate, 2007).

**Conroy J**, *Unspeakable Acts, Ordinary People: The Dynamics of Torture* (London: Vision Paperbacks, 2001).

**Conte A**, *Counter-Terrorism and Human Rights in New Zealand* (Wellington: New Zealand Law Foundation, 2007).

**Cook D**, *Understanding Jihad* (Berkley, Los Angeles, London: University of California Press, 2005).

**Cook R J** (ed), *Human Rights of Women* (Pennsylvania: University of Pennsylvania Press, 1994).

**Coomans F** and **Kamminga M** (eds), *Extraterritorial Application of Human Rights Treaties* (Antwerp: Intersentia, 2004).

**Cooper R**, *The Breaking of Nations — Order and Chaos in the Twenty First Century* (London: Atlantic, 2004).

**Copelon R**, 'Intimate Terror: Understanding Domestic Violence as Torture' in R J Cook (ed), *Human Rights of Women* (Pennsylvania: University of Pennsylvania Press, 1994).

**Curtin D** and **Heukels T** (eds), *Institutional Dynamics of European Integration (Essays in Honour of Henry G. Schermers)* (Dordrecht, Boston: M Nijhoff, 1994).

**Dalacoura K**, *Islam, Liberalism and Human Rights* (London, New York: I B Tauris, 2003).

**Daniels R J**, **Macklem P**, and **Roach K** (eds), *The Security of Freedom: Essays on Canada's Anti-Terrorism Bill* (Toronto: University of Toronto Press, 2001).

**Danner M**, *Torture and Truth: America, Abu Ghraib, and the War on Terror* (London: Granta Books, 2005).

**Dashti A**, *23 Years: A Study of the Prophetic Career of Mohammad* (Costa Mesa: Mazda Publishers, 1994).

**Delpech T**, *International Terrorism and Europe* Chaillot Paper No 56, Paris: Institute for Security Studies (2002).

**Dershowitz A**, *Why Terrorism Works: Understanding the Threat, Responding to the Challenge* (New Haven: Yale University Press, 2002).

**Dixon D**, *Law in Policing: Legal Regulation and Police Practices* (Oxford, New York: Clarendon Press, 1997).

**Donohue L** 'Terrorism and Counter-Terrorist Discourse' in V Ramraj, M Hor and K Roach (eds), *Global Anti-Terrorism Law and Policy* (Cambridge, New York: Cambridge University Press, 2005).

**Donohue L K**, *Emergency Powers and Counter-Terrorist Law in the United Kingdom 1922–2000* (Dublin: Irish Academic Press, 2000).

**Douzinas C**, *The End of Human Rights* (Oxford: Hart, 2000).

**duBois P**, *Torture and Truth* (New York: Routledge, 1991).

**Duffy H**, *The 'War on Terror' and the Framework of International Law* (Cambridge; Cambridge University Press, 2005).

**Dyzenhaus D** (ed), *Law as Politics: Carl Schmitt's Critique of Liberalism* (Durham, NC: Duke University Press, 1997).

**Easteal P** (ed), *Balancing the Scales: Rape, Law Reform and Australian Culture* (Sydney: Federation Press, 1998).

**Easteal P**, 'Beyond Balancing' in P Easteal (ed), *Balancing the Scales: Rape, Law Reform and Australian Culture* (Sydney: Federation Press, 1998).

**Eissen M**, 'The Principle of Proportionality in the Case-Law of the European Court of Human Rights' in R St J Macdonald, F Matscher and H Petzold (eds), *The European System for the Protection of Human Rights* (Dordrecht, Boston: Martinus Nijhoff, 1993).

**El Fadl K A**, *Speaking in God's Name: Islamic Law, Authority and Women* (Oxford: Oneworld, 2001).

**Elsass P**, *Treating Victims of Torture and Violence: Theoretical, Cross-cultural, and Clinical Implications* (New York: New York University Press, 1997).

**Ergec R**, *Les droits de l'homme à l'épreuve des circonstances exceptionnelles: étude sur l'article 15 de la Convention européenne des droits de l'homme* (Brussels: Editions de l'Universite libre de Bruxelle, 1987).

**Erikson P et al** (eds), *Harm Reduction: A New Direction for Drug Policies and Programs* (Toronto: University of Toronto Press, 1997).

**Esack F**, *Qur'an, Liberation and Pluralism: An Islamic Perspective of Interreligious Solidarity Against Oppression* (Oxford: Oneworld, 1997).

**Esposito J J**, *Terror in the Name of Islam* (Oxford, New York: Oxford University Press, 2002).

**Falk R**, 'Human Rights: a Descending Spiral' in R A Wilson (ed), *Human Rights in the 'War on Terror'* (Cambridge: Cambridge University Press, 2005).

**Farrall J**, *United Nations Sanctions and the Rule of Law* (Cambridge: Cambridge University Press, 2007).

**Fawkner P** (ed), *A Fair Go in an Age of Terror* (Victoria: David Lovell Publishing, 2004).

**Fitzpatrick J**, *Human Rights in Crisis: the International System for Protecting Rights During States of Emergency* (Philadelphia: University of Pennsylvania Press, 1994).

**Foucault M**, *Discipline and Punish: the Birth of the Prison* (trans A Sheridan) (NY: Pantheon Books, 1977).

**Freeman M**, 'Order, Rights, and Threats: Terrorism and Global Justice' in R A Wilson (ed), *Human Rights in the 'War on Terror'* (Cambridge: Cambridge University Press, 2005).

**Frowein J A** and **Peukert W**, *Kommentar – Europäische Menschenrechtskonvention* (2$^{nd}$ ed, 1996).

**Fuller L L**, *The Morality of Law* (New Haven: Yale U P, revised ed, 1969).

**Gani M**, 'Codifying the Criminal Law: Issues of Interpretation' in S Bottomley and S Corcoran, *Interpreting Statutes* (Sydney: Federation Press, 2005).

**Gani M**, 'Upping the Ante in the "War on Terror"' in P Fawkner (ed), *A Fair Go in an Age of Terror* (Victoria: David Lovell Publishing, 2004).

**Gearty C**, *Terror* (London: Faber and Faber, 1991).

**Gearty C**, *Can Human Rights Survive?* (Cambridge: Cambridge University Press, 2006).

**Gearty C**, *Principles of Human Rights Adjudication* (Oxford: Oxford University Press, 2004).

**Geyer F**, 'The European Arrest Warrant in Germany: Constitutional Mistrust Towards the Concept of Mutual Trust' in E Guild (ed), *Constitutional Challenges to the European Arrest Warrant* (Nijmegen: Wolf Publishers, 2006).

**Glendon M**, *Rights Talk: The Impoverishment of Political Discourse* (New York: Maxwell Macmillan, 1990).

**Goldsmith J**, *The Terror Presidency: Law and Judgment Inside the Bush Administration* (New York and London: W W Norton & Co, 2007).

Goold B and Lazarus L (eds) *Security and Human Rights* (Oxford: Hart Publishing, 2007).

Gowlland-Debbas V (ed), *United Nations Sanctions and International Law* (The Netherlands: Kluwer Law International, 2001).

Greenberg K (ed), *Al Qaeda Now: Understanding Today's Terrorists* (Cambridge: Cambridge University Press, 2005).

Greenberg K and Dratel J (eds), *The Torture Papers: The Road to Abu Ghraib* (New York: Cambridge University Press, 2005).

Grey S, *Ghost Plane: the True Story of the CIA Torture Program* (New York: St Martin's Press, 2006).

Gross O and Ní Aoláin F, *Law in Times of Crisis: Emergency Powers in Theory and Practice* (Cambridge: Cambridge University Press, 2006).

Guild E (ed), *Constitutional Challenges to the European Arrest Warrant* (Nijmegen: Wolf Publishers, 2006).

Guild E and Carrera S, 'No Constitutional Treaty? Implications for the Area of Freedom, Security and Justice' (CEPS Working Document No 231, Centre for European Policy Studies, Brussels, 2005).

Gutter J, *Thematic Procedures of the United Nations Commission on Human Rights and International Law: In Search of a Sense of Community* (Antwerp: Intersentia, 2006).

Hallaq W H B, *A History of Islamic Legal Theories* (Cambridge: Cambridge University Press, 1997).

Halliday F, *Islam and the Myth of Confrontation: Religion and Politics in the Middle East* (London, New York: I B Tauris, 1996).

Hamilton M et al (eds), *Drug Use in Australia: A Harm Minimisation Approach* (Melbourne: Oxford University Press, 1998).

Harlow C, 'Access to Justice as a Human Right: The European Convention and the European Union' in P Alston (ed), *The EU and Human Rights* (Oxford, New York: Oxford University Press, 1999).

Harris D J, O'Boyle M and Warbrick C, *Law of the European Convention on Human Rights* (London: Butterworths, 1995).

Hay D, 'Property, Authority and the Criminal Law' in D Hay et al, *Albion's Fatal Tree* (London: Allen Lane, 1975).

Henkin L (ed), *The International Bill of Rights: The Covenant on Civil and Political Rights* (New York: Columbia University Press, 1981).

Herrick J, *Against the Faith: Essays on Deists, Skeptics, and Atheists* (Buffalo, NY: Prometheus Books, 1985, ch 3: Voltaire: *Écrasez l'infâme*, 56).

**Hocking J**, *Terror Laws — ASIO, Counter-terrorism and the Threat to Democracy* (Sydney: UNSW Press, 2004).

**Hogan G** and **Walker C**, *Political Violence and the Law in Ireland* (Manchester: Manchester University Press, 1989).

**Hogg R** and **Brown >D**, *Rethinking Law and Order* (Sydney: Pluto Press, 1998).

**Honderich T**, *Humanity, Terrorism, Terrorist War: Palestine, 9/11, 7/7* (London, New York: Continuum Books, 2006).

**Hope R M**, *Protective Security Review* (Canberra: Commonwealth of Australia, 1979).

**Hroub K**, *Hamas — A Beginner's Guide* (London: Pluto Press, 2006).

**Human Rights Watch**, *The Security Council's Counter-Terrorism Effort* (10 August 2004).

**Husain E**, *The Islamist: Why I Joined Radical Islam in Britain, What I Saw Inside and Why I Left* (London: Penguin Books, 2007).

**Hussein N**, *The Jurisprudence of Emergency: Colonialism and the Rule of Law* (Ann Arbor, MA: University of Michigan Press, 2003).

**Ignatieff M**, *The Lesser Evil — Political Ethics in an Age of Terror*, (Edinburgh: Edinburgh University Press, 2005).

**Ingles K S**, 'Bean, Charles Edwin Woodrow (1879-1968)', *Australian Dictionary of Biography vol 7* (1979).

**Jacobs F G**, 'European Community Law and the European Convention on Human Rights' in D Curtin and T Heukels (eds), *Institutional Dynamics of European Integration (Essays in Honour of Henry G. Schermers)* (Dordrecht, Boston: M Nijhoff, 1994).

**Joseph S**, **Schultz J** and **Castan M**, *The International Covenant on Civil and Political Rights, Cases and Commentary* (Oxford: Oxford University Press, 2$^{nd}$ ed, 2004).

**Kepel G**, *Jihad, The Trail of Political Islam* (London: I B Tauris, 2006).

**Khadduri M** (ed), *Al-Shafi'i's Risala: Treatise on the Foundation of Islamic Jurisprudence* (Cambridge: Islamic Texts Society, 1987).

**Khadduri M**, *The Islamic Law of Nations: Shaybani's Siyar* (Baltimore: The Johns Hopkins Press, 1966).

**Lawrence B**, *Messages to the World — the Statements of Osama bin Laden* (US: Verso, 2005).

**Leigh L**, 'The Right to a Fair Trial and the European Convention on Human Rights' in D Weissbrodt and R Wolfrum (eds), *The Right to a Fair Trial* (Berlin, New York: Springer, 1997).

**Levinas E**, *Otherwise Than Being* (A Lingis trans of *Autrement qu'être* (2$^{nd}$ ed, 1978) Hague; Boston: M Nijhoff; Hingham, MA: Distributors for the US and Canada, Kluwer Boston, 1981).

**Levinas E**, *Totality and Infinity* (A Lingis trans of *Totalite et infin* (first published 1961, Pittsburgh: Duquesne University, 1969).

**Loader I** and **Walker N**, *Civilising Security* (Cambridge: Cambridge University Press, 2007).

**Loveland I** (ed), *Frontiers of Criminality* (London: Sweet & Maxwell, 1995).

**Luban D**, 'Eight Fallacies About Liberty and Security' in R A Wilson (ed), *Human Rights in the 'War on Terror'* (Cambridge: Cambridge University Press, 2005).

**Lynch A** and **Williams G**, *What Price Security? Taking Stock of Australia's Anti-Terrorism Laws* (Sydney: UNSW Press, 2006).

**MacDonald R St J** (ed), *Essays in Honour of Wang Tieya* (Dordrecht, Boston: Martinus Nijhoff, 1993).

**Macdonald R St J**, 'The Margin of Appreciation' in R St J Macdonald, F Matscher and H Petzold (eds), *The European System for the Protection of Human Rights* (Dordrecht, Boston: Martinus Nijhoff, 1993).

**Macdonald R St J**, **Matscher F** and **Petzold H** (eds), *The European System for the Protection of Human Rights* (Dordrecht, Boston: Martinus Nijhoff, 1993).

**Macovei M**, *The Right To Liberty and Security of the Person*, Human Rights Handbooks, No 5 (Strasbourg: Council of Europe, 2002).

**Manderson D**, *From Mr Sin to Mr Big: A History of Australian Drug Laws* (Melbourne: Oxford University Press, 1993).

**Manderson D**, *Proximity, Levinas and the Soul of Law* (Montreal; Ithaca: McGill–Queen's University Press, 2006).

**Margulies J**, *Guantánamo and the Abuse of Presidential Power* (New York: Simon & Schuster, 2006).

**Martin R I**, *The Most Dangerous Branch: How the Supreme Court of Canada Has Undermined Our Law and Our Democracy* (Montreal: McGill-Queen's University Press, 2005).

Mathew P, 'Resolution 1373 — a Call to Preempt Asylum Seekers? (or, "Osama the Asylum Seeker")', in J McAdam (ed), *Forced Migration, Human Rights and Security* (Oxford: Hart Publishing, 2008).

McAdam J (ed), *Forced Migration, Human Rights and Security* (Oxford: Hart Publishing 2008).

McCormick J P, 'The Dilemmas of Dictatorship: Carl Schmitt and Constitutional Emergency Powers', in D Dyzenhaus (ed), *Law as Politics: Carl Schmitt's Critique of Liberalism* (Durham, NC: Duke University Press, 1997).

McEvoy K, *Paramilitary Imprisonment in Northern Ireland: Resistance, Management, and Release* (Oxford: Oxford University Press, 2001).

McNamara L, *Human Rights Controversies: The Impact of Legal Form* (Abingdon & New York: Routledge-Cavendish, 2007).

McWhinney E, *Aerial Piracy and International Terrorism* (Dordrecht, Boston: Martinus Nijhoff, 1987).

Merrills J G, *The Development of International Law by the European Court of Human Rights* (Manchester, New York: Manchester University Press, 1988).

Miles S, *Oath Betrayed: Torture, Medical Complicity and the War on Terror* (New York: Random House, 2006).

Milgram N (ed), *Stress and Coping in Time of War* (New York: Brunnor/Mazel, 1986).

Mill J S, *Utilitarianism* (G Sher (ed), Indianapolis: Hackett, 2001, original work published 1861).

Mishal S and Sela A, *The Palestinian Hamas: Vision, Violence and Coexistence* (New York: Columbia University Press, 2006).

Morton F L and Knopff R, *The Charter Revolution and the Court Party* (Peterborough, Ontario: Broadview Press, 2000).

Moussalli A S, *The Islamic Quest for Democracy, Pluralism and Human Rights* (Gainesville: University Press of Florida, 2001).

Ní Aoláin F, *The Politics of Force: Conflict Management and State Violence in Northern Ireland* (Belfast: Blackstaff Press, 2000).

Nolan M A and Oakes P J, 'Human Rights Concepts in Australian Political Debate' in T Campbell, J Goldsworthy and A Stone (eds), *Protecting Human Rights: Instruments and Institutions* (Oxford: Oxford University Press, 2003).

**Nolan M A**, *Construals of Human Rights Law: Protecting Subgroups as well as Individual Humans* (unpublished doctoral thesis, the Australian National University, 2003).

**Nowak M**, *UN Covenant on Civil and Political Rights: CCPR Commentary*, 1st ed, (Strasbourg: NP Engel, 1993).

**Nussbaum M**, *Hiding from Humanity: Disgust, Shame and the Law* (Princeton, NJ: Princeton University Press, 2004).

**O'Leary B** and **McGarry J**, *The Politics of Antagonism: Understanding Northern Ireland* (London: Athlone Press, 1997).

**O'Neill N**, **Rice S** and **Douglas R**, *Retreat from Injustice: Human Rights in Australia* (Sydney: Federation Press, 2nd ed, 2004).

**Packer H**, *The Limits of the Criminal Sanction* (Stanford, Cal: Stanford University Press, 1968).

**Paglen T** and **Thompson A C**, *Torture Taxi: On the Trail of the CIA's Rendition Flights* (Hoboken, NJ: Melville House, 2006).

**Pearson R**, *Voltaire Almighty: A Life in Pursuit of Freedom* (London: Bloomsbury, 2005).

**Pipes D**, *The Path of God: Islam and Political Power* (New Brunswick and London: Transaction Publishers, 2003).

**Posner R**, *Not a Suicide Pact: The Constitution in Times of Emergency* (New York: Oxford University Press, 2006).

**Qutb S**, *Milestones* (Dehli: Markazi Maktaba Islami, first published 1964, 1991 ed).

**Rahnema A** (ed), *Pioneers of Islamic Revival* (London: Zed Press, 1994).

**Ramraj V**, **Hor M** and **Roach K** (eds), *Global Anti-Terrorism Law and Policy* (Cambridge, New York: Cambridge University Press, 2005).

**Rawls J**, *A Theory of Justice* (Oxford: Oxford University Press, 1971).

**Redman B R** (ed), *The Portable Voltaire* (New York: Viking Press 1949 ed).

**Rees W**, *Transatlantic-Counter Terrorism Cooperation: The New Imperative* (Abingdon/New York: Routledge, 2006).

**Reich W T** (ed), *Encyclopedia of Bioethics* vol 4 (New York: Macmillan Library References USA, 1994).

**Reinisch A**, 'The Action of the European Union to Combat International Terrorism' in A Bianchi (ed), *Enforcing International Law Norms against Terrorism* (Oxford: Hart Publishing, 2004).

**Ribeiro M**, *Limiting Arbitrary Power* (Vancouver: UBC Press, 2004).

Roach K, *September 11: Consequences for Canada* (Montreal, Quebec & Kingston, Ontario: McGill-Queen's University Press, 2003).

Robertson G, 'Fair Trials for Terrorists' in R A Wilson (ed), *Human Rights in the 'War on Terror'* (Cambridge: Cambridge University Press, 2005).

Robertson G, *The Tyrannicide Brief* (London: Chatto & Windus, 2005).

Robinson M, 'Connecting Human Rights, Development and Human Security' in R A Wilson (ed), *Human Rights in the 'War on Terror'* (Cambridge: Cambridge University Press, 2005).

Ronzitti N (ed), *Maritime Terrorism and International Law* (1990).

Rosen S and Frank R, 'Measures against International Terrorism', in D Carlton and C Schaerf (eds), *International Terrorism and World Security* (1975).

Rudolf B, *Die thematischne Berichterstatter und Arbeitsgruppen der UN-Menschenrechskommission – Ihr Beitrag zur Fortentwicklung des internationalen Menschenrechtsschutzes* (Berlin: Springer, 2000).

Rushd I, *The Distinguished Jurist's Primer*, (I A K Nyaze trans, Reading: Garnet, 1994) vol 1, 454–78 [trans of: *Bidayat al-Mujtiahid*].

Sacerdoti G, 'States' Agreements with Terrorists in Order to Save Hostages: Non-Binding, Void or Justified by Necessity?' in N Ronzitti (ed), *Maritime Terrorism and International Law* (1990).

Said E W, *Culture and Imperialism* (London: Chatto and Windus, 1993).

Said E W, *Orientalism: Western Conceptions of the Orient* (London: Routledge and Kegan Paul, 1978).

Sajo A (ed), *Militant Democracy* (Amsterdam: Eleven International Publishing, 2004).

Saul B, *Defining Terrorism in International Law* (Oxford: Oxford University Press, 2006).

Scarry E, *The Body in Pain: The Making and Unmaking of the World* (New York: Oxford University Press, 1987 ed) .

Schabas W, *An Introduction to the International Criminal Court* (Cambridge: Cambridge University Press, 2002).

Schmitt C, *Legality and Legitimacy* [1932], trans Jeffrey Seitzer (Durham, NC: Duke University Press, 2003).

Singer P, *Practical Ethics* (Cambridge: Cambridge University Press, 1993).

Smith M (ed), *Human Rights 2005 – The Year in Review* (Melbourne: Castan Centre for Human Rights, 2006).

**Steiner J**, **Woods L** and **Twigg-Flesner C**, *EU Law* (Oxford: Oxford University Press, 9th ed, 2006).

**Strawson J** (ed), *Law after Ground Zero* (London: Routledge-Cavendish, 2002).

**Strawson J**, 'Holy War in the Media: Images of Jihad' in S Chermak, F Y Bailey, and M Brown (eds), *Media Images of September 11* (Westport and London: Praeger, 2003).

**Strawson J**, 'Islamic Law and the English Press', in J Strawson (ed), *Law after Ground Zero* (London: Routledge-Cavendish, 2002).

**Sunstein C**, *Laws of Fear: Beyond the Precautionary Principle* (Cambridge: Cambridge University Press, 2005).

**Svensson-McCarthy A-L**, *The International Law of Human Rights and States of Exception: With Special Reference to the "Travaux Préparatoires" and Case Law of the International Monitoring Organs* (The Hague, Boston: Martinus Nijhoff, 1998).

**Swift J**, 'A Modest Proposal' (1729) in *A Modest Proposal and Other Satires* (Amherst, MA: Prometheus Books, 1994).

**Touzé S**, *La Protection des Droits des Nationaux à l'Étranger – Recherches sur la Protection Diplomatique*, PhD thesis, University of Paris II Panthéon-Assas (2006).

**Tyler T**, *Why People Obey the Law* (New Haven: Yale University Press, 1990).

**Van Dijk P et al** (ed), *Theory and Practice of the European Convention on Human Rights* (Deventer, London: Kluwer Law and Taxation, 4th ed, 2006).

**Vennemann N**, 'Country Report on the European Union' in C Walter et al (ed), *Terrorism as a Challenge for National and International Law: Security versus Liberty?* (Berlin, London, New York: Springer, 2004).

**Viswanathan G** (ed), *Power, Politics and Culture: Interviews with Edward Said* (New York: Vintage, 2001).

**Voltaire**, *Questions sur les Miracles* (1765) (Louis Moland (ed), *OEuvres complètes de Voltaire*, Paris: Garnier, 1877–1885, tome 25 (357-450)).

**Von Clausewitz C**, *On War* (UK: Penguin Classics, first published 1832, 1982).

**Waldron J** (ed), *'Nonsense upon Stilts', Bentham, Burke and the Rights of Man* (London, New York: Methuen, 1987).

**Walker C**, *The Prevention of Terrorism in British Law* (2nd ed) (Manchester: Manchester University Press, 1992).

**Walsh D**, *The Use and Abuse of Emergency Legislation in Northern Ireland* (London: Cobden Trust, 1983).

Walter C (ed), *Terrorism as a Challenge for National and International Law: Security Versus Liberty* (Berlin: Springer, 2004).

Walter C et al (ed), *Terrorism as a Challenge for National and International Law: Security versus Liberty?* (Berlin, London, New York: Springer, 2004).

Weatherburn D, *Law and Order in Australia: Rhetoric and Reality* (Sydney: Federation Press, 2004).

Weissbrodt D and Wolfrum R (eds), *The Right to a Fair Trial* (Berlin, New York: Springer, 1997.

White T H, *The Making of the President, 1960* (New York: Atheneum Publishers, 1961).

Williams B, *Ethics and the Limits of Philosophy* (Cambridge, Mass: Harvard University Press, 1985).

Williams G, *A Bill of Rights for Australia* (Sydney: UNSW Press, 2000).

Williams G, *A Charter of Rights for Australia* (Sydney: UNSW Press, 2007).

Williams G, *The Case For An Australian Bill of Rights: Freedom in the War on Terror* (Sydney: UNSW Press, 2004).

Wilson R A (ed), *Human Rights in the 'War on Terror'* (Cambridge: Cambridge University Press, 2005).

Wodak A and Moore T, *Modernising Australia's Drug Policy* (Sydney: UNSW Press, 2002).

Wodak A and Owens R, *Drug Prohibition: A Call for Change* (Sydney: UNSW Press, 1996).

Yoo J, *War By Other Means* (New York: Atlantic Monthly Press, 2006).

Zawati H M, *Is Jihad a Just War? War Peace, and Human Rights under Islamic and Public International Law* (Lewiston, Queenston, Lampeter: The Edwin Mellen Press, 2001).

Zedner L, 'Seeking Security by Eroding Rights: The Side-Stepping of Due Process' in B Goold and L Lazarus (eds), *Security and Human Rights* (Oxford: Hart Publishing, 2007).

Zedner L, 'Seeking Security by Eroding Rights: The Side-Stepping of Due Process' in B Goold and L Lazarus (eds) *Security and Human Rights* (Oxford: Hart Publishing, 2007).

Zubaida S, *Law and Power in the Islamic World* (London: I B Tauris, 2003).

## Journal Articles

Ahmed T and de Jesús Butler I, 'The European Union and Human Rights: An International Law Perspective' (2006) *European Journal of International Law* 771.

Arbour L, 'In Our Name and on Our Behalf' (2006) 4 *European Human Rights Law Review* 371.

Ashworth A, 'Crime, Community and Creeping Consequentialism' [1996] 43 *Criminal Law Review* 220.

Ashworth A, 'What Have Human Rights Done for Criminal Justice in the UK?' (2004) 23 *University of Tasmania Law Review* 151.

**Australian Human Rights Centre**, 'The Anti-Terrorism Bill (No 2) 2005' *Human Rights Defender* (2005 Special Issue).

Bagaric M and Clarke J, 'Not Enough Official Torture in the World? The Circumstances in Which Torture is Morally Justifiable' (2005) 39(3) *University of San Francisco Law Review* 1.

Bagaric M and Clarke J, 'Not Enough Official Torture in the World? The Circumstances in which Torture is Morally Justifiable' (2005) 39 *University of San Francisco Law Review* 3.

Bakker C, 'A Full Stop to Amnesty in Argentina' (2005) 3 *Journal of International Criminal Justice* 1106.

Balassa B, 'Towards a Theory of Economic Integration' (1961) 14(1) *Kyklos* 1.

Balzaq T, Bigo D, Carerra S and Guild E, *Security and the Two-Level Game: The Treaty of Prüm, the EU and the Management of Threats* (CEPS Working Paper No 234, Centre for European Policy Studies, Brussels, 2006).

Barnes T, 'Star Chamber Mythology' (1961) 5(2) *American Journal of Legal History* 1.

Barnum D, 'Indirect Incitement and Freedom of Speech in Anglo-American Law' [2006] *European Human Rights Law Review* 258.

Bar-Tal D and Antebi D, 'Beliefs about Negative Intentions of the World: A Study of the Israeli Siege Mentality' (1992) 13(4) *Political Psychology* 633.

Bar-Tal D and Antebi D, 'Siege Mentality in Israel' (1992) 16(3) *International Journal of Intercultural Relations* 251.

Bianchi A, 'Assessing the Effectiveness of the UN Security Council's Anti-Terrorism Measures: The Quest for Legitimacy and Cohesion' (2006) 17 *European Journal of International Law* 881.

**Bianchi A**, 'Security Council's Anti-terror Resolutions and their Implementation by Member States: An Overview' (2006) 4 *Journal of International Criminal Justice* 1044.

**Bilder R B** and **Vagts D F**, 'Speaking Law to Power: Lawyers and Torture' (2004) 98 *American Journal of International Law* 689.

**Bohlander M**, 'In Extremis – Hijacked Airplanes, "Collateral Damage" and the Limits of Criminal Law' [2006] *Criminal Law Review* 579.

**Bohr S**, 'Sanctions by the UN Security Council and the EC' (1993) 4 *European Journal of International Law* 256.

**Bonner D**, 'Checking the Executive? Detention without Trial, Control Orders, Due Process and Human Rights' (2006) 12 *European Public Law* 45.

**Bowring B** and **Korff D**, 'Terrorist Designation with Regard to European and International Law: The Case of the PMOI', (Paper presented at the International Conference of Jurists in Paris, 10 November 2004) 30 (2005) *Statewatch* online.

**Braithwaite J**, 'Crime in A Convict Republic' [2001] 64(1) *Modern Law Review* 11.

**Brighton S**, 'British Muslims, Multiculturalism and UK Foreign Policy: "Integration" and "Cohesion" in and beyond the State' (2007) 83(1) *International Affairs* 1.

**Bronitt S** and **Stellios J**, 'Regulating Telecommunications Interception and Access in the Twenty-First Century: Technological Evolution or Legal Revolution?' (2006) 24(4) *Prometheus* 413.

**Bronitt S** and **Stellios J**, 'Sedition, Security and Human Rights: 'Unbalanced' Law Reform in the "War on Terror"' (2006) 30(3) *Melbourne University Law Review* 923.

**Bronitt S** and **Stephens D**, '"Flying Under the Radar" — The Use of Lethal Force Against Hijacked Aircraft: Recent Australian Developments' (2007) 7(2) *Oxford University Commonwealth Law Review* 265.

**Bronitt S**, 'Constitutional Rhetoric v Criminal Justice Realities: Unbalanced Responses to Terrorism?' (2003) 14 *Public Law Review* 76.

**Bronitt S**, 'Electronic Surveillance, Human Rights and Criminal Justice' (1997) 3(2) *Australian Journal of Human Rights* 183.

**Burke J**, 'Think Again: Al Qaeda' (2004) 142 *Foreign Policy* 18.

**Burke-White W**, 'Reframing Impunity: Applying Liberal International Law Theory to an Analysis of Amnesty Legislation' (2001) 42 *Harvard International Law Journal* 467.

**Cameron I**, 'European Union Anti-Terrorist Blacklisting' (2003) 3 *Human Rights Law Review* 225.

**Campbell C** and **Connolly I**, 'Making War on Terror? Global Lessons from Northern Ireland' (2006) 69(6) *Modern Law Review* 935.

**Canor I**, 'Can Two Walk Together, except they Be Agreed? The Relationship between International Law and European Law: The Incorporation of UN Sanctions against Yugoslavia into European Community Law through the Perspective of the ECJ' (1998) 35 *Common Market Law Review* 137.

**Carne G**, 'Brigitte and the French Connection: Security Carte Blanche or A La Carte' (2004) 9(2) *Deakin Law Review* 604.

**Carne G**, 'Reconstituting "Human Security" in a New Security Environment: One Australian, Two Canadians and Article 3 of the Universal Declaration of Human Rights' (2006) 25 *Australian Year Book of International Law* 1.

**Cassel D**, 'Lessons From the Americas: Guidelines for International Response to Amnesties for Atrocities' (1996) 59 *Law and Contemporary Problems* 197.

**Cavanaugh K**, 'Policing the Margins: Rights Protection and the European Court of Human Rights' (2006) 4 *European Human Rights Law Review* 422.

**Charlesworth H**, 'The Australian Reluctance about Rights' (1993) 30 *Osgoode Hall Law Journal* 195.

**Cole D**, 'Judging the Next Emergency: Judicial Review and Individual Rights in Time of Crisis' (2003) 101 *Michigan Law Review* 2565.

**Cole D**, 'The Priority of Morality: The Emergency Constitution's Blind Spot' (2004) 113 *Yale Law Journal* 1753.

**Conforti B**, 'Decisioni del Consiglio di sicurezza e diritti fondamentali in una bizzarra sentenza del Tribunale comunitario di primo grado' (2006) 11 *Il Diritto dell'Unione Europea* 333.

**Conforti B**, 'The Activities of National Judges and the International Relations of their State' (1993) 65 *Annuaire de l'Institut de Droit International* I.

**Crenshaw M**, 'The Psychology of Terrorism: An Agenda for the 21$^{st}$ Century' (2000) 21 *Political Psychology* 405.

**Davis F**, 'Internment Without Trial; The Lessons from the United States, Northern Ireland & Israel' (August 2004), available at SSRN online.

**de Wet E**, 'Human Rights Limitations to Economic Enforcement Measures Under Article 41 of the United Nations Charter and the Iraqi Sanctions Regime' (2001) 14 *Leiden Journal of International Law* 277.

de Wet E and Nollkaemper A, 'Review of Security Council Resolutions by National Courts' (2002) 45 *German Yearbook of International Law* 166.

Dershowitz A, 'The Torture Warrant: A response to Professor Strauss' (2004) 48 *New York Law School Review* 275.

Dickson B, 'Law Versus Terrorism: Can Law Win?' [2005] *European Human Rights Law Review* 11.

Doehring K, 'Unlawful Resolutions of the Security Council and their Legal Consequences' (1997) 1 *Max Planck Yearbook of United Nations Law* 91.

Donohue L K, 'Regulating Northern Ireland: The Special Powers Acts, 1922–1972' (1998) 41(4) *Historical Journal* 1089.

Doran M, 'Somebody Else's Civil War' (2002) 81(1) *Foreign Affairs* 22.

Dorling K, 'An Exceptional Situation? A Comparative Assessment of Anti-Terrorism Arrest and Detention Powers in the UK and Spain and of their Compliance with the European Convention on Human Rights' (2007) 4(1) *Essex Human Rights Review* 1.

Dugard J, 'Dealing with Crimes of a Past Regime: Is Amnesty still an Option?' (2000) 12 *Leiden Journal of International Law* 1001.

Dugard J, 'Diplomatic Protection and Human Rights: The Draft Articles of the International Law Commission' (2005) 24 *Australian Year Book of International Law* 75.

Dumitriu E, 'The E.U.'s Definition of Terrorism: The Council Framework Decision on Combating Terrorism' (2004) 5 *German Law Journal* 585.

Dyzenhaus D, 'Intimations of Legality Amid the Clash of Arms' (2004) 2(2) *International Journal of Comparative Constitutional Law* 244.

Emsley C, 'Repression, "Terror" and the Rule of Law in England during the Decade of the French Revolution' (1985) 100 *English Historical Review* 801.

Evans C, 'Legislative Scrutiny Committees and Parliamentary Conceptions of Human Rights' (2006) *Public Law* 785.

Evans C, 'Responsibility for Rights: the ACT Human Rights Act' (2004) 32 *Federal Law Review* 291.

Ewing K D, 'The Futility of the Human Rights Act' [2004] *Public Law* 829.

Farer T J, 'The Two Faces of Terror' (2007) 101 *American Journal of International Law* 363.

Feldman D, 'Deprivation of Liberty in Anti-Terrorism Law' (2008) 67(1) *Cambridge Law Journal* 4.

**Feldman D**, 'Human Rights, Terrorism and Risk: The Roles of Politicians and Judges' (2006) *Public Law* 364.

**Fenwick H**, 'The Anti-Terrorism, Crime and Security Act 2001: A Proportionate Response to September 11?' (2002) 65 *Modern Law Review* 724.

**Fitzpatrick J**, 'Speaking Law to Power: The War Against Terrorism and Human Rights' (2003) 14 *European Journal of International Law* 241.

**Flynn E J**, 'The Security Council's Counter-Terrorism Committee and Human Rights' (2007) 7 *Human Rights Law Review* 371.

**Foot R**, 'Human Rights and Counterterrorism in Global Governance: Reputation and Resistance' (2005) 11 *Global Governance* 291.

**Foot R**, 'The United Nations, Counter Terrorism and Human Rights: Institutional Adaptation and Embedded Ideas' (2007) 29 *Human Rights Quarterly* 489.

**Forsyth C**, 'Control Orders, Conditions Precedent and Compliance with Article 6(1)' (2008) 67(1) *Cambridge Law Journal* 1.

**Franck T** and **Niedermeyer D**, 'Accommodating Terrorism: An Offence against the Law of Nations' (1989) 19 *Israeli Yearbook on Human Rights* 75.

**Franck T M**, 'Criminals, Combatants, or What? An Examination of the Role of Law in Responding to the Threat of Terror' (2004) 98 *American Journal of International Law* 686.

**Fuller L**, 'The Case of the Speluncean Explorers' (1949) 62 *Harvard Law Review* 616.

**Gani M** and **Urbas G**, 'Alert or Alarmed? Recent Legislative Reforms Directed at Terrorist Organisations and Persons Supporting or Assisting Terrorist Acts' (2004) 8(1) *Newcastle Law Review* 23.

**Garapon A**, 'Three Challenges for International Criminal Justice' (2004) 2 *Journal of International Criminal Justice* 716.

**Gavron J**, 'Amnesties in the Light of Developments in International Law and the Establishment of the International Criminal Court' (2002) 51 *International and Comparative Law Quarterly* 91.

**Gearty C**, 'Human Rights in an Age of Counter-Terrorism: Injurious, Irrelevant or Indispensable?' (2005) 58 *Current Legal Problems* 25.

**Gearty C**, 'Rethinking Civil Liberties in a Counter-Terrorism World' (2007) 2 *European Human Rights Law Review* 111.

**Gearty C**, 'Terrorism and Human Rights: A Case Study in Impending Legal Realities' (1999) 19 *Legal Studies* 367.

**Gearty C**, 'Terrorism and Morality' [2003] *European Human Rights Law Review* 377.

Gianelli A, 'Il rapporto tra diritto internazionale e diritto comunitario secondo il Tribunale di primo grado delle Comunità Europee' (2006) 89 *Rivista di diritto internazionale* 131.

Golder B and Williams G, 'What is "Terrorism"? Problems of Legal Definition' (2004) 27 *University of New South Wales Law Journal* 270.

Goldstone R, 'Past Human Rights Violations: Truth Commissions and Amnesties or Prosecutions' (2000) 51 *Northern Ireland Legal Quarterly* 164.

Gooding G, 'Fighting Terrorism in the 1980s: The Interception of the Achille Lauro Hijackers' (1987) 12 *Yale Journal of International Law* 158.

Gross O and Ní Aoláin F, 'From Discretion to Scrutiny: Revisiting the Application of the Margin of Appreciation Doctrine in the Context of Article 15 of the European Convention of Human Rights' (2001) 23 *Human Rights Quarterly* 625.

Gross O, '"Once More unto the Breach": The Systemic Failure of Applying the European Convention on Human Rights to Entrenched Emergencies' (1998) 23 *Yale Journal of International Law* 437.

Gross O, 'The Normless And Exceptionless Exception: Carl Schmitt's Theory Of Emergency Powers and The "Norm-Exception" Dichotomy' (2000) 21 *Cardozo Law Review* 1825.

Hakimi M, 'The Council of Europe Addresses CIA Rendition and Detention Program' (2007) 101 *American Journal of International Law* 442.

Hartman J F, 'Working Paper for the Committee of Experts on the Article 4 Derogation Provision' (1985) 7 *Human Rights Quarterly* 89.

Head M, 'Australia's Expanded Military Call-Out Powers: Causes for Concern' (2006) 3 *University of New England Law Journal* 125.

Henrard K, 'The Viability of National Amnesties in View of the Increasing Recognition of Individual Criminal Responsibility at International Law' (1987) 8 *Michigan Yearbook of International Legal Studies* 595.

Hepple B, 'Race and Law in Fortress Europe' (2004) 67(1) *Modern Law Review* 1.

Hickman T R, 'Between Human Rights and the Rule of Law: Indefinite Detention and the Derogation Model of Constitutionalism' (2005) 68(4) *Modern Law Review* 655.

Higgins R, 'Derogations Under Human Rights Treaties' (1976–77) 48 *British Yearbook of International Law* 281.

Hocking J, 'Counter-Terrorism and the Criminalisation of Politics: Australia's New Security Powers of Detention, Proscription and Control' (2003) 49(2) *Australian Journal of Politics and History* 355.

**Hoffman B**, 'Al Qaeda, Trends in Terrorism, and Future Potentialities: An Assessment' (2003) 26(6) *Studies in Conflict & Terrorism* 588.

**Hoffman B**, 'The Changing Face of Al Qaeda and the Global War on Terrorism' (2004) 27(5) *Studies in Conflict & Terrorism* 549.

**Hufnagel S**, 'German Perspectives on the Right to Life and Human Dignity in the "War on Terror"' (2008) 32 *Criminal Law Journal* 100.

**Jackson V C**, 'Proconstitutional Behaviour, Political Actors and Independent Courts: A Comment on Geoffrey Stone's Paper' (2004) 2 *International Journal of Constitutional Law* 368.

**Klaaren J** and **Varney H**, 'A Second Bite at the Amnesty Cherry? Constitutional and Policy Issues around Legislation for a Second Amnesty' (2000) 117 *South African Law Journal* 572.

**Kleinig J**, 'Ticking Bombs and Torture Warrants' (2005) 10(2) *Deakin Law Review* 614.

**Kokott J** and **Schlölch R**, *Dorsch Consult Case*, 'International Decisions' (1999) 93 *American Journal of International Law* 688.

**Labayle H**, 'Architecte ou Spectatrice, la Cour de Justice de l'Union dans l'espace de Liberté, Sécurité et Justice, à Paraître' (2006) *Revue trimestrielle de Droit Européen* 1.

**Lavranos N**, 'Judicial Review of UN Sanctions by the Court of First Instance' (2006) 11 *European Foreign Affairs Review* 471.

**Leader-Elliott I**, 'Elements of Liability in the Commonwealth Criminal Code' (2002) 26 *Criminal Law Journal* 28.

**Lehnardt C**, 'European Court Rules on UN and EU Terrorist Suspect Blacklists' (2007) 11 *ASIL Insight* online.

**Lepsius O**, 'Human Dignity and the Downing of Aircraft: The German Federal Constitutional Court Strikes Down a Prominent Anti-terrorism Provision in the New Air-transport Security Act' (2006) 7(9) *German Law Journal* 761.

**Lord Steyn**, 'Guantánamo Bay: The Legal Black Hole' (2004) 53 *International and Comparative Law Quarterly* 1.

**Lord Steyn**, Democracy, the Rule of Law and the Role of Judges' (2006) 3 *European Human Rights Law Review* 243.

**Lubell N**, 'Challenges in Applying Human Rights Law to Armed Conflict' (2005) 87 *International Review of the Red Cross* 860.

**Lustgarten L**, 'National Security, Terrorism and Constitutional Balance' (2004) 75(1) *The Political Quarterly* 4.

Lynch A and Reilly A, 'The Constitutional Validity of Terrorism Orders of Control and Preventative Detention' (2007) 10 *Flinders Journal of Law Reform* 105.

Lynch A, 'Legislating with Urgency — the Enactment of the Anti-Terrorism Act [No 1] 2005' (2006) 30 *Melbourne University Law Review* 747.

Majzub D, 'Peace or Justice: Amnesties and the International Criminal Court' (2002) 3 *Melbourne Journal of International Law* 247.

Manderson D, 'Another Modest Proposal' (2005) 10(2) *Deakin Law Review* 640.

Manderson D, 'Apocryphal Jurisprudence' (2001) 26 *Australian Journal of Legal Philosophy* 27.

Marks J H, '9/11+3/11+7/7=? What Counts in Counterterrorism?' (2006) 37 *Columbia Human Rights Law Review* 559.

Marks S, 'Civil Liberties at the Margin: The UK Derogation and the ECHR' (1995) 15 *Oxford Journal of Legal Studies* 69.

McCulloch J, 'Australia's Anti-Terrorism Legislation and the Jack Thomas Case' (2006) 18(2) *Current Issues in Criminal Justice* 357.

McInnes C, 'A Different Kind of War? September 11 and the United States' Afghan War' (2003) 29 *Review of International Studies* 165.

McSherry B, 'Terrorism Offences in the Criminal Code: Broadening the Boundaries of Australian Criminal Laws' (2004) 27(2) *University of New South Wales Law Journal* 354.

McSherry B, 'The Introduction of Terrorism-Related Offences in Australia: Comfort or Concern' (2005) 12(2) *Psychiatry, Psychology and Law* 279.

Meisenberg S, 'Legality of Amnesties in International Humanitarian Law: The Lomé Amnesty Decision of the Special Court for Sierra Leone' (2004) 856 *International Review of the Red Cross* 837.

Michaelsen C, 'Antiterrorism Legislation in Australia: A Proportionate Response to the Terrorist Threat?' (2005) 28(4) *Studies in Conflict & Terrorism* 321.

Michaelsen C, 'Balancing Civil Liberties against National Security? A Critique of Counterterrorism Rhetoric' (2006) 29 *University of New South Wales Law Journal* 1.

Michaelsen C, 'International Human Rights on Trial – The United Kingdom's and Australia's Legal Response to 9/11' (2003) 25(3) *Sydney Law Review* 275.

Modood T, 'Muslims and the Politics of Difference' (2003) 74(1) *Political Quarterly* 100.

Monar J, 'Common Threat and Common Response? The European Union's Counter-Terrorism Strategy and Its Problems' (2007) 42(3) *Government and Opposition* 292.

Nadery A N, 'Peace or Justice? Transitional Justice in Afghanistan' (2007) 1 *International Journal of Transitional Justice* 173.

Naqvi Y, 'Amnesty for War Crimes: Defining the Limits of International Recognition' (2003) 85 *International Review of the Red Cross* 583.

Neumann P, 'Negotiating with Terrorists' (2007) 86(1) *Foreign Affairs* 128.

O'Boyle M, 'Torture and Emergency Powers under the European Convention on Human Rights: Ireland v the United Kingdom' (1977) 71 *American Journal of International Law* 705.

O'Brien R, 'Amnesty and International Law' (2005) 74 *Nordic Journal of International Law* 261.

O'Cinneide C, 'Controlling the "Gorgon" of State Power in the State of Exception: A Reply to Professor Tushnet' (2008) 3(4) *International Journal of Law in Context* 15.

O'Cinneide C, 'Democracy and Rights: New Directions in the Human Rights Era' (2004) 57 *Current Legal Problems* 175.

O'Connell M E, 'Affirming the Ban on Harsh Interrogation' (2005) 66 *Ohio State Law Journal* 1231.

O'Connell M E, 'Debating the Law of Sanctions' (2002) 13 *European Journal of International Law* 63.

O'Connor M and Rumann C, 'Into the Fire: How to Avoid Getting Burned by the Same Mistakes Made Fighting Terrorism in Northern Ireland' (2003) 24 *Cardozo Law Review* 1657.

O'Donnell T A, 'The Margin of Appreciation Doctrine: Standards in the Jurisprudence of the European Court of Human Rights' (1982) 4(4) *Human Rights Quarterly* 474.

O'Boyle K, 'Torture and Emergency Powers under the ECHR: Ireland v. the United Kingdom' (1977) 71(4) *American Journal of International Law* 674.

Orakhelashvili A, 'The Impact of Peremptory Norms on the Interpretation and Application of United Nations Security Council Resolutions' (2005) 16 *European Journal of International Law* 59.

Orentlicher D, 'Settling Accounts' Revisited: Reconciling Global Norms with Local Agency' (2007) 1 *International Journal of Transitional Justice* 10.

Pavoni, R 'UN Sanctions in EU and National Law: The Centro-Com Case' (1999) 48 *International and Comparative Law Quarterly* 582.

Pech L, 'Trying to Have it Both Ways — On the First Judgments of the Court of First Instance Concerning EC Acts Adopted in the Fight against International Terrorism' (2007) 1 *Irish Human Rights Law Review* 1.

Peers S, 'EU Responses to Terrorism' (2003) 51 *International and Comparative Law Quarterly* 227.

Peers S, 'First EU Court Ruling on Terrorist Lists' (2005) *Statewatch* online.

Peers S, 'Limited responsibility of European Union member States for actions within the scope of Community Law' (2006) 2 *European Constitutional Law Review* 443.

Phillipson G P, 'Deference, Discretion and Democracy in the Human Rights Act Era' (2007) 60 *Current Legal Problems* 40.

Posner E A and Vermeule A, 'Emergencies and Democratic Failure' (2006) 92 *Virginia Law Review* 1091.

Pue W W, 'War on Terror: Constitutional Governance in a State of Permanent Warfare' (2003) 41 *Osgoode Hall Law Journal* (Special Issue on Civil Disobedience, Civil Liberties, and Civil Resistance, edited by H Glasbeek and J Fudge) 267.

Reinisch A, 'Developing Human Rights and Humanitarian Law Accountability of the Security Council for the Imposition of Economic Sanctions' (2001) 95 *American Journal of International Law* 851.

Roach K, 'A Comparison of Australian and Canadian Anti-Terrorism Laws' (2007) 30(1) *University of New South Wales Law Journal* 53.

Robert I et al, 'Psychiatric Problems of Detainees under the Anti-Terrorism Crime and Security Act 2001' (2005) 29 *Psychiatric Bulletin* 407.

Rosand E, 'Security Council Resolution 1373, the Counter-Terrorism Committee, and the Fight against Terrorism' (2003) 97 *American Journal of International Law* 333.

Rosand E, 'The Security Council's Efforts to Monitor the Implementation of Al-Qaida/Taliban Sanctions', (2004) 98 *American Journal of International Law* 745.

Rose G and Nestorovska D, 'Australian Counter-Terrorism Offences: Necessity and Clarity in Federal Criminal Law Reforms' (2007) 31 *Criminal Law Journal* 20.

Ruddock P, 'A New Framework – Counter-Terrorism and the Rule of Law' (2005) 16 *The Sydney Papers* 113.

Ruddock P, 'Australia's Legislative Response to the Ongoing Threat of Terrorism' (2004) 27(2) *University of New South Wales Law Journal* 254.

**Ruddock P**, 'National Security and Human Rights' (2004) *Deakin Law Review* 14.

**Rumney P N S**, 'Is Coercive Interrogation of Terrorist Suspects Effective? A response to Bagaric and Clarke' (2006) 40 *University of San Francisco Law Review* 479.

**Ryan C R**, 'Jordan: Islamic Action Front Presses for Role in Governing' (2006) 4(3) *Arab Reform Bulletin* online.

**Sands P**, 'The International Rule of Law: Extraordinary Rendition, Complicity and its Consequences' (2006) 4 *European Human Rights Law Review* 408.

**Satterthwaite M**, 'Rendered Meaningless: Extraordinary Rendition and the Rule of Law' (2006) *NYU Public Law and Legal Theory Working Papers* 43.

**Scheuerman W E**, 'Survey Article: Emergency Powers and the Rule of Law After 9/11' (2006) 14(1) *Journal of Political Philosophy* 61.

**Schreuer C**, 'Derogation of Human Rights in Situations of Public Emergency' (1982) 9 *Yale Journal of World Public Order* 113.

**Shay G** and **Kalb J**, 'More Stories of Jurisdiction-Stripping and Executive Power: Interpreting the Prison Litigation Reform Act (PLRA)' (2007) (29)(1) *Cardozo Law Review* 291.

**Simmond N E**, 'Law as a Moral Idea' (2005) 55 *University of Toronto Law Journal* 61.

**Simon D** and **Mariatte F**, 'Le Tribunal de première instance des Communautés: Professeur de droit international' (2005) *Europe* 12.

**Slye R**, 'The Legitimacy of Amnesties under International Law and General Principles of Anglo-American Law: Is a Legitimate Amnesty Possible?' (2003) 43 *Vanderbilt Journal of International Law* 173.

**Spencer J**, 'The European Arrest Warrant' (2005) 6 *The Cambridge Yearbook of European Legal Studies* 201.

**Spjut R J**, 'Internment and Detention without Trial in Northern Ireland 1971-1975: Ministerial Policy and Practice' (1986) 49(6) *Modern Law Review* 712.

**Stahn C**, 'Complementarity, Amnesties and Alternative Forms of Justice: Some Interpretative Guidelines for the International Criminal Court' (2005) 3 *Journal of International Criminal Justice* 695.

**Stahn C**, 'United Nations Peace-Building, Amnesties and Alternative Justice: A Change in Practice?' (2002) 845 *International Review of the Red Cross* 193.

Stanhope J, 'The Human Rights Act 2004 (ACT): Making a Stand in the ACT' (2005) 30 *Alternative Law Journal* 54.

Stellios J 'Federal Dimensions to the ACT Human Rights Act' (2005) 47 *AIAL Forum* 33.

Stevenson J, 'How Europe and America Defend Themselves' (2003) 82 *Foreign Affairs* 75.

Stone G R, 'Free Speech in World War II: "When Are You Going to Indict the Seditionists?"' (2004) 2 *International Journal of Constitutional Law* 334.

Strawson J, 'A Western Question to the Middle East: Is There a Human Rights Discourse in Islam?' (1997) 1 *Arab Studies Quarterly* 10.

Symeonidou-Kastanidou E, 'Defining Terrorism' (2004) 12 *European Journal of Crime, Criminal Law and Criminal Justice* 14.

Tappeiner I, 'The Fight against Terrorism. The List and the Gaps' (2005) 1 *Utrecht Law Review* 97.

Tham J, 'Possible Constitutional Objections to the Powers to Ban "Terrorist" Organisations' (2004) 27(2) *University of New South Wales Law Journal* 482.

Tierney S, 'Determining the State of Exception: What Role for Parliament and the Courts?' (2005) 68(4) *Modern Law Review* 668.

Tomkins A, 'Legislating against Terror: the Anti-Terrorism, Crime and Security Act 2001' (2002) (Summer) *Public Law* 205.

Tomkins A, 'Readings of A v Secretary of State for the Home Department' [2005] *Public Law* 259.

Tomuschat C, 'Ahmed Ali Yusuf and Al Barakaat International Foundation v. Council and Commission: Case Note' (2006) 43 *Common Market Law Review* 537.

Tushnet M, 'Controlling Executive Power in the War on Terrorism' (2005) 118 *Harvard Law Review* 2673.

Tushnet M, 'Defending Korematsu?: Reflections on Civil Liberties in Wartime' (2003) *Wisconsin Law Review* 273.

Tushnet M, 'The Political Constitution of Emergency Powers: Parliamentary and Separation of Powers Regulation' (2007) 3 *International Journal of Law in Context* 275.

Twining W and Twining P, 'Bentham on Torture' (1973) 24 *Northern Ireland Law Quarterly* 307.

**Vierucci L**, 'Prisoners of War or Protected Persons qua Unlawful Combatants? The Judicial Safeguards to which Guantanamo Bay Detainees are entitled' (2003) 1 *Journal of International Criminal Justice* 284.

**Vlcek W**, 'Acts to Combat the Financing of Terrorism: Common Foreign and Security Policy at the European Court of Justice' (2006) 11 *European Foreign Affairs Review* 491.

**Waddington P A J**, 'Slippery Slopes and Civil Libertarian Pessimism' (2005) 15(3) *Policing and Society* 353.

**Waldron J**, 'Security and Liberty: The Image of Balance' (2003) 11(2) *The Journal of Political Philosophy* 191.

**Waldron J**, 'Terrorism and the Use of Terror' (2004) 8(1) *Journal of Ethics* 5.

**Walker C**, ' Keeping Control of Terrorists without Losing Control of Constitutionalism' (2007) 59 *Stanford Law Review* 1395.

**Walker C**, 'Prisoners of "War All the Time"' (2005) *European Human Rights Law Review* 50.

**Walker C**, 'Terrorism and Criminal Justice: Past, Present and Future' [2004] *Criminal Law Review* 311.

**Walker C**, 'The Legal Definition of "Terrorism" in United Kingdom Law and Beyond' [2007] *Public Law* 331.

**Walker C**, 'The Treatment of Foreign Terror Suspects' (2007) 70(3) *Modern Law Review* 427.

**Warbrick C**, 'The European Response to Terrorism in an Age of Human Rights' (2004) 15 *European Journal of International Law* 989.

**White H**, Judge Who Gave Canada Homosexual 'Marriage' Had Conflict of Interest Says Women's Rights Group (2006) *LiveSiteNews* online.

**Williams G**, 'Australian Values and the War against Terrorism' (2003) 26(1) *University of New South Wales Law Journal* 191.

**Williams G**, 'The Victorian Charter of Rights and Responsibilities: Origins and Scope' (2007) 26 *Melbourne University Law Review* 880.

**Williams, G**, 'Balancing National Security and Human Rights: Assessing the Legal Response of Common Law Nations to the Threat of Terrorism' (2006) 8(1) *Journal of Comparative Policy Analysis* 43.

**Wilson N** and **Thomson G**, 'Deaths from International Terrorism Compared to Road Crash Deaths in OECD Countries' (2005) 11 *Injury Prevention* 332.

**Wilson N** and **Thomson G**, 'Policy Lessons from Comparing Mortality from Two Global Forces: International Terrorism and Tobacco' (2005) 1 *Global Health* 18.

Wilson N and **Thomson G**, 'The Epidemiology of International Terrorism Involving Fatal Outcomes in Developed Countries (1994–2003)' (2005) 20 *European Journal of Epidemiology* 375.

Zedner L, 'Preventive Justice or Pre-Punishment? The Case of Control Orders' (2007) *Current Legal Problems* 174.

Zedner L, 'Securing Liberty in the Face of Terror: Reflections from Criminal Justice' (2005) 32(4) *Journal of Law and Society* 507.

Zolo D, 'Peace through Criminal Law?' (2004) 2 *Journal of International Criminal Justice* 727.

## Reports / Reviews / International Documents

**ACT Legislative Assembly Standing Committee on Legal Affairs**, *Report on Terrorism (Extraordinary Temporary Powers) Bill 2005 – Exposure Draft* (2006) Report 3.

**ACT Scrutiny Committee**, *Scrutiny Report No 21* (2006).

**American Commission on Human Rights**, 'Pertinent Parts of July 23, 2002 Reiteration of Precautionary Measures regarding Detainees in Guantanamo Bay, Cuba' (2006) 45(3) *International Legal Materials* 667.

**American Commission on Human Rights**, 'Pertinent Parts of July 29, 2004 Reiteration and Amplification of Precautionary Measures and Request for Additional Information: (Detainees In Guantanamo Bay, Cuba)' (2006) 45(3) *International Legal Materials* 671.

**American Commission on Human Rights**, 'Pertinent Parts of March 18, 2003 Reiteration of Precautionary Measures and Request for Additional Information (Detainees In Guantanamo Bay, Cuba)' (2006) 45(3) *International Legal Materials* 669.

**American Commission on Human Rights**, 'Pertinent Parts of October 28, 2005 Reiteration and further Amplification of Precautionary Measures (Detainees In Guantanamo Bay, Cuba)' (2006) 45(3) *International Legal Materials* 673.

**Amnesty Committee, Truth and Reconciliation Commission of South Africa**, 'Some Reflections on the Amnesty Process' *Report* vol 6, s 1, ch 5 (2003).

**Amnesty International**, 'Close Guantánamo. Guantánamo — Torture and other ill-treatment' AMR 51/189/2006.

**Amnesty International**, 'International Criminal Court: The Unlawful Attempt by the Security Council to Give US Citizens Permanent Impunity From International Justice', May 2003, AI Index: IOR 40/006/2003.

**Amnesty International**, 'Off the Record: U.S. Responsibility for Enforced Disappearances in the "War on Terror"', June 2007, AI Index: AMR 51/093/2007.

**Amnesty International**, *Guantanamo and Beyond: The Continuing Pursuit of Unchecked Executive Power (Report on the United States)* (2005).

**Australian Law Reform Commission**, *Fighting Words: A Review of Sedition Laws in Australia*, Report No 104 (2006).

**Biersteker T** and **Eckert S**, *Strengthening Targeted Sanctions Through Fair and Clear Procedures*. White Paper prepared by the Watson Institute for International Studies Targeted Sanctions Project, Brown University, Providence (2006) online.

**Bybee J S**, 'Memorandum for Alberto Gonzales: Application of Treaties and Laws to al Qaeda and Taliban Detainees', 22 January 2002, in K Greenberg and J Dratel (eds), *The Torture Papers: The Road to Abu Ghraib* (New York: Cambridge University Press, 2005).

**Byrnes A**, 'United Nations Reform and Human Rights' in M Smith (ed), *Human Rights 2005 – The Year in Review* (Melbourne: Castan Centre for Human Rights, 2006).

**Cameron I**, 'The European Convention on Human Rights, Due Process and United Nations Security Council Counter-Terrorism Sanctions' *Report to Council of Europe* (2006).

**Lord Carlile**, *The Definition of Terrorism: A Report*, Cm 7052 (London: Home Office, 2007).

**Commission on Human Security**, *Human Security Now. Protecting and Empowering People* (New York: United Nations Human Security Unit, 2003).

**Committee on Legal Affairs and Human Rights of the Parliamentary Assembly of the Council of Europe**, 'Alleged Secret Detention Centres in Council of Europe Member States, Information Memorandum (Revised)' (2005) AS/Jur (2005) 52 rev 2, 22 November 2005.

**Committee on Legal Affairs and Human Rights of the Parliamentary Assembly of the Council of Europe**, 'Alleged Secret Detentions and Unlawful Inter-State Transfers Involving Council of Europe Member States', Draft report – Part II (explanatory memorandum), Doc 10957, 12 June 2006.

**Committee on Legal Affairs and Human Rights of the Parliamentary Assembly of the Council of Europe**, 'Secret Detentions and Unlawful Inter-State Transfers Involving Council of Europe Member States', Second report, Doc 11302 rev, 11 June 2007.

**Constitutional Affairs Select Committee**, *The Operation of the Special Immigration Appeals Commission (SIAC) and the Use of Special Advocates*, HC 323-I (London: The Stationery Office, 2005).

**Council of Australian Governments**, *Communiqué, Special Meeting on Counter-Terrorism*, (27 September 2005).

**Council of the European Union**, *A Secure Europe in a Better World. European Security Strategy* (Paris: Institute for Security Studies, 2003).

**Counter-Terrorism Committee**, Report to the Security Council for its consideration as part of its comprehensive review of the Counter-Terrorism Committee Executive Directorate, UN Doc S/2006/989.

**Department for Education and Skills (UK)**, *Promoting Good Campus Relations: Working with Staff and Students to Build Community Cohesion and Tackle Violent Extremism in the Name of Islam at Universities and Colleges* (2006).

**Department of Foreign Affairs and Trade**, *Transnational Terrorism: the Threat to Australia* (Canberra: Commonwealth of Australia).

**Department of Foreign Affairs and Trade**, *Transnational Terrorism: Why Australia is a Terrorist Target* (2004).

**Europol**, *EU Terrorism Situation and Trend Report (TESAT) 2007* (The Hague: Europol, 2007).

**Europol**, *Terrorist Activity in the European Union: Terrorism Situation and Trend Report (TESAT) 2004–2005* (The Hague: Europol, 2006).

**Fassbender B**, *Targeted Sanctions and Due Process* (Study commissioned by United Nations Office of Legal Affairs, Office of the Legal Counsel, 2006).

**Gil-Robles A**, *Report by Mr Alvaro Gil-Robles, Commissioner for Human Rights on his visit to the United Kingdom* Comm DH (2005) 6 (Strasbourg: Council of Europe, 2004).

**Gonzales A**, 'Memorandum for the President: Decision Re Application of the Geneva Conventions on Prisoners of War', 25 January 2002, in K Greenberg and J Dratel (eds), *The Torture Papers: The Road to Abu Ghraib* (New York: Cambridge University Press, 2005).

**Hampson F** and **Salama I**, 'Working Paper on the Relationship Between Human Rights Law and International Humanitarian Law', UN Doc E/CN.4/Sub.2/2005/14.

**Human Rights Committee**, 'Concluding Observations on the Second and Third Periodic Reports of the United States of America' (2006) CCPR/C/USA/CO/3/Rev.1, 18 December 2006.

**Human Rights Committee**, General Comment No 29, UN Doc CCPR/C/21/Rev.1/Add.11, 31 August 2001.

**Human Rights Committee**, General Comment No 31, The Nature of the General Legal Obligation Imposed on States Parties to the Covenant, CCPR/C/21/Rev.1/Add. 13.

**Inter-American Commission on Human Rights**, *Report on Terrorism and Human Rights*, OEA/Ser.L/V/II.116 Doc 5 rev. 1 (2002).

**Lord Lloyd**, *Inquiry into Legislation against Terrorism*, Cm. 3420 (London: Stationery Office, 1996).

**Mayor of London**, *Why the Mayor of London will Maintain Dialogue with all London's Faiths and Communities: A Reply to the Dossier Against the Mayor's Meeting with Dr Yusuf Al Qaradawi* (London: Greater London Authority, 2005).

**Parliament of the Commonwealth of Australia** *Review of the Listing of Four Terrorist Organisations* (2005).

**Parliament of the Commonwealth of Australia**, *Inquiry into the proscription of 'terrorist organisations' under the Australian Criminal Code* (2007).

**Parliament of the Commonwealth of Australia**, *Review of Security and Counter Terrorism Legislation* (2006).

**Parliament of the Commonwealth of Australia**, *Review of the Listing of Six Terrorist Organisations* (2005).

**Parliament of the Commonwealth of Australia**, *Review of the Listing of the Kurdistan Workers' Party (PKK)* (2006).

**Parliament of the Commonwealth of Australia**, *Review of the Listing of the Palestinian Islamic Jihad (PIJ)* (2004).

**Parliament of the Commonwealth of Australia**, *Review of the Listing of Four Terrorist Organisations* (2005).

**Parliament of the Commonwealth of Australia**, *Review of the Listing of Seven Terrorist Organisations* (2005).

**Parliament of the Commonwealth of Australia**, *Review of the Re-Listing of ASG, JuA, GIA and GSPC* (2007).

**Parliament of the Commonwealth of Australia**, *Review of the Re-Listing of Al Qa'ida and Jemaah Islamiyah as Terrorist Organisations* (2006).

**Parliamentary Joint Committee on ASIO, ASIS and DSD, Parliament of the Commonwealth of Australia**, *Review of the Listing of Six Terrorist Organisations* (2005).

**Parliamentary Joint Committee on Intelligence and Security, Parliament of the Commonwealth of Australia**, *Review of the Listing of the Palestinian Islamic Jihad PIJ* (2004).

Parliamentary Joint Committee on Intelligence and Security, Parliament of the Commonwealth of Australia, *Review of the Re-Listing of Al Qa'ida and Jemaah Islamiyah as Terrorist Organisations under the Criminal Code Act 1995* (2006).

Parliamentary Joint Committee on Intelligence and Security, Parliament of the Commonwealth of Australia, *Review of the Listing of Four Terrorist Organisations* (2005).

Parliamentary Joint Committee on Intelligence and Security, Parliament of the Commonwealth of Australia, *Review of the Listing Provisions of the Criminal Code Act 1995* (2007).

Parliamentary Joint Committee on Intelligence and Security, *Review of Security and Counter Terrorism Legislation* (December 2006).

Privy Counsellor Review Committee, *Anti-Terrorism, Crime and Security Act 2001 Review Report*, Session 2003–4, HC 100 (London: Stationery Office, 2004).

Security Legislation Review Committee, *Report of the Security Legislation Review Committee* (2006).

Security Legislation Review Committee, *Report of the Security Legislation Review Committee* (2006).

Senate Standing Committee on Constitutional and Legal Affairs, *Report of Inquiry into the Security Legislation Amendment (Terrorism) Bill 2002 [No 2] and Related Bills - Interim Report* (3 May 2002).

Tasmanian Law Reform Institute, *A Charter of Rights for Tasmania*, Issues Paper No 11 (August 2006).

Tasmanian Law Reform Institute, *A Charter of Rights for Tasmania*, Report No 10 (October 2007).

United Kingdom, Foreign and Commonwealth Office, *Counter-Terrorism Legislation and Practice: a Survey of Selected Countries* (2005).

United Kingdom, HM Government, *Countering International Terrorism: The United Kingdom's Strategy: July 2006*, HMSO, London, 2006.

United Kingdom, Home Office, *Asylum Policy Instructions on the Cessation, Cancellation and Revocation of Refugee Status* (London, 2005).

United Kingdom, Home Office, *Counter-Terrorism Powers: Reconciling Security and Liberty in an Open Society*, Cm. 6147 (London: Home Office, 2004).

United Kingdom, Home Office, *Exclusion or Deportation from the UK on Non-Conducive Grounds* (London: Home Office, 2005).

**United Kingdom, Joint Committee on Human Rights**, 10th Report, Session 2005-06, *Government Response to the Committee's Third Report of this Session: Counter-Terrorism Policy and Human Rights: Terrorism Bill and Related Matters* HL 114/HC 888, (London: Stationery Office, 2005).

**United Kingdom, Joint Committee on Human Rights**, 10th Report, Session 2007–2008, *Counter-Terrorism Policy and Human Rights: Annual Renewal of Control Orders Legislation 2008*, HL 57/HC 356 (London: The Stationery Office, 2008).

**United Kingdom, Joint Committee on Human Rights**, 10th Report, Session 2004–05, *Prevention of Terrorism Bill*, HL68/HC334 (London: The Stationery Office, 2005).

**United Kingdom, Joint Committee on Human Rights**, 12th Report, Session 2005–2006, *Counter-Terrorism Policy and Human Rights: Draft Prevention of Terrorism Act 2005 (Continuance in force of sections 1 to 9) Order* 2006, HL122/HC915 (London: The Stationery Office, 2006).

**United Kingdom, Joint Committee on Human Rights**, 24th Report, *Counter-Terrorism Policy and Human Rights: Prosecution and Pre-Charge Detention*, HL 240/HC 1576 (London: Stationery Office, 2006).

**United Kingdom, Joint Committee on Human Rights**, 3rd Report, Session 2005-06, *Counter-Terrorism Policy and Human Rights: Terrorism Bill and Related Matters*, HL75/HC 561, (London: Stationery Office, 2005).

**United Kingdom, Joint Committee on Human Rights**, 8th Report, Session 2006–2007, *Counter-Terrorism Policy and Human Rights: Draft Prevention of Terrorism Act 2005 (Continuance in force of sections 1 to 9) Order* 2007, HL60/HC365 (London: The Stationery Office, 2006).

**United Kingdom, Joint Committee on Human Rights**, 9th Report, Session 2004–05, *Prevention of Terrorism Bill: Preliminary Report*, HL61/HC389 (London: The Stationery Office, 2005).

**United Kingdom**, *Report of the Official Account of the Bombings in London on 7th July 2005* (2006).

**United Nations**, *Report of the Committee against Torture*, UN GAOR Supp. No 44 (A/55/44) (2000).

**United Nations**, *Report of the International Law Commission, 55th sess*, UN GAOR, 58th sess, Supp. 10, UN Doc A/58/10 (2003).

**United Nations**, *Report of the Working Group on Arbitrary Detention*, UN Doc E/CN.4/2003/8 (2003).

**United Nations**, *Report of the Working Group on Arbitrary Detention*, UN Doc E/CN.4/2004/3 (2004).

**United Nations**, *Report of the Working Group on Arbitrary Detention*, UN Doc E/CN.4/2005/6 (2005).

**United States, Department of Defense**, *Working Group Report on Detainee Interrogations in the Global War on Terrorism: Assessment of Legal, Historical, Policy and Operational Considerations,* 6 March 2003.

**United States, Office of Legal Counsel US Department of Justice**, *Memorandum For Alberto R. Gonzalez, Counsel to the President, and William J. Haynes II General Counsel of the Department of Defense, Re: Application of Treaties and Laws to Al Qaeda and Taliban Detainees,* 22 January 2002.

# Acronyms and Abbreviations

| | |
|---|---|
| 9/11 | September 11, 2001 terrorist attacks on targets in New York and Washington DC, USA |
| AC | Law Reports, House of Lords, Appeal Cases (United Kingdom) |
| ACT | Australian Capital Territory |
| ADF | Australian Defence Force |
| AFP | Australian Federal Police |
| AFSJ | Area of freedom, security and justice |
| ASEM | Asia-Europe-Meeting |
| ASIO | Australian Security Intelligence Organisation |
| ASIS | Australian Secret Intelligence Service |
| CAT | Committee Against Torture (United Nations) |
| CEPOL | European Police College |
| CFI | Court of First Instance |
| CFSP | Common Foreign and Security Policy (European Union) |
| CIA | Central Intelligence Agency |
| COAG | Council of Australian Governments |
| CTC | Counter-Terrorism Committee (United Nations) |
| CTED | Counter-Terrorism Executive Directorate (United Nations) |
| DFAT | Department of Foreign Affairs and Trade (Australian Government) |
| DSD | Defence Signals Directorate (Australia) |
| EC | European Community |
| ECHR | European Convention on Human Rights |
| ECJ | European Court of Justice |
| ECrtHR | European Court of Human Rights |
| EHRR | European Human Rights Reports (European Union) |
| ESDP | European Security and Defence Policy |
| EU | European Union |
| GAM | Free Aceh Movement |
| HVD | High-value detainees |
| ICC | International Criminal Court |
| ICCPR | International Covenant on Civil and Political Rights |
| ICESCR | International Covenant on Economic, Social and Cultural Rights |
| ICJ | International Court of Justice |
| ICRC | International Committee of the Red Cross |
| IHL | International Humanitarian Law |

| | |
|---|---|
| IPCC | Independent Police Complaints Commission (United Kingdom) |
| IRA | Irish Republican Army |
| JCHR | Joint Committee on Human Rights (United Kingdom Parliament) |
| LRA | Lord's Resistance Army |
| LTTE | Liberation Tigers of Tamil Eelam |
| MP | Member of Parliament |
| NATO | North Atlantic Treaty Organization |
| NGO | Non-government organisation |
| NSW | New South Wales, Australia |
| OHCHR | Office of the High Commissioner for Human Rights |
| PCTF | Police Chiefs Task Force (European Union) |
| PDOs | Preventative detention orders |
| PIJ | Palestinian Islamic Jihad |
| PJCIS | Parliamentary Joint Committee on Intelligence and Security (Australian Parliament). Formerly known as the Parliamentary Joint Committee on ASIO, ASIS and DSD |
| PKK | Kurdistan Workers' Party |
| PTA | *Prevention of Terrorism (Temporary Provisions) Act 1974* (United Kingdom) |
| PVA | *Prevention of Violence (Temporary Provisions) Act 1939* (United Kingdom) |
| SCAG | Standing Committee of Attorneys General (Australia) |
| Sheller Committee | Security Legislation Review Committee (Australia) |
| SIAC | Special Immigration Appeals Commission (United Kingdom) |
| TEC | Treaty Establishing the European Community |
| TEU | Treaty on European Union |
| TREVI | Terrorisme, Radicalisme, Extremisme et Violence Internationale |
| UDHR | Universal Declaration of Human Rights |
| UK | United Kingdom |
| UN | United Nations |
| US | United States |

# Index

**A**

Afghanistan, 1, 17, 18, 23, 143, 145, 163, 164, 189, 197, 198, 199, 239, 241, 242, 248, 288
    Independent Human Rights Commission, 198
Al Qa'ida, 22, 23, 24, 118, 121, 164, 211, 213, 214, 236, 237, 241, 242, 243, 244, 276, 277, 287, 288, 289, 290, 304, 307, 308, 309, 319
    *See also* Islam, Osama bin Laden
Albania, 220
Algeria, 190, 200, 201, 214, 220, 221, 307, 339, 340, 343, 344
    African Union Counter-Terrorism Centre, 220
Amnesty International, 32, 36, 134
Angola, 197
Argentina, 192, 193
Australia, 53, 58, 65, 70, 74, 77, 80, 81, 82, 85, 89, 93, 94, 96, 97, 98, 159, 177, 183, 184, 273, 274, 277, 285, 287, 289, 292, 294, 297, 300, 302, 303, 306, 307, 308, 309, 310, 311, 315, 316, 317, 318, 320, 321, 361, 362, 363, 364, 365, 369, 374
    Andrews, Kevin, Minister for Immigration 2006-2007, 185
    Attorney-General's Department, 73, 272, 307, 310, 314
    Australian Capital Territory, 70, 76, 77, 183, 184, 361, 363, 365, 366, 367, 368, 369, 370, 371, 372, 373, 374, 375, 376, 377
    Australian Defence Force, 79, 291
    Australian Federal Police, 75, 77, 178, 183, 288, 289, 371
    Australian Law Reform Commission, 66
    Australian Secret Intelligence Service (ASIS), 281, 300
    Australian Security Intelligence Organisation (ASIO), 53, 77, 97, 281, 284, 285, 286, 289, 300, 304, 311, 312, 313, 315, 318, 366
    Council of Australian Governments (COAG), 74, 77, 93, 96, 364, 365, 366, 367, 368, 369, 370, 371, 374, 377
    Defence Signals Directorate, 281, 300
    Department of Foreign Affairs and Trade (DFAT), 284, 285, 286, 309, 313, 318
    Federal Court of Australia, 186, 282
    Habib, Mamdouh, 33
    Haneef, Mohamed, 96, 98, 185, 186, 376
    High Court of Australia, 53, 183, 187, 278, 288, 290, 298, 299, 358, 376
    Howard government 1996-2007, 181, 309, 310, 312, 314, 322, 368, 369, 371
    Howard, John, Prime Minister 1996-2007, 86, 287, 368
    Lodhi, Faheem, 98, 270, 271, 273, 276, 278, 283, 290-3
    Mallah, Zak (Zeky), 270, 271, 273, 276, 277, 283, 284-7, 291
    National Crime Authority, 29, 40
    Parliamentary Joint Committee on Intelligence and Security, 269, 281, 282, 297, 300, 305, 309, 311, 313, 314, 315, 318, 322
    Refugee Review Tribunal, 316
    Roche, Jack, 98
    Ruddock, Philip, Attorney-General 2003-2007, 65, 68, 78, 85, 181
    Security Legislation Review Committee (Sheller Committee), 65, 76, 269, 282, 294, 314, 315
    Standing Committee of Attorneys-General (SCAG), 364, 365
    Thomas, Jack, 73, 270, 271, 277, 278, 283, 287-90

**B**

Bahrain, 13, 24
Bangladesh, 17
Bar-Tal, Daniel, 86, 87, 88, 89, 92, 106
Belgium, 212
Bosnia, 19, 163

**C**

Cambodia, 193
    Khmer Rouge, 193
Canada, 48, 50, 51, 52, 54, 55, 56, 57, 58 , 59, 60, 61, 62
    Khawaja, Mohammad Momin, 59
Chechnya, 117, 293
Chile, 134
Council of Europe, 117, 130, 152, 153, 154, 155, 157, 256, 266, 337
    Marty, Dick, 152, 153, 154, 155, 156
Cuba, 154, 166
Cyprus, 19, 225

**E**

East Timor, 196
Egypt, 13, 17, 18, 19, 24, 36, 189
European Community, 209, 235, 240, 241, 260, 261, 262, 263, 268

415

European Union, 153, 209, 210, 211, 212, 213, 214, 215, 216, 217, 218, 219, 220, 221, 222, 223, 224, 225, 226, 227, 228, 229, 230, 231, 232, 235, 236, 237, 238, 239, 240, 241, 244, 245, 246, 248, 249, 252, 258, 260, 262, 263, 267
   Common Foreign and Security Policy, 215, 220, 228, 240, 241, 242, 244, 245, 262
   Court of First Instance, 228, 229, 230, 236, 237, 238, 239, 240, 244, 245, 246, 247, 248, 249, 250, 251, 252, 253, 255, 257, 258, 259, 262, 263, 265, 266, 267
   European Commission on Human Rights, 112, 114, 222, 226
   European Council, 211, 212, 232, 237, 241, 242, 243, 244, 245, 247, 249, 254, 263, 265, 267
   European Court of Justice, 210, 219, 226, 227, 228, 229, 230, 231, 232, 233, 236, 237, 238, 239, 240, 244, 245, 246, 251, 252, 256, 258, 264, 267, 268
   European Court of Human Rights, 70, 77, 110, 112, 114, 115, 116, 118, 119, 120, 121, 122, 123, 124, 144, 176, 180, 182, 214, 236, 238, 239, 245, 246, 251, 253, 256, 257, 264, 330, 333, 334, 336, 338, 339, 344, 354, 358
      Macdonald, Ronald St James, 114
   European Parliament, 219, 227, 230, 232, 233, 240
   European Police College, 222
   European Police Office (Europol), 213, 218, 219, 221, 222, 223, 224, 225, 226
   European Security and Defence Policy, 215, 220
   Monitoring Centre on Racism and Xenophobia, 221

F
Fiji, 197, 198
Finland, 171, 225
France, 27, 28, 121, 175, 190, 214, 262, 292

G
Germany, 134, 212, 214, 225
   Baader-Meinhof Gang, 191

H
Human Rights Watch, 133, 197

I
India, 17, 22, 25, 182, 186, 220
Indonesia, 196, 221
   Free Aceh Movement, 196
   Jakarta Centre for Law Enforcement, 220
   Jamaat-e-Islami, 17, 24
   Jemaah Islamiyah, 307
Inter-American Commission on Human Rights, 138, 142, 144, 147, 165
International Bar Association, 197, 198, 206
International Commission of Jurists, 69, 83, 113, 283
International Committee of the Red Cross, 144, 151
International Court of Justice, 144, 148, 171, 202, 203, 237, 251, 252
International Criminal Court, 177, 191, 199, 202, 203, 204, 205
International Law Association, 113
International Law Commission, 170, 260
Iran, 11, 17, 18, 24, 189
   Islamic Human Rights Commission, 17
Iraq, 1, 18, 19, 23, 24, 143, 144, 146, 159, 189, 192, 196, 239, 307, 345, 358
   Abu Ghraib, 30, 32, 186
   al-Kubaisi, Abdul Jaber, 146
Ireland, 42, 190, 239, 251, 327, 332
Irish Republican Army, 190, 327, 332
   Adams, Gerry, 190
Islam, 9, 10, 11, 12, 13, 14, 15, 16, 17, 18, 19, 20, 21, 22, 23, 24, 25, 26, 175, 198, 200, 213, 214, 221, 232, 293, 298, 304, 307, 308, 309, 327
   bin Laden, Osama, 21, 22, 236, 237, 241, 242, 243, 244, 258, 319
   Islamism, 11, 13, 19, 20, 21, 23, 24, 26, 309
   Islamists, 11, 19, 20, 21, 22, 25, 200
   Jihad, 16, 21, 22, 285
   Qur'an, 19
   Shari'a (Islamic law), 16, 19, 20, 21
   Siyar (Islamic international law), 21
Israel, 14, 15, 19, 22, 24, 88, 92, 107, 144, 148, 149, 172, 189, 198, 199, 303, 308, 311, 317, 321
Italy, 189, 212, 214, 338, 344

J
Jordan, 18, 339, 343, 344

K
Kashmir, 18, 307
Kenya, 220

Kosovo, 19
Kurdistan Workers Party, 307
Kuwait, 239

L
League of Nations, 201
Lebanon, 18, 24, 25, 199, 303, 308, 321
   Hezbollah, 24
Liberia, 194
   Taylor, Charles, President, 194
Libya, 74, 202, 203, 259, 339, 344
   Gaddafi, Muammar Abu Minyar al-, 74

M
Macedonia, 220
Mexico, 134
Morocco, 19, 200, 220, 221
Muslims, 9, 10, 14, 15, 16, 17, 18, 19, 21, 24, 185, 350
   Hizb-ut-Tahrir (Party of Liberation), 17, 18
   Hizballah, 199, 214, 280, 303, 307, 308, 321, 345
   Jahilliyyah, 15, 16
   Mawdudi, Sayyid Abdul Ala, 17
   Muslim Brotherhood, 13, 14, 15, 17, 21, 24, 309
   Muslim World League, 17
   Palestinian Islamic Jihad, 307
   Shi'a, 17, 19
   Shi'ite, 196, 308
   Sunnis, 19, 196, 307, 308
   Taliban, 22, 51, 199, 236, 237, 239, 241, 242, 243, 244, 248
   World Assembly of Muslim Youth, 17

N
Netherlands, 171
New Zealand, 53
Nigeria, 194
non-governmental organisations, 133, 137, 151, 152, 153, 155, 157, 159, 330, 337, 352, 354, 355, 357, 358
North Atlantic Treaty Organization, 155, 156

O
Office of the High Commissioner for Human Rights, 133, 134, 135, 136, 163
Organisation of American States, 130
Organization for Security and Co-operation in Europe (OSCE) Action Against Terrorism Unit, 123

P
Pakistan, 17, 18, 22, 145, 189, 220, 288, 289, 291, 292
   Lashkar-e-Tayyiba, 278, 280, 292
Palestine, 13, 15, 18, 24, 189, 190, 300, 198
   Arafat, Yasser, 190
   Gaza, 149, 199, 311
   Hamas, 13, 17, 24, 199, 280, 307, 308, 309, 321
Palestinians, 14, 15, 17, 19, 24, 87, 148, 307, 308, 311, 317, 321
People's Republic of China, 220
Philippines, 307
Poland, 155, 225

Q
Qutb, Sayyid, 15, 16, 17, 19

R
Robertson, Geoffrey, 72, 73
Romania, 155
Russia, 51, 220, 293
Rwanda, 195

S
Saudi Arabia, 17, 21, 24, 244
   Wahabis, 17, 21, 23, 24
Sierra Leone, 192, 193, 194
South Africa, 196, 206, 261, 320
   African National Congress, 190
   Mandela, Nelson, 51, 190
   South African Amnesty Committee, 206
Spain, 47, 122, 190, 212, 214, 360
   Euskadi Ta Askatasuna (Basque separatist group), 190
Sri Lanka, 91, 190, 191, 317
   Liberation Tigers of Tamil Eelam, 190, 191, 276, 277, 317, 318
Sudan, 24, 205
   Darfur, 19
Sweden, 171, 236, 244
Syria, 18, 36

T
Tanzania, 220
terrorism, 9, 10, 12, 13, 14, 20, 23, 24, 25, 26, 28, 30, 31, 47, 49, 50, 51, 59, 62, 65, 66, 67, 68, 69, 71, 73, 74, 75, 76, 78, 79, 82, 83, 88, 89, 91, 92, 93, 95, 97, 99, 100, 101, 102, 103, 105, 106, 107, 110, 111, 117, 118, 119, 120, 121, 122, 124, 127, 128, 129, 130, 131, 133, 134, 135, 136, 137, 139, 140, 141, 142, 146,

150, 156, 157, 158, 159, 171, 173, 174, 175, 176, 180, 186, 187, 189, 190, 191, 194, 199, 200, 201, 202, 203, 204, 209, 211, 212, 213, 214, 215, 216, 217, 218, 219, 220, 221, 222, 224, 225, 226, 230, 231, 232, 233, 236, 242, 259, 265, 266, 269, 270, 271, 273, 274, 283, 285, 286, 287, 292, 294, 302, 303, 304, 311, 312, 315, 316, 318, 319, 320, 321, 327, 331, 334, 336, 337, 344, 345, 346, 356, 360, 364, 366, 376
   anti-terrorism, 48, 49, 50, 51, 52, 53, 55, 58, 59, 61, 62, 66, 78, 109, 110, 111, 130, 134, 177, 184, 199, 202, 204, 210, 217, 219, 220, 222, 223, 224, 225, 226, 227, 228, 229, 230, 232, 233, 269, 271, 273, 277, 294, 298, 311, 317, 353, 362, 364, 366, 367, 375, 376
   counter-terrorism, 31, 34, 65, 66, 70, 74, 75, 76, 77, 78, 79, 81, 82, 83, 85, 86, 88, 92, 93, 95, 99, 100, 101, 103, 104, 106, 107, 109, 110, 118, 127, 128, 129, 130, 133, 134, 135, 136, 137, 141, 142, 150, 157, 158, 184, 185, 213, 216, 217, 218, 219, 220, 222, 223, 224, 225, 227, 231, 233, 235, 236, 237, 239, 240, 244, 248, 249, 252, 253, 258, 259, 261, 263, 264, 265, 267, 268, 294, 305, 315, 328, 329, 330, 332, 334, 340, 344, 345, 347, 348, 349, 350, 351, 352, 353, 354, 355, 356, 357, 358, 359, 360, 364, 366, 369
   global, 30, 31, 50, 164, 215, 298, 304
   international, 109, 110, 117, 118, 123, 127, 201, 203, 257, 266
   war on terror, 1, 2, 3, 31, 46, 47, 48, 49, 58, 91, 127, 128, 139, 141, 143, 144, 153, 159, 164, 165, 174, 214, 231, 235, 237, 310, 322, 329, 347
Turkey, 18, 117, 317, 318

U
Uganda, 205
   Lord's Resistance Army, 205
United Kingdom, 11, 17, 24, 48, 66, 70, 71, 74, 82, 111, 119, 120, 121, 122, 123, 124, 132, 159, 174, 175, 176, 177, 180, 183, 184, 186, 202, 212, 214, 244, 257, 259, 265, 266, 327, 329, 330, 331, 333, 334, 335, 336, 338, 339, 340, 343, 344, 345, 346, 347, 348, 350, 351, 352, 353, 354, 356, 357, 358, 359, 360
   Al Qaradawi, Sheikh Yusef, 14, 15, 17, 22, 24
   Blair, Tony, Prime Minister 1997-2007, 1, 10, 329, 347, 348
   Brown, Gordon, Prime Minister, 348
   Dawatul Islam, 17
   House of Commons, 336, 338, 346
   House of Lords, 110, 111, 119, 120, 122, 123, 173, 174, 331, 335, 336, 337, 338, 339, 341, 342, 343, 352, 357
      Baroness Hale, 120, 175
      Lord Atkin, 331, 357
      Lord Bingham, 120, 121, 122, 124, 349
      Lord Carlile, 340, 353
      Lord Carswell, 120
      Lord Denning, 357
      Lord Hoffmann, 120, 122, 123, 124, 174, 335, 342, 347, 357
      Lord Hope, 120
      Lord Lloyd, 353
      Lord Nicholls, 120
      Lord Rodger, 120
      Lord Scott, 120
      Lord Steyn, 31, 160, 161, 358
   Islamic Forum Europe, 17
   Joint Select Committee on Human Rights, 330, 338, 340, 346, 354, 358
   Liberty, 330, 353, 358
   Muslim Association of Britain, 13
   Muslim Council of Britain, 13
   Northern Ireland, 82, 190, 214, 327, 329, 330, 331, 332, 333, 335, 340, 350, 352
   United Kingdom Islamic Missions, 17
   Young Muslims Organisation, 17
United Nations, 127, 130, 131, 132, 137, 138, 140, 141, 144, 147, 148, 155, 159, 163, 173, 176, 192, 193, 197, 200, 202, 216, 220, 227, 230, 235, 236, 237, 238, 239, 240, 241, 243, 246, 248, 249, 250, 251, 252, 254, 255, 258, 260, 262, 264, 267, 280, 299, 300
   Annan, Kofi, Secretary-General 1997-2007, 202
   Commission on Human Rights, 135, 140, 163, 172, 175
   Committee against Torture, 138, 147, 148, 149, 150, 170, 171, 172
   Counter-Terrorism Committee, 131, 132, 133, 134, 135, 136, 137, 236, 237
      Greenstock, Sir Jeremy, UK Ambassador 1998-2003, 132, 133
      Løj, Ellen Margrethe, Danish

Ambassador 2001-2007, 136
Counter-Terrorism Executive Directorate, 132, 135, 136, 137, 220
High Commissioner for Human Rights, 133, 134, 135, 136
    Arbour, Louise, High Commissioner for Human Rights, 134
    Robinson, Mary, High Commissioner for Human Rights 1997-2002, 133
    Vieira de Mello, Sergio, High Commissioner for Human Rights 2002-2003, 134
Human Rights Committee, 77, 114, 117, 121, 123, 134, 138, 147, 148, 149, 165, 166, 169, 172, 174, 180, 181, 184, 256
    Rodley, Sir Nigel, 134, 149
Security Council, 131, 132, 133, 136, 137, 146, 176, 192, 200, 201, 202, 203, 227, 230, 235, 236, 237, 238, 239, 240, 241, 242, 243, 244, 245, 248, 250, 251, 252, 253, 254, 255, 256, 257, 258, 259, 260, 262, 265, 267, 280, 299, 300
United Nations Counter-Terrorism Implementation Task Force, 127
Working Group on Arbitrary Detention, 138, 140, 144
United States of America, 1, 14, 24, 29, 30, 31, 32, 33, 36, 38, 53, 55, 56, 57, 58, 66, 67, 82, 127, 128, 131, 138, 139, 141, 142, 143, 144, 145, 146, 147, 148, 149, 150, 151, 152, 153, 154, 155, 156, 159, 160, 161, 162, 163, 164, 165, 166, 167, 168, 169, 170, 171, 172, 174, 177, 184, 187, 189, 196, 199, 202, 203, 211, 214, 215, 219, 224, 230, 289, 351
    11 September 2001 (9/11), 1, 9, 22, 26, 30, 49, 51, 65, 66, 76, 77, 78, 82, 83, 86, 88, 89, 90, 95, 101, 107, 111, 118, 119, 122, 123, 124, 127, 130, 131, 133, 139, 141, 142, 145, 150, 153, 156, 158, 189, 200, 209, 211, 212, 214, 216, 219, 220, 222, 223, 224, 231, 232, 241, 242, 288, 297, 299, 304, 320, 327, 329, 330, 334, 339, 351, 356, 357, 360
    Bush, George W, President, 1, 2, 31, 46, 50, 152, 156
    Bybee, Jay S, Assistant Attorney-General 2001-2002, 167, 171, 172
    Central Intelligence Agency (CIA), 152, 153, 154, 155, 156
    Gonzales, Alberto, Attorney-General 2005-2007, 31, 32, 40, 167, 171, 172
    Guantánamo Bay, 31, 36, 145, 147, 148, 150, 154, 159, 160, 161, 162, 163, 165, 166, 172, 174, 175, 183, 358, 368
    Rumsfeld, Donald, Secretary of Defense, 2001-2006, 31
    Working Group Report on Detainee Interrogations in the Global War on Terrorism, 31

Y

Yugoslavia, former Federal Republic of, 25, 203, 238

www.ingramcontent.com/pod-product-compliance
Lightning Source LLC
Chambersburg PA
CBHW040934240426
43670CB00033B/2971